Drugs
issues for today
THIRD EDITION

ROBERT R. PINGER, PH.D.
Department of Physiology and Health Science,
Ball State University

WAYNE A. PAYNE, ED.D.
Department of Physiology and Health Science,
Ball State University

DALE B. HAHN, PH.D.
Department of Physiology and Health Science,
Ball State University

ELLEN J. HAHN, D.N.S., R.N.
College of Nursing
University of Kentucky

WCB
McGraw-Hill

Boston   Burr Ridge, IL   Dubuque, IA   Madison, WI   New York   San Francisco   St Louis
Bangkok   Bogotá   Caracas   Lisbon   London   Madrid
Mexico City   Milan   New Delhi   Seoul   Singapore   Sydney   Taipei   Toronto

**TO OUR STUDENTS, PAST, PRESENT, AND FUTURE,
WITH THE HOPE THAT THE DECISIONS THEY MAKE
WILL BE HEALTHY ONES.**

WCB/McGraw-Hill

A Division of The McGraw-Hill Companies

DRUGS: ISSUES FOR TODAY

3 4 5 6 7 8 9 0 QPD/QPD 9 0

ISBN 0-8151-2937-8

Vice president and editorial director: *Kevin T. Kane*
Publisher: *Edward E. Bartell*
Executive editor: *Vicki Malinee*
Developmental editor: *Melissa Martin*
Marketing manager: *Pamela S. Cooper*
Project manager: *Cathy Ford Smith*
Production supervisor: *Deborah Donner*
Designer: *Crispin Prebys/Ellen Pettengell*
Compositor: *Shepard Poorman Communications Corp.*
Typeface: *Janson Text*
Printer: Quebecor/Dubuque

Library of Congress Cataloging-in-Publication Data:

Drugs : issues for today / Robert R. Pinger . . . [et al.]. – 3rd ed.
   p. cm.
   Includes index.
   ISBN 0-8151-2937-8
   1. Drug abuse—United States.   2. Drug utilization—United States.
3. Substance abuse—United States.   I. Pinger, R. R.
HV5825.D85 1998
362.29′0973—do21
                                        97-35943
                                           CIP

www.mhhe.com

PREFACE

What a difference a few years can make. In the second edition of *Drugs: Issues for Today*, we indicated that overall drug use in America was declining. Now that trend has reversed and drug use has actually increased, particularly in America's cities. The nation's public health focus has broadened to encompass other concerns, such as gun violence and the reemergence of infectious diseases. However, polls still confirm what news magazines and television reports announce—that the abuse of alcohol, tobacco, and other drugs is still the nation's number one problem.

The daily headlines tell the story: "Drug abuse among American teens continues to rise," "Assaults linked to date-rape drug," and "Methamphetamine abuse spreads to the Midwest." In addition, binge drinking among high school and college students is a widespread and serious problem. The proportion of youth smoking cigarettes has risen in recent years. Over-the-counter medications and prescription drugs are too often misused and abused. Trafficking and abuse of illegal drugs, such as cocaine, heroin, and methamphetamine, continue to be significant problems in our society so that everyone, from the unborn child to the elderly adult, is affected by the drug problem.

Understanding the nature of drugs and the issues surrounding drug abuse is the first step toward finding solutions to the problems. It is important for students to have accurate, up-to-date, clearly presented information so that they can make informed and wise decisions about drugs. The third edition of *Drugs: Issues for Today* provides this information for today's college and university students.

AUDIENCE

Drugs: Issues for Today has been written for use in introductory drugs courses aimed at students who have a limited background in the life sciences. The vocabulary and level of reading difficulty have been carefully monitored to ensure that the content will be understandable to all readers.

NEW ORGANIZATION

We have reorganized the chapters in this new edition of *Drugs: Issues for Today* to emphasize important issues and topics and to make the book more useful for students and instructors. These organizational changes are summarized in the following list:

- The book begins with a new introduction that precedes the first chapter. This introduction is intended to pique students' interest about drug abuse and help them understand how the drug problem affects each of us.
- Nicotine and caffeine are now covered in separate chapters. Increasing rates of smoking among children and teenagers and growing interest in the health effects of caffeine warranted more comprehensive chapters on each of these drugs.
- Inhalants, which were previously presented in the hallucinogens chapter, are now discussed separately. This allows us to provide more complete coverage of these two dangerous drugs.
- Prevention, education, and treatment are introduced early in the book (chapter 2) and given comprehensive coverage in a separate chapter near the end of the text.
- The critical topic of drugs and public policy is now presented in a separate chapter that encourages students to stay informed about legislative issues and become involved in local prevention and education programs.
- Limiting the availability of drugs on the street and punishing drug-related offenses has been an important aspect of our national drug policy. Accordingly, law enforcement is covered in a separate chapter to highlight its integral role in a comprehensive drug policy.

- Some scientific and technical material, such as a more detailed explanation of nervous system function and chemical formulas, has been moved to the appendices. This information is thus available if you wish to cover it, but it is no longer prominently featured.

NEW OR EXPANDED TOPICS

We are committed to making *Drugs: Issues for Today* the most up-to-date drugs textbook available. The following is a sampling of topics that are either completely new to this edition or covered in greater depth than in the previous edition:

Chapter 1   Drugs and Drug Use in America
Classification of controlled substances
Workplace drug abuse and testing

**Chapter 2   Determinants of Drug Abuse and
                Elements of Prevention**
Reward deficiency syndrome
Addictive behaviors and addictive disorders
Disease model vs. adaptive model of drug
   dependence
Gateway drugs
Advertising and promotion of social drugs
Primary, secondary, and tertiary prevention
Four major concepts of prevention: education,
   treatment, public policy, and law enforcement
Self-assessment activity to determine risk for
   drug abuse

**Chapter 3   Neurophysiology: How Drugs
                Affect the Nervous System**
Simplified discussion of the brain and nervous
   system
Clarified discussion of nerve impulse
   transmission and synaptic function
New figures to illustrate anatomy and function
   of the nervous system

**Chapter 4   Pharmacology: How the Body
                Processes Drugs**
Expanded discussion of psychological and
   physical dependence
Drug testing technology

**Chapter 5   The Stimulants: Cocaine,
                the Amphetamines,
                and the Cathinoids**
Signs and symptoms of cocaine abuse
Treatment for cocaine abuse
Treatment for pregnant substance-abusing
   women
Ritalin for treatment of ADHD
Amphetamines and violence

Chapter 6   Depressants
Triazolam (Halcion) for treatment of insomnia
Stress, stressors, eustress, and distress
Flunitrazepam (Rohypnol), the "date-rape drug"
New uses for thalidomide

Chapter 7   Narcotics
Heroin snorting
Self-assessment activity to identify drug
   addiction
Syringe sale and exchange programs

Chapter 8   Marijuana
Legalization of marijuana for medical purposes
   in Arizona and California
Medical uses of marijuana
Controversy about marijuana laws

Chapter 9   Hallucinogens
Brief discussion of neurotransmitters affected by
   each group of hallucinogens
Rights of Native Americans to use peyote in
   religious ceremonies

**Chapter 10   Over-the-Counter Drugs
                 (Nonprescription Drugs)**
OTC labeling
Homeopathic and herbal medicines
Use of botanicals in the development of new
   pharmaceutical medications
Rational herbalism and paraherbalism
Dietary supplements
Self-assessment activity on proper use of OTC
   medications
The hormone DHEA and the aging process

Chapter 11   Prescription Drugs
Historically important regulations for
   prescription medications
Patient compliance
Role of children in drug testing
Prescription drugs for the treatment of
   depression and psychosis
Clinical trials
HIV/AIDS medications

Chapter 12   Nicotine
Marketing of tobacco products, including
   international sales
Restrictions on cigarette advertising
Theories of nicotine addiction
Current trends in cigarette smoking
Smoking cessation
Tobacco industry liability

**Chapter 13   The Methylxanthines and
                 Related Compounds**
Caffeine intoxication
Safe caffeine dosage for adults

Health consequences of caffeine use, including
   effects on women, adolescents, and children
Caffeine and athletic performance
Caffeine and suicidal behavior
Tips for breaking the caffeine habit

Chapter 14   Anabolic Drugs
Anabolic drugs and fair competition
Prevention and control of anabolic drug use
Treatment of anabolic drug use
Professional organizations that prohibit steroid
   use

Chapter 15   Inhalants
School-based inhalant abuse prevention
Prevention of inhalant abuse
Updated statistics on inhalant abuse

**Chapter 16   Alcohol: History, Physiology,
   Pharmacology**
Dangers of nonalcoholic beer for people in
   recovery
Heavy drinkers' ability to mask symptoms of
   alcohol intake
Tougher drunk driving laws, including lower
   legal BAC limits
Fetal alcohol syndrome

**Chapter 17   Alcohol: Social, Economic and Legal
   Issues**
Liquor advertising on television
New drug (naltrexone) for treating alcoholism
Social consequences of alcoholism
Intensive outpatient treatment services

**Chapter 18   Drug Abuse Prevention: Education
   and Treatment**
Chapter devoted solely to education and
   treatment; public policy covered in a new,
   separate chapter
Community-based education and treatment
   programs
Treatment settings and approaches for alcohol
   and other drug dependence
Unique treatment issues for women
Expanded *Sources for Help* box

Chapter 19   Drugs and Public Policy
How public policy affects drug use
Healthy People 2000 objectives related to drug
   use
Counteradvertising
Controversial public policies, including harm
   reduction
How drug testing programs work
Grassroots and grasstops community coalitions

Chapter 20   Law Enforcement
Table of federal drug trafficking penalties

Table of federal agencies that enforce drug
   control laws
Current national drug control strategy
Role of gangs in drug distribution
Expanded discussion of alcohol, tobacco, and
   illegal drug laws, with special emphasis on
   tobacco laws

PEDAGOGY

Each chapter of *Drugs: Issues for Today* highlights elements designed to enhance students' understanding of the content. The following pedagogical features are included:

- *Chapter Objectives* appear at the beginning of each chapter and give the student stated learning objectives.
- *Boxed Definitions* of key terms appear near the terms themselves to facilitate learning and retention.
- *Review Questions* give students an opportunity to test their understanding of chapter content and its application to their lives.
- Each chapter includes complete documentation of *References* cited in the body of the chapter.
- A *Summary* concludes each chapter by recapping the main points.

ISSUES BOXES

To present the most current issues related to drug use and abuse, we've often supplemented the chapter content with boxed material:

- *Alternative Choices* boxes suggest useful alternatives to drug use in various situations. The goal of this feature is to encourage students to consider healthier alternatives to drug use.
- *Drugs in Your World* boxes describe the impact, both negative and positive, drugs have on society.
- *Self-Assessment* boxes encourage students to reflect on their own values and lifestyle and make health-enhancing behavior changes when necessary.
- *What Do You Think?* boxes ask students to consider contrasting viewpoints about drug-related issues.
- *Profile* and *Solutions* boxes are a new feature in this edition. A Profile box at the beginning of each relevant chapter presents a sketch of a person who uses the drug covered in the chapter. A corresponding Solutions box at the end of the chapter shows how secondary or tertiary prevention strategies or treatment programs were effective in helping the user recover from his or her addiction. The goal of these boxes is to send a positive message about the power of intervention in overcoming drug abuse.

DESIGN AND ILLUSTRATION PROGRAM

The attractive new design of *Drugs: Issues for Today*, combined with its interesting and useful illustrations, will draw students in with every turn of the page. We have included many new photographs and skillfully executed illustrations that highlight important concepts.

INTERNET WEBSITE ACTIVITIES

Prepared by Jerome Kotecki, of Ball State University, a new section placed at the end of the book will help students learn about drugs by using the most accurate, up-to-date information available on the Internet. Three activities for each chapter direct students to important drug-related websites, such as the web pages for the National Institute for Drug Abuse, the Addiction Research Foundation, Narcotics Anonymous, and the Drug Enforcement Administration. For each activity, students explore the website and then answer a specific question, write a summary of what they learned, or complete a quiz or self-assessment offered at the site. These activities help students think critically about valuable drug-related information.

EXAM PREP GUIDE

A perforated exam preparation section is now included in the back of the book. Multiple-choice questions for each chapter test students' retention of the material they have read. Critical thinking questions allow them to integrate the concepts introduced in the text with the information presented in class lectures and discussions.

APPENDICES

- Appendix A comprises the federal government's schedule of controlled substances.
- Appendix B contains a photograph and description of the structure and function of the brain.
- Appendix C contains a list of the most well-known neurotransmitters, their location, function, and examples of interacting drugs.
- Appendix D is an extended explanation of dose-response formulas.
- Appendix E is a short discussion of inhibitory interactions between drugs.
- Appendix F is a table of the duration of detectability of drugs in the urine.
- Appendix G is a list of common OTC drug interactions.

GLOSSARY

The glossary contains all of the boldfaced key terms defined in the text and enables students to quickly check their understanding of these terms.

INDEX

The index for this edition has been enlarged to include some of the street names for illegal drugs.

SUPPLEMENTARY MATERIALS

Instructor's Manual and Test Bank

Prepared by Rebecca Brey, of Ball State University, the *Instructor's Manual* includes outlines of each chapter, suggested activities to encourage student involvement, discussion questions, and annotated readings related to chapter topics. The *Test Bank* contains about 50 test items (multiple choice, true/false, matching, and critical thinking) for each chapter. In addition, 25 transparency masters are provided in the *Instructor's Manual*. These include important illustrations from *Drugs: Issues for Today* and several supplemental illustrations not found in the textbook.

Computerized Test Bank

The test bank software provides unique user-friendly aids that enable the instructor to select, edit, delete, or add questions, as well as construct and print tests and answer keys. The computerized test bank package is available for Windows or Macintosh.

HealthQuest Interactive CD-ROM*

This CD-ROM by Robert Gold, Nancy Atkinson, Kathleen Mullen, and Robert McDermott contains many assessment activities with customized feedback, activities to assess readiness for behavior change, a risk analysis component, many articles from journals and other sources, and video and animation. Units on illegal drug use, alcohol, tobacco, and related topics make this a useful resource for your drugs course. An accompanying *Instructor's Manual* is included.

WCB/McGraw-Hill Drugs Transparency Set*

This set of acetates contains more than 40 key illustrations from several WCB/McGraw-Hill texts and from other sources.

WCB/McGraw-Hill Drugs Photo CD*

This photo CD contains more than 40 colorful illustrations to enhance your class presentations.

Taking Sides: Clashing Views on Controversial Issues in Drugs and Society*

This *Taking Sides* title examines both sides of 17 important issues related to causes and effects of drug use, prevention and treatment of drug abuse, and public drug policy.

Annual Editions: Drugs, Society, and Behavior*

This book contains a broad selection of current articles that address the widespread use and abuse of drugs in society. The physical, social, and psychological effects of drug abuse are highlighted in this new edition.

Health Exchange Online Newsletter

This online newsletter provides instructors with the latest information about "hot" health topics to supplement WCB/McGraw-Hill health, fitness, drugs, and wellness textbooks. The newsletter is a useful resource for instructors.

ACKNOWLEDGMENTS

We are grateful for the careful and constructive guidance offered by the expert reviewers, who are themselves teachers of courses on drug issues. We would like to acknowledge the help of the following people:

For the third edition:

Michael Berghoef, Ferris State University
Robert Blackburn, Gardner Webb University
James Forsting, College of St. Benedict
John R. Harvey, Western Illinois University
Georgia L. Keeney, University of Minnesota-Duluth
Steven A. Stokely, Lamar University
Barbara Vesely, St. Cloud State University
Nadine M. Wood, Western Oregon State College

* These supplementary materials can be packaged with the text at a discount to your students. Contact your WCB/McGraw-Hill sales representative for details or call 1-800-338-3987.

For the second edition:

Dorothy J. Downey, West Texas State University
Denise Fandel, University of Nebraska at Omaha
Kay E. Krasin, Austin Community College
Phillip J. Levine, Drake University College of Pharmacy and Health Sciences
Warren McNab, University of Nevada
Patty Murray, Fort Peck Community College
Karen Novara, Cazenovia College
Peter E. Russel, Chappey College

For the first edition:

Marley S. Barduhn, State University of New York—Cortland
Judy L. Billman, Illinois State University
Ida J. Cook, University of Central Florida
Dale W. Evans, California State University—Long Beach
Marc Gellman, University of Miami
Michael G. Horton, Pensacola Junior College
Gay James, Southwest Texas State University
Georgia L. Keeney, University of Minnesota—Duluth
William M. London, Kent State University
Rustem S. Medora, University of Montana
Rick Nelson, Northland Community College
David Strobel, University of Montana
David M. White, East Carolina University

Our special thanks go to Barbara Howes, Science Librarian, Butler University, and Dr. James Comes, University of Massachusetts Medical School Library, for assistance in locating critical information and references.

We were the recipients of a significant amount of guidance from people at WCB/McGraw-Hill, including Melissa Martin, Cathy Smith, and Vicki Malinee. Without their assistance, this book could not have been completed.

Finally, we wish to acknowledge the contributions of our parents, Elizabeth Reaugh, Will and Marty Hahn, and Bernie and Ruth Covitch. Their support, guidance, and encouragement made it possible for us to write this book.

Robert R. Pinger
Wayne A. Payne
Ellen J. Hahn
Dale B. Hahn

CONTENTS IN BRIEF

CONTENTS

12   NICOTINE 200

13   THE METHYLXANTHINES AND RELATED COMPOUNDS 223

14   ANABOLIC DRUGS 234

15   INHALANTS 247

INTRODUCTION: A LOOK AT DRUG USE IN AMERICA

Years ago, health educators had to make a concerted effort to sell students on the importance of a college course on drugs and drug abuse. This is no longer the case. Today's students are much more inquisitive about drug abuse. They see friends (or themselves) getting drunk regularly. They watch disturbing stories on television about drug-related violence, child abuse, and homicide. For students who are about to graduate, the likelihood of a pre-employment drug test becomes very real, and commuter students sometimes worry about drivers who have been drinking or using illegal drugs.

Other students are concerned about their personal safety, especially when walking around campus during the evening or late night hours. They fear being confronted by an assailant who is high on drugs. Occasionally, a student will remind the class that every day in the United States 1,100 people die of tobacco-related illness—about as many people daily as would be in four jumbo-jet airplane crashes. Some students worry about friends or relatives who abuse drugs while they are pregnant, and others wonder if they should seek treatment for spouses, friends, or even themselves.

All of these thoughts are racing through students' minds on the first day of class, making them eager to learn about drug use and abuse. They want to know more about effective drug enforcement, prevention, and treatment programs. They want to know more about newly approved drugs for the treatment of AIDS, heart disease, and cancer. They also want to know more about drugs they've been hearing about: Are the products sold in health food stores, such as Herbal Ecstasy, safe and effective? Do the different penalties for possession of powder cocaine and crack cocaine reflect racial discrimination? Why has Rohypnol ("roofies") become known as "the date-rape drug"? Other topics students are curious about include abuse of the prescription stimulant Ritalin, the

continued rise in methamphetamine use, the increase in marijuana use, new laws legalizing the medicinal use of marijuana in some states, and the possible health dangers of using the two new prescription weight-loss drugs fenfluramine and phentermine, or "phen-fen."

Our interest in drug abuse is often piqued by the highly publicized drug problems of certain celebrities and famous sports figures. Hardly a week goes by in which we do not hear news of another athlete, musician, or actor who is struggling with drug abuse. The drug abuse rate among people in these fields is probably about the same as that of people in more mundane jobs. However, because they are so visible, they attract the media's attention.

Take, for example, the trials and tribulations of golf pro John Daly. When he joined the Professional Golf Association (PGA) tour in the early 1990s, Daly quickly established a reputation as a force to be reckoned with when he won two of golf's major tournaments: the PGA and the British Open. With his down-home style and straightforward approach to golf, Daly was a breath of fresh air to the sometimes stodgy PGA tour. Daly appeared to play the game because, quite simply, it was fun. His "grip it and rip it" stance made him an instant celebrity on the golf circuit.

Off the golf course, however, Daly was controlled by alcohol. Once he started to drink, he could rarely stop. Drunken scuffles escalated into barroom brawls. He trashed hotel rooms. His personal life was in shambles. Some of his corporate sponsors were so embarrassed by his conduct that they eventually dropped Daly as a spokesman.

Daly's difficulties came to a head in the spring of 1997, when he checked himself into an alcohol rehab program. This was not the first time Daly had sought help, but this time something was different—he appeared to be much more committed to getting and staying sober. Daly is convinced that he is ill and, indeed, that he is an alcoholic. He plans to take a 12-step approach to recovery, in which he can take "one day at a time."

Other well-known personalities have not been so fortunate. Your professors and parents will tell you that many 1960s rock icons died as a result of their drug abuse. Jimi Hendrix, Janis Joplin, and Jim Morrison headline a long list of rock musicians who died from drug overdoses. In country music, Hank Williams and Keith Whitley died of alcohol-related illness. In the 1990s, the most famous musician to die from drug-related difficulties was Kurt Cobain, charismatic leader of the group Nirvana. Cobain shot himself after repeated problems with cocaine abuse and with his personal life.

Recent headlines reported two unusual stories with connections to drug involvement. The first report came from Mexico in July 1997. An infamous drug warlord, Amado Carillo, died while undergoing cosmetic surgery to conceal his identity from authorities. Drug agents were closing in on this drug kingpin, and in a desperate move to alter his appearance, Carillo planned to completely restructure his facial features to evade capture. Unfortunately for Carillo, he did not survive the operation.

The second event also occurred in July 1997. Carroll O'Connor, the instantly recognizable "Archie Bunker" from the *All in the Family* television sitcom of the 1970s, was declared not guilty in a defamation of character suit. This legal action was taken against O'Connor because of comments he made after his son's suicide. O'Connor had publicly identified and pilloried a person he believed to be the principal supplier of the drugs that fed his son's addiction. A jury, however, found the popular actor not guilty of making slanderous remarks about the reputed drug dealer.

By the time you read this, there will certainly be many new headlines that relate to drug use in America and around the world. Although many of these news stories will be alarming, others will announce new medicines and more effective ways to prevent and treat drug abuse. We hope that your venture into this book will be an interesting one that will give you new insights into many aspects of America's drug problem. This book should reinforce the assertion that each of us is affected by drug use, whether or not we ourselves use or abuse drugs. By understanding the content presented in this text, we believe that you will be better prepared to become an active partner in the search for solutions to drug issues, which will not just go away by themselves. So let's get started with the third edition of *Drugs: Issues for Today*.

DRUGS AND DRUG USE IN AMERICA

1. Explain why drug misuse and abuse are significant social and health problems in the United States.

2. Define the terms *drug, drug use, drug misuse,* and *drug abuse,* and give examples of each.

3. Develop and defend a system for the classification of drugs based upon their legality, safety of use, potential for abuse, and ability to produce dependence.

4. Describe recent and current trends in drug abuse in the United States by age group and type of drug.

Crank, crack, ecstasy, and ice are just some of the drug-related words that appear daily in newspapers and magazines. They are heard on news broadcasts and special reports, in school yards, and in the workplace. Abuse of legal and illegal drugs has become a national problem that costs this country thousands of lives and billions of dollars each year. Alcohol and other drugs are often associated with unintentional injuries, domestic violence, and violent crimes (fig. 1.1).

Billions of dollars are also spent for both nonprescription and prescription drugs that, although legal, are subject to considerable misuse and abuse. We cannot watch television or pick up a newspaper or magazine without seeing advertisements for these products, some of which we know to be of little or no value to our health. Clearly, Americans in the 1990s belong to a society in which drugs and drug-taking behavior have become major concerns. *Drugs: Issues for Today* presents accurate and up-to-date information about drugs and drug-related issues in a clear and straightforward way, so you can make informed decisions about drug-related matters in your life.

DEFINITION OF DRUGS

The term **drug** refers to any substance, used as a medicine or as an ingredient in a medicine, that kills or inactivates germs or affects any body function or structure. Penicillin is an example of a drug that kills germs. Aspirin is an example of a drug that alters body function. A drug that alters sensory perceptions, mood, thought processes, or behavior is known as a **psychoactive drug.** Nicotine, alcohol, and marijuana are psychoactive drugs.

Drugs may be **legal (licit) or illegal (illicit).** Prescription and nonprescription medications are examples of legal drugs, as are alcohol and tobacco when purchased and used within the bounds of the law. Drugs which, in the government's view, are without medical value and dangerous can be declared illegal. Examples are heroin, cocaine, marijuana, and LSD (lysergic acid diethylamide). Whether a drug is legal or illegal may depend upon historical events or the physical properties of the drug itself. For example, tobacco cultivation is historically linked to the birth of our nation. Revenue from tobacco farming helped to pay for our war supplies to fight the British. Thus, in spite of the fact that tobacco is extremely harmful to health, it is legal in the United States. Drugs can be further classified on their potential for abuse, accepted medical use, degree of safety for use, and their **psychological** and **physical dependence** potential.

DEFINITION OF DRUG USE, MISUSE, AND ABUSE

Because *Drugs: Issues for Today* provides information on a wide variety of drugs, including nonprescription and prescription medications, as well as legal and illegal psychoactive drugs, it is important to define terms that accurately describe drug-taking behavior. The terms use, misuse, and abuse are defined differently by different authors. The following definitions are clear and unchanging throughout the entire text.

Drug Use

Drug use is an all-encompassing term to describe drug taking in the most general way. We employ this term when the term drug misuse or drug abuse is incorrect or

Many people are able to meet the demands of everyday life without the use of drugs.

FIGURE 1.1

Violent events and deaths associated with alcohol and drug abuse.

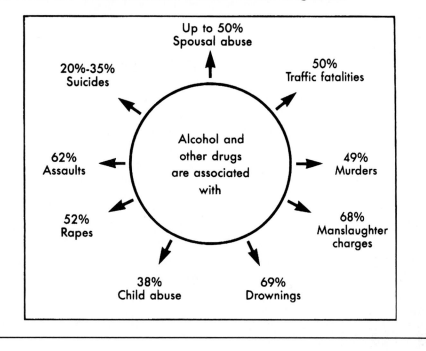

Drug Misuse

Drug misuse is the inappropriate use of legal drugs intended to be medications. Drug misuse occurs when a person fails to use a drug in the approved manner. This could occur, for example, if a patient takes the incorrect dose of a prescription or nonprescription (over-the-counter) drug or when a patient shares a prescription drug with a friend or family member for whom the drug was not prescribed. Misuse also occurs when a patient takes a prescription or over-the-counter (OTC) drug for a purpose or condition other than that for which it was intended or discontinues use of a drug before the completion of the prescribed treatment.

Drug Abuse

The spectrum of drug use ranges from abstinence (no drug use) to dependence (fig. 1.2). It is not always easy to determine precisely when drug use or misuse becomes abuse. In this text, we use the term **drug abuse** for any use of an illegal drug, or any use of a legal drug when it is detrimental to one's physical, emotional, social, intellectual, spiritual, or occupational health. Thus, drinking alcohol in excessive quantities ("getting drunk") is an example of drug abuse because it places one's health in jeopardy.

drug any substance that kills germs in the body or affects body function or structure

psychoactive drug a drug that alters sensory perceptions, mood, thought processes, or behavior

legal (licit) drugs drugs that can be manufactured, distributed, and sold legally

illegal (illicit) drugs drugs that cannot be manufactured, distributed, or sold legally and that usually lack recognized medical value

psychological dependence a psychological state of mind characterized by an overwhelming desire to continue taking a drug even though clinical signs of physical illness may not be apparent

physical dependence a physiological state in which clinical signs of illness appear when one abstains from a drug

drug use a general term to describe drug-taking behavior

drug misuse inappropriate use of a prescription or nonprescription drug

drug abuse any use of an illegal drug or the use of a legal drug when it is detrimental to one's health or the health of others

SELF-ASSESSMENT

Personal Consequences of Drug Abuse

The misuse and abuse of drugs can exert negative influences on many aspects of young adulthood. Assess the extent to which your drug misuse and abuse put you at risk for adverse personal consequences. Select the number that best describes the consequences you have experienced as a result of drug use.

1 = never
2 = once or twice
3 = three or more times

Because of alcohol or other drug use, have you ever:

missed work or class?	1	2	3
been late for work or scored lower on an exam?	1	2	3
lost a job, or dropped or failed a course?	1	2	3
lost a girl- or boyfriend, or angered a relative?	1	2	3
risked getting an infection or become infected (hepatitis, STD, HIV)?	1	2	3
damaged a car or other property?	1	2	3
been in a fight?	1	2	3
injured another person?	1	2	3
suffered financial problems?	1	2	3
stolen something?	1	2	3
been fined, arrested, or incarcerated?	1	2	3
become ill?	1	2	3
put a fetus at risk?	1	2	3
experienced depression or low self-esteem?	1	2	3
thought about suicide?	1	2	3

Your score on this self-assessment should help you determine whether your drug-taking behavior is putting your chances for a healthy and productive life at risk.

Score	Risk
15–18	low
19–22	moderate
23+	high

The costs of drug abuse extend beyond the failure to achieve optimal health. Potential consequences of drug abuse include underachievement in school or at work, failed personal relationships, financial and legal problems, and harm to others in the community. To assess the extent to which your drug use behavior may be putting you at risk for adverse consequences, take the self-assessment survey on this page.

HISTORY OF DRUG USE

The history of drug use, and of efforts to prevent drug misuse and abuse, is not only interesting, it is also important, because a knowledge of past use is helpful as we make personal and community decisions about drug use issues today. For example, our nation's experience with prohibition during the 1920s taught us much about ourselves and about that particular approach to controlling alcohol use and abuse.

Drug use undoubtedly began before recorded history, perhaps with the consumption of fermented fruit by our distant ancestors. It can probably be said that as *Homo sapiens* evolved, their drug behaviors evolved with them. Archeological evidence of drug use dates back nearly 5,000 years. Therefore, with the possible exception of isolated populations, humans have never known the absence of drugs and drug use.

FIGURE 1.2

The spectrum of drug abuse.

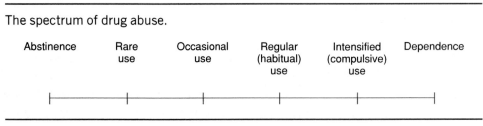

| Abstinence | Rare use | Occasional use | Regular (habitual) use | Intensified (compulsive) use | Dependence |

DRUGS IN YOUR WORLD

The Spawning of a Drug Epidemic

Stage	Example
1. Use of a specific drug is confined to small isolated communities or subcultures.	1. Cocaine was used in the early 1970s by a subculture of well-to-do groups in the entertainment industry.
2. Users switch to various types of drugs or preparations.	2. Some users found that smoking "base" cocaine was more desirable.
3. Local opinion coalesces around a specific drug preparation.	3. "Freebasing" was deemed less harmful than snorting cocaine. Demand became high.
4. Distribution by enterprising drug dealers accelerates.	4. Dealers organized "rock houses" and distributed crack cocaine on the streets.
5. Drug use increases precipitously.	5. Crack use increased because of ample supply, low cost, and high demand. Easy money drew more suppliers to the crack market.
6. Drug use becomes epidemic, overloading public agencies and health systems.	6. Number of users spiraled upward and dose levels increased. Emergency rooms and treatment facilities were overwhelmed. Police and court systems became overwhelmed.
7. The media report on the drug and the epidemic, often suggesting a "new" drug is involved.	7. Newspapers and television news programs reported a growing problem, using the term *crack* to denote a "new" drug.

Modified from Chaiken MR: Can drug epidemics be anticipated? *National Institute of Justice Journal* 226:23, 1993.

Today, new drugs are reaching the marketplace almost daily. New over-the-counter (OTC) drugs and prescription drugs are regularly discovered through field research, developed in the laboratory, and approved for use.

"New" illegal drugs seem to appear on the street each year, as well. Are all of these "new" drugs really new, or are they old drugs dressed up in new clothes and given new names to entice a new generation of our youth into drug experimentation? How is it that new drug epidemics seem to occur every few years? See the box on this page for a discussion of these questions.

DRUG CLASSIFICATIONS

There are a great many ways to classify drugs today—legal and illegal, natural and synthetic, addicting and nonaddicting, and so on. Drugs can be classified by their routes of administration, for example, whether they are ingestible, inhalable, injectable, or absorbed. Drugs are often classified by their effects on physiology—stimulation, depression, hallucinating, and so on. Within each of these systems of classification there is some overlap, because there are always some drugs that can be assigned to more than one class.

One classification system, used by those charged with regulating the distribution and sales of potentially dangerous drugs, is based on the **Comprehensive Drug Abuse Control Act of 1970.** This act, more commonly referred to as the **Controlled Substance Act,** provides for the classification of narcotics and other dangerous drugs based upon their approved medical uses, potential for abuse, and their potential for producing psychological dependence and/or physical dependence.

Controlled Substance Act (Comprehensive Drug Abuse Control Act of 1970) key federal legislation that provides the legal basis by which access to certain substances is controlled by the federal government

Excluded from this classification scheme are alcoholic beverages and tobacco products (table 1.1).

Schedule I drugs are those with no approved medical use and high potential for abuse. These drugs are said to lack accepted safety standards for use, even under medical supervision. Examples include heroin, marijuana, and LSD.

All drugs in schedules II to V have approved medical uses. Schedule II drugs, however, have a high potential for abuse. Abuse of these drugs may lead to severe psychological and physical dependence. Examples of schedule II drugs include cocaine, morphine, dextroamphetamine, and methamphetamine. Schedule III drugs are those that have less potential for abuse than

TABLE 1.1   Schedule of Controlled Substances

Schedule I

Guidelines

- The drug or other substance has a high potential for abuse.
- The drug or other substance has no currently accepted medical use in treatment in the United States.
- There is a lack of accepted safety for use of the drug or other substance under medical supervision.

Examples

Type of Drug	Name	Trade or Common Name	Dependence Physical	Psychological	Tolerance
Narcotic	Heroin	Horse, Smack	High	High	Yes
Depressant	Methaqualone	Quaalude	High	High	Yes
Hallucinogen	LSD	Acid	None	Unknown	Yes

Marijuana

Schedule II

Guidelines

- The drug or other substance has a high potential for abuse.
- The drug or other substance has no currently accepted medical use in treatment in the United States or has a currently accepted medical use with severe restrictions.
- Abuse of the drug or other substance may lead to severe psychological or physical dependence.

Examples

Type of Drug	Name	Trade Name	Dependence Physical	Psychological	Tolerance
Narcotic	Morphine	Morphine	High	High	Yes
Stimulant	Cocaine	Cocaine	Possible	High	Yes
Stimulant	Methamphetamine	Desoxyn	High	High	Yes
Narcotic	Methadone	Dolophine	High	High	Yes
Stimulant	Methylphenidate	Ritalin	High	High	Yes

Schedule III

Guidelines

- The drug or other substance has a potential for abuse less than the drugs or other substances in schedules I and II.
- The drug or other substance has a currently accepted medical use in treatment in the United States.
- Abuse of the drug or other substance may lead to moderate or low physical dependence or high psychological dependence.

Examples

Type of Drug	Name	Trade Name	Dependence Physical	Psychological	Tolerance
Narcotic	Codeine	Tylenol with Codeine	Moderate	Moderate	Yes
Stimulant	Phendimetrazine	Trimstat	Moderate	Moderate	Yes
Depressant	Glutethimide	Doriden	High	Moderate	Yes
Anabolic-Androgenic Steroid	Oxymetholone	Anadrol	Moderate	Moderate	Yes

TABLE 1.1 (continued) Schedule of Controlled Substances

Schedule IV

Guidelines

- The drug or other substance has a low potential for abuse relative to the drugs or other substances in schedule III.
- The drug or other substance has a currently accepted medical use in treatment in the United States.
- Abuse of the drug or other substance may lead to limited physical dependence or psychological dependence relative to the drugs or other substances in schedule III.

Examples

Type of Drug	Name	Trade Name	Dependence Physical	Psychological	Tolerance
Depressant	Barbiturate	Phenobarbital	High-Moderate	High-Moderate	Yes
Depressant	Diazepam	Valium	Moderate	Moderate	Yes
Stimulant	Pemoline	Cylert	Possible	Possible	Yes
Narcotic	Propoxyphene	Darvon	High-Moderate	High-Moderate	Yes

Schedule V

Guidelines

- The drug or other substance has a low potential for abuse relative to the drugs or other substances in schedule IV.
- The drug or other substance has a currently accepted medical use in treatment in the United States.
- Abuse of the drug or other substance may lead to limited physical dependence or psychological dependence relative to the drugs or other substances in schedule IV.

Examples

Type of Drug	Name	Trade Name	Dependence Physical	Psychological	Tolerance
Narcotic	Codeine	Pediacof	Moderate	Moderate	Yes

Data from *Physicians' Desk Reference*, ed. 50, Montvale, NJ, 1995, Medical Economics Data Production; and Indiana Board of Pharmacy.

schedule I or II drugs. Abuse of schedule III drugs can lead to moderate physical dependence or severe psychological dependence. Schedule III includes most barbiturates and most anabolic-androgenic steroids. Schedule IV drugs have a relatively low potential for abuse. Their abuse can cause limited physical or psychological dependence. Examples of schedule IV drugs include phenobarbital, chloral hydrate, and paraldehyde. Schedule V drugs have a low potential for abuse relative to schedule IV drugs and are less likely to produce dependence. Examples include mixtures containing small amounts of opium or codeine. For more examples of scheduled drugs, see Appendix A.

In *Drugs: Issues for Today*, we divide drugs into two major classes: legal and illegal drugs. Legal drugs include drugs that are manufactured, produced, bought, and sold within the confines of the law: (1) nonprescription drugs (also known as OTC drugs), (2) prescription drugs, and (3) social drugs—nicotine, caffeine, and alcohol.

Illegal drugs are those that have either no medical use or very restricted medical use and are subject to widespread abuse. We have further subdivided this class of drugs into two groups. The first contains those with a

higher potential for producing dependence: amphetamines, cocaine, depressants, and narcotics. The second group includes drugs that have a lower capacity for producing dependence: marijuana and hallucinogens. Although marijuana has been shown to produce dependence in some individuals, it does not do so in most, and its dependence-producing capability is much less predictable than that of the strongly dependence-producing drugs previously listed. The fact that marijuana produces hallucinations at high doses provides a second reason for classifying it with the hallucinogens.

Legal Drugs

Legal drugs can be classified as being nonprescription, prescription, or social drugs. Many familiar examples of each category exist.

Nonprescription (Over-the-Counter) Drugs. In drug stores, supermarkets, convenience stores, and even vending machines, thousands of choices of drugs are available for purchase without a physician's prescription. Examples

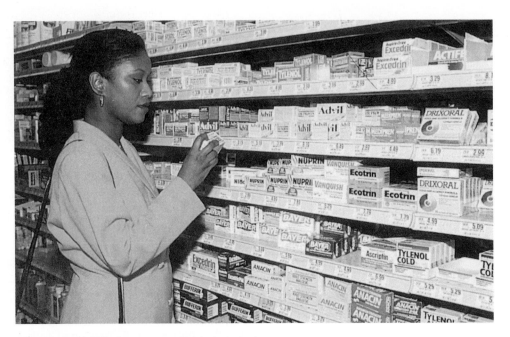

Thousands of OTC drugs are available to today's consumer.

include aspirin, cough syrups, laxatives, certain contraceptives, antacids, and vitamin supplements. These **nonprescription** or **over-the-counter (OTC) drugs** are taken for an endless variety of reasons, including pain relief, hunger control, sedation, stimulation, dandruff control, constipation, and nasal congestion. The national and multinational corporations that make up the OTC drug industry produce 250,000 to 300,000 products that generate billions of dollars in sales each year.

Although physicians' prescriptions are not required for OTC drugs, the federal government's **Food and Drug Administration (FDA)** has undertaken an evaluation of the safety and effectiveness of all active ingredients in these products. With thousands of products in each of the 26 classes of OTCs, this FDA evaluation is time-consuming and costly but has resulted in making America's nonprescription drug products among the safest in the world. Nonetheless, appropriate and careful use of these drugs is largely the responsibility of the consumer. Understanding the OTC classification system, labeling guidelines, and marketing strategies are keys to the intelligent use of these products. For more information on OTC drugs, please read chapter 10.

Prescription Drugs. Today, physicians have an ever-expanding list of pharmaceutical agents they can prescribe for their patients. All available **prescription drugs,** more than 2,500 specific pharmaceutical products, are listed in an annual publication, *Physicians' Desk Reference (PDR).*[1] Some of the types of prescription drugs included in this reference are antibiotics, analgesics, contraceptives, medicated shampoos, sedatives, stimulants, antidepressants, and anesthetics. Many of the psychoactive prescription drugs, such as amphetamines, barbiturates, and narcotics, are subject to abuse because they produce desirable short-term changes in mood, states of consciousness, or sensitivity to pain.

Use of prescription drugs in this country is noteworthy. In 1988, Americans spent approximately $17.8 billion for 1.5 billion prescriptions.[2] In 1995, Americans spent $55 billion for 2 billion prescriptions.[3] For more information on prescription drugs, please see chapter 11.

Social Drugs. The annual consumption of huge quantities of alcoholic beverages, tobacco products, and coffee and tea in this country is evidence that these **social drugs** are basic to our culture. Use levels of these drugs vary from light and experimental to heavy and chronic. Products containing alcohol and nicotine produce physical dependence in a large number of people who use them.

Obviously, social drug use is related to health risks and economic loss. Cigarette smoking causes more than 400,000 deaths in the United States each year; one in every four American adults smokes and one of every five deaths in this country is the result of smoking.[4] The annual health care cost resulting from tobacco use and abuse in the United States may exceed $100 billion.[5] The cost for alcohol-related problems in 1995 is projected to be $150 billion.[6] The social drugs are examined in more detail in chapter 12 (tobacco), chapter 13 (caffeine), and chapters 16 and 17 (alcohol).

Illegal Drugs

The wide variety of illegal drugs can be classified in terms of the strength of their ability to produce chemical dependence in users.

Strongly Dependence-Producing Drugs. Heroin, cocaine, amphetamines, barbiturates, and some inhalants are examples of drugs that interact with the body in such a way as to make it very difficult to discontinue taking them. Because these substances have either no approved medical uses or very restricted approved uses, it is illegal for the general population to buy, sell, possess, or use them. Despite their limited legal availability, these **strongly dependence-producing drugs** are subject to widespread abuse. For some legal drugs, such as sedatives and minor tranquilizers, abuse may occur when more than one drug is taken at a time, known as polydrug abuse. Polydrug abuse may include both legal and illegal drugs. With other strongly dependence-producing drugs, such as heroin and crack cocaine, any use is illegal. Strongly dependence-producing drugs are discussed in chapter 5 (cocaine and amphetamines), chapter 6 (barbiturates and other depressants), and chapter 7 (narcotics).

Weakly Dependence-Producing Drugs. Marijuana and the hallucinogens, such as LSD, peyote, and psilocybin, are **weakly dependence-producing drugs.** (Recently, marijuana has been shown to produce dependence in some individuals after long-term abuse.) For the majority of abusers, however, neither marijuana nor the hallucinogens interact with the body chemistry in such a way as to produce serious physical symptoms of discomfort upon discontinuation of abuse. Research data on some of the newer substances in this group are incomplete, however, and therefore, caution about the dependence-producing nature of some of these substances is advised.

Although early proponents of the use of hallucinogenic substances believed that they would prove useful in medicine, particularly psychiatry, scientific research has thus far failed to document any significant medical usefulness for the hallucinogens. The medical use of marijuana is highly controversial and has resulted in a number of legal battles. Nonetheless, it remains a schedule I drug. For more information on marijuana, please read chapter 8. For more information on the hallucinogens, please see chapter 9.

DRUG ABUSE PATTERNS

Drug abuse permeates all aspects of our society, cutting across all age levels, occupations, and social settings. Data on drug use patterns by people in the United States

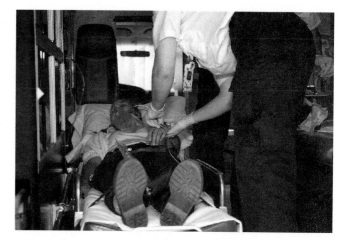

Drug abuse can be life-threatening.

are available from a variety of sources. Two of the more useful resources are the *National Household Survey on Drug Abuse*, published by the Substance Abuse and Mental Health Services Administration of the United States Public Health Service, and the *National Survey Results on Drug Use from the Monitoring the Future Study*, published by the National Institutes of Health, also part of the Public Health Service.

Age

Approximately 72.4 million Americans (34%) have used an illegal substance at least once in their lives, and 12.8 million (6%) have used one in the past month (table 1.2).[7]

nonprescription drugs drugs that can be legally purchased without a physician's prescription (for example: aspirin)

over-the-counter (OTC) drugs a term interchangeable with nonprescription drugs

Food and Drug Administration (FDA) federal agency charged with overseeing the safety and effectiveness of drugs and medications

prescription drugs drugs and medications dispensed by pharmacists on orders from a physician or dentist

social drugs legally available psychoactive drugs that are used by a large proportion of society (for example: alcohol, nicotine, caffeine)

strongly dependence-producing drugs illegal drugs that produce chemical dependence in a high proportion of those who abuse them

weakly dependence-producing drugs illegal drugs that do not produce chemical dependence in a high proportion of those who abuse them

TABLE 1.2 Illegal Drug Use in 1988, 1992, and 1995, by Age Group and for Total Population

Age Group	Time Frame	Percentage Who Have Used			Estimated Number of Users in Millions		
		1988	1992	1995	1988	1992	1995
12–17							
	Ever used	24.7	16.5	22.2	5.0	3.4	4.9
	Past month	9.2	6.1	10.9	1.9	1.3	2.4
18–25							
	Ever used	58.9	51.7	45.8	17.5	14.4	12.7
	Past month	17.8	13.0	14.2	5.2	3.6	4.0
26–34							
	Ever used	64.2	60.8	54.8	24.8	23.2	19.7
	Past month	13.0	10.1	8.3	5.0	3.9	3.0
35+							
	Ever used	23.0	28.0	27.9	25.2	33.3	35.0
	Past month	2.1	2.2	2.8	2.3	2.6	3.5
Total population							
	Ever used	36.6	36.2	34.2	72.5	74.4	72.4
	Past month	7.3	5.5	6.1	14.5	11.4	12.8

National Household Survey on Drug Abuse: Population Estimates, 1995. DHHS Pub. No. (ADM) 96-3095 (Rockville, Md.: National Institute on Drug Abuse, 1996); *National Household Survey on Drug Abuse: Population Estimates, 1988,* DHHS Pub. No. (SMA) 89-1636, (Rockville, Md.: Office of Applied Studies, SAMHSA, 1989); *National Household Survey on Drug Abuse: Population Estimates, 1992,* DHHS Pub. No. (SMA) 93-2053 (Rockville, Md.: Office of Applied Studies, SAMHSA, 1993).

The National Household Survey on Drug Abuse, which is carried out annually by the Substance Abuse and Mental Health Services Administration, indicated a decline in lifetime and past-30-day illicit drug use between 1988 to 1992 in most age groups.[8] However, between 1992 and 1995, there has been an increase in illicit drug use among 12 to 17 year olds. Use of an illicit drug in the previous month is also up in the 35-years-and-older age group and for the total population. The age group with the highest percentage of those reporting illicit drug use within the past 30 days is the 18- to 25-year-old age group (14%), while the highest lifetime use was reported among the 26 to 34-year-old age group (54.8).[9]

Use of selected legal and illegal drugs is shown in table 1.3. Alcohol and tobacco were the most popular drugs. More than half of all Americans aged 12 years and older had drunk alcohol, and more than 60 million Americans had smoked cigarettes within the past 30 days. Nearly one-third (31%) of the 12-years-and-older population had tried marijuana, and one in ten (10.3%) had tried cocaine.[10]

A major concern in 1996 was the continued rise in drug use among American teens. The proportion of eighth graders using any illicit drug in the prior 12 months more than doubled between 1991 and 1996 (from 11% to 24%), and since 1992, it has nearly doubled among tenth graders (from 20% to 38%). Marijuana accounted for much of this increase, but there were also increases in the annual use rates of other drugs, such as

LSD and other hallucinogens.[11] Drug use trends for each drug will be discussed in the respective chapters.

Environment

Drug abuse occurs almost everywhere, in homes and schools, on the assembly line, backstage, and in executive office suites. There is no place that is unaffected by drugs. Even those who feel unaffected may be experiencing the economic pinch caused by government decisions aimed at controlling drug abuse, because money spent to combat drug problems cannot be spent on education, national parks, or other desirable programs.

Home. One need only look at the home for examples of drug misuse and abuse. The father or husband who stops for "a beer" on the way home from work but drinks several and comes home drunk; the couple who smokes marijuana to mellow out after the kids are in bed; and the daughter who takes oral contraceptives prescribed for her mother or older sister are all examples of drug problems at home.

Of particular concern is drug abuse by pregnant and breast-feeding women. More than 6 million (10%) of the 60 million women in their childbearing years, ages 15 to 44, are current abusers of illegal drugs. One survey on drug use estimated that 375,000 infants may be affected by their mothers' drug abuse.[12] If the effects of alcohol and nicotine are included, the number of affected infants

TABLE 1.3 Percentage and Estimated Number of Users of Selected Drugs in the U.S. Household Population, Aged 12 and Older, 1988, 1992, and 1995

Drug Type	Time Frame	Percentage Who Have Used			Estimated Number of Users in Millions		
		1988	1992	1995	1988	1992	1995
Alcoholic beverages							
	Lifetime	85.0	83.0	82.3	168.5	170.7	174.2
	Past month	53.4	47.8	52.2	105.9	98.4	110.5
Cigarettes							
	Lifetime	75.1	71.0	71.8	149.0	146.0	151.9
	Past month	28.8	26.2	28.8	57.1	53.9	60.9
Cocaine							
	Lifetime	10.7	11.0	10.3	21.2	22.6	21.7
	Past month	1.5	0.6	0.7	2.9	1.3	1.5
Crack							
	Lifetime	1.3	1.4	1.8	2.5	2.8	3.9
	Past month	*	0.2	0.2	0.5	0.3	0.4
Hallucinogens							
	Lifetime	7.4	8.0	9.5	14.6	16.4	20.1
	Past month	*	0.3	0.7	0.8	0.5	1.5
Heroin							
	Lifetime	1.0	0.9	1.2	1.9	1.8	2.5
	Past month	*	0.2	0.2	0.6	0.3	0.4
Inhalants							
	Lifetime	5.7	4.8	5.7	11.3	9.8	12.0
	Past month	.6	0.4	0.4	1.2	0.9	0.9
Marijuana							
	Lifetime	33.2	32.8	31.0	65.7	67.5	65.5
	Past month	5.9	4.4	4.7	11.6	8.4	9.8
PCP							
	Lifetime	3.1	4.0	3.2	6.1	8.2	6.7
	Past month[†]	*	0.2	0.2	0.4	0.5	0.3
Sedatives							
	Lifetime	3.5	3.5	2.7	7.6	7.1	5.8
	Past month	*	0.4	0.2	0.8	0.7	0.4
Smokeless tobacco							
	Lifetime	14.9	14.7	17.0	29.5	30.3	35.9
	Past month	3.6	3.7	3.3	7.1	7.5	6.9
Stimulants							
	Lifetime	7.1	6.3	4.9	14.1	12.9	10.3
	Past month	0.9	0.2	0.4	1.7	0.5	0.8
Tranquilizers							
	Lifetime	4.8	5.0	3.9	9.5	10.6	8.3
	Past month	0.6	0.4	0.4	1.2	0.8	0.8

National Household Survey on Drug Abuse: Population Estimates, 1995, DHHS Pub. No. (ADM) 96-3095 (Rockville, Md.: National Institute on Drug Abuse, 1996); *National Household Survey on Drug Abuse: Population Estimates, 1988*, DHHS Pub. No. (SMA) 89-1636 (Rockville, Md.: Office of Applied Studies, SAMHSA, 1989); *National Household Survey on Drug Abuse: Population Estimates, 1992*, DHHS Pub. No. (SMA) 93-2053 (Rockville, Md.: Office of Applied Studies, SAMHSA, 1993).

*Less than .5%.

[†]No data available for past month.

Lifetime use means the person used the drug at least once in his/her lifetime.

would be much higher. More than 50% of women of childbearing age report using alcohol within the past month and nearly one-third of them smoke.[13] The effects these drugs have on the developing fetus, should these women continue to use these drugs during pregnancy, will be discussed in later chapters.

Two other concerns are the accidental taking of drugs by young children in the home and unintended drug

TABLE 1.4 When High School Students Use Drugs and Alcohol*

| | Type of Drug | | | | | |
| | Alcohol | | Marijuana | | Cocaine | |
Time of Use	1988–89	1994–95	1988–89	1994–95	1988–89	1994–95
Before school	2.0%	2.2	3.9%	5.8	0.8%	0.9
During school	1.5%	2.0	2.7%	4.2	0.8%	1.0
After school	5.1%	5.6	5.6%	8.7	1.0%	1.1
Weeknights	8.7%	9.3	7.0%	10.7	1.3%	1.3
Weekends	43.9%	42.2	17.0%	22.2	3.2%	2.9

From National Parent's Resource Institute for Drug Education (PRIDE), September 1989, August 1996.

*Students could choose more than one time. Table does not include students who reported no drug use.

misuse by senior citizens. While child-resistant safety caps have greatly reduced accidental child poisonings, these still occasionally occur. There are many seniors who have multiple health conditions for which they have been prescribed separate medications. These drugs can interact with each other or with nonprescription drugs and produce unintended effects. More will be said about prescription drug safety in chapter 11.

School. Alcohol is the drug of choice for many of the nation's school-age children, and many of these children start drinking before the end of the eighth grade. First alcohol use by the end of the eighth grade was reported by 55% of 1996 eighth graders, about the same as was reported by 1993 eighth graders. Likewise, there was no progress in reducing the number of eighth graders who reported having been drunk at least once (26.8%) between 1991 and 1996.[14] By the end of high school, 79% of seniors graduating in 1996 reported having consumed alcohol at least once in their lives, a figure virtually unchanged from 1993.[15] Edging up from the 1992 figures, to just over 30%, is the percentage of 1996 high school seniors who report having consumed five or more drinks in a row within the past two weeks.[16] Approximately 3.5% of graduating seniors in 1995 (5.5% of graduating males and 1.6% of graduating females) reported using alcohol on a daily basis.[17]

Marijuana use has increased since 1992 after declining between 1988 and 1992. In 1992, 33% of high school seniors had tried this drug, down from the 47% reported in 1988.[18] By 1996, the percentage of high school seniors who had tried marijuana had rebounded to 45%. Twelve percent of high school seniors reported having smoked marijuana within the past month in 1992, down from the 18% who reported having done so in 1988. By 1996, this figure had rebounded to 22%, or more than one in five.[19]

By their senior year, 20% of high school students reported having used an illicit drug other than marijuana within the past year. Cocaine and crack cocaine use, which declined significantly among high school seniors between 1988 and 1992, has edged up in 1996. In 1988, slightly over 12% of high school students had tried cocaine in

some form; 5% had tried crack. In 1992, only 6% of high school seniors had ever tried cocaine, and 3% had smoked crack.[20] However, the 1996 survey data indicate that 7% of high school seniors have tried cocaine, and 3.3% have smoked crack cocaine.[21] The biggest increase in cocaine use among school-aged children occurred in the eighth and tenth graders. Both of these groups showed a significant increase in reported lifetime and annual use rates between 1992 and 1996.[22] As these children age in the next few years, use rates among high school seniors and college students can be expected to rise.

When we consider illicit drug use, along with the reported use of alcohol (already discussed) and tobacco use (22% of high school students smoke cigarettes on a daily basis), it becomes apparent that drug-taking behavior is well entrenched in our school-aged population.[23] While most drug and alcohol use occurs on the weekends, a growing percentage of students use drugs before, during and after school during the week (table 1.4).

Colleges. Drug abuse among the college student population is similar in most regards to that reported for high school seniors. Lifetime marijuana use levels, which declined from 54% in 1988 to 44% in 1992, stabilized at 42% in 1993 and 1994. Reports of use in the past year, which declined from 35% in 1988 to 28% in 1992, have since rebounded to 29% in 1994. In 1988, 16% of college students had tried cocaine at least once in their lives, but by 1992 only 8% had, and by 1994 only 5% had. In 1988, 4% of college students reported using cocaine within the previous 30 days, while in 1992, only 1% used cocaine, and in 1994, only 0.6% did.[24]

Alcohol remains the favored drug of college students, although there have been slight declines in recent years. In 1994, 88% of college students reported having drunk alcohol at least once in their lifetimes, 83% within the past year, and 67% within the past month. These figures are slightly lower than the figures of 95%, 90%, and 77%, respectively, reported in 1988.[25] Still troubling is the fact that 40% of college students interviewed in 1994 reported **binge drinking** (the consumption of five or more drinks in a row) at least once in the previous two-

TABLE 1.5 Occupation Categories with the Highest and Lowest Rates of Current Illicit Drug Use, Full-Time Workers, Ages 18–49, 1991–1993

Ten Highest Rates of Current Illicit Drug Use			Ten Lowest Rates of Current Illicit Drug Use		
Rank	Occupation Category	Percentage Reporting Drug Use	Rank	Occupation Category	Percentage Reporting Drug Use
1	Other construction (563–566,573,588–599)	17.3	1	Police and detectives (418–424)	1.0
2	Construction supervisors (553–558)	17.2	2	Administrative support (389)	2.2
3	Food preparation (436–444)	16.3	3	Teachers (113–159)	2.3
4	Waiters and waitresses (435)	15.4	4	Child care workers (406,468)	2.6
5	Helpers and laborers (864–873)	13.1	5	Dental and health aides (445–446)	2.8
6	Writers, designers, artists, and athletes (183,185–188,193–194,199)	13.1	6	Data clerks (384–386)	3.2
7	Janitors (453)	13.0	7	Records processing clerks (326–336)	3.5
8	Purchasing agents and buyers (028–033)	12.9	8	Computer programmers and operators (229,308–309)	3.6
9	Auto mechanics (505)	12.8	9	Engineers (044–059)	3.9
10	Construction laborers (865,869)	12.8	10	Therapists (098–106)	4.0
	Other laborers (889)	12.8			

Source: Office of Applied Studies, SAMHSA, National Household Survey on Drug Abuse, 1991–1993.

Note: Standard occupation codes appear in parentheses. Occupation categories that had equal percentages of current illicit drug use were assigned rank order alphabetically.

week period.[26] Binge drinking among college students often results in unplanned sexual intercourse, rape, unwanted pregnancies, unexpected diseases, and unintentional injuries. Furthermore, an inverse relationship has been found between the amount of alcohol consumed and grade point average.[27]

Heavy alcohol use in the form of binge drinking can be a serious problem for high school and college students.

Like their high school counterparts, college students take illicit drugs other than marijuana, but the overall use of illicit drugs among college students has declined since 1988. In 1994, only 12% of college students reported having used an illicit drug other than marijuana in the previous year, a drop from the 19% reported in 1988.[28]

Workplaces. While the rate of illicit drug use among the unemployed is often twice the rate for full-time workers (14% vs. 7%), three-quarters of adult illicit drug users are employed.[29] Drug abuse in the workplace appears to be broadly distributed across occupation categories, but reported rates of use of illicit drugs are higher in some occupations than in others. For example, among full-time workers ages 18 to 49 (1991–1993), construction workers had the highest percentage reporting illicit drug use (17.3%), while police and detectives had the lowest percentage (1%) (table 1.5). Heavy alcohol use is also distributed among categories of workers, and again,

binge drinking the consumption of five or more alcoholic drinks in a row

TABLE 1.6 Occupation Categories with the Highest and Lowest Rates of Heavy Alcohol Use, Full-Time Workers, Ages 18–49, 1991–1993

Ten Highest Rates of Heavy Alcohol Use			Ten Lowest Rates of Heavy Alcohol Use		
Rank	Occupation Category	Percentage Reporting Heavy Alcohol Use	Rank	Occupation Category	Percentage Reporting Heavy Alcohol Use
1	Other construction (563–566,573,588–599)	20.6	1	Data clerks (384–386)	0.8
2	Construction laborers (865,869)	19.9	2	Personnel and training specialists (008,027)	1.1
3	Helpers and laborers (864–873)	19.5	3	Secretaries and typists (313–315)	1.4
4	Auto mechanics (505)	16.3	4	Bank tellers (383)	1.5
5	Food preparation (436–444)	16.3	5	Bookkeepers (337)	1.7
6	Truck drivers, light (805–806)	15.1	6	Clinical laboratory and technologists (203,208)	2.2
7	Vehicle and mobile equipment mechanics and repairers (505–519)	14.9	7	Teachers (113–159)	2.2
8	Painters, plasterers, and plumbers (579–587)	14.8	8	Dental and health aides (445–446)	2.3
9	Carpenters (567–569)	13.8	9	Computer scientists and analysts (064–065)	2.4
10	Material moving operators (844–859)	13.8	10	Child care workers (406,408)	2.6

Source: Office of Applied Studies, SAMHSA, National Household Survey on Drug Abuse, 1991–1993.

Note: Standard occupation codes appear in parentheses. Heavy alcohol use is defined as drinking five or more drinks on five or more occasions during the past 30 days.

contract workers led the way (table 1.6). Category of job is not always an accurate predictor of risk for drug use. Instead, a lack of commitment to social institutions, such as school or marriage, is a stronger predictor of drug abuse than type of employment.[30]

The good news is that a significant decline in workplace drug use has occurred over the past eight years. According to a report by SmithKline Beecham Clinical Laboratories, positive drug tests in the workplace declined each year between 1987 and 1995. In 1987, the first year of workplace testing, 18.1% of all tests were positive; in 1995, only 6.7% of all tests were positive.[31]

The proportion of major U.S. businesses that test for drugs has risen steadily, from 21.5% in 1987 to 81.1% in 1996.[32] There is an inverse relationship between the amount of drug testing and the rate of positive tests during 1987–1995 (fig. 1.3). That is, as the number of firms testing their employees for drugs increased, the number of samples found to contain evidence of drug use declined. Drug testing serves multiple purposes: (1) it

weeds out drug abusers at the time of initial hiring, (2) it detects drug abuse among current employees, (3) it deters employees who might be considering using a drug because of the increased likelihood of their being caught, and (4) it ensures the firm's customers will receive quality workmanship or services.

One of the key industries with regard to drug testing is the transportation industry because drug abuse by members of this industry puts the lives of the general public at increased risk. For people in these occupations, drug testing has been mandated and supported by court decisions. Among safety-sensitive transportation workers, the rate of positive drug tests in 1995 was 3.5%, less than half that of the nontransportation general workforce, 7.5%.[33]

The current widespread use of drug testing in the workplace and the importance of being drug free at the time of application for employment reflect the relationship of drug-taking behavior to job opportunities. Students preparing to enter the job market should be aware of the relevance of their drug use status to their ability to

FIGURE 1.3

The relationship between the prevalence of workplace drug testing and the rate of positive test results. As the percentage of U.S. firms testing for drugs increased between 1987 and 1995, the rate of positive test results declined.

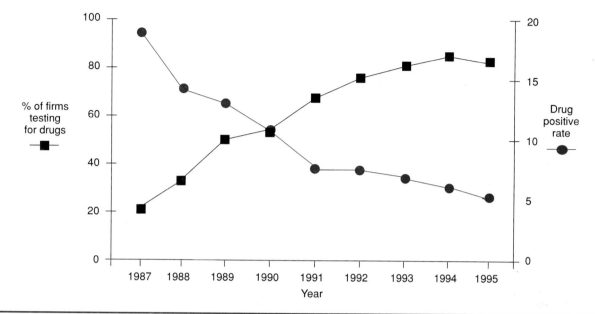

(Data from the 1996 American Management Association survey of workplace drug testing and drug abuse policies)

be hired and to maintain employment. Perhaps no occupation receives as much public exposure as athletics. After all, professional athletes are actually in the entertainment business. Drug abuse among athletes and other entertainers is reported widely in the press. The drugs abused are many, ranging from dangerous anabolic steroids to alcohol, amphetamines, and cocaine. Factors that may place professional athletes and entertainers at risk for drug abuse are the intensity of their work schedules, the rapid change in their lifestyles, and the large amounts of money available to them. Some athletes and other entertainers turn to drugs hoping to improve performance. Others do so to help deal with success or failure. Because these people are role models for millions of children, their drug abuse problems are a public concern.

The abuse of drugs in our society is so pervasive that few people are left untouched. Many people can name a friend, neighbor, or relative whose life has been damaged by drug use. Drug use by others may affect you (See the box on page 16.) Even those who do not feel affected on a personal level feel the effects of the financial costs of the drug problem in America. President Clinton's request for Federal Drug Control Spending for the fiscal year 1997 was more than $15 billion.[34] That comes to about $240 for a family of four, but if you count in all the costs associated with alcohol, tobacco, and other drug use in the United States, the cost per individual is much higher.

One figure often cited is $177 billion, or $756 for each man, woman, and child.[35] Obviously, this is money that could have been put toward education, parks, or other programs of national interest.

Locally, addressing drug abuse could mean spending more money on policing and less on other programs. For example, a school district might have to hire an extra custodian to clean drug gang graffiti off of school property with funds that could have been used to hire another teacher. Clearly, the drug problem is one of the most economically pervasive issues facing America in this decade.

SUMMARY

A drug is any substance that kills germs or affects the function or structure of the body. Psychoactive drugs are drugs that alter perceptions, mood, and thought processes or behavior. The misuse and abuse of legal and illegal drugs results in major social and economic problems, costing thousands of lives and billions of dollars each year.

Drugs can be classified in various ways. Legal (licit) drugs are those that can be bought, sold, and used in our society within the bounds of the law. Illegal (illicit) drugs are those that cannot. Legal drugs include

WHAT DO YOU THINK?

Is Injection Drug Use by Others Putting Your Health at Risk?

As the HIV/AIDS epidemic continues to grow, the proportion of cases in which injection drug use is cited as the only source of exposure also grows. Public health officials are now concerned about the deadly link between drug abuse, HIV/AIDS, and the renewed spread of tuberculosis (TB), a phenomenon that has been called the public health equivalent of the "three-headed dog from hell" by Joseph A. Califano, Jr., president of the Center on Addiction and Substance Abuse, Columbia University.[a]

Of the 334,344 adult and adolescent cases of AIDS reported through September 1993, 68,029 (20%) were in people who reported injected drugs as their only source of exposure.[b] The proportion of people with AIDS that are

[a]Substance Abuse and Mental Health Services, "SAMHSA Fights 'Three-Headed Dog from Hell,'" *SAMHSA News* 1, no. 3(1993):17.

[b]Centers for Disease Control and Prevention, *HIV/AIDS Surveillance Report,* Third Quarter Ed., Atlanta, 1993.

drug abusers has increased from one in six in 1989 to one in five in 1993. Injection drug use is helping to fuel the HIV/AIDS epidemic, and the human immunodeficiency virus (HIV) provides major fuel for the resurgence of TB by compromising the immune system. TB, once called the white plague, was a leading cause of death in the United States 100 years ago and remains one of the world's deadliest plagues. The incidence of active TB in HIV/AIDS patients is nearly 500 times the rate in the general population.

The number of new cases of TB are increasing again in the United States; 26,283 new, active cases were reported in 1991—one case in every 10,000 Americans. More active cases of TB means that more uninfected people will be exposed to this serious disease. An increasing number of the active cases are drug resistant forms of the disease—that is, incurable with currently available antibiotics. This is an example of how injection drug use increases the health risk of the entire community.

prescription and nonprescription medications, caffeine, tobacco, and alcohol products. Illegal drugs can be further divided into those that produce a strong state of chemical dependence in most people—amphetamines, cocaine, depressants, and narcotics—and those that are less strongly dependence producing—marijuana and hallucinogens.

Drug abuse is pervasive, affecting all age groups and occupations. While the use of some illicit drugs in high schools and colleges has declined, the use of others has not. Alcohol use is beginning at a younger age, and heavy alcohol use, in the form of binge drinking, is prevalent in young adults. The cost of drug abuse to health and to social institutions is significant.

REVIEW QUESTIONS

1. How do your authors differentiate between the terms drug use, misuse, and abuse? Which relates primarily to prescription medications and OTC drugs? Which term describes drug-taking behavior involving risks to one's health?
2. What are the two major categories of drugs? What are examples of legal drugs? Which legal drugs do your authors refer to as social drugs?

3. How do your authors classify illegal drugs? Which illegal drugs are described as being weakly dependence producing?
4. How would you describe current drug use patterns for high school and college students in terms of incidence of use? In which occupational groups is drug abuse a particular concern? Why? What is accomplished by drug testing in the workplace?

REFERENCES

1. *Physician's Desk Reference,* 51 ed. (Montvale, N.J.: Medical Economics Company, Inc., 1997).
2. "50th Annual Rx Review: A Vintage Year," *Drug Topics* 133 (1989):32.
3. Sutton, S., "Pharmacy: Annual Report Part 2," *Drug Store News,* 20 May, 1996, p. 31.
4. Bartecchi, C. E., T. D. Mackenzie, and R. W. Schrier, "The Human Costs of Tobacco Use, Part I, *N. Engl. J. Med.* 330, no. 13 (1994), 907–12.
5. Mackenzie, T. D., C. E. Bartecchi, and R. W. Schrier, "The Human Costs of Tobacco Use, Part II, *N. Engl. J. Med.* 330, no. 14 (1994):975–80.
6. U.S. Department of Health and Human Services, *Alcohol and Health: Seventh Special Report to the U.S. Congress,* DHHS Pub. No. (ADM) 90-1656 (Washington, D.C.: U.S. Government Printing Office, 1990).

7. *National Household Survey on Drug Abuse: Population Estimates, 1995,* DHHS Pub. No. (ADM) 96-3095 (Rockville, Md.: National Institute on Drug Abuse, 1996); *National Household Survey on Drug Abuse: Population Estimates, 1988,* DHHS Pub. No. (SMA) 89-1636 (Rockville, Md.: Office of Applied Studies, SAMHSA, 1989); *National Household Survey on Drug Abuse: Population Estimates, 1992,* DHHS Pub. No. (SMA) 93-2053 (Rockville, Md.: Office of Applied Studies, SAMHSA, 1993).

8. *Survey on Drug Abuse, 1988; Survey on Drug Abuse, 1992.*

9. *Survey on Drug Abuse, 1995.*

10. Ibid.

11. "The Rise in Drug Use Among American Teens Continues in 1996," The University of Michigan News and Information Services, Ann Arbor, Michigan, 19 December, 1996. Press Release.

12. Substance Abuse and Mental Health Services Administration, *Pregnant, Substance-Using Women: Treatment Improvement Protocol (TIP), Series 2,* DHHS Pub. No. (SMA) 93-1998 (Washington, D.C.: U.S. Government Printing Office, 1993).

13. *Survey on Drug Abuse, 1992.*

14. "Drug Use among American Teens."

15. Ibid.

16. Ibid.

17. Johnston, L. D., P. M. O'Malley, and J. G. Bachman, *National Survey Results on Drug Use from Monitoring the Future Study, 1975–1995,* NIH Publication No. 96-4139 (Rockville, Md.: National Institute on Drug Abuse, 1996).

18. Johnston, L. D., P. M. O'Malley, and J. G. Bachman, *Drug Use, Drinking, and Smoking: National Survey Results from High School, College, and Young Adult Populations, 1975–1988,* NIH Publication No. 89-1638 (Rockville, Md.: National Institute on Drug Abuse, 1989); Johnston, L. D., P. M. O'Malley, and J. G. Bachman, *Drug Use, Drinking, and Smoking: National Survey Results from High School, College, and Young Adult Populations, 1975–1992,* NIH Publication No. 93-3597 (Rockville, Md.: National Institute on Drug Abuse, 1993).

19. "Drug Use among American Teens."

20. Johnston, O'Malley, and Bachman, *Drug Use, Drinking, and Smoking, 1975–1988;* Johnston, O'Malley, and Bachman, *Drug Use, Drinking, and Smoking, 1975–1992.*

21. "Drug Use among American Teens."

22. Ibid.

23. Ibid.

24. *National Survey Results on Drug Use from the Monitoring the Future Study, 1975–1994,* vol. II, *College Students and Young Adults* (Rockville, Md.: National Institute on Drug Abuse, 1996).

25. Ibid.

26. Ibid.

27. Presley, C. A., and P. W. Meilman, *Alcohol and Drugs on American College Campuses: A Report to College Presidents, 1992* (Carbondale, Ill.: Student Health Program, Wellness Center, Southern Illinois University).

28. *Survey Results on Drug Use, 1975–1994.*

29. *Drug Use among U.S. Workers: Prevalence and Trends by Occupation and Industry Categories, 1996* (Rockville, Md.: Substance Abuse and Mental Health Services Administration).

30. Mensch, B. S., and D. B. Kendel, "Do Job Conditions Influence the Use of Drugs?" *Health Soc Behav* 9(1988):169.

31. "Drug Detection in Workplace in 1995 Declines for Eighth Straight Year SmithKline Beecham Data Shows," Smithkline Beecham Clinical Laboratories, Collegeville, Pennsylvania, 29 February, 1996. Press Release.

32. *1996 AMA Survey: Workplace Drug Testing and Drug Abuse Policy-Summary of Reg Findings* (New York, N.Y.: American Management Associates, 1996).

33. "Drug Detection in Workplace."

34. Office of National Drug Control Policy, *The National Drug Control Strategy, 1996.* Executive Office of the President, The White House, Washington D.C., 1996. NCJ 160086.

35. *Prevention Plus II: Tools for Creating and Sustaining Drug-Free Communities.* Office for Substance Abuse Prevention, DHHS Publication No. (ADM) 89-1649. Distributed by the National Clearinghouse for Alcohol and Drug Information, Rockville, Md.

SOURCES FOR HELP

Institute on Black Chemical Abuse (IBCA)
2614 Nicollet Ave.
Minneapolis, MN 55408
(612) 871–7878

National Association of State Alcohol and Drug Abuse Directors (NASADAD)
444 N. Capitol St., N.W., Suite 520
Washington, D.C. 20001
(202) 783–6868
http://www.social.com/health/nhic/data/

National Clearinghouse for Alcohol and Drug Information (NCADI)
P.O. Box 2345
Rockville, MD 20852
(301) 468–2600
http://www.health.org

Office for Substance Abuse Prevention (OSAP)
5600 Fishers Lane, Parklawn Bldg.
Rockville, MD 20852
(301) 443–0365

Alcoholics Anonymous
General Service Office
(212) 870–3400
http://www.alcoholics_anonymous.org

DETERMINANTS OF DRUG ABUSE AND ELEMENTS OF PREVENTION

CHAPTER OBJECTIVES

After studying this chapter, you will be able to:

1. Define the terms *risk factors* and *protective factors* as they relate to vulnerability to drug abuse, and list at least ten examples of risk factors and ten protective factors.

2. Explain how genetic factors can influence drug-taking behavior.

3. Explain what is meant by the terms *addictive behavior* and *reward deficiency syndrome.*

4. Describe the relationship between the successful development of interpersonal skills and one's risk for drug abuse and between the successful mastery of developmental tasks and the risk for drug abuse.

5. Explain how home and family life can influence one's drug-taking behavior.

6. Discuss the influence of the school environment and peers on one's choices about drugs.

7. Outline some ways in which our society and culture encourage drug use.

8. Define the terms *primary prevention*, *secondary prevention*, and *tertiary prevention* as they relate to drug-taking behavior and give an example of an activity at each level of prevention.

9. Define the terms *education*, *treatment*, *public policy*, and *law enforcement* as they relate to drug abuse prevention.

The focus of this chapter is twofold: (1) to describe and explain the determinants of (factors that influence decisions about) alcohol and other drug use, misuse, and abuse, and (2) to introduce the major elements of drug abuse prevention.

While it is true that the ultimate decision to use mind-altering drugs lies with the individual, evidence shows that individuals are differentially at risk for engaging in drug-taking behavior. For example, some people never experiment with drugs, while others who do experiment discontinue use after only a few experiences. Still others continue to use drugs on an irregular basis or become regular users. Finally, there are some people who develop use patterns that can be characterized as intensive or compulsive (abusive) patterns that may result in dependence. In the section that follows, we discuss the factors that contribute to drug abuse and dependence.

DETERMINANTS OF DRUG ABUSE

Several types of factors influence drug-taking behavior. One type includes individual influences, such as genetic predisposition, personality traits, attitudes and beliefs, interpersonal skills, and unmet developmental needs. A second type of influences includes family, school, peers, and community setting. Finally, there are the influences of cultural, economic, and social environments (fig. 2.1). Knowledge of these influences and how they shape an individual's decisions about drugs are important for understanding drug abuse in our society. Complete the self-assessment on page 21 to see whether you are at risk for drug abuse.

The term **vulnerability** has been used to describe the concept that individuals are differentially at risk for engaging in drug-taking behavior, for making the transition from drug use to drug abuse, and for becoming drug

FIGURE 2.1

Factors that influence the use and abuse of alcohol, tobacco, and other drugs.

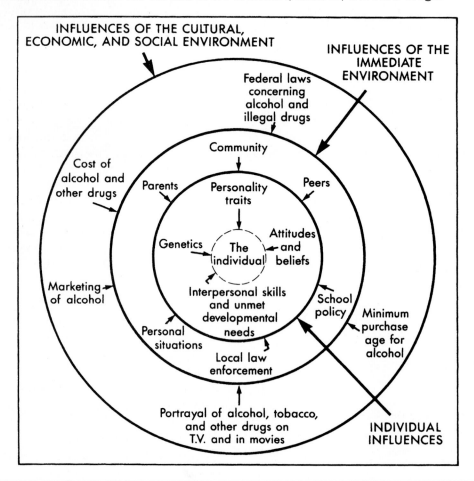

SELF-ASSESSMENT

Are You at Risk for Drug Abuse?

A number of the risk factors discussed in this chapter have been incorporated in the following self-assessment instrument.

	Yes	No
I have a parent or grandparent who is (was) an alcoholic.	☐	☐
I have tried inhalants.	☐	☐
The first time I got drunk was before I entered high school.	☐	☐
I know at least two adults who have used marijuana, cocaine, or heroin.	☐	☐
Being able to drink on weekends is very important to me.	☐	☐
I have friends who get drunk or high two to three times a week.	☐	☐
I smoked a cigarette or used smokeless tobacco in the last month.	☐	☐

	Yes	No
I often feel that there is something missing in my life.	☐	☐
I often feel that others have advantages I do not have.	☐	☐
I was glad to finally be away from my family.	☐	☐
Getting drunk or getting high makes me feel really great.	☐	☐
It is important to me to be able to drive very fast (above the speed limit).	☐	☐
Religion is not a very important part of my life.	☐	☐
I have been called impulsive.	☐	☐
My close friends know more about drugs than I do.	☐	☐
I feel that my life is restricted by too many rules.	☐	☐

Scoring: If you answered yes to 8 or more of these statements, you are at high risk; 4–6 moderate risk; 3 or below, low risk.

dependent.[1] Individual attributes, characteristics, situational conditions, or environmental contexts that promote or increase the probability of drug use, abuse, or transition of involvement with drugs are known as **risk factors.** The opposite of vulnerability is **resistance.** Individual attributes, characteristics, situational conditions, or environmental contexts that inhibit, reduce, or buffer the probability of drug involvement, and thus strengthen one's resistance, are called **protective factors.**[2] The relationship between risk factors and protective factors is illustrated in fig. 2.2.

INDIVIDUAL FACTORS

Risk and protective factors that can be traced to traits of an individual are classified as individual factors. These factors include genetics, personality traits, personal attitudes and beliefs, interpersonal skills or skill deficiencies, and met or unmet developmental needs.

Genetic Factors

Research has demonstrated that factors that influence vulnerability to drug involvement are either genetic or environmental.[3] The importance of genetic risk factors when compared with environmental factors, such as home life, friends, and school, has not been precisely determined. However, studies with alcoholics have demonstrated that genetic factors can sometimes play a role in the eventual development of alcohol abuse patterns. Research with identical twins born to an alcoholic parent, then separately adopted by different families at birth and raised without knowledge of the biological parent's alcoholism, illustrates the presence of some inherited traits.[4]

How these inherited factors actually work is still being studied. For example, recent studies suggest that genetically predisposed people show less intense responses to low doses of alcohol than subjects with no genetic predisposition.[5] Therefore, they may be less able to

vulnerability the concept that people are differentially at risk for drug abuse

risk factors genetic or environmental factors that increase the probability of drug use, abuse, or dependence

resistance the concept that individuals are endowed with attributes that lower their susceptibility to drug involvement

protective factors genetic or environmental factors that decrease the probability of drug use, abuse, or dependence

FIGURE 2.2

Risk factors for drug abuse may be counterbalanced by protective factors.

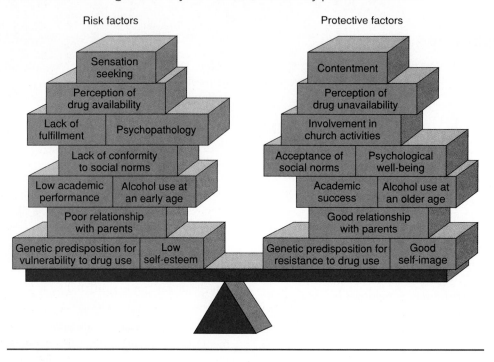

estimate how intoxicated they are becoming when they are drinking. This could make it more difficult for them to know when to stop drinking. Other differences in the physiological responses to alcohol have been noted between children of alcoholics and children of nonalcoholics. After only one drink, some alcoholics have significantly different brain wave patterns than nonalcoholics, suggesting that alcohol affects each group differently.[6]

Recent studies have found that addictive, impulsive, and compulsive disorders, such as alcoholism, attention deficit disorder, drug abuse, and food binging, may share a common genetic origin.[7] While there is no such thing as an "alcohol gene" or an "obesity gene," a statistical association has been found between the frequency of certain genetic variants in populations of those with a particular disease and control populations. Some scientists believe that a genetic abnormality previously found to be associated with alcoholism may also be related to a larger group of addictive, compulsive, or impulsive disorders. Included in this group of disorders are substance abuse, smoking, compulsive overeating and obesity, attention deficit disorder, Tourette's syndrome, and pathological gambling.[8] The disorders seem to result from a failed linkage between cells and signaling molecules in the brain's reward system. The proposed name for a manifestation of one or more of these behavioral disorders is **reward deficiency syndrome.**[9]

People with reward deficiency syndrome suffer from sensory deprivation of the brain's pleasure mechanisms. While normal people are rewarded by a full stomach, a warm fire, or a comfortable chair, those with reward deficiency syndrome have a chemical imbalance that supplants feelings of well being with anxiety, anger, or a craving for a substance that can relieve these negative feelings. Dopamine is a neurotransmitter (a chemical substance) associated with the brain's reward system. Studies have found that a variant of the gene for the D2 dopamine receptor is more likely to occur in those who have reward deficiency syndrome. Expression of the variant is thought to result in deficient D2 dopamine receptors in the brain, causing unpleasant emotions or cravings for substances that can provide temporary relief by releasing dopamine. Alcohol, cocaine, and nicotine have been shown to cause the release of dopamine.[10] The released dopamine provides temporary relief of the reward deficiency.

Although there is now substantial evidence that genetic factors play a role in the vulnerability of certain people to alcohol, tobacco, and other drug abuse, they constitute only one set of contributing factors. There are other determinants, both inherited and environmental, that influence one's decisions about alcohol, tobacco, or other drug use (see figs. 2.1 and 2.2).

Personality Traits

In addition to the physiologically expressed genetic factors discussed previously, personality type, temperament, and attitudes and beliefs may also contribute to one's vulnerability to drug use. These factors, unique to each individual, are of interest to those who attempt to understand why particular people abuse drugs, even when they come from apparently healthy environments. However, like genetic factors, they are only partial contributors to one's overall vulnerability.

In the simplest of terms, *personality* refers to a person's skills in relating to other people. To psychologists, however, personality includes a wide range of personal characteristics. The term *addictive personality* is a product of psychoanalytical explanations of deviant human behavior that were popular in the early decades of this century.[11] Today, the term *addictive personality* has been replaced by *addictive behavior*, a term based upon observable events. **Addictive behavior** is behavior that is excessive, compulsive, and destructive psychologically and physically.[12] A person who exhibits addictive behavior is said to have an **addictive disorder**.[13]

Although one cannot predict a person's degree of vulnerability to drug dependence exclusively on the basis of personality traits and temperament, correlations have been noted between certain of these traits and the progression from drug experimentation to regular drug use, drug abuse, and eventually drug dependence. For example, it has been found that in comparison with adolescents who do not regularly use drugs, those who do, display one or more of a cluster of personality traits, including rebelliousness, resistance to authority, independence, and lowered self-esteem.[14] Further, they often have a high tolerance for deviance in others, do not value education and religion, and display low levels of competence in task performance, low degrees of obedience, and an inferior sense of diligence.[15]

Despite evidence that certain personality traits are associated with addictive behavior, controversy exists over the nature of this association. To what extent is drug abuse and dependence fostered by the presence of these personality traits? To what extent do these traits emerge during the progression from drug use to abuse and from drug abuse to dependence? Extensive studies are needed to answer these questions.

Another controversy exists over whether alcoholism and other drug dependence constitute a "disease." According to the **disease model of drug dependence**, alcoholism or other drug dependence is a primary disease over which an individual has no control and not a manifestation of some other, psychological disorder. In this model, the "victim" of the disease may require help to recover. This is the position of the well-known support group Alcoholics Anonymous. Others subscribe to the **adaptive model of drug dependence**, which posits that drug dependence results from an individual's efforts to adapt to the influences of environmental stressors (fig. 2.3).[16]

Whether viewed as a disease or as a consequence of a series of freewill choices, substance dependence constitutes a serious threat to one's health and life. Therefore, each person must take personal responsibility for his or her actions. For those who subscribe to the disease model, taking responsibility can be viewed in the context of managing one's disease, just as adult diabetics must take responsibility for their own care. For others, taking responsibility means becoming informed, learning from mistakes, and making mature and wise choices in one's life.

Ignorance and rationalization often give rise to poor choices. In the box on page 25 are several "poor choice" rationales that sometimes enable individuals to intensify their drug use. Collectively, these are referred to as **compensatory behaviors** because they are used to compensate for shortcomings in one's personality development. After reading about self-indulgence, escape, coping, naïveté, faulty compliance, and self-destruction, think about how these behaviors and their rationales contribute to one's vulnerability toward drug abuse and dependence.

reward deficiency syndrome the manifestation of one or more addictive, impulsive, or compulsive behavioral disorders, including drug abuse or dependence

addictive behavior behavior that is excessive, compulsive, and destructive psychologically and physically

addictive disorder a physical or psychological abnormality that results in a pattern of addictive behavior

disease model of drug dependence the concept that alcohol or other drug dependence is a primary disease over which an individual has no control and not the manifestation of some other, psychological disorder

adaptive model of drug dependence drug dependence that results from an individual's efforts to adapt to the influences of environmental stressors

compensatory behavior behavior that results from "poor choice" rationales used to compensate for shortcomings in one's personality development

FIGURE 2.3

Competing models of addiction: (*a*) Disease model and (*b*) adaptive model.

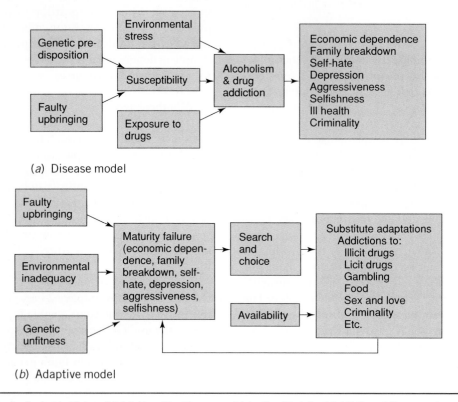

(*a*) Disease model

(*b*) Adaptive model

(Peele, S., (ed.), *Vision of Addiction: The Disease and Adaptive Models of Addiction: A Framework Evaluation,* 46–47; 1988. Lexington, MA: Lexington Books.)

Interpersonal Skills Development and Developmental Task Mastery

In addition to the personality-related aspects of vulnerability mentioned earlier, youthful drug abusers are usually deficient in **interpersonal skills.** They generally score poorly on tests that measure well-being, responsibility, social skills, tolerance, and achievement. Additionally, their level of competence in task performance, degree of obedience, and sense of diligence are lower than those of peers who do not use drugs on a regular basis. Again, the degree to which these traits existed before the onset of drug involvement is a topic of some controversy. However, some experts are convinced that certain individuals are at risk for making the transition from drug use to abuse even before they use drugs for the first time.[17]

The process of personal growth throughout the course of adulthood is supported by the successful mastery of **developmental tasks,** including independent living, social skills development, assumption of responsibility, pursuit of intimacy, and repayment of society for its past and future support.[18] People deficient in the mastery of these tasks sometimes attempt to compensate for or escape from their deficiencies through regular drug use. When regular drug use results in drug dependence, the opportunity and ability to pursue normal adult growth and development falter. Those in recovery often discover that they must still complete one or more of these developmental tasks in order to remain in recovery.

ENVIRONMENTAL FACTORS

The importance of environmental factors in drug-taking behavior cannot be overemphasized. These include influences of the **immediate environment** and those of society at large. The immediate environment includes home and family, school, peers, and community. It is usually from the people in one's immediate environment that a person first learns about drugs.

Home and Family

Studies have shown that when drug abuse begins in childhood, it is often associated with a group of home and family conditions.[19] The earlier in one's life that drug involvement begins, the greater one's vulnerability.[20] While all children can be considered vulnerable at least

DRUGS IN YOUR WORLD

Examples of Compensatory Behavior

Self-Indulgence. The term *self-indulgence* means the rewarding of oneself in ways that foster feelings of pleasure, importance, or acceptance by others. When the reward is a psychoactive drug, misuse or abuse can occur.

Cigarette smoking is a prime example. Advertising suggests that smoking offers the rewards of pleasure, acceptance, and importance. By the time smokers realize that cigarettes do not provide these rewards, dependence upon nicotine has been established, making it difficult to quit smoking.

Escape. Life is for most people only occasionally as exciting, glamorous, and fulfilling as they would like it to be. As a result, drug users seek mechanisms through which they think they can experience a world more like their expectations.

Escape through chemically induced intoxication can become the only option for a "better life." Getting drunk on alcohol or getting high on marijuana or crack are, for some, attempts to escape to a fantasy world.

Coping with Stress. Change is a reality in the lives of busy people. The rigors of school, work, and family confront people on a daily basis. For most people, these demands are met in a reasonably straightforward manner. Sharing time with friends, play, study, reflection, and physical activity are among the more familiar coping strategies.

For some people, reliance on drugs becomes a method of coping with stress. Examples include minor tranquilizers prescribed by physicians or alcohol purchased at a liquor store. It is now recognized that these chemical approaches to coping with stressful situations are temporary and nonproductive. The use of the more powerful illicit drugs reflects faulty coping carried to an extreme. When dependence on a drug is fully developed, the original stressors cease and more narrowly defined drug-related stressors

(such as maintaining an adequate drug supply) become all-encompassing.

Naïveté. Naïveté can be defined as a state in which one lacks intellectual awareness. With regard to drugs, this could be ignorance about the properties of a drug or acceptance of misinformation about the drug. For people who do not clearly understand the potential dangers of drug use, drug experimentation can quickly turn to habitual use.

For some drug users, a kind of "contrived naïveté" is used to rationalize drug use. Such statements as "If I had known how hard it is to stop using drugs, . . ." or "I never would have started if . . ." are commonly heard.

Compliance. Compliant people are those who follow the advice of experts in various fields. The strict adherence to the doctor's orders for use of a prescription medication represents the ideal concept of compliance. The use of alcohol and caffeine in a responsible manner and the discontinuation of tobacco use on the advice of a physician are further examples of positive compliant behavior.

In contrast, some people are compliant, but their compliance is toward poor information that is provided by people lacking expertise. Drug experimentation resulting from the encouragement of or pressure by peers represents compliance that is unlikely to result in improved health.

Self-Destruction. Some believe that the desire for self-destruction causes some people to abuse drugs. People who were unloved as children or who were otherwise abused or neglected may have negative feelings about themselves. They may turn to self-destructive behaviors, including the abuse of drugs.

Tragically, this symbolic death that some people intend to express through their abuse of drugs frequently becomes death in the most literal sense. Death from suicide, infectious disease, neglect, accidents, and of course, overdose can occur with drug abuse.

---

to some degree, those at greatest risk are the children whose parents exhibit poor management skills, antisocial behavior, or criminality. These families are often disorganized and have poorly defined roles for adults and children. Low educational hopes for children and a lack of family closeness also seem to contribute to the early onset of drug-taking behavior among children. Some experts believe that if these home conditions develop when the children are older, their effects upon the drug-taking behavior of the children are not as great.[21]

In some cases, heads of the family use drugs or are tolerant of use by others. A survey published in 1996

found that parents who used marijuana and whose teens know they used marijuana have teens at much higher risk

interpersonal skills communicative and behavioral skills needed to interact successfully with others

developmental tasks processes involved in developing an adult self-identity, independence, responsibility, and social skills that occur during maturation from child to adult

immediate environment home and family, school, peers, and the community

of drug use than other teens.[22] This suggests that parental ambivalence about the use of marijuana results in the absence of a clear message that marijuana use is wrong. The study also found that 40% of parents think they have little influence over their adolescent's decision whether to use drugs or not. Another troubling finding is that 46% of parents expect that their teens will try illegal drugs.[23] While parental risk factors (characteristics and views of parents) are less correlated with a teen's risk for using drugs than the teen's own individual risk factors, they are, nonetheless, important. Some of the parental risk factors are (1) no specified curfew, (2) disapproval of teen's friends, (3) parental expectation their teen will try drugs and (4) family rarely has dinner together.[24] Table 2.1 lists eight parental risk factors.

Family socialization and child-rearing methods may play a role in determining a child's vulnerability toward drug use. Although home and family life can affect one's perceptions about drug use and abuse, it is only one of many influences. Individuals from high-risk family environments may choose not to become involved with drugs, while people from apparently low-risk homes occasionally develop alcohol or other drug problems. See the self-assessment on page 28 to consider whether your family's patterns made you more vulnerable or more resistant to drug abuse.

To varying degrees, people adopt behavioral patterns that they see and admire in older family members or other people older than themselves. This purposeful incorporation of the behavioral patterns of others into one's own behavior is called **modeling.** When a person dresses, talks, or otherwise behaves like a parent, older sibling, movie star, or sports figure, modeling is occurring. Modeling can be constructive or destructive, depending upon the qualities of the behavior being modeled. It has been shown that modeling plays an important role in fostering drug abuse among adolescents.[25] For example, children who observe their parents drinking alcohol or taking other drugs get the message that this behavior is normal and appropriate for them to emulate (or model).

A negative image, while perhaps less effective than a positive image, also has the power to influence behavior. This theory has been put to use in the design of a number of drug abuse prevention posters that show very unattractive people using drugs. The idea is that the image is so unattractive that behavioral urges to experiment with drugs will be extinguished. Statements such as "My mother smoked and I hated it; I vow to never smoke," are sometimes heard. The conscious decision to exclude from one's behavior an observed behavioral pattern judged to be undesirable is called **reverse modeling.** The goal of testimonials of recovering drug abusers, whether they are athletes, entertainers, or common citizens, is to elicit reverse modeling behavior among members of the audience.

School

Outside of the home, young people spend the greatest amount of time in school. Children from disorganized or socially maladjusted families frequently have more difficulty adjusting to the organized environment of a school. Many such children lack essential academic skills, such as vocabulary development and verbal reasoning. These children, who perform poorly in the classroom and often have difficulty socially, may lose interest in school and become at risk for compensatory behavior, including drug experimentation.[26] In older students (junior/senior high school), a low level of commitment to education is related to drug use. Failure to complete homework assignments and frequent absences from school are symptomatic of social problems, including drug abuse.[27]

A chain of events has been described to explain the relationship of poor home environment and weak academic performance to drug abuse (fig. 2.4). An undesirable home environment contributes to poor school performance and poor social development. Failure at school leads to loss of self-esteem, aggressive behavior, and loss of interest in school. These factors, in turn, may foster truancy and drug experimentation during later grades. Drug problems arising from difficulties in the home and school environments may be further complicated by underlying genetic or personality factors discussed earlier in this chapter.

In contrast to the students just described, well-adjusted students may experiment with drugs without developing subsequent patterns of drug abuse behavior. This finding suggests that a subtle but important difference exists between the two groups.[28]

Peers

Conventional wisdom suggests that **peer groups** are influential in determining whether adolescents experiment with drugs. Research confirms that a clear relationship exists between peer group drug-taking behavior and the drug-taking behavior of individual members.[29] That is, if

modeling adoption of one person's behavior by another, usually younger, person

reverse modeling conscious or unconscious decision to exclude from one's own behavior an observed behavioral pattern judged undesirable

peer groups people of the same age or social status (age-mates)

TABLE 2.1 Parental Risk Factors

(attributes and attitudes of the parent and the household that increase the risk of substance abuse)

1. **There is no specified curfew for the teen.** The fact of a curfew indicates parental attention to the teen's comings and goings. It also implies a household with standards of behavior. It is the highest scoring risk factor over which a parent has direct control (13% of parents report their teens do not have a curfew; 3% don't know if their teens have a curfew).
2. **The parent disapproves of the teen's friends.** We have made the point repeatedly here that parents are not naive; this is an excellent example. If a parent does not like a teen's friends, they are probably right to be concerned. The teen is, according to our data, hanging with substance abusers and is at high risk himself or herself. The question, then, is what will the parent do to act on his or her apprehensions (13% of parents disapprove of their teen's friends)?
3. **The parent expects their teen will try drugs.** Again, if parents thinks their kid will try illegal drugs, they are probably right. Most parents know, at some level, when their kids are at risk. The issue is whether they will act on their intuitions in a purposeful manner to reduce their teen's risk of drug use, rather than hide behind a veil of nonresponsibility and inefficacy (46% of parents expect their teen to try illegal drugs).
4. **The teen's family rarely has dinner together.** It probably isn't just the fact of sitting down to dinner as a family that reduces drug use risk, but what the fact of having dinner together says about the character of the family environment. In any case, the pattern is clear: for each additional dinner a family has together in a typical week, the teen's risk score declines (29% of parents say their family has dinner together fewer than four nights a week.)
5. **The parents do not attend religious services and do not take the teen with them if they do.** It is not simply the act of going to church or synagogue several times a month, it is the code of conduct in evidence in the household that emerges from religious commitment and religion being a factor in the teen's moral formation (27% of parents do not attend religious services in a typical month). Corroborating this finding is the fact that teens who say drug abstinence by their peers occurs because drug use is morally wrong are less at risk than teens who give other responses to that question. This raises a side point: parents will be more effective as advocates of drug abstinence if they can say, with credibility, that drug use is morally flawed behavior.
6. **The parent smoked marijuana and the teen knows.** Many of today's parents of teenagers are themselves children of the sixties and seventies. Nearly half admitted to us they had tried marijuana or used it regularly, yet this finding struck us initially as counterintuitive in that we assumed parents who were hiding their youthful dalliances would have teens at greater risk than parents who admitted their drug "experimentation" forthrightly. Not so. For a teen to know (correctly) that their parent used drugs contributes substantially to their own risk score.

   Why? It appears that those parents may be conveying the message that drugs generally and marijuana specifically are benign. Plus, to concede prior use certainly can undercut the claim drug use is morally wrong. As an illustration of how prior marijuana use affects parents' perceptions of marijuana, 83% of parents who did not smoke in their youth say they would regard the use of marijuana by their teen as a "crisis," but only 58% of past regular pot users would be similarly alarmed.
7. **The parent really thinks that marijuana is benign.** If a parent does not regard marijuana as a big deal, they cannot or will not persuade their teenagers that it is a big deal. The view of marijuana as benign emerges from questions concerning its effect on health and performance.
8. **The parent feels powerless, blames drug use on others, or does not assume responsibility.** A parent must believe that he or she can make a difference. Parents who feel they have little influence over their teen's decision regarding the use of illegal drugs are probably right; it's a self-fulfilling prophecy. Parents who say parents are to blame for drug-infested schools have less at risk kids. Activism, diligence, certitude, confidence—these are the characteristics a parent needs to be successful in keeping the drug culture at bay. Most of all, they must embrace responsibility for keeping their teens off drugs in the first place.

The National Center on Addiction and Substance Abuse at Columbia University. Conducted by Luntz Research Companies: *National Survey of American Attitudes on Substance Abuse II: Teens and Their Parents, The Parental Risk Factors.* September 1996, pp. 24–25.

SELF-ASSESSMENT

Family Socialization and the Abuse of Drugs

The family is one of the most important environmental influences on drug-taking behavior. As discussed on pages 25–26, adolescents who are likely to abuse drugs often come from families who foster the abuse of drugs.

Which of the following family characteristics would minimize drug abuse? To help you consider this question further, contrasting patterns of child rearing are outlined below. As you read through this list, think about which patterns prevailed in your family as *you* were growing up.

"Traditional" or Status-Centered	**"Modern" or Person-Centered**
Each member's place in family is a function of age and sex status	Emphasis on selfhood and individuality of each member
Father is defined as boss and, more important, as agent of discipline; he receives "respect" and deference from mother and children	Father is more affectionate, less authoritative; mother becomes more important as agent of discipline
Emphasis on overt acts—what child does rather than why	Emphasis on motives and feelings—why child does what he or she does
Valued qualities of child are obedience, cleanliness	Valued qualities of child are happiness, achievement, consideration, curiosity, self-control
Emphasis on "direct" discipline: physical punishment, scolding, threats	Discipline based on reasoning, isolation, guilt, threat of loss of love
Social consensus and solidarity in communication; emphasis on "we"	Communication used to express individual experience and perspectives; emphasis on "I"
Emphasis on communication from parent to child	Emphasis on two-way communication between parent and child; parent open to persuasion
Parents feels little need to justify demands to child; commands are followed with "because I say so"	Parent gives good reasons for demands, e.g., not "Shut up" but "Please keep quiet or go into the other room; I'm trying to talk on the telephone"
Emphasis on conforming to rules, respecting authority, maintaining conventional social order	Emphasis on reasons for rules; particular rules can be criticized in the name of "higher" rational or ethical principles
Child may attain a strong sense of social identity at the cost of loss of individuality and poor academic performance	Child may attain strong sense of selfhood but may have identity problems and feel guilt, alienation

In light of your own drug use history, did your family pattern increase your vulnerability or your resistance? Which characteristics are you most likely to incorporate into the family pattern you establish if you have children? Will this pattern foster vulnerability or resistance in your children?

your friends experiment with or abuse drugs, it is likely that you too will engage in this behavior. Interestingly, it also has been shown that one's perceptions of the drinking behavior of close friends is a strong predictor of certain aspects of adolescent alcohol use.[30]

In addition to the perceptions of friends' involvement with alcohol or other drugs, one's self-image can affect one's vulnerability to drug involvement. Adolescents who perceived themselves as unattractive in the eyes of their peers were found to be four times more likely to abuse drugs than their counterparts who felt adequately attractive. When the basis for this perception of unattractive-ness was being underweight, the risk of drug abuse was even higher.[31] Clearly, self-perception and peer group approval are important determinants of drug abuse.

Young people who display a greater-than-normal orientation toward the values of their peers, relative to those of their families, are more likely to opt for drug experimentation if their peers use drugs. When friends serve as models for drug-related, peer-based drug prevention programs, such as Students Against Driving Drunk, in high schools and colleges, it is evidence for the strength of peer influence on drug-using behavior. Peers can influence people in both positive and negative directions.

FIGURE 2.4

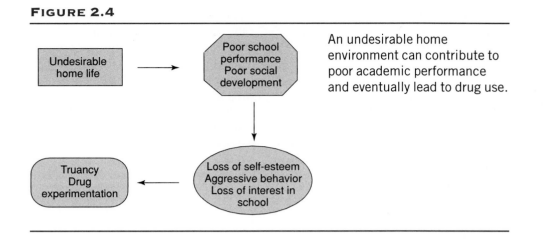

An undesirable home environment can contribute to poor academic performance and eventually lead to drug use.

Community

One's community is an important influencing factor in a person's decisions about drugs because communities set the norms for the behavior of their citizens. For example, it is up to the local community to limit the availability and supply of drugs in the community. Communities can do this by restricting the sale of tobacco and alcohol to minors, enacting local zoning laws to limit the number and location of liquor stores and bars, and enforcing federal, state, and local drug laws. Communities that are lax in these areas are guilty of **institutional enabling,** encouraging continued abuse of alcohol, tobacco, and other drugs. Descriptions of successful community-based drug prevention programs will be presented and discussed in chapters 18, 19, and 20.

INFLUENCES OF CULTURE, ECONOMICS, AND MODERN SOCIETY

Societal norms and expectations are another set of forces that influence behavior. Such factors as the youth subculture, advertising and promotion, legislation, economics, and advanced technology in our society all influence decisions about drug abuse.

Youth Subculture

Because most states mandate formal education until the age of 16 to 18 years, young people are kept apart from the general population for much of their waking hours. As a result, they are members of an American subculture often called the *youth subculture.* This subculture has its own expectations, roles, and standards, as well as its own language, dress code, and behavior.

Although drug misuse and abuse are not limited to a single age group, drug use prevalence rates among 12 to 17 year olds have increased significantly in the past three years. In 1992, just over 6% of young people in this age group had used an illicit drug in the past month; in 1995, nearly 11% had (see table 1.2).[32]

One attempt to explain the processes that occur during the development of one's final status as a drug user is based on the concept of entry or gateway drugs. **Gateway drugs** are easily obtainable legal or illegal drugs (alcohol, tobacco, or marijuana) that serve as the drug user's first experience with a mind-altering drug. The concept of gateway drugs arose from a study of New York high school students in the 1970s. The study found that the majority of these adolescents who eventually took illegal drugs had first engaged in the use of legal drugs, such as beer, wine, tobacco, and hard liquor. Of those few who eventually used illegal drugs, almost all smoked marijuana before using any other illegal drug. Only 1% of students who used an illegal drug other than marijuana, such as heroin or cocaine, had not first used a legal drug and then marijuana.[33] Later studies have essentially confirmed this phenomenon. In one study, for example, of the high school seniors who used crack cocaine, only 10% used it before they had first tried marijuana.[34]

Another report found that 89% of those individuals who use cocaine first used all three gateway substances (cigarettes, alcohol, and marijuana), and 99.9% of individuals who use cocaine first used a gateway drug.[35] Also, 90% of children and adults who use marijuana first

institutional enabling failure of official or unofficial community organizations to discourage alcohol, tobacco, and other drug misuse and abuse

gateway drugs easily obtainable legal or illegal drugs (alcohol, tobacco, and marijuana) that represent the drug user's first experience with a mind-altering drug

smoked cigarettes or drank alcohol and "children 12–17 years old who use marijuana are 85 times more likely, who drink are 50 times more likely, and who smoke are 19 times more likely, to use cocaine than children who have never used those substances."[36] The report also found that the younger children begin with gateway drugs, the more likely they are to use cocaine, heroin, hallucinogens and other illicit drugs. For example, "60% of children who smoke pot before age 15 move on to cocaine; only 20% of those who smoke pot after age 17 use cocaine."[37]

Figure 2.5 suggests that there are several paths to cocaine use. Fifty-two percent of all cocaine users began their drug use by smoking cigarettes first, then drank alcohol and used marijuana before using cocaine. Sixty-five percent first smoked cigarettes or drank alcohol and then used marijuana before using cocaine. While this chart does not show every possible combination of gateway drug use, 89% of all cocaine users first used all three gateway drugs before using cocaine.[38] As you can see, it would be extremely rare for someone to use cocaine who had not first used at least one of the gateway drugs.

FIGURE 2.5

Paths to cocaine use.

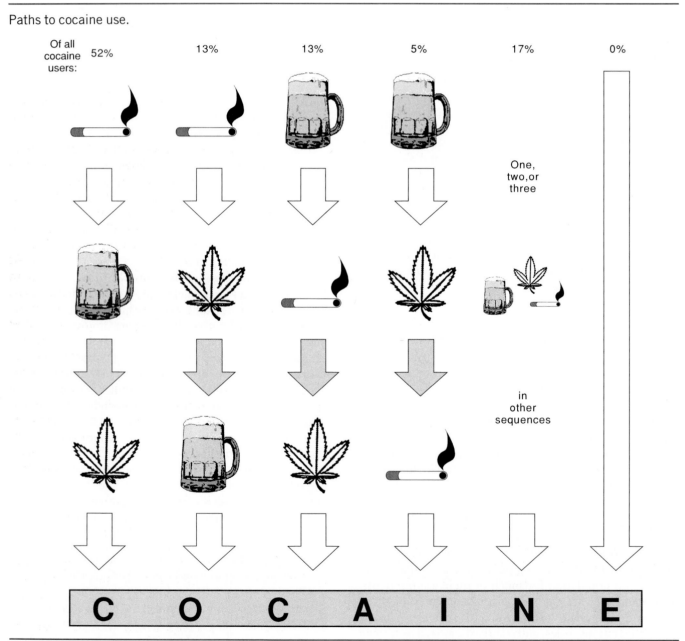

These percentages have been rounded to the nearest whole number.

(Center on Addiction and Substance Abuse at Columbia University, Cigarettes, Alcohol, Marijuana: Gateways to Illicit Drug Use, October, 1994, New York, N.Y.).

Recently, much concern has been expressed over tobacco as a gateway drug. Studies have shown that 82% of adults who ever smoked had their first cigarette before age 18, and more than half of them had become regular smokers by that age.[39] Reports such as this have led the United States Food and Drug Administration (FDA) to look for ways to limit youth access to tobacco.[40]

While national surveys indicate that the highest incidence of illegal drug abuse occurs in the 18- to 24-year-old age group, there is cause for concern. As stated, the prevalence of reported illicit drug use in the past month increased more rapidly in the 12- to 17-year-old group between 1992 and 1995 than in any other age group (see table 1.2). Among eighth graders, annual prevalence of marijuana use (use in the past 12 months) tripled from 6% in 1991 to 18% in 1996.[41] Experts are concerned because patterns of behavior established in youth often continue into later life.

Advertising and Promotion

The advertising industry is well aware of the power of certain images to entice modeling behavior by people of all ages but particularly the young. Images of rich and attractive people appear on television and print media in an effort to alter the viewer's behavior. The goal is to get the viewer to model the behavior they see in these advertisements. The marketing of alcohol and tobacco products in this manner is perhaps the best example of the use of attractive images in advertising to induce modeling behavior. "Beautiful people" are depicted enjoying industry products in pleasant surroundings that some viewers can only hope to experience at some future time. Well-known celebrities participate in concerts and athletic events sponsored by the alcohol and tobacco industries. Company logos are seen on every item that appears on television, including the clothing and equipment of the participants, outfield walls, scoreboards, and race cars. Clearly, the marketing departments of these firms and the advertising industry in general understand the power of modeling in influencing behavior.

Until recently, the mandated removal of cigarette advertisements from television in the early 1970s remained the clearest example of the "respect" that health authorities have for the power of media modeling, but tobacco companies are resourceful. Print advertising has overcome the loss of television advertising, and these ads have been successful in reaching our youth. For example, teens are twice as likely as adults to smoke the three most heavily advertised brands of cigarettes (Marlboro, Camel, and Newport).[42] As a result, in August 1995, the FDA proposed new regulations restricting the sale and distribution of cigarettes and smokeless tobacco to protect children and adolescents.[43] The final regulations were issued in August 1996.

Briefly, the final regulation generally limits tobacco advertising in all existing forms to a black-and-white, text-only format. Outdoor advertising is prohibited within 1,000 feet of public playgrounds, elementary schools or secondary schools. Advertisements in publications read primarily by adults and advertisements placed in adult-only locations are exempt from any advertising restrictions.

Tobacco companies will not be permitted to sell or distribute promotional items such as tee shirts, caps, and sporting goods identified with tobacco products, for example through use of a brand name or logo. Similarly, logos, brand names, and other identifiers of tobacco products cannot be used in sponsorship of musical, cultural, and other events or on teams and entries. However, sponsored events and entries in the name of a tobacco company may continue.[44]

Economics

Today, in some areas of the country, both urban and rural, there are declining opportunities for employment. Many families are experiencing a loss of income, and for some, this leads to marital instability. Approximately 31% of all children (67% of African-American children) under the age of 18 grow up in single-parent homes,[45] many with limited income. Many children grow up in homes where they are abused or neglected.

Drug abuse and drug dealing are all too common responses to harsh conditions of economic deprivation. Imagine, for example, the problems of a 17-year-old teenager who has been kicked out of the home and onto the street to survive. Suppose this young person must choose between making $750 per day selling drugs or $5.00 per hour flipping hamburgers? Suppose further that this person is the sole or primary provider for younger brothers and sisters. This teenager might be tempted to deal drugs, at least temporarily, to provide food, shelter, or other care for younger siblings. He or she soon becomes accustomed to a lifestyle in which there is more money than was ever expected. Younger children in the neighborhood now show respect; it becomes difficult for the teenager to return to a lifestyle below the poverty level. This scenario illustrates how economic deprivation can influence drug use.

On the other hand, wealth can foster thrill seeking that may include drug experimentation. The prevalence of drug abuse among certain highly paid professional athletes and entertainers attests to the fact that wealth is not a protective factor for drug abuse. High school teachers report that some of their students routinely carry more money than is necessary for everyday expenses. This behavior is evidence that some of our youth have the means to purchase drugs. The availability of drugs in this atmosphere represents an enticing and dangerous situation in which drug experimentation and abuse can easily occur.

Modern Society

Certain aspects of our contemporary society make drug taking easier and more socially acceptable than in the past. Two such aspects are the concept of self-care and our reliance on technology.

Self-Care. A form of drug experimentation practiced by young and old alike often occurs when a person is suffering from illness. In the past decade, a self-care movement has become solidly established in this country. Americans self-diagnose and self-prescribe a wide variety of medications without consulting either a doctor or a pharmacist.

The medications most often used in self-care are the over-the-counter (OTC) products with which the consumer can often obtain relief for almost any day-to-day health concern. Although drugs that relieve pain, congestion, diarrhea, and constipation are still the mainstay of the OTC market, consumers can now purchase an ever-growing variety of products. While OTC products are seldom harmful when used according to their directions, many do contain ingredients that hold the potential for misuse and abuse.

Misuse of prescription medications can result in serious health consequences more quickly than the misuse of OTC drugs. Misuse of prescription medications occurs when individuals discontinue use too early, use previously prescribed medications to treat a self-diagnosed condition, or use medications prescribed for another person. It also occurs when people, especially the elderly, forget whether they took their medication and take extra doses unintentionally or take the wrong medicine in the dark. Certain types of prescription medications, such as those that alter mood (for example, barbiturates and amphetamines), are subject to greater abuse than others.

The attitude of self-care extends to social and illicit drugs. Alcoholics frequently prescribe drinks for themselves, and smokers (nicotine addicts) smoke to feel better (gain relief from nicotine withdrawal). Heroin addicts undergoing withdrawal illness become "sick" and take the cure (more heroin).

Reliance on Technology. For people of any age, drug misuse can occur in the context of attempting to maintain health. Americans have great faith and high expectations that scientific research and technological advances will provide answers for their health problems. These expectations are a result, in part, of the marvelous medical advances of the recent past, such as life-saving antibiotics and vaccines. Sensational announcements in newspapers about modern drugs give Americans every reason to believe that these advances will continue to occur at a rapid pace.

One of the unfortunate results of these technological advances is that Americans have come to expect a life without problems or pain, one in which relief from all health problems is immediate and easy. Evidence of these expectations can be observed in drug-taking behavior. People take aspirin or ibuprofen at the first sign of a headache, cold medicine when they sneeze, and laxatives at the first hint of irregularity. Many are not shy about asking their physician for stronger medicines, such as pain relievers and sedatives, when there are other solutions that would be better choices. A few will even change doctors in order to obtain a desired prescription drug. These people, with unrealistic expectations about modern medicine and the role of drugs, are at risk for developing a drug dependence problem.

In spite of the influencing factors that could, and often do, lead to drug use, people must take responsibility for their own lives to the extent that they are able. This means making the best possible choices about their drug-taking behavior, with particular attention paid to avoiding drug misuse and abuse that could result in dependence.

Unfortunately, drug abuse and dependence do occur, and occur all too often. In chapter 1, we discussed the costs of drug abuse and dependence in terms of lives and dollars. It is only natural, for both moral and economic reasons, that many public and private organizations are involved in drug abuse prevention activities. We will now introduce the four essential elements of prevention—education, treatment, public policy, and law enforcement. We expand our discussion of these elements in chapters 18, 19, and 20.

ELEMENTS OF DRUG ABUSE PREVENTION

Prevention can be considered "the sum of our actions to ensure healthy, safe and productive lives for all Americans."[46] Prevention of drug abuse and dependence has many benefits, including (1) saving lives, (2) containing health care costs, and (3) reducing social costs, such as those stemming from violence, crime, unemployment, and lost productivity.[47]

The four major elements of alcohol, tobacco, and other drug abuse prevention are (1) education, (2) treatment, (3) public policy, and (4) law enforcement. Education and treatment have as their primary goal a reduction in the demand for drugs. Public policy and law enforcement are aimed primarily at reducing the supply of drugs. To be truly effective, a drug abuse prevention program must be comprehensive, that is, it must incorporate several or all of the elements listed.

From a public health standpoint, preventing drug abuse and dependence involves primary, secondary, and tertiary prevention strategies. The concept of prevention can be best understood when it is viewed as occurring at three different levels. **Primary prevention** includes measures aimed at preventing the onset of drug use. **Secondary prevention** involves detection, screening, intervention, and treatment of early drug abuse so that those who are just beginning to use drugs can avoid further use. **Tertiary prevention** includes treatment and rehabilitation of people with more serious or chronic drug problems so that they will no longer need or want drugs.

As discussed in the first part of this chapter, a variety of individual and environmental risk factors increase one's vulnerability to drug abuse. The more risk factors present in a person, the greater his or her vulnerability. A comprehensive drug abuse prevention program combines primary, secondary, and tertiary prevention strategies to limit these risk factors and thus reduce vulnerability. Primary prevention strategies (aimed at forestalling the initiation of drug use) promote protective factors by distributing information through media campaigns; character-building efforts, such as the YMCA, Boy Scouts, and Girl Scouts; and educational programs, particularly those aimed at children. Secondary prevention strategies involve early detection and intervention, before the effects of drug abuse become severe. Alternative programs, such as alcohol-free parties, and intervention approaches, such as ToughLove, are examples of secondary prevention measures. Tertiary prevention strategies aim to encourage recovery from drug dependence and maintenance of drug-free lifestyles. Treatment, including detoxification and counseling, and relapse prevention programs, such as support groups, are examples of tertiary prevention measures.

Education

Education is the process of not only providing knowledge and skills but also changing beliefs and behavior. Drug abuse prevention education is aimed at limiting the demand for drugs by providing information about drugs of abuse, changing attitudes and beliefs about drugs, providing the skills necessary to abstain from using drugs, and ultimately changing drug abuse behavior.

Drug abuse prevention education is a crucial element of any comprehensive, community-based drug abuse prevention program. To be effective, drug abuse prevention education must target people of all ages, those who are in school and those who are not. The message must be clear and consistent throughout the entire community. More information about drug abuse prevention education is presented in chapter 18.

Treatment

Treatment is the act of providing medical and/or psychological care to someone with an injury, illness, or disorder. Treatment of drug abuse or dependence can occur through a variety of approaches in either inpatient or outpatient settings. One of the keys to providing the appropriate treatment in the correct setting is an accurate diagnosis. Among the most widely used criteria for the diagnosis of drug dependence and abuse are those published by the American Psychiatric Association.[48] These are reproduced in the box on page 34.

Treatment for drug dependence normally involves a progression through three stages. These are detoxification, active treatment, and aftercare.[49] Treatment will be discussed in chapter 18.

Public Policy

Public policy comprises the principles and courses of action pursued by governments to solve practical problems affecting society. With respect to drug abuse prevention, public policy includes the enactment of drug laws and zoning ordinances, the regulation of advertising and labeling of legal drugs, and the regulation of over-the-counter and prescription drugs. Public policy also has to do with what proportion of the federal, state, or local government's budget will be used to address drug problems. Public policy plays a major role in drug abuse prevention. Public policy will be the subject of chapter 20.

Law Enforcement

Law enforcement is the application of federal, state, and local laws to arrest, jail, bring to trial, convict, and sentence those who break laws. The goal of drug law enforcement is to control the supply of illegal drugs by interrupting the source, transit, and distribution of drugs. Law enforcement will be discussed in chapter 19.

prevention the sum of all efforts to reduce drug abuse and dependence

primary prevention measures aimed at preventing the onset of drug use

secondary prevention detection, screening, intervention, and treatment of early drug abuse to avoid further use

tertiary prevention treatment and rehabilitation of people with more serious or chronic drug problems so they no longer need or want drugs

education the process of providing knowledge, changing attitudes and beliefs, and altering behavior

treatment the act of providing medical and/or psychological care to someone with an injury, illness, or disorder

public policy principles and courses of action pursued by governments to solve practical problems that affect society

law enforcement the application of federal, state, and local laws to arrest, jail, bring to trial, and sentence those who break laws

DRUGS IN YOUR WORLD

Psychiatric Diagnosis of Substance Disorders

Diagnostic Criteria for Substance Dependence

A maladaptive pattern of substance use, leading to clinically significant impairment or distress, as manifested by three (or more) of the following, occurring at any time in the same 12-month period:

1. Tolerance, as defined by either of the following:
   a. A need for markedly increased amounts of the substance to achieve intoxication or desired effect
   b. Markedly diminished effect with continued use of the same amount of the substance
2. Withdrawal, as manifested by either of the following:
   a. The characteristic withdrawal syndrome for the substance
   b. The same (or closely related) substance is taken to relieve or avoid withdrawal symptoms
3. The substance is often taken in larger amounts or over a longer period than was intended
4. There is a persistent desire or unsuccessful effort to cut down or control substance use
5. A great deal of time is spent in activities necessary to obtain the substance
6. Important social, occupational, or recreational activities are given up or reduced because of substance use
7. The substance use is continued despite knowledge of having a persistent or recurrent physical or psychological problem that is likely to have been caused or exacerbated by the substance

Diagnostic Criteria for Substance Abuse

1. A maladaptive pattern of substance use leading to clinically significant impairment or distress, as manifested by one (or more) of the following, occurring within a 12-month period:
   a. Recurrent substance use resulting in failure to fulfill major role obligations at work, school, or home
   b. Recurrent substance use in situations in which it is physically hazardous
   c. Recurrent substance-related legal problems
   d. Continued substance use despite having persistent or recurrent social or interpersonal problems caused or exacerbated by the effects of the substance
2. The symptoms have never met the criteria for Substance Dependence for this class of substance[a]

[a]American Psychiatric Association, *Diagnostic and Statistical Manual of Mental Disorders,* 4th ed. (Washington, D.C.: The Association, 1994).

SUMMARY

The determinants of drug abuse and dependence include those factors associated with the individual, including genetic factors, personality traits, attitudes and beliefs, and interpersonal skills, factors associated with one's family, peer group, school, and community environment, and factors associated with American culture and society.

The terms *vulnerability* and *resistance* are used to describe the concept that individuals are differentially at risk for engaging in drug use and abuse. Evidence of genetic vulnerability toward drug abuse includes the discovery that one genetic variant occurs more frequently in people with addictive, impulsive, and compulsive behavioral disorders than in normal populations. The proposed term for the manifestation of these disorders is *reward deficiency syndrome.*

Proponents of the disease model of drug dependence consider alcohol or other drug dependence to be a primary disease, not a symptom of some other, underlying disorder. Proponents of the adaptive model view drug dependence as a result of an individual's effort to adapt to influences and stressors in the environment.

Gateway drugs are easily attainable legal or illegal drugs that provide the user with a first experience with a mind-altering drug. The primary gateway drugs are tobacco, alcohol, and marijuana. Modeling, the conscious or unconscious incorporation of someone else's behavioral pattern into one's own behavior, is a powerful force in drug use by young people. Reverse modeling is the conscious or unconscious exclusion of someone else's behavioral patterns from one's own behavior.

Americans of all ages willingly participate in self-care. Many believe that there are new drugs and technological advances to solve every real or imagined health problem. This view may contribute to drug overuse, misuse, and even abuse and dependence.

The four major elements of drug abuse prevention are education, treatment, public policy, and law enforcement. Prevention can be thought of as primary, secondary, and tertiary. Comprehensive drug abuse prevention education is aimed at limiting the demand for drugs by providing information, changing attitudes and beliefs, and providing skills necessary to abstain from drugs.

Drug abuse treatment, the care given to someone with a drug dependence disorder, can occur in different settings and employ a variety of approaches. The stages of drug abuse treatment are detoxification, active treatment, and aftercare.

Public policy and law enforcement are activities aimed at reducing the supply of drugs. Public policy comprises principles and actions by governments aimed at solving societal problems. Law enforcement is the application of laws to arrest, jail, and prosecute those who break laws.

REVIEW QUESTIONS

1. Define the terms *vulnerability* and *resistance* as they relate to drug abuse.
2. List ten "risk factors" and ten "protective factors" for drug abuse.
3. What is the state of our current understanding of genetic predisposition to drug misuse and abuse?
4. What is reward deficiency syndrome?
5. List at least four personality traits that are most strongly associated with drug abuse.
6. Explain the disease model of drug dependence.
7. Describe the role that drug abuse can play in each of the following: self-indulgence, escape, naïveté, coping with stress, compliance, and self-destructive behavior.
8. Describe the manner in which home and family, school, and peer groups function as immediate environmental influences that encourage or discourage drug-taking behavior among adolescents.
9. Explain *institutional enabling* and give some examples.
10. What is the basis of the gateway drug theory?
11. Explain the difference between modeling and reverse modeling.
12. In what ways can economic conditions foster drug use?
13. Describe how the self-care movement and aggressive marketing tactics have encouraged drug misuse and abuse.
14. Your textbook suggests that our growing reliance on technology has contributed to drug misuse and abuse. How has this occurred?
15. Name the four main elements of drug abuse prevention. Which are aimed primarily at demand reduction? Which are aimed primarily at supply reduction?
16. Define drug abuse prevention education.
17. Define the terms *public policy* and *law enforcement*.

REFERENCES

1. Glantz, M., and R. Pickens, "Vulnerability to Drug Abuse: Introduction and Overview," *Vulnerability to Drug Abuse*, eds. M. Glantz and R. Pickens (Washington, D.C.: American Psychological Association, 1992).
2. Clayton, R. R., " Transitions in Drug Use: Risk and Protective Factors," *Vulnerability to Drug Abuse*, eds. M. Glantz and R. Pickens (Washington, D.C.: American Psychological Association, 1992).
3. U.S. Department of Health and Human Services, *Alcohol and Health: Seventh Special Report to the U.S. Congress*, DHHS Pub. No. (ADM) 90-1656 (Washington, D.C.: U.S. Government Printing Office, 1990).
4. Schuckit, M. A., *Genetics and the Specific Dimensions of Risk for Alcoholism*, National Institute on Drug Abuse Research Monograph, no. 81 (1987); Pickens, R. W., and D. S. Svikis, "Genetic Vulnerability to Drug Abuse," National Institute on Drug Abuse Research Monograph, no. 89, (1988); Comings, D., "Genetic Factors in Drug Abuse and Dependence," in *Individual Differences in the Biobehavioral Etiology of Drug Abuse*, eds. H. W. Gordon and M. D. Glantz, National Institute on Drug Abuse, Research Monograph, no. 159, (1996).
5. Schuckit, M. A., "Genetics and the Risk for Alcoholism," *JAMA* 254 no. 18 (1985): 2614; Schuckit, M. A., S. C. Risch, and E. O. Gold, "Alcohol Consumption, ACTH Level, and Family History of Alcoholism," *Am J Psychiatry* 145 no. 11 (1988):1391.
6. Purvis, A., "DNA and the Desire to Drink," *Time*, 30 April, 1990, p. 88.
7. Blum, K., J. G. Cull, E. R. Braverman, and D. E. Comings, "Reward Deficiency Syndrome," *Amer. Scientist* 84 (1996):132–145.
8. Ibid.
9. Ibid.
10. Ibid.
11. Cox, W. M., *The Encyclopedia of Psychoactive Drugs: The Addictive Personality* (New York: Chelsea House (1986).
12. Ibid.
13. Fleming, M. F., and K. L. Barry, *Addictive Disorders* (St. Louis: Mosby-Year Book, Inc., 1992).
14. Hawkins, J. D., D. M. Lishner, and R. F. Catalano, *Childhood Predictors and the Prevention of Adolescent Substance Abuse*, National Institute on Drug Abuse Research Monograph, no. 56 (DHHS Pub. no. (ADM) 87-1335, Rockville, MD, 1985).

15. Ibid.
16. Alexander, B. K., "The Disease and Adaptive Models of Addiction: A Framework Evaluation, *Visions of Addiction*, ed. S. Peele (Lexington, Mass.: Lexington Books, 1988).
17. Glantz and Pickens, "Vulnerability to Drug Abuse."
18. Payne, W. A., and D. B. Hahn, *Understanding Your Health*, 3 ed. St. Louis, MO: Mosby, 1995.
19. Hawkins, Lishner, and Catalano, *Childhood Predictors*.
20. Glantz and Pickens, "Vulnerability to Drug Abuse."
21. Hawkins, Lishner, and Catalano, *Childhood Predictors*.
22. The National Center on Addiction and Substance Abuse at Columbia University, *National Survey of American Attitudes on Substance Abuse II: Teens and Their Parents*, CASA, 152 West 57th Street, New York, NY, 1996.
23. Ibid.
24. Ibid.
25. Baumrind, D., *Familial Antecedents of Adolescent Drug Use: A Developmental Perspective.* National Institute on Drug Abuse Research Monograph, no. 56 (DHHS pub. no. (ADM) 87-1335. Rockville, MD, 1985).
26. Loeber, R. T., and J. Dishion, "Early Predictors of Male Delinquency: A Review," *Psychol Bull* 93 (1983):68.
27. Hawkins, Lishner, and Catalano, *Childhood Predictors*.
28. Shore, M. F., *Correlates and Concepts: Are We Chasing our Tail*, National Institute on Drug Abuse Research Monograph, no. 56 (DHHS pub. no. (ADM) 87-1335. Rockville, MD, 1985).
29. Cox, *Encyclopedia of Psychoactive Drugs*.
30. Wilks, J., V. J. Callan, and D. A. Austin, "Parent, Peer and Personal Determinants of Adolescent Drinking," *Br J of Addic* 84 (1989):619.
31. Page, R. M., "Perceived Physical Attractiveness and Frequency of Substance Use Among Male and Female Adolescents," *J Alcohol and Drug Educ* 38 no. 2 (1993): 81.
32. *National Household Survey on Drug Abuse: Population Estimates, 1994*, DHHS Publ. No. (SMA) 95-3063 (Rockville, Md.: Office of Applied Studies, SAMHSA, 1994.)
33. Kandel, D., and R. Faust, "Sequences and Stages in the Patterns of Adolescent Drug Use." *Arch. Gen. Psychiatry* 32 (1975):923–29.
34. Kandel, D., and K. Yamaguchi, "From Beer to Crack: Developmental Patterns of Drug Involvement," *Amer. J. Public Health* 83 no. 6 (1993): 851–55.
35. Center on Addiction and Substance Abuse at Columbia University, *Cigarettes, Alcohol, Marijuana: Gateways to Illicit Drug Use*, CASA, 152 West 57th Street, New York, N.Y., 1994.
36. Ibid.
37. Ibid.
38. Ibid.
39. Centers for Disease Control and Prevention, *Preventing Tobacco Use Among Young People: A report of the Surgeon General* (Washington, D.C.: U.S. Government Printing Office, 1994).
40. U.S. Food and Drug Administration, DHHS, *The Regulations Restricting the Sale and Distribution of Cigarettes and Smokeless Tobacco to Protect Children and Adolescents*, Executive Summary, Rockville, Md., 23 August, 1996.
41. "Cigarette Smoking Continues to Rise among American Teen-Ages in 1996," The University of Michigan, News and Information Services, Press Release, 19 December, 1996, Ann Arbor, Mich.
42. Ibid.
43. Centers for Disease Control and Prevention, "Changes in the Cigarette Brand Preferences of Adolescent Smokers—United States, 1989–1993." MMWR, 43 no. 32 (1994): 577–81.
44. U.S. Food and Drug Administration, "Regulations Restricting."
45. U.S. Department of Commerce, Bureau of the Census, *Statistical Abstract of the United States 1995*, 115 ed. (Washington, D.C.: U.S. Government Printing Office, 1995).
46. *Prevention Works: A Discussion Paper on Preventing Alcohol, Tobacco and Other Drug Problems*, Rockville, Md.: Center for Substance Abuse Prevention, DHHS, PHS, SAMHSA, 1993.
47. Ibid.
48. American Psychiatric Association, *Diagnostic and Statistical Manual of Mental Disorders*, 4th ed. (Washington, D.C.: The Association, 1994).
49. Ray, O., and C. Ksir, *Drugs, Society and Human Behavior*, (St. Louis, Mo.: Mosby, 1996).

SOURCES FOR HELP

National Drug Information Center of Families in Action, Inc.
2296 Henderson Mill Rd., Suite 204
Atlanta, GA 30345
(404) 934–6364

National Federation of Parents for a Drug-Free Youth
P.O. Box 3878
St. Louis, MO 63122
(314) 968–1322

Parents' Resource Institute for Drug Education
   (PRIDE)
50 Hunt Plaza, Suite 210
Atlanta, GA 30303
(404) 577–4500

Smart Moves
Boys Clubs of America
771 First Ave.
New York, NY 10017
(212) 351–5900

World Youth Against Drugs (WYAD)
100 Edgewood Ave., Suite 1216
Atlanta, GA 30303
(800) 241–9746

ToughLove
Doylestown, PA
(215) 348–7090

National Institute on Alcohol and Drug Abuse Hot
   Line
(800) 662–HELP

National Federation of State High School
   Associations
Target Program
Kansas City, MO
(816) 464–5400

NEUROPHYSIOLOGY: HOW DRUGS AFFECT THE NERVOUS SYSTEM

CHAPTER OBJECTIVES

After studying this chapter, you will be able to:

1. Describe the general organization and function of the nervous system and explain the difference between the central nervous system and the peripheral nervous system.

2. Outline the major components of the central nervous system.

3. Describe the major anatomical parts of the brain and some of their functions.

4. Explain the role of the spinal cord as a passageway for the flow of information between the brain and the peripheral nervous system.

5. Outline the division of the peripheral nervous system into the voluntary and involuntary nervous systems.

6. Explain how the division of the peripheral nervous system into the sympathetic and parasympathetic branches enables the body to respond appropriately to environmental stimuli.

7. Describe the structure and function of the nervous system at the cellular level.

8. Explain three major ways that psychoactive drugs can affect the transmission of information between nerve cells.

From cellular telephones to highly sophisticated military networks, our society depends on communication systems that can distribute information quickly and accurately. In the human body, this task is accomplished by the nervous system, a complex communication network. Specific lines and networks allow an exchange of electrical messages within the body and permit the body to respond to both the internal and the external environment. The control center for most of this activity is the brain. This chapter explores the organization, structure, and function of the nervous system and describes in a general way how drugs alter the functioning of this complex system.

Human behavior is the outwardly observable evidence of nervous system function. A response is generated when internal or external stimuli are received by sensory receptors (such as the eyes or ears), transmitted to the brain for interpretation, and transformed into mental or physical activity. Activity observable by others is termed *behavior.*

The continuously healthy functioning of the nervous system allows individuals to monitor their environment and respond appropriately. The tendency of the body's physiological system to maintain internal stability is called **homeostasis.** This homeostatic mechanism results from the coordinated response of the parts of the physiological system to any situation or stimulus that disturbs its normal condition. Psychoactive drugs that affect brain chemistry disrupt homeostasis by altering the accuracy of monitoring, interpretation, and response to internal and external stimuli. When homeostasis is disrupted, illness or death can result.

GENERAL ORGANIZATION OF THE NERVOUS SYSTEM

The nervous system is organized into two subsystems, the central nervous system (CNS) and the peripheral nervous system (PNS). The nervous system functions like a two-way communication system: information from outside the CNS is transmitted to it by the PNS. Responses to these stimuli are transmitted back to the PNS from the CNS.

Central Nervous System

The **central nervous system (CNS)** is made up of all the nerve cells (neurons) of the brain and spinal cord, which are discussed in the sections that follow. For more information about the nervous system, see appendix B.

Brain. The single most familiar and important anatomical structure of the nervous system is the **brain.** The brain contains some 100 billion nerve cells, or neurons,

and about 900 billion glia, or non-conducting support cells.[1] This highly complex organ monitors, analyzes, and interprets stimuli. The brain controls human behavior. No computer has been developed that coordinates so completely the many functions that can be performed by the human brain.

The brain is located entirely within the skull. Through its connection with the spinal cord, the brain acts with the PNS to monitor and control the body. The sensory organs (such as the eyes, ears, and skin) supply the brain with information from outside the body. Sensory cells within the body supply information about the body's internal environment, such as levels of chemicals within the blood. The brain processes and interprets both internal and external information.

The structures and functions of the brain are complex and have long been the subject of intense investigation. The following overview should help you understand some of the effects of drugs on the brain and, thus, on human behavior. This overview is not meant to be a technical or in-depth explanation, although some of the terms may be new to you.

There are four major structures of the brain.[2] From the top and proceeding downward, they are the cerebrum, diencephalon, cerebellum, and the brain stem (fig. 3.1). The brainstem is attached to the spinal cord, which lies outside of the skull.

The **cerebrum,** sometimes referred to as the *upper brain,* consists of two halves, the right and left cerebral hemispheres. Among the functions associated with the cerebrum are vision, hearing, speech, sensory perception, memory, emotional states, and higher intellectual function. There is little doubt that psychoactive drugs affect the cerebrum, but because of the complexity of this part of the brain, understanding these effects is difficult. We know that depressant drugs, such as alcohol, slow the functioning of some portions of the cerebrum, while stimulants increase activity.

The central area of the brain enclosed by the cerebral hemispheres and lying above the brainstem is called the **diencephalon.** In this critical region are found several

---

homeostasis the tendency of the body's physiological system to maintain internal stability

central nervous system (CNS) the brain and spinal cord

brain the portion of the central nervous system enclosed in the skull; includes the cerebrum, diencephalon, cerebellum, and brainstem

cerebrum the uppermost part of the brain, consisting of two halves, the right and left cerebral hemispheres; the center for higher intellectual thought

diencephalon the portion of the brain that lies above the brainstem and is enclosed by the cerebral hemisphere

FIGURE 3.1

Cross-section of the human brain, with major areas identified.

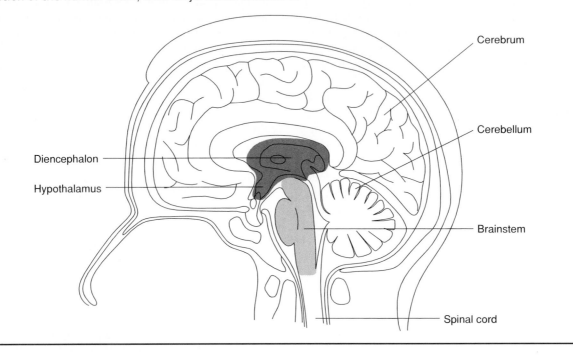

structures that coordinate the distinctively human thoughts of the cerebrum with the vital functions in the brainstem below. Major structures of the diencephalon are the thalamus, the hypothalamus, and the limbic system.

The **cerebellum,** the second largest part of the brain, is located below the posterior portion of the cerebrum and is connected to the brainstem. The cerebellum coordinates movement with spatial judgment. The effects of certain drugs on the cerebellum become evident when people stagger and lose coordination after taking these drugs. Alcohol is one such drug.

The **brainstem,** which lies below the diencephalon and connects the rest of the brain with the spinal cord, is a passageway for information from the spinal cord to the diencephalon, the cerebrum, and the cerebellum. Parts of the brainstem have control over basic physiological functions, such as respiration, heart rate, and sleeping/waking. Complex networks of nerve fibers pass through the brainstem and extend to the cerebrum. Narcotic drugs, which depress respiration, do so in part by affecting parts of the brainstem.

Spinal Cord.   The **spinal cord** serves as the passageway for information between the brain and most portions of the PNS. A second function of the spinal cord is the conduction of spinal reflexes. This is accomplished by an arrangement of neurons called the **reflex arc.**[3] When an individual touches something hot, receptors of sensory neurons are stimulated. Information is transmitted to the spinal cord, where a motor neuron (a neuron that can cause a muscle to contract) is excited. Electrical messages return from motor neurons to muscle cells, which then contract. Thus, the reflex arc of the spinal cord permits the rapid withdrawal of the hand, perhaps before severe burning occurs. This movement takes place at almost the same time the brain registers the feelings of heat.

Information from the brain also reaches the spinal cord, thereby stimulating or depressing motor neuron activity. Strychnine, and certain other drugs, influence motor neurons in particular. Its presence produces overstimulation at the junction between the neuron and the muscle such that muscles are unable to relax. Continuous muscular contractions result in muscle rigidity. Depressants, such as alcohol and barbiturates, decrease the flow of information from the brain to the spinal cord and produce sedation.

Peripheral Nervous System

The **peripheral nervous system (PNS),** the second major division of the nervous system, lies completely outside of the brain and spinal cord but is connected to and functions with the CNS. The PNS receives information from the outside world and from within the body and transmits this information along sensory nerve fibers to the CNS. In turn, information from the brain pertaining to an appropriate response is transmitted on motor fibers

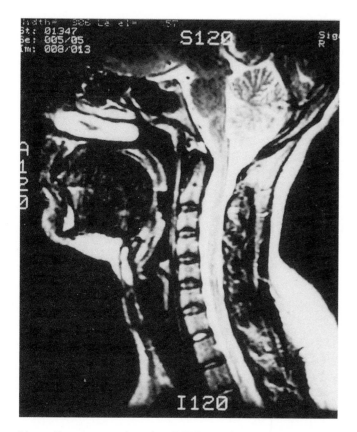

Magnetic resonance imaging (MRI) showing the brain stem and spinal cord.

The involuntary nervous system has the ability to increase or decrease the intensity of both muscle contractions and glandular secretions. When directed by the CNS to prepare the body for increased regulatory activities (such as heart function or breathing), the **sympathetic branch** of the involuntary nervous system is activated. By stimulating the release of epinephrine from the adrenal gland and norepinephrine from neurons, the sympathetic branch is able to increase the intensity of the body's responses necessary to expend energy. This could happen when you are confronted with a stressor, such as an angry dog. The sympathetic branch of the involuntary nervous system increases your ability to fight off the dog or run away from the dog. This response has been termed the *general alarm reaction*, also known as the "fight-or-flight reaction."[4]

In contrast, the **parasympathetic branch** of the involuntary nervous system decreases the intensity of muscular and glandular responses and helps the body return to a resting state. Parasympathetic responses are generally less widely distributed than the dominant

of the PNS to skeletal muscles, smooth muscles within vessels and major organs, and glandular tissues (fig. 3.2).

The PNS is actually made up of two completely different systems, the voluntary nervous system and the involuntary nervous system.

Voluntary Nervous System. The **voluntary nervous system** (also known as the *somatic nervous system*) is the part of the nervous system that enables us to move our bodies as we choose. We can "will" our skeletal muscles to contract in order for a body part to move. As a consequence, we are able to work, play, and engage in a full range of chosen activities.

Involuntary Nervous System. Many of the body's activities, such as breathing, glandular secretion, and heart function, are regulatory in nature. That is, they work to maintain homeostasis, the relative constancy of the body's normal internal environment, and therefore must continue to function without our conscious control or awareness. Thus, it is essential that the body be equipped with an automatic capability within the nervous system. This portion of the PNS is most often referred to as the **involuntary nervous system** (or *autonomic nervous system*).

cerebellum the second largest part of the brain; lies below the cerebrum at the back of the head; coordinates movement with spatial judgment

brainstem the portion of the brain that lies below the diencephalon and connects the brain to the spinal cord

spinal cord the part of the central nervous system that lies outside the skull and serves as a passageway for information between the brain and peripheral nervous system

reflex arc a special arrangement of neurons in the spinal cord that allows for a direct transfer of impulses from sensory to motor neurons

peripheral nervous system (PNS) the portion of the nervous system that lies outside the skull and spinal cord

voluntary (somatic) nervous system a division of the peripheral nervous system through which willful control of voluntary (skeletal) muscles occurs

involuntary (autonomic) nervous system a division of the peripheral nervous system that controls glands and involuntary muscles

sympathetic branch that portion of the involuntary nervous system, mediated by the neurotransmitters, epinephrine and norepinephrine that increases the intensity of muscular contractions and glandular secretions

parasympathetic branch that portion of the involuntary nervous system, mediated by acetylcholine, that decreases the intensity of muscular contractions and glandular secretions

FIGURE 3.2

Sensory nerve fibers of the peripheral nervous system (*a*) receive stimuli from the external environment and relay them to the central nervous system (*b*) for integration. Motor pathways carry the information from the central nervous system to muscles and glands (*c*) for appropriate responses (*d*).

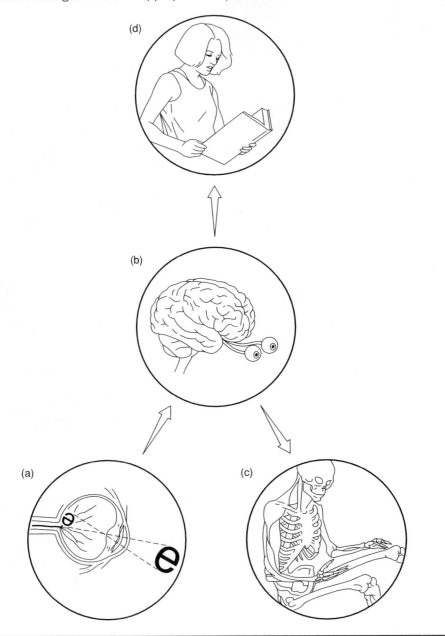

sympathetic responses and are not brought about by the action of epinephrine or norepinephrine. As a rule, the neurotransmitter acetylcholine is responsible for the parasympathetic activity of the involuntary nervous system.[5] Drugs like nicotine affect the parasympathetic nervous system by increasing the activity of the neurotransmitter acetylcholine.

STRUCTURE OF NEURONS (NERVE CELLS)

To appreciate the effects that psychoactive drugs have on the nervous system, it is necessary to examine structure and function at the level of the cells. The smallest func-

FIGURE 3.3

Diagram of a nerve cell (neuron).

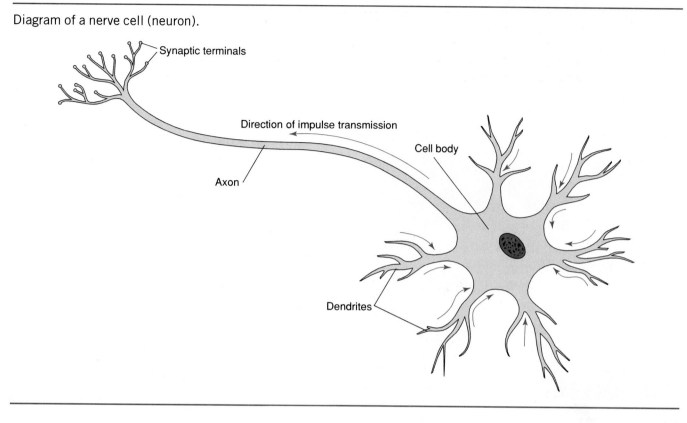

tional unit of the system is the nerve cell, or **neuron.** Although neurons vary in structure on the basis of their location within the system, the basic components of any neuron—dendrites, cell body, and axon—are the same (fig. 3.3).

Dendrites

Dendrites are the portions of a neuron designed to receive chemical messages from the axons of adjacent neurons. The dendrites of a single neuron have been shown to connect with the axons (nerve cell endings) of as many as 50,000 other neurons.

Cell Body (Soma)

Essentially, each neuron functions like an on/off switch: either it "fires"—that is, transmits the action potential—or it doesn't. Information from adjacent neurons can be either inhibitory or excitatory. Because a particular neuron has multiple dendrites, each of which is in contact with a different neuron, excitatory and inhibitory impulses may reach the cell body simultaneously. The function of the **cell body,** or **soma,** of a particular neuron, therefore, is to "summarize" these multiple messages into a single action potential for transmission through the axon. If excitatory impulses that reach the soma are

more prevalent than are inhibitory impulses, an action potential is directed down the axon. When more inhibitory impulses than excitatory impulses reach the soma, no action potential is generated.

Axon

The **axon** is the portion of the neuron designed to transmit a single specific action potential to another neuron, muscle, or gland. This transmission occurs as a result of changes in the electrical charges in the outer membrane of the neuron. At the end of the axon, the impulse must be converted from electrical to chemical form to be transmitted to an adjacent neuron. This transformation occurs at the synapse.

neuron a single nerve cell; the smallest functional unit of the nervous system

dendrite a nerve cell component that receives chemical impulses and conducts impulses toward the cell body

cell body (soma) a central nerve cell component that summarizes many impulses into a single action potential

axon a nerve cell component that conducts electrical impulses (action potentials) away from the cell body and toward the synapses

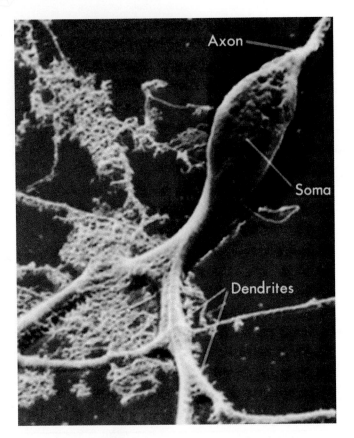

Scanning electron micrograph of a neuron, showing the soma, dendrites, and a small portion of the axon.

Synapses

The junctions between axons and dendrites are called **synapses.** Depending on the specific type of neuron, there may be a few hundred or as many as 200,000 synapses per single sensory input fiber to the brain.[6] Synapses occur between neurons and other neurons, between neurons and muscle cells, and between neurons and gland cells.

FUNCTION OF NEURONS

Communication occurs when impulses travel the length of the neuron and are transmitted to one or more adjacent neurons. Information is transmitted through the nervous system in the form of an electrochemical signal, or impulse, the **action potential.**[7] This action potential exists because of a difference in the electrical charge between the inside, which is more negatively charged, and the outside of the cell, which is positively charged. When the cell membrane is stimulated in such a way that positively charged sodium or calcium ions flow into the cell, an electrical impulse is created. The impulse travels along the membrane of the neuron until it reaches the membranes at the axon, where the electrical impulse is translated into a chemical message (described in the following section).

Communication between adjacent neurons and between neurons and muscle or gland cells occurs at synapses. A drawing of a synapse is shown in figure 3.4. The important components of the synapse are (1) the **presynaptic membrane,** the cellular membrane of the axon, (2) the **synaptic vesicles,** in which a chemical known as a neurotransmitter is stored; (3) the **synaptic cleft,** the space that separates the presynaptic membrane of one neuron from the postsynaptic membrane of an adjacent neuron; and (4) the **postsynaptic membrane,** the cellular membrane of the dendrites on the adjacent neuron, where receptor sites for the neurotransmitter are located.

When the action potential reaches the terminal of the axon, it is converted into a chemical message that is released into the synaptic cleft. The message is transmitted by the neurotransmitter molecules. These neurotransmitters then spread across the synaptic cleft and chemically excite the dendrite of an adjacent neuron.

NEUROTRANSMITTERS

Neurotransmitters are chemicals contained within synaptic vesicles in nerve cell endings. Neurotransmitters are released into the synaptic cleft and stimulate the production of either excitatory or inhibitory postsynaptic potentials. There are many chemicals in the CNS and PNS that may serve as neurotransmitters. These include acetylcholine, epinephrine, gamma-aminobutyric acid (GABA), dopamine, glutamic acid, serotonin, and histamine.[8]

There is a lack of agreement among scientists concerning whether neurotransmitters should be classified on the basis of structure or function. This disagreement results from the fact that (1) some neurotransmitters have chemical structures that allow them to be classified in more than one way, and (2) the function of a neurotransmitter may be related to the type of receptor it reaches, as well as the neurotransmitter concentration at a receptor site. A list of some of the more common neurotransmitters, their locations and functions, and the drugs that affect their activity can be found in appendix C.

SYNAPTIC FUNCTION

The following is a brief description of how messages are transmitted by cells of the nervous system. Refer to

FIGURE 3.4

Diagram of a neural synapse (the point at which two neurons exchange information).

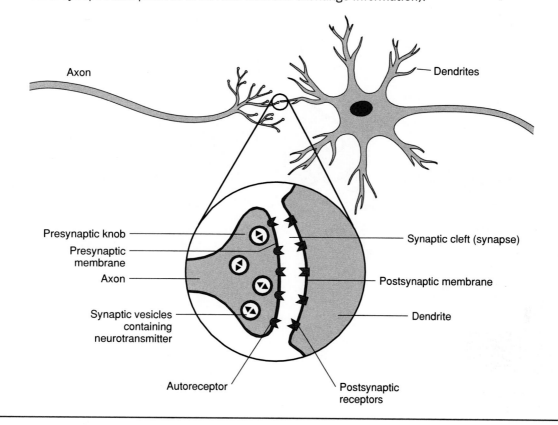

figure 3.5 as you read this description. When an impulse reaches the cellular membrane in the vicinity of an axon, synaptic vesicles containing neurotransmitters fuse with the presynaptic, or axonic, membrane. An electrical excitation of the presynaptic region of the axon occurs, stimulating the release of a chemical substance (the neurotransmitter) from the synaptic vesicles. The release is the result of subtle changes in the composition of the vesicular membrane brought about by the electrical stimulation. Upon their release into the synaptic cleft, neurotransmitter molecules diffuse throughout the width of the cleft (about 5 millionths of an inch). Some neurotransmitter molecules reach the postsynaptic, or dendritic, membranes, where they bind with receptors specifically designed to receive them, much as a key is designed to fit into a specific lock.

The binding of the neurotransmitter (the key) to these receptors (the locks) results in a change in the membrane potential, or voltage difference across the membrane. If the neurotransmitter reaching the dendritic membrane is *excitatory*, it produces a **depolarization** of the membrane that, in turn, can lead to generation of an action

synapse the junction between adjacent neurons or between neurons and muscle or gland cells

action potential the electrical impulse that travels within a neuron

presynaptic membrane the cellular membrane of the axon

synaptic vesicles membranous globules containing neurotransmitter molecules

synaptic cleft the space that separates the presynaptic membrane of one neuron from the postsynaptic membrane of an adjacent neuron

postsynaptic membrane the cellular membrane of the dendrite

neurotransmitters chemical messengers within nerve cells that, when released into the synaptic cleft, diffuse across the cleft and produce a postsynaptic response

depolarization a loss of electrical potential between the inside and the outside of a cell, resulting in impulse transmission

FIGURE 3.5

Diagram showing release, reception, and reabsorption of a neurotransmitter at the synapse.

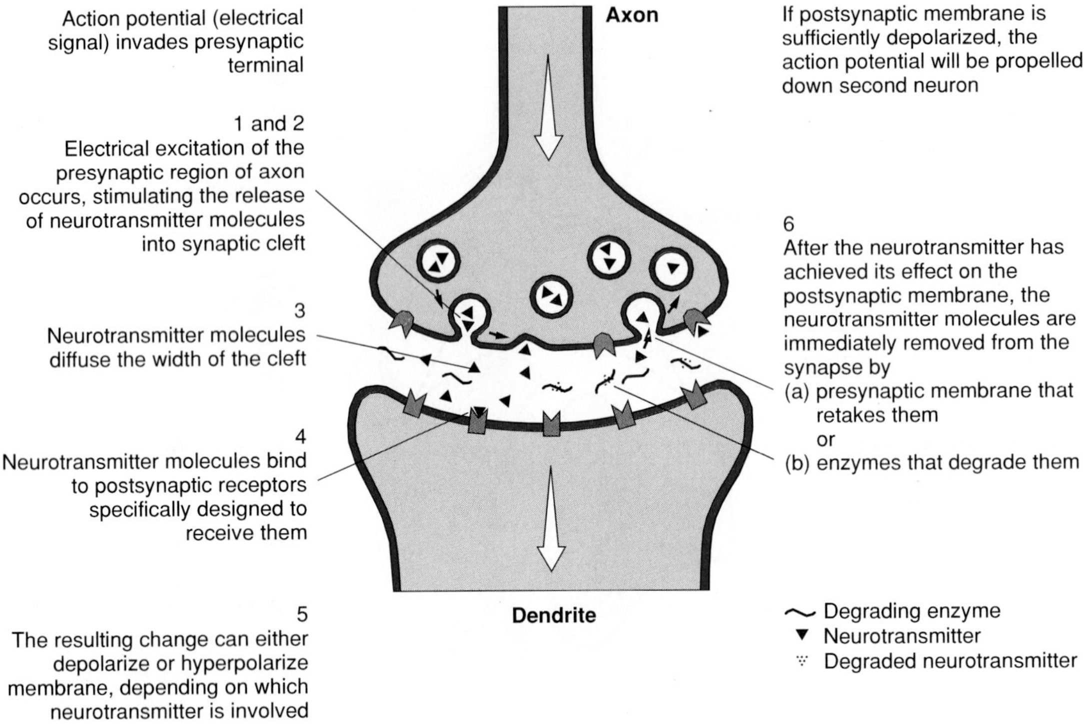

Action potential (electrical signal) invades presynaptic terminal

1 and 2
Electrical excitation of the presynaptic region of axon occurs, stimulating the release of neurotransmitter molecules into synaptic cleft

3
Neurotransmitter molecules diffuse the width of the cleft

4
Neurotransmitter molecules bind to postsynaptic receptors specifically designed to receive them

5
The resulting change can either depolarize or hyperpolarize membrane, depending on which neurotransmitter is involved

Axon

If postsynaptic membrane is sufficiently depolarized, the action potential will be propelled down second neuron

6
After the neurotransmitter has achieved its effect on the postsynaptic membrane, the neurotransmitter molecules are immediately removed from the synapse by
(a) presynaptic membrane that retakes them
or
(b) enzymes that degrade them

Dendrite

~ Degrading enzyme
▼ Neurotransmitter
˅ Degraded neurotransmitter

---

potential. If the neurotransmitters reaching the dendrite are *inhibitory* overall, **hyperpolarization** occurs, resulting in no action potential and no impulse transmission.[9]

After the neurotransmitter has achieved its effect on the postsynaptic membrane, the neurotransmitter molecules are immediately removed from the synapse to prevent their continued action, which could be toxic. This occurs in three different ways: (1) by diffusion into surrounding areas, (2) by enzymatic breakdown within the synaptic cleft, or (3) by active transport back into the presynaptic axon (fig. 3.6). The entire process takes place in a few thousandths of a second.[10]

DRUGS AND THE NERVOUS SYSTEM

The influence of psychoactive drugs on the nervous system is almost entirely caused by changes produced at the synapse (fig. 3.7). Drugs can modify the transmission of impulses in any of three major ways:

1. By binding with the receptors on the postsynaptic membrane, thus altering the membrane potential of the postsynaptic cell.
2. By destroying the enzymes that break down neuro-

transmitter molecules, thus allowing these molecules to continue to affect the postsynaptic receptor sites for longer than they normally would.
3. By binding with the receptor sites on the presynaptic membrane that are involved with actively transporting neurotransmitters back into the presynaptic terminal (a process sometimes referred to as neurotransmitter reuptake or *reabsorption*).

The degree to which each of these processes of neurotransmitter removal occurs depends on the type of neurotransmitter molecule involved. In later chapters, the proposed action of various drugs on the nervous system and synaptic function will be presented. The purpose of this chapter has been to lay a foundation for understanding these drug actions.

As we approach the end of this century, the structure and function of the nervous system is becoming increasingly better understood. Research continues to refine our understanding of this complex body system. Progress has also been made in our understanding of the

hyperpolarization an increase in electrical potential between the inside and the outside of cell, resulting in no impulse transmission

FIGURE 3.6

Representation of the ways neurotransmitter concentration can be reduced following its release: (*1*) diffusion into surrounding areas, (*2*) enzymatic breakdown within the synaptic cleft, and (*3*) reuptake into presynaptic axon. Typically only one mechanism is utilized in a given synapse.

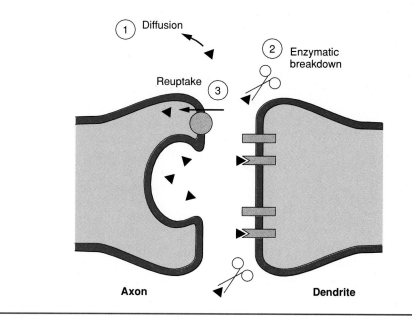

FIGURE 3.7

(*a*) A drug is shown blocking postsynaptic receptors. (*b*) Drugs destroy enzymes that degrade the excess neurotransmitter, which then remains in the synapse too long and acts as a poison. (*c*) A drug is shown blocking some of the presynaptic receptors, preventing the normal reabsorption of the neurotransmitter back into the presynaptic cell.

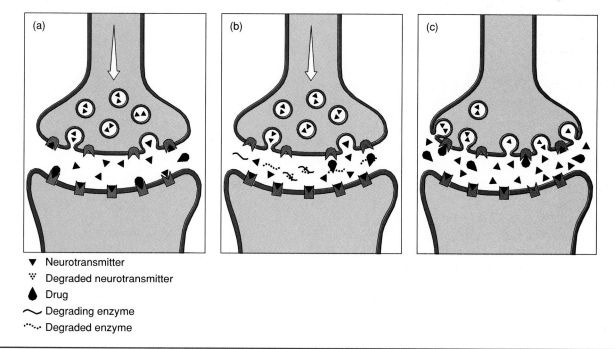

▼ Neurotransmitter

⋯ Degraded neurotransmitter

🌢 Drug

⌢ Degrading enzyme

⋯⋯ Degraded enzyme

WHAT DO YOU THINK?

Should Fetal Tissue Be Used as a Source of Neurotransmitters?

Parkinson's disease is a neurological disorder in which the loss of dopamine production within substantia nigra of the brain leads to a gradual loss of motor control. Symptoms of Parkinson's disease include the slowing of voluntary movement, muscular rigidity, and tremors. The disease is progressive, debilitating, and in many cases emotionally depressing. Death from complications usually occurs within a decade of initial diagnosis. Various causes for the condition have been suggested, including toxic chemicals, viral infections, encephalitis, and hardening of the arteries that carry blood to the brain.[a]

For the past 30 years, the treatment of Parkinson's disease has been centered on the use of the drug l-dopa. In the brain, l-dopa stimulates dying dopamine-producing cells to increase their production. However, within a decade of use, l-dopa loses its effectiveness, and the disease progresses rapidly. In addition, the side effects associated with l-dopa use are marked, including uncontrolled repetitive movements, weight loss, and psychosis.

In an attempt to find a cure for Parkinson's disease, researchers began in the early 1980s to implant cells from fetal substantia nigra into the corresponding areas of the brains of people with Parkinson's disease. Findings from studies begun in 1988 have been encouraging, including evidence that not only do symptoms diminish but that fetal cells actually become established and grow as normal tissue.[b] Despite early progress in fetal tissue research, in 1988 the Reagan administration barred the use of federal funding for further fetal tissue research. The relatively few studies that continued after the ban were funded privately. With the advent of the Clinton administration in 1993, the ban on fetal tissue research was lifted, and research into both basic and applied aspects of fetal tissue use is now increasing. In January 1994, the federal government approved the first federal grant to study the effects of fetal tissue implantation into the brains of patients with Parkinson's disease.[c] Today, scientists are searching for new sources of neurotransmitters. This research could affect the prognoses of people with such conditions as Alzheimer's disease and Huntington's chorea.

As might well be imagined, the use of fetal tissue in this manner has generated a great deal of controversy, because the source of this fetal tissue is aborted fetuses. Concerns over the "ownership" of fetal tissue, the appropriateness of federal funding for this research, and the "harvesting" of fetal tissue have been expressed by both medical professionals and the general public.[d] What are your feelings on this topic? What if you or someone you loved had Parkinson's disease?

[a]Walton, J., *Brain Diseases of the Nervous System* (Oxford: Oxford University Press, 1985).

[b]Spencer, D. D. et al. "Unilateral Transplantation of Human Fetal Mesencephalic Tissue into the Caudate Nucleus of Patients with Parkinson's Disease," *N Engl J Med* 327 no. 22 (1992): 1541; Freed, C. R. et al., "Survival of Implanted Fetal Dopamine Cells and Neurological Improvement 12 to 46 Months after Transplantation for Parkinson's Disease," *N Engl J Med* 327 no. 22 (1992): 1549.

[c]Langston, J. W., and J. Palfreman, *The Case of the Frozen Addicts* (New York: Pantheon Books, 1995).

[d]Council on Scientific Affairs, Council on Ethical and Judicial Affairs, "Medical Applications of Fetal Tissue Transplantation," *JAMA* 263 no. 4 (1990): 565; Kassever, J. P. and M. Augella, "The Use of Fetal Tissue in Research on Parkinson's Disease," *N Engl J Med* 327 no. 22 (1992): 1591.

influences of psychoactive drugs on the nervous system. Scientists conducting this research continue to discover new pathways and effects. The goal, of course, is a full understanding of the structure and function of the nervous system and of the interaction between a drug and its user. Until that time, however, students should realize that even the most innocent use of psychoactive drugs disrupts homeostasis. Drug abuse lessens the quality of life for the user and often for those around him or her.

SUMMARY

The nervous system is a complex communication network for the body, with the brain as the control center. The nervous system is organized into two primary divisions: the central nervous system (CNS) and the peripheral nervous system (PNS). The CNS is made up of the brain and the spinal cord, while the PNS consists of all nervous tissue outside the CNS. Psychoactive drugs influence behavior by altering the function of the nervous system.

The brain is a complex organ that analyzes, interprets, and responds to internal and external stimuli. The brain comprises four major structures—the cerebrum, the diencephalon, the cerebellum, and the brainstem. The diencephalon includes three major components: the thalamus, the hypothalamus, and the limbic system. Parts of the brainstem have control over basic physiological functions, such as respiration, heart rate, and sleeping/waking.

The spinal cord, the second principal structure of the CNS, serves as a passageway for the flow of information between the brain and the PNS. The two primary divisions of the PNS are the voluntary nervous system and the involuntary nervous system, which permit voluntary and involuntary control over bodily functions, respectively. Drugs can affect the function of these systems.

The overall function of the nervous system is better understood by studying the functions of its individual cells, the neurons. Each neuron has dendrites, which collect information from adjacent neurons; a soma (or cell body), which summarizes this information into an impulse, or action potential; and a single axon, which carries the action potential to neighboring neurons or other cells.

Neurons are connected to other neurons, muscle cells, or gland cells by tiny junctions called synapses. When an impulse reaches the end of an axon, it is converted into a chemical message for transmission across the synaptic cleft. This occurs when neurotransmitters are released from presynaptic vesicles, diffuse across the synapse, and bind with receptor sites on the postsynaptic membranes of dendrites of adjacent cells. The chemical message is then translated into an electrical message by the receiving neuron. The result could be depolarization of the membrane resulting in an impulse, or a hyperpolarization of the membrane, resulting in no impulse.

Psychoactive drugs produce their effects by binding with presynaptic receptor sites or postsynaptic receptor sites or by destroying enzymes that break down neurotransmitters. These effects can result in changes in perception, mood, thinking, and activity level and, ultimately, changes in behavior.

REVIEW QUESTIONS

1. What are the two major divisions of the nervous system? Which is confined to the brain and spinal cord? Which extends outward to muscles, internal organs, and sensory organs?
2. Name four major areas of the brain, and describe the location and function of each.
3. Describe a simple reflex arc as it occurs in the spinal cord.

4. Contrast voluntary and involuntary functions of the peripheral nervous system.
5. The involuntary nervous system is divided into sympathetic and parasympathetic branches. Which branch is responsible for increasing involuntary activity and which for decreasing the level of involuntary activity? Which neurotransmitters are associated with each system?
6. Name each of the major components of a neuron. What is the role of the soma, or cell body, in electrical impulse transmission? Upon leaving the cell body, on which part of the neuron will the action potential travel?
7. Diagram a synapse and label its structures. Explain what occurs, step by step, when an action potential traveling along the membrane of the axon of a neuron reaches a synapse.
8. Describe the three important ways that drugs can alter normal neurotransmitter function at the synapse.

REFERENCES

1. Thibodeau, G. A., and K. T. Patton. *Anatomy and Physiology*, 2d ed. (St. Louis: Mosby, 1996). Guyton, A. C., and J. E. Hall, *Textbook of Medical Physiology*, 9th ed. (Philadelphia: W. B. Saunders Company, 1996).
2. Moffett, D. F., S. B. Moffett, and C. L. Schauf, *Human Physiology: Foundations and Frontiers*, 2d ed. (St. Louis: Mosby, 1993).
3. Guyton and Hall, *Medical Physiology*.
4. Selye, H., *Stress Without Distress* (New York: New American Library, 1975).
5. Guyton and Hall, *Medical Physiology*.
6. Ibid.
7. Ibid.
8. Ibid.
9. Thibodeau and Patton, *Anatomy and Physiology*; Moffett, Moffett, and Schauf, *Human Physiology*.
10. Guyton and Hall, *Medical Physiology*; Julien, R. M., *A primer of Drug Action*, 6th ed. (New York: W. H. Freeman, 1992).

SOURCES FOR HELP

National Institutes of Health
http://www.nih.gov

National Heart, Lung, and Blood Institute
P.O. Box 30105
Bethesda, MD 20824–0105
(301)-251–1222
http://www.nhlbi.nih.gov/nhlbi/nhlbi.htm

American Medical Association
http://www.ama-assn.org/

PHARMACOLOGY: HOW THE BODY PROCESSES DRUGS

CHAPTER OBJECTIVES

After studying this chapter, you will be able to:

1. Define the term *pharmacology.*
2. Describe four ways in which drugs can enter the body.
3. Explain how absorbed drugs are distributed to the brain and throughout the body.
4. Explain how drugs and their metabolites are stored by the body.
5. List and describe several different types of effects drugs can produce.
6. Explain the dose-response curve.
7. Discuss various types of drug interactions.
8. Explain how chronic drug use results in tolerance and dependence.
9. Distinguish between physical and psychological dependence and give an example of each.
10. Explain how drugs are altered by the body's chemistry and how they are excreted.
11. Describe how drug testing can detect drugs and their metabolites in urine, blood, and hair.

Before drugs can interact with the body in any way, beneficially or detrimentally, they must enter the body, be distributed by the bloodstream, and move or be carried across cell membranes. During this process, the drugs are subject to actions by the body that alter their form and eliminate them. **Pharmacology** is the science that studies these interactions, including the absorption, distribution, action, biotransformation (see p. 63), and excretion of drugs.

ENTRY OF DRUGS INTO THE BODY

With the exception of those that are injected, drugs must penetrate the body's natural barriers and enter the bloodstream to exert their effects. The bloodstream then delivers them to the brain and throughout the body. The natural barriers of the body include the skin, mucous membranes (such as those of the eyes, nose, mouth, and genitals), and linings of the alimentary canal (esophagus, stomach, and intestines). Two factors that influence the capacity of a substance to penetrate these natural barriers and gain access to the bloodstream are (1) the route of administration and (2) the characteristics of the drug itself.

Routes of Administration

The effectiveness of a particular drug depends to some degree on its **route of administration.** Drugs can enter the body in a variety of ways, including ingestion (by mouth), injection (by hypodermic needle), inhalation (by breathing), and absorption (through the skin or mucous membranes) (fig. 4.1).

Inhalation and intravenous injection are the quickest routes of administration. Because of the rapid action of drugs taken by these routes, inhalation and injection are the preferred routes of administration by physicians administering lifesaving drugs, as well as by many chronic drug abusers. Absorption through the mucous membranes is slightly slower. Oral ingestion is slower still, and transdermal absorption (from an application on top of the skin) is the slowest.[1]

The preferred route of administration may depend on the characteristics of a particular drug, since some drugs are effective only by certain routes. For example, aspirin is an effective pain reliever when administered orally but totally ineffective when applied dermally (to the skin). Some hallucinogenic drugs, such as dimethyltryptamine (DMT), have no effect in oral administration but are very potent if inhaled, whereas others, like lysergic acid diethylamide (LSD), are most effective when taken orally. Some drugs, such as cocaine, which can be injected, absorbed through mucous membranes, or inhaled into the lungs, are effective by more than one route.

pharmacology the study of interactions of drugs with the physiology of the body

route of administration the pathway by which a drug enters the body

FIGURE 4.1

The four routes of drug administration: ingestion (oral administration); injection (intravenous, subcutaneous, or intramuscular); inhalation; and absorption (transdermal).

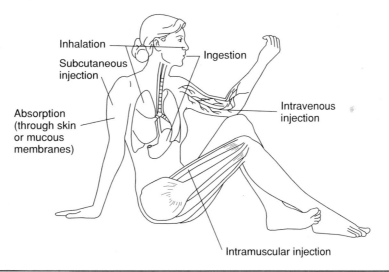

Ingestion. **Ingestion,** or oral administration, is a familiar way to introduce drugs into the body, since it is also through this route that food enters the body. Ingested drugs enter the bloodstream when they are absorbed through the cells that line the stomach or small intestine. The advantages of ingestion as a route of administration are (1) convenience, since there is no need for **drug paraphernalia** (such as a pipe or syringe) and (2) safety, since the drug does not have to be sterile and the stomach can sometimes be emptied in case of an overdose.

The disadvantages of ingestion include occasional nausea and frequent incomplete absorption. Failure to absorb significant portions of the administered dose can be the result of the breakdown of the drug by acids in the stomach or the binding of the drug to other contents in the digestive tract and eventual excretion in the feces.

In spite of its disadvantages, because the oral route is a natural one, it is used by commercial drug manufacturers. Commercially prepared drugs are often formulated as tablets, capsules, caplets, and fluid suspensions. Amateur laboratories often prepare illicit drug products that are administered in this same way.

Injection. **Injection** offers several important advantages over other routes. Injected drugs need not be absorbed; instead, they bypass the body's defense layers (skin, mucous membranes, and linings of the alimentary canal) and are able to reach sites of action very rapidly. The three most common routes of injection, in order of rapidity of effect, are **intravenous, intramuscular,** and **subcutaneous** (injection into the layer of tissue immediately under the skin).

There are advantages and disadvantages to injection as a route of administration of drugs. Injection permits an accurate measurement of the dosage, assuming the concentration of the drug is known and the syringe is a familiar size. The amount of drug administered is more closely related to the amount that actually reaches the site of action, in contrast to ingestion. Injection also permits the delivery of more than one drug at a time.

Disadvantages to the injection method, beyond the slight pain associated with the hypodermic needle, include the limited time for dealing with overdoses or allergic responses and, on the street, the risk of infection with a variety of diseases. Among the most serious agents transmitted through shared needles are HIV and hepatitis B virus (table 4.1).

Recently, a new, high-speed injector system has been introduced on the market by Bioject, Inc. (Portland, Oregon). Medications can be injected intramuscularly or subcutaneously without a needle. The Biojector employs compressed carbon dioxide as a power source to penetrate the skin, creating a tiny orifice through which medication can be injected in a fraction of a second. This system virtually eliminates the risk of infection with blood-borne pathogens for patients and healthcare workers.

Inhalation. Because the body absorbs oxygen and releases carbon dioxide by diffusion across the vast surface area of the lungs, an important pathway exists for the administration of drugs in their gaseous or vaporous state. Like oxygen, drugs contained in inhaled gaseous mixtures will diffuse from areas of higher concentration to areas of lower concentration. Thus, in the lungs, inhaled gases diffuse from the alveoli (tiny air sacs) into the capillaries that surround the alveoli. Once in the bloodstream, the drugs are distributed throughout the body.

Inhalation is one of the most rapid methods by which certain drugs can be introduced into the body. The rate of absorption into the bloodstream is related to the concentration of the drug in the mixture inhaled, the solubility of the compound in the blood, and the rate at which the lungs are supplied with unsaturated blood.[2] Since it is possible, in the hospital or laboratory, to measure precisely the concentration of drugs introduced through inhalation, this is a frequent route for the administration of general anesthetics for surgery. Examples include nitrous oxide used in dentists' offices and halothane used in surgical operating rooms.

Inhalation is the normal route of administration for many different medications. These include medications for asthma and hay fever; recently, insulin for noninsulin-dependent diabetes mellitus has been

TABLE 4.1 Some Agents and Diseases Transmissible by Hypodermic Needles

Agent	Disease
Human immunodeficiency virus (HIV)	Acquired immunodeficiency syndrome (AIDS)
Heptatitis B virus (HBV)	Viral hepatitis B
Hepatitis D virus (HDV)	Viral hepatitis D
Plasmodium parasites	Malaria
Staphylococcus bacteria	Staphylococcal septicemia (a blood infection) and endocarditis (inflammation of the sac that surrounds the heart)

successfully administered by inhalation.[3] Administration through inhalation eliminates the pain and discomfort associated with injections.

Because of its rapid action, inhalation is a favored route of self-administration by users of psychoactive drugs. Examples of psychoactive drugs that are rapidly absorbed into the blood from the lungs are nicotine (from tobacco smoke); tetrahydrocannabinol, or THC, (from marijuana smoke); cocaine (crack); and methamphetamine (crank or ice). Other substances that are abused in this manner are petroleum products and solvents, such as toluene and gasoline; and vapors from airplane glue, rubber cement, hair spray, Scotch Guard®, and Freon gas. A disadvantage to inhalation is the irritation to the throat and lungs or deterioration of the linings or membranes caused by the drug itself and also, in the case of ignited materials, by the products of combustion.

Absorption. **Absorption** describes a process by which a substance applied to a membrane crosses that membrane and eventually enters the bloodstream. The two most important surfaces across which drugs are absorbed are the mucous membranes (mucosa) that line the body openings and the skin. Of primary importance are the linings of the respiratory tract (nose, mouth, and throat). The snorting or sniffing of cocaine or methamphetamine crystals is an example of drugs entering the body by absorption through mucous membranes. Another popular drug taken through absorption is the nicotine in smokeless tobacco. This nicotine enters the bloodstream through the mucous membranes of the mouth. An example of a therapeutic drug that is absorbed through the mucosa of the mouth is nitroglycerin for heart patients.

Of secondary importance are the mucous membranes of the rectum, vagina, urethra, bladder, and eyes. When the rectum is used as the site of drug absorption, suppositories containing the drug are inserted into the rectum and then melt to release the active ingredient, which is absorbed through the lining of the rectum. This method is commonly used for the administration of medication to young children and the elderly. The introduction of cocaine into the vagina or rectum during sexual intercourse has been practiced by some drug-abusing thrill seekers.[4] This practice is risky because tissues numbed by the cocaine could become abraded or torn, increasing the risk of infection. An example of a drug that can be absorbed through the bladder is dimethyl sulfoxide (DMSO), prescribed for the treatment of bladder inflammation.[5]

Whereas absorption of drugs through the mucous membranes is moderately rapid, absorption through the skin is quite slow. Absorption rates vary depending on the thickness of the skin. Thus, absorption is more rapid

A poison control center in operation.

in the genital area, where the skin is thin, and slower near the back of the neck, where the skin is thick. Examples of therapeutic drugs administered transdermally include the antihistamine scopolamine (for motion sickness), nicotine (for smoking cessation), the stimulant nitroglycerin (for chest pain associated with coronary artery disease), and the narcotic fentanyl (for chronic pain). See the box on page 54 for more information about transdermal patches.[6]

In comparison with the other routes, the skin is a barrier that permits drugs to cross very slowly. For this reason, it is rarely the route of choice for those who self-administer drugs for pleasure, escape, or mood changes. Nevertheless, the skin is an important route of entry for many foreign substances and is of prime importance in workplace poisoning. One example of a workplace poisoning is green tobacco sickness. It occurs when dew containing nicotine from tobacco leaves soaks workers' clothes and skin.[7] Other toxic chemicals that can be absorbed through the skin are solvents, pesticides, and certain heavy metals, such as mercury. The box on page 55 presents guidelines for preventing accidental poisoning and overdose.

ingestion entry of a drug through the mouth into the digestive tract

drug paraphernalia various devices used to administer drugs

injection use of a needle to insert a drug into the body

intravenous into a vein

intramuscular into a muscle

subcutaneous under the skin

inhalation administration of a drug through the lungs

absorption administration of a drug through the skin or mucous membranes

ALTERNATIVE CHOICES

Transdermal Patches: An Alternative Method of Drug Delivery

In recent years, there has been rapid growth in the number of therapeutic drugs administered transdermally. This growth has followed the development of the patch technique for delivering a steady, dependable supply of active drug at the proper dose for effective therapy.[a]

Patches are normally designed in four layers. Beginning at the outer surface, there are (1) a transparent polyester film, (2) a drug reservoir, (3) a rate-controlling membrane, and (4) an adhesive. The first such patch, approved by the FDA in 1979, was the scopolamine patch, worn behind the ear for motion sickness.[b] Next came the nitroglycerine patch, worn on the chest for angina pectoris (heart pain). The nitroglycerin dilates blood vessels, increasing the heart's oxygen supply. In 1986, clonidine, a blood pressure medication, became available in a dermal patch. The first nicotine patch, Nicoderm, was approved in November 1991, and similar products soon followed. In 1996, the nicotine patch became available as an over-the-counter drug. It provides a steady release of nicotine into the bloodstream of former smokers. Other drugs that are now administered by patch include the hormones testosterone, estrogen, and progesterone.

The future of patch technology is bright. A birth control patch is currently under development, and there is hope that patches can be developed for the treatment of diabetes, osteoporosis, Alzheimer's disease, and growth deficiencies. There soon may be electronic patches that will permit hydrophilic molecules to penetrate the skin.[c] In addition to the therapeutic effect of the medications contained in patches, transdermal delivery provides an attractive alternative to more traditional routes for the following reasons:

[a]*Physician's Desk Reference,* 50th ed. (Montvale, N.J.: Medical Economics Data Production, 1996); M. Segal, "Patches, Pumps, and Time Release: New Ways to Deliver Drugs," *FDA Consumer* 25, no. 8 (1991): 13.

[b]M. Segal, "Patches, Pumps, and Time Release: New Ways to Deliver Drugs," *FDA Consumer* 25, no. 8 (1991): 13.

[c]N. Bodor, et al. "A Strategy for Delivering Peptides into the Central Nervous System by Sequential Metabolism," *Science* 257 (1992): 1698.

1. The use of transdermal patches virtually eliminates noncompliance (failure of the patient to follow the doctor's or pharmacist's instructions for proper use). It is difficult to not "take your medicine" when it is continuously introduced into the body through contact with the skin.

2. The use of transdermal patches minimizes the chance that inappropriate amounts of a medication will be taken, as absorption occurs at a constant rate. Dosage can be effectively regulated by the amount or concentration of nicotine contained in the patch. Multistep patches allow the user to gradually step down to lower doses of the drug until he or she is able to stop using the patch completely.

3. For nicotine-dependent people, transdermal delivery eliminates exposure to the toxic components of cigarette smoke. Of course, secondhand smoke is nonexistent.

4. For drugs traditionally administered by injection, transdermal delivery eliminates contact with needles and thus the risk of blood-borne infections, including HIV.

5. Should birth control become available through transdermal delivery, another nonmechanical method of birth control would be available for those who want protection but have little access to the various devices now available that are intended to prevent pregnancy.

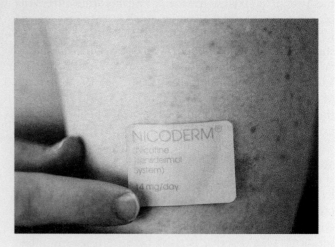

The use of dermal patches for the delivery of drugs is becoming increasingly common.

A variation of the absorption route is **implantation,** in which a drug is surgically placed under the skin so that it can be absorbed into the blood at a controlled rate over a long period of time. The birth control drug Norplant (levonorgestrel) is an example of such a drug. Once the Norplant capsules are implanted subdermally, the drug is absorbed at a constant, effective rate for about five years.

DRUGS IN YOUR WORLD

Preventing Poisoning and Accidental Overdose

Key things to remember to prevent poisonings:

- Keep all medications and household products well out of the reach of children.
- Install special latches to keep children from opening cabinets and drawers.

A brightly colored Mr. Yuk sticker is a poison symbol any child could understand.

- Use childproof safety caps on containers of drugs and medicine.
- Keep products in their original containers.
- Use poison symbols, such as Mr. Yuk stickers, to identify dangerous substances.
- Be sure to explain to children the meaning of any poison symbols you use.
- *Never* tell children that medicine is a treat in order to encourage them to take it.
- Dispose of all outdated drugs promptly and properly, by flushing them down the toilet.

Tips for preventing accidental overdose:

- Read the package instructions each time you take medicine, especially when opening a container for the first time.
- Never take medication in the dark.
- Keep drugs for adults and children in separate locations or on different shelves.

Adapted from: The American National Red Cross, *First Aid: Responding to Emergencies,* 2d ed. (St. Louis: Mosby Lifeline, 1996).

Characteristics of Drugs That Influence Absorption

To a significant degree, a drug's physical characteristics dictate its capacity to enter the body and be absorbed into the bloodstream. These characteristics include its solubility in fats, molecular size, formulation, purity, and stability.

Lipid Solubility. The solubility of a substance is a measure of its ability to become dissolved in a liquid, such as water or oil. Most substances are more soluble in one of these liquids than in the other. Oil and vinegar salad dressing is an example of a mixture in which some ingredients are dissolved in the oil, or **lipid** portion, whereas other ingredients are dissolved in the vinegar, or **aqueous** (waterlike) portion. Substances that are easily dissolved in oils or fats are called **lipophilic** (fat loving), whereas substances that dissolve more quickly in water are called **hydrophilic** (water loving).

The human body is made up of cells, the membranes of which contain a high lipid, or fat, content. These cells and their membranes make up the skin, mucous membranes, alimentary canal, and blood vessels. Even the cells of the nervous system have lipophilic membranes. Therefore, lipophilic drug molecules are attracted to and penetrate cellular membranes much more rapidly than hydrophilic (water-soluble) drugs.

For example, heroin is a very lipophilic, or fat-soluble, drug and thus is absorbed extremely rapidly. Penicillin, on the other hand, is highly water soluble and is absorbed slowly. Some drugs have molecules with both lipophilic and hydrophilic properties. Alcohol, a drug that is rapidly absorbed, is soluble in both oil and water.

Molecular Size. A second factor in the rate of absorption is molecular size. Small molecules diffuse more rapidly than large molecules. That is, the time between the

---

implantation a variation of the absorption route of administration in which a drug is surgically placed under the skin so that the drug can be absorbed into the bloodstream at a controlled rate

lipid oil or fat

aqueous having the properties of water

lipophilic "fat loving," a substance that binds easily with oils and fat

hydrophilic "water loving," a substance that binds easily with water molecules

Norplant rods allow contraceptive hormones to be absorbed at a controlled rate.

administration of a dose and the observation of a response is generally shorter for drugs with small molecules than for drugs with large ones. Of the inhalable drugs, ether is one of the smallest and most rapidly absorbed molecules, while THC (tetrahydrocannabinol, found in marijuana) is much larger and absorbed much more slowly. The time required for the body to rid itself of the quicker-acting drugs is also shorter, although other factors, such as lipid solubility, may affect this process also.

Formulation, Purity, and Stability. *Formulation* refers to the physical state of a drug. For fluids, there are oil- or water-based solutions; dry formulations include dusts, powders, granules, tablets, and capsules. Oils are absorbed more quickly than water-based solutions. Drugs in the form of finely ground powders expose more surface area of an active ingredient than drugs in a granular form and are, therefore, absorbed more quickly.

The effectiveness of a drug also depends on its purity and stability. Drugs that contain several less potent compounds in addition to the primary psychoactive ingredient, or that contain other, unrelated, nonreactive compounds, are less effective than the pure drug substances. The stability of a drug refers to its resistance to chemical deterioration in storage before use. Drugs that are unstable lose their purity and become less potent with time. The heart drug nitroglycerin is an example of a drug that is unstable and is chemically altered when exposed to light. For this reason, it must be stored in dark-colored bottles.

DISTRIBUTION OF DRUGS
WITHIN THE BODY

Once drugs reach the bloodstream, they are rapidly distributed throughout the body by the circulatory system. Portions of a drug may reach several sites at once, including (1) sites of action, (2) sites of storage, (3) sites of biotransformation (where drugs are chemically altered before elimination), and (4) sites of excretion.

Sites of Action

As a drug is distributed throughout the body, some of it begins to appear at **sites of action,** specific locations where the drug interacts with the biochemistry of the body to produce physiological or psychological changes. The quantity of drug that reaches these sites influences the strength of the response.

The primary sites of action for most of the drugs discussed in this book are the synapses between neurons of the central nervous system, which were described in detail in chapter 3. After leaving the circulatory system, drugs may come into contact with cells of the nervous system and affect the functioning of these cells.

Sites of Storage

One of the primary ways in which the body defends itself against the action of toxic substances is by means of **storage.** The portion of a drug stored and its storage location(s) depend on its chemical structure. Stored drugs are unable to reach sites of action until they are released from storage. This protection mechanism also delays the rate at which the body is able to biotransform and excrete certain drugs.[8]

Storage in the Blood. One of the most important storage sites is the blood itself. Here, some of the drug molecules become bound to proteins in the blood called **plasma proteins,** thereby becoming unavailable for further distribution. The amount of a drug that becomes bound to plasma proteins is different for each drug. Some drugs are not bound to plasma proteins to any degree, whereas others are bound quite significantly. Seconal (a sleeping compound), for example, is about 50% bound to plasma proteins.[9] Protein-bound drugs are distributed throughout the body as part of the blood plasma but are unable to react until they become unbound.

An equilibrium is established between the bound and unbound portions of a drug such that bound molecules are freed in response to the departure of unbound molecules from the blood. Unbound drug molecules are less restricted in their movement out of the circulatory system and are available to influence sites of action, to undergo biotransformation (metabolic) reactions (see p. 65), to be stored elsewhere, or to be excreted.

Storage in the Liver and Kidneys. Two of the most important storage depots are the liver and kidneys. Many toxic substances are bound in these organs, perhaps because these are the primary organs for the metabolism

FIGURE 4.2

Capillaries carrying blood to the brain restrict the entry of certain drugs into the brain.

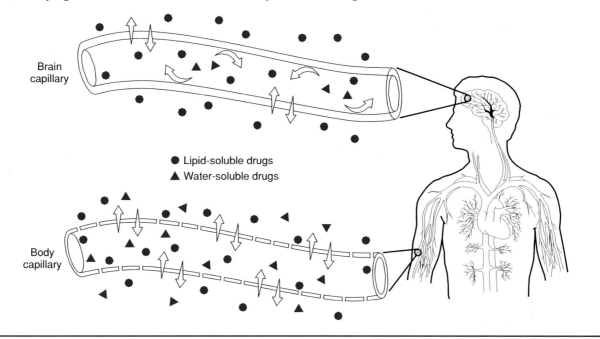

Brain capillary

● Lipid-soluble drugs
▲ Water-soluble drugs

Body capillary

---

and excretion of foreign chemicals. As sites of storage and metabolism for foreign substances, these organs are at special risk for damage by drugs. For example, chronic, heavy alcohol abuse often results in severe liver damage, whereas amphetamine abuse can destroy the kidneys. Unaltered drugs that are bound in these organs may become unbound and return to the bloodstream.

Storage in Fatty Tissues.   Some drugs are stored to a significant degree in the body fat. As one would expect, lipophilic (fat loving) molecules are readily stored in the fat. As with other storage depots, the stored drug is in balance with the portion circulating in the bloodstream. An example of a drug that is heavily stored in the fat is THC, the psychoactive ingredient in marijuana. The high degree of fat storage of THC explains why the drug and its metabolites remain in the body for up to six weeks.[10] Because of this, drug tests are able to detect THC in the body long after marijuana use.

Barriers to Distribution

Although the blood distributes oxygen and nutrients throughout the body, barriers exist that restrict the free flow of other substances to certain areas of the body. Two important barriers are the blood-brain barrier and the placental barrier.

Blood-Brain Barrier.   A unique feature of the capillaries of the brain is that they lack the pores found in capillaries

throughout the rest of the body.[11] These uniquely structured capillaries restrict some drugs, especially the water-soluble drugs, from entering the fluid surrounding the cells of the brain. This structural feature of the central nervous system circulation is known as the **blood-brain barrier.** Lipid-soluble drug molecules are less likely to be hindered by the blood-brain barrier. Caffeine, nicotine, alcohol, and cocaine, for example, easily pass through the blood-brain barrier because they are lipid soluble and diffuse directly through the brain's capillary walls[12] (see fig. 4.2). New technology may soon permit the delivery[13] of water-soluble drugs across the blood-brain barrier (see the box on p. 58).

Placental Barrier.   A second barrier found within the human body is the placenta. This unique structure found in pregnant women allows the fetus to receive oxygen and

---

site of action body location at which a drug exerts its effects

storage drug deposition in tissue away from the site(s) of action

plasma proteins proteins circulating in the blood that bind drugs, thereby preventing them from reaching sites of action or from being excreted

blood-brain barrier uniquely structured capillaries of the brain that lack pores and thus restrict the movement of some drugs into the brain

DRUGS IN YOUR WORLD

Delivery of Water-Soluble Peptides into the Brain

Normally, hydrophilic (water-soluble) peptides, such as insulin, insulinlike growth factor, transferrin, and albumin, cannot cross the blood-brain barrier (BBB) into the central nervous system (CNS). They are blocked by (1) the lipid (fat-soluble) nature of the membranes that make up the BBB and (2) the presence of peptide-destroying enzymes located on the membranes.

Recently, scientists have developed a way to chemically transport these peptides through the BBB and deliver them to the CNS. This is accomplished by packaging the peptide, in this case an enkephalin, in a "molecular environment" that hides its hydrophilic nature and enables it to penetrate the BBB as if it were lipophilic. Once it reaches the CNS, the molecular packaging is discarded, trapping the peptide behind the BBB. The residue of the "packaging" molecule is then degraded into harmless chemicals that are rapidly excreted from the body.

The developers of this delivery system suggest that the capability of delivering biologically active, water-soluble peptides, such as opioid pain-killing enkephalins, to the brain, will foster the development of a new generation of high-efficiency neuropharmaceuticals[a].

[a]N. Bodor, et al. "A Strategy for Delivering Peptides into the Central Nervous System by Sequential Metabolism," *Science* 257 (1992): 1698.

nutrients from the maternal blood supply. The **placental barrier** also keeps many larger cells and organisms from entering the fetal bloodstream. Projections containing capillaries from the fetus (chorionic villi) make contact with the uterine wall, thus bringing the fetal circulation close to the mother's. Nutrients, oxygen, carbon dioxide, wastes, and drugs move back and forth between the maternal and fetal circulatory systems, although maternal and fetal blood never mix (fig. 4.3).

Fetal capillary composition permits movement of lipid-soluble drug molecules into the fetal circulation, and any drug that can pass the mother's blood-brain barrier can also pass through the placenta to the fetus. The permeability of the placenta to drugs of abuse has been recently reviewed.[14] Alcohol, cocaine, morphine, and nicotine all readily cross the placenta. Studies of the contents of the umbilical cords of newborns also demonstrate this fact.[15] Therefore, the "placental barrier" is actually a myth, as far as psychoactive drugs are concerned. There are few drugs, if any, to which the placenta is known to be an effective barrier.

Two well-documented phenomena that illustrate the ability of drugs to cross the placenta (with disastrous results for the fetus) are fetal alcohol syndrome and heroin dependence in newborns whose mothers used these substances during pregnancy. More recently, similar disturbances have been described in babies of mothers who have abused cocaine.[16]

DRUG ACTION

Drug action refers to observed responses that occur as drug molecules interact with and alter the biochemistry of the body. Five types of drug actions have been identified for psychoactive drugs. These are (1) stimulative, (2) depressive (sedative/hypnotic), (3) antidepressive and antipsychotic, (4) narcotic (analgesic), and (5) hallucinogenic (psychedelic). It is important to note that many drugs produce more than one effect. For example, at relatively low concentrations, nicotine is a stimulant, whereas at higher concentrations, nicotine acts as a depressant. Drug actions can be classified as (a) acute or (b) chronic.

Acute Drug Action

Acute drug action refers to the immediate effects of a drug and to the responses that occur minutes, hours, or even several days after the entry of a drug into the body. Acute drug action is best described in terms of dose-response relationships.

Dose-Response Principles.   Central to a basic understanding of drug action is a thorough familiarity with dose-response principles. For a given drug to produce an observable effect, molecules of the drug must arrive at the site of action and exert their influence on a particular physiological function. As soon as the concentration of drug molecules is high enough for the drug's effect to be observed, a threshold response has been reached. As additional drug molecules arrive, that is, as the drug concentration increases, the intensity of the effect increases. As the concentration of molecules at the site of action continues to increase, a point of maximum response is achieved, beyond which the delivery of additional drug molecules will not heighten the effect.

The chronological sequence of events that occurs following the administration of a drug dose is described in the following list and illustrated in figure 4.4:

FIGURE 4.3

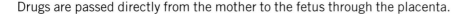

Drugs are passed directly from the mother to the fetus through the placenta.

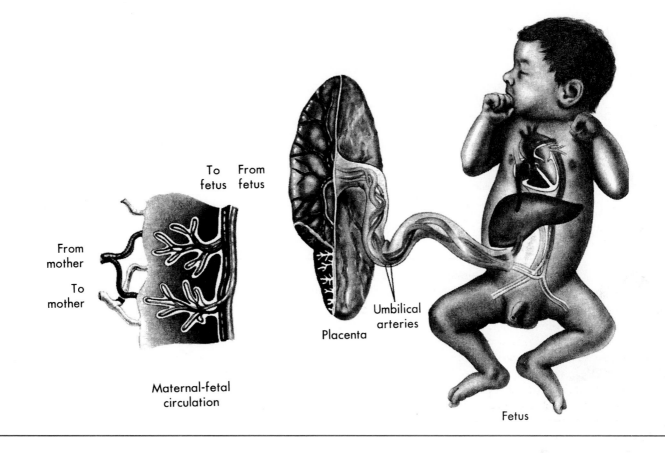

To fetus   From fetus

From mother

To mother

Placenta

Umbilical arteries

Maternal-fetal circulation

Fetus

Point 1: A drug is administered.

Point 2: The first sign of the drug's effect is observed (threshold).

Point 3: The maximum effect of the drug is first observed.

Point 4: The concentration of the drug in the bloodstream reaches its maximum point.

Point 5: The concentration of the drug begins to fall (although the maximum effect continues for some time).

Point 6: The level of effectiveness drops below maximum.

Point 7: The concentration drops below the threshold level; drug effect is no longer observable (level observed at Point 2).

Point 8: The drug can no longer be detected in the body.

Dose-Response Curve.   If a drug were to be administered to a large population, some of the people would respond to low doses or concentrations of the drug, whereas others would respond only to higher doses. The number of people, or cases, responding at each dose can be plotted as a graph and usually yields the typical **dose-response**

curve seen in figure 4.5. For more details about the dose-response curve and other measurements of acute drug action, see appendix D.

The shape of the dose-response time curve is affected not only by the physical characteristics of the drug and the route of administration (factors discussed earlier in this chapter), but also by the physiological characteristics of the user. Physiological conditions that can affect drug action include age, sex, weight, blood volume, nutritional state, pregnancy, health, and

placental barrier the unique circulatory structures of the placenta that restrict the passage of some substances into the fetal bloodstream

drug action the observed response that occurs as drug molecules exert their influence on particular body tissues

acute drug action the immediate (short-term) result of a drug's presence in the body

dose-response curve a graphic depiction of the response range of a test population to a drug

FIGURE 4.4

The events that occur when a drug enters the body (refer to the text for explanation).

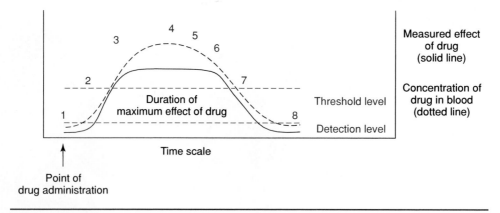

FIGURE 4.5

A simplified dose-response curve. As the dose increases, the percentage of the population responding increases. ED50 is the dose that is effective for 50% of the population.

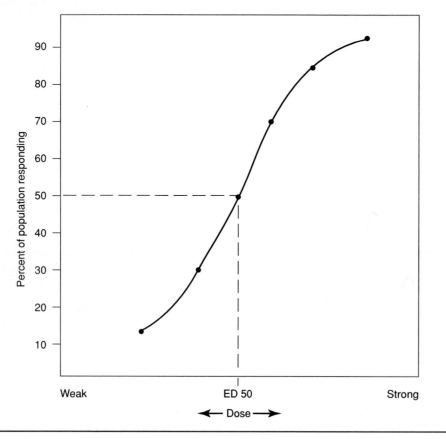

history of previous drug abuse. Psychological and social factors, such as mood and social setting, can also affect the outcome of drug use. A summary of all factors that can influence the outcome of drug use is presented in the box on page 61.

DRUG INTERACTION

Recent studies suggest that many drug users take more than one drug at a time. For example, many people who drink alcohol also use marijuana. Other combinations in-

DRUGS IN YOUR WORLD

Factors that Increase or Decrease the Speed of Drug Action

While the effect of a drug depends primarily on its chemical structure, such factors as the drug's form, the route of administration, and characteristics of the user can influence the speed of onset of drug action. The following are examples of the ways these factors affect the speed of drug action. An up arrow indicates a directly proportional effect: the greater the influencing factor, the faster the onset of drug action. A down arrow indicates an inversely proportional effect: the greater the influencing factor, the slower the onset of drug action.

Drug Form	Increases Action	Decreases Action
High concentration	↗	
Greater lipid solubility	↗	
Larger molecular size		↘
Larger particle size (smaller surface area)		↘

Drug Form	Increases Action	Decreases Action
Higher purity	↗	
Greater stability	↗	
Route of Administration		
Intravenous injection	↗	
Inhalation	↗	
Oral ingestion		↘
Absorption (skin or mucous membranes)		↘
Characteristics of the User		
Prior use		↘
Large body size (larger volume of distribution)		↘
Young age (infant or child)	↗	
Old age	↗	
Food in stomach (in oral drug ingestion)		↘

clude coffee and cigarettes (caffeine and nicotine), alcohol and sleeping pills, and narcotics and stimulants. Also, many elderly people have several diagnosed health conditions and, therefore, take several prescription and OTC medications every day. The term for this behavior is **polydrug use.**

The effects that the action of one drug can have on the action of another are collectively referred to as **drug interactions.** Although it may be true in some cases that there are no drug interactions, these cases are the exceptions. Polydrug use can be dangerous because the effects of drug interactions are difficult to predict. In general, interactions can result in increasing effects (enhancing interactions) or in lowering effects (inhibitory interactions).

Polydrug use can result in serious health problems for the drug abuser because drug interaction can cause increased effects and because polydrug users are at an increased risk for developing infections and chronic diseases. Perhaps the primary polydrug use problem in the United States involves alcohol used with other drugs. Among the drugs most commonly used with alcohol are marijuana, benzodiazepines (tranquilizers), cocaine, and narcotics. Many of the "overdose" cases seen in emergency rooms are the result of polydrug use. Drug interactions not only cloud the pharmacological picture, but they also complicate the processes of drug detoxification and treatment.[17]

Enhancing Interactions

Enhancing interactions are those in which the effects of one drug increase the effects of another. This increase may be additive, synergistic, or potentiating in nature. *Additive interaction* describes the situation in which the total effect of both drugs is equal to what it would be if either of the drugs was taken alone at a dose equal to the total dose. Mathematically, this can be visualized as $2 + 3 = 5$, meaning that two doses of drug A and three doses of drug B are equal to five doses of either drug. An obvious example would be mixing different types of alcoholic beverages, such as wine and beer. Two standard glasses of wine and three 12-ounce cans of beer would have the same effect as five cans of beer. Also, two similar but different barbiturates taken together usually produce an additive effect.

Synergistic interaction occurs when the effects of polydrug use are more than additive; this can be visualized as $1 + 2 = 5$. For example, one dose of a barbiturate swallowed with two servings of alcohol results in a greater than expected depression of the central nervous system because of their synergistic interaction. *Potentiation*

polydrug use use of two or more drugs at the same time

drug interaction the effect that the action of one drug can have on the action of other drugs

occurs when a drug that does not exhibit a significant effect by itself enhances the effects of another drug. Potentiation can be visualized by the equation $0 + 2 = 4$. For example, consumption of small quantities of isopropyl alcohol alone does not cause liver damage, but when consumed in addition to the inhalation of carbon tetrachloride (used as a solvent and in fire extinguishers), the liver damage produced by the latter is greatly increased.

Inhibitory Interactions

Inhibitory interaction refers to the counteraction of drugs in polydrug use. A knowledge of inhibitory interactions is useful for emergency room physicians, who are often confronted with cases of acute overdose. For example, a patient who is unconscious with a heroin overdose can be given an injection of naloxone, an inhibitory narcotic, which counteracts (inhibits) the effects of heroin (depression of the respiratory system).[18] For more information on this phenomenon, see chapter 7 on the narcotics. For further information on types of inhibitory drug interactions, see appendix E.

Chronic Drug Action

Chronic (long-term) drug abuse often upsets the body's normal balance, or homeostasis. This occurs as the body's chemical pathways change to adjust to the presence of a drug. As a result, tolerance and psychological and physical dependence with withdrawal symptoms often develop during a period of extended use. These phenomena are responsible for the great difficulties encountered in the treatment and rehabilitation of chronic drug abusers.

Tolerance. **Tolerance** can be described as the body's ability to adjust to the continued use of a drug in such a way that ever-increasing doses are required to reproduce the previous experience. Tolerance can result from two different mechanisms. The first occurs when regular amounts of a drug stimulate the liver to produce continually increasing levels of the enzyme that biotransforms the drug for excretion. Through this **enzymatic tolerance,** the longer the drug is taken, the more efficient enzyme production becomes and the more quickly the drug is deactivated. Since the drug is removed at a continuously increasing rate, the user must increase the dose to have the same effects experienced previously.

A second mechanism, **neural adaptation** (dispositional tolerance), occurs as the drug user's body makes other physiological adjustments to the presence of a drug. For example, the nervous system can increase the production of a neurotransmitter to offset the inhibiting influence of a particular drug. Conversely, the production of a specific neurotransmitter might be curtailed in response to a similar compound provided artificially as a drug. It is probable that for many drugs both enzymatic and neural mechanisms are activated during chronic drug use.

A noteworthy phenomenon is **reverse tolerance,** in which the chronic user experiences the effects of a drug at lower doses than expected. This is not a true reversal of physiological tolerance at all. Two explanations have been proposed. One is that experienced users become familiar with the effects of a drug and anticipate and then "play out" its effects. A second explanation involves the storage phenomenon, whereby a drug already stored in the body might contribute to that available at the sites of action. Marijuana is an example of a drug that has been said to produce "reverse tolerance."

Dependence. **Drug dependence** (chemical dependence) is a psychological and sometimes physical state resulting from the interaction between the user and a drug. Drug dependence is characterized by a compulsion to take the drug on a continuous or periodic basis to experience its psychic effects and sometimes to avoid the discomfort of its absence.[18] Drug dependence is often called **addiction,** especially in scientific writings that deal with narcotics.

Psychological Dependence. **Psychological dependence** describes a condition in which purely emotional or psychological components of the desire to take a drug are present, but no physical signs are observed with abstinence or withdrawal from the drug. The emotions experienced range from mild feelings of pleasure or relief of tension through stronger emotional drives that lead to persistent use, to changes in lifestyle and personal commitments, including keeping the company of those who are similarly involved with the drug.[19] A good example of psychological dependence can be seen in the recovering crack cocaine user who has already completed a period of abstinence of perhaps one week. At this point, all of the cocaine has been eliminated from the body, and there are no measurable clinical signs of withdrawal, such as abnormal pulse, high temperature, or chills. Nonetheless, the individual may experience an overwhelming desire to continue to use the drug, based purely on a memory of the previous experience. This is psychological dependence.

Beyond this, users may develop deviant lifestyles outside the norms of society and become members of a subculture of drug users, alienated by their behavior from the law and from normal society. Some authorities use the term *habituation* to describe psychological dependence.

Physical Dependence. **Physical dependence** is a condition in which a drug, or one of its products, has become necessary for the continual function of certain body processes. Upon abstinence from the drug, true physically manifested and clinically recognized signs and symptoms occur. The illness that results from drug withdrawal is called withdrawal illness or abstinence syndrome. Withdrawal illness associated with quitting heroin includes the following symptoms in addition to craving for the drug: restlessness and extreme anxiety, sweating, chills and fever, violent retching and vomiting, increased rate of breathing, cramps, sleeplessness, explosive diarrhea, and intense aches and pains.[20]

Sometimes it is difficult to separate psychological and physical dependence, and usually, dependence comprises both psychological and physical components. An alcoholic's psychological dependence is normally sufficient to keep the alcoholic drinking, but during the initiation of abstinence, the effects of physical dependence are added to those of the psychological dependence, making it very difficult to maintain abstinence.

Withdrawal Illness. **Withdrawal illness,** or **abstinence syndrome,** is the development of unpleasant symptoms when drug use is discontinued. This phenomenon is a direct result of the development of the physical tolerance discussed previously. The appearance of withdrawal illness can occur within hours of discontinuation of drug use or may take days to develop. The type and severity of symptoms vary with the type of drug, the strength of the usual dose, and the length of abuse. The physical symptoms eventually subside if abstinence continues, although the psychological desire to take the drug may linger for weeks, months, or even years.

If individuals return to their previous drug use pattern while experiencing withdrawal illness, the symptoms subside immediately. In some instances, symptoms of withdrawal illness can also be relieved with different but related drugs. Since the use of these related drugs may allow the drug-dependent user to function more normally in society, they form an important component of some drug treatment programs. Methadone therapy for heroin addicts is the prime example of this practice. It is clear that drugs that produce withdrawal illness are among the most difficult for the user to stop using.

BIOTRANSFORMATION AND EXCRETION OF DRUGS

As they enter the body, drugs and other foreign compounds immediately begin to undergo biochemical reactions that result in alterations or transformations into new compounds. These new compounds may be transformed again and again, each time into a compound more easily excreted (removed) from the body. This process is called **biotransformation.** A specific example is the biotransformation of alcohol, first to acetaldehyde, then to acetic acid, and finally to carbon dioxide and water (see chapter 15 for more details).

Drugs and their biotransformed products, sometimes referred to as *metabolites,* are then removed from the body by **excretion** in the urine and feces and, to a lesser extent, through the lungs, perspiration, and in nursing mothers, breast milk.

Biotransformation

Biotransformation reactions occur constantly as part of the normal biochemical functioning of the body. These reactions rid the body of its own natural waste products. Some of these biotransformation reactions result in less active compounds **(biodeactivation),** whereas others result in metabolites that are more active than the original compounds **(bioactivation).** An example of a drug that is biodeactivated is the depressant triazolam (Halcion). It takes the body only about two and one half hours to eliminate one-half of the triazolam remaining in the body. An example of bioactivation can be seen in another depressant, diazepam (Valium). Some of the diazepam taken is

chronic lasting a long time or recurring often

tolerance physiological and enzymatic adjustments made in response to a chronic presence of a drug in the body such that ever-increasing doses are required to produce the same intensity of effect

enzymatic tolerance tolerance resulting from increased enzyme production

neural adaptation tolerance resulting from adjustments in neurotransmitter production or release

reverse tolerance a phenomenon in which a chronic drug user experiences the effects of a drug at a lower dose than expected

drug dependence a psychological and sometimes physical state resulting from interaction between the body and a drug

addiction a condition characterized by the compulsive abuse of a drug or drugs; drug dependence

psychological dependence the emotional or psychological drive to continue drug use; habituation

physical dependence state of drug dependence in which abstinence from a particular drug results in clinical signs and symptoms of withdrawal illness

withdrawal illness (abstinence syndrome) occurrence of unpleasant or painful, clinically recognizable symptoms when drug use is discontinued

biotransformation the chemical alteration of drugs into various metabolites before excretion

excretion the removal of drug metabolites and other waste products from the body through urine, feces, exhaled air, perspiration, or breast milk

biodeactivation a biotransformation reaction that results in the alteration of the drug into a less active compound

bioactivation a biotransformation reaction that results in compounds more active than the original drug

converted to nordiazepam, a longer-acting depressant that is eliminated five times more slowly than the original compound.[21] Thus, the metabolite is more active than the original compound. The sum total of these reactions is what is actually meant by the term *biotransformation.*[22]

Although it is true that some drugs are excreted unchanged, the lipid-soluble nature of most psychoactive drugs requires that they be biotransformed into more water-soluble products before they can be efficiently removed from the body. This biotransformation is accomplished through the action of enzymes, many of which originate in the liver. There are usually two stages involved. The first stage involves the removal of small portions of the drug molecule or the addition of small portions to it; the second stage involves a joining of the altered drug molecule to a larger molecule in the body. The products of these biotransformation reactions are more water soluble than the original drug and thus can be excreted more quickly.

Excretion

The two primary organs of excretion are the kidneys and the liver. Once biotransformed into more water-soluble compounds by liver enzymes, many of the smaller drug metabolites are filtered from the blood by the kidneys and excreted in the urine. Many of the larger metabolites are secreted with the liver bile into the intestines and may then pass from the body through the feces.[23]

The lungs are an extremely important organ of excretion for certain volatile drugs (drugs made of substances that evaporate quickly). Air passes over the membranes of the lungs, and molecules of the volatile substances diffuse from the blood into the air, which is then exhaled. Anesthetic gases and a portion of ethyl alcohol leave the blood and are exhaled in this manner. The exhaled air contains a concentration of alcohol molecules directly proportional to the concentration of alcohol in the blood. Therefore, by measuring the amount of alcohol in the exhaled air, it is possible to accurately determine the concentration of alcohol in the blood. This is the basis for the breathalyser test for alcohol. A less important route of excretion is skin, particularly in breast milk and perspiration.

Half-Life

The time required for a drug to be eliminated from the body is of interest to physiologists, pharmacologists, doctors, and law enforcement officials. The *rate* of elimination varies depending on the type of drug and the extent to which the drug becomes distributed around the body. Drugs are detoxified by liver enzymes and excreted by the kidneys faster when the concentration of the drug in the bloodstream is high and slower when the concentration of the drug in the bloodstream is lower. There is an equilibrium between the bound and unbound portions of the drug such that, as free (unbound) drug molecules are biotransformed and excreted, other molecules that were bound and distributed to other sites in the body become unbound and begin to appear in the blood. These, too, then become available for excretion. Thus, the *rate* at which a drug is excreted slows down. What remains constant for a given drug is the *time* required to eliminate one-half of the remaining drug from the body. This time period, the drug's **half-life,** can be determined by monitoring the drug's concentration in the blood. Some drugs, such as cocaine, have a half-life of only 30 to 90 minutes, while other drugs, such as THC (the active ingredient in marijuana), have a much longer half-life—30 hours to 4 days.

DRUG TESTING TECHNOLOGY

The half-life of drugs is an important consideration in **drug testing** because the presence of even minute quantities of drugs or their metabolites can be detected in the urine, blood, or hair through the technology of drug testing.

Drug testing technology has evolved rapidly in the past two decades, and it is now possible to identify the use of a large variety of drugs, both legal and illegal. Specific substances that can be detected in the urine, blood, and hair include but are not limited to alcohol, amphetamines, barbiturates, benzodiazepines, marijuana, cocaine, methadone, methaqualone, opiates, phencyclidine, and testosteronelike anabolic steroids.[24]

Although urine testing has been the most common method used in drug testing, urine may not be the most accurate source of testing for drug use. The lengths of times during which certain drugs can be detected in the urine are listed in appendix F. Opiates and cocaine are rapidly excreted through the urine, usually within 48 to 72 hours. Only marijuana has a relatively long urine excretion rate (it can take several weeks). Thus, urine testing may actually underestimate true drug use. Hair is

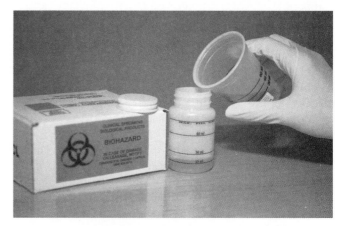

Drug tests can detect minute quantities of drugs or their metabolites in the urine.

becoming a more reliable source for drug testing, since hair analysis can detect drug use that occurred several months before or even longer. [25]

As is true with other areas of technology, drug testing technology is constantly evolving. New tests capable of identifying more compounds with increasing sensitivity appear regularly. Advances in genetic engineering, the development of sophisticated equipment, and improved technician training have all contributed to advancements in drug testing technologies. The Naval Research Laboratory in Washington, D.C., is testing a new portable, high-tech flow immunosensor that would detect within 45 seconds small amounts of cocaine and heroin in the blood, urine, or saliva.[26]

On the basis of present technology, drug testing is conducted at two levels—an initial **drug screening** and a more sensitive **confirmatory drug test.** There are two methods used to test both urine and hair for drugs: immunoassay and chromatography. **Immunoassay** tests use antibodies to detect the presence or absence of drugs in urine or hair. An antibody is a protein that reacts only with a specific substance, or antigen. Immunoassay testing involves adding a "tagged" antigen that can be measured after the antibody and antigen react. Commonly used "tagged" antigens include radioactive materials, as in **radioimmunoassay, or RIA;** enzymes, as in **enzyme-multiplied immunoassay test, or EMIT;** or fluorescent materials, as in **fluorescent polarization immunoassay, or FPIA.**

The results of the RIA and EMIT are usually read with a machine, so the readings are usually objective. Nonetheless, immunoassay for drug testing is not error free. It is estimated that 1 to 2 out of every 100 negative urine or hair samples may actually test positive (false positive).[27] Therefore, immunoassay is most commonly used only as a screening test for drugs. Screening tests alone are not capable of diagnosing drug use, but they are useful in sorting out those who are probably positive from those who are probably negative. The cost of these screening tests runs from $5.00 to $30.00 for each sample screened.[28] Problems arise when agencies use results from screening tests as evidence that an individual is "guilty" of using drugs.

Gas chromatography/mass spectrometry (GC/MS) is a more accurate drug testing method. Gas chromatography uses a nonreactive gas and a special instrument to vaporize the test sample. The sample is then put into a detector, or mass spectrometer, that identifies the drug and specifies what amount of the drug is present. GC/MS is the most accurate drug testing method and also the most expensive and time-consuming. GC/MS is 99.9% accurate and is the only test that is accepted in most courts of law as proof of drug use beyond reasonable doubt.[29] Thus GC/MS is often used as a confirmatory test, not as a screening method.[30] Machines that carry out these tests cost approximately $200,000, so it is not surprising that the test itself costs $100 per sample.[31] For a discussion of workplace drug testing and drug testing as a public policy, see chapter 19.

SUMMARY

Pharmacology is the study of the interaction between drugs and the physiology of the body. Drugs can enter the body through ingestion, injection, inhalation, and absorption. Each route offers certain advantages and disadvantages in regard to the speed of onset of drug action, effectiveness, and safety. Once in the body, drugs are distributed rapidly throughout the body by the bloodstream. The lipid solubility of each drug influences its movement across cellular membranes to sites of action or storage. Drugs can be stored in the blood, kidneys, liver or within fatty tissue deposits. The blood-brain barrier limits the passage of some drugs into the brain.

Upon reaching their sites of action, drugs exert their acute effects in a manner consistent with recognized dose-response dynamics. Regardless of the specific nature of their effects, psychoactive drugs influence normal function by altering the communication patterns normally present in the nervous system.

Chronic drug use places individuals at risk of developing drug dependence. Physical dependence is characterized by tolerance and withdrawal, whereas psychological dependence reflects a growing compulsion to use drugs to experience their particular effects on normal function. Some drugs can be stored in the body for an extended period of time, but all drugs are eventually removed from the body. This process

half-life the length of time required for the body to excrete one-half of remaining drug, as measured by the drug's concentration in the blood

drug testing the use of chemical analysis to examine urine, hair, blood, or other body fluids or tissues for the presence of drugs or their metabolites

radioimmunoassay (RIA) the use of small amounts of radioactive material to detect antibodies to drugs in an immunoassay

enzyme-multiplied immunoassay test (EMIT) the use of an enzyme system to detect antibodies to drugs in an immunoassay

fluorescent polarization immunoassay (FPIA) the use of a fluorescent dye to detect the presence of antibodies in an immunoassay

gas chromatography/mass spectrometry (GC/MS) a highly technical method of drug detection that is 99.9% accurate and involves identifying minute quantities of drugs or drug byproducts in a machine called a mass spectrometer

involves biotransformation of the drug into water-soluble metabolites, followed by excretion of the drug through urine, feces, lungs, perspiration, or breast milk. Minute quantities of drugs and their metabolites can be detected by drug testing, the chemical analysis of body fluids or tissues for the presence of drugs.

REVIEW QUESTIONS

1. Identify the four primary routes through which drugs can enter the body. What are the advantages/disadvantages of each in terms of speed of onset, effectiveness, and safety? Name a drug or medication that is administered through each route.
2. Differentiate between the terms *lipophilic* and *hydrophilic* as they apply to drugs. Which form passes most readily through cell membranes? Which is most easily excreted?
3. Name three important storage sites for drugs within the body. What role do the plasma proteins play in fostering movement of drugs in and out of the circulatory system?
4. In regard to restricting drug movement, contrast the effectiveness of the blood-brain barrier and the placental barrier.
5. Psychotropic drugs exert one or more influences on the function of the nervous system. Name the five primary types of influences.
6. Using the eight points that describe the dose-response relationships (p. 61), visually depict a hypothetical dose-response curve.
7. Differentiate between physical and psychological dependence. Which equates with "addiction" and which with "habituation?"
8. Consult the first chapter on alcohol (chapter 16) regarding the biotransformation of ethyl alcohol to carbon dioxide and water. How many enzymes are required? How long does it take the body to biotransform and excrete one standard-size serving of an alcoholic beverage?
9. Explain how drug testing can detect small quantities of drugs in body fluids or tissues hours, days, or even weeks after drug use. Which drugs do you think can be detected for the longest period after use?

REFERENCES

1. Klaassen, C. D., "Absorption, Distribution, and Excretion of Toxicants," in Casarett and Doull's *Toxicology: The Basic Science of Poisons*, 4th ed. (New York: McGraw-Hill, 1993).
2. Gordon, T., and M. O. Amdur, "Toxic Responses of the Respiratory System to Toxic Agents," in Casarett and Doull's *Toxicology: The Basic Science of Poisons*, 4th ed. (New York: McGraw-Hill, 1993).
3. Laube, B. L., A. Georgopoulos, and G. K. Adams, "Preliminary Study of the Efficacy of Insulin Aerosol Delivered by Oral Inhalation in Diabetic Patients," *JAMA* 269 no. 16 (1993):2106.
4. Ettinger, T. B., "Sudden Death Temporally Related to Vaginal Cocaine Abuse," *Am J Emerg Med* 7 no. 1 (1989):129; Doss, P. L., and G. T. Gowitt, Investigation of a Death Caused by Rectal Insertion of Cocaine. *Am J Forensic Med Pathol* 9 no. 4 (1988):336.
5. *Physicians' Desk Reference*, 50th ed. (Montvale, N.J.: Medical Economics Data Production, 1996).
6. Ibid.; Segal, M., "Patches, Pumps and Timed Release: New Ways to Deliver Drugs, *FDA Consumer* 25, no. 8 (1991):13.
7. Centers for Disease Control and Prevention, "Green Tobacco Sickness in Tobacco Harvesters—Kentucky, 1992," *MMWR* 42 no. 13 (1993):237.
8. Klaassen, "Toxicants."
9. Ibid.
10. Julien, R. M., *A Primer of Drug Action*, 6th ed. (New York: W. H. Freeman, 1992).
11. Schauf, C. L., D. F. Moffett, and S. B. Moffett, *Human Physiology: Foundations and Frontiers*, (St. Louis, MO.: Mosby, 1990).
12. Ibid.
13. Bodor, N. et al., "A Strategy for Delivering Peptides into the Central Nervous System by Sequential Metabolism, *Science* 257 (1992):1698.
14. Olsen, G. D., "Placental Permeability for Drugs of Abuse and Their Metabolites," in R. S. Rapaka *Membranes and Barriers: Targeted Drug Delivery*, National Institute on Drug Abuse, Research Monogram No. 154, NIH Publ. No. 95-3889, Rockville, Md., 1995, 152–62.
15. Szeto, H. H., "Maternal-Fetal Pharmacokinetics and Fetal Dose-Response Relationships," in *Prenatal Abuse of Licit and Illicit Drugs*, Ann N Y Acad Sci 562 (1989):42.
16. Spear, L. P., C. L. Kristein, and N. A. Frambes, "Cocaine's Effects on the Developing Central Nervous System: Behavioral, Psychopharmacological, and Neurochemical Studies," in *Prenatal Abuse of Licit and Illicit Drugs*, Ann N Y Acad Sci 562 (1989):290.
17. Mayer, J. M., "Mechanisms of Drug Interactions with Alcohol," in *Dual Addiction: Pharmacological Issues in the Treatment of Concomitant Alcoholism and Drug Abuse* (New York: Haworth, 1984); Novick, D. M. "Major Medical Problems and Detoxification Treatment of Parenteral Drug-Abusing Alcoholics," in *Dual Addiction: Pharmacological Issues in the Treatment of Concomitant Alcoholism and Drug Abuse* (New York: Haworth, 1984).
18. Platt, J. J., *Heroin Addiction: Theory, Research, and Treatment* (Malabar, Fla.: Robert E. Krieger, 1986).
19. World Health Organization, *A Manual on Drug Dependence* (Geneva, 1975).
20. Julien, *Primer of Drug Action*.

21. Julien, *Primer of Drug Action.*
22. Sipes, I. G., and A. J. Gandolfi, "Biotransformation of Toxicants," in Casarett and Doull's *Toxicology: The Basic Science of Poisons* (New York: McGraw-Hill, 1993).
23. Klaassen, "Toxicants."
24. Ackerman, S., "Drug Testing: The State of the Art," *American Scientist* 77 (1989):19.
25. Mieczkowski, T., H. J. Landress, R. Newel, and S. D. Coletti, *Testing Hair for Illicit Drug Use*, National Institute of Justice: Research in Brief 138539:1, 1993.
26. "Next, a 45-Second Drug Test," *USA Today,* 16 April, 1991.
27. Visher, C., and K. McFadden, K., *A comparison of Urinalysis Technologies for Drug Testing in Criminal Justice*, National Institute of Justice: Research in Action, 129292:1, June 1991.
28. Ackerman, "Drug Testing."
29. Berges, G., *Drug Testing Impact Book* (New York: Grolier's, 1987).
30. "Testing Technologies," *National Institute of Justice Journal* 226 (1993):13.
31. Ackerman, "Drug Testing"; Berges, *Drug Testing Impact Book.*

SOURCES FOR HELP

Check your local telephone directory for the nearest poison control center.

Los Angeles Regional Drug and Poison Information Center
LAC & USC Medical Center
7 days a week, 24 hours a day
(213) 226–2622
(800) 777–6476 (in California only)

Drug Information Center
Memorial Sloan-Kettering Cancer Center
New York, NY
(212) 639–7552

Drug Information Services
University of Chicago
Chicago, IL
(312) 702–1388

Drug Information Center
University of Colorado Health Science Center
Denver, CO
(303) 270–8489

Drug Information Center
Miami VA Medical Center
Miami, FL
(305) 324–3237

New Mexico Poison and Drug Information Center
University of New Mexico
Albuquerque, NM
7 days a week, 24 hours a day
(505) 843–2551
(800) 432–6866 (in New Mexico only)

American Society of Addiction Medicine
12 West 21st St.
New York, NY 10010
(212) 848–6050

Office on Smoking and Health
Centers for Disease Control and Prevention
4770 Buford Highway, N.E.
Mailstop K-50
Atlanta, GA 30341–3724
(404) 488–5708

THE STIMULANTS:
COCAINE, THE AMPHETAMINES,
AND THE CATHINOIDS

CHAPTER OBJECTIVES

After studying this chapter, you will be able to:

1. Define the term *stimulants* and give examples of three different kinds.

2. Describe the discovery and early use of cocaine, including early medical and social uses in Europe and the United States.

3. Describe the factors that led to the American cocaine epidemic of the 1970s and 1980s and describe the contemporary patterns of use and abuse.

4. Describe the various ways cocaine can be administered and the time required for it to reach the brain by each route.

5. Define the terms *crack, free-basing,* and *speedballing.*

6. Describe how cocaine alters neurotransmitter activity at the synapse and how this affects the nervous system.

7. Describe the acute and chronic effects of cocaine abuse.

8. List and describe the health problems that result from cocaine abuse.

9. List the approved medical uses for cocaine.

10. Describe a typical cocaine addiction cycle and a typical cocaine treatment program.

11. Describe the discovery and early history of amphetamine use and abuse.

12. Explain how amphetamines can be administered and how they work to alter brain function, including the neurotransmitters affected during amphetamine intoxication.

13. Describe the acute and chronic physiological and psychological effects of amphetamine abuse.

14. List the approved medical uses for the amphetamines.

15. Describe the factors that contributed to the increase in methamphetamine abuse in the United States in the 1980s, and describe the abuse trends of the mid- to late 1990s.

16. Explain what *cathinone* and *cathine* are and where they come from.

17. Explain what methcathinone is, what its effects are, and why it is classified as a schedule I drug.

PROFILE

At 17, Jeff's life was a mess. He had dropped out of high school and was working at a low-paying job flipping burgers. He wasn't a bad kid—in fact, most of the money he made went to help his mother pay rent and the other bills they owed.

When he wasn't working, he was hanging out with his friends. One hot, steamy Saturday, just to shake things up, they tried some speed. Jeff liked the way it made him feel—more confident, smarter, and just plain good. Jeff started using more and more of his money to buy "crystal." He covered up his spending by telling his mother that the burger shack had cut his hours again.

As time went on, Jeff bought even larger amounts of "crystal." He began to resell it to support his own habit. The long hours at work standing over the spitting hot grill seemed to go by faster when he was high. Soon he began using more and more of the crystal he had intended to resell.

When Jeff came home one evening, he saw his mother crying in the entry hall with a slip of paper in her hand—it was an eviction notice. Without Jeff's contribution to their living expenses, his mother hadn't been able to make ends meet. The sight of his mother's distress tore Jeff apart. Later that night he stole $2,000 from the restaurant where he worked. He planned to make a really big buy and then sell most of the speed to some kids he knew. If all went well, he could replace the money the next day. This time, he vowed, he would use the profits to help his mother.

What do you think were the consequences of Jeff's impulsive actions? How might he pull out of this downward spiral of drug abuse, fulfill his responsibility to his mother, and turn his own life around? Think about Jeff's situation as you read this chapter, and then read the solutions box on page 91.

In this chapter we discuss the stimulants—substances that increase central nervous system activity. They increase heart rate, induce wakefulness, reduce fatigue, elevate mood, and produce euphoria. These powerful drugs grew in popularity in the 1980s, and while their abuse has declined somewhat, they remain popular in the late 1990s. We first discuss cocaine, then the amphetamines, and lastly the cathinones, the newest stimulant to appear on the American drug scene. Each of these stimulants has its own history, pharmacology, and usage trends; the feature they share is their high potential for abuse.

COCAINE

History

Cocaine is the primary psychoactive substance found in the leaves of the coca plant (*Erythroxylon coca*). It is generally agreed that the native people who inhabited the Andes Mountains of South America were chewing coca leaves for many centuries before the Spanish arrived to begin their conquest of the Inca civilization in the sixteenth century. Perhaps the earliest uses of cocaine were associated with religious ceremonies and spiritual beliefs. The chewing of coca leaves was said to have produced an "exaltation of spirit, freedom from fatigue, and a sense of well being."[1] Over time, however, the chewing of coca leaves became a common and widespread practice, and by the time the Spanish arrived, the plant was being cul-

tivated by the Indians and even used as a unit of exchange.

In the nineteenth century, coca leaves were taken to Europe, where they were studied in the laboratory. The earliest record of the isolation of purified cocaine was made by Gaedken in 1844.[2] It was not until 1923 that total synthesis of cocaine was achieved in the laboratory. (This process is a fairly difficult one, though. Consequently, all of the cocaine used for medical purposes today is still derived from coca leaves.)

During the latter decades of the 1800s, some members of the medical community believed that cocaine was a new wonder drug. Early medical uses for cocaine included use as a local anesthetic for surgery and as a medication for the relief of depression and indigestion. One of cocaine's early proponents was Austria's Dr. Sigmund Freud, the father of psychoanalysis. Freud, who initially spoke of cocaine in glowing terms, also attempted to use the drug to relieve the withdrawal symptoms of morphine addicts. This soon proved to be disastrous, and he eventually recanted his praise of cocaine.[3] Thus, by 1890, the dangerous side of cocaine had been well exposed.

From 1890 to 1906, coca leaf extracts were also used in various tonics, nostrums, elixirs, and patent medicines that were sold to anyone willing to buy. One of the products containing such extracts was Mariani's coca wine,

---

cocaine a potent peripheral and central nervous system stimulant found in the leaves of the coca plant, *Erythroxylon coca*

A native South American woman chewing coca leaves.

A Colombian man stirs coca leaves over a fire to dry them.

and another was "America's favorite soft drink," Coca-Cola. Many unsuspecting consumers became dependent on these and other products.[4] In 1906 the Pure Food and Drugs Act was passed by Congress. This law, which regulated the labeling of patent medicines, and the Harrison Act of 1914, which classified cocaine as a narcotic for the purpose of law enforcement, ended the nonprescription use of cocaine in America.[5] By the 1920s, enforcement of the Harrison Act had made cocaine more expensive and less available for the remaining users. General interest in the drug began to decline. The introduction of the amphetamines in the 1930s caused a continued decline in cocaine use among both cocaine abusers and heroin addicts.

A renewal of interest in cocaine as a pleasure drug began in the 1960s, when the amphetamines became the target of greater and greater governmental regulation. The problems associated with cocaine use, documented at the beginning of the twentieth century, were all but forgotten. Since physical withdrawal symptoms, such as those produced by the withdrawal from alcohol, heroin, morphine, and the barbiturates, were not observed with

cocaine, its potential to produce a state of dependence went unrecognized during the 1970s.

However, cocaine was still expensive and difficult to obtain in the early 1970s, a fact that helped create its status as a glamour drug of the rich, including entertainers and professional athletes. *Modeling*, the imitation of behaviors of another, usually older person, undoubtedly helped the practice of cocaine abuse spread to youth and to "wannabes" who rushed to emulate the lifestyles of the rich and famous. Cocaine's popularity also increased because many abusers in the early 1970s believed that cocaine was a safe recreational drug.

Rise of the Drug Cartels. The increase in demand for cocaine was soon met with an increase in supply. The amount seized by customs agents quadrupled between 1967 and 1969 and continued to increase in the 1970s and 1980s. In 1988, record seizures of cocaine hydrochloride were made, but wholesale and retail prices continued to decline while purity improved. In 1985, 1 g of cocaine sold for about $100; by 1988, prices for the same quantity

FIGURE 5.1

Cocaine smuggling routes into the United States. (Data from the Drug Enforcement Administration)

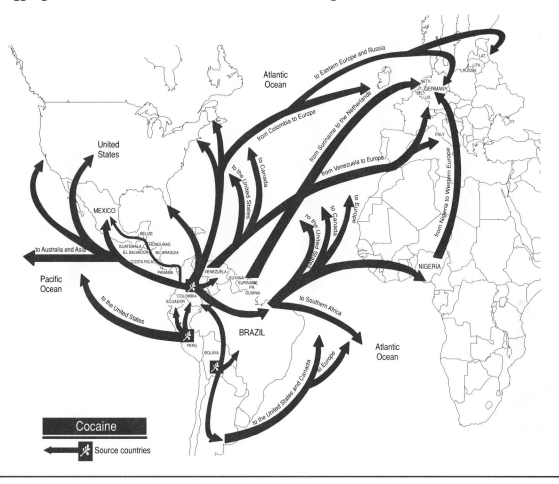

(Source: The NNICC Report 1995: The supply of illicit drugs to the United States, Drug Enforcement Adminstration, Washington, D.C.)

had dropped in some locations to as low as $50. Since 1988, the wholesale price and purity of cocaine have not changed significantly.[6]

The abundance of cocaine is the result of powerful and illegal independent drug dealers who have joined forces to form **drug cartels** that control the production, refining, and smuggling of cocaine into the United States (fig. 5.1) and to the rest of the world. To continue the trafficking of cocaine, two of the most powerful drug cartels, one centered in Cali, Colombia, and the other in Medellin, Colombia, have murdered thousands of their countrymen with their own private armies.[7] Judges and other government officials have been assassinated and elections threatened.

Despite some highly publicized arrests and many large seizures of cocaine, the Colombian drug traffickers continue to ship cocaine in metric ton amounts into the United States by way of the Caribbean, Central America, and Mexico (fig. 5.2). Mexico is the major transit country

for cocaine shipments into the United States, but some of the shipments arrive from other transit countries, such as Brazil, Ecuador, and Argentina. Even the United States serves as a transit country for shipments destined for Canada. Increasingly, shipments are destined for European countries, and there is evidence that Australia is now being targeted.[8]

President Clinton has pledged to continue the efforts to combat the influx of cocaine into the United States through an international cocaine strategy that "focuses on the growing and processing areas of the source countries."[9] This strategy involves efforts to "eradicate production, arrest drug kingpins and destroy their organizations, and interdict drug flow." While the Clinton

> **drug cartels** groups of illegal independent drug dealers who join forces for the purpose of controlling the production, distribution, and marketing of illegal drugs

FIGURE 5.2

Cocaine seizures (metric tons) in the United States, 1990–1995.

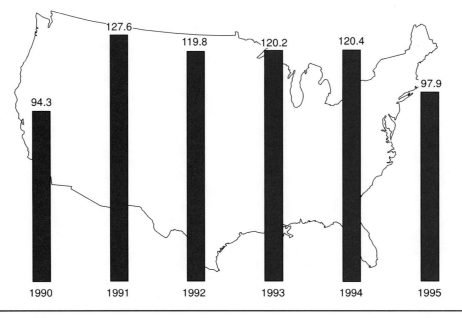

(Source: The NNICC Report 1995: The supply of illicit drugs to the United States, Drug Enforcement Adminstration, Washington, D.C.)

administration points to some recent successes—the disruption of air drug traffic between Peru, where most of the cocaine is grown, and Colombia, where most of the processing takes place, the arrest of major drug traffickers in Colombia and Mexico, and the largest maritime seizure in U.S. history—only time will tell if this approach will change the following statistics. In the meantime, some South American drug mafia have begun to export another profitable drug, heroin (see chapter 6).

Cocaine Epidemic in the United States. In 1975, 5.6% of high school seniors reported using cocaine at least once in the previous year. Between 1975 and 1985 the annual prevalence of cocaine abuse among high school seniors continued to increase to 13.1%, after which the annual prevalence rate began to decline.[10] This decline continued through 1992, when only 3.1% of seniors indicated they had used cocaine in the past year.[11] Beginning in 1993, there was a slight upward trend in cocaine use among high school seniors; in 1995, 4% of high school seniors reported at least one use in the previous year (fig. 5.3).[12] Accompanying this upward trend in cocaine use among twelfth graders was a decline in the perceived risk of harm in trying cocaine, while availability remained relatively steady (fig. 5.3).[13]

Another indicator of the prevalence of cocaine abuse is available through a tabulation of emergency room mentions of cocaine over the past eight years. In 1988, cocaine was mentioned 101,578 times as the reason for an emergency room visit. By 1992, the number of ER mentions had increased to 119,843, an 18% increase. By 1995, the number of mentions was 142,494, another 19% increase (fig. 5.4).[14] Clearly, cocaine remains an important drug problem for our society in the late 1990s.

Pharmacology

The pharmacology of cocaine is influenced by the route of administration, rate of absorption, distribution, and elimination. Cocaine is rapidly distributed throughout the body to the nervous system, where it produces potent stimulatory effects. It is quickly inactivated and excreted. Therefore, it remains in the body for only a short time.

Administration. There are four commonly used routes of cocaine administration. These are oral (ingestion), snorting (absorption), smoking (inhalation), and intravenous administration (injection). The rate of movement of cocaine into the bloodstream, and hence, its rate of arrival at the sites of action in the brain, depends on the route of administration.

Oral administration is perhaps the oldest route and is still used by (and primarily confined to) the South American Indians. Leaves of the coca plant are rolled into a

FIGURE 5.3

Trends in cocaine use among high school seniors, 1985–1995.[10,11]

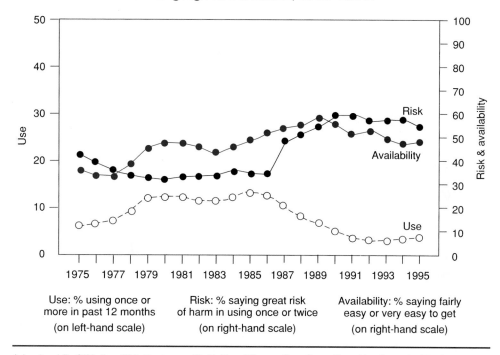

Use: % using once or more in past 12 months (on left-hand scale)

Risk: % saying great risk of harm in using once or twice (on right-hand scale)

Availability: % saying fairly easy or very easy to get (on right-hand scale)

Johnston LD, O'Malley, PM, Bachman JG: National Survey Results on Drug Use from the Monitoring the Future Study, 1975–1995. Vol. 1. Secondary School Students, NIH Pub. No (96-4139) Rockville, Md, 1996, USDHHS.

ball and tucked into the cheek and occasionally chewed. This results in a slow release of juices containing, among other chemicals, active cocaine, which begins to reach the brain in 15 to 20 minutes (fig. 5.5). As mentioned earlier in this chapter, cocaine has also been ingested in the form of tonics and drinks. Recently, there has been a renewed interest in the oral administration of cocaine in herbal teas.

The second route is that of snorting or sniffing the purified powder (cocaine hydrochloride crystals). Throughout most of the 1920s and again in the 1960s and early 1970s, a majority of those seeking pleasure from cocaine employed this method. The cocaine crystals are arranged in lines on a smooth surface, such as a mirror, and sniffed using a small tube or a rolled-up dollar bill. Cocaine crystals are deposited on the mucous membranes of the nasal passages and throat, where they dissolve and are absorbed into the bloodstream. They are distributed to the brain within several minutes. This method continues to find favor among some social abusers.

Because cocaine is absorbed so readily through the mucous membranes and because it has a reputation as an aphrodisiac, some bizarre and dangerous routes of administration have recently appeared in the medical literature. In one case, cocaine was applied to the vagina before vaginal intercourse.[15] In another case, cocaine was inserted into the rectum for the purpose of relaxing the anal sphincter and increasing pleasure during male homosexual anal intercourse.[16] Both of these cases resulted in the death of the abuser. These practices are dangerous because the highly vascular nature of the vaginal and rectal mucosa provide rapid absorption of the drug into the bloodstream.

Smoking (inhalation), a third route of administration, became popular first in the 1920s and then again in the 1970s. **Free-basing** has been a method of choice for those who want to inhale cocaine vapors. In this method, the crystals of cocaine hydrochloride are dissolved in ether (a highly flammable liquid) and then applied to a cigarette (tobacco or marijuana) or allowed to dry and then smoked through a water pipe. The effect is an almost immediate high, or "rush," that occurs much more rapidly than through ingestion, absorption, or even injection—perhaps as fast as 8 seconds (see fig. 5.5).

> **free-basing** the act of preparing smokable cocaine from cocaine hydrochloride crystals by dissolving them in ether or mixing them with baking soda or ammonia and water and then smoking (inhaling) the vapors produced from heating the mixture

FIGURE 5.4

Trends in emergency room mentions of cocaine, 1988–1995.[14]

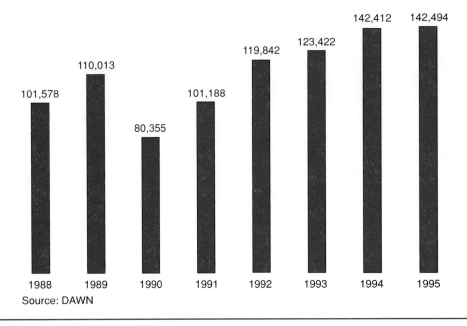

Source: DAWN

Preliminary Estimates from the Drug Abuse Warning Network: 1995 Preliminary Estimates of Drug-Related Emergency Department Episodes. SAMHSA Advance Report No. 17 Aug. 1996. USDHHS. PHS, Rockville MD. Office of Applied Studies.

However, this method of free-basing can cause explosions and fires, as comedian Richard Prior learned in 1980 when his clothes caught fire and he was severely burned. A safer method of making free-base cocaine involves the use of baking soda or ammonia in water to make smokable cocaine. This method of making smokable cocaine led to a new epidemic of cocaine abuse, smoking "crack."

"**Crack**" and "rock" are nicknames for a stable, smokable lump composed of cocaine mixed with baking soda or ammonia. These ready-to-use chunks of free-base cocaine allow the user to quickly repeat dose after dose of the drug. Because of its ease of preparation, its stability, and its cost, crack smoking had become epidemic in many parts of the United States by the mid-1980s. Cocaine in this form is available to anyone with $5 or $10. Even though the price seems cheaper, buying cocaine this way is more expensive when calculated on a cost per gram of cocaine basis. Crack is often smoked close to the point of its sale, often in an abandoned building known as a "crack house."

Unfortunately, smoking crack increases the likelihood that the abuser will develop an uncontrollable dependence on cocaine. The abuser gets an almost immediate high (within 8 seconds) that lasts only a few minutes. The depression that follows deepens with each subsequent use and is accompanied by an intense desire to repeat the use.

The result is the rapid onset of dependence and the equally rapid loss of the user's financial resources.

Intravenous administration has been the preferred route for cocaine abusers who are also regular abusers of heroin or other injectable drugs. Intravenous injections result in an almost immediate high, or "rush," which begins within 15 seconds after injection, lasts about 10 minutes, and is followed by an unpleasant period of depression, or "crash." A "smoother ride" is said to be obtained from a "**speedball**," the injectable mixture of heroin and cocaine (or methamphetamine). The price for this experience is an increased risk for a drug overdose and a more rapid onset of drug dependence. Comedian John Belushi died while doing speedballs.

Absorption, Distribution, and Excretion. Intravenous injection and inhalation of smoked crystals bring cocaine directly in contact with the blood and bypass the normal routes usually described by the term *absorption*. Each of these direct routes provides an almost immediate physiological response. Sniffed or snorted cocaine is absorbed through the mucous linings of the nose and throat into the bloodstream, whereas ingested cocaine enters the bloodstream after being absorbed through the stomach wall. The cocaine is transported throughout the body by the blood.

FIGURE 5.5

FIGURE 5.5

The method of administration determines the speed of the drug's effect on the brain. The more rapid the means of administration, the greater the potential for addiction.

How Fast Does Cocaine Affect the Brain?

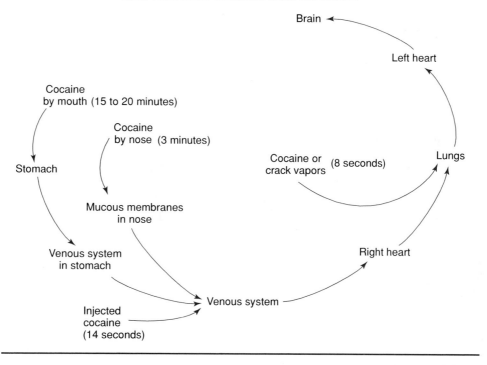

Cocaine rapidly crosses the blood-brain barrier and is found in the fluids that bathe the brain. It also crosses the membranes in the placenta and is distributed by the fetal circulation to the developing nervous system. Cocaine's effects continue until its concentration in these tissues is reduced by enzymatic biodeactivation. Enzymes that detoxify cocaine are present in the liver and in the bloodstream itself. The compounds resulting from enzymatic action are somewhat more water soluble than cocaine and are more easily excreted by the kidneys. The half-life of cocaine in the body is short, lasting only one to two hours.

Neurohormonal Influences of Cocaine

The chemical name for cocaine is **benzoylmethylecgonine.** Although cocaine's chemical structure is markedly different from those of the amphetamines and dopamine and norepinephrine, its effects are virtually identical. In blind trials, experienced users were unable to distinguish between cocaine and dextroamphetamine (d-amphetamine).

Mode of Action.   The sites of action of cocaine are the synapses between nerve fibers of both the central nervous system (CNS) and the peripheral nervous system (PNS). The mode of action is not clearly understood and is currently the topic of intense investigation. There is evidence, however, that cocaine molecules interfere with the reuptake of the neurotransmitter dopamine into the presynaptic nerve terminals (fig. 5.6). The continued presence of this neurotransmitter at the postsynaptic receptors produces an elevation of mood and increased mental and physical alertness.

Physiological Effects.   Cocaine affects both the PNS and the CNS. Although cocaine's acute effects are highly stimulatory, they are very brief. The chronic physiological effects can result in serious medical complications and death.

> **crack** a chunk of solid, smokable, free-base cocaine
> **speedball** an injectable mixture of heroin and cocaine (or, alternatively, heroin and amphetamine)
> **benzoylmethylecgonine** the chemical name for cocaine

FIGURE 5.6

(*a*) In a normal synapse, dopamine is reabsorbed into the nerve cell. (*b*) When cocaine is present, the dopamine remains in the synaptic cleft, thus increasing the pleasure sensation.

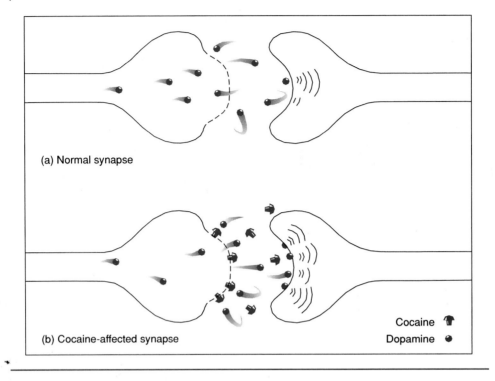

Acute Effects. Cocaine's effects on the sympathetic nervous system include an increase in respiration and heart rate and a loss of appetite. Heartbeats may be irregular and extremely rapid. As blood vessels constrict, blood pressure and body temperature rise. The rise in blood pressure may cause hemorrhaging or congestive heart failure. Other symptoms include sweating and a pale appearance. Cocaine's effects on the voluntary branch of the PNS include increased motor activity but no increase in physical strength or improvement in coordination.

Cocaine's effects on the CNS include euphoria, increased alertness and mental awareness, and a corresponding reduction in fatigue. At exceedingly high (toxic) doses, convulsions and seizures may occur.

Chronic Effects. In addition to the primary physiological responses listed earlier, cocaine abusers experience a number of undesirable side effects associated with chronic abuse. These include dizziness, irregular heartbeat, sleeping disturbances, nasal burns and sores, chest pains, and coughing. Although cocaine is touted as having aphrodisiac properties, chronic abuse can actually lead to impotence and a loss of sex drive.[17]

As with other drugs, chronic cocaine abuse results in tolerance. More and more cocaine is needed with each successive use to achieve the same level of euphoria achieved by a previous dose. Unfortunately for the abuser, tolerance with regard to the euphoric feeling increases rapidly, whereas tolerance against serious physiological reactions does not. Therefore, as cocaine abuse intensifies, abusers may be steadily increasing their risks of heart attack, seizure, and stroke.

Psychological Effects. Cocaine produces acute and chronic psychological effects that are similar to those produced by the amphetamines. Reported feelings range from euphoria and exhilaration immediately after administration to **anhedonia** (inability to experience pleasure) and depression as the drug is eliminated. Dependence is firmly established in a significant proportion of abusers.

Acute Effects. Cocaine's acute psychological effects depend to some degree on the route of administration. Administration by any route results in an elevation of mood and feelings of energy, optimism, confidence, and euphoria. Administration by inhalation or injection results in the rapid delivery of large quantities of cocaine to the brain all at once, resulting in a shortening and intensifying of these feelings. Sometimes referred to as a "rush," these effects have been described as "the best bodily feel-

Cocaine's only legitimate medical use is as a topical anesthetic for examination and surgery of the oral, nasal, and laryngeal cavities.

no physical dep – strong craving

ing you can get on earth" and "a major-league orgasm." Many abusers recount experiencing these intense feelings with their first experimental uses of cocaine and end up spending a great deal of time and money trying, but failing, to recapture those same feelings.

As cocaine levels in the blood fall, the mood returns to normal, and then to below normal. At this point, there are feelings of dysphoria, despondency, depression, and even thoughts of suicide, all of which entice the abuser to pursue further cocaine use.

In this regard, cocaine and amphetamines share several behavioral similarities. For example, human research subjects with a history of cocaine use often mistake dextroamphetamine for cocaine during trials. Other experiments have been designed in which laboratory animals can self-administer cocaine or dextroamphetamine. The cocaine-addicted animals show no withdrawal signs when they self-administer dextroamphetamine. Both cocaine and dextroamphetamine have been shown to be powerful **reinforcers**—that is, they quickly produce a self-administration response in laboratory animals.[18]

Some researchers believe that the rate of change that occurs at the cellular level is directly related to the strength of reinforcement. Evidence from long-term studies indicates that users who self-administer cocaine by methods resulting in rapid infusion (intravenous injection and smoking) are more likely to develop compulsive abuse than those who take it by routes allowing slower rates of infusion (ingestion and snorting).[19]

Chronic Effects. Chronic cocaine abuse can produce psychological disturbances, such as irritable and violent behavior, depression, confusion, impaired thinking, anxiety, paranoia, memory loss, cocaine psychosis, halluci-

nations, and suicidal tendencies. Until recently, it was believed that cocaine did not produce physical dependence because the classic physical withdrawal symptoms, such as those observed in withdrawal from alcohol, barbiturates, and heroin, could not be detected. However, it was soon found that the intense desire to repeat the experience of euphoria and the profound depression that immediately follows the high produce an extremely high potential for abuse. That is, the primary withdrawal symptoms are psychological, including craving and depression. The depression and the irritable feeling of a need for another dose (craving) often result in a loss of control in spite of serious consequences for one's health, family, financial well-being, or life.

Current Use Patterns

Although current medical uses of cocaine are quite limited, nonmedical uses, as we have already mentioned, seem to be unlimited. Even though cocaine abuse seems to be slowing, new users experiment for the first time each day, and many of these will lose control to the drug.

Medical Uses. Today, cocaine's only legitimate medical use is as a local anesthetic used before examination or surgery of oral, nasal, or laryngeal cavities.[20] It can be

> **tolerance** physiological and enzymatic adjustments made in response to the chronic presence of a drug
>
> **anhedonia** feelings of emptiness, meaninglessness, and lack of pleasure
>
> **reinforcers** drugs that are capable of generating a self-administration response in laboratory animals

Modified from Chatlos C, *Crack: What You Should Know About the Cocaine Epidemic* (New York: Putnam, 1987).

SELF-ASSESSMENT

Are You at Risk for Crack Addiction?

The following are some steps toward crack dependence. Many experts agree that dependence progresses more rapidly with crack than with most other drugs. Are you on this path?

1. *Experimentation.* Peer pressure, availability, lack of information, misinformation, and prior use of gateway drugs, such as nicotine, alcohol, or marijuana, contribute to first or experimental use of crack.

   Do you follow advice from friends about trying new and dangerous experiences? How available is crack in your neighborhood, school, or college? What are your use habits with tobacco, alcohol, and marijuana? How would you rate your risk for experimentation with crack?

2. *Social recreational use.* If you have used crack more than once, you know that the absence of tolerance at first use leads to an immediate euphoria and a quick return to normal. You probably felt that no harm was done. You may have begun recreational use of crack. If you continue to smoke crack, perhaps along with continued use of other drugs, tolerance will develop and you will soon need to increase your dose.

   If you have smoked crack more than once, have you increased your dose? Have you missed a class or other school or social activity? Are you having trouble obtaining enough money to buy crack? Are you spending more time with different friends? Do people say you have changed?

3. *Preoccupation.* In this stage, crack smoking becomes intensified, occurring on a more than regular basis. Other drugs, such as amphetamines, PCP, and heroin, may be tried. Although still in school, the crack smoker is preoccupied with planning and thinking about crack or other drugs. Rationalization about the need for these activities becomes second nature. Drug use may even be considered self-medication needed just to feel normal.

   Are you often thinking about where or from whom you can buy more crack, how much to buy, and with whom to smoke it? Have you had to do something dishonest, such as lie, cheat, or steal, in order to buy crack? Do you often find yourself explaining to yourself and to others why you are smoking crack? Do you feel that you need to smoke crack in order to feel better?

4. *Dependence.* In this stage, drug use has become compulsive. The crack smoker has become addicted to crack and perhaps to other drugs. Drug use becomes the primary focus of life. The crack smoker doesn't know what normal is any more. Because self-image is connected with drugs, the crack smoker feels guilty. This poor self-image results in the perception that suicide is now a possible escape route. It is estimated that as many as 36% of crack users think about suicide and 18% attempt it.

   Do you smoke crack just to feel normal? Do you seek out other drugs to relieve the feelings that occur when there is no more crack? Have you thought about your situation as being hopeless? Have you considered suicide? Have you thought about seeking help?

---

applied topically or injected with a hypodermic needle into the mucous membranes of the nose, throat, or bronchi, where it produces rapid vasoconstriction and local anesthesia (numbing). Such local use may, nonetheless, result in a certain level of systemic intoxication. Cocaine is no longer used to ease the withdrawal symptoms of opiate addicts or for the treatment of depression. The reasons for this discontinuation are the fleeting nature of cocaine's stimulatory effects and the subsequent period of depression.

Patterns of Abuse

Going by such street names as "blow," "C," "coke," "cola," "flake," "golddust," "happydust," "leaf," "pearl," "rock," "snow," "stardust," "toot," "white girl," and many other descriptive names, cocaine became America's fastest growing illicit drug during the 1970s and 1980s, particularly among teenagers and young adults. Even though polls show that abuse has declined since 1986, cocaine use is still a serious problem in the United States.

Many new users begin as experimental or social users and progress through a series of stages to compulsive abuse or addiction (see the box above). For some, cocaine use represents the addition of yet another drug to their previously established usage of marijuana and alcohol. Results from a long-term study indicate that although some users are able to remain classified as **recreational users** (including experimental and social users), others become **intensified users,** who abuse cocaine daily. Still others become **compulsive users,** whose abuse has become even more frequent and intense, resulting in disruption of their lives and deterioration of their health.[21] This study was completed before the advent of crack cocaine, but it is instructive to note that all of the compulsive users in this study were free-base cocaine smokers. Dependence on cocaine occurs more rapidly when smoking is the route of administration. Earley has proposed a five-stage cycle to explain the development of dependence on cocaine. This cycle is outlined in the following section.[22]

The Cocaine Addiction Cycle.   A model of the **cocaine addiction cycle** as described by Earley is illustrated in figure 5.7.[23] The cycle is divided into five distinct stages. Stage I begins with cocaine use, which may be the result of an almost casual decision early in the addiction process or the result of craving and rationalization when dependence has become severe. When the initial euphoria caused by the drug wears off, there is an immediate craving or intense desire for more cocaine. Use continues until all of the addict's cocaine or money is gone, even though continued use fails to fully meet the user's expectations for euphoria. Later in the binge, side effects may occur, including the appearance of small, flashing flicks of light, paranoia, a racing heart, and chest pains. The addict may renew the search for more cocaine or the money to buy it. If more cocaine is obtained, the addict may consume huge quantities in an attempt to recapture the euphoric effects of the first dose. If the addict is unable to find more cocaine, he or she may consume large amounts of other drugs, such as alcohol, barbiturates, or other depressants, to temper the effects of the falling levels of cocaine in the bloodstream. This is called modulator drug use. Stage I, which lasts from 1 to 48 hours, ends with the end of the cocaine binge.

Stage II, early crash, is characterized by extreme cravings for cocaine, agitation, and paranoia. The addict searches everywhere for more cocaine (or money), including old hiding places, and fantasizes about obtaining more. The addict in this stage has no appetite and finds food revolting. The addict's body temperature is high, and he or she sweats profusely. The addict uses other drugs to modulate the effects of the cocaine crash. Feelings of remorse over cocaine use mark the transition from stage II to stage III. Stage II lasts from 1 to 4 hours.

Stage III, late crash, begins when intense cravings for cocaine diminish. This occurs over a period of about 30 minutes; the addict feels at once less anxious and more remorseful. Appetite returns, and the addict becomes sleepy. The addict may sleep or eat voraciously. Feelings of guilt, shame, self-reproach, or even suicide occur at this stage. Addicts may consider entering a treatment program and sometimes call emergency rooms or hot-

lines during this stage. Consumption of other drugs stops, and the addict promises never to use cocaine again. Stage III can last from 4 to 36 hours.

Stage IV is the time between binges, when the addict feels good about having survived the horrors of the cocaine binge. There is relief, an improving mood, and a self-confidence about one's ability to avoid relapse. While the addict feels normal, especially compared with the recent experiences in stages II and III, there remains a restlessness and emptiness. This empty or flat feeling, when there is no pleasure and a lack of meaning in one's life, is called *anhedonia.* Although the addict feels he or she has won the battle over cocaine, there are intermittent episodes of craving. These episodes can be brought on by exposure to cocaine or by other cues that remind the addict of cocaine. For many, the memories of the intense pleasure overwhelm the memories of stages II and III, and the addict decides that he or she needs cocaine, thus entering stage V. Nevertheless, it is at stage IV that the addict can take the other fork in the road, the path to recovery. This occurs as the result of the **recovery response,** a natural response to the trauma of being chemically dependent. The recovery response can be nurtured and strengthened through counseling, a treatment program, or a support group, such as a 12-step program like Cocaine Anonymous. Recovery can occur only when the addict removes himself or herself completely from the cycle. Stage IV can last from 4 hours to 45 days.

Stage V is characterized by drug seeking. The addict rationalizes this behavior, which is easy to do because of the growing intensity of the craving and the overwhelming anticipation, the latter often manifested in the "pre-cocaine jitters" (dry mouth, racing pulse, sweaty palms, and diarrhea). Once the addict obtains and uses cocaine again, he or she returns to stage I, and the cocaine addiction cycle continues. Stage V lasts from 30 minutes to 4 hours.

recreational users those with a cocaine use pattern that includes experimental and social use and that does not cause significant deterioration in function for the user

intensified users those with a cocaine use pattern involving daily use over a long period of time and who, therefore, are more likely to have deterioration of function

compulsive users those with a cocaine use pattern characterized by high-frequency and high-dosage use

cocaine addiction cycle a theoretical cyclical model that describes five stages of drug addiction as they relate specifically to cocaine dependence

recovery response a natural reflex of the mind that occurs when specific obstacles are removed from the addict's path to recovery

FIGURE 5.7

The cocaine addiction cycle (*top*) depicts the cyclic behavioral pattern exhibited by cocaine addicts. Specific events mark the transition from one stage to the next (*bottom*).

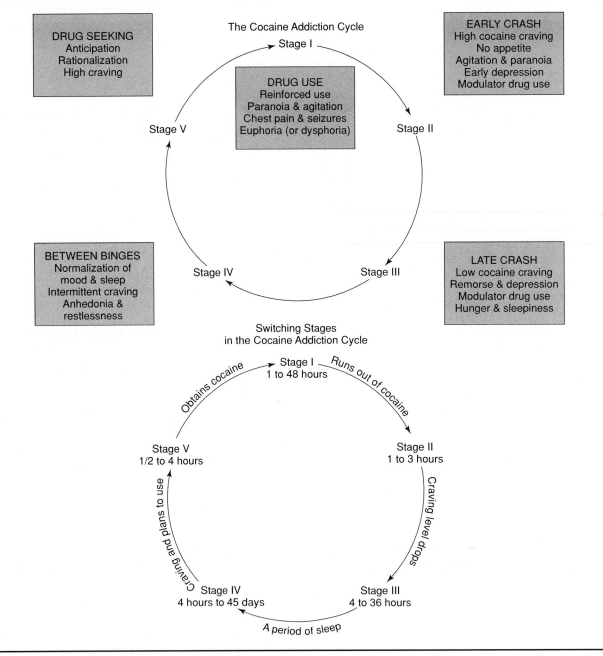

(Modified from Earley, P.H.: *The cocaine recovery book,* Newbury Park, Calif, 1991, Safe Publications.)

Health Consequences of Cocaine Abuse

Cocaine is one of the most destructive drugs known. Its abuse has resulted in untold misery for millions by causing death and loss of both physical and mental health. These deaths and health problems affect not only the abuser but often the abuser's family. In this respect, cocaine represents not only a personal health problem, but also a major social and economic problem for our community.

Deaths. Many deaths have been associated with cocaine abuse. Death can be caused directly by the drug, such as

DRUGS IN YOUR WORLD

The Dangers of Cocaine

Cocaine can be harmful or fatal in a number of ways, many of which you may not know about. Read about the dangerous effects of cocaine below—then think twice before you roll the dice with cocaine.

- **Cardiovascular toxicity.** Cocaine can impair heart functioning in a number of ways. It increases blood pressure and heart rate. It also causes coronary arteries to constrict, which can cut off adequate blood flow to the heart. In addition, cocaine can slow the electrical activity of the heart. Any of these changes can contribute to potentially lethal cardiovascular events, such as a heart attack.[a]

- **HIV/AIDS infection.** According to the Centers for Disease Control and Prevention, drug abuse is the largest single contributing factor to the spread of HIV infection and AIDS in the United States.[b] An analysis of data gathered in the nation's 96 largest cities showed that nearly half of all newly diagnosed cases of AIDS and HIV infection were linked to drug abuse. The virus is transmitted when users share needles, syringes, or other drug paraphernalia.

- **Tuberculosis infection.** "Shotgunning," a practice in which a crack user inhales smoke and then exhales it into another person's mouth, has the potential for efficient transmission of respiratory pathogens, including the tuberculosis bacterium. Reasons users cite for engaging in this risky practice include fostering intimacy, conserving drugs, and getting a better high.[c]

- **Accidental overdose.** One study showed that mortality rates associated with overdoses of cocaine and opiates were linked to the user's economic status.[d] Users living in poverty were more likely to die from overdose. However, death from overdose is a risk that all cocaine users take.

- **Asthma attacks and seizures.** Smoking cocaine can cause acute constriction of the airways, leading to crack-induced wheezing and asthma attacks. It can also cause epileptic seizures that can lead to fatal convulsions.

- **Violent death.** Cocaine use is linked to an increased incidence of murder, suicide, and accidental death, such as falls and automobile crashes.

- **Severe emotional and behavioral problems.** Many cocaine users show aggressive behavior, anxiety (including panic attacks), attention problems, delinquency, depression, social withdrawal, other social problems, and thought problems.[e] These behavioral difficulties make it extremely unlikely that the user will be able to function adequately in mainstream society.

- **Adulterated drugs.** The origin and purity of street drugs are always questionable. Cocaine is sometimes diluted, or "cut," with dangerous agents, such as cleaning powders, brick dust, and rat poison.

[a]Schindler C: Cocaine and cardiovascular toxicity, *Addiction Biology* 1(3):31–47, 1996.

[b]Swann N: CDC report highlights link between drug abuse and spread of HIV, *NIDA Notes* Mar/Apr 1997, p. 7.

[c]Perlman D et al: "Shotgunning" as a drug use practice and its relationship to tuberculosis, *NIDA Research Monograph Series 174*. Washington, DC: US Government Printing Office, 1997, p. 196.

[d]Marzuk P et al: Poverty and fatal accidental drug overdoses of cocaine and opiates in New York City: An ecological study, *American Journal of Drug and Alcohol Abuse* 23(2):221–228, 1997.

[e]USDHHS: SAMHSA study of co-occurence between mental syndromes and substance abuse, *DAWN Briefings,* Mar 1997, pp. 3–4.

---

when a user dies of an overdose, heart attack, or seizure, or indirectly, such as when a user contracts HIV or tuberculosis after engaging in unsafe drug use practices. These and other dangers of cocaine are outlined in the Drugs in Your World box above.

Serious Health Problems. A number of serious problems are associated with each route of administration, whether it be snorting, smoking, or intravenous use. Medical problems associated with snorting cocaine include nasal sores, bleeding, congestion and discharge, sinus congestion and headaches, and perforation of the nasal septum (the cartilage between nostrils).

Free-base smoking can cause chest congestion, wheezing, coughing, and the production of black phlegm. There can also be lung damage from the intense heat of the smoke, burns of the lips, mouth, tongue, and throat, and hoarseness. Intravenous administration carries with it the risk of infections at the site of injection, as well as systemic infections that may result in hepatitis, septicemia (a blood infection), endocarditis (inflammation of the sac that surrounds the heart), and AIDS.[24]

Complications during Pregnancy.   A study of illicit drug abuse among arrestees in 21 major cities during 1994 revealed that cocaine was the most prevalent drug abused among female arrestees, ranging from 18% in San Diego to 80% in Manhattan.[25] Medical records from eight Philadelphia hospitals revealed that 16.3% of women in 1989 (the last year for which statistics are available) had used cocaine while pregnant.[26] The abuse of cocaine by women of childbearing age is particularly disturbing because of the effects cocaine can have on the fetus.

Higher rates of spontaneous abortion, detached placentas, and babies with neonatal neurobehavioral deficiencies have been reported in babies born to women who used cocaine while pregnant. Cocaine has also been reported to cause a greater number of premature deliveries, sudden infant deaths, fetal urogenital tract malformations, and low-birth weight babies.[27] One study found that babies born to cocaine abusers are four to five times more likely to be low-birth weight babies (babies weighing less than 2500 g, or 5 lbs) than babies born to noncocaine-using mothers.[28] This study has been confirmed by a second study that also found that cocaine use in the prenatal period was associated with babies of younger gestational age and smaller size at birth and with an increased risk for detached placentas and sudden infant death.[29] In spite of these reports, it is also possible that no ill effects will be detected.[30]

Despite the valid concerns about the prevalence of cocaine use among pregnant women and the consequences outlined above, several authorities have cautioned against drawing firm conclusions too quickly.[31] There are a number of complicating factors that make interpretation of studies in this field difficult. For example, the study populations have not always been adequately defined; that is, the sample studied may not be representative of the entire population. Second, the identification of women using cocaine during pregnancy, the amounts used, and the time periods of cocaine use may have varied. Furthermore, babies born to cocaine-addicted mothers may have also been exposed to a number of other drugs, to infectious diseases, and to inadequate prenatal care.[32] The cocaine-addicted mother is likely to be less able to care for her baby properly, so the baby and other children of the mother are at risk of neglect and abuse. Thus, the extent and permanence of specific effects of intrauterine cocaine exposure on newborns require further study.[33]

Cost to Society

The eventual plight of those who lose control over their cocaine use is clear. They use up all immediate resources, including personal financial assets and perhaps those of family or friends. They may then turn to crime (such as dealing in drugs, prostitution, or stealing) to pay for cocaine. The abusers cease to be productive members of society and become detriments. While cocaine use has declined since 1986, recent data indicate that there are currently 1 to 2 million regular cocaine users in the United States.[34] The cost of America's experiment with cocaine has run into the trillions of dollars.

Signs and Symptoms of Abuse

The signs and symptoms of *early* cocaine abuse are subtle. Someone you know, such as a spouse, roommate, or child, may be using cocaine if you notice:[35]

- A change in sleeping patterns, such as staying up late and sleeping during the day
- Unusual moodiness or irritability
- Frequent "cold" symptoms, or sinus problems, hoarseness, difficulty swallowing
- Runny, bleeding, or sore nose (from snorting cocaine)
- Loss of appetite and/or weight; loss of interest in sex
- Unexplained depletion of money or other resources (spent on cocaine)
- Frequent trips to the restroom (to snort or inject cocaine or to smoke crack)
- Frequent absences from home, school, or work (to buy cocaine)
- Problems in school or at work
- An attitude of distrust or secretiveness
- An unexplained, newfound fear of police or authority
- Avoidance of a drug test or failing to pass a drug test

Signs and symptoms of *chronic* cocaine abuse include:

- Chest pain, breathing difficulties, and respiratory failure
- Bleeding in the lungs, coughing up black phlegm or blood
- Anxiety, depression, loss of pleasure in acts normally pleasurable
- Lack of energy
- Paranoia, hallucinations
- Craving

Treatment

There is no antidote for cocaine dependence, although the search for such a drug is under way. The rapid rise in cocaine abuse in the early 1980s and the subsequent need for treatment facilities caught most communities by surprise. In the early 1980s, many professionals with experience in directing drug treatment programs for other types of dependence began to try to treat cocaine addicts. By the mid-1980s, the treatment of cocaine abuse was identified as a "growth industry."[36]

In response to the need, new treatment programs were developed, but in the 1990s, changes in the health care delivery system resulted in a shift from inpatient care, in which the patient lives in the treatment facility, to primarily outpatient care, in which the patient lives outside the facility. Under managed care, reimbursements from health care insurance will usually not cover inpatient care after the initial period of intake and detoxification, which usually lasts a maximum of 28 days.

It is generally thought that broad-based treatment programs that include medical, psychiatric, pharmacological, and psychosocial elements are the most successful. There have been a few reports of new and successful treatment methods. One method that shows some promise over the standard drug abuse counseling approach is a behavioral approach that involves immediate reward for each urine sample a patient gives that is negative for cocaine. Cocaine abusers receive points recorded on vouchers, which can be exchanged for money, state lottery tickets, or items that promote healthy living, such as ski lift passes, fishing licenses, bicycle equipment, and continuing education materials. It was found that abusers in this behavioral treatment program accepted the program better, stayed in treatment longer, and achieved higher levels of abstinence than those in traditional drug abuse counseling programs.[37] For a discussion of different kinds of treatment programs, see chapter 17.

Treatment for Pregnant Substance-Abusing Women

Society hasn't completely made up its mind about how to view pregnant women who abuse drugs. In some states, such as South Carolina, a woman who gives birth to a baby with cocaine in its body can be sentenced to a prison term for child abuse.[38] Others view the mother, as well as the baby, as a patient, if not a victim. Regardless of the point of view, there is little doubt that pregnant substance-abusing women have special treatment needs based upon their particular characteristics as a population. For example, many share the traits listed in the Centers for Substance Abuse Treatment's (CSAT) publication *Pregnant, Substance-Using Women*:[39]

- Function as single parents and receive little or no financial support from birth fathers
- Lack employment skills and education and are unemployed or underemployed
- Live in unstable or unsafe environments, including households where others use alcohol and other drugs
- Many women are at risk of being homeless and some are homeless
- Lack transportation and face extreme difficulty getting to and from appointments/treatment centers
- Lack child care and baby-sitting options and are unable to enroll in treatment programs
- Experience special therapeutic needs, including problems with codependence, incest, abuse, victimization,

sexuality, and relationships involving significant others
- Experience special medical needs, including gynecological problems

Because of these special characteristics and special needs, gender-specific treatment services are recommended for pregnant substance-abusing women. These should include:[40]

- Comprehensive inpatient and outpatient treatment on demand
- Comprehensive medical services
- Gender-specific services that are also ethnically and culturally sensitive
- Transportation services
- Child care, baby-sitting, and therapeutic day care services for children
- Counseling services
- Vocational and educational services leading to training for meaningful employment, the General Equivalency Diploma (GED), and higher education
- Drug-free, safe housing
- Financial support services
- Case management services
- Pediatric follow-up and early intervention services
- Services that recognize the unique needs of pregnant adolescent substance users

The counseling services listed above should cover the full range of reproductive options, including preconceptional counseling. Preconceptional counseling should include a discussion of (1) the various methods of contraception and the attitudes of the woman, her significant others, and her community regarding their use, (2) the impact on the woman and the fetus of alcohol and other drug use during pregnancy, (3) the potential for prescribed medications, such as Antabuse and various anticonvulsants, to cause birth defects, and (4) alternative

Pregnant substance-abusing women require comprehensive medical care.

medication, with reduced or no potential to cause birth defects, to treat common problems, such as seizure disorders.[41]

Cocaine Hotline: 800–COCAINE

Because of the broadening and deepening epidemic of cocaine abuse in the early 1980s, a cocaine hotline was established in May 1983 to provide counseling and information for those affected by the epidemic. While this number, 800–COCAINE, is still operating, it is now part of a network of national help lines that make up the Nationwide Family Support Group and Crisis Center. Other numbers that reach the same network are 1–800–9HEROIN, 1–800–CRISIS9, and 1–800–HELP111. These numbers can be dialed toll-free from anywhere in the country, 24 hours a day, 7 days a week. Professional counseling services are no longer offered over the phone, but callers can receive information about treatment centers and support groups in the caller's immediate geographic area, information about signs and symptoms of cocaine or other drug abuse, and instructions about how to obtain help for themselves or for others. This telephone service is sponsored by the Phoenix House and the American Council for Drug Education, two private nonprofit organizations dedicated to substance abuse prevention education and treatment.

AMPHETAMINES

The **amphetamines** are synthetic drugs that produce an increase in CNS activity and an elevation of mood. They include several closely related compounds: amphetamine (formerly Benzedrine), dextroamphetamine (Dexedrine), and methamphetamine (Desoxyn).[42] These compounds do not have a natural source and are completely manufactured in the laboratory. On the street, these drugs are known as "bennies," "dexies," or "meth," respectively, or simply as "uppers" or "speed." In addition to these three amphetamines, there are several chemical derivatives of amphetamines that enjoy restricted use as prescription medications. The best known are methylphenidate (Ritalin), phenmetrazine (Preludin), and pemoline (Cylert).

History

The amphetamines were discovered during a search for a synthetic drug with the properties of ephedrine, the active ingredient in a Chinese medicinal tea prepared from the Ephedra plant. The first synthesis of amphetamine was in 1887, but its medical properties were not noted until 1927. Amphetamine was shown to raise blood pressure and effectively dilate bronchial passages of asthmatics when administered as an inhalant.[43] It was marketed in 1932 under the trade name Benzedrine.

In 1935, oral administration of amphetamine was successfully used in the treatment of **narcolepsy**, a disorder characterized by the rapid and uncontrolled onset of sleep.[44] In 1937, amphetamine was shown to be effective in the treatment of hyperactivity in children. In the early 1940s, orally administered amphetamine was used by the Americans as well as the Germans and the Japanese in World War II to promote wakefulness, stimulate activity, and elevate mood. One estimate was that 200 million tablets were supplied to U.S. troops.[45]

Between 1939 and 1947, amphetamines were used without much criticism. Benzedrine (amphetamine) was a common ingredient in OTC inhalers. The inhalers could be disassembled and the amphetamine could be extracted from the paper core and taken orally. College students also used "bennies" to cram for examinations, and truck drivers took them to stay awake at the wheel. Heroin addicts discovered that amphetamines were cheaper and more easily obtainable than cocaine and could be used to replace cocaine in a "speedball," a mixture of speed and heroin injected intravenously.

By 1947, the medical community had become aware of the ongoing abuse of amphetamines, but it was not until 1959 that the Food and Drug Administration banned the use of Benzedrine in OTC inhalers. Other early medical uses of amphetamines in the 1950s and 1960s included treatment for chronic fatigue, chronic depression, and weight control. For 20 years, prescription amphetamines found a large market in America, where overweight and obese people make up nearly half of the adult population.

Pharmacology

Amphetamines can be administered by a variety of routes and are rapidly distributed throughout the body, where they produce effects on the central and peripheral nervous systems. Because they are structurally similar to the neurotransmitters norepinephrine and dopamine, they stimulate the sympathetic branch of the peripheral nervous system and the reward center of the brain.

Administration. Amphetamines are effective whether ingested, injected, snorted, or inhaled. For the purposes of prescription medication, amphetamines are available only as an oral preparation (tablets or capsules). Intravenous injection of amphetamines (principally methamphetamine), either alone or mixed with heroin in a speedball, continues to be a favored route for many who abuse amphetamines. Data on emergency room patients recorded by the Drug Abuse Warning Network (DAWN) reported the following routes of administration of methamphetamine, the primary amphetamine of abuse: intravenous, 35%; snorting, 22%; oral, 10%; smoking, 7%; and unknown routes, 26%.[46]

Methamphetamine smoking, relatively rare before the late 1980s, differs from cocaine smoking in that a glass pipe is used. One or two crystals of methamphetamine are placed inside the glass bowl of the pipe, and the pipe is heated from the bottom. The smoker then removes his or her finger from the hole on the roof of the pipe and inhales the vapors.

Smoking methamphetamine has two perceived advantages. First, inhaling methamphetamine vapors delivers the drug with extreme rapidity to the blood and hence to the brain. Secondly, smoking "meth" is seen as safer since, unlike the hypodermic needle used for intravenous administration, the pipe cannot transmit HIV or hepatitis virus. Methamphetamine smoked in this way is called **"ice."**

Absorption, Distribution, and Excretion.
Amphetamines are quickly absorbed into the blood and rapidly distributed throughout the body. Their molecular structures are sufficiently nonpolar so that they readily cross the blood-brain barrier (see chapter 4 for more information on the distribution of drugs in the body). Inhalation (7–8 seconds) and intravenous injection (15 seconds) produce effects on the central nervous system almost immediately. Snorting (5–10 minutes) and ingestion (20–30 minutes) produce a much slower onset of action.

Elimination of amphetamines involves their biotransformation (by liver enzymes) to other compounds, followed by excretion in the urine. Another metabolic pathway involves the deactivation of amphetamines by the attachment of additional molecules to the original structure for excretion by the digestive system. The removal of amphetamines by these two methods occurs at rates such that about half of the drug is removed from the body every 8 to 12 hours.

Neurohormonal Influences

At low to moderate doses, amphetamines elevate mood and increase alertness and feelings of energy. They do this by interfering with the normal activities of neurotransmitters. They also decrease activities of the stomach and intestine and decrease hunger. At high doses, amphetamines can increase heart rate and blood pressure to dangerous levels. Many other side effects also occur in those who use amphetamines. As amphetamines are eliminated from the body, fatigue sets in, sometimes accompanied by depression.

Mode of Action.
The mode of action of the amphetamines is directly related to their structures, which are very similar to those of the neurotransmitters norepinephrine and dopamine. It is thought that amphetamines produce their stimulatory effects by intensifying the effects of these two neurotransmitters. There is also evidence that they cause the release of norepinephrine from presynaptic nerve terminals. Lastly, it has been suggested that amphetamines might block the active uptake of norepinephrine and dopamine back into their presynaptic nerve terminals.

All of these proposed modes of action produce the same result: stimulation of the norepinephrine receptors. This produces alertness and wakefulness in the person who has taken amphetamines. Amphetamines also stimulate the dopamine receptors and thereby produce increased motor activity and feelings of euphoria.

Acute Effects.
The acute physiological effects of amphetamines depend to some degree on the dose taken. For example, at normal oral doses (5–15 mg), amphetamines increase blood pressure, relax bronchial muscles, increase blood sugar, increase blood flow to muscles, and decrease blood flow to internal organs.[47] At high doses or in susceptible individuals, rapid heartbeat and palpitations of the heart can occur.

Because amphetamines stimulate the sympathetic nervous system, they are sometimes referred to as *sympathomimetics*. They produce a slowing of activity in the stomach and intestines, resulting in the suppression of appetite. Overstimulation of the nervous system by amphetamines can cause dizziness, restlessness, insomnia, dryness of the mouth, and other gastrointestinal disturbances.

Chronic Effects.
Chronic physiological and psychological effects of amphetamine abuse include rapid tolerance and strong psychological dependence. Other chronic effects are impotence and episodes of paranoia and psychosis. Once the stimulating effects diminish, chronic users frequently enter into periods of depression that can be severe.

Tolerance.
Tolerance to amphetamines develops fairly rapidly in regular users, but tolerance develops more rapidly to some of amphetamine's effects than to others. For

---

amphetamines drugs, related in structure to the neurotransmitters norepinephrine and dopamine, which produce stimulatory effects on the nervous system

narcolepsy a disorder characterized by the rapid and uncontrollable onset of sleep

ice highly purified methamphetamine crystals that can be dissolved and injected or "smoked" as heated vapors in a glass pipe; also called "crystal meth" or "crank"

example, tolerance quickly develops to its appetite-suppressing effects, but more slowly to its mood-elevating effects.[48] When used to treat **attention deficit/hyperactivity disorder (ADHD)** in children, tolerance to the therapeutic effects develops very slowly. On the other hand, tolerance to psychological effects sought by amphetamine abusers, such as the rush of intense pleasure after an injected, snorted, or smoked dose, develops so rapidly that the habitual user, or **"speed freak,"** may soon need to increase his or her dose to one or two hundred times a normally prescribed dose.

The route of administration of amphetamines is an important factor in the development of tolerance. Oral administration and snorting produce a slower onset of effects and a slower development of tolerance. Inhalation of vapors and intravenous injection of dissolved crystals produce a more rapid build-up of tolerance.

Dependence.   As tolerance develops, it is often accompanied by a strong psychological dependence. Amphetamine abusers feel they cannot face the day without the drug, and they experience a strong desire to take the drug to reverse the feelings of depression that occur as the body eliminates the drug. This desire to repeat amphetamine use is most intense in those who inject or inhale it. In some cases, postabuse depression can be severe and may be accompanied by fatigue and lethargy and the need for long periods of sleep. Classic withdrawal symptoms, such as the shaking, convulsions, and coma that can occur during alcohol or barbiturate withdrawal, are not seen in amphetamine withdrawal.

Medical Uses

Valid and appropriate medical uses for amphetamines are currently limited to three conditions: obesity (caused by overeating, not endocrine imbalances), narcolepsy, and ADHD in children.[49]

The usefulness of amphetamines for the treatment of obesity is somewhat limited. Controlled studies have demonstrated that small (but significant) weight loss is achieved in short-term weight loss programs when amphetamines are prescribed. However, the effectiveness of amphetamines in weight loss programs is short-lived because patients develop a tolerance to the drug in two to three weeks, and this tolerance severely limits the drug's long-term value in weight reduction programs. Moreover, amphetamines do not alter eating behaviors, a process necessary for long-term weight control. The indiscriminate use of these drugs for weight control received much public criticism during the 1980s, yet amphetamines are still approved in some states for obesity and prescribed by some physicians for patients on short-term weight loss programs.

Dextroamphetamine sulfate (Dexedrine) and methylphenidate (Ritalin) are still routinely prescribed for the management of narcolepsy, a sleep disorder described earlier. Obviously, it is appropriate to prescribe this medication only when this condition has been accurately diagnosed. Successful management of narcolepsy with amphetamines also requires the patient's strict compliance with both the manufacturer's recommendations for use and the prescribing physician's directions.

Amphetamines have also proven useful in the management of ADHD in children. The prevalence of ADHD is estimated at 3% to 5% in school aged children (about 2 million children).[50] Prescribing a stimulant drug to reduce excess physical activity may sound paradoxical. (Drugs do not produce opposite effects in adults and children, as commonly believed.) Stimulants taken for ADHD work by causing the reticular activating system in the brain to filter out insignificant stimuli. By not being bombarded with excessive visual or auditory stimuli, a child is better able to focus on a given task. Only a doctor can determine whether your child has ADHD. However, "the essential feature of attention deficit/hyperactivity disorder is a persistent pattern of inattention and/or hyperactivity-impulsivity that is more frequent and severe than is typically observed in individuals at a comparable level of development."[51]

In 1996, more than 1 million children took Ritalin regularly.[52] This was two and a half times more than took the drug in 1990. The question being asked in many magazine articles and televised investigative reports is whether the drug is being overprescribed. That is, how many children should be included in that group who exhibit "a pattern of inattention and/or hyperactivity-impulsivity that is more frequent and severe than is typically observed?" As with any drug, there are side effects that accompany the use of Ritalin and other amphetamines for the treatment of ADHD. The advantages and disadvantages of amphetamine use for the treatment of ADHD are discussed further in the box on page 87.

With so much Ritalin around, it is no surprise that some of it is being diverted for unintended uses. Older siblings who have discovered the stimulatory effects of Ritalin, referred to on the street as "Vitamin R," sometimes take them to school to sell them or to share at parties. Even school officials have been caught with their hands in the "cookie jar." When younger children bring their medications to school, the drugs are often stored by the nurse or health teacher until time for use. In one case, a coach was actually caught stealing the Ritalin.[53]

Abuse

Amphetamines have been used for nonmedical purposes since the earliest days of their marketing. Because of their

WHAT DO YOU THINK?

Treatment of Children with Attention Deficit/Hyperactivity Disorder Using Amphetamines: The Ritalin Riddle

One of the medical conditions for which amphetamines are prescribed is attention deficit/hyperactivity disorder (ADHD). The most common of these are Ritalin (methylphenidate), Dexedrine (dextroamphetamine), and Cylert (pemoline). One of the potential side effects of treatment with these medications is growth inhibition; that is, the child undergoing long-term therapy with either of these drugs could fail to reach predicted growth, either in weight or height.[a] Other side effects may be loss of sleep, headaches, dizziness, nausea, stomach pains, irritability, and facial tics.

The potential benefits are that the child is able to control himself or herself when taking the medication; the child is in a sense "available to learn." Moreover, the child is not yelled at, threatened, and punished as frequently, a situation that can lead to better performance in school and greater self-esteem. Because of their calmer demeanor, many children gain friends and peer acceptance.

[a]Physicians' Desk Reference, 51st ed. (Montvale, N.J.: Medical Economics Company, Inc., 1997).

For some parents these benefits far outweigh the consequences of a child's taking the medication. What would you do if you had to make this decision for your child?

Amphetamines have proven useful in the medical management of attention deficit/hyperactivity disorder in children.

great potential for abuse, they are classified as schedule II substances by the Controlled Substances Act of 1970. Their abuse stems from the feelings of euphoria the user experiences as a result of the activity of these drugs on the central nervous system or from the performance-enhancing effects that result from their activity on the peripheral nervous system. Indeed, there is evidence that amphetamines can slightly enhance the performance of physical tasks, such as running, jumping, and swimming. In a world where time is measured in hundredths of a second, the temptation is great for an athlete to try to improve his or her performance by any method, including drugs.

Abuse of "stimulants" by high school seniors declined annually between 1981 and 1992 and then began to increase.[54] Record keeping for the prevalence of use of "crystal" methamphetamine (also known as "crank," "gofast," or "ice") among high school seniors and young adults began in 1990. Between 1990 and 1995, the percentage of high school seniors reporting at least one use in the previous year nearly doubled to 2.5%.[55] One reason for initiating record keeping on crystal metham-

phetamine abuse was the 19% increase in 1988 of methamphetamine-related hospital emergencies reported by DAWN. Another reason was the persistently high number of seizures of clandestine methamphetamine laboratories in the late 1980s (see the following discussion).[56] The number of illegal methamphetamine labs seized declined each year until 1993, when only 218 were seized, and then began to increase again; in 1995, 327 were seized.[57] The number of methamphetamine and amphetamine-related emergency department episodes also rose significantly in 1994 and remained high in 1995 (fig. 5.8).[58]

attention deficit/hyperactivity disorder (ADHD) a neurological disorder in which stimulating sensory input is not filtered out by the brain's reticular system, resulting in exaggerated behavioral responses; formerly called *hyperactivity*

speed freak a person who injects or inhales large amounts of amphetamines

FIGURE 5.8

Methamphetamine and amphetamine emergency room episodes, 1988–1995.[14]

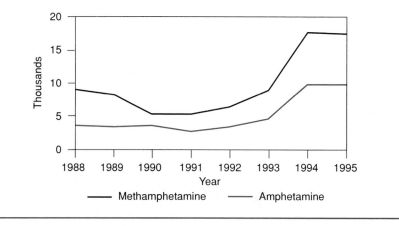

METHAMPHETAMINE

Methamphetamine goes by the street names "crank," "ice," "crystal," "meth," "speed," "go-fast," "go," "crystal meth," "zip," "chris," and "christy." Beginning in the latter half of the 1980s, there was a rapid increase in the abuse of all forms of methamphetamine in Hawaii and in the western continental United States. Experts predicted that this new wave of methamphetamine abuse would spread to the rest of the country, but this did not occur immediately. Figure 5.9 shows the number of illegal methamphetamine laboratories seized from 1988 to 1995.[59] The number of labs seized increased through 1988, decreased during 1989–1993, and then increased through 1995, when 327 labs were seized. Methamphetamine labs accounted for 90% of all the illegal laboratories seized in 1995.[60]

Through 1995, 92% of illegal methamphetamine labs seized were in the West or Midwest.[61] One-third of all labs seized were in California. The prevalence of methamphetamine abuse is also higher in the West[62] and is reported to be more popular than cocaine in some areas of Los Angeles.[63] However, just as experts predicted it would, methamphetamine abuse is now spreading to new parts of the country. In 1995, Missouri was second only to California in the number of illegal meth labs seized, with 374.[64] In 1996, the DEA seized 303 meth labs in the Midwest compared with only six in 1992. The bulk of them (250) were in Missouri.[65]

Traditionally, outlaw motorcycle gangs have been involved in the manufacture and distribution of methamphetamine, especially in the Western states. While these groups and other independent trafficking groups are still involved, organized crime drug groups operating in Mexico currently dominate wholesale methamphetamine trafficking in the United States. The reason organized

crime has become a major player in methamphetamine trafficking is that they have developed international wholesale supply sources for ephedrine, an important precursor for methamphetamine production. Methamphetamine production is increasingly occurring in Mexico. The drug is then smuggled into the United States.[66]

Ice

"Ice" is a form of methamphetamine that first appeared in Hawaii in 1985 and quickly surpassed cocaine as the drug of choice in Honolulu. Between January 1988 and October 1989, there were two methamphetamine arrests for every cocaine arrest in Honolulu.[67] Sold under the street names "crystal meth," "crack meth," "quartz," "glass," "shabu," and "batu," ice continues to be the drug of choice in Hawaii.[68]

Ice in Hawaii is a very pure form of methamphetamine (98% to 100% pure) and looks like rock candy. (It should be noted that the term "ice" has been used for other drugs and drug combinations, depending on user group and geographic location.) The production of the pure crystal methamphetamine used in Hawaii traditionally takes place in the far east, in South Korea, Taiwan, and the Philippines. Mainland China has also been confirmed as yet another source.[69] The chemical method necessary to produce this form of methamphetamine has apparently not reached the United States, so the methamphetamine manufactured on the U.S. mainland is not of the same purity as Hawaiian ice. Most recently, methamphetamine traffickers from Mexico have replaced the traditional Asian suppliers as the primary source of methamphetamine to Hawaii.[70]

Crystal methamphetamine abuse has been a long-standing problem for the Japanese. In Japan, however,

FIGURE 5.9

Methamphetamine laboratory seizures, 1988–1995.[6]

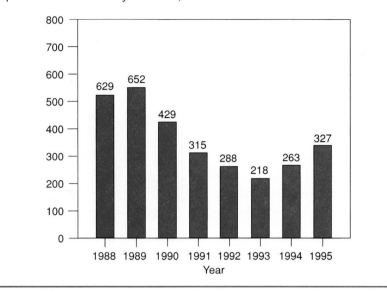

the crystals were usually dissolved in water and injected.[71] Soon after ice was introduced into Hawaii, it was sold as the only smokable form of methamphetamine. The high profile of "crack" (smokable cocaine) and the fear of the spread of AIDS through shared needle use added to crystal methamphetamine's appeal.

When crystal methamphetamine is smoked, its effects are felt in 7 to 8 seconds as a wave of intense physical and psychological exhilaration. The effects may last from 4 to 14 hours, much longer than the effects from crack. The drug keeps the user awake and alert but eventually causes a depletion of the body's stored energy, which can only be restored with sleep. Physically, the body burns itself up while depleting itself of vitamins and nutrients. Chronic users exhibit weight loss; reduced resistance to disease; damage to the lungs, liver, and kidneys; and behavioral problems.[72]

Psychological dependence on methamphetamine deepens with intensified use. Insomnia, anxiety, depression, fatigue, and a psychotic state develop. Toxic psychosis, similar to paranoid schizophrenia, and delusions may also occur. Withdrawal results in acute depression and fatigue but not physical discomfort. However, the depression can be severe and, therefore, dangerous. Other dangers associated with the use of ice are the effects of toxic (poisonous) doses that can cause convulsions, coma, and death. Methamphetamine can pass from mother to fetus and has been found in newborn babies.[73] Concern has been expressed about the possible long-term effects of amphetamine abuse on the neurotransmitter systems of developing fetuses, particularly during the later stages of gestation.[74] However, more research is

needed to determine more precisely the type and degree of damage that could occur.

Amphetamines and Violence

Violence can be associated with drug use in three ways: (1) users can become violent under the influence of the drug, (2) users can use violence to get the drug or money to buy the drug, and (3) traffickers can use violence in the course of their business. There is some evidence that violence attends methamphetamine abuse more than certain other drugs because the effects of chronic use include delusions, hallucinations, paranoia, and extreme agitation. Police in Contra Costa County, California, report that methamphetamine is involved in almost 90% of the cases of domestic violence they investigate. Drug enforcement officials report that seizures of illegal labs often include the capture of numerous weapons and armaments. Many gang-style killings have also been reported in southern California and elsewhere.[75]

THE CATHINOIDS

The **cathinoids** are alkaloids derived from the khat plant, *Catha edulis*. Khat is native to east Africa and the southern part of the Arabian Peninsula, where it grows as an evergreen shrub or small tree. The primary

> **cathinoids** alkaloid chemicals that are unique to the khat plant, *Catha edulis*

psychoactive ingredients in khat are **cathinone** and **cathine,** two central nervous system stimulants. **Methcathinone,** a synthetic structural analog of cathinone (and also of methamphetamine), appeared in the United States for the first time in 1991.[76]

History

Khat has been used for social and medicinal purposes in East Africa for centuries, perhaps longer than coffee. It is grown in Kenya, Ethiopia, and North Yeman and imported into the nearby desertlike country of Somalia, where it is enjoys popular use. The Somalian khat trade began in the 1960s but was outlawed by the Somalian government in 1983. When the warlords took over, the khat trade resumed.[77] Most Americans first learned about khat from press reports about the United States' humanitarian action in Somalia in 1993.[78]

Cathinone is about 10 times more potent than cathine but loses its potency quickly as its leaves age. This explains why, unlike coffee, the use of khat remained a local phenomenon until recently, when air transport made it possible to export the drug to Europe and the United States. Shipments were seized in Finland, Italy, Norway, Sweden, and Switzerland in the early 1990s. In 1991 and 1992, approximately 800 kg of khat were seized in the United States by the U.S. Customs Service.[79] In 1994, 6.3 metric tons of the plant were seized, and through June 1995, 7 metric tons were seized.[80]

Methcathinone is also known as "cat," "goob," "sniff," "stat," and "wonder star" and is sometimes passed off as methamphetamine, using the names "speed" and "crank." The drug was first encountered in the United States in February 1991 in Marquette, Michigan, where it was being produced in an apartment laboratory. It is believed that the recipe originally came from Ann Arbor, Michigan.[81] Since the drug was new, and technically not illegal, there were delays while the justice system resolved legal questions. Thus, when the police net finally dropped on this lab, some of those involved escaped capture, taking with them the simple procedure for producing cat. Cat production spread to other states. Between June 1991 and August 1993, 27 cat labs were seized. By October 1993, five cat labs had been seized in Wisconsin, one in Washington, one in Illinois, and four in Indiana.[82] Cat is also reported to be a drug of abuse in the former Soviet Union, where it is also known as *ephedrone.*[83]

Pharmacology

Chemically the cathinoids are very similar to the amphetamines and are, in fact, considered to be amphetamines by some authorities. Methcathinone is related to cathinone in the same manner that methamphetamine is related to amphetamine. That is, each is the methylated form of its related compound and thus is more fat soluble and more potent. They are all powerful central nervous system stimulants.

One of more than 25 methcathinone labs seized in the United States in the early 1990s.

Administration. Cathinoids can enter the body by ingestion, snorting, injection, or smoking. In Somalia and other areas of East Africa, leaves and tender stems are chewed and retained in the cheek as a ball, dried and drunk as a tea, or crushed into a paste and smoked like tobacco.[84] The most common route of administration for methcathinone is by snorting, but it can also be ingested, injected intravenously, or smoked.[85]

Absorption, Distribution, and Excretion. To date, few studies have been completed on the absorption, distribution, and excretion of these drugs. It is likely that the cathinoids are biotransformed and excreted along the same metabolic pathways as the amphetamines.

Neurohormonal Influences

The cathinoids are powerful CNS stimulants that produce effects similar to cocaine and the amphetamines.

Mode of Action and Acute Effects. Oral ingestion of cathinone by chewing khat leaves provides a temporary sense of exhilaration, energy, hyperactivity, wakefulness, talkativeness, thirst, and appetite suppression. Continued use may result in psychological dependence.

Although no studies have been published on the effects of methcathinone on humans, preclinical trials in

SOLUTIONS

Things didn't go as Jeff had planned. He was arrested for theft before he could make the big buy. At his juvenile court hearing, the judge suspended Jeff's sentence conditional on his entrance into an outpatient drug treatment program, regular attendance at support group meetings, obtaining his GED, and completing 100 hours of community service.

Although he was relieved to avoid prison, Jeff thought at first the outpatient treatment program was unnecessary. After the first few weeks, however, he began to participate in the group therapy sessions. His counselor, Tony, didn't lead the group discussions but acted as more of a moderator who kept things on track. Jeff responded well to this hands-off leadership approach and felt comfortable enough to share some of his problems. Talking with other members of the group, Jeff began to see some of the ways he might be able to avoid getting himself back into trouble.

Jeff's counselor also helped him get a better-paying job with medical benefits and enroll in a GED program at night. Despite his initial reluctance to participate in the treatment program, Jeff was able to complete it—with continual support from Tony and his mother. To fulfill his 100 hours of community service, Tony put Jeff in touch with an elementary school drug prevention program for which he could volunteer. Today, Jeff has not used drugs for the past six months. After staying with relatives for a while, Jeff and his mother were able to find a small apartment in a neighborhood close to his new job. Jeff's not just killing time anymore—he's looking forward to the future.

rodents have shown that the drug increases spontaneous physical activity, causing the release of dopamine from dopaminergic nerve terminals in the brain, and suppresses appetite.[86] According to reports, methcathinone appears to produce methamphetamine-like effects, including a burst of energy, a speeding of the mind, a feeling of increased self-confidence, feelings of euphoria, and a head or body "rush."[87]

Chronic Effects.   Some very unpleasant effects begin to appear with habitual abuse of the cathinoids. Chronic idleness has been reported as a side effect of long-term khat use in East Africa. Chronic effects reported for methcathinone snorting include paranoia, hallucinations, anxiety, tremor, insomnia, malnutrition, weight loss, dehydration, sweating, stomach pains, nose bleeding, and body aches. Also reported are depression and thoughts of suicide. Little is known about tolerance and dependence, but it can be assumed that tolerance develops quickly, as it does with the amphetamines, and that psychological dependence also develops.

Medical Uses

Neither cathinone nor methcathinone has been approved for any medical use in the United States, and both have been shown to have a high potential for abuse. Thus, both have been placed on schedule I of the Controlled Substances Act (CSA).[88] Cathine is not considered to have significant potential for abuse and has been placed on schedule IV of the CSA.[89]

Abuse

The abuse patterns of methcathinone parallel those of methamphetamine and cocaine—that is, it is abused in binges that last from two to six days. Over this period, methcathinone is continuously self-administered, and the abuser does not sleep or eat and ingests only small amounts of liquids.[90] The binge is followed by a crash in which the abuser eats and/or sleeps. Depression and thoughts of suicide may follow.

Long-term methcathinone abuse by a middle-class youth was reported as follows:

> [The abuser] . . . felt paranoid. Unable to eat, he dropped 40 pounds. His sinuses became caked with blood from snorting the drug. His mouth always felt dry, and thumbnail-size flakes of skin hung from his lips. Even his perspiration smelled of cat. In spite of his condition, only running out of money forced this addict to seek help.[91]

Our knowledge of the chronic effects of abusing the cathinoids is in its infancy. Until scientists have had a chance to carry out more studies, there is little to report. What will become of the budding methcathinone epidemic? Will methcathinone abuse become as widespread as the abuse of methamphetamine or cocaine, or will it be contained? Will international criminals become deeply involved in cat trafficking as they have with heroin and cocaine? Stay tuned.

---

cathinone the primary central nervous system stimulant found in fresh leaves and stems of the khat plant, *Catha edulis*

cathine a secondary (and weaker) stimulant found in leaves and stems of the khat plant, *Catha edulis*

methcathinone a synthetic, structural analog of cathinone, manufactured in illegal laboratories; a powerful CNS stimulant, subject to abuse

SUMMARY

In this chapter, three groups of powerful central nervous system stimulants were discussed—cocaine, the amphetamines, and the cathinoids. Cocaine is derived from leaves of the coca plant, native to parts of the Andes mountains of South America. Although chewing the leaves was a centuries-old custom among the native peoples of South America, the introduction of cocaine into Europe during the 1800s led to its widespread use as an ingredient in over-the-counter medications. This widespread use was discontinued by the close of the nineteenth century, but renewed interest in cocaine arose during the 1960s. Abuse of cocaine grew rapidly in the 1970s and early 1980s and then declined. The epidemic was fueled by international drug cartels operating in South America and the development and popularity of a new, smokable form of cocaine—crack. In the late 1990s, there has once again been a slight increase in the reported use of cocaine.

The pharmacology of cocaine is influenced by the route of administration. Cocaine can be ingested, absorbed, inhaled, or injected. Little ingestion of cocaine occurs in this country. Absorption is through the mucous membranes of the nasal passages and throat. Inhalation of cocaine vapors and injection of dissolved cocaine crystals rapidly produce tolerance and often establish compulsive abuse and dependence. There are five stages in the cocaine addiction cycle.

Cocaine inhibits the reuptake of the excitatory neurotransmitters, principally norepinephrine and dopamine. Acute physiological and psychological effects include an increase in heart rate, body temperature, and blood pressure, as well as mood elevation and feelings of energy and euphoria. Chronic cocaine abuse results in the development of tolerance and dependence. Abstinence results in cravings, paranoia, rapid heart rate, and chest pains. Later psychological disturbances include remorse, guilt, depression, and suicidal thoughts. Other acute health consequences of cocaine abuse include possible cardiovascular or respiratory emergencies that sometimes result in death. The impact of cocaine abuse by women of childbearing age is a particularly disturbing public health problem.

The amphetamines were first marketed in the 1930s as bronchial dilators for asthmatics. Because they produce mood elevation and feelings of euphoria, the amphetamines soon became subject to widespread abuse. The amphetamines can be administered in a variety of ways. Injection and inhalation of heated vapors produce the most rapid onset of stimulation. Amphetamines pass easily through the blood-brain barrier and quickly influence the action of the neurotransmitters norepinephrine and dopamine, producing feelings of wakefulness, energy, and euphoria, among other effects. Tolerance develops rapidly to the amphetamines, and chronic abusers develop strong psychological dependence accompanied by feelings of paranoia and, upon abstinence, severe depression.

Recognized medical uses of amphetamines include short-term weight reduction, the treatment of narcolepsy, and the treatment of attention deficit/hyperactivity disorder (ADHD) in children. Recently, there has been concern about its overuse for this last purpose.

Methamphetamine abuse among high school and college students has declined throughout most of the United States since 1982 but remains a problem in the western states. The number of illicit methamphetamine labs declined each year during the period 1989–1992 and then began to increase again. Approximately 90% of all illicit drug labs seized in the United States are methamphetamine labs. Violence is a by-product of methamphetamine trafficking and abuse.

The cathinoids include such natural compounds as cathine and cathinone, which are derived from the khat plant, and such synthetic compounds as methcathinone, which mimics the stimulatory effects of the natural cathinoids. The khat plant has long been used in its native lands as a stimulant, in the same way that coffee and tea have been used elsewhere. Recently, illegal shipments of khat leaves have been intercepted in a number of Western countries, including the United States.

Cathinone and methcathinone are strong central nervous system stimulants with a structure and pharmacology similar to the amphetamines. Because they have no approved medical uses and high potential for abuse, they have been classified as schedule I drugs in accordance with the Controlled Substances Act.

REVIEW QUESTIONS

1. Define the term *stimulant*. Give three examples of stimulants discussed in this chapter.
2. Where exactly does cocaine come from? What were the early medical uses of cocaine? What famous nineteenth century physician advocated cocaine use as a treatment for morphine addiction? What popular beverage was at one time formulated with a cocaine extract?
3. What factors led to the increase in cocaine abuse in the 1970s? During what year did cocaine abuse among high school seniors reach a peak? How would you describe the cocaine abuse patterns among high school seniors who graduated in 1995? What percentage have ever used cocaine (lifetime)? What percentage are currently using cocaine (past 30 days), according to the most recently available statistics? Has cocaine abuse increased or decreased since 1992?
4. Name the four routes through which cocaine can be

administered. Which route is rarely used in America today? Which route delivers cocaine to the brain most quickly? Which routes are most likely to be associated with the development of physical dependence?

5. Differentiate between free-basing cocaine and using crack cocaine. What is a speedball?

6. Describe cocaine's action at the synapse and how this action affects the nervous system.

7. List three acute and three chronic physiological effects of cocaine abuse. How is the cocaine rush described? List several chronic psychological effects of cocaine abuse.

8. List at least six health risks associated with cocaine abuse.

9. What uses, if any, does cocaine have in the practice of modern medicine?

10. Describe the cocaine addiction cycle.

11. Describe a typical cocaine treatment program. How would you describe the effectiveness of such a treatment program?

12. Describe the discovery and early history of the amphetamines. In what OTC device did the amphetamines first appear? Who were some of the first groups of people to abuse amphetamines?

13. What are the primary routes of administration of amphetamines? How do amphetamines affect the brain? The actions of which two neurotransmitters are affected?

14. What are the acute physiological and psychological effects of amphetamines? Describe the chronic physiological and psychological effects, including tolerance and dependence.

15. For which specific medical conditions are amphetamines currently prescribed?

16. Describe the factors that contributed to the epidemic of methamphetamine abuse in the United States in the 1980s, and describe the trends in methamphetamine abuse in the mid- to late 1990s?

17. What are the cathinoids? Where do they come from? List three of them.

18. What group of drugs are the cathinoids similar to?

19. What medical uses do the cathinoids have?

20. What are the acute and chronic effects of abusing methcathinone?

REFERENCES

1. N. Taylor, *Plant Drugs that Changed the World* (New York: Dodd, Mead, 1965).

2. *Remmington's Pharmaceutical Sciences*, 17th ed. (Easton, Penn.: Mack Publishing, 1985).

3. E. M. Breecher, "Licit and Illicit Drugs." in *The Consumer Union's Report* (Boston: Little, Brown, 1972).

4. Ibid.

5. Ibid.

6. National Narcotics Intelligence Consumer's Committee, *The NNICC Report 1992: The Supply of Illicit Drugs to the United States* (DEA-93051) (Arlington, Va.: Drug Enforcement Administration, 1993); National Narcotics Intelligence Consumer's Committee, *The NNICC Report 1995: The Supply of Illicit Drugs to the United States* (DEA-96024) (Arlington, Va.: Drug Enforcement Administration, 1996).

7. T. Squiteri, and J. Kelley, "Colombians Say They Can Win Drug War," *USA Today*, 9 February 1990, p. 3A.

8. NNICC, *Report 1992*.

9. Office of National Drug Control Policy, *The National Drug Control Strategy, 1996*. Executive Office of the President, The White House, Washington, D.C., 1996, NCJ 160086.

10. L. D. Johnston, P. M. O'Malley, and J. G. Bachman, *Drug Use, Drinking, and Smoking: National Survey Results from High School, College, and Young Adult Populations, 1975–1988* (Rockville, Md.: National Institute on Drug Abuse, 1989).

11. L. D. Johnston, P. M. O'Malley, and J. G. Bachman, *National Survey Results on Drug Use from the Monitoring the Future Study, 1975–1994*, NIH Pub. No. 95-4026 (Rockville, Md.: Public Health Service, National Institutes of Health, 1993).

12. Johnston, O'Malley, and Bachman, *National Survey Results, 1975–1994*; L. D. Johnston, P. M. O'Malley, and J. G. Bachman, *National Survey Results on Drug Use from the Monitoring the Future Study, 1975–1995*, vol I, Secondary School Students. NIH Pub. No. 96-4139 (Rockville, Md.: Public Health Service, National Institutes of Health, 1996).

13. Johnston, O'Malley, and Bachman, *National Survey Results, 1975–1995*.

14. Substance Abuse and Mental Health Services Administration, Office of Applied Studies, *Preliminary Estimates from the Drug Abuse Warning Network (DAWN): 1995 Preliminary Estimates of Drug-Related Emergency Department Episodes*. Advance Rept. No. 17, August, 1996. Rockville, Md.

15. T. B. Ettinger, "Sudden Death Temporarily Related to Vaginal Cocaine Abuse," *Am J Emerg Med* 7, no. 1 (1989):129.

16. P. I. Doss, and G. T. Gowitt, "Investigation of a Death Caused by Rectal Insertion of Cocaine," *Am J Forensic Med Path* 9, no. 4 (1988):336.

17. R. K. Siegel, *Changing Patterns of Cocaine Use: Longitudinal Observations, Consequences, and Treatment*, Research Monograph 50 (Washington, D.C.: National Institute of Drug Abuse, 1984).

18. R. A. Wise, *Neural Mechanisms of the Reinforcing Action of Cocaine*, Research Monograph 50 (Washington, D.C.: National Institute of Drug Abuse, 1984).

19. Siegel, *Changing Patterns.*
20. *Physicians' Desk Reference*, 51st ed. (Montvale, N.J.: Medical Economics Company, Inc., 1997).
21. Ettinger, "Sudden Death."
22. P. H. Earley, *The Cocaine Recovery Book* (Newbury Park, Calif: Safe Publications, 1991).
23. Ibid.
24. Ibid.
25. National Institute of Justice, *Drug Use Forecasting: 1994 Annual Report on Adult and Juvenile Arrestees*, NCJ 157644 (Washington, D.C.: U.S. Department of Justice, 1995).
26. J. L. Mitchell, *Pregnant, Substance-Using Women: Treatment Improvement Protocol (TIP) Series 2*, DHHS Publ. No. (SMA) 93-1998. Rockville, Md.: SAMHSA, DHHS, PHS, 1993.
27. I. Chasnoff, and D. R. Griffith, "Cocaine: Clinical Studies of Pregnancy and the Newborn." in *Prenatal Use of Licit and Illicit Drugs, Ann N Y Acad Sci* 562 (1989):260; D. B. Pettitti, and C. Coleman, "Cocaine and the Risk of Low Birth Weight," *Am J Public Health* 80, no. 1 (1990):25.
28. Pettitti and Coleman, "Cocaine and the Risk."
29. J. J. Volpe, "Effect of Cocaine on the Fetus," *N Engl J Med* 327, no. 6 (1992):399.
30. Mitchell, *Pregnant, Substance-Using Women.*
31. L. C. Mayes, R. H. Granger, M. H. Bornstein, and B. Zuckerman, "The Problem of Prenatal Cocaine Exposure: A Rush to Judgment." *JAMA* 267 (1992): 406–8; B. Zuckerman, and D. A. Frank, "Prenatal cocaine exposure: Nine years later," *The Journal of Pediatrics* 124, no. 5(1992): 731–33.
32. L. Finnegan, *Management of Maternal and Neonatal Substance Abuse Problems*, Research Monograph 90 (Rockville, Md.: National Institute of Drug Abuse, 1988).
33. Mayes, et al., "Problem of Prenatal Cocaine Exposure"; Zuckerman and Frank, "Prenatal Cocaine Exposure"; L. C. Mayes, "Exposure to Cocaine: Behavioral Outcomes in Preschool and School-Age Children," in *Behavioral Studies of Drug-Exposed Offspring: Methodological Issues in Human and Animal Research*, DHHS, NIH, NIDA Research Monograph 164, 1996.
34. Substance Abuse and Mental Health Administration, *National Household Survey on Drug Abuse: Population Estimates, 1995*, DHHS Pub. No. (SMA) 96-3095, Rockville, Md., 1996.
35. Center for Substance Abuse Prevention (CSAP), "Tips for Teens: About Crack and Cocaine," DHHS, PHS, SAMHSA, Rockville, Md. (Pamphlet/no date); Drug Enforcement Administration, "It's Your Business: Drug Awareness—Cocaine and Crack," U.S. Department of Justice, Washington, D.C. (Pamphlet/no date).
36. T. J. Crowley, "Clinical Issues in Cocaine Abuse," in Fisher S, Raskin A, Uhlenhuth EH: *Cocaine: Clinical and Biobehavioral Aspects* (New York: Oxford University Press, 1987).
37. Ibid.; S. T. Higgins, D. D. Delaney, A. J. Budney, W. K. Bickel, J. R. Hughes, F. Foerg, and J. W. Fenwick, "A Behavioral Approach to Achieving Initial Cocaine Abstinence." *Am J Psychiatry* 148, no. 9 (1991):1218–24. S. T. Higgins, A. J. Budney, W. K. Bickel, J. R. Hughes, F. Foerg, and G. Badger, "Achieving Cocaine Abstinence with a Behavioral Approach." *Am J Psychiatry* 150, no. 5 (1993): 763–69.
38. "Cocaine babies" USA Today, 16 July 1996, 3A.
39. Mitchell, *Pregnant, Substance-Using Women.*
40. Ibid.
41. Ibid.
42. "Amphetamines." *The Harvard Medical School Mental Health Letter*, 6, no. 10 (1990):1–4.
43. Breecher, "Licit and Illicit Drugs."
44. Ibid.
45. S. E. Lukas, "Amphetamines: Danger in the Fast Lane," in *The Encyclopedia of Psychoactive Drugs* (New York: Chelsea House, 1985).
46. U.S. Department of Justice, Drug Enforcement Agency, Intelligence Division, *Methamphetamine: 1992–1993 Threat Assessment*, DEA-94002, June, 1994, Washington, D.C., the DEA.
47. R. M. Julien, *A Primer of Drug Action*, 6th ed. (New York: W. H. Freeman, 1992).
48. Ibid.
49. *Physicians' Desk Reference.*
50. L. Hancock, P. Wingert, M. Hager, C. Kalb, K. Springen, and D. Chinni, "Mother's Little Helper." *Newsweek*, 18 March 1996, 51–56.
51. American Psychiatric Association, *Diagnostic and statistical manual of mental disorders*, 4th ed. (Washington D.C.: the Association, 1994).
52. Hancock, et al., "Mother's Little Helper."
53. "Hooked on Ritalin," *20/20* broadcast of 20 October 1995, Hugh Downs, Barbara Walters, and Tom Jarriel (Segment host), 1995, Liviona, MI, ABC News.
54. Johnston, O'Malley, and Bachman, *National Survey Results, 1975–1994*; Johnston, O'Malley, and Bachman, *National Survey Results, 1975–1995.*
55. Johnston, O'Malley, and Bachman, *National Survey Results, 1975–1995.*
56. NNICC, *Report 1992*; National Narcotics Intelligence Consumer's Committee, *The NNICC Report 1987: The Supply of Illicit Drugs to the United States* (Arlington, Va.: Drug Enforcement Administration, 1988).
57. NNICC, *Report 1995.*
58. Substance Abuse and Mental Health Services Administration, *1995 Preliminary Estimates.*
59. NNICC, *Report 1992*; NNICC, *Report 1995*; NNICC, *Report 1987.*
60. NNICC, *Report 1995.*
61. NNICC, *Report 1995.*

62. Substance Abuse and Mental Health Administration, *Household Survey, 1995.*
63. DOJ, DEA, *Methamphetamine Situation.*
64. NNICC, *Report 1995.*
65. "Drug Epidemic Grips the Heartland." *Muncie Star-Press,* 9 March 1997, 5A.
66. DOJ, DEA, *Methamphetamine Situation.*
67. *A Special Report: Ice (d-methamphetamine hydrochloride)* (Arlington, Va.: Drug Enforcement Administration, 1989).
68. NNICC, *Report 1992.*
69. Ibid.
70. DOJ, DEA, *Methamphetamine Situation.*
71. DEA, *A Special Report.*
72. D. G. Gibb, (Chief of Police, Honolulu Police Department), Testimony before Select Committee on Narcotics Abuse and Control, House of Representatives, 24 October 1989.
73. Ibid.
74. L. D. Middaugh, "Prenatal Amphetamine Effects on Behavior: Possible Mediation by Brain Monoamines," *Ann N Y Acad Sci* 562 (1989):308.
75. DOJ, DEA, *Methamphetamine Situation.*
76. "Khat Factsheet," (DEA-92064), March, 1993, Drug Enforcement Administration, Intelligence Division.
77. P. Kalix, "Chewing Khat," *World Health,* June 1986: 24–25.
78. NNICC, *Report 1992.*
79. Kalix, "Somalia Khat Use."
80. NNICC, *Report 1995.*
81. J. Keen, "Drug Addiction Enslaves a Starving Nation: Somalia Plagued by Khat Use," *USA Today,* 22 December 1992. 5A.
82. P. Glastris, "The New Drug in Town," *U.S. News and World Report,* 26 April 1993.
83. Department of Justice, Drug Enforcement Administration, "Schedules of Controlled Substances: Placement of Methcathinone into Schedule I," *Federal Register* 58, no. 198 (1993):53404.
84. NNICC, *Report 1995.*
85. Glastis, "New Drug."
86. Department of Justice, Drug Enforcement Administration, "Schedules of Controlled Substances: Extension of Temporary Placement of Methcathinone into Schedule I," *Federal Register* 58, no. 81 (1993): 25934.
87. DOJ, DEA, "Placement of Methcathinone."
88. Department of Justice, Drug Enforcement Administration, *Methcathinone (CAT).* February, 1994, DEA-94007, Washington, DC, DOJ, DEA.
89. DOJ, DEA, "Placement of Methcathinone"; Department of Justice, Drug Enforcement Administration, "Schedules of Controlled Substances: Placement of Cathinone and 2, 5-dimethoxy-4-ethylamphetamine (DOET) into Schedule I," *Federal Register* 58, no. 9 (1993):4316.
90. DOJ, DEA, *Threat Assessment.*
91. DOJ, DEA, *Methcathinone.*

SOURCES FOR HELP

American Council for Drug Education
204 Monroe Street, Suite 110
Rockville, MD 20850
(800) 488–DRUG (3784) or (310) 294–0600

CSAP National Resource Center for the Prevention of Perinatal Abuse of Alcohol and other Drugs
9300 Lee Highway
Fairfax, VA 22031
(800) 354–8824 or (703) 218–5600

Center for Substance Abuse Treatment
Substance Abuse and Mental Health Services Administration
Public Health Service, USDHHS
Rockwall II, 5600 Fishers Lane
Rockville, MD 20857

National Clearinghouse for Alcohol and Drug Information
P.O. Box 2345
Rockville, MD 20852
(800) 729–6686 or (301) 468–2345

Alcohol and Other Drug Use and Pregnancy

Public Health Advisor
Division of Clinical and Prevention Research
National Institute on Alcohol Abuse and Alcoholism
5600 Fishers Lane
Room 14C-20
Rockville, MD 29857
(301) 443–1207

National Maternal and Child Health Clearinghouse
8201 Greensboro Drive
Suite 600
McLean, VA 22102
(703) 821–8955, ext. 254

Hotlines: 1–800–COCAINE (262–2463) or 1–800–788–2800

Cocaine Anonymous (For groups in your area, please consult your local telephone directory.)

DEPRESSANTS 6

1. Explain what depressants are, how they affect the central nervous system, and how they alter behavior.

2. Give five examples of depressant drugs.

3. Explain the mode of action of the most common types of depressant drugs.

4. Describe the acute effects of depressants at different dosage levels.

5. Describe the effects of chronic depressant abuse, including tolerance, dependence, and withdrawal symptoms for both barbiturates and benzodiazepines.

6. Discuss the medical uses of barbiturates, benzodiazepines, and other depressant drugs, including the advantages and disadvantages of the different kinds of depressants.

7. Describe the misuse and abuse of depressants in America.

8. Explain the risks and hazards associated with depressant abuse.

PROFILE

With three small children and an elderly mother to care for, Dolores had been close to having a nervous breakdown. Her doctor gave her a prescription for Valium. After a few months, however, the doctor was reluctant to renew the prescription, and it was only after Dolores insisted that she was not going to be able to cope with the family's upcoming move to Chicago and the responsibilities of a new job that he agreed to continue the prescription for three more months.

When Dolores settled in Chicago, she found a new doctor, from whom she obtained another prescription for Valium. She realized that she was taking more Valium tablets daily than she was supposed to take, but she continued to do so to cope with the overwhelming stress she felt. Dolores was concerned that she might be addicted to Valium.

One day she decided to stop taking the tablets altogether. By late afternoon, she had become nervous and irritable. She snapped at her children and was impatient with her mother. Nevertheless, she refrained from taking any medication the rest of the day. That night she was unable to sleep, even though she had drunk several glasses of wine before going to bed. Frustrated, she took a Valium tablet at about midnight. She tossed and turned until 2 A.M., when she took another Valium tablet. When her alarm when off at 6:30 A.M., she felt drugged and was unable to get up.

What signs of dependence does Dolores show? Is it too late for her to stop using Valium? As you read this chapter, think about drug-free ways Dolores might have coped with her stressful daily routine. Then read the solutions box on page 109.

Depressants are drugs that produce a slowing of physical and mental activities, reduce anxiety, and sedate. In this chapter, we discuss the depressant drugs, except for alcohol, which we discuss in chapters 16 and 17. These substances produce effects similar to those of alcohol but are legally available only through a doctor's prescription. The depressants covered in this chapter include the barbiturates, the benzodiazepines, meprobamate, methaqualone, and several other miscellaneous substances.

Depressant drugs are often referred to as *sedative-hypnotic agents* because they produce a calming effect on behavior (sedation) and induce a state of sleep (hypnosis). The range of physiological responses that can result from the use of depressants depends, in part, on the dosage and includes relief from anxiety, **disinhibition,** sedation, hypnosis, general anesthesia, coma, and death (fig. 6.1).

BARBITURATES

The barbiturates are among the most familiar of the depressant drugs and continue to play an important role in modern medical care. Because of their potential for misuse and abuse, however, barbiturates are among the most dangerous of all prescription medications. The following is a brief discussion of the history, uses, and physiological actions of the barbiturates.

History

Barbiturates are sedative-hypnotic compounds whose central chemical structure is barbituric acid. The discovery of barbituric acid dates back to 1863, when Dr.

A. Baeyer, the German founder of the Bayer Company, first produced it.[1] Although barbituric acid itself does not produce depressant effects, some of its 2,500 derivatives do, and as a group, they comprise some of our most commonly used (and abused) drugs. Barbital, the first synthetic barbiturate, was produced in 1903 by German chemists and given the trade name Veronal. The second barbiturate to be introduced for medical use was phenobarbital (Luminal), which became available in 1912. Secobarbital (Seconal) and pentobarbital (Nembutal) appeared in 1930. More than 25 barbiturates are currently in use today.

Classification

Barbiturates can be subclassified into three groups based on the rapidity of the onset of their effects and the duration of these effects (table 6.1).[2] Ultrashort-acting barbiturates can be felt in 15 minutes or less (in seconds with an intravenous injection), and their duration of action lasts only 2 to 3 hours. Intermediate-acting barbiturates have an onset of approximately one-half hour and a duration of action of 5 to 6 hours. Long-acting barbiturates require approximately 1 hour before the onset of action and have a duration of activity lasting from 6 to 10 hours.

---

depressants drugs that produce slowing of mental and physical activity, reduce anxiety, and sedate

disinhibition the removal of social and personal controls on behavior

barbiturates depressant drugs that share the central chemical structure of barbituric acid

FIGURE 6.1

The range of psychological responses to depressants from mildest (relief of anxiety) to most severe (death).

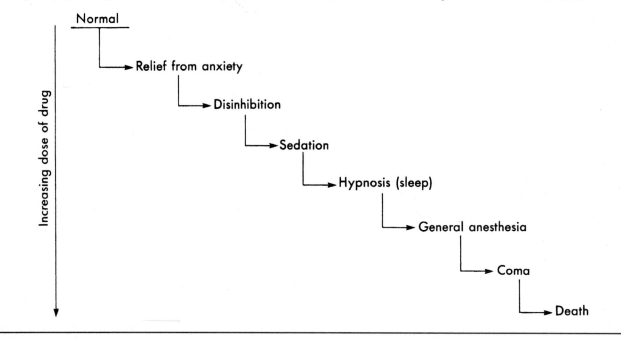

The characteristic bioactivities of barbiturates, and hence their groupings, are directly related to their lipid solubilities (see chapter 4). The ultrashort-acting barbiturates are very soluble in lipids, rapidly enter the bloodstream through the stomach (when taken orally), and quickly cross the blood-brain barrier. These compounds are also cleared from the bloodstream more quickly than the intermediate-acting and long-acting barbiturates, hence, their shorter duration of action.

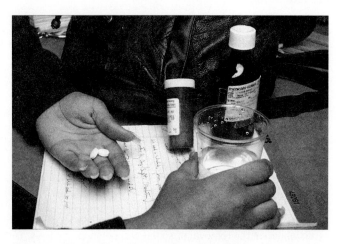

Depressants are drugs that produce sedation and induce sleep.

Pharmacology

The administration, distribution, biodeactivation, and excretion of the various barbiturates are similar. Their rates of distribution are, however, influenced by the degree of lipid (fat) solubility that each possesses.

Administration. Barbiturates are usually taken orally because they are easily absorbed through the gastrointestinal tract. Thiopental and methohexital are administered by intravenous injection as anesthetics for surgery.[3] The result of intravenous injection of these is an almost immediate sleep. Specialized medical training in anesthesiology and careful monitoring of patients are required to safely use barbiturates under these conditions.

Illegal barbiturates are usually taken orally. Abuse of injectable barbiturates, prevalent in the 1960s, is much less common today.[4]

Distribution. Barbiturates are distributed throughout the body by the bloodstream at rates that are dependent on their solubility in lipids or fats. In the bloodstream, a substantial portion of some barbiturates is bound by plasma proteins. Secobarbital, for example, is about 50% bound by plasma proteins.[5] The bound portion of the dose is not immediately available to produce a reaction (see chapter 4). In addition to storage by the plasma pro-

TABLE 6.1 Barbiturates: Elimination Time (Half-Life) and Clinical Data

Generic Name	Trade Name	Elimination Half-Life (hr)	Clinical Use	Route of Administration
Long-Acting				
Butabarbital	Butisol	34–42	Hypnotic	Oral
Phenobarbital	Luminal	24–140	Hypnotic	Oral
Intermediate-Acting				
Amobarbital	Amytal	8–42	Hypnotic	Oral
Aprobarbital	Alurate	14–34	Hypnotic	Oral
Pentobarbital	Nembutal	20–25	Hypnotic	Oral
Secobarbital	Seconal	19–34	Hypnotic	Oral
Ultrashort-Acting				
Thiopental	Pentothal	3–8	Anesthetic	Intravenous
Methohexital	Brevital	4–8	Anesthetic	Intravenous

Modified from W. Clark, D. C. Brater, and A. R. Johnson, *Goth's Medical Pharmacology*, 13th ed. (St Louis: Mosby, 1992).

teins, barbiturates are stored in muscle and adipose (fat) cells. Significant amounts of barbiturates can also be found in the liver, where the concentration ratio (liver: blood) may reach 4:1.[6]

Biodeactivation and Excretion. Barbiturates are biodeactivated by enzymes produced in the liver. Studies have shown that the presence of barbiturates in the blood stimulates the liver to increase production of these enzymes. This, in turn, increases the liver's ability to deactivate any barbiturates present. This process is responsible for the rapid development of tolerance seen in barbiturate use.

As the free (unbound) barbiturate compounds are metabolized and excreted by the kidneys, bound and stored portions of the drug become free and available for metabolism. The equilibria existing among fat-stored, plasma-bound, and free forms of the drug are responsible for the various durations of action observed for the different barbiturates and for their half-lives, the time required for one-half of the drug remaining in the body to be excreted. (For a review of the concept of drug half-life, see chapter 4.) The effective half-life of the fastest of the ultrashort-acting barbiturates is only 1 to 2 hours, although grogginess may continue for hours as fat-stored material is redistributed into the blood and eventually excreted.[7] The long-acting barbiturates are less soluble in lipids and more soluble in water. Therefore, they enter the bloodstream from the stomach much more slowly. They also reach the brain with more difficulty and are redistributed to and from storage sites more slowly. The effective half-life of some of these substances is between 80 and 100 hours. The intermediate-acting barbiturates have half-lives that fall between these extremes.

Neurohormonal Influences

Barbiturates produce general depression of the central nervous system (CNS) by affecting postsynaptic receptor sites at the synapses of brain cells. That is, there is no reduction of the speed of impulse transmission within neurons; rather, there is an inhibition of impulse transmission at the synapses between neurons. The result is sedation and sleep.

Mode of Action. Barbiturates (and the benzodiazepines, discussed later) enhance the activity of the inhibitory neurotransmitter **gamma-aminobutyric acid (GABA).** They do this not by binding with the neuron's receptor sites for GABA, but by binding at sites nearby and somehow enhancing the binding of GABA at its binding site. The result is a greater inhibitory effect of GABA on the neuron.

Acute Effects of Barbiturates. The psychological and physiological responses to the presence of barbiturates in the brain are dose-dependent and are similar to those produced by alcohol. At low doses, behavioral disinhibition and slight sedation are produced first. These effects may be accompanied by a reduction in anxiety, and the result can be mild feelings of euphoria. The observed behavior, however, may depend on such factors as the individual's mood and the social-environmental setting in which the drug is taken. For example, in an exciting setting, uninhibited behavior might be observed,

> **gamma-aminobutyric acid (GABA)** an inhibitory neurotransmitter whose action is enhanced by depressant drugs

whereas in a quiet setting the same individual would probably just fall asleep. Higher doses produce sleep rapidly, and very high doses produce general anesthesia (loss of consciousness), coma, and death. Deaths from barbiturate overdoses are caused by depression of the respiratory system.

Chronic Effects of Barbiturates. Chronic use of barbiturates carries with it the risk of development of both psychological and physical dependence. Studies have shown that ultrashort-acting barbiturates are **reinforcing agents**; that is, test subjects (usually animals) will repeatedly administer these drugs to themselves without any other associated reinforcement.[8] Tolerance rapidly develops with chronic use. This tolerance results from two biochemical phenomena: **microsomal induction** and an adaptation of neurons in the brain to the presence of the drug. Hence, ever-increasing doses of barbiturates are needed to achieve the same level of effects felt initially.

The physical dependence that results from chronic barbiturate use is seen in the withdrawal illnesses that are observed on abrupt abstinence. For example, withdrawal from secobarbital is characterized at first (after 8–12 hours) by the disappearance of barbiturate intoxication and by signs of clinical improvement. Then, however, signs of anxiety, insomnia (sleeplessness), tremulousness, and weakness appear. Difficulty in cardiovascular adjustment is experienced on standing, and anorexia (loss of appetite), nausea, and vomiting also may be experienced.

One or more *grand mal*-type convulsions usually occur during the second or third day of abstinence from barbiturates. Following the seizures, a psychosis characterized by confusion, disorientation to time and place, agitation, tremulousness, insomnia, delusions, and visual and auditory hallucinations may occur.[9] The mortality rate from untreated, abrupt withdrawal from barbiturates is about 5%. In general, the withdrawal syndrome is similar to that observed in alcoholics during abstinence after chronic alcohol intoxication. Partial relief from the symptoms of barbiturate (and alcohol) withdrawal can be achieved by the administration of alternative depressants, the benzodiazepines.

Medical Uses

Many of the barbiturates have beneficial uses in modern medical practice as **anesthetic, preanesthetic,** and **antiepileptic agents.** They are also used for the treatment of sleep disorders, for anxiety reduction, and in therapy for some neuroses. Thiopental and methohexital are used as general anesthetics for surgery because of their rapid action and short half-lives. Amobarbital is sometimes administered as a preanesthetic medication. Butabarbital, aprobarbital, pentobarbital sodium, and secobarbital are prescribed for insomnia. Butabarbital and phenobarbital are also prescribed as **anxiolytic agents** because of their long half-lives. Phenobarbital and mephobarbital are used as antiepileptic drugs because they prevent the onset of seizures.

The overuse of barbiturates for the treatment of insomnia has come under criticism recently. The use of barbiturates may be appropriate as a temporary remedy for the abrupt onset of insomnia caused by a painful event, such as loss of a loved one, hospitalization, or severe pain. However, it is important to note that barbiturate-induced sleep differs from normal, physiological sleep in that the time spent in the rapid eye movement (REM) phase, or dreaming sleep, is less. Following the cessation of regularly used barbiturates, a person may experience markedly increased dreaming, nightmares and/or insomnia.[10] Barbiturates should not be prescribed indiscriminately for long-term or chronic cases of insomnia. Instead, the exact cause of the insomnia should be determined and treated.[11] Long-term use of barbiturates results in the development of tolerance and an increased risk of polydrug use, especially with alcohol.

Fortunately, there are better ways to deal with most sleep problems. The suggestions outlined in the box on page 101 will help many people achieve a restful night's sleep.

Barbiturates and the other depressant drugs discussed in this chapter have very limited use in the treatment of psychoses (major mental disorders characterized by loss of contact with reality). Although they are useful in treating neuroses (anxiety disorders), they are ineffective in the management of more severe conditions, such as manic-depressive psychosis and schizophrenia. Also, it is important to note that the barbiturates and the other depressants discussed in this chapter are not **analgesic agents**; that is, they do not relieve pain.

Barbiturates are useful in the management of certain sleep disorders because they produce sleep.

ALTERNATIVE CHOICES

To Help You Sleep

Can we work at being better sleepers? The answer is yes. Many activities, when done at the appropriate time, will aid you in your quest for sound sleep.

Activities for the Day

Schedule. Maintain a consistent schedule of daily activities; a disrupted day makes sleeping difficult.

Physical activity. Regular vigorous activity promotes sleep; exercising too near bedtime, however, can make you too energized to sleep soundly.

Eating. A large meal taken late in the evening interferes with sleeping; avoid heavy late-night snacks as well.

Alcohol use. A single drink in the evening may be relaxing, but too many drinks during the day make sleeping difficult.

CNS stimulants. Coffee, tea, caffeinated soft drinks, and some medications can disrupt normal sleeping patterns.

Worry. Problems and concerns should be put behind you by the time you retire; practice leaving your concerns at the office or in the classroom.

Rituals. A ritualistic "winding down" over the course of the evening promotes sleep; watching television, listening to records, and reading during the evening are excellent ways to prepare the body for sleep.

Activities for the End of the Day

Bathing. For many people, a warm bath immediately before retiring promotes sleep.

Yoga. The quiet, relaxing exercises of yoga promote sleep by slowing the body's activity level.

Snack or nightcap. A light snack of foods high in l-tryptophan (eggs, tuna, and turkey) and a glass of milk will help you fall asleep.

Muscular relaxation. Alternating contraction and relaxation of the large muscles of the extremities aids the body in falling asleep.

Imaging. Quieting images can distract the mind, allowing sleep to occur more easily.

Fantasies. Escape into fantasies slows the mind and facilitates the onset of sleep.

Breathing. Slow, deep breaths set a restful rhythm the body can "ride" into sleep.

Thinking. By envisioning yourself sleeping soundly, you may in fact fall asleep more quickly.

Abuse of Barbiturates

Barbiturates are subject to abuse because, like alcohol, they provide temporary relief from anxiety and, like alcohol, they quickly produce disinhibition. This effect is believed by some authorities to be responsible for the brief feelings of euphoria and stimulation felt as one of the first actions of depressants. Because of the high potential for abuse, they are classified as schedule II drugs by the Controlled Substances Act (CSA) of 1970.

Most barbiturate abuse occurs in two groups of people. The first are those who seek out barbiturates to get "high." The high, as mentioned above, results from the disinhibition that occurs soon after ingestion of the drug. This pattern of abuse parallels the binge drinking pattern exhibited by those who abuse alcohol. For this group, acute overdose (perhaps from mixing barbiturates with alcohol) rather than the development of physical dependence constitutes the primary health risk.

This group of abusers may obtain barbiturates from a dealer on the street. The street names for barbiturates are many. As a group, they are known as "dolls," "goofballs," or "downers," but specific brands are referred to by names that describe their appearance rather than their effects. For example, Seconal (secobarbital) capsules are

reinforcing agent a drug that produces self-administration, usually demonstrated in laboratory animals

microsomal induction a phenomenon in which the presence of a foreign substance increases the number of microsomes (in the liver), which produce enzymes that detoxify the foreign substance

anesthetics depressant drugs used in medical practice to induce a state of general anesthesia, including the loss of sensation and consciousness

preanesthetic agents depressant drugs given before administration of anesthetic drugs

antiepileptic agents depressant drugs used to minimize the occurrence of epileptic seizures

anxiolytic agents depressant drugs, usually with long durations of action, that reduce anxiety

analgesic agents drugs that relieve pain

called "red birds," "red devils," or "reds." Nembutal (pentobarbital) capsules are referred to as "yellow dolls," "yellow bullets," "yellow jackets," or "yellows." Amytal (amobarbital) capsules are known as "blue angels," "bluebirds," "blue heaven," or "blues," and Tuinal (secobarbital and amobarbital combination) capsules are called "rainbows" or "gorilla pills."[12]

The second group of people who abuse barbiturates are those who obtain unnecessary prescriptions from physicians for daytime sedatives or nighttime sleeping pills. As tolerance occurs, some of these individuals try to obtain duplicate prescriptions from more than one physician to overcome the effects of tolerance. These individuals risk the development of physical dependence.

Trends in Barbiturate Abuse. Barbiturate abuse in high school seniors declined from 1975 to 1992 and then began to increase again. Among 1995 high school seniors, 10.7% reported having taken barbiturates within the previous year, compared with only 2.8% in 1992 and 4.7% in 1995.[13] Only 1.2% of college students surveyed in 1994 reported barbiturate use in the previous year, compared with a high of 3.2% in 1982.[14] While the annual prevalence rate of barbiturate abuse by American high school students has increased since 1992, abuse of barbiturates is less of a problem than abuse of most other drugs.

BENZODIAZEPINES

Although unrelated in chemical structure to the barbiturates, the **benzodiazepines** function in much the same manner. In the sections that follow, the history, pharmacology, physiological influences, and use and misuse of the benzodiazepines are described.

History

Before 1960, when the first of the benzodiazepines became available, the only sedative-hypnotic prescription drugs on the market were the barbiturates and the nonbarbiturate drugs meprobamate (Miltown, Equanil), glutethimide (Doriden), and methyprylon (Noludar). Because of some of the undesirable effects of these drugs and the problems of abuse, the medical community welcomed the arrival of the benzodiazepines. Chlordiazepoxide (Librium), the first member of the benzodiazepines to be marketed, appeared in 1960. Because of its perceived benefits, such as the reduction of anxiety without producing undue drowsiness and the large margin of safety from overdose, chlordiazepoxide rapidly became the most prescribed drug in America. In the early 1970s, chlordiazepoxide was surpassed by another

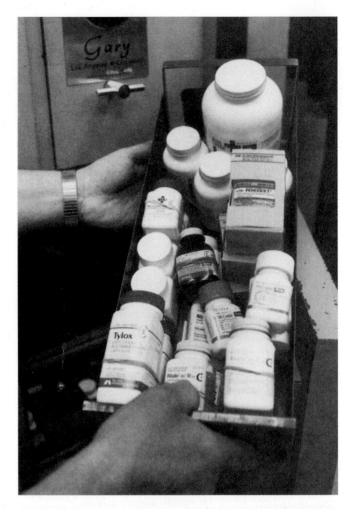

Many barbiturates are Schedule II drugs and must be stored in secured cabinets in hospital pharmacies.

benzodiazepine, diazepam (Valium). Benzodiazepines remain among the most widely used drugs; more than 55 million prescriptions are filled each year.[15]

Currently, about 13 benzodiazepines are available on the U.S. market (table 6.2). As stated, their structure is unrelated to that of the barbiturates, but they produce a similar sedation. It was noted in early studies, however, that when given at doses effective in reducing anxiety, the hypnotic (sleep-producing) effects of the benzodiazepines were somewhat less than those produced by the barbiturates. It was at first thought that the benzodiazepines were superior to the barbiturates because they seemed to produce physical dependence only rarely and to produce little if any psychological dependence. It has since been shown that physical and psychological dependence can occur but that the symptoms of withdrawal illness are less severe than those seen in barbiturate withdrawal. This is believed to be the result, in part, of the longer time required for the body to excrete benzodiazepines.

TABLE 6.2 Depressant Drugs: Uses and Elimination Time (Half-Life)

Generic Names (Trade Names)	Antianxiety	Insomnia	Alcohol Withdrawal	Antiepileptic	Anesthetic	Preanesthetic	Elimination Half-Life (Hours)
Barbiturates							
Phenobarbital (Luminal)	x	x		x			24–140
Mephobarbital (Mebaral)				x			50–120
Amobarbital (Amytal)		x				x	10–40
Pentobarbital (Nembutal)		x					15–50
Secobarbital (Seconal)		x					15–40
Thiopental (Pentothal)					x		3–6
Methohexital (Brevital)					x		1–2
Benzodiazepines							
Alprazolam (Xanax)	x						4–28
Chlordiazepoxide (Librium)	x		x			x	8–24
Clonazepam (Klonopin)				x			15–30
Clorazepate (Tranxene)	x		x	x			50–100
Diazepam (Valium)	x		x	x		x	20–90
Flurazepam (Dalmane)		x					50–100
Halazepam (Paxipam)	x						14–30
Lorazepam (Ativan)	x	x	x	x		x	10–20
Oxazepam (Serax)	x		x				10–25
Prazepam (Centrax)	x						20–100
Temazepam (Restoril)		x					10–20
Triazolam (Halcion)		x					2–5
Midazolam (Versed)					x	x	1–2
Miscellaneous Depressants							
Meprobamate (Equanil)	x						10–24
Methaqualone (Parest, Quaalude)*		x					19–41
Glutethimide (Doriden)		x					5–22
Methyprylon (Noludar)		x					4–8
Ethchlorvynol (Placidyl)		x					10–25
Chloral hydrate (Noctec)		x					4–7

From R. M. Julien, *A Primer of Drug Action,* 5th ed. (New York: W. H. Freeman, 1989).

*Removed from licit market but widely available on illicit market.

Pharmacology

In comparison to the barbiturates, absorption of the benzodiazepines occurs from the small intestine rather than from the stomach. Therefore, absorption occurs more slowly. Administration, distribution, and excretion, however, occur in a manner similar to that seen with the barbiturates.

Administration. For anxiety reduction and daytime sedation, the benzodiazepines are usually administered orally. For the relief of the acute symptoms of alcohol withdrawal, injectable formulations of chlordiazepoxide (Librium) and diazepam (Valium) are also available. Injectable diazepam is also used as an anticonvulsant and as a preanesthetic for surgery. Injecting the drug directly into the muscles speeds up the process of absorption; hence, the onset of the drug's effects begins within minutes.

benzodiazepines a group of sedative-hypnotic compounds that includes chlordiazepoxide (Librium) and diazepam (Valium)

WHAT DO YOU THINK?

Marketing Drugs

Benzodiazepines have been marketed as a new type of depressant that is different and much safer than barbiturates. While this is true in some cases, benzodiazepines have been shown to have many similar characteristics of barbiturates in that they produce tolerance and dependence and are dangerous when taken with alcohol. How much of what we know about drugs is based on information provided by drug companies' marketing divisions?

Heroin, now an illegal narcotic, was originally marketed as a cough remedy, while methaqualone, now an illegal depressant, was originally marketed as a cure for malaria. How were these marketing errors made?

A drug company is in business to make money. In order to do this, it must find and develop a drug that meets the needs of patients and their physicians, and then sell enough of that drug to recover costs and make a profit. When a company finds a drug that produces physiological or psychological effects, what is the primary factor it takes into account in reaching its marketing decisions? Patient need, market demand, or the properties of the drug itself? What do YOU think?

Absorption, Distribution, and Excretion.   As a group the benzodiazepines are more water soluble than the barbiturates and, therefore, are absorbed more slowly. The absorption of an oral dose does not occur to any significant degree until the drug reaches the small intestine. Onset of physiological effects begins 2 to 4 hours after ingestion. Maximum levels of the compound appear in the bloodstream in 8 to 24 hours, and the drug is distributed only slowly to the brain. The half-lives of these drugs range from 5 to 250 hours (averaging 24 to 48 hours), and effective levels of these drugs may remain in the blood for up to a week. (See chapter 4 for a discussion of drug half-lives.)

Metabolism of some of the benzodiazepines involves their biotransformation to intermediate compounds that are pharmacologically as active as the original drug. For example, diazepam and chlorazepate are metabolized to nordiazepam and then to oxazepam, both of which are potent sedative-hypnotics.[16] This phenomenon, which is not unusual in pharmacology, prolongs the duration of activity of these benzodiazepines. The benzodiazepines and their metabolites are eventually excreted by the kidneys.

Neurohormonal Influences and Mode of Action

As mentioned earlier, the benzodiazepines produce a depressing effect on the activity of the nervous system that results in a calming of anxiety feelings. The mode of action of the benzodiazepines is centered in the enhancement of GABA's inhibitory influence on the nervous system; thus, they function in a manner that is similar to that of the barbiturates. Despite the fact that these compounds have been marketed as "new and different" (from the barbiturates), the differences between benzodiazepines and the barbiturates may not be as great as the marketing materials for these drugs suggest. For more thoughts on the marketing of drugs, read the box above.

Acute Effects of Benzodiazepines.   Because of their slow absorption rates, their long onset of action, and their weak effect on the sleep centers compared to the barbiturates, the acute effects of the benzodiazepines are less pronounced than those of the barbiturates. In fact, although overdoses with benzodiazepines are not uncommon, deaths are extremely rare.[17]

Chronic Effects of Benzodiazepines.   The benzodiazepines produce tolerance with long-term use, although this occurs less dramatically than with the barbiturates. Dependence on benzodiazepines occurs rapidly and frequently. Physical dependence often occurs within 4 to 6 weeks of daily use.[18] The clinical signs exhibited with abstinence, although similar to those for barbiturate withdrawal, are shorter in duration and milder in degree. The difference is believed to be related to the relatively longer half-lives of the benzodiazepines and, hence, the slow reduction in the blood levels of these compounds.

Physiological responses to withdrawal include tremors, shakiness, headache, profuse sweating, heart palpitations, and insomnia. Psychological effects include irritability, increased anxiety, tension, agitation, restlessness, difficulty in concentration, feelings of foreboding, and panic attacks. Other physical reactions may include muscle twitching, muscular aches and pains, and sensitivity to light, sound, touch, pain, and smell. There may be nausea, vomiting, loss of appetite, weight loss, and flulike symptoms. On rare occasions, seizures and psychotic reactions occur.[19] Unlike in withdrawal from narcotics, symptoms do not include preoccupation, cravings, or drug-seeking behavior.[20]

FIGURE 6.2

The effects of depressant drugs on the body.

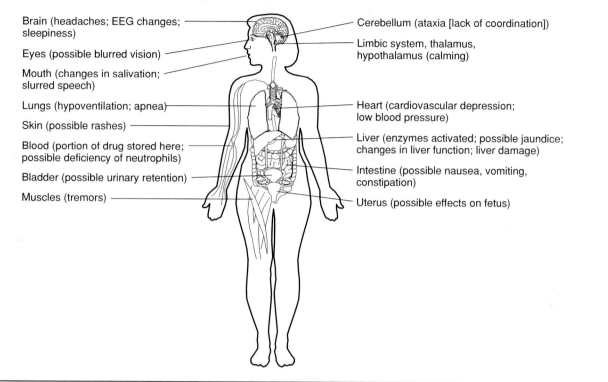

Brain (headaches; EEG changes; sleepiness)

Eyes (possible blurred vision)

Mouth (changes in salivation; slurred speech)

Lungs (hypoventilation; apnea)

Skin (possible rashes)

Blood (portion of drug stored here; possible deficiency of neutrophils)

Bladder (possible urinary retention)

Muscles (tremors)

Cerebellum (ataxia [lack of coordination])

Limbic system, thalamus, hypothalamus (calming)

Heart (cardiovascular depression; low blood pressure)

Liver (enzymes activated; possible jaundice; changes in liver function; liver damage)

Intestine (possible nausea, vomiting, constipation)

Uterus (possible effects on fetus)

In spite of the withdrawal symptoms previously listed, the benzodiazepines are relatively safe compounds when taken for a limited time as a prescribed medication under a physician's supervision. However, there are two situations in which they are definitely dangerous. The first involves their use during pregnancy, particularly during the first trimester, a time when these drugs have been associated with congenital malformations (birth defects) (Fig. 6.2). The second involves their additive or synergistic action when used with alcohol. The combined effect of these drugs produces severe sedation, resulting in significant physical and mental impairment that is especially dangerous when operating a vehicle or dangerous machinery. Polydrug use also increases the likelihood of developing dependence and the risk of an accidental overdose.

Medical Uses

In terms of clinical application, the "uniqueness" of the benzodiazepines has resulted in uses somewhat different from those assigned to the barbiturates (see the box on p. 106). For example, some of the benzodiazepines are faster-acting than others, and some of these are marketed as hypnotics (sleeping compounds). Examples are temazepam (Restoril), which has a half-life of 5 to 25 hours, and triazolam (Halcion), which has a half-life of 1.7 to 3 hours.

Triazolam is the most frequently prescribed sleeping medication in the United States today. More than 7 million prescriptions were written in 1990,[21] earning the Upjohn company more than 250 million dollars. What makes triazolam different from most other sleeping aids is that while other sleeping medications may leave a patient feeling groggy, triazolam does not. Instead, it may leave people feeling more anxious and sometimes confused the following day. There have also been reports of memory loss, sometimes called "traveler's amnesia" because it can occur on airplane flights. It is believed to occur when someone is awakened before the entire effect of the drug is gone. It should also be noted that elderly patients are especially susceptible to dose-related adverse effects.[22] Many have questioned the drug's safety, and there have been some highly publicized lawsuits.[23]

Many experts feel that the drug's adverse effects are a result of overuse. This occurs when tolerance to the drug develops (usually within two weeks), and the dose must be increased for the drug to remain effective. Increasing the dose increases the risk of side effects. Many of the patients who have suffered serious side effects had been taking higher than normal dosages over long periods of time.

Benzodiazepines are often prescribed for anxiety and for relief from stress. Diazepam, with a half-life of 20 to 100 hours, and lorazepam (Ativan), with a half-life of

ALTERNATIVE CHOICES

The Strange Case of Thalidomide

In 1962, thalidomide became the world's most infamous drug when it was found to be responsible for causing about 12,000 cases of severely malformed babies. At that time, the drug was sold as a sleeping pill and also for relief of morning sickness associated with pregnancy. Its use often resulted in babies being born with missing or malformed limbs and sometimes other birth defects. The drug was never approved for sale in the United States, but was sold in 48 other counties.

In spite of the problems with thalidomide, research on the drug has continued. One of the diseases for which thalidomide has proven most useful is leprosy. More recently, it was discovered that the drug is also useful against some of the potentially fatal side effects of bone marrow surgery. Other reports suggest that it might be useful in fighting tuberculosis; macular degeneration (which can lead to blindness); and even AIDS.

It is obvious that thalidomide has multiple effects in addition to sedation. Scientists are now trying to determine exactly how the drug works. So far, they have found that it blocks tumor necrosis factor, which fights both malignant cells and infections but in large quantities worsens the symptoms of leprosy, tuberculosis, and AIDS. Thalidomide also inhibits the formation of new blood vessels, a feature that leads to the birth defects mentioned previously.

Currently, two U.S. drug companies are expected to seek FDA approval for thalidomide's use in treating lesions associated with leprosy and in treating the mouth, throat, and rectal ulcers afflicting AIDS patients. Clearly, patients will have to take precautions against becoming pregnant while taking thalidomide if the FDA approves this drug for use, even restricted use, in the United States.

C. Gorman, "Thalidomide's Return," *Time* 143(24): 67. "FDA weighs approval of thalidomide," *USA Today,* 13 November 1996, 9D.

---

10 to 20 hours, have been marketed primarily as anxiolytic agents or sedatives. However, mental health experts believe it is important that people learn alternative ways to deal with stressful situations instead of using drugs. This is particularly true on college campuses, where many students report that their number one health problem is stress—stress related to financial matters, classes and grades, and personal and family relationships.

What is stress and how does it relate to anxiety and impairment of health? **Stress** is a natural psychological and physiological response to **stressors,** environmental stimuli that produce feelings of tension and strain. Among the physiological changes that accompany stress are an increase in heart rate, respiration, and blood pressure. Stress that results from planned experiences, such as jogging, has been referred to as **eustress**; stress resulting from unpleasant situations, such as receiving a personal insult or being fired, is called **distress.** Even people who consider themselves to be in good mental health carry out their everyday activities under considerable stress. Unrelenting exposure to stressors can cause anxiety or other mental health problems.

Some college students learn to develop very effective and healthy ways to reduce their stress. Some of these include relaxation training, physical exercise, social programs, meditation, biofeedback, and yoga. Many colleges and universities offer stress management programs through their counseling centers, wellness centers, or health centers. Some departments (such as psychology, health education, and physical education) have short courses to help students deal with stress more effectively. Habits that students establish in college to reduce stress often stay with them for a lifetime.

Benzodiazepines are the preferred drug type for the treatment of alcohol withdrawal syndrome.[24] Injectable diazepam (Valium) can be useful in the symptomatic relief of acute agitation, tremor, impending or acute delirium tremens, and hallucinations.[25] However, routine use of benzodiazepines in the long-term treatment of alcoholism is not recommended, because these drugs

Valium is often prescribed to reduce the stress of day to day living.

Barbs = Schedule II   Benzos - Schedule IV

might produce a state of dependence that is just as devastating as that caused by alcohol.

Abuse of the Benzodiazepines

Considering the large number of prescriptions issued for benzodiazepines each year in the United States, the number of people abusing these drugs is relatively small. The reasons, in part, are the slow onset of action and long half-lives of most of the benzodiazepines when compared to the barbiturates. Chlordiazepoxide (Librium), the first benzodiazepine marketed, is rarely abused. Diazepam (Valium), a stronger drug, has been linked to abuse. However, abuse of diazepam is less frequent than abuse of the barbiturates and is of a different type. The barbiturates, especially the ultrashort-acting ones, have been shown to be powerful reinforcers of behavior in both human and animal studies[26] and, thus, are sometimes abused for their acute effects in much the same way that alcohol is abused. The benzodiazepines are only weak reinforcers and, therefore, less subject to this type of abuse.

Accordingly, the benzodiazepines are classified under the CSA as schedule IV drugs, whereas the barbiturates are classified as schedule II drugs.[27] When a benzodiazepine is the primary drug of abuse, it is usually abused by those who either obtain prescriptions from multiple doctors, forge prescriptions, or purchase drugs diverted from legitimate pharmaceutical companies. Benzodiazepines are a secondary drug of abuse for heroin and cocaine abusers who use them to extend the effects of, or modulate the withdrawal symptoms associated with, their primary drugs of abuse. Approximately 50% of people entering treatment for narcotics or cocaine addiction also report abusing benzodiazepines.[28]

Flunitrazepam (Rohypnol). In the early 1990s, a new benzodiazepine, **flunitrazepam (Rohypnol),** was detected by officials in Florida, Texas, and southern California. Rohypnol came to the attention of officials not only because American youth were mixing the drug with alcohol to "get roached," but because some individuals and groups were using the drug to incapacitate young women before raping them. This resulted in Rohypnol's reputation as the "date rape drug."[29]

The drug, also known as "roofies" or "roaches," is legally prescribed as a depressant in 60 European and Latin American countries but has not been approved for medical use in the United States.[30] The drug is produced by the Roche company in Switzerland and its subsidiaries, including Hoffmann-LaRoche, which makes the drug in South America, Europe, Mexico, and Asia. The drug was initially brought into the United States legally from these sources in small amounts (three months' supply) for personal use, but in March 1996, Treasury Secretary Robert Rubin ordered U.S. Customs officials to confiscate all imports of Rohypnol.[31]

By March 1, 1996, the Drug Enforcement Administration had documented 2,460 federal, state, and local cases involving Rohypnol in 32 states.[32] There had also been numerous seizures of Rohypnol tablets by U.S. Customs officials. In one three-week period, more than 100,000 tablets were confiscated in Laredo, Texas.[33] The drug has become so available that it has been called the "lunch money drug" because it can be bought at school for $1 or $2.

Since Rohypnol is a benzodiazepine, it would normally fall into schedule IV of the CSA classification system, but a report by the DEA indicates that the drug meets all the requirements for declaring it a schedule I drug (refer to chapter 1 for a review of this classification system).[34] In October 1996, President Clinton signed a federal law strengthening the penalties for using Rohypnol to facilitate violent crimes, such as rape, to a maximum of life in prison, for other uses to a maximum of 20 years, and for simple possession to a maximum of 3 years.[35]

MEPROBAMATE

Meprobamate (Miltown, Equanil) was actually the first of the "modern" antianxiety agents. It was approved for use in 1955 and immediately became very popular. At first, it was believed that meprobamate, unlike the barbiturates, produced no physical dependence. This assumption soon proved to be false, and meprobamate was eventually classified as a schedule IV controlled substance, its use being restricted to temporary situations. (See chapter 1 for a discussion of the scheduling of controlled substances.)

During its most popular period, in the late 1950s, meprobamate was used only for daytime sedation and not as a hypnotic. Its duration of action is very short. When evidence was presented associating it with physical and

stress a natural psychological and physiological response resulting from exposure to stressors

stressors environmental stimuli that produce tension and strain

eustress stress that results from planned experiences, such as physical exercise or friendly competition

distress unhealthy stress; results from unpleasant and unplanned situations

flunitrazepam (Rohypnol) a benzodiazepine, illegal in the United States, that has achieved notoriety as the modern "date rape drug"

meprobamate a sedative-hypnotic drug used as an antianxiety agent under the brand names Equanil and Miltown

psychological dependence, and after the benzodiazepines became available, meprobamate lost its popularity.

METHAQUALONE

Methaqualone (Quaalude) was first synthesized in 1955 in India, where it was thought for a short time to be useful in the treatment of malaria. It was soon introduced into Europe and Japan as a hypnotic (sleeping pill), unlike meprobamate, which had been marketed as a sedative. As with other new drugs, methaqualone was advertised as "nonaddictive." By 1972, seven years after its introduction into the United States, it had become the sixth best-selling sedative-hypnotic drug on the market.[36]

The first U.S. company to manufacture methaqualone was the William H. Rorer Company, in 1965, which used the trade name Quaalude. However, other pharmaceutical companies soon entered the profitable market of methaqualone with such trade names as Sopor, Optimil, Parest, and Somnofac. The introduction of this drug into the United States as a nonscheduled prescription drug was allowed to occur despite accumulating evidence from abroad that methaqualone was being used to commit suicide and was also being otherwise abused.

Abuse occurred not only through overprescription but also in the street, where the drug went by such names as "ludes," "sopors," "sopes," "714s," "Dr. Jekyll and Mr. Hyde," "mandrakes," and "quacks." As evidence against its medical value mounted and the number of prescriptions fell, street use became epidemic, bolstered by the drug's unfounded reputation as an **aphrodisiac.** It was known as the "love drug" and "heroin for lovers," both of which were undeserved titles.

In 1973, as a result of U.S. Senate hearings, methaqualone became classified as a schedule II substance—a drug with medical use but high potential for abuse. Drugs in this category are subject to strict controls and record keeping. One result of this regulation was the emergence of "stress clinics" in some states, including Florida. For $75 to $100, individuals could attend one of these "clinics" and, after a brief physical examination and counseling session, obtain a prescription for methaqualone. Because of the difficulty of obtaining the drug by other methods, a portion of the prescribed medication could be sold in the street for a profit. Another result was the increased amount of smuggling of methaqualone from Colombia, through Panama, to the United States. The U.S. Drug Enforcement Agency seized 57,173 kg of methaqualone in 1981.[37] In addition to this illegally imported product, illegal laboratories in the United States produced significant quantities of "bootleg" methaqualone.

In 1984, the U.S. Congress reclassified methaqualone as a schedule I substance—one having high potential for abuse and no accepted medical use. The drug had previously been banned in a number of foreign countries, and all commercial manufacturing had ceased the year before. Successful enforcement operations have reduced the abundance of methaqualone on the streets, and what sells illegally as methaqualone is of questionable identity and quality.

Methaqualone was shown to produce both psychological and physical dependence and became one of the leading causes of drug-related deaths during its peak popularity. Used concurrently with alcohol, methaqualone causes the same impairment of motor coordination as that produced by other depressants. In summary, it was never shown that methaqualone had any of the distinguishing or valuable characteristics of other sedative-hypnotics, but it did have at least as many negative features as the others. The sleeping pill market, for which it was a candidate, remains the domain of the barbiturates.

Currently, abuse of methaqualone is rare in the United States because there is very little methaqualone to be found. Only one illegal laboratory has been seized by the DEA in each of the past three years (compared with more than 1,000 methamphetamine laboratories), and cooperation among various countries has virtually shut down international trafficking in this drug. Most of the confiscated "Quaaludes" that are smuggled into this country are counterfeit; that is, they contain barbiturates, benzodiazepines, or other sedative-hypnotic substances, not methaqualone.[38]

OTHER DEPRESSANT DRUGS

In addition to those already discussed, several other depressant drugs have been developed over the years. Each of these has enjoyed popularity at some time; hence, each warrants brief mention.

Glutethimide, Methyprylon, and Ethchlorvynol

Glutethimide (Doriden) and methyprylon (Noludar) are two nonbarbiturate depressants that were introduced in the early 1950s to produce sedation and sleep. Although not technically barbiturates, the chemical structure of these substances is so similar to those of the barbituric acid derivatives that the modes of actions are thought to be the same. Nevertheless, drug companies marketed these compounds as "new drugs" at the time of their introduction. They are not prescribed very often because of their toxic effects and the fact that they are now deemed less safe than the barbiturates. The medical use

SOLUTIONS

Dolores realized that she needed help discontinuing the use of her prescription depressant. She was reluctant to call Dr. Velasquez, her new doctor, because she was afraid that she would take her off Valium immediately. However, when Dolores explained her experiences to her, including the precipitating crises and prescriptions from her previous physician, Dr. Velasquez was very understanding.

She renewed Dolores's current prescription at a lower dose. She explained that a gradual withdrawal would be less unpleasant than stopping "cold turkey" and told Dolores to call her immediately if she experienced any distressing symptoms. She warned her not to drink alcohol while taking benzodiazepines. She also indicated that within three months Dolores should be able to stop taking Valium altogether.

Dolores felt normal for the first two days she was on the lower dose but didn't sleep as well the second night. She began to feel a little more anxious on the third day and then became restless and irritable. A few times she yelled at the children, who had done nothing unusual to provoke the outburst. She began to question herself: Was she being too harsh? Or was she just more involved with them now that she was taking a lower dose of the depressant?

Dolores called Dr. Velasquez to discuss her concerns. She reassured Dolores that her patience would return and suggested some techniques for keeping her temper in check. She continued to work with her as she tapered off the medication. Over the next year, Dolores became a completely drug-free mother. She began to attend a support group for women in the "sandwich generation," who must care for both their children and their aging parents. Finding out that she was not alone eased the burden of caregiving and helped Dolores move toward better managing the many demands on her time and emotions.

---

for ethchlorvynol (Placidyl), another nonbarbiturate, is as a hypnotic, but the drug carries with it a significant risk of death by overdose.

Chloral Hydrate, Paraldehyde, and the Bromides

Chloral hydrate, one of the oldest known CNS depressants, was first synthesized in 1832. Although rarely prescribed today, it originally was used for inducing sleep, which occurs 30 to 60 minutes after taking a 1 to 2 g dose. Although this drug does not depress respiration as the barbiturates do and has few after effects, it does produce dependence. Chloral hydrate is often marketed in a liquid or syrup and achieved notoriety as "knock-out drops," or a "Mickey Finn," when added to the beverage of an unsuspecting person. Chloral hydrate produces gastric irritation, a characteristic unpleasant side effect.

Paraldehyde shares the advantages of chloral hydrate (CNS depression with rapid onset and little depression of respiration) but has two very unpleasant characteristics: its odor and taste. It is sometimes used as an anticonvulsant and in the treatment of withdrawal symptoms from chronic alcohol use.

The bromides were among the first sedative-hypnotics to be used in medicine. Introduced in 1860 as an anticonvulsant, potassium bromide was shown to produce a number of unpleasant side effects, such as dermatitis, constipation, and, more serious, motor disturbances, delirium, and psychosis. Bromides were also found to accumulate in the body, producing chronic intoxication. The advent of the barbiturates spelled the end of any significant use of the bromides.

Similarities among Depressant Drugs

Whereas the discussion in this chapter is organized by classes of depressants, the similarities rather than the differences of these groups of drugs should be considered. Although novel and sometimes spectacular claims were originally made for most of these substances, their effects are all quite similar. Observed differences in physiological response to these drugs, and to alcohol, often correlate more closely to dosage levels than to any differences in chemical structure. In general, these drugs produce sedation at low doses and hypnosis at high doses. The mood of the user, the social or environmental setting in which use occurs, and the user's expectations of the experience all influence the actual behavioral outcome of depressant drug use.

methaqualone a sedative-hypnotic drug with no currently accepted medical use in the United States; formerly sold under the brand name Quaalude

aphrodisiac a drug that arouses or increases sexual desire

It should be remembered that, unlike the narcotics (discussed in chapter 7), sedative-hypnotic drugs do not specifically relieve pain. Last, this group of drugs is particularly dangerous because of the potential for synergism resulting from polydrug use.

SUMMARY

The depressants, or sedative-hypnotic drugs, are drugs that slow CNS activity, reduce anxiety, and sedate. Unlike alcohol, which is sold over the counter, these drugs can be legally purchased only with a physician's prescription.

Barbiturates are depressant drugs that share the same basic structure, that of barbituric acid. Barbiturates can be classified into three categories according to their onset and duration of action: ultrashort-acting, intermediate-acting, and long-acting.

Administration of depressants, with few exceptions, is by the oral route. The barbiturates and the benzodiazepines are distributed, stored, and excreted on the basis of their lipid solubility. The biodeactivation of barbiturates takes place in the liver, where microsomal induction helps the process. Microsomal induction contributes to the rapid development of tolerance to the barbiturates.

Abuse of barbiturates has increased among high school students since 1992 but remains relatively low in comparison to most other drugs and in comparison to abuse levels of the early 1980s.

The benzodiazepines are structurally different from the barbiturates, but their action is similar. Both increase the activity or effects of the inhibitory neurotransmitter GABA. The benzodiazepines produce sedation as do the barbiturates, but without the respiratory depression associated with the barbiturates. Librium, Valium, and Halcion are the most familiar of the many benzodiazepines.

Medically, benzodiazepines are used as hypnotics, sedatives, and anxiolytics, depending on the unique character of the drug. Overdose deaths from benzodiazepines alone rarely occur. Abstinence by chronic users results in a withdrawal illness that progresses more slowly than that for barbiturates and is not life threatening. Benzodiazepines should not be taken by pregnant women or by those who use alcohol.

Considering the large number of prescriptions issued for the benzodiazepines each year, the number of people abusing them is relatively small. Because they are not as subject to abuse as barbiturates, they are classified as schedule IV drugs by the Controlled Substances Act of 1970. One benzodiazepine that is illegal in the United States is flunitrazepam (Rohypnol). This drug, manufactured in foreign countries, was first discovered in the United States in the early 1990s. It is a powerful sedative that has achieved notoriety as a modern "date-rape drug."

Meprobamate was the first of the "modern" antianxiety agents marketed. Today, the use of meprobamate as a sedative is very limited. Methaqualone was medically important only briefly as a hypnotic. Its reputation among those who use street drugs, although unwarranted, made it a popular illegal drug during the 1970s and early 1980s. Because of effective legislation, enforcement, and international cooperation, the abuse of methaqualone has decreased to a very low level.

Glutethimide, methyprylon, and ethchlorvynol are all nonbarbiturate sedatives whose medical use is limited because of strong toxic effects. Three older depressant drugs, chloral hydrate, paraldehyde, and the bromides, were used in the past but today are largely of only historical interest.

REVIEW QUESTIONS

1. What effect do the depressants have on central nervous system function? How are these effects reflected in observable behavior? Explain the difference between sedation and hypnosis.
2. Which two groups of depressant drugs dominate the market today? Give several examples of each.
3. Describe in your own words the mode of action of depressants; that is, how do they work?
4. Describe the acute physiological and psychological effects of depressant use. How is dosage level related to effect?
5. What are the effects of chronic use/abuse of depressant drugs? Contrast the barbiturates and benzodiazepines with reference to the establishment of tolerance and dependence and their characteristic withdrawal symptoms.
6. What are some of the medical uses of the barbiturates? What is the likely consequence of combining barbiturates with alcohol?
7. What is the primary advantage of the benzodiazepines over the barbiturates? Why are overdoses of benzodiazepines rare?
8. Why were the meprobamates thought at one time to be superior to the barbiturates for use as sedatives?
9. What was the first intended role of methaqualone in medical practice? For what purpose was methaqualone marketed in the United States? Why has abuse of this drug declined?
10. Why were chloral hydrate, paraldehyde, and the bromides initially thought to be valuable sedatives? What was the historically notable use of chloral hydrate?
11. What is Rohypnol? How does it reach the United States? How is it abused?
12. In general, describe the misuse and abuse of depressant drugs in the United States in the 1990s. How does the abuse of depressants compare with the

abuse of other drugs we will be studying in this book? (See chapter 1 for a clue.) Who is at risk for depressant abuse?

13. Are there any special risks associated with depressant abuse?

REFERENCES

1. J. E. Henningfield, and N. A. Ator, *Barbiturates: Sleeping Potion or Intoxicant?* (New York: Chelsea House, 1986).

2. W. Clark, D. C. Brater, and A. R. Johnson, *Goth's Medical Pharmacology*, 13th ed. (St Louis: Mosby, 1992).

3. R. M. Julian, *A Primer of Drug Action*, 6th ed. (New York: W. H. Freeman, 1992).

4. Henningfield and Ator, *Barbiturates*; L. D. Johnson, P. M. O'Malley, and J. G. Bachman, *National Survey Results on Drug Use from Monitoring the Future Study, 1975–1995*, Vol. 1, *Secondary School Students*, NIH Pub. No. 96-4139 (Rockville, Md.: National Institute for Drug Abuse, 1996).

5. M. O. Amdur, J. Doull, and C. D. Klaassen, *Casarett and Doull's Toxicology: The Basic Science of Poisons*, 4th ed. (New York: McGraw Hill, 1993).

6. Ibid.

7. Julian, *Primer of Drug Action*.

8. O. Ray, and C. Ksir, *Drugs, Society, and Human Behavior*, 6th ed. (St Louis: Mosby, 1993).

9. Henningfield and Ator, *Barbiturates*.

10. *Physicians' Desk Reference*, 51st ed. (Montvale, N.J.: Medical Economics Company, Inc., 1997).

11. J. C. Gillin, "Sleeping Pills," in *Harvard Medical School Health Letter*, Boston, 7 May 1990, President and Fellows of Harvard College.

12. Henningfield and Ator, *Barbiturates*.

13. Johnson, O'Malley, and Bachman, *Survey Results, 1975–1995*.

14. L. D. Johnston, P. M. O'Malley, and J. G. Bachman, *National Survey Results on Drug Use from the Monitoring the Future Study, 1975–1994*, Vol. 2, *College Students and Young Adults*, NIH Pub. No. 96-4027 (Rockville, Md.: National Institute for Drug Abuse, 1996).

15. Julian, *Primer of Drug Action*.

16. Ibid.

17. J. Marks, *The Benzodiazepines: Use, Overuse, Misuse and Abuse*, 2nd ed. (Boston: MTP Press, 1975).

18. N. S. Miller, and M. S. Gold, "Benzodiazepines: Tolerance, Dependence, Abuse, and Addiction, *Psychoactive Drugs* 22, no. 1 (1990):23.

19. Mark, *Benzodiazepines*.

20. Miller and Gold, *Benzodiazepines*.

21. "Safe Use of Sleeping Pills," in *The Johns Hopkins Medical Letter: Health After 50* 3, no. 11 (1992):1.

22. *Physicians' Desk Reference*.

23. G. Cowley, et al., "Sweet Dreams or Nightmare?" *Newsweek*, 19 August 1991, p. 44.

24. M. K. Romach, and E. M. Sellers, "Management of the Alcohol Withdrawal Syndrome," *Annu Rev Med* 42 (1991):323.

25. Ibid.

26. Ray and Ksir, *Drugs*.

27. Department of Justice, Drug Enforcement Administration, *Drugs of Abuse* (Arlington, Va.: DOJ, DEA, 1996).

28. Ibid.

29. "Assaults Linked to New Drug in U.S.," *The Muncie Star*, 15 February 1995, p. 4C; T. Henry, and C. Hedges, "Date-Rape Drug Target of New Law," *USA Today*, 14 October 1996, p. 1A.

30. "Assaults Linked."

31. C. Kriss, "Date Rape Pill Banned from USA," *USA Today*, 6 March 1996, p. 1A.

32. T. Friend, "Monster Drug Soon to be on Same List as LSD, Heroin," *USA Today*, 20 June 1996, p. 1A.

33. Kriss, "Date Rape Pill."

34. Friend, "Monster Drug."

35. Henry and Hedges, "Date-Rape Drug."

36. M. Carroll, and G. Gallo, "Quaaludes: The Quest for Oblivion," in *The Encyclopedia of Psychoactive Drugs* (New York: Chelsea House, 1985).

37. Ibid.

38. National Narcotics Intelligence Consumer's Committee, *The NNICC Report 1991: The Supply of Illicit Drugs to the United States*, DEA-92032 (Arlington, Va.: Drug Enforcement Administration, 1992); National Narcotics Intelligence Consumer's Committee, *The NNICC Report 1992: The Supply of Illicit Drugs to the United States*, DEA-93051 (Arlington, Va.: Drug Enforcement Administration, 1993).

SOURCES FOR HELP

National Mental Health Association
1021 Prince St.
Alexandria, VA 22314
(703) 684–7722
(800) 969–HMHA (for brochure)

National Institute for Mental Health
14C-02 Park Lawn Building
5600 Fishers Lane
Rockville, MD 20857
(301) 443–4515

NARCOTICS

7

1. Explain what narcotics are and where they come from.

2. Briefly recount important events in the history of the opium trade and opium use in past centuries. Comment on current patterns of narcotics abuse.

3. Explain how narcotics can be classified and give examples.

4. Describe the various ways that narcotics can be administered.

5. Explain the mode of action of narcotic drugs.

6. Explain how heroin is biotransformed into morphine and how it is excreted.

7. Describe the acute physiological and psychological effects of narcotics.

8. Explain the effects of chronic narcotic abuse, including tolerance, dependence, and withdrawal illness.

9. List the medical uses of narcotics.

10. Discuss the characteristics of heroin abuse, including typical first use, controlled use, and addiction. Describe the "cycle of addiction" typical for many heroin abusers.

11. Discuss the factors that cause heroin addicts to seek treatment and the factors that affect success rates.

12. Distinguish between methadone maintenance and heroin maintenance programs.

PROFILE

Yung, the youngest of four boys in an immigrant family, grew up in an ethnic neighborhood in a large city. His parents were strict disciplinarians who had high expectations for their sons. No matter what Yung did, he couldn't seem to do it as well as his older brothers. Searching for acceptance and a feeling of pride, he joined a street gang when he was 13. The gang gave him a sense of honor that his family didn't.

Soon Yung began to "huff" spray paint vapors or solvents with some of the other younger gang members. Then some of the older teens showed them how to snort heroin. It made Yung sick the first time, but after that it became pretty much a regular thing. As heroin is a bit more expensive than spray paint, Yung and a few of the other younger gang members began to take part in the older boys' "fund raising" activities.

When he was 16, Yung quit school because it interfered with his delivery job. Two to three times a week, he delivered drugs and sometimes drug money. Now he had graduated to shooting heroin. At first he was careful to use a clean syringe and needle. By the time he was 18, he had a $100-a-day habit and could no longer support it by delivering drugs. Yung grew careless and occasionally shot up with used syringes.

Yung's thin frame, hollow cheeks, and unkempt appearance had attracted his family's notice. At his father's birthday party, Yung's oldest brother took him aside and told him how worried his father was about him. Yung had not yet been able to score a hit that day and was already short tempered. Yung shoved his brother away and stormed out of the party. His family received no word from him for two weeks after that.

Narcotics, or narcotic analgesics, are drugs that relieve pain and produce sedation. The word *narcotic* comes from the Greek word *narke*, meaning numbness or stupor. The term *opioid*, or *opioid analgesic*, is also used to describe this group of drugs including natural narcotics, which are derivatives of opium; quasi-synthetic narcotics, made by chemically altering natural opiates; and synthetic narcotics, opiatelike drugs manufactured by drug companies. This classification scheme is discussed beginning on page 116.

Unlike the sedative-hypnotic drugs discussed in chapter 8, narcotics are true **analgesics**; that is, they relieve pain without producing sleep. Some of the narcotic analgesics are counted among the most powerful and useful medications available. However, they are also among the most deadly of abused substances. Those who become dependent on these substances risk death from overdose and from infection with potential fatal diseases, such as hepatitis and AIDS.

HISTORY OF OPIUM AND NARCOTICS

Opium and narcotics have a long and interesting history that spans thousands of years. Although opiate use in the United States remained relatively stable from 1975 to 1994, a recent study established an increase in both its perceived availability and its use among certain segments of the U.S. population.[1] Clearly, abuse of opiates is still a serious concern in the late 1990s.

Early History

The substance **opium** is derived from the dried juice of the oriental poppy plant, *Papaver somniferum*. The geographic origin of the oriental poppy appears to be the Middle East, where hot, dry summers prevail. The use of opium began at least 6,000 years ago. By A.D. 1000, opium had reached India, China, and other parts of Southeast Asia.

Probably the earliest medical use of opium was for the treatment of diarrhea, which in severe cases can cause dehydration and death. Opium provides relief from the pain of "stomach cramps" by reducing the strength of smooth muscle contractions in the intestines and permitting the reabsorption of water. Opiates (derivatives of opium) are still among the most effective antidiarrheal drugs.

Later, opium came to be used as a sedative and as a euphoriant. Consequently, nonmedical use of opium also became well established. Opium gained a reputation as a cure-all for everything from snakebite to leprosy.

In 1806, a young German pharmacist, Frederick Serturner, isolated the primary pharmacological component in opium and called it morphine, after Morpheus,

narcotic a morphinelike drug that relieves pain and induces a stuporous state

analgesics drugs that relieve pain (usually without excessive sedation)

opium the primary psychoactive substance, or "mother drug," extracted from the oriental poppy plant

The drug opium is derived from the oriental poppy plant, *Papaver somniferum.*

the Greek god of dreams.[2] **Morphine** is about 10 times as powerful as opium. In all, about 30 different compounds have been isolated from natural opium, but the only other one with real medical significance is **codeine,** a component in many present-day **antitussives** (cough medicines) and analgesics (pain killers).

During the mid-1800s, two historical events occurred in which opium figured prominently. The first was the Opium Wars, which occurred between Great Britain and China from 1839 to 1842. The British won these wars, which allowed them to expand their opium trade in Asia until the early 1900s.

The second event was the American Civil War (1861 to 1865). The Civil War was the first war in which morphine was available for the treatment of pain. The invention of the hypodermic syringe in 1853 by Dr. Alexander Wood permitted the direct injection of morphine into the body. The widespread use of morphine during the

American Civil War (as well as wars in nineteenth-century Europe) caused many soldiers to become dependent on morphine. Morphine addiction became known as "army disease."[3]

In another chapter of American drug history, the practice of opium smoking was brought to the United States by the thousands of Chinese laborers who were imported to build railroads in the West. These laborers eventually migrated to San Francisco and other West Coast cities, where opium smoking became popular. Fearing that the practice was spreading to include non-Orientals, voters in San Francisco in 1875 passed an ordinance outlawing opium smoking.[4] Other cities soon followed suit.

By the end of the 1800s, scientists at Bayer Laboratories had developed what they thought was a safer drug, but one that still had morphine's qualities. By chemically altering morphine, they produced a drug three times as potent as morphine.[5] The new drug was originally introduced as a cough suppressant, a substitute for codeine. Because it was thought to have wonderful, even heroic properties, it was named **heroin.** Heroin's potency results from its relatively high lipid solubility and hence its rapid absorption into the brain. Unfortunately, heroin proved to be even more addicting than morphine and was eventually withdrawn from the market.

Recent History

At the turn of this century, at least 200,000 Americans (perhaps as many as 1% of the U.S. population) had become dependent on one of the opiates. Opium addicts fell into three groups: (1) long-time users of patent medicines containing opiates, a majority of whom were women; (2) opium smokers, mostly residing in such cities as San Francisco and New York; and (3) those who injected morphine.[6]

In 1906, the first legislation was passed that helped to stem further increase in the number of patent medicine addicts. The Pure Food and Drugs Act of 1906 established the requirement of accurate labels on all drugs sold in interstate commerce, specifically referring to heroin, morphine, opium, and cocaine. The Harrison Act of 1914 was aimed specifically at making illegal the unregistered sale of any of the narcotics or cocaine. Immediately following the passage of this act, addicts could still legally use morphine, but they could legally obtain it only through a physician. Subsequently, the Supreme Court declared it illegal to possess illegally obtained opiates. Eventually, in the 1920s, it became illegal for addicts to obtain these drugs even from physicians.

This criminalization of opiate possession and use resulted in changes in both the population of addicts and the attitude of the public toward those addicted. The number of people who were dependent on the opiates in patent medicines and the number of opium smokers diminished. Those injecting opiates became the main com-

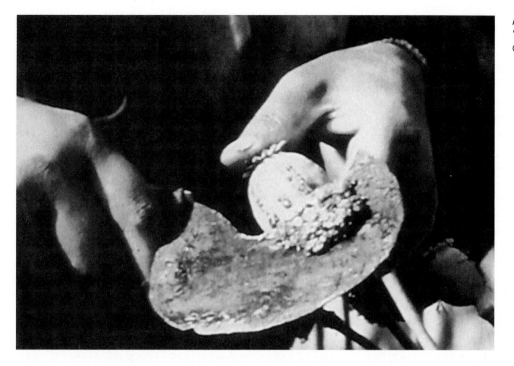

An opium farmer scrapes opium "gum" from the surface of an opium poppy pod during harvest.

By the end of the nineteenth century, thousands of Americans had become dependent upon one of the opiates through the use of patent medicines such as these.

ponent of the addicted population. For these addicts, heroin had become the most popular abused drug.

With the end of the availability of legal drugs, the price of illegal opiates rose, and addicts turned to crime to support their habits. These addicts were not master criminals, and most of their crimes were burglary, prostitution, and low-level drug dealing. Before the passage of legislation that made obtaining and using narcotics illegal, drug addicts were often pitied as victims. Afterward, they became scorned as moral deviates and despised in the public eye.

morphine a natural narcotic, the primary psychoactive ingredient in opium

codeine a natural narcotic with antitussive properties; a component in many prescription cough medicines

antitussive a drug that acts on the central and peripheral nervous systems to suppress the cough reflex

heroin a highly addictive, quasi-synthetic narcotic produced by chemically altering morphine

Heroin abuse continued at a relatively low level until after World War II, when it began to increase, particularly in the inner city ghettos. From 1945 to 1960, there were periods of high and low availability, which resulted in corresponding changes in the purity and price of heroin on the street. The general trend, however, was toward higher prices and lower purity. Heroin abuse accelerated in the 1960s when other drugs, such as the hallucinogens, became popular.

When large numbers of American soldiers were sent to the Vietnam War in the 1960s, some of them experimented with opiates. One study reported traces of opiates in the urine of 1 in 20 returning servicemen. Fortunately, only 1% to 2% of these individuals continued to abuse opiates after returning home.[7] This discovery supports the belief that environmental conditions are a predisposing factor in drug abuse. It also demonstrates that, for many, occasional or experimental use of narcotics does not necessarily lead to addiction. Of course, this should not be considered an endorsement for experimentation.

The first of several heroin epidemics in the United States occurred between 1967 and 1971, when heroin processed from Turkish opium and supplied through the "French Connection" was prevalent in the United States. Aggressive law enforcement, along with international cooperation among law enforcement agencies and successful diplomacy leading to a ban on opium poppy cultivation in Turkey, ended this epidemic.[8] Recent political changes in Turkish leadership have raised concerns about whether the ban on poppy cultivation will continue to be enforced.

Another epidemic occurred from 1974 to 1978, when Mexican heroin became widely available. Poppy eradication efforts by the Mexican government and a drought ended that epidemic.[9]

During most of the 1980s, heroin in the United States came from Southwest Asia, Pakistan, Iran, Afghanistan, and Lebanon. In the early 1990s, the U.S. heroin market was dominated by the presence of high-purity Southeast Asian heroin.

Current Trends

It is estimated that 2.4 million Americans have used heroin at some point in their lifetime and that more than 400,000 Americans have used it in the past year.[10] Although annual use of heroin and other opiates by young adults has remained stable and relatively low (around 2.5%) over the past 20 years, there is evidence that heroin use is once again on the rise.

Heroin arrives in the United States from four sources: (1) Southwest Asia, the "golden crescent" of Afghanistan, Pakistan, and Iran; (2) Southeast Asia, the "golden triangle" of Thailand, Laos, and Myanmar (Burma); (3) Mexico; and (4) Colombia (fig. 7.1). In 1992, there was an upward trend in the availability of heroin on the east coast of the United States because of the increased supply of highly purified heroin from Southeast Asia, the source of 58% of the heroin seized and purchased in the United States that year.[11] By 1995, however, the Colombian drug cartel had become a major player in the U.S. heroin market. According to an intelligence bulletin published by the Drug Enforcement Administration, 62% of the total weight of the heroin seized that year came from South America, compared with 17% from Southeast Asia, 16% from Southwest Asia, and 5% from Mexico (fig. 7.2).[12]

An increased availability of purified heroin has been determined not only by analysis of seizures and purchases but also by the number of emergency room mentions of heroin in the Drug Abuse Warning Network (DAWN) reports, which rose between 1985 and 1988 and rose again between 1990 and 1992.[13] Heroin-related emergencies in 1995 were at their highest ever and twice the level reported in 1988.[14]

Perhaps a more significant statistic is that availability and perceived availability of heroin have risen steadily among high school seniors and young adults over the past 10 years. In 1995, 35% of twelfth graders perceived that heroin was fairly easy to get. This perceived availability rate is the highest since the study began in 1975. Lastly, the number of twelfth graders reporting having used heroin in the past year or in the past month doubled between 1994 and 1995.[15]

There has been some concern that a segment of the drug-using subculture may be turning away from cocaine, realizing the true nature of that drug and turning toward heroin. High-purity heroin from Southeast Asia has made it possible for young people who fear or disdain needle use to be initiated into heroin use through snorting or smoking it. National surveys provide evidence of a decline in the annual prevalence of needle use between 1993 and 1996,[16] perhaps because of the fear of contracting HIV/AIDS or other blood-borne disease (see the box on p. 119). However, there are reports that at least some of those who begin their heroin use by snorting or smoking soon shift to injecting it when they no longer get the desired effect from snorting or smoking it.[17] These young people are on their way to becoming the next generation of hard-core heroin addicts.

CLASSIFICATION OF NARCOTICS

Narcotics can be subgrouped on the basis of their origin into the natural, quasi-synthetic, and synthetic narcotics (fig. 7.3).

Natural Narcotics

Naturally occurring substances derived from the Asian poppy plant include opium (the "mother drug," or the

FIGURE 7.1

The primary sources of heroin are the Golden Triangle countries of Thailand, Laos, and Myanmar (Burma), the Golden Crescent countries of Iran, Afghanistan, and Pakistan; Mexico; and most recently, Colombia.

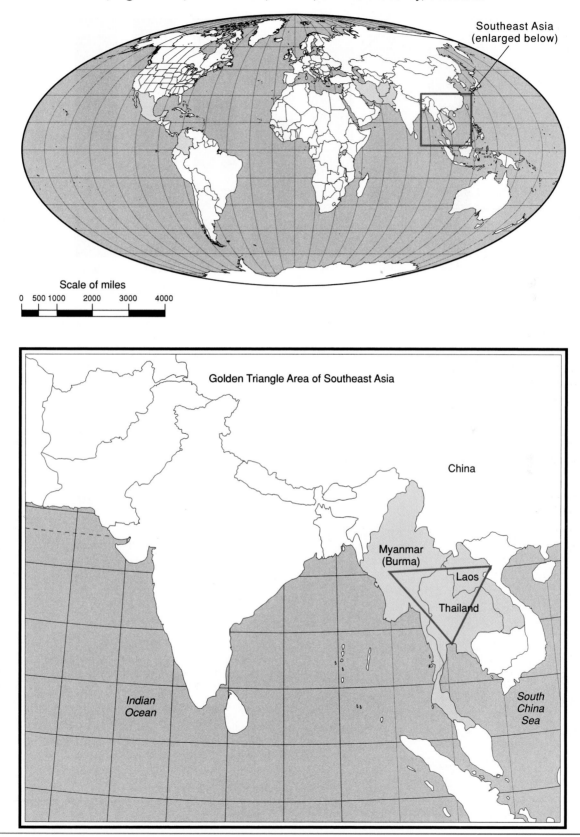

FIGURE 7.2

Geographic source area distribution based on net weight of heroin seized (percent)—1983 to 1995.[a,b]

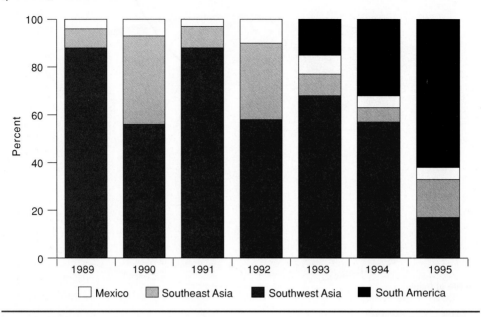

(a) Drug Enforcement Administration, Intelligence Division, National Narcotics Intelligence Consumers Committee (NNICC): *The NNICC Report 1995: The Supply of Illicit Drugs to the United States.* August, 1996, Washington, D.C., DEA-96024.

(b) Drug Enforcement Administration, Intelligence Division, *Intelligence Bulletin: The 1995 Heroin Signature Program,* DEA-96042, August 1996, Washington D.C.

FIGURE 7.3

Opium and related drugs: natural, quasi-synthetic, and synthetic narcotics.

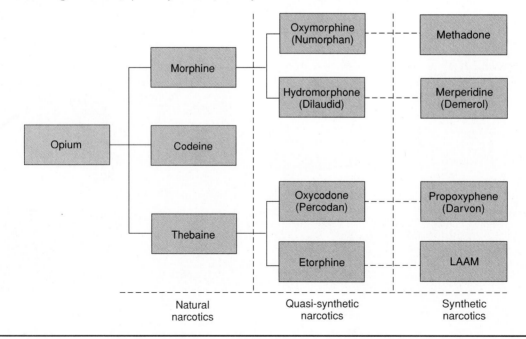

WHAT DO YOU THINK?

Drug Dependence versus HIV/AIDS: Promoting Health and Safety in America Through a Reasonable Syringe Sale and Possession Policy

The dual epidemics of drug use and the human immunodeficiency virus and acquired immunodeficiency syndrome (HIV/AIDS) are significant threats to the health and safety of Americans. There are between one and two million injection drug users (IDUs) in the United States who are at risk for acquiring a variety of blood-borne pathogens, such as hepatitis B and C, HIV/AIDS, endocarditis (inflammation of the sac surrounding the heart), and malaria. Furthermore, illegal drug use results in the destruction of families, domestic abuse and neglect, and a variety of social and economic problems. Drug abuse is also associated with higher rates of crimes against people and property. The annual cost to society of drug abuse has been estimated at nearly $60 billion.

Injection drug use is also the second most frequently reported risk factor for AIDS, accounting for 184,359 cases through December 1995. In 1995, 36% of all AIDS cases occurred among IDUs, their heterosexual sex partners, and children whose mothers were IDUs or sex partners of IDUs. Transmission of HIV infection by IDUs occurs primarily through multiperson use of syringes—needle sharing. (In our discussion here, the term *syringe* includes both syringe and needle). When an IDU injects drugs, the syringe becomes contaminated with that person's blood and blood-borne pathogens, which can then be transmitted to another IDU who uses the same syringe.

In an effort to control the widespread use of opium, morphine, cocaine, and heroin in the late nineteenth and early twentieth centuries, states passed laws restricting physicians' freedom to dispense the drugs and also regulating the sale and distribution of syringes. In 1979, the Drug Enforcement Administration wrote the Model Drug Paraphernalia Act, versions of which were adopted by many states. These laws were adopted in response to the proliferation of the drug paraphernalia industry and the numerous "head shops" operated nationwide. Included as drug paraphernalia are "hypodermic syringes, needles, and other objects used, intended for use, and designed for use in parenterally injecting controlled substances into the human body."

A recent survey reveals that 47 states and the District of Columbia have passed drug paraphernalia statutes. Ten states have laws, regulations, or ordinances that require a prescription for the purchase of syringes, and 16 additional states have laws or regulations that can otherwise limit the sale and purchase of syringes. To the extent that these laws, regulations, and ordinances restrict access to sterile syringes, they contribute to the spread of blood-borne diseases among IDUs, their sexual contacts, and their children. Some, but not all of these states, have carved out some provisions to exempt operators and participants of syringe exchange programs from prosecution under these laws.

Pharmacists face substantial legal and professional hurdles if they sell syringes to IDUs. Physicians and other health professionals face potentially dire legal consequences when they prescribe syringes or otherwise directly assist IDUs in obtaining sterile syringes. Criminal and professional sanctions prevent these professionals from providing important HIV prevention services to people who continue to inject drugs. Most of the laws that restrict the sale, possession, or distribution of syringes were promulgated before the HIV/AIDS epidemic.

Many public health, medical, and legal organizations have supported the deregulation of syringes as a strategy to prevent HIV/AIDS and other blood-borne diseases among IDUs. What do you think? Consider the following questions:

1. What are the legitimate medical (public health) purposes of sterile syringes?
2. Should drug paraphernalia laws be modified?
3. Should syringe prescription laws be changed to permit the over-the-counter sales of syringes in pharmacies?
4. Should pharmacy regulations that prevent pharmacists from dispensing sterile needles to IDUs be repealed?
5. Should there be in-service training for pharmacists and other health professionals and criminal justice personnel so that they can advance public health goals?
6. Should states allow local discretion in establishing syringe exchange programs?
7. What kinds of programs should be developed to reduce the number of contaminated syringes in circulation and reduce health risks to the public?

L. O. Gostin, Z. Lazzarini, T. S. Jones, and K. Flaherty, "Prevention of HIV/AIDS and Other Blood-Borne Diseases among Injection Drug Users: A National Survey on the Regulation of Syringes and Needles," *JAMA* 277, no. 1 (1997): 53–62.

unpurified mixture of drugs collected directly from the plant), morphine (the primary active ingredient in opium), codeine (an antitussive), and thebaine (a compound not used as a drug itself but as a basic structure in the synthesis of certain quasi-synthetic drugs). Most of the 30 or so other compounds that make up opium do not produce significant effects.

Quasi-Synthetic Narcotics

In the search for an even better analgesic drug, one that would not produce tolerance and dependence, a number of quasi-synthetic and synthetic narcotics have been developed (fig. 7.3). **Quasi-synthetic narcotics** are those that are manufactured by chemically altering morphine or one of its related compounds in the laboratory. Unfortunately, little if any improvement has been made to the natural substance. In some cases in which improvements were found in analgesic qualities, the margin of safety between the therapeutic and toxic doses was reduced. In other cases, new drugs showed dangerously strong dependence-producing characteristics.

The best-known example of a quasi-synthetic narcotic, and of the failure to improve on the usefulness of morphine, is heroin. Although heroin is a faster acting and more effective analgesic than morphine, it is more addictive and thus less useful. Other quasi-synthetic narcotics include hydromorphone (Dilaudid), dihydromorphone, and oxymorphone, all derived from morphine, and oxycodone (Percodan) and etorphine, derived from thebaine.

Synthetic Narcotics

Synthetic narcotics are compounds synthesized entirely in the laboratory to copy the activity of the natural opiates. Examples include such substances as meperidine (Demerol), methadone (Dolophine), levo-acetyl-alpha-methadol (LAAM), and propoxyphene (Darvon). Meperidine, first introduced in 1939, has become widely used in modern medicine as an analgesic.[18] Its effects do not include the relief of coughing or diarrhea. Its pain-relieving strength is about one-tenth that of morphine. Meperidine has also been subject to abuse. Propoxyphene, an analgesic even weaker than meperidine but still stronger than aspirin, is available only in oral preparations.

Another synthetic narcotic is methadone, first developed in Germany during World War II as a morphine substitute.[19] Its primary advantages over morphine are its effectiveness by the oral route and its longer duration of activity (about 24 hours). Methadone suppresses withdrawal symptoms in people physically dependent on morphine or heroin. Because methadone use results in the cessation of the endless cycle of alternating highs and desperate lows associated with heroin addiction, it is widely used in withdrawal and maintenance programs for heroin dependence. (Treatment approaches are discussed later in this chapter.)

LAAM, a substance chemically related to methadone, has an even longer duration of action (48 to 72 hours) and represents an improvement for some patients in heroin treatment programs. Opiate-dependent patients on LAAM maintenance are able to reduce the frequency of their maintenance dose from daily to three times per week.

PHARMACOLOGY OF NARCOTICS

As with other drugs, the rate of absorption and distribution of narcotics depends on the route of administration, the degree of protein binding, and lipid solubility. The effects of various routes of administration on the absorption and distribution of narcotics has been much studied. Likewise, the metabolism (biotransformation), excretion, and mode of action of narcotics have been the subject of intensive research.

Administration

Opiates can be ingested, inhaled as smoke, snorted, or injected, either under the skin or into a vein. In general, opium and its derivatives are poorly absorbed when taken orally, methadone being a well-known exception. Inhalation of smoke containing the products of opium combustion results in the rapid and almost complete absorption of the drug. Opium smoking has a long and colorful history in Eastern cultures, but smoking heroin has not been a popular form of use in the United States.

Snorting heroin places the drug on the mucous linings of the nose and throat, where it is absorbed into the bloodstream. This is often the way people begin their heroin use. Heroin may also be injected subcutaneously ("skin-popping"), intramuscularly (primarily for medical purposes), and intravenously ("mainlining").

In the late 1980s, the practice of snorting heroin began to increase in New York and New Jersey,[20] undoubtedly as a result of the increased availability of high-purity heroin from Southeast Asia and the fear of HIV transmission from hypodermic needle sharing. According to one report, the percentage of patients reporting injection as their primary means of administration had fallen from 73.3% in 1989 to 58.6% in 1994, while the number of patients snorting rose from 3.9% in 1989 to 12% in 1994.[21] Snorting heroin is not always safe; intranasal use was involved in several deaths in 1994 and 1995. Intranasal use (snorting or sniffing) of heroin was the most common primary route of administration in several major cities in 1994 and 1995, including Newark, Chicago, and New York City. The percentage of those reporting intranasal use is also very large in Detroit and Boston

TABLE 7.1 Route of Administration Among Addicts Admitted for Heroin Treatment in Major U.S. Cities

Area	Smoking	Sniffing	Injecting
Atlanta	4	12	75
Boston	2	32	61
Denver	1	3	92
Detroit	2	46	50
Los Angeles	4	3	92
Miami	1	28	70
Minneapolis/St. Paul	2	22	76
Newark	1	71	28
New York City	—	53	45
Philadelphia	1	24	73
St. Louis	—	—	90
San Diego	3	2	95
San Francisco	5	6	88
Texas	1	3	93

(Data from CEWG, December 1995)

(table 7.1).[22] Use of heroin without a needle is now more prevalent at each grade level (eighth, tenth, and twelfth) than with a needle.[23]

Absorption

Most of the opium derivatives are only slowly and incompletely absorbed after taking an oral dose because of their poor lipid solubility (see chapter 4). They are poorly absorbed through the stomach wall. Most of the absorption occurs in the large intestine. Peak blood concentrations after taking an oral dose are usually half those after an injected dose. Absorption of opiates through the mucous lining of the nose and throat is faster than through the intestinal tract but slower than by inhalation or injection. Absorption of a subcutaneous injection is also faster than by the oral route but slower than intravenous injection. Intravenous injection produces an almost immediate effect, often referred to as a "rush."

Distribution

After absorption into the bloodstream, narcotics are distributed throughout the body within minutes. Narcotics not bound to plasma proteins cross the blood-brain barrier by simple diffusion (see chapter 4). Morphine, which is more water soluble, penetrates the blood-brain barrier more slowly than heroin, which is more fat soluble. Heroin reaches the brain so quickly that its effects are felt by the user as a rush. Although the immediate effects of morphine are much less intense, its duration of action is longer, since it is absorbed and distributed more slowly. It has been estimated that less than 0.1% of any adminis-

tered narcotic reaches an active site in the CNS.[24] The remainder is broken down, bound, stored, or excreted before it reaches sites of action.

Opiates, including heroin, readily cross the placenta and are distributed by fetal circulation to all tissues of the developing fetus. The CNS of the fetus is especially vulnerable, since the blood-brain barrier is imperfectly developed. Newborn babies of drug-dependent mothers are themselves dependent and undergo withdrawal symptoms after birth if the drug is withheld.

Biotransformation and Excretion

Opiates are biotransformed into products that are usually more water soluble than the original compound and thus easier to excrete. It is important to note, however, that not all biotransformation reactions result in less active compounds. Foreign substances may undergo several, or even many, different biochemical reactions at once. Processes that result in more active compounds are called *bioactivation*; those that result in compounds less active than the parent compound are known as *biodeactivation*. (See chapter 4 for a review of these terms.)

An example of a narcotic that is bioactivated is heroin. Heroin itself produces minimal CNS effects but, because of its high lipid solubility, is transported quickly to the

---

quasi-synthetic narcotics drugs formed by chemically modifying one of the naturally occurring narcotics

synthetic narcotics drugs produced entirely in the laboratory and thus not occurring naturally

brain. In the brain, it is rapidly biotransformed into morphine, which produces narcotic effects. Heroin, therefore, can be thought of as a carrier for the active opiate morphine.[25]

Excretion routes for biodeactivated products include the kidneys, intestines, lungs, saliva, and perspiration. The primary route is the kidneys; it is estimated that 50% to 57% of the original dose is excreted in the urine. Of this, approximately 50% is bound to other molecules, and approximately 7% is free morphine.[26] Urine tests used to screen athletes and others for the use of illicit drugs are capable of detecting minute quantities of opiates up to 2 to 4 days after use. (Drug testing was discussed in chapter 4.)

Another important pathway of opiate excretion involves the liver and alimentary canal (digestive tract). Here biodeactivated products are attached to larger molecules and excreted with the bile into the intestines. The duration of action of many opiates, such as the heroin-morphine complex, is 4 to 5 hours. As mentioned previously, the duration of methadone activity is about 24 hours.

Neurohormonal Influences

Narcotics produce their numbing effects by altering neurotransmitter function at synapses of the nervous system. Their greatest effect is on the CNS. Chronic abuse of narcotics results in tolerance and physical and psychological dependence.

Mode of Action

Opiates act at specific receptor sites around synapses of the brain. Of course, these receptor sites do not exist solely for the purpose of attracting foreign substances, but rather for the attachment of the body's own (endogenous) morphinelike substances, called **endorphins.** Endorphins and a second group of natural substances, **enkephalins,** neuromodulators of pain, reside within the neurons and are released from terminals. Enkephalins have an effect on the intensity with which pain messages are transmitted to higher brain centers.[27] It is at the receptor sites for these substances that the opiates produce their numbing effects. In fact, it has been proposed that opiates may act by stimulating the release of endorphins and enkephalins, which in turn produce analgesic effects.[28]

Narcotic Antagonists and Agonists

There are some compounds that bind with the receptor sites for morphinelike substances but have no intrinsic pharmacological activity. These compounds produce no CNS depression and no euphoria. These substances, called **antagonists,** rapidly reverse the effects of **agonists,** in this case, opioid analgesics, which produce effects by interacting with the body's cell physiology. Antagonists can be used to diagnose and treat individuals who have become dependent on narcotics. They are also useful in the emergency room to counteract the effects of a narcotic overdose. The best examples of antagonists are naloxone (Narcan), which is used clinically to reverse heroin overdoses and sometimes save lives, and naltrexone (Revia, Trexan), used in the treatment of heroin dependence.[29] (Naltrexone can also be use for treatment of alcohol dependence; refer to chapter 17).

Physiological Effects

Narcotics produce their most pronounced effects on the CNS; however, they also influence the PNS, particularly the smooth muscles of the intestinal tract and the eyes. As with other drugs, both acute and chronic effects have been demonstrated.

Acute Effects. Narcotics produce analgesia, euphoria, drowsiness, and depression of mental faculties. They do not depress motor activity or cause the slurring of speech to the degree that alcohol and barbiturates do, but they do depress respiration. Opiates appear to reduce the sensitivity of the brainstem to levels of carbon dioxide that may be building up in the body. At high doses, breathing becomes irregular and slow. The primary cause of death in cases of narcotic overdoses is respiratory arrest. In this regard, narcotics are the leading cause of deaths from unintentional drug poisonings.[30]

Fortunately, the analgesic properties are usually felt at doses below those that seriously depress respiration. Interestingly, morphine alters the perception or interpretation of pain rather than eliminating the pain itself. Patients who have been given morphine report that they are still aware of the pain, but they do not suffer because of it. It is as if pain messages continue to be sent and received, but the interpretation of these messages is garbled.

Other undesirable effects of narcotics include constipation, stimulation of the "vomiting center" in the medulla, and suppression of rapid eye movement (REM) sleep. Since REM sleep is associated with memory formation, narcotics are detrimental to this physiological process. The specific depression of the cough center of the brain also occurs, and this is regarded as a therapeutically desirable effect of opiates. Codeine is the narcotic that is most effective as an antitussive (cough suppressant).

Chronic Effects. Tolerance to most of the effects of narcotics, including the analgesic and euphoric properties, develops when the administration of a certain amount of a drug fails to produce the same effects as the initial dose.

Tolerance seems to develop most rapidly to morphine's euphoric effects, less rapidly to its analgesic effects, and never to its effects on the smooth muscles, such as those in the eye and in the intestines. **Cross tolerance,** the phenomenon in which tolerance developed against one member of a particular group of drugs also reduces the effectiveness of all others in that group, is a well-established phenomenon of narcotic usage. For example, people who abuse Darvon, a synthetic narcotic, would not experience a numbing effect from codeine administered for dental work.

Symptoms of physical dependence on opiates appear with the abrupt termination of chronic opiate abuse. The physical signs and symptoms that appear after a period of abstinence are referred to as *abstinence syndrome* or *withdrawal illness* (see chapter 4 for review of these terms). In the case of opiates, the signs and symptoms of withdrawal illness may include anxiety, restlessness, irritability, general body aches, insomnia, runny nose and eyes, perspiration, fever and chills, hot flashes, dilated pupils, nausea, gagging, vomiting, diarrhea, increased heart rate, increased blood pressure, and abdominal and other muscle cramps.[31] The peak of symptoms occurs in 24 to 48 hours, and severe discomfort seldom lasts longer than 96 hours. Some reports, however, indicate that certain physiological changes, such as suppression of REM sleep patterns, continue to occur for weeks or months after the beginning of abstinence.

An important concern related to long-term opiate abuse is that of prenatal exposure. The developing fetus of a pregnant heroin addict becomes physically dependent on heroin and undergoes a period of withdrawal illness after birth. There have been numerous studies attempting to show developmental differences between these children and children of nonaddicted mothers. According to a recent review, the results of most of these studies were inconclusive, because although differences did exist, these differences could have been caused by the home environment or other postnatal differences between groups.[32] While fetal alcohol syndrome, which is sometimes seen in the offspring of mothers who consume excessive amounts of alcohol during pregnancy, can produce permanent mental retardation, such effects have not yet been reported from heroin abuse.

Psychological Effects

The psychological effects of narcotics vary with individuals, their moods, and social or environmental settings. As with the physiological effects, both acute and chronic psychological effects of narcotics occur.

Acute Effects. Acute effects of narcotic use can be observed outwardly as a behavioral pattern of lethargy, lack of concern, and inability to concentrate. Inwardly, users report peacefulness, feelings of well-being, and even eu-

phoria. Others, especially intravenous users, describe the rush in sexually pleasurable terms, followed by the sensations mentioned previously. These highs last only a short time, however, and are followed by a period of increasing anxiety. Because tolerance develops, those who continue to abuse the drug are invariably disappointed in their attempts to repeat the same high level of pleasure achieved in earlier usages.

Chronic Effects. The existence of psychological dependence, as evidenced by **craving,** is well established for narcotic use. Morphine and heroin are strong positive reinforcers; that is, animals will self-administer continual doses of these substances without the need for other rewards, such as food or water. If the drug is then withheld and the animal experiences elements of abstinence syndrome, the effects of negative reinforcement are added to those of positive reinforcement. The result is a strong desire to repeat the experience, both to enjoy the positive effects and to avoid the negative ones.

The user's mood and the social or environmental setting in which the drug is taken are important in the establishment of psychological dependence in intravenous heroin users. Experiments have shown that physiological responses can be produced just by placing an addicted person or animal in an environment in which the drug is habitually administered. Thus, heroin is strongly addictive, both physically and psychologically.

CURRENT USE PATTERNS

The narcotics now include a large number of natural, quasi-synthetic, and synthetic compounds. Some of these still have important medical uses. Misuse and abuse occur when prescription narcotics are illegally diverted to nonmedical use or when illicit narcotics that have no medical use are imported and distributed illegally.

endorphins morphinelike substances produced and released naturally in the human body

enkephalins substances produced and released naturally that influence the way pain messages are perceived or transmitted

antagonists nonpsychoactive compounds that compete with other compounds, such as the narcotics, for receptor sites

agonists drugs, including narcotics, that produce effects by interacting with cell physiology

cross tolerance a condition in which tolerance to one drug results in tolerance to other, related drugs

craving an overwhelming desire or perceived need to take a drug to feel its positive effects and avoid the negative effects of withdrawal

WHAT DO YOU THINK?

Are Physicians Too Cautious in Prescribing Narcotics for Pain Relief?

In the practice of medicine, physicians sometimes must treat patients experiencing excruciating pain. These patients fall into two categories—those with severe post-operative pain and those with long-term pain, such as burn victims and terminally ill cancer patients.

When dealing with patients suffering from pain, physicians have a variety of analgesics from which to select. These include narcotics, such as morphine, Darvocet-N, Demerol, and Percodan, and nonnarcotic analgesics, including acetaminophen (Tylenol, Talacen), ibuprofen (Advil, Motrin, Mediprin), and aspirin. Nonnarcotic pain relievers are less effective than narcotic pain relievers but are sometimes prescribed out of fear that the patient might become addicted to a narcotic analgesic. Is this fear justified?

In an article titled "The Tragedy of Needless Pain," Dr. Ronald Melzack, Professor of Neurophysiology at McGill University and research director of the Pain Clinic at Montreal General Hospital, states that morphine given solely for the control of pain is not addictive.[a] He maintains that society's failure to distinguish between the emotionally impaired addict and the psychologically healthy pain sufferer has meant needless suffering for millions of people over the years.

Dr. Melzack cites numerous studies that support his belief. In one study, 38 patients were placed on long-term narcotic therapy for severe, chronic noncancer-type pain. This therapy was helpful for 60% of the patients, who reported that their pain was eliminated or reduced to a tolerable level. During this study, only two patients developed problems related to drug dependence, and both of these people had a history of drug abuse.

Another study cited in this article indicated that many children who had major surgery received no postoperative pain relief, perhaps because of the mistaken belief that young children do not feel pain as much as adults. In another study, elderly patients, who recover more slowly than younger patients and suffer from pain over a longer period, were found to receive no more narcotic pain relief than their younger counterparts.

[a]R. Melzack, "The Tragedy of Needless Pain," *Sci. Am.* 262, no. 2 (1990):27.

In reviewing these and other studies, Dr. Melzack found no evidence that narcotics given solely for the relief of pain cause addiction in otherwise healthy people. Instead, he found a good deal of evidence to suggest that we need an enlightened view of the use of narcotics for pain relief.

Since Dr. Melzack's article was written, many articles have been published on pain management. A study by the Department of Health and Human Services found that half of all the patients undergoing the 23 million surgical procedures performed each year suffered unnecessary pain after surgery.[b] Expressions like "no pain, no gain," "pain builds character," and "pain is necessary," have been all too common and are simply not true. Furthermore, unrelieved pain only stalls the healing process. In fact, adequate pain control is so important that the American Board of Anesthesiology is considering certifying the specialty of pain management.[c] Other studies have confirmed that children and elderly adults often do not receive sufficient medication for pain control.[d] Finally, there is a better understanding that dosages should be tailored to fit each patient's underlying medical condition and that control of pain needs to begin at the time of surgery, not after surgery.[e]

What do you think? Why have physicians sometimes been too cautious in prescribing narcotic pain killers? Is it because they fear that their patients will become dependent on pain medication? Is it because they fear state or federal drug control agencies who, after examining prescription records for schedule II drugs, might question their professional judgment? Is it because they want to avoid a reputation among their colleagues as a physician who prescribes pain killers too often?

[b]J. J. Clinton, "Acute Pain Management Can Be Improved," JAMA, 267, no. 19 (1992): 2580; "Speeding Recovery with Pain Control," *The Johns Hopkins Medical Newsletter, Health after 50* (October 1992); 7.

[c]M. F. Goldsmith, "Pain Speaking—and Anesthesiologists Answer," *JAMA* 267, no. 12 (1992): 1578.

[d]G. A. Walco, R. C. Cassidy, and N. L. Schechter, "Pain, Hurt and Harm: The Ethics of Pain Control in Infants and Children," *N. Engl. J. Med.* 331, no. 8 (1994): 541; Anonymous, "Pain Control Falls Short in Nursing Homes," *Amer. J. Nursing* 96, no. 2 (1996): 10.

[e]L. J. Saidman, "Anesthesiology," *JAMA* 275, no. 23 (1996): 1795.

Medical Uses

Morphine and related narcotics are prescribed for moderate to severe pain. Their analgesic qualities are unsurpassed, and they cause no reduction in motor or sensory function. Demerol (meperidine), for example, is used for treatment of moderate to severe pain, as a preoperative anesthetic, and for obstetrical analgesia (see the box on p. 124). A second important use of opiates is as antidiarrheal drugs. The antidiarrheal drug Lomotil, for example, contains the narcotic diphenoxylate hydrochloride, which is closely related to Demerol.[33] Still another common medical use is cough suppression, for which codeine is still the standard by which other antitussives are judged.

Narcotics are useful in the medical management of heroin addiction itself. Methadone is prescribed for treatment of narcotic addiction and for maintenance treatment. Narcan (naloxone hydrochloride) is used for diagnosis and treatment of acute narcotic overdose.[34]

Patterns of Abuse

In addition to their medical uses as analgesics, antidiarrheals, and antitussives, opiates are subject to widespread misuse and abuse. As with other drugs, there are varied abuse patterns ranging from experimental to occasional to compulsive. These are accompanied by complex physiological changes and psychosocial adjustments.

First Use. It is a common misbelief that one use of heroin produces a binding physical dependence. This is almost never the case, and in truth, the length of time involved between first use and addiction is reported to be from 5 to 18 months.[35] A more likely result from first use is nausea and vomiting.

Curiosity, the influence of others, relief of personal problems, and the seeking of a mood change ("high") are among the reasons heroin addicts give when asked about their first use of heroin.[36] Studies aimed at isolating the factors associated with personal decision making, however, suggest that other influences, unidentified by the user, are often present. These include (1) low self-esteem (resulting from poor education, lack of vocational skills and work habits, absence of a role model for success, family disruption, and general lack of social skills), (2) the belief that the opiates will solve interpersonal problems, (3) ignorance of the opiate's chronic effects, (4) a quest for a mystical or transcendental experience, and (5) relief from anxiety or pain.

Peer influence is undoubtedly an important factor in initial use. Studies indicate that a significant percentage of addicts were introduced to heroin by friends.[37] In this regard, it is interesting to note that a heroin user is most "contagious" during his first year of use, when he or she is still a member of the nonusing culture. After about a year, the user is more likely to become a member of the addict culture and is isolated from former friends whom he or she could perhaps influence.

Nonaddictive Opiate Abuse. Although addiction is a clear risk for abusers of opiates, some are able to control their use even after a considerable duration of exposure to the drug. These **controlled users,** sometimes called "chippers," fall into various use patterns with regard to frequency and intensity of use and whether they were previously addicted. The weekend user, for example, may use heroin only to relax or "get high" on weekends. There is a clear risk, however, that this person might discover that weekends begin earlier on Fridays and last through Monday mornings and that one or two midweek highs help make the week pass a little more quickly. Still, there is evidence that for some, controlled use is a stable situation. For others, controlled use is only a stage on the pathway to addiction. The risk is always there. Complete the self-assessment on page 126 to see whether you should be concerned about your risk for addiction.

Heroin Addiction. **Drug addiction** can be defined as the surrendering of oneself to the compulsive or obsessive abuse of drugs. Although the term *addiction* is still used extensively in the professional literature on narcotics and also by the media, it has fallen into disfavor with some public health officials and health educators because it means different things to different people. It is often replaced by the terms *drug dependence* or *chemical dependence.*

Where possible, distinctions are made between the two types of dependence: physical dependence (as evidenced by an abstinence or withdrawal syndrome) and psychological dependence, the emotional component of dependence. These more precise terms are used extensively throughout this book in keeping with current terminology. Unfortunately, even experts disagree about the relative importance of physical and psychological dependence in relation to heroin abuse.

Furthermore, the use of these precise terms does not seem to account for all of the psychosocial problems that occur during the course of addiction. For these reasons, and for historical reasons, the term *addiction* is still used in narcotics literature. In this chapter, we have used the

---

controlled users those who practice a narcotics use pattern characterized by the absence over time of an increase either in dose or frequency; sometimes called "chippers"

drug addiction a condition characterized by the compulsive abuse of a drug or drugs; drug dependence or chemical dependence

SELF-ASSESSMENT

Am I An Addict?

Only you can answer this question.

1. Do you ever use drugs alone?
2. Have you ever substituted one drug for another, thinking that one particular drug was the problem?
3. Have you ever manipulated or lied to a doctor to obtain prescription drugs?
4. Have you ever taken one drug to overcome the effects of another?
5. Do you avoid people that do not approve of you using drugs?
6. Have you ever used a drug without knowing what it was or what it would do to you?
7. Has your job or school performance ever suffered from the effects of your drug use?
8. Have you ever lied about what or how much you use?
9. Do you put the purchase of drugs ahead of your financial responsibilities?
10. Does the thought of running out of drugs terrify you?
11. Do you ever question your own sanity?
12. Have you ever felt defensive, guilty, or ashamed about your using?
13. Have you ever taken drugs you didn't prefer?
14. Do you continue to use despite the negative consequences?
15. Do you think you might have a drug problem?

If your answer to more than one of these questions is yes, you should be concerned about your risk for drug addiction.

Modified from Narcotics Anonymous, *Am I an addict?*, pamphlet no. 7, Revised, 1996 (Van Nuys, Calif.: World Service Office, 1986).

---

term *addiction* in accord with the existing literature, but the term *drug dependence* can be substituted.

Cycle of Addiction.   A great many theories of addiction have been proposed by those who have studied this phenomenon. These include conditioning theories, metabolic theories, sociological theories, and psychoanalytic and psychosocial theories. Each of these theories attempts to explain the course of addiction. Researchers have tried to incorporate these theories into a conceptual model of the **cycle of addiction** (fig. 7.4). This cycle of addiction describes changes in self identity and behavior of an addict over a period of several to many years, not just from one binge to the next, as in the cocaine addiction cycle discussed in chapter 5.

Several cycles have been proposed; the following is offered as an example.[38] Interwoven into the context of the cycle are two preconditions for addiction: a personality, or psychiatric, component and a sociological component. Phase I of the cycle is called *tolerance for potential addiction* and is characterized by experimentation. At the beginning of this phase, the user may not use heroin intravenously, since this method is associated with "junkies." However, as tolerance develops and the user needs to maximize the effect of the drug and to obtain greater quantities of the drug in his body, he learns the techniques necessary for the intravenous administration of heroin.

Intravenous injection speeds the onset of physical dependence and involves the user more closely with the addict population. Experiencing the symptoms of absti-

nence and then the relief of these symptoms by more heroin reinforces the user's desire for the drug. This starts him or her on a never-ending search for the next dose. The user may attempt to abstain from the drug during this phase to avoid addiction, but these attempts fail. After this, he or she undergoes changes in self-image that eventually allow him or her to enter phase II of the cycle, tolerance of the addiction system.

In phase II, the new addict has entered the drug-using subculture and become a member of this deviate population. Although drug acquiring skills have become more sophisticated and most of the user's activities are directed toward this goal, there are eventually other attempts at

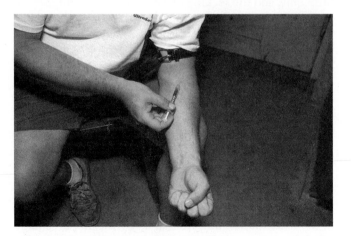

Despite the risk of HIV/AIDS, injection remains the primary route of administration of heroin in virtually all American cities.

FIGURE 7.4

The cycle of heroin addiction.

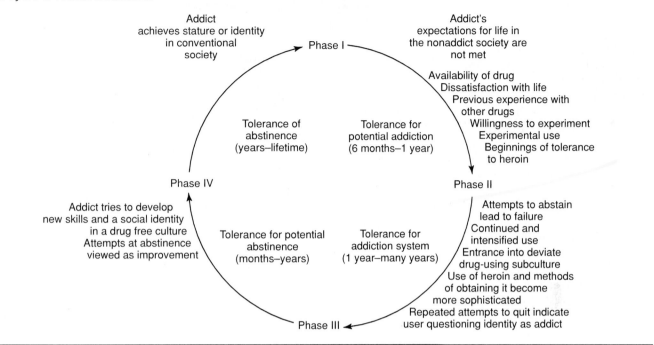

(Data from Alksne, Lieberman, and Brill, A conceptual model of the life cycle of addiction, *International Journal of the Addictions,* 2:2, 1967.)

withdrawal. In these attempts, the user is questioning his or her identity as an addict. When the addict begins to reject this identity, he or she may be ready to enter phase III, tolerance for potential abstinence.

During phase III, a failed withdrawal is not considered a total failure because any such experience is regarded as an improvement. However, it is recognized that there must be a modification of the emotional component before a drug-free state is achieved. The addict must develop new skills and make new associations before supportive chemotherapy, such as methadone maintenance, or detoxification will be truly effective. He must also develop a social identity in the drug-free culture. This is the most difficult stage for an addict. If a former addict can achieve membership in conventional society, he or she has entered phase IV, tolerance of abstinence.

Relapses occur when the former addict's expectations for life in the nonaddict society are not met. The addict may have difficulty maintaining his or her identity as a nonaddict, particularly if he or she perceives that he or she has been granted only marginal status in conventional society. A relapse at this point encourages self-identity as a chronic addict.

TREATMENT FOR NARCOTICS ADDICTION

Most addicts will eventually seek treatment at some time. They do so for various reasons, including the high cost of their habit, their desire to reduce or stop drug abuse, anxiety over drug-related physical problems, a decision to attempt to change their overall lifestyle, or a court order requiring them to do so. Interestingly, fear of arrest and punishment is almost never mentioned as a reason for seeking treatment. Reasons reported for not seeking treatment earlier include the users' infrequent abuse of narcotics and their desire not to become involved with official agencies or clinics.

There are as many approaches to treatment as there are theories of addiction. These will be discussed in

cycle of addiction a conceptual model that describes changes in self identity and behavior of an addict in relation to drug use and the addict's social setting

ALTERNATIVE CHOICES

Just for Today

For most of us, the thought of stopping any habit forever can seem insurmountable. The 12-step programs encourage people to concentrate on the present, not the nightmare of a past or the uncertainty of the future. One of their slogans reminds addicts that the way to stay drug-free forever is to stay clean "just for today."

"When we focus our thoughts on today the nightmare of drugs fades away overshadowed by the dawn of a new reality. We find that when we are troubled we can trust our feelings to another recovering addict. In sharing our past with other addicts we discover we are not unique, that we share common bonds.

Perfection is no longer a goal today; we can achieve adequacy. It is important to remember that any addict who can stay clean for one day is a miracle. 'Just for Today' applies to all areas of our life, not just abstinence from drugs. Reality has to be dealt with on a daily basis. A lot happens in one day, both negative and positive. If we do not take time to appreciate both, perhaps we will miss something that will help us grow."

Modified from Narcotics Anonymous, *Just for today,* pamphlet no. 8 (Van Nuys, Calif.: World Service Office, 1983).

chapter 18. Most programs involve three phases: detoxification (with or without medication), active treatment, and aftercare. In this chapter, discussion will be limited to treatment information that is unique to dependence on narcotics. One such program is a form of substitute dependence called methadone maintenance.

Methadone Maintenance

Methadone maintenance is a unique form of **substitute dependence treatment** in which a safer drug and/or route of administration is substituted for a more dangerous drug or route of administration. A familiar example of substitute dependence treatment is the nicotine patch. In this case, the treatment involves a safer route of administration of nicotine—one that does not endanger the mouth, throat, and lungs of the user. The drug-dependent person is still physically dependent on the drug but is not at risk for some of the health hazards associated with abusing the original drug. With regard to methadone maintenance, the goal is not abstinence from narcotics but rather retention in treatment, successful employment experiences for the client, cessation of illegal drug abuse, and the elimination of criminal behavior. Methadone maintenance therapy is based on the phenomenon of cross tolerance, defined on page 123. In this form of therapy, a legal prescription narcotic, methadone, is prescribed for use by the addict as a substitute for the illegal drug, heroin.

Methadone provides relief from the alternating periods of highs and sickness that preoccupy the thoughts and actions of the heroin addict. Relief from this cycle sometimes allows the addict to gather the resources nec-

essary to restructure his or her life. In support of this program is the belief that addicts on methadone maintenance commit fewer crimes because they do not need money for heroin. Proponents of methadone maintenance programs point to this reduction in crime as a key benefit to society. They also assert that methadone maintenance improves the general health of the patient and slows the spread of AIDS. An advancement over methadone is levo-acetyl-alpha-methadol (LAAM). As described earlier, LAAM has an even slower and longer-lasting effect than methadone, about 72 hours, reducing the number of patient visits by half.[39]

Detoxification, as defined in chapters 2 and 18, refers to the elimination of a drug from the body with or without treatment for the relief of symptoms associated with abstinence syndrome. In a standard heroin detoxification program, methadone is used to suppress the abstinence syndrome. After stabilization on methadone, detoxification can be completed by a gradual reduction of methadone dosage. To test the success of detoxification, a narcotic antagonist, such as naloxone hydrochloride (Narcan), is administered. If the person is still chemically dependent on narcotics, the naloxone will compete with and replace the narcotic (agonist) at the receptor sites, causing withdrawal symptoms. If the patient experiences no discomfort, he or she is "free" of narcotics.

Once detoxification is completed, the patient can be given another antagonist, naltrexone (Revia, Trexan), which neutralizes the reinforcing characteristics of heroin and other opiates. It should be noted here that naltrexone has not been shown to provide any therapeutic benefit except as part of an appropriate plan of management for the addictions.[40] Unlike a patient taking Antabuse (disulfiram), used in alcohol treatment, the pa-

ALTERNATIVE CHOICES

The Twelve Steps of Narcotics Anonymous

1. We admitted that we were powerless over our addiction—that our lives had become unmanageable.
2. We came to believe that a Power greater than ourselves could restore us to sanity.
3. We made a decision to turn our will and our lives over to the care of God as we understood Him.
4. We made a searching and fearless moral inventory of ourselves.
5. We admitted to God, to ourselves, and to another human being the exact nature of our wrongs.
6. We were entirely ready to have God remove all these defects of character.
7. We humbly asked Him to remove our shortcomings.
8. We made a list of all persons we had harmed and became willing to make amends to them all.
9. We made direct amends to such people wherever possible, except when to do so would injure them or others.
10. We continued to take personal inventory and when we were wrong, promptly admitted it.
11. We sought through prayer and meditation to improve our conscious contact with God as we understood Him, praying only for knowledge of His will for us and the power to carry that out.
12. Having had a spiritual awakening as a result of these steps, we tried to carry this message to addicts and to practice these principles in all our affairs.

From Hazelden Educational Materials, *What is NA?* (Center City, Minn.: Hazelden Foundation, 1985).

---

tient will not experience any serious symptoms if heroin is administered.

Detoxification and antagonist maintenance alone offer the addict little more than an opportunity to explore an alternative lifestyle. Posttreatment success (continued abstinence) in detoxification and antagonist therapy depends on social support systems such as Narcotics Anonymous (NA). One NA approach toward successful recovery is to stay clean "just for today" (see the box on p. 128).

Heroin Maintenance

Finally, there are those who have proposed that heroin be made available to addicts in some legal way. The proponents of **heroin maintenance** point out that more addicts could be reached (only about 10% are involved in treatment programs currently) and that the crime rate would drop. Proponents also believe that this would be a blow to organized crime and those groups responsible for supplying most of the illicit narcotics.

The Drug Abuse Council has studied this alternative solution in some detail. Perhaps the most serious problem with heroin maintenance lies in the pharmacological traits of heroin itself, which require the addict to secure repeat doses three to five times per day. There are also the problems of individual dosage and the continual cycles of highs and sickness. The individual addicted to heroin is usually in no condition to seek employment or otherwise get his or her life together. Also, the availability of heroin in clinics might undermine the work of detoxification and other treatment programs. Lastly, there

is the possibility that in the absence of careful screening, the number of new addicts might even increase. For these reasons, official support for heroin maintenance has not been forthcoming.

The primary support group for those who are recovering from dependence on narcotics is Narcotics Anonymous (NA). This nonprofit fellowship, formed in 1953, is modeled after Alcoholics Anonymous, including a 12-step creed (see the boxes on p. 128 and above). NA is an important part of aftercare for those who have successfully completed either inpatient or outpatient treatment for narcotics abuse.

Treatment Outcomes. Success rates for various treatment programs vary from 2% to 25%, depending on the type of program and the profile of the client group. The highest rate of success was reported for white male volunteers over the age of 30 years who were involved in a

methadone maintenance a form of therapy in which a legal narcotic, methadone, is prescribed for an addict to replace heroin

substitute dependence treatment a component of a drug abuse treatment program in which a safer drug and/or a safer route of administration is substituted for a more dangerous drug or route of administration.

heroin maintenance a proposed program through which heroin addicts would be supplied heroin by a governmental agency in an attempt to assist them in better managing their condition and to reduce drug-related crimes

SOLUTIONS

When Yung finally came home, disheveled and broke, his parents pleaded with him to stop using heroin, but it was impossible for him to think about quitting when he needed to shoot up. Yung often told himself, "I'll quit forever, tomorrow."

Yung was arrested four times over the next six years for possession of heroin and a number of other crimes. He received probation twice and two short jail sentences. Somehow, he avoided a long prison term. In between the times he was incarcerated, he tried several treatment programs, but he couldn't shake his well-established addiction.

Yung is now on a new, enhanced methadone maintenance program and works for a construction company as an unskilled laborer. His boss knows about his drug use history but believes in giving him a chance. Yung would like to get off narcotics altogether but doesn't think he is ready to try that yet. He does seem to be making progress. For the first three months of treatment, he had to visit the clinic each day in order to be observed taking his methadone dose. He now visits the clinic three times a week and is allowed to take one or two doses home with him. He has received helpful advice from his drug counselor and from an employment counselor. The program even provided a psychiatrist for several sessions. These enhanced methadone treatment services seem to have made a difference for Yung. He has had four months of clean urine samples. He likes his job and plans to start night school to get his GED. Only time will tell whether Yung has kicked his addiction for good this time.

multimodality program of treatment. Success with this particular population group may have been attributable to a phenomenon known as maturing out.[41] It has been observed that many addicts over 30 years of age quit using heroin even in the absence of treatment. It is postulated that they no longer need opiates to cope with the demands of living or have developed other coping skills. Also, it may be that in the fourth decade of life, male addicts experience less need to quench a sex drive that is now diminishing.

In summary, there is an unimpressive level of success in most of the treatment programs. Though abstinence rates seem to increase with time, these successes usually cannot be linked to any particular aspect of the treatment programs, but rather with the profiles of the patients. Better methods are needed to categorize treatment services so that outcomes can be accurately evaluated.

SUMMARY

Narcotics are drugs that are derived from or are chemically related to opium. They relieve pain and produce a numbing effect without producing sleep. The narcotics can be classified as natural, quasi-synthetic, and synthetic drugs. Opium, morphine, and codeine are nat-

urally occurring narcotics, whereas heroin is a quasi-synthetic narcotic. Meperidine (Demerol), methadone, and propoxyphene (Darvon) are classified as synthetic narcotics.

Narcotics are highly subject to abuse and are smuggled into the United States from Southeast Asia, Southwest Asia, Mexico, and more recently, South America. While injection is still the primary route of administration for those abusing heroin, intranasal administration is becoming more common and has become the primary route of administration in some major cities.

Narcotics produce a number of acute and chronic physiological and psychological effects. They act at specific receptor sites for endogenous morphinelike substances in the CNS. They also influence the autonomic branch of the PNS. Narcotic antagonists and partial antagonists interfere with the action of narcotics, and some of these have medical and treatment uses.

Chronic abuse of narcotics results in tolerance and physical dependence. Cross tolerance between narcotics has been demonstrated and is the basis of substitute dependence treatment programs for heroin addicts.

Opiates are used medically as analgesics, antitussives, and antidiarrheals. Illicit use patterns range from experimental to compulsive. First use is experimental and generally involves friends. Chronic regular abuse often results in compulsive use or addiction. A cycle of addiction involving four distinct phases can be used to explain opiate addiction and recovery.

Treatment theories and programs for heroin addiction abound. Treatment programs for heroin dependence involve detoxification, active treatment, and aftercare. A special form of treatment that does not involve immediate detoxification from narcotics is substitute depen-

multimodality programs treatment programs that combine several different treatment approaches

maturing out an observed phenomenon in which older heroin addicts discontinue drug use even in the absence of treatment

dence treatment. The most popular narcotic substituted for heroin is methadone. Success rates for heroin addiction treatment programs are low. For those heroin addicts who are not ready to give up their drug use, no treatment program will work. Others, who no longer feel the desire for heroin or simply become tired of using heroin, may discontinue using heroin without treatment through a process called "maturing out."

REVIEW QUESTIONS

1. Where does the word *narcotic* come from and what does it mean?
2. How do narcotics differ from anesthetics (sedative-hypnotics)?
3. From a historical perspective, what is the relationship between the opiates and the Opium Wars, the American Civil War, the building of the transcontinental railway, and the Vietnam War?
4. What impact did the Harrison Act of 1914 have on the availability of opiates in this country?
5. What are the three major classifications of narcotic drugs? Give two examples of each class.
6. Briefly review the administration, absorption, and distribution of the opiates. Name four routes through which heroin is administered. Why is heroin more addictive than morphine?
7. What are endorphins? Enkephalins?
8. Identify three acute and three chronic physiological effects of opiate use.
9. List three major medical uses of narcotics.
10. Who is most likely to "assist" someone with the first use of heroin?
11. What is meant by the term *controlled use* as it applies to narcotic use?
12. Define each phase associated with the "cycle of addiction."
13. What are the primary steps undertaken during narcotic addiction treatment? How would you describe the success of current treatment programs?
14. What is meant by the term *heroin maintenance*, and how does this differ from substitute dependence?
15. Explain the term *maturing out.*

REFERENCES

1. L. D. Johnston, P. M. O'Malley, and J. G. Bachman, *National Survey Results on Drug Use from the Monitoring the Future Study, 1975–1995,* NIH Pub. No. 96-4139 (Rockville, Md.: Public Health Service, National Institutes of Health, 1996).
2. F. Zackon, "Heroin: The Street Narcotic," in *The Encyclopedia of Psychoactive Drugs* (New York: Chelsea House, 1986).
3. Ibid.
4. E. M. Breecher, "Licit and Illicit Drugs," in *The Consumer's Union Report* (Boston: Little Brown, 1972).
5. O. Ray, and C. Ksir, *Drugs, Society and Human Behavior,* 6th ed. (St Louis: Mosby, 1993).
6. Ibid.
7. Ibid.
8. Drug Enforcement Administration, *Worldwide Heroin Situation Report—1992.* Drug Intelligence Report, March, 1994, Publications Unit, Intelligence Division, DEA Headquarters, Washington, D.C.
9. Ibid.
10. Substance Abuse and Mental Health Administration, *National Household Survey on Drug Abuse: Population Estimates, 1995.* DHHS Pub. No. (SMA 96-3095) (Rockville, Md.: USDHHS, 1996).
11. National Narcotics Intelligence Consumers Committee, *The NNICC Report 1988: The Supply of Illicit Drugs to the United States* (Arlington, Va.: Drug Enforcement Administration, Department of Justice, 1989); National Narcotics Intelligence Consumer's Committee, *The NNICC Report 1991: The Supply of Illicit Drugs to the United States* (Arlington, Va.: Drug Enforcement Administration, Department of Justice, 1992); National Narcotics Intelligence Consumer's Committee, *The NNICC Report 1992: The Supply of Illicit Drugs to the United States* (Arlington, Va.: Drug Enforcement Administration, 1993).
12. Drug Enforcement Administration, *Intelligence Bulletin: The 1995 Heroin Signature Program,* DEA, Intelligence Division, August, 1996, DEA-96042, USDOJ, DEA, Washington, D.C.
13. Substance Abuse and Mental Health Services Administration, Office of Applied Studies, *Estimates from the Drug Abuse Warning Network: 1992 Estimates of Drug-Related Emergency Room Episodes,* Advance Report No. 4 (Rockville, Md.: Department of Health and Human Services, 1993).
14. Substance Abuse and Mental Health Services Administration, Office of Applied Studies, *Preliminary Estimates from the Drug Abuse Warning Network: 1995 Preliminary Estimates of Drug-Related Emergency Department Episodes,* Advance Report No. 17, (Rockville, Md.: Department of Health and Human Services, 1996).
15. Johnston, O'Malley, and Bachman, *Survey Results 1975–1995.*
16. Substance Abuse and Mental Health Services Administration, Office of Applied Studies, *National Household Survey on Drug Abuse: Population Estimates, 1993.* DHHS Publ. No. (SMA) 95-3063 (Rockville, Md.: USDHHS, 1994); Substance Abuse and Mental Health Services Administration, Office of Applied Studies, *National Household Survey on Drug Abuse: Population Estimates, 1994.* DHHS

Publ. No. (SMA) 95-3063 (Rockville, Md.: USDHHS, 1995); Substance Abuse and Mental Health Services Administration, Office of Applied Studies, *National Household Survey on Drug Abuse: Population Estimates, 1995.* DHHS Publ. No. (SMA) 96-3095 (Rockville, Md.: USDHHS, 1996).

17. National Institute on Drug Abuse, *Epidemiological Trends in Drug Abuse*, Vol. 1, *Highlights and Executive Summary. 1996.* Community Epidemiology Work Group, December, 1995. NIH Publ. No. 96-4128 (Rockville, Md.: USDHHS, December 1995).

18. D. Hutchings, "Methadone: Treatment for Addiction," in *The Encyclopedia of Psychoactive Drugs*, (New York: Chelsea House, 1985).

19. Ibid.

20. NNICC, *Report 1988.*

21. National Narcotics Intelligence Consumer's Committee, *The NNICC Report 1995: The Supply of Illicit Drugs to the United States*, Drug Enforcement Administration, DEA-96024 (Arlington, Va.: Drug Enforcement Administration, 1996).

22. National Institute on Drug Abuse.

23. "The Rise in Drug Use among American Teens Continues in 1996," The University of Michigan, News and Information Services, Ann Arbor, Michigan, 19 December 1996. Press Release.

24. S. J. Mule, "Physiological Disposition of Narcotic Agonists and Antagonists," in Narcotics: biochemical pharmacology, ed. D. H. Clouet (New York: Plenum Press, 1971).

25. J. J. Platt, *Heroin Addiction: Theory, Research, Treatment*, 2nd ed. (Malabar, Fla.: Krieger Publishing, 1986).

26. Ibid.

27. D. E. Moffett, S. B. Moffett, C. L. Schauf, *Human Physiology: Foundations and Frontiers*, 2nd ed. (St. Louis, Mo.: Mosby, 1993).

28. Platt, *Heroin Addiction.*

29. *Physicians' Desk Reference*, 51st ed. (Montville, N.J.: Medical Economics Company, Inc., 1997).

30. Centers for Disease Control and Prevention, "Current Trends: Unintentional Poisoning Mortality— United States, 1980–1986," *MMWR* 38, no. 10 (1989):153.

31. Platt, *Heroin Addiction.*

32. G. Wilson, "Clinical Studies of Infants and Children Exposed Prenatally to Heroin," *Ann N Y Acad Sci* 562 (1989):183.

33. *Physicians' Desk Reference.*

34. Ibid.

35. Platt, *Heroin Addiction.*

36. Ibid.

37. Ibid.

38. H. Alksne, L. Lieberman, and L. Brill, "A Conceptual Model of the Life Cycle of Addiction," *Int J Addict* 2 (1967):221.

39. "LAAM Approved to Treat Drug Dependence," *FDA Consumer* (October 1993): 4.

40. *Physicians' Desk Reference.*

41. Ray and Ksir, *Drugs, Society and Human Behavior.*

SOURCES FOR HELP

Narcotics Anonymous (NA)
World Service Office, Inc.
P.O. Box 9999
Van Nuys, CA 91409
(818) 780–3951

Narcotic Educational Foundation of America
5055 Sunset Blvd.
Los Angeles, CA 90027
(213) 663–5171

Websites

Addiction Research Foundation (Canada)
http://www.arf.org/

Drug Enforcement Administration (DEA)
http://www.usdoj/gov/dea/deahome.html

MARIJUANA

8

1. Give the scientific name of the marijuana plant and describe its various uses throughout history.

2. Describe the various usable forms and products of the plant.

3. Explain how THC, the primary psychoactive compound in marijuana, is absorbed and distributed throughout the body and how it is biotransformed and excreted.

4. Describe marijuana's acute and chronic physiological effects, including its anesthetic, analgesic, and hallucinogenic effects.

5. Discuss the acute and chronic psychological effects of marijuana use.

6. Discuss the possible medical usefulness of marijuana and the controversies surrounding such uses.

7. Describe past and current trends in marijuana use by the nation's youth.

8. Discuss what is known about the health risks associated with smoking marijuana.

9. Discuss the pros and cons of current marijuana laws in America.

PROFILE

Bill was wild kid even in junior high school. He was bright and quick witted and determined never to let anyone get the best of him. He was on a select soccer team and was an excellent goalie and fullback. Off the field he spent his time with a group of friends from his neighborhood. To fit in with this older crowd, Bill began drinking beer and smoking marijuana when he was 12 years old.

When Bill sprained his ankle and had to miss the second half of the winter soccer season, he stopped hanging out with his teammates altogether. He began using marijuana every day. He gained a reputation as a troublemaker in class, neglected his studies, and became more of a loner at school. Bill quit the soccer team the next year.

One afternoon when he came home, he couldn't walk straight and was talking excitedly and incoherently. He fell onto the sofa in the family room and began to gaze distractedly at the T.V. His older brother noticed that something wasn't right. He pulled Bill from the sofa and took him back to his room. Bill became belligerent, and an argument ensued.

"I don't know, they must have laced it with something," was all Bill could communicate between swirling delusions and paranoia.

What do you think caused Bill's erratic behavior? To find out, turn to the solutions box after you read this chapter.

In chapters 8 and 9, substances that produce hallucinations are discussed. Products of the **marijuana** plant, *Cannabis sativa,* are sometimes grouped with the hallucinogens because they can, when administered at high doses, produce hallucinations. Marijuana is unique, however. At lower doses, the active ingredients of *C. sativa* produce a variety of other effects, including sedation, mild euphoria, and mild analgesia. Because of its uniqueness, its current widespread use in the United States, and its controversial status as a **decriminalized** but illicit drug, marijuana is covered in a chapter separate from the more powerful hallucinogens discussed in chapter 9.

HISTORY

The marijuana plant, *Cannabis sativa,* has been cultivated for thousands of years for use in making rope, for the oil in its seed, for medicinal purposes, and for its psychoactive properties.[1] Through cultivation, at least two varieties have been developed: a tall, thin plant and a shorter, bushier plant. Although some authors suggest that these are separate species, hybridization studies suggest that all varieties are cross-fertile and, therefore, represent a single species.[2]

The taller variety, *C. sativa* variety *sativa,* was imported to North America in the 1700s as a source of hemp for making rope. This variety soon spread throughout much of this country as a weed, except during World War II, when serious efforts were made to grow it for fiber. Today, it is still found growing in ditches along roads and highways of the upper Midwest, where it is called "ditchweed" (see the box on p. 135). The shorter, bushier variety, sometimes called *C. sativa* variety *indica,*

was cultivated, principally in tropical countries, for its psychoactive properties.

Early History

The use of *Cannabis* can be traced to China nearly 5,000 years ago, when it was used for both its fiber and its medicinal properties.[3] By 1000 B.C., it had spread to India, and by the fifth century B.C., it had become familiar to the inhabitants of ancient Greece. By A.D. 1000, it had spread to the Middle East and the eastern

A marijuana plant,*Cannabis sativa.*

DRUGS IN YOUR WORLD

In Search of "Ditchweed"

Soldiers who clambered down cargo nets into landing crafts during the Normandy invasion of World War II were using marijuana differently from how it is used today. The cargo net's hemp rope was made from fibers extracted from the stems of marijuana plants. Indiana was among the leading producers of the hemp used in the production of rope. Today, the descendants of those "war effort" pot plants grow wild in most of the northwestern counties of the Hoosier state, where they are referred to as "ditchweed."

With the growth of marijuana's popularity during the 1970s and early 1980s, the harvesting of "ditchweed" in Indiana and other states became a popular approach to obtaining an inexpensive supply of marijuana for personal use as well as for sale. Harvesters roamed freely along fence rows, drainage ditch banks, and fallow fields looking for the low-grade but readily available ditchweed. Gradually, however, local residents and law enforcement agencies grew tired of the annual summer harvest.

Today in the "pot counties" of Indiana, the eradication of ditchweed has taken on the characteristics of a crusade. County and state marijuana eradication programs employ teams of high school and college students, who spend their summers eradicating marijuana plants by pulling, burning, or spraying. In Indiana alone, 39.91 million plants were eradicated by burning through the first half of 1990.[a] The

cost of this effort is, of course, borne by Indiana taxpayers. Other economic setbacks of eradication efforts are reduced sales of garbage bags in local hardware stores and an increase in vacancies in the area's few motels during the ditchweed harvest season.

The success of county and state governments in eradicating the low-grade ditchweed marijuana has driven growers indoors. In 1992, law enforcement officials in Indiana seized 178 indoor growing operations through October 15, twice the number seized in all of 1991.[b] In 1995, 370.2 million of the 373.5 million marijuana plants eradicated nationwide by law enforcement officials were low-potency, wild marijuana (ditchweed).[c] Because indoor plants are usually more potent than ditchweed plants, is the ditchweed eradication program effective in reducing the availability and use of marijuana? Will controlling ditchweed that has a THC content of about 1% foster the use of more potent varieties of marijuana that may contain 6% to 10% THC?

[b]M. Olsen, "We're Number One!," *Indiana's Finest,* 8, no. 4 (1992):39.

[c]National Narcotics Intelligence Consumers Committee, *The NNICC Report 1995: The Supply of Illicit Drugs to the United States,* Pub. No. (DEA) 96024 (Arlington, Va.: Drug Enforcement Administration, 1996).

[a]J. Grass, "Roadside Pot Lures 'Pickers' to Indiana," *USA Today,* 26 July 1990, p. 8A.

Mediterranean and by the fifteenth century A.D. to western Europe. *Cannabis* was introduced to South America by the Spanish conquistadores and to North America by the English. These introductions were made principally for the fiber and not for any medicinal or psychoactive value.[4]

In America, the psychoactive properties of *Cannabis* created little interest until about 1920. During Prohibition, when the price of alcohol rose while its quality fell, marijuana use increased in some areas of the country. Marijuana was thrust into the limelight in 1926 by a series of articles published in a New Orleans newspaper that associated marijuana with crime.[5] Over the next 10 years, many articles appeared in the popular press blaming marijuana for violent acts and horrible crimes. Few if any of these articles were based on scientific studies, and many of the articles referred to just one questionable incident.

As a result of this negative publicity, Congress enacted the Marijuana Tax Act in 1937. This act taxed the culti-

vation, distribution, sale, and purchase of marijuana, thereby making it unfeasible for anyone to do business in this commodity.[6] After this, the Bureau of Narcotics wrote and distributed to the states a sample of legislation that could be enacted by individual states that would actually make the possession or use of marijuana illegal. Many states passed this law, which referred specifically to the leaves of *C. sativa.* As one would expect, the price of marijuana increased after passage of this act, and

marijuana the dried parts or extracts of the *Cannabis sativa* plant, capable of producing a psychoactive effect in the user

Cannabis sativa the scientific name for the marijuana plant

decriminalize to lessen the criminal penalties for possession of small quantities of a drug

DRUGS IN YOUR WORLD

Marijuana Subculture

There is an entire subculture in America that centers on the smoking of "pot." Members of this subculture include aging hippies, military veterans, young people in search of an alternative lifestyle, some totally lost individuals, and some very astute entrepreneurs. In the "pot subculture," smoking marijuana is not merely acceptable. It is celebrated as an unalienable right, on par with the right to assemble in peace and freedom of the press.

Speaking of freedom of the press, the pop culture's organ is *High Times*, a monthly magazine that carries a variety of pro-marijuana articles, news, and advertisements. Examples of articles that might be found in a single issue are "*Cannabis* Spirituality," excerpts from a forthcoming book; "Third World Growing in the First World," an article about the Spartan life of marijuana growers in the Pacific Northwest, and "The High Times Interview: Barbara Marciniak," an interview with the New Age author of *Bringers of the Dawn*, a book about Pleiadians, extraterrestrials from the Pleiades star cluster. In addition to articles and regular features, the magazine offers tips for growing marijuana and making hashish out of crushed buds, legislative news items, and lots of advertisements for pot literature, drug paraphernalia, and a variety of "life-enhancing pharmaceuticals," including ephedrine-containing products and the popular Herbal Ecstacy™.

Of course, *High Times*, published by Trans-High Corporation, 235 Park Avenue South, 5th floor, New York, NY, assumes "no responsibility for any claims or representations contained in this magazine or in any advertisement nor do they encourage the illegal use of any of the products advertised within." Yet glossy photos of succulent *Cannabis sativa* plants are abundant throughout the magazine, and instructions for growing marijuana abound. Clearly freedom of the press is alive and well in America. The magazine's web site is: http://www.hightimes.com.

Are the claims the magazine makes about marijuana objective and accurate or do the claims seem one-sided?

marijuana use remained unpopular except on the fringes of society until the early 1960s.

Recent History

In the 1960s, drug use increased among American middle- and upper-class youths. The reasons for this will always be debated. Much of the younger generation was strongly dissatisfied with governmental decisions affecting the environment, social injustices, and especially the war in Vietnam. A particularly prominent feature of this "antiestablishment" sentiment was the perception that the government was lying about many things, ranging from official body counts in the Vietnam War to the dangers of marijuana use.

This well-educated generation was capable of finding and reading scientific reports on the effects of marijuana, comparing them with their own experiences, and deciding that the existing laws were at best out of date and inconsistent with current knowledge and at worst a governmental conspiracy to deprive the youth of its right to enjoy this gift of nature. Many youths also wished to disengage from society, and drugs, including marijuana, seemed to be a way of temporarily disengaging, or "dropping out."

For whatever reason, marijuana use increased steadily during the 1960s and 1970s, whereas the popularity of hallucinogenic drugs, such as LSD, waxed and waned. By 1972, about 2 million Americans were using marijuana daily, and an even greater number were using it on a less regular basis.[7] This level of consumption of an illegal drug was bound to produce many arrests. Indeed, 1973 saw 420,700 marijuana arrests, more than for all other drug offenses combined.[8] Even nonusers had to admit that many state marijuana laws were antiquated and inappropriate.

In 1973, Oregon became the first state to decriminalize the use of marijuana, making possession of small amounts a finable offense, not unlike failure to stop at a stoplight. Several other states followed Oregon's lead. Several studies in the 1980s supported the findings of earlier studies, which concluded that the use of marijuana is much less dangerous than was previously thought.[9] Paradoxically, by the time these reports became available, the upward trend in marijuana smoking had reversed, and its popularity had begun to decline. This decline ended in 1992, and marijuana is again gaining popularity among secondary school students.[10] Popular opinion about how marijuana should be regulated continues to be divided in the 1990s. While the federal government's Drug Enforcement Administration continues to classify marijuana as a Schedule I drug, an entire subculture in America believes marijuana should be legal (see the box above).

In 1996, California and Arizona passed state laws permitting the medical use of marijuana. In California, proposition 215 exempted from criminal laws patients and defined caregivers who possess or cultivate mari-

Schedule I.

An entire subculture in America believes that marijuana should be legal.

juana for medical treatment recommended by a physician. California and Arizona are now among the 26 states and the District of Columbia that "have passed various laws and resolutions establishing therapeutic-research programs, allowing doctors to prescribe marijuana, or asking the federal government to lift the ban on medical use."[11]

Opponents view the movement to legalize marijuana for medical use as a thinly veiled push for legalization of all drugs. They worry that any acceptance of marijuana as legitimate medicine will be used to rationalize continued use by millions of current users and experimental use by millions of young people who have not begun to use it. They also remind those who will listen that there is no sound scientific evidence to support the medical claims made for marijuana.[12]

THE PRODUCTS OF *CANNABIS*

Preparations made from *Cannabis* include marijuana, the dried plant material; **hashish,** the dried resin from the flowers and associated leaves; and **hash oil,** an oily solution of resins and other plant juices extracted in alcohol, filtered, and reduced by evaporation. Marijuana is the form most commonly used because it requires little or no processing. It is known on the street by such names as "pot," "grass," or "weed." Imported varieties go by such colorful labels as "Acapulco Gold," "Colombian Gold," and "Panama Red."

The quality of marijuana varies in two ways: (1) the composition of plant parts and (2) the concentration of the primary active ingredient, **tetrahydrocannabinol (THC).** The best-quality marijuana, referred to in Asia as *ganja,*[13] includes only the tops of the plant—the

flowers and young leaves. Poorer quality marijuana, known in Asia as *bhang,* is made up of the lower leaves, stems, and seeds. The concentration of THC in the leaves and buds of a *Cannabis* plant depends on the variety of the plant and the growing conditions, including the temperature and amount of sunshine and moisture.

In recent years, modern cultivation techniques have increased the potency of *Cannabis* plants from less than 1% THC by weight to, on some occasions, nearly 30%.[14] This is achieved through modern plant breeding and horticultural techniques. For example, by continually removing male plants from the vicinity of young female plants, growers prevent fertilization and the formation of seeds. The resulting plant, called **sinsemilla,** "without seeds," is a female plant that produces an increased amount of resin. In nature, this would increase the likelihood of fertilization. Many of those who cultivate sinsemilla marijuana also use another technique to increase THC levels. By pinching off some of the buds, growers can increase the number of branches and, thus, the number of flowers. The result is a shorter, bushier plant that produces more resin than plants that are left to grow naturally. Finally, by growing *Cannabis* as a potted plant, soil and lighting conditions can be set and maintained to maximize plant growth and resin production.

More than 400 chemicals have been isolated from *Cannabis.* Those that are particular to this plant, about 61, are known as **cannabinoids.** Among these is tetrahydrocannabinol (THC), the primary psychoactive ingredient in marijuana. Other cannabinoids that have been isolated are cannabinol and cannabidiol.

PHARMACOLOGY

Because THC and related cannabinoids are very soluble in lipids, they are rapidly absorbed and distributed throughout the body. (Refer to chapter 4 for a review of this topic.) These products readily cross the blood-brain barrier and the placenta. The products of marijuana biodeactivation are excreted through the feces and urine.

hashish dried, smokeable resin from marijuana flowers and leaves

hash oil oily solution of marijuana resins extracted in alcohol, filtered, and reduced by evaporation

tetrahydrocannabinol (THC) primary active compound in marijuana

sinsemilla female plants that have been protected against fertilization and are, therefore, without seeds; they produce increased amounts of resin, and therefore more THC, than plants with seeds

cannabinoids chemical compounds unique to the plant genus *Cannabis*; THC is the most familiar cannabinoid

Marijuana can be smoked either as hand-rolled cigarettes, as shown here, through a pipe, or by stuffing it into a hollowed out cigar.

Administration of Cannabinoids

In the United States, the products of *Cannabis* are usually smoked. Marijuana is smoked either as a hand-rolled cigarette (joint), or through a pipe or water pipe (bong). In a current trend, marijuana is stuffed into a hollowed-out commercial cigar. These marijuana cigars are called "blunts," "vegas," or "swishers."[15] In other countries, where *Cannabis* may be used as an herb or spice, it is ingested. Ingestion of marijuana in the United States is uncommon, but not rare. Smoking is about three times as effective in delivering THC to the bloodstream as is ingestion.[16] Hashish is smoked in pipes specially designed for this purpose; hash oil is usually applied to a marijuana or tobacco cigarette, which is then smoked. Use of hashish and hash oil is popular with some groups in Canada, although it is uncommon in the United States because most American users prefer marijuana.[17]

Absorption

The inhaled smoke from marijuana brings THC into contact with the blood in the alveoli of the lungs, where the THC is rapidly absorbed because of its high lipid solubility. Experienced users develop the habit of inhaling deeply and then holding the smoke in the lungs for several moments to permit a more complete absorption of the THC. The rate of absorption also depends on the concentration of THC in the inhaled smoke. According to an analysis of samples from drug seizures and street buys in the United States in 1995, the concentration of THC for that year averaged nearly 6% for marijuana, nearly 11% for sinsemilla marijuana, only 3.6% for hashish, and about 16% for hash oil.[18]

Distribution

The THC concentration in the blood peaks 10 to 30 minutes after smoking begins.[19] Because of its high lipid solubility, THC does not remain in the bloodstream for long. Most of it is absorbed out of the bloodstream within 30 minutes after the cessation of smoking. THC rapidly moves across the blood-brain barrier to the brain and across the placenta to the fetus, where THC levels are about the same as those for the mother.

The small amount of THC remaining in the bloodstream has a half-life of about 19 hours. This long half-life results because levels of THC in the plasma equal those in the fatty storage tissues in the liver and elsewhere. The deposition of THC and its metabolites into fat lengthens the time necessary to clear THC from the body. This is because THC and its metabolites are released slowly into the bloodstream from the fat as levels of these compounds in the bloodstream drop.

Enzymes in the liver biodeactivate THC to several compounds. The long-term storage of THC and its metabolites in the tissues is probably the reason that regular marijuana users seem to experience its effects more quickly than novice users.

With today's drug testing technology, the presence of THC and its metabolites can be detected in the blood and urine for up to 6 weeks after last use of marijuana.

Biotransformation and Excretion

About 80 compounds result from the biotransformation of THC. The primary one has a half-life of about 50 hours.[20] Because of this long half-life, up to 50% of the original marijuana dose can be detected in the body for up to a week; its complete elimination can take as long as six weeks.[21] The major pathways for elimination of the products of THC biotransformation are the feces (about two-thirds) and the urine (about one-third). THC and its metabolites have been detected in the breast milk of lactating mothers. In some cases, the amounts excreted in this manner could be enough to affect the alertness of a nursing infant.

elmination
1° = feces 2° = urine

NEUROHORMONAL INFLUENCES

THC (the primary active compound in marijuana) produces several physiological and psychological changes. Both acute and chronic effects have been noted.

Mode of Action

THC produces many physiological and psychological effects, including sedation, mild euphoria, and mild analgesia. At high doses, THC may produce hallucinations and heightened sensations.[22] Eventually, several modes of action for these effects will probably be discovered. In 1988, studies found evidence for a receptor binding site with characteristics similar to those observed for known neurotransmitter receptor systems.[23] The pres-

ence of such a binding site suggested the existence of an endogenous substance similar to THC. In 1992, scientists isolated from pig brains a natural, endogenous THC-like substance that they named **anandamide.** This discovery was similar to the discovery a few years ago of natural opiates in humans, the endorphins and enkephalins.[24] In addition, evidence suggests that THC affects cell membranes that are known to have lipophilic properties. The isolation of a natural THC-like substance provides hope that the mode of action of THC will eventually be understood.

Physiological Effects

The acute physiological effects of *Cannabis* appear moments after smoking begins. Serious acute reactions to toxic doses of marijuana are rare but have increased in recent years. Physical health problems associated with chronic use have not been determined with complete certainty, but most authorities expect these problems to become evident as large numbers of long-term marijuana users continue to age. *B.S.!*

Acute Physiological Effects. Because THC is rapidly absorbed and distributed, its acute effects can be detected within a few seconds after smoking begins. These effects include changes in both the cardiovascular system and the CNS. The pulse rate and blood pressure increase.

anandamide a natural, endogenous cannabinoid

Pulse ; BP ↑

Bronchodilation

The eyes redden as blood vessels of the cornea dilate, and the throat and mouth become dry.[25] Other effects often reported include dizziness and nausea. Bronchodilation also occurs, leading to the occasional suggestion that marijuana should be prescribed for the treatment of asthma.

Balance and stability of stance may be affected, particularly when the eyes are closed. Muscular strength and hand steadiness decrease. Information processing and the ability to perform sequential tasks in the proper order become impaired.[26] At higher doses, simple motor tasks and reaction times are also impaired.

Chronic Physiological Effects.   The chronic effects of marijuana use are similar to those that result from smoking tobacco, namely, assaults on the respiratory system. Except for the absence of nicotine and the presence of THC, the constituents (gases and particulate matter) of the inhaled smokes of marijuana and tobacco are very similar. As a rule, a marijuana smoker consumes fewer cigarettes in a day than a tobacco smoker, so the burden on the throat and lungs may be somewhat less. Marijuana smoke contains more carcinogens and is inhaled more deeply, however, so puff for puff, marijuana is probably more dangerous.

Although marijuana use and cancer or heart disease have not been definitely linked yet, studies aimed at doing so are under way. One study reported that 92% of young (median age 36 years) head and neck cancer patients used marijuana.[27] Other studies are under way to examine whether THC suppresses the immune system.[28] Many years of research were needed to establish the links between tobacco use and disease. One might logically suppose that someday marijuana use and disease also might be linked. Recent evidence has linked marijuana use and time lost at work. In a study that measured the number of restricted activity days (days in which less than one-half day was worked), those who used marijuana within the past year reported more restricted days than those who never used marijuana.[29]

Tolerance.   Both human and animal research has shown the development of physiological tolerance to THC. Tolerance has been demonstrated through both performance and physiological measurements, including heart rate and electroencephalogram (EEG) measurements of alpha rhythm.[30] Clinical evidence suggests that tolerance is more likely to develop in the high-dose daily user. The development of such tolerance might cause the user to increase the dose or switch to a more powerful drug that can provide the desired high. As with other drugs, tolerance to THC results from increased metabolic rates and from decreased sensitivity of the target cells.

Dependence.   The question of whether *Cannabis* produces physiological dependence is clouded. Studies with dogs resulted in no observable withdrawal symptoms.

The cessation of *Cannabis* use in humans produces a desire to resume use, but this alone is not a demonstration of physical dependence. For now, the question of physical dependence must remain open.

Psychological Effects

The psychological effects of marijuana are both acute and chronic. Acute psychological effects are influenced not only by dose, but also by the user's mood and the setting in which the drug is used. Chronic psychological effects are a matter of continuing concern, because, although classic physical dependence does not develop, psychological dependence may develop. Long-term marijuana use can result in chronic apathy and a loss of important developmental time.

Acute Effects.   Some users describe the acute psychological effects of mild THC intoxication as similar to a state of daydreaming, or the way one feels just before falling asleep. Mood and setting are important variables in the psychological outcome. In a friendly social setting, users may feel tense at first as they feel the onset of physiological changes but then develop feelings of hilarity, followed by a mood of carefree relaxation, sleepiness (sedation), and mild euphoria. Of course, there are alternatives to using marijuana as a social lubricant (see the box on p. 141). Similar effects are reported by subjects who use the drug when alone, except that the sleepiness may be more pronounced. These feelings are accompanied by enhanced gustatory, tactile, olfactory, visual, and auditory perceptions. Thought formation and the perception of time also change. Food, especially sweets, is sometimes craved.[31] The outward behavior of an individual experiencing these feelings in most cases would not appear unusual to the nonusing observer.

Experienced users often report the onset of the effects of THC before novice users. This may occur because the practiced user recognizes the onset of psychological effects. The experienced user can also inhale more deeply and hold the THC in his or her lungs longer than the novice. Lastly, the habitual user may already have a base level of THC in the bloodstream from previous uses.

At high doses, hallucinations, delusions, paranoia, disorientation, and confusion have been reported.[32] These may become intensified and more vivid at even higher doses. The user may fear that these states will worsen or never end, resulting in reports of medical emergencies.[33] Although some of these emergencies are traceable to adulterated THC or other drugs, such as phencyclidine (PCP), other emergencies might be caused by the greater concentration of THC in today's marijuana.

Chronic Effects.   Perhaps the most serious of the psychological effects of chronic marijuana use is the phenomenon called **amotivational syndrome.**[34] Characterized by apathy, lack of motivation, loss of interest in achievement

ALTERNATIVE CHOICES

Reaching New Heights

Although some prefer to experience the mind-altering effects of marijuana in seclusion, most use it in the context of social interaction, in much the same way others use alcohol. In this context, it is intended to help establish a bond between smokers and to facilitate conversation within the group.

Are there, however, other ways of "bonding" with friends and acquaintances without using an illegal drug whose short- and long-term use can cause a variety of physiological and psychological problems? Consider these suggestions:

1. Simply think about the enjoyable aspects of being in the company of good friends, without the "assistance"

of, and potential problems associated with, smoking marijuana.

2. Work to improve your social skills to become more comfortable in the presence of others, thereby reducing your feelings of need for a "social lubricant."

3. Seek out new friends with whom you can enjoy social interaction without the use of marijuana.

4. Engage in a competitive activity, such as a board game, a card game, or sports.

5. Eating and preparing food is another good alternative to smoking marijuana. Preparing a salad, tacos, or even a more elaborate meal allows everyone to join in the fun of cooking.

6. Listen to music with your friends.

---

and in the future, diminished scholastic or job performance, and introversion, this condition usually disappears several weeks after detoxification. In some cases, however, it may linger for months or years.

There is no solid evidence that marijuana causes mental illness or insanity. Clearly, however, for young people the time spent "getting high" on marijuana is time that could be better spent developing the coping skills needed to deal with the problems of living.[35] In this sense, marijuana represents a poor choice, particularly for those who may never develop these necessary coping skills or problem-solving techniques.

Although the question of physical dependence remains unanswered, clearly *Cannabis* users develop a strong desire to continue use and for many, quitting is very difficult. Most experts view the difficulty in quitting as a psychosocial problem and not an inevitable consequence of marijuana use.[36]

PATTERNS OF USE

Currently, marijuana (THC) enjoys limited use in modern medicine and is prescribed by some physicians despite the fact that the federal government's Drug Enforcement Administration continues to classify it as a schedule I drug. Marijuana is the most widely used illicit drug in the United States and the fourth most popular of all drugs, after alcohol, tobacco, and caffeine.

Medical Uses

Although the prescription form of THC, Marinol (dronabinol) has several approved medical uses, the medical use of crude preparations of *Cannabis sativa* remains

highly controversial. The proposed medical uses for marijuana include the relief of uncontrolled vomiting and nausea associated with chemotherapy in cancer treatment, the relief of anorexia associated with weight loss in AIDS patients, the relief of pain and muscle spasms in people with epilepsy and multiple sclerosis, and the reduction in eye pressure in people with glaucoma. It has also been used in the past to prevent convulsions, sedate, treat asthma, and relieve the symptoms of alcohol, opiate, or barbiturate withdrawal.[37]

Currently, the only prescription medication containing THC is Marinol.[38] Some who have tried Marinol for extreme nausea and vomiting associated with cancer therapy say that the pill is hard to swallow when you are vomiting and that it is easy to take an overdose, which results in a drugged feeling. In contrast, regulating dosage is much easier when smoking marijuana. Another drug used to stop vomiting is ondansetron (Zofran), but this drug is expensive. Marinol for wasting and low appetite in AIDS patients has the same shortcoming—difficulty in taking the right dose. A new drug, megestrol acetate (Megase), is being tested for this purpose. Two drugs commonly prescribed to reduce muscle spasms and pain are dantrolene sodium (Dantrium) and bactofen (Lioresal). Both of these have significant side effects. Finally, a new medication seems to be as effective as or more effective than smoking marijuana in relieving

amotivational syndrome symptoms or a behavior pattern characterized by apathy, loss of effectiveness, and a more passive, introverted personality, this syndrome can result from chronic marijuana abuse

WHAT DO YOU THINK?

Should the Use of Marijuana for Medical Purposes Be Legal?

Marijuana is currently classified as a schedule I drug, meaning that it has no currently accepted medical use, carries a potential risk for abuse, and may produce dependence. However, many people believe that marijuana has significant medical use for the prevention of nausea and vomiting during chemotherapy for cancer, for relief of anorexia in AIDS patients, for the treatment of glaucoma, and for relief of spasticity in people with amputated limbs and those with multiple sclerosis. Past and currently proposed medical uses for *Cannabis* are the subject of a new book, *Marijuana, the Forbidden Medicine.*[a]

The book recounts much of the testimony presented in hearings held by the Drug Enforcement Administration. Testimony was given both for and against the rescheduling of marijuana as a schedule II drug. Schedule II includes drugs that have medical uses but carry a high potential for abuse. Much of the testimony was forceful and touching, particularly testimony from families with suffering, terminally ill children and from cancer and AIDS patients for whom the smoking of marijuana seemed to make all the difference in the world.

Although an administrative law judge who listened to arguments from both sides recommended the rescheduling

[a]L. Grinspoon, and J. B. Bakalar, *Marijuana, the Forbidden Medicine* (New Haven, Conn.: Yale University Press, 1993).

of marijuana, the administrator of the Drug Enforcement Administration rejected the ruling, citing the lack of scientifically controlled studies supporting the usefulness of such treatment. He also cited statements from the American Medical Association and other societies that marijuana has not been demonstrated as suitable for medicinal use.[b] This position was reaffirmed by Drug Czar Gen. Barry McCaffrey in 1997.[c]

However, citizens in California and Arizona think differently and have voted to allow the use of marijuana for medical treatment.[d] Some medical authorities agree with them.[e] What do you think? If a drug seems to help a very ill person, should he or she be allowed to use it, even if it is illegal? Is the DEA worried about a few thousand cancer patients or about the increase in drug trafficking that might occur if marijuana is rescheduled? If someone you knew was very sick from chemotherapy, would you try to obtain some marijuana for him or her? *absolutely!*

[b]J. C. Lawn, "Their Government Tells Them All to Get Lost," *Federal Register* 44(249):53767, December 1989.

[c]B. McCaffrey, "We're on a Perilous Path," *Newsweek*, 3 February 1997.

[d]T. Morganthau, "The War over Weed," *Newsweek*, 3 February 1997, pp. 20–22.

[e]M. Conant, "This Is Smart Medicine," *Newsweek*, 3 February 1997, p. 26; J. P. Kassirer, "Federal Foolishness and Marijuana," *The New England Journal of Medicine* 336(5): 366–67, 30 January 1997.

pressure within the eye in glaucoma patients. This drug is called latanoprost (Xalantan) and is a once-a-day eye drop.[39]

The federal government has moved slowly on expanding the role of THC as a prescription drug for several reasons. First, the method of action for THC is not clearly known, although as discussed earlier, researchers clearly are making progress. Second, other drugs are effective for treatment of each of the conditions for which THC is used. Third, in controlled studies, THC therapy yielded inconsistent results, and because of its side effects, it seems to be a less-than-perfect drug, even for the prevention of vomiting.[40] Opponents of the use of crude preparations of *Cannabis* (marijuana cigarettes) point to the availability of purer drugs and the health risk involved in inhaling the 400 other chemicals that make up the marijuana smoke.[41] Proponents of its medical use point out the high cost of purified THC and other similar prescription drugs and the fact that smoking marijuana enables the patient to adjust the dose better than taking pills.

In response to a well-run campaign that focused on "compassionate medical use," voters in California and Arizona passed state propositions in November 1996, allowing the medical use of marijuana in those states. In California, the law permits its use for almost any complaint if a doctor recommends it. A prescription is not required. The Arizona law also "permits the use of heroin, LSD and methamphetamines if the user gets prescriptions from two doctors."[42] In January 1997, an editorial in the highly regarded *New England Journal of Medicine* recommended that the federal government change marijuana's status to schedule II (drugs that are potentially addictive but with some accepted medical use).[43] Only time will tell how this controversial issue will be resolved (for more thoughts, see the box above).

Misuse and Abuse

Marijuana remains the most popular illegal drug in the United States. Current use trends show that the long de-

Indiana is a leader in the eradication of naturally growing marijuana plants.

cline in marijuana use during the 1980s and early 1990s ended in 1992. The widespread availability of marijuana in the United States is the result of increased domestic production, as well as substantial importation of foreign-grown product. Thus, availability increased despite substantial eradication and interdiction efforts.

Availability Trends. Estimating the actual net marijuana production in the United States is extremely difficult, particularly now that much of the growing has moved indoors. However, federal seizures in 1995 increased to 480 metric tons from 363 metric tons in 1994. Some 3.27 million cultivated plants were eradicated in 1995.[44] The perceived availability of marijuana among young people, which had remained fairly level between 1975 and 1992, has increased in each of the last four years. In 1996, 52% of eighth graders, 78% of tenth graders, and 89% of twelfth graders reported that marijuana was "fairly easy" or "very easy" to get.[45]

As mentioned previously, two types of marijuana are sold in the United States—commercial grade and sinsemilla. Data on the percentages of domestically eradicated *Cannabis* that were commercial grade and the sinsemilla type are not available for recent years. Another statistic, however, reflects the increase in marijuana's potency, namely, emergency room visits. The rate of emergency room mentions of marijuana/hashish per 100,000 population has doubled, from 9.2 in 1988 to 20.2 in 1995.[46] These emergency room reports may result partly from the higher THC content in marijuana.

Use Trends. The popularity of marijuana use among high school seniors peaked in 1978 and 1979 and declined through 1992 as more students perceived harmfulness in its use. Although lifetime, annual, and 30-day drug use patterns all declined substantially during that period, the daily use patterns declined the most. In 1978, 10.7% of high school seniors reported using the drug daily or nearly daily, whereas by 1992 only 1.9% reported similar usage. Since 1992, the percentage of seniors reporting daily use has risen to 4.9% (nearly one in 20), and 22% (one in five) report use within the previous 30 days (table 8.1).[47]

This increase in marijuana use among high school seniors, although disappointing to many of those working in drug education and prevention efforts, was predicted several years ago when it was shown that lifetime, annual, and 30-day use of marijuana in eighth graders increased in 1992.[48] This was an obvious warning sign, because approximately half of all high school marijuana users began using before high school. The 1992 eighth graders are the 1996 twelfth graders in the 1996 Monitoring the Future Report.[49] Furthermore, in 1996, marijuana use increased more among eighth and tenth graders than among twelfth graders. Eleven percent of eighth graders and 20% of tenth graders reported marijuana use within the past 30 days.[50]

Lifetime, annual, 30-day, and daily use patterns among college students declined substantially between 1980, the first year data were collected for this group, and 1992, then steadied or began to increase in 1993 and 1994 (table 8.2). Male college students are four times

TABLE 8.1 Trends in Marijuana Use among High School Seniors, 1978–1996

	Percentage of Seniors Reporting Use (by Year)																		
Frequency of Use	1978	1979	1980	1981	1982	1983	1984	1985	1986	1987	1988	1989	1990	1991	1992	1993	1994	1995	1996
Ever used	59.2	60.4	60.3	59.5	58.7	57.0	54.9	54.2	50.9	50.2	47.2	43.7	40.7	36.7	32.6	35.3	38.2	41.7	44.9
Within past year	50.2	50.8	48.8	46.1	44.3	42.3	40.0	40.6	38.8	36.3	33.1	29.6	27.0	23.9	21.9	26.0	30.7	34.7	35.8
Within past 30 days	37.1	36.5	33.7	31.6	28.5	27.0	25.2	25.7	23.4	21.0	18.0	16.7	14.0	13.8	11.9	15.5	19.0	21.2	21.9
Daily (within past 30 days)	10.7	10.3	9.1	7.0	6.3	5.5	5.0	4.9	4.0	3.3	2.7	2.9	2.2	2.0	1.9	2.4	3.6	4.6	4.9

L. D. Johnston, P. M. O'Malley, and J. G. Bachman, *National Survey Results on Drug Use from Monitoring the Future Study, 1975–1995,* vol. 1, Secondary School Students. NIH Pub. No. (PHS) 99-4139 (Rockville, Md.: USDHHS, 1996); *The Rise in Drug Use among American Teens Continues in 1996.* Press Release. 19 December 1996, University of Michigan, Ann Arbor.

TABLE 8.2 Trends in Marijuana Use among College Students, 1980–1994

	Percentage of Students Reporting Use (by Year)														
Frequency of Use	1980	1981	1982	1983	1984	1985	1986	1987	1988	1989	1990	1991	1992	1993	1994
Ever used	65.0	63.3	60.5	63.1	59.0	60.6	57.9	55.8	54.3	51.3	49.1	46.3	44.1	42.0	42.2
Within past year	51.2	51.3	44.7	45.2	40.7	41.7	40.9	37.0	34.6	33.6	29.4	26.5	27.7	27.9	29.3
Within past 30 days	34.0	33.2	26.8	26.2	23.0	23.6	22.3	20.3	16.8	16.3	14.0	14.1	14.6	14.2	15.1
Daily (within past 30 days)	7.2	5.6	4.2	3.8	3.6	3.1	2.1	2.3	1.8	2.6	1.7	1.8	1.6	1.9	1.8

L. D. Johnston, P. M. O'Malley, and J. G. Bachman, *National Survey Results on Drug Use from Monitoring the Future Study, 1975–1994,* vol. 2, College Students and Young Adults, NIH Pub. No. (PHS) 96-4027 (Rockville, Md.: USDHHS, 1996).

Male 4y more than female to use daily

more likely than female college students to be daily smokers of marijuana. Daily marijuana use was reported by only 1.8% of college students in 1994, the most recent year for which data are available; this was less than half the rate of daily use among noncollege-attending young adults.[51]

Attitudes and beliefs are often a key to drug-taking behavior. In 1991, 78.6% of high school seniors said they believed that those who smoke marijuana regularly risk harming themselves. This compares with only 35% who felt that way in 1978.[52] Beginning in 1992, the perceived harmfulness associated with smoking marijuana regularly decreased to less than 60% of seniors. This occurred while marijuana was perceived to be more available. In 1996, perceived availability reached a 15-year high among twelfth graders and record highs among eighth and tenth graders.[53] By plotting survey data on levels of use against responses about perceived health risk and the perceived availability of marijuana, we see an interesting trend (fig. 8.1).[54] Marijuana use declined as perceived risk grew, in spite of steady availability. How-

ever, as the perception of the health risk of occasional or regular marijuana use declines, use increases. Similar declines in the perception of harmfulness also occurred among eighth graders and tenth graders.

Another factor that may have contributed to the decline in marijuana use during the 1980s was increasing rates of disapproval by peers. The percentage of students at all three grade levels who said they disapproved of people who smoked marijuana has decreased significantly. This decrease in disapproval rates, which began in 1991 and 1992, foretold the current increase in use.

MARIJUANA AND HEALTH

Acute toxic doses of marijuana are rarely serious when compared with those of other illicit drugs. The health effects from long-term marijuana use are still under investigation. Several major problems resulting from intense marijuana use have been noted, including the use

FIGURE 8.1

Marijuana trends.[54]

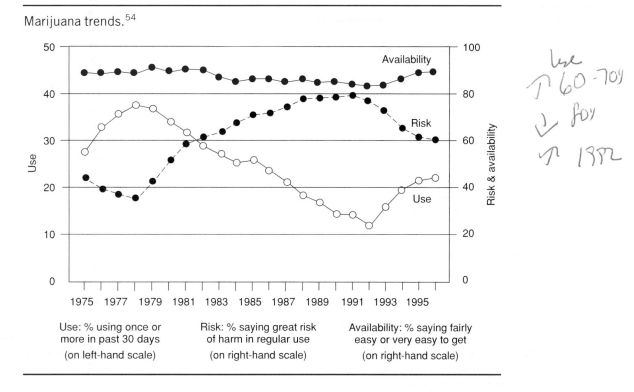

Use: % using once or
more in past 30 days
(on left-hand scale)

Risk: % saying great risk
of harm in regular use
(on right-hand scale)

Availability: % saying fairly
easy or very easy to get
(on right-hand scale)

of marijuana in combination with other drugs (primarily alcohol) and marijuana use and driving. Medical problems associated with chronic use are diseases of the respiratory system and psychological problems.

Acute Health Risks

Serious acute physiological responses to high doses of marijuana are rare, and no overdose deaths have been reported in the United States.[55] Recently though, the number of emergency room reports naming marijuana/ hashish as the precipitating cause of distress has increased.[56] As stated earlier, this increase may be the result of the higher THC concentrations being seen in *Cannabis*; or they may be a consequence of polydrug use.

Studies have demonstrated that alpha brain waves of subjects given alcohol-marijuana combinations are increased when compared with those of subjects given placebo-marijuana combinations. Because alpha brain waves are associated with pleasant mood states, the alcohol-marijuana combination may be reinforcing and, therefore, may encourage abuse.[57]

Marijuana, either alone or in combination with alcohol, has been proven detrimental to automobile driving ability. Impairments include reduced concentration, slowed reaction time, and impaired judgment. In this regard the effects of marijuana and alcohol are additive.[58]

Another health risk from an acute dose of marijuana is the so-called **panic reaction.** This is most likely to

occur in the novice user who may be seized by guilt feelings associated with using an illicit drug, by fear of loss of control, or by fear of being arrested. This panic reaction may sometimes result from fear that the marijuana was contaminated or otherwise unsafe.

Chronic Health Risks

Health concerns resulting from long-term use of marijuana include those associated with route of exposure (smoking), reproduction physiology, neonatal problems, and possible problems with the immune system. Inhaling smoke of any type is an assault on the respiratory system. Because marijuana smoke contains more than 400 chemicals, including several known to be dangerous (such as carbon monoxide, nitrosamines, and benzopyrene), long-term marijuana smoking obviously represents a significant health risk. The health effects of long-term marijuana smoking are now under study, and within the next 5 to 10 years, we should know more about the actual disease rates of this widespread practice. For now, we must assume that the nonnicotine-induced ill effects of tobacco smoking, such as chronic bronchitis, cancer, and

panic reaction sudden exaggerated response to initial use of an illicit drug; associated with fear or feeling of loss of control

emphysema, will also result from marijuana smoking. Because marijuana smoke enters the lungs unfiltered, the chronic health risks from marijuana, puff for puff, probably are greater than those from tobacco.

We know surprisingly little about another concern associated with chronic marijuana use, its effects on the fetus. One study found that newborn babies who were prenatally exposed to marijuana because their mothers smoked showed an increased incidence of fine tremors, exaggerated and prolonged startles, and poorer habituation to visual stimuli compared with nonexposed babies. In general, offspring exposed to marijuana seemed less mature than the nonexposed infants during the early part of the postnatal period.[59] Although maternal-fetal studies were carefully controlled for other drug use (nicotine and alcohol), this is not usually the case in everyday life, where polydrug use is often the rule. As we have stated throughout this text, one should always avoid all psychoactive drugs during pregnancy.

Chronic marijuana use has been shown in some studies to reduce testosterone (male hormone) levels and sperm counts, but results are inconsistent; thus, their usefulness may be in doubt.[60] Some reports suggest that marijuana smoking compromises the immune system. Further studies are needed before these ideas are proven.

SHOULD MARIJUANA LAWS BE REFORMED?

One of the most controversial issues surrounding *C. sativa* is whether marijuana laws should be changed. Proponents of such reform argue that the products of the marijuana plant are less harmful than those of the tobacco plant and less harmful than alcohol. Observers estimate that 90% of the illegal drug use in the United States is marijuana use.[61]

Marijuana trafficking has changed in the last 30 years. In 1969, when the so-called "drug war" began, most of the marijuana smoked in this country was imported. Today most of the marijuana smoked here is grown in the United States. State laws vary greatly in the severity of the penalties for marijuana growing or trafficking, and many enforcement agencies are so understaffed that enforcing marijuana laws is a low priority. "Why don't you catch that serial killer instead of arresting Jethro for smoking marijuana again?" might be a familiar question. The same argument is often made about the use of our scarce prison space to hold marijuana growers while violent offenders are given mandatory release.

In Bacon County, Georgia, citizens refused to elect to the office of sheriff a deputy who had strictly enforced marijuana laws. Instead they elected his opponent, who

made no arrests and eradicated no marijuana plants during his first year in office.[62]

Opponents argue that marijuana alters brain waves, produces a variety of health problems, including amotivational syndrome and impaired driving ability, and is a gateway drug that leads to further drug use (see chapter 2 for a discussion of the gateway drug theory). It has been classified as a schedule I drug (high risk for abuse and no medical value) and, therefore, is illegal. Under this view, state and federal laws would probably have to be tightened, more funds made available for enforcement, and more prisons made available to house those arrested.

Most Americans are willing to concede that smoking marijuana is unhealthy and at the very least a terrible waste of time, especially for youth. Many Americans, however, do not seem to have "the stomach" for an all-out war on marijuana. Without popular support, waging such a war would not be successful. After all, in a democracy, you can police people only as much as they are willing to be policed and, when it comes to marijuana, just how much is that? Asset seizure laws allow the government to seize personal property, including cars, boats, homes, and farms, used for drug trafficking, including marijuana growing. In 1995, more than $42 million worth of personal assets were seized.[63] Assets can be seized before the suspect has been proven guilty and even if the owner did not know the property was being used for this purpose. Are such asset seizure laws too invasive for most Americans?

One group in favor of changing marijuana laws is the National Organization for the Reform of Marijuana Laws (**NORML**). Members of this group are often invited to speak on college campuses. Perhaps, in the more liberal social and political climate of the 1990s, the reform of marijuana laws can be seriously debated. Currently, however, college students and others perceive the risk to health to be high enough that any serious bid for legal reform is unlikely.

One outcome of the passage of the California and Arizona initiatives mentioned previously is that $1 million of federal funds has been made available to study the potential benefits of marijuana.[64] The goals of this study are to determine what elements in marijuana smoke might be beneficial and to make those elements available for medical use—not to make smoking marijuana an acceptable medical treatment.

Other research efforts seek to further characterize the nature of specific receptor sites for THC on certain neurons in the central nervous system. These studies may reveal the mechanism of the analgesic properties of

NORML National Organization for the Reform of Marijuana Laws

SOLUTIONS

Bill's experience with the PCP-laced joint didn't turn him off to marijuana, but it did sever his relationship with his group of older friends. He felt they had taken advantage of him by making him the butt of their "experiment" or joke. Bill made a few close friends his own age and continued to party, with marijuana and alcohol being an important part of the social interaction.

Bill finished high school and then went out of state for college. His best friend Ian stayed home to pursue a career as a musician. Later that year, while Bill was away at school, Ian was killed in an early morning house fire after a party. One of the guests had passed out on the sofa while smoking. Ian had awakened to cries for help and had helped a number of people climb out a basement window before being overcome by smoke himself.

The shock of this loss and its circumstances made Bill vow never to smoke marijuana again. He applied himself both mentally and physically as he had never done before. He began to pay attention in class and took up running as a way to be alone and work off his stress. When he was back in shape, he decided to join his college rugby team. Bill could no longer help his friend, but he had found a way to help himself.

THC, which seem to be different from those of the narcotics, and lead the way to the development of a new set of painkillers. In other research, public health epidemiologists are expected to report on data being gathered on America's experiment with long-term use of marijuana. Results of these studies may help lawmakers decide whether to legalize this drug.

Lastly, because we are currently unable to significantly reduce the supply of marijuana to our youth, reducing demand seems logical and wise. Demand reduction (decreasing the interest in and desire for drugs) has the advantage that one comprehensive program can be effective against various substances. That is, you do not need separate programs to control use of crack cocaine, marijuana, heroin, LSD, and so on. You need only a program that instills a belief in young people that using drugs of any kind is wasteful and often dangerous.

SUMMARY

Marijuana has been cultivated in Asia for thousands of years for use in making rope, for its oil, for medicinal uses, and for its psychoactive properties. It was first used in the United States for making rope. The drug was used widely for its psychoactive properties in this country in the 1920s during Prohibition. Marijuana's reported association with crime and bizarre behavior resulted in the Marijuana Tax Act of 1937. During the 1960s and 1970s, marijuana use became popular among American youths. In the 1980s, the popularity of marijuana declined, but in the first half of the 1990s, marijuana use increased again.

The psychoactive products of *C. sativa* include marijuana, hashish, and hash oil. The strength of the product is determined by the percentage of THC in the plant parts being used. Modern cultivation techniques have increased the potency of marijuana by increasing the THC content.

Marijuana is most often administered through the inhalation of marijuana cigarette smoke. High lipid solubility assures rapid absorption of THC. THC can be found in the brain and other tissues within 10 to 30 minutes after use. Evidence of marijuana use can be detected for up to 6 weeks after use.

The THC in marijuana produces a multitude of physiological and psychological effects. Chronic respiratory effects of marijuana smoking resemble those of chronic tobacco smoking. Tolerance to THC develops, but classic withdrawal symptoms have not been observed. Acute psychological effects of marijuana use depend on dosage, mood, and setting. Amotivational syndrome is one of the possible outcomes of chronic marijuana use.

Medical use of marijuana is more controversial than ever before. Two states, California and Arizona, have legalized marijuana for medical use even though it is still classified by the Drug Enforcement Administration as a schedule I drug. Illicit use among high school students and young adults, which declined in the 1980s, has increased again in the 1990s, as perceived health risk has declined. Perceived availability has also increased in the past few years, suggesting that interdiction to stop marijuana from entering our borders and the eradication of domestic plants to reduce supply is not working.

Marijuana use clearly causes impaired driving ability and may carry other significant health risks. Alterations to the reproductive and immune systems as a result of chronic use are still under investigation. Attempts by NORML to reform marijuana laws continue, but the public has not given this proposal broad-based support.

And there has been no broad support for tightening these laws further.

REVIEW QUESTIONS

1. What is the scientific name of the marijuana plant? In which country are the earliest records of its use found?

2. List and describe the past and current uses of *Cannabis sativa*. When did the psychoactive properties of marijuana first become of interest in this country? When did marijuana smoking become widespread in American life?

3. What is the primary psychoactive compound in marijuana? How is its concentration measured? What is the range of concentrations of THC in marijuana plants? How has the average concentration of THC in marijuana changed over the past 20 years? What is the sinsemilla form of marijuana?

4. List the various routes of administration of marijuana. Which is the most common route in America? How does THC's high lipid solubility influence its absorption, distribution, and storage? Where does the biotransformation of THC occur?

5. What are the acute physiological effects associated with marijuana use?

6. What are the chronic physiological effects of marijuana use? To what extent are tolerance and withdrawal associated with marijuana use?

7. What are the acute psychological effects associated with marijuana use? What are the chronic psychological effects of marijuana use? What is amotivational syndrome?

8. What are the recognized medical uses for (1) THC, and (2) marijuana?

9. Among high school and college students, how have marijuana use patterns changed over the past two decades? What roles have perceived risk and peer approval played in altering marijuana use patterns? How has the availability of marijuana affected use patterns? How does marijuana use vary between the sexes in college students; between college and non-college youth of the same age?

10. What are the primary health concerns associated with short-term marijuana use? With chronic use? In terms of health dangers, how does smoking marijuana compare with cigarette smoking? (You may wish to refer to chapter 12.)

11. What reasons are given in support of reforming marijuana laws? What arguments are given by those who oppose changing the laws?

REFERENCES

1. G. G. Nahas, *Marijuana in Science and Medicine* (New York: Raven Press, 1984); L. Grinspoon, and J. B. Bakalar, *Marijuana, the Forbidden Medicine* (New Haven, Conn.: Yale, University Press, 1993).

2. E. Small, and A. Cronquist, "A Practical and Natural Taxonomy for *Cannabis*," *Taxon* 25, no. 4 (1976):405.

3. Grinspoon and Bakalar, *Forbidden Medicine*; E. M. Breecher, "Licit and Illicit Drugs," in *The Consumer's Union Report* (Boston: Little, Brown, 1972).

4. Breecher, "Drugs."

5. Breecher, "Drugs"; O. Ray, and C. Ksir, *Drugs, Society, and Human Behavior*, 6th ed. (St Louis: Mosby, 1993); R. M. Julien, *A Primer of Drug Action*, 6th ed. (New York: W. H. Freeman, 1992).

6. Grinspoon and Bakalar, *Forbidden Medicine*; Ray and Ksir, *Human Behavior*.

7. Ray and Ksir, *Human Behavior*.

8. Ibid.

9. Ibid.

10. L. D. Johnston, P. M. O'Malley, and J. G. Bachman, *National Survey Results on Drug Use from Monitoring the Future Study, 1975–1995*, vol. 1, *Secondary School Students*. NIH Pub. No. (PHS), 99-4139 (Rockville, Md.: USDHHS, 1996).

11. G. Cowley, "Can Marijuana Be Medicine?" *Newsweek*, 3 February 1997.

12. B. McCaffrey, "We're on a Perilous Path," *Newsweek*, 3 February 1997.

13. Small and Cronquist, "Taxonomy for *Cannabis*"; R. E. Shultes, and A. Hofmann, *The Botany and Chemistry of the Hallucinogens* (Springfield, Ill.: Charles C. Thomas, 1973).

14. Drug Enforcement Administration, *Illegal Drug Price/Purity Report—United States: January 1990–September 1993*, Pub. No. (DEA) 93074 (Arlington, Va.: Department of Justice, 1993).

15. National Narcotics Intelligence Consumers Committee, *The NNICC Report 1992: The Supply of Illicit Drugs to the United States*, Pub. No. (DEA) 93051 (Arlington, Va.: Drug Enforcement Administration, 1993); National Narcotics Intelligence Consumers Committee, *The NNICC Report 1995: The Supply of Illicit Drugs to the United States*, Pub. No. (DEA) 96024 (Arlington, Va.: Drug Enforcement Administration, 1996); Community Epidemiology Work Group, *Epidemiologic Trends in Drug Abuse*, vol. 1, *Highlights and Executive Summary*, NIH Pub. No. 96-4128 (Rockville, Md.: NIDA, 1996).

16. Julien, *Drug Action*.

17. United States Department of Justice, Drug Enforcement Administration, *Source to the Street*, Pub. No.

(DEA) 93036 (Arlington, Va.: Department of Justice, 1993).

18. Drug Enforcement Administration, *Illegal Drug Price/Purity Report—United States: January 1992– March 1995*, Pub. No. (DEA) 95063 (Arlington, Va.: Department of Justice, 1995).

19. Julien, *Drug Action.*

20. Ray and Ksir, *Human Behavior.*

21. Julien, *Drug Action.*

22. Ibid.

23. M. Johnson, et al., *Structural Studies Leading to the Discovery of a Cannabinoid Binding Site*, Research Monograph 90 (Rockville, Md.: National Institute for Drug Abuse, 1988).

24. W. A. Devane, et al., "Isolation and Structure of a Brain Constituent That Binds to the Cannabinoid Receptor," *Science* 258 (1992):1946; K. A. Fackelmann, "Marijuana and the Brain," *Science News* 143 (1993):88.

25. Breecher, "Drugs."

26. Julien, *Drug Action.*

27. J. N. Endicott, P. Skipper, and L. Hernandez, "Marijuana and Head and Neck Cancer," in *Drugs of Abuse, Immunity, and AIDS. Advances in Experimental Medicine and Biology*, ed. T. W. Klein and S. Spector (New York: Plenum Press, 1993).

28. T. W. Klein, et al., "Marijuana and Bacterial Infections," in *Drugs of Abuse, Immunity, and AIDS. Advances in Experimental Medicine and Biology*, ed. T. W. Klein and S. Spector (New York: Plenum Press, 1993); L. J. Paradise, and H. Friedman, "Syphilis and Drugs of Abuse," in *Drugs of Abuse, Immunity, and AIDS. Advances in Experimental Medicine and Biology*, ed. T. W. Klein and S. Spector (New York: 1993).

29. D. W. Keer, et al., "Restricted Activity Days and Other Problems Associated with Use of Marijuana or Cocaine among Persons 18–44 Years of Age: United States, 1991," *Advance Data* 246 (April 1994):1.

30. Nahas, *Marijuana.*

31. Ray and Ksir, *Human Behavior.*

32. Julien, *Drug Action.*

33. Substance Abuse and Mental Health Services Administration, Office of Applied Studies, *Estimates from the Drug Abuse Warning Network—1992 Estimates of Drug-Related Emergency Room Episodes*, Advance Report Number 4 (Rockville, Md.: USDHHS, 1993).

34. Nahas, *Marijuana.*

35. S. Cohen, "Adverse Effects of Marijuana," in "Selected Issues in Research Development in Drug and Alcohol Use," *Ann N Y Acad Sci* 362 (1981):119.

36. Ray and Ksir, *Human Behavior.*

37. Nahas, *Marijuana.*

38. *Physicians' Desk Reference*, 51st ed. (Montvale, N.J.: Medical Economics Company, Inc, 1997).

39. Cowley, "Medicine."

40. Nahas, *Marijuana.*

41. Ibid.

42. T. Morganthau, "The War over Weed," *Newsweek*, 3 February 1997, pp 20–22.

43. J. P. Kassirer, "Federal Foolishness and Marijuana," *The New England Journal of Medicine* 336(5): 366–67, 30 January 1997.

44. NNICC, *Report 1995.*

45. *The Rise in Drug Use among American Teens Continues in 1996.* Press Release, 19 December 1996, University of Michigan, Ann Arbor.

46. Substance Abuse and Mental Health Services Administration, Office of Applied Studies, *Preliminary Estimates from the Drug Abuse Warning Network, 1995 Preliminary Estimates of Drug-Related Emergency Room Episodes.* Advance Report number 17, August 1996, Pub. No. (SMA) 96-3106 (Rockville, Md.: USDHHS, 1996).

47. Johnston, O'Malley, and Bachman, *Survey Results 1975–1995; Rise in Drug Use*, Press Release.

48. L. D. Johnston, P. M. O'Malley, and J. G. Bachman, *National Survey Results on Drug Use from Monitoring the Future Study, 1975–1992*, NIH Pub. No. (PHS), 93-3597, 93-3598 (Rockville, Md.: USDHHS, 1993).

49. Johnston, O'Malley, and Bachman, *Survey Results 1975–1995;* SAMHSA, *1995 Preliminary Estimates.*

50. *Marijuana and Tobacco Use Still Rising among 8th and 10th Graders.* HHS News Press Release, 19 December 1996, U.S. Department of Health and Human Services.

51. L. D. Johnston, P. M. O'Malley, and J. G. Bachman, *National Survey Results on Drug Use from Monitoring the Future Study, 1975–1994*, vol. 2 College Students and Young Adults, NIH Pub. No. (PHS), 96-4027 (Rockville, Md.: USDHHS, 1996).

52. Johnston, O'Malley, and Bachman, *Survey Results 1975–1995.*

53. Johnston, O'Malley, and Bachman, *Survey Results 1975–1995; Rise in Drug Use*, Press Release.

54. Ibid.

55. Nahas, *Marijuana;* Ray and Ksir, *Human Behavior.*

56. SAMHSA, *DAWN 1992 Estimates.*

57. S. Lucas, et al., *Ethanol Effects on Marijuana-Induced Intoxication and Electroencephalographic Activity*, Research Monograph Series, no. 90 (Rockville, Md.: National Institute on Drug Abuse, 1988).

58. Nahas, *Marijuana.*

59. P. A. Fried, "Postnatal Consequences of Maternal Marijuana Use in Homes," in "Prenatal Abuse of

Licit and Illicit Drugs," *Ann N Y Acad Sci* 562 (1989):123.

60. Nahas, *Marijuana*.
61. *Pot of Gold*, Peter Jennings Reports, ABC News, aired 13 March 1997.
62. Ibid.
63. NNIC, *Report 1995*.
64. McCaffery, "Perilous Path."

SOURCES FOR HELP

AAA Foundation for Traffic Safety
2990 Telestar Court
Falls Church, VA 22042
(703) 222–2060

NORML (National Organization for the Reform
    of Marijuana Laws)
2001 South St, N.W., Suite 640
Washington, D.C. 20009
(202) 483–5500
http://www.norml.org/

9 HALLUCINOGENS

1. Define the term *hallucinogen* and provide six examples.

2. Describe how hallucinogenic drugs can be classified based on their interaction with one or more neurotransmitters and give examples.

3. Give a brief history and explain the origin of each of the hallucinogens.

4. Describe the acute physiological and psychological effects of LSD.

5. Discuss the health and legal risks associated with using each hallucinogenic drug.

6. Explain the special risks associated with the use of phencyclidine.

7. Describe the recent and current trends in hallucinogenic drug use in the United States.

PROFILE

Rick looked out the window of the tractor-trailer as he and his trucking partner descended the mountain highway into the desert. "One hit? Why not—what else have I got to do?" he said to his partner, a middle-aged man with a receding hairline. "It's going to be another long night, huh?"

"This stuff's not too strong. It's laced with strychnine to keep the eyes open, know what I mean?"

Rick took the small piece of paper from him and put it under his tongue. The truck continued to roll into the night. Occasionally, the hair on the back of his neck stood up or pinwheels raced before his eyes. He didn't sleep that night. No matter how tired he got, his eyes just wouldn't close.

When Rick returned to college that fall after working with the trucking company all summer, he continued to experiment with a range of hallucinogens. He justified his increased drug use with his belief that he was on a noble quest to tap into the limitless potential of his unconscious mind.

Soon he was tripping two or three times a week. He lacked motivation in every aspect of his life and, instead, lived for the world he experienced within the chemical firing of his brain during his trips. Various notes and writings he completed while on his "journeys" made no sense to him until he tripped again—then his words seemed profoundly insightful.

Could Rick find a more positive way to explore the reaches of his mind? Is his drug use related to his lack of motivation in other areas of his life? Think about these questions as you learn about hallucinogens in this chapter. Then, read the solutions box on page 163.

[handwritten: taken orally] [handwritten: ↓ Physical dependence −(+)tolerance.] [handwritten: Schedule I – LSD]

In this chapter, we discuss substances that produce hallucinations. These drugs include LSD, psilocybin, mescaline, and several other hallucinogenic substances of natural and synthetic origin. **Hallucinogens,** also known as psychedelics, are substances that produce (1) distortions in perceptions of reality and (2) hallucinations characterized by **synesthesia,** the blending of perceptions and interpretations of visual and auditory images. Most hallucinogens are effective when taken orally and do not produce physical dependence, although tolerance and cross tolerance develop.

The use of hallucinogenic drugs peaked in American society in the 1960s, when these substances were touted as "mind expanding." Although they are somewhat less popular today, they continue to be used by many. Marijuana, sometimes considered hallucinogenic, was covered in the previous chapter (chapter 8) because of important differences in its physiological effects and its unique status as America's most popular illicit drug.

The history of each hallucinogen is unique, and although some of the hallucinogens were discovered only recently, others have been used for centuries. A brief outline of the history of each hallucinogenic drug precedes the discussion of its pharmacology and its physiological and psychological effects. This chapter concludes with a discussion of the health concerns associated with the use of hallucinogenic drugs.

Hallucinogenic drugs are either natural or synthetic in origin. The **natural hallucinogens** are those that are derived entirely from nature. They include psilocybin from mushrooms, peyote from cacti, dimethyltryptamine (DMT) from plants that occur in South and Central America, myristicin and mace from the nutmeg plant, and several others. The **synthetic hallucinogens** include lysergic acid diethylamide (LSD), phencyclidine (PCP), 3,4-methylenedioxymethamphetamine (MDMA), and several other manufactured drugs sometimes referred to as designer drugs.

[handwritten: LSD, PCP, MDMA]

CLASSIFICATION

Each of the hallucinogens interacts with one or more groups of neurotransmitters, which were discussed in chapter 3 (serotonin, norepinephrine, dopamine, and acetylcholine). In this chapter, we use these interactions as a basis for classification.

HALLUCINOGENS THAT AFFECT SEROTONIN ACTIVITY

The neurotransmitter serotonin alters pain perception, helps control mood, focuses attention, influences sleep, and does much more. LSD, psilocybin, and DMT are among the hallucinogens that affect serotonin.

Lysergic Acid Diethylamide (LSD)

There are many hallucinogenic substances, but the one against which all others are measured is **d-lysergic acid diethylamide** (LSD). This was the first produced, and perhaps the best known, synthetic hallucinogen. It is the most powerful of all known hallucinogenic substances.

[handwritten: LSD, Psilocybin, DMT – affect serotonin.]

LSD is the most powerful hallucinogen known. There is more than enough of it on one of these pieces of blotter paper for a 6- to 9-hour "trip."

History. When LSD was isolated in 1938, Albert Hofmann was studying a group of chemicals that were extracted from the ergot fungus *Claviceps purpurea*, which infects rye and other cereal grains. The fungus was of interest because it produces ergotism, an illness in people who eat bread made from the infected grain. Although the fungus does not contain LSD, it does contain related compounds that share the basic structure of LSD. One of the substances that Hofmann synthesized for Sandoz Laboratories in Basel, Switzerland, turned out to be LSD.[1] In 1943, five years later, he accidentally discovered its hallucinogenic effects. On April 16, 1993, the fiftieth anniversary of Hofmann's discovery was marked in San Francisco with a three-day "Psychedelic Summit" to celebrate the discovery. The summit was attended by Timothy Leary, who helped spread the use of LSD in the 1960s, and by Laura Huxley, wife of the late author and LSD experimenter Aldous Huxley.[2]

Between the mid-1950s and the mid-1970s, LSD was the subject of extensive biochemical and behavioral research.[3] Some thought LSD could be used to produce a model of psychosis that could be used for the study of psychiatric treatment methods. Others thought that LSD would allow researchers to view the "subconscious mind," that it could be used in the treatment of alcohol-

ism, or that it would prove useful in counseling terminal cancer patients. Because of concern about possible unpredictable side effects and growing abuse by American youth, LSD research came to a virtual standstill in the mid-1970s. It became socially unacceptable to do LSD research.

The popularity of individual experimental use of LSD can be traced to counterculture Harvard professor Timothy Leary and his colleagues during the early 1960s. LSD replaced the less powerful psilocybin among his group and became the sacrament in religious ceremonies of their "League of Spiritual Discovery."

In the mid-1990s, research on LSD and other hallucinogenic drugs, including federally funded research, has begun again. One reason for this is the increased interest in brain research. There is also some evidence from studies done in the 1960s that LSD treatment might have actually benefited alcoholics.[4]

Pharmacology. LSD, like most of the hallucinogens, is almost always administered orally, usually on a piece of blotter paper or in a sugar cube. However, it can be administered through the skin or through the conjunctiva of the eye. Because it is so powerful, only tiny amounts of LSD (several doses can be placed on the head of a pin) need to be ingested to produce **psychedelic effects.** LSD is absorbed rapidly from the gastrointestinal tract and then distributed throughout the body. Although a less effective route, LSD also can be absorbed through the skin. There does not appear to be any selective distribution or concentration in the brain. LSD is similar in structure to the neurotransmitter serotonin and produces psychedelic effects by interfering with the normal activity of this neurotransmitter.

LSD is metabolized in the liver and excreted. The half-life of LSD in the bloodstream is about 3 hours. Its effects last an average of 10 to 12 hours.[5]

hallucinogens drugs that produce distortions in perceptions of reality, hallucinations, and blending of perceptions of visual and auditory images

synesthesia blending of sensory inputs

natural hallucinogens hallucinogenic drugs derived from natural sources, such as plants

synthetic hallucinogens hallucinogenic drugs that are formulated in a laboratory

d-lysergic acid diethylamide the chemical name for the hallucinogen LSD, the most potent known hallucinogen

psychedelic effects variety of psychological changes produced by hallucinogenic drugs, including heightened perception of sensory input, vivid imagery, and an enhanced sense of awareness

ALTERNATIVE CHOICES

Digital Reality

The attractiveness of a hallucinogen rests in its ability to alter sensory perceptions, but we now have many nondrug-based alternatives. Among these is the rapidly developing world of "virtual reality." With this technology, computer programs present an array of "other worlds" with which the participant can interact. Through the use of sensors, the participant's movements in response to the sounds, colors, and movements of the virtual world (generated by a computer signal) produce responses that produce a constantly changing "virtual reality." So sophisticated is this interaction between the computer and the participants that the "real world" is left behind without the risks associated with LSD and other hallucinogenic drugs.

Physiological Effects. Although its psychological effects are the most dramatic, LSD does produce physiological changes that are detectable approximately 20 minutes after ingestion. These effects include dilated pupils, elevated temperature, an increase in heart rate and blood pressure, and an elevation in the level of glucose in the blood. Sometimes the user also experiences sweating and chills, dry mouth or excessive salivation, headache, nausea, and vomiting. These effects are usually mild and short term, and the user's attention is soon directed to the psychological effects.

Psychological Effects. Psychological events soon follow physiological changes, occurring approximately 40 minutes after ingestion of an effective dose. LSD produces mood changes, changes in bodily sensations, and abnormal perceptions of color, space, and time. Those taking the drug report that their bodies feel as though they had turned into lead or that they feel as though they were outside their bodies. Distortions of scenery and objects are reported. Spoken words may be visualized in colors that defy description. This blending of sensory response is called synesthesia.

LSD experiences may be deemed by users as positive or "mind expanding" or negative or "mind constricting," depending on one's mind-set and the social setting in which the drug is taken. Positive sensations include feelings of creativity, deep understanding of self and the universe, and feelings of grandeur.

Although LSD users report feelings of insight and creativity, a real increase in these skills has never been demonstrated. Negative feelings, collectively called a "bad trip," include fear, feelings of persecution, and paranoia. Although bad trips occasionally occur with LSD, some of those reported to be caused by LSD might have been caused by ingestion of other substances, such as PCP, that were sold to the user as LSD. Careful studies of those using LSD under experimental and therapeutic conditions have revealed that serious negative reactions (such as attempted suicide) are very infrequent. Furthermore, the margin for safety between effective and toxic doses is extremely high; apparently, there has never been a documented overdose death from LSD. Of course, deaths resulting from bizarre behavior after taking LSD have been reported. Perhaps the behavior reported to be "bizarre" by an outside observer is viewed as a "sensible" response to the hallucinations being experienced by the LSD user.

There is one frequently reported adverse reaction to LSD use—**flashbacks.** Flashbacks are the unanticipated return of visions or other symptoms of an LSD trip weeks or months after LSD use. These disturbing experiences occur in about 15% of LSD users.[6] While flashbacks may last from several minutes to several hours, they can be unnerving enough that a second drug, Valium, is sometimes prescribed to relieve the anxiety. There have been cases in which the LSD users experience periodic visual distortions more than 20 years after last use.[7]

Psilocybin and Psilocin

Psilocybin and **psilocin** are the primary psychoactive ingredients in a group of mushrooms that includes the species *Psilocybe mexicana* and its relatives. These substances also affect serotonin activity.

History. Archeological evidence suggests that primitive cultures in Central America used mushrooms ceremonially 3,500 years ago.[8] Spanish priests arriving in the New World several hundred years ago tried to eliminate the

---

flashbacks recurrences of visions or other symptoms associated with earlier use of a hallucinogen

psilocybin and psilocin primary psychoactive ingredients in the *Psilocybe mexicana* mushroom

ALTERNATIVE CHOICES

Timothy Leary's New Drug: Digital Technology

Dr. Timothy Leary directed the Harvard Psychedelic Research Project in the early 1960s. Throughout the 1960s, Leary served as a radical spokesperson for the counterculture movement. As such, he encouraged people to think for themselves and to question authority.

Leary challenged young people to be receptive to all avenues of personal discovery, even if this included experimentation with various drugs. At the top of Leary's list of enlightening drugs was LSD. As an advocate for this drug, Leary directly opposed established medical, legal, and social opinions.

During his 70s, Leary no longer advocated the use of illegal drugs. He had replaced psychedelic drugs with a new alternative mood modifier: digital technology. Leary contended that the new digital technology used in video and sound production permits a person to experience sensations similar to those produced by psychedelic drugs.

Timothy Leary, then (1960s) and shortly before his death in May, 1996. By then, Leary had shunned his old drug habits in favor of technotrips.

Today's evolving digital technology allows people to access enormous amounts of information, edit it, and send it to others instantly. Users of this technology can interact directly with various computer software programs (especially CD-ROM programs). This personal interaction allows a measure of control over the "medium" that is unavailable to users of illegal drugs.

Leary was such a believer in the value of this technology that he started his own computer programming company, called Futique. Do you think that Leary was correct in believing that interactive digital technology could be a viable alternative to drug use? Have you been exposed to this technology? In what forms have you experienced computer technology?

Modified from N. Szymanski, "The psychedelic guru," *Expo*, (Ball State student magazine)(Fall 1993)17.

use of "sacred mushrooms" called *teonanacatl*, or "God's flesh," but succeeded only in suppressing the practice. In 1955, investigators discovered that these mushrooms were still being used in religious ceremonies, and in 1958, the active ingredient was isolated for the first time by the Swiss chemist Albert Hofmann.

In 1960, Dr. Timothy Leary, of Harvard University, discovered for himself the use of psilocybin in Mexico. During the 1960–61 school year, he and several colleagues and students experimented with it at Harvard and in his home, before switching to LSD. The pronouncements of Leary, who was eventually dismissed from the university, and his associates resulted in the spread of psilocybin use on college campuses in the early 1960s. With the entry of LSD into the college drug scene in the mid-1960s, psilocybin use in America began to decline. Today, while cocaine, heroin, methamphetamine, and even LSD are still widespread, psilocybin use hardly receives a mention in drug surveys.

Pharmacology. After oral ingestion, psilocybin is converted to the more lipophilic psilocin, which is rapidly distributed throughout the body, including the central nervous system (CNS). Its duration of action is from two to four hours, much shorter than that for LSD.

Effects. Like LSD, psilocybin and psilocin affect the action of the neurotransmitter serotonin. Psilocin produces characteristic physiological effects that precede the psychological ones. These may include the dilation of pupils and an elevation of temperature and blood pressure. When taken in sufficient quantities, psilocybin and its more active metabolite, psilocin, produce changes in the perceptions of one's body (reportedly one's "spirit" seems to leave the body and take flight). There are also distortions in time and space perception and hallucinations similar to those experienced under LSD.[9] Psilocin is about 200 times weaker than LSD, however.

Dimethyltryptamine

Dimethyltryptamine (DMT) is derived from the bark, seeds, and leaves of plants in South America and islands in the Caribbean. The bark or seeds, which also contain quantities of another hallucinogen, bufotenin, are dried and ground into a powder known as *cohoba* or *yopo*.[10]

History. No one actually knows when the use of DMT began. It is not widely used in the United States but is an important part of the spiritual rituals of many of the South American tribes, such as the Yanomamo of northern Brazil. Among these peoples, DMT is used by the medicine man and other tribe elders to help them communicate with the spiritual world. While experiencing the drug's effects, users appeal to the spirits for deliverance from such miseries as an impacted tooth or malaria or for victory over rival tribes.

Recently, enterprising chemists have developed the capability to manufacture DMT (and DET [diethyltryptamine]) inexpensively in a laboratory. This has resulted in its appearance on the street. In this form, it is usually smoked, although it can be injected. Its duration of effect is only one to two hours, leading to its title, the "businessman's LSD."[11]

Pharmacology. In its powdered form, DMT is ineffective when taken orally. Members of the Indian tribes either snort it or blow it into each others' nostrils, where it is absorbed through the mucous linings of the nose and throat.

Effects. DMT affects the action of serotonin, producing both physiological and psychological effects. These include stimulatory effects characterized by behavioral excitability accompanied by visual distortions, hallucinations, and euphoria.

HALLUCINOGENS THAT AFFECT NOREPINEPHRINE AND DOPAMINE

The neurotransmitter norepinephrine helps control the overall activity and mood of the mind, working to regulate emotion and arousal responses of the body. Dopamine is also involved in emotional behavior, physiology of the brain's reward center, and motor control. Mescaline and the hallucinogenic amphetamines DOM, MDA, and MDMA imitate or otherwise affect the action of these two neurotransmitters.

Mescaline

Mescaline is derived from the peyote cactus, *Lophophora williamsii* Lemaire, which can be found in Mexico and in parts of the United States along its border with Mexico.[12]

History. The use of the peyote cactus by Native Americans dates to the pre-Columbian period of American history. Its effects, which include kaleidoscopic displays of vivid colors, auditory and tactile hallucinations, and synesthetic experiences, were seen as "communion with the gods"; thus, peyote was regarded as a sacred substance.[13] As with mushrooms, the use of peyote by some tribes survived attempts to stamp it out, and in the latter part of the nineteenth century, peyote use spread from northern Mexico to many of the remaining Indian tribes in the

WHAT DO YOU THINK?

Should the Use of Certain Drugs Be Legal for Religious Ceremonies?

Peyote is sacred to many Native Americans. It has been used for centuries as an integral part of many of their religious ceremonies. Until a 1990 U.S. Supreme Court ruling, Native American Church members believed that their right to use peyote in religious ceremonies was protected under the U.S. Constitution.[a] The Supreme Court, however, upheld an Oregon state law that declared the use of the hallucinogen for any purpose illegal in that state. (The federal government and 23 states make exceptions for the use of peyote by the Native American Church). The Court, by a six-to-three majority, ruled in favor of Oregon and against Indian traditions, stating that an individual's religious beliefs do not excuse him or her from compliance with an otherwise valid law prohibiting conduct that the state is

[a]"High Court to Rule on Religious Use of Peyote," *USA Today,* 6 November, 1989, p.3A.

free to regulate. The Native Americans have pointed out that their practice predates the U.S. Constitution.[b] In 1994, Senator Daniel Inouye introduced legislation in the U.S. Senate to protect the sovereignty of the Indian nations. On October 6, 1994, President Clinton signed legislation that prevents the federal and state governments from prohibiting the use, possession, or transportation of peyote by Native Americans for traditional religious purposes.[c] What do you think? Should Native Americans who wish to practice ceremonial peyote use be allowed to do so even in states with laws that explicitly forbid its use? Could a religion hold the use of marijuana sacred?

[b]"Religious Liberties," *Time,* 30 April, 1990, p. 85.

[c]R. M. Peregoy, W. R. Echo-Hawk, and J. Botsford, "Congress Overturns Supreme Court's Peyote Ruling," *NARF Legal Review* 20, no. 10 (1997):1–31. The Native American Rights Fund, 1506 Broadway St., Boulder, CO 80302, http://www.narf.org/archives/nlr/nlr20aen.htm

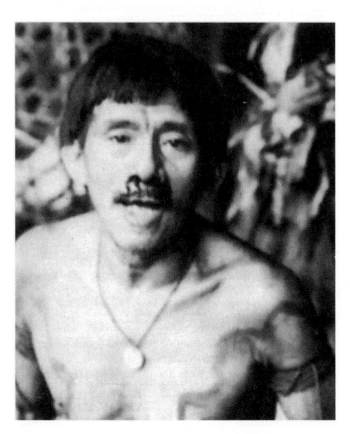

This Yanomamo Indian from Brazil is intoxicated with cohoba. Notice excess of the drug dripping from his nostrils.

United States. Peyote use is now an important part of religious ceremonies of the Native American Church of North America.

Pharmacology. The crown of the peyote cactus is harvested and sliced into circular "mescal buttons" that are eaten.[14] The mescaline is readily absorbed into the bloodstream from the gastrointestinal tract but crosses the blood-brain barrier much more slowly. Therefore, relatively high doses of mescaline are necessary to produce hallucinogenic effects. The need for high doses and the relative impermeability of the blood-brain barrier to mescaline account for the drug's long duration of activity (as long as 12 hours). Mescaline does not appear to be metabolized before it is excreted.[15]

Effects. Mescaline produces physiological and psychological responses similar to LSD. Unlike LSD, however, its action seems to be on the norepinephrine neurotransmitter system. Physiological responses include the

dimethyltryptamine (DMT) hallucinogen derived from the powdered bark, seeds, and leaves of several South and Central American plants

cohoba (yopo) native terms for dimethyltryptamine

mescaline hallucinogen derived from the peyote cactus

WHAT DO YOU THINK?

Designer Drugs: The Role of Bulk Suppliers

Designer drugs, the legal and sometimes illegal versions of known, regulated psychotropic drugs, are the handiwork of amateur chemists working out of laboratories set up in homes, apartments, warehouses, and even motel rooms. Because the "street life" for designer drugs is short (before they are identified and added to the controlled substance list), it is necessary for these chemists to make their drugs quickly and distribute them as widely as possible in a short time. In fact, when designer drug laboratories are discovered by police, the production has usually ceased, the chemist has gone, and the only materials remaining are pieces of discarded laboratory equipment and empty containers for the raw chemical ingredients used to synthesize the designer drug. From the size of these containers, it is obvious that ingredients were purchased in bulk from legitimate chemical suppliers.

The fact that large quantities of specific chemicals known to be precursors of illicit drugs are sold to people not associated with reputable manufacturers and delivered to job sites in homes, warehouses, and other unsafe places raises questions about the role of legitimate chemical suppliers in the development of the designer drugs.

Is it conceivable that some suppliers know (or are highly suspicious of) the people buying these materials? Recently, certain chemicals used in the manufacture of mind-altering drugs have come under scrutiny. Should suppliers of such materials be under any legal obligation to report all purchases of certain chemicals? When designer drug chemists are apprehended, should the bulk suppliers be arrested too?

dilation of pupils, the elevation of temperature, and an increase in heart rate and blood pressure. The slightly greater behavioral arousal, reflecting CNS stimulation, is not surprising given the structural similarities between mescaline and the amphetamines. Psychological effects include hallucinations in vivid colors of designs, flowers, and animals. There are also distortions in the perception of colors, time, and space.[16] Some individuals experience serious nausea and vomiting with mescaline. In spite of these common side effects, a large dose is needed to produce a severely toxic response or cause death.

Hallucinogenic Amphetamines (Designer Drugs)

Still other synthetic hallucinogens share the same basic chemical structure with norepinephrine, dopamine, and the amphetamines. These drugs, the **hallucinogenic amphetamines,** are manufactured in illegal laboratories and belong to a group of substances called **designer drugs.** Designer drugs are either newly synthesized products that are similar to already outlawed drugs, but which have not been outlawed, or reconstituted or renamed illicit substances marketed for certain income groups. To combat the designer-drug chemists and their products, the federal government passed the Anti-Drug Abuse Act of 1986, sometimes called the analog drug act. This act permitted drugs that are structurally or pharmacologically similar to schedule I or schedule II controlled substances and that have no approved medical use to be treated by the Drug Enforcement Administration as if they were controlled substances in schedule I.[17]

The force driving the development and production of these new drugs is money, of course, and the belief that initially these drugs are neither illegal nor detectable by methods currently available to those in drug enforcement. Therefore, there is an unavoidable "grace period" as legislation and enforcement catch up to production. As the nature of these new synthetic drugs becomes known, they are usually added to the controlled sub-

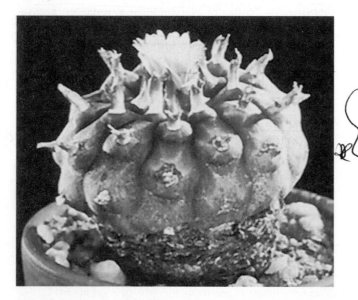

Mescaline is derived from the peyote cactus, found in Mexico and parts of southern Texas.

ALTERNATIVE CHOICES

A New Rave

Today in the United States a "rave" refers to an all night dance party. Drug-free raves began in the early 1990s in San Francisco and New York as an alternative to parties characterized by heavy drug use. Potential participants sometimes follow clues or call a special phone number that leads them to the secret location of the party.

When the participants arrive, they often find bowlfuls of sugar candy and blended fruit drinks known as "smart drinks." Fortified with high protein drinks and lots of sugar (but no drugs) participants dance all night into a wild frenzy. This gives young people, especially those under 21, a safer outlet for their extra energy.

stance schedules. By the time this occurs, the chemist who designed the drug may be concocting an entirely different substance for the market. Some of these synthetic drugs have been shown to be dangerous. Not all designer drugs are hallucinogens. For example, China white, a designer heroin, is a derivative of the narcotic fentanyl.

DOM, MDA, and **MDMA** are examples of hallucinogenic amphetamines once considered to be designer drugs. They are capable of producing euphoria at low doses and hallucinations at high doses, and being more potent than mescaline, each produces more unpleasant side effects than mescaline.

DOM first appeared in the late 1960s under its nickname "STP," so named perhaps because it was supposed to "make your engine run smoother." Others said it stood for "serenity, tranquility, and peace." It is perhaps 100 times more powerful than mescaline and at high doses produces effects not unlike those a user would feel after taking LSD and an amphetamine at the same time. Unfortunately, acute and chronic toxic reactions are not uncommon among DOM users.

MDA and MDMA are slightly more potent than mescaline and produce similar effects. MDA, sometimes called "speed for lovers" or the "hug drug," occurs naturally in sassafras and other plant oils. For the most part, though, it is synthesized as a white powder, which is sniffed, injected, or taken orally. MDA induces a response similar to that of mescaline, but one that purportedly is characterized by empathy and sensitivity to others. Unfortunately, the continued abuse of MDA carries a high cost. Studies with rats have determined that MDA selectively destroys nerve terminals associated with serotonin activity.[18] Similar research has confirmed that this also occurs in primates.[19] It seems logical that a substance that is this toxic could also damage human brain cells.

MDMA, known on the street as "ecstasy," "The Big E," "Adam," "the love drug," or "XTC," induces a five to six hour euphoric effect characterized by increased activity, mood alteration, and alterations in perception.[20] It has been a schedule I controlled substance since July 1, 1985.[21] Before it was scheduled, some psychiatric patients used MDMA as an adjunct to therapy.

Analysis showed MDMA to be very similar to MDA, which is known to be toxic. Furthermore, a recent study has shown that a volunteer who received only MDMA excreted both MDMA and MDA, indicating that the toxic MDA is one of the products of biotransformation of MDMA.[22]

In spite of the potential dangers associated with MDMA use, the drug became the controlled substance of choice among those attending "raves" (all-night techno-music dance parties) in the early 1990s.[23] Today MDMA is sold at raves, night clubs, and bars, where a single tablet costs $6 to $30. MDMA is produced in clandestine laboratories in the United States, Mexico, Belgium, and the Netherlands. The number of doses seized increased from 196 in 1993 to 27,760 in 1995.[24]

Unfortunately, ecstasy use resulted in at least 15 deaths in England, where raves were popular in the late 1980s. Deaths were caused by hyperthermia (overheating of the body), which sometimes resulted in coagulation of the blood and kidney failure. How the drug elevates the body's temperature is not known, but it may have to do with the drug's effect on the serotonin system.[25]

hallucinogenic amphetamines synthetic hallucinogens that share the same chemical structure with norepinephrine, dopamine, and the amphetamines

designer drugs psychoactive drugs whose chemical formulations are very similar to controlled substances

DOM hallucinogenic amphetamine with a potency approximately 100 times that of mescaline; also known as STP

MDA and MDMA hallucinogenic amphetamines similar in formulation to mescaline but much more powerful; MDMA is also known as "ecstasy"

The list of synthetic amphetamine hallucinogens includes other substances of dubious value, such as DOB, MMDA, PMA, and DET. Experimentation with these substances is dangerous because the origin, strength, and purity are usually unknown.

Phencyclidine *PCP* *Ketamine Special K*

Phencyclidine (PCP) is one of two substances that were originally produced and marketed as anesthetics but were later found to produce hallucinations. The other, **ketamine hydrochloride** (Ketalar, Ketaset), sometimes known as "special K" on the street, is less frequently abused than PCP.[26] These anesthetic substances make the user feel removed from his or her body and from the nearby environment, resulting in the label of *dissociative anesthetics* for these drugs.[27] As a hallucinogen, PCP is unique in its effects and is, therefore, classified as a **hallucinogenic anesthetic.**

History. PCP first appeared in the late 1950s as a new type of anesthetic. Animal trials demonstrated remarkable results. While anesthetized with phencyclidine (the generic name for PCP), the animals' eyes remained open and their heart and lung functions were slightly elevated. Human trials, which began in 1957, yielded disappointing results. Patients suffered psychological disturbances that did not occur with other established anesthetics. These disturbances included agitation, excitement, disorientation, delirium, and hallucinations.

Further studies demonstrated that PCP produced schizophrenic behavior in normal patients and intensified schizophrenia in disturbed patients.[28] In 1965, Parke, Davis and Company withdrew Sernyl (phencyclidine) as an investigational drug. It is currently marketed only for veterinary purposes under the trade name Sernylan.

In the mid-1960s, clinical workers in San Francisco obtained samples of the "PeaCe Pill" (hence the nickname PCP) that was being widely distributed among the "hippies." They determined that these pills contained phencyclidine. The drug surfaced again in New York in 1968, where it was called "hog" or "trank," for tranquilizer. Altogether, more than 130 street names for PCP have been recorded.[29]

Despite bad publicity, abuse of the drug continued. In the 1970s, PCP crystals, "angel dust," were sprinkled on herbs, such as parsley and oregano, or on marijuana, which was then smoked. Because PCP is very inexpensive to produce, limiting its supply has been difficult. It appears in many colors and forms, including powder, tablet, capsule, leaf mixture, liquid, crystal, and granule.[30] It has often been sold to unsuspecting buyers as LSD, THC, mescaline, amphetamine, or cocaine. The purity and strength of any street drug are questionable, and this is especially true for PCP.

Smoking most common

Pharmacology. PCP can be smoked, snorted, ingested in food or drink, or injected. Smoking is the most common method of PCP use, with approximately 73% of users preferring this method. According to some reports, PCP powder is mixed with herbal leaves for smoking or dissolved into a liquid, which is then rubbed on thick brown-papered cigarettes.[31] A small percentage of users (13%) report sniffing or snorting PCP powder, and even fewer (12%) consume it by first dissolving it in lemonade or another drink. PCP may also be found in the form of 1-gram "rocks" or pills. Injection of PCP is a method of administration employed by less than 2% of users. Accidental intoxication sometimes occurs in home PCP laboratories when volatile solvents, such as PCP-containing ether, are inhaled.[32]

The precise mode of action of PCP remains unclear. At least three types of receptor binding sites in the brain have been identified, including an acetylcholine-type binding site, an opium-type binding site, and a potassium-ion-channel binding site.[33] (Refer to chapter 3 for a review of neurophysiology). Interestingly, these sites have different distributions in the brain, perhaps explaining different behaviors resulting from PCP intoxication.

Effects. *Unpredictable effect* PCP is unique not only because it produces hallucinogenic effects, but also because it acts as an analgesic, a depressant, a stimulant, and an anesthetic. This makes the typical PCP experience impossible to describe. The effects of PCP begin within a few minutes after consumption and last for four to six hours. Physical effects include a slight increase in body temperature, respiration, heart rate, and blood pressure. Also reported are muscle rigidity, rapid and uncontrolled eye movements, decreased sensitivity to pain, and changes in intake and output of fluids. The user may have increased

Quick action - lasts 4-6 hr.

PCP, a hallucinogenic anesthetic, has a reputation as a particularly unpredictable and dangerous drug.

sensitivity to outside stimuli but also may experience relaxation or sedation. The psychological effects of low doses may include mild to intense feelings of euphoria, unreality, separation from one's environment, distortions of seeing and hearing, and decreased ability to concentrate. At high doses, these feelings may progress to restlessness, disorientation, confusion, anxiety, paranoia, panic, and fear of dying. Reports abound of bizarre, even homicidal, behavior by those intoxicated with PCP.[34]

Users who experience favorable reactions on first use may continue to abuse the drug. Because of tolerance, abusers eventually increase their dosage even though the favorable effects become less frequent and negative experiences occur more often. Unfortunately, the search for the occasional good experience, coupled with the low cost and high availability of PCP, perpetuates its abuse to the point where severe reactions become commonplace.[35] In some medical centers, PCP intoxication is the number-one cause of drug abuse emergencies.[36]

Experts estimate that there may be as many as 125 analogues to PCP (drugs that have the same basic structure as PCP but differ slightly). Some of these have found their way to the street. Those that have been placed on schedule I as controlled substances are TCP, PCE, PCC, and PHP.[37]

HALLUCINOGENS THAT PRIMARILY AFFECT THE ACETYLCHOLINE SYSTEM

The neurotransmitter acetylcholine has both excitatory and inhibitory effects in the brain. It works reciprocally with norepinephrine. Destruction of acetylcholine-producing cells in the brain has been linked to Alzheimer's disease. In the peripheral nervous system, acetylcholine is the neurotransmitter that functions between motor neurons and skeletal muscle. Three hallucinogenic drugs that influence acetylcholine pathways are atropine, scopolamine, and muscarine.[38]

Atropine and Scopolamine

Atropine and **scopolamine,** which block acetylcholine receptor sites, can be found in four genera of the plant family Solanaceae. They occur in high concentrations in the *Atropa belladonna* (deadly nightshade). They also occur in *Datura stramonium* (jimsonweed) and in *Mandragora officinarum* (mandrake). Atropine sulfate is used medically as an aid in the treatment of disturbances of the gastrointestinal tract. Scopolamine is used medically to prevent nausea and vomiting associated with motion sickness.[39]

These natural hallucinogens depress salivation, causing a dry mouth and difficulty in swallowing; reduce sweating; dilate the pupils; and increase heart rate. In general, these substances depress and sedate, although sometimes they produce euphoria. Although they do not increase or alter sensory perceptions, they do result in a loss of attention, a clouded consciousness, and amnesia for the period of intoxication. In these respects, they are different from the hallucinogens that were discussed earlier. Each of these natural plant products has a long and interesting history of use as poison, in rituals, or both.

Muscarine

The third hallucinogen that affects the acetylcholine system is **muscarine,** which occurs in the mushrooms *Amanita muscaria* (Agaricaceae).[40] Muscarine acts to increase the effects of acetylcholine rather than depressing them as the preceding drugs do. Ingestion results in profuse sweating and salivation, constriction of the pupils, decreased heart rate, and increased blood pressure. Muscarine may produce depression and stupor, followed by excitement, hallucinations, delirium, and muscle spasms. Because of its profound side effects, muscarine is rarely used as a social drug. Likewise, atropine and scopolamine are seldom chosen for individual experimentation.

MISCELLANEOUS NATURAL HALLUCINOGENS

Three other natural hallucinogens are less common and, therefore, are mentioned only briefly here. These are **bufotenin** (from *Amanita muscaria* and *A. peregrina*), **ololiuqui** (from morning glory, *Rivea corymbosa*), and **harmine** (from *Peganum harmala* and other plants). All

---

phencyclidine (PCP) hallucinogenic drug initially developed as a veterinary anesthetic

ketamine hydrochloride dissociative anesthetic or hallucinogenic anesthetic chemically related to PCP

hallucinogenic anesthetic anesthetic that produces hallucinations as a part of its pharmacological effect

atropine and scopolamine hallucinogens derived from *Atropa belladonna* (deadly nightshade), *Datura stramonium* (jimsonweed), and *Mandragora officinarum* (mandrake)

muscarine hallucinogen derived from *Amanita muscaria*

bufotenin hallucinogen derived from *Amanita muscaria* and other plants

ololiuqui hallucinogen derived from *Rivea corymbosa* (morning glory)

harmine hallucinogen derived from *Peganum harmala* and other plants

of these cause physiological changes that include initial excitement, dilation of the pupils, increased blood pressure, headache, and perhaps nausea and vomiting. These are followed by psychological effects that include distortions in perceptions of space and time, change in body perception, and hallucinations.[41] These three natural hallucinogens produce their effects by interfering with the neurotransmitter serotonin.

PATTERNS OF USE

Currently, the hallucinogenic drugs discussed in this chapter have no approved medical uses. The nonmedical use of these drugs increases and decreases over the years. For example, LSD use increased in the 1970s, declined in the 1980s, and increased again in the 1990s.[42] While 9.9% of 18-to-25-year-olds reported using a hallucinogen within the previous year in 1979, only 3.9% reported doing so in 1990. By 1995, however, this figure had increased to 5.3%, more than 1 in 20.[43] Observers estimate that, in 1995, approximately 20 million Americans had used a hallucinogen (including LSD and PCP) at least once in their lives and nearly 1.5 million had used a hallucinogen at least once during the previous month.[44]

Among college students one to four years beyond high school, use of a hallucinogen within the past year increased to 6.2% in 1994 from 5.1% in 1989.[45] Much of this increase can be attributed to an increase in the annual use of LSD, which rose to 5.2% in 1994 from 2.2% in 1985.

The outlook for a decline in use anytime soon is not particularly bright. Among twelfth graders, the percentage who perceived that trying LSD once or twice was harmful declined from 46.6% in 1991 to only 36.2% in 1996. The percentage who disapproved of others using LSD likewise declined. Furthermore, between 1991 and 1996, the percentage of twelfth graders who said that it would be fairly easy or very easy to get LSD increased significantly, from 39.5% to 51.3%.[46] The percentage of high school seniors who reported using LSD at least once in the past year in 1996 reached an all-time high, 8.8%, and the percentages of eighth and tenth graders who reported having used LSD in the past 30 days, past year, or ever were also at all-time highs.[47]

PCP use has also increased in recent years; in 1996, 2.6% of high school seniors reported using PCP at least once in the past year.[48] Unlike LSD, PCP is often used in combination with other drugs. PCP and marijuana, perhaps in a hollowed-out "blunt" cigar, are often mixed in a combination called "love boat," "wet," or "illies." There are also reports of PCP-crack mixtures; this combination is called a "spaceball."[49]

HALLUCINOGENS AND HEALTH

With the possible exception of PCP, there is no evidence that any of the hallucinogens produce physical dependence. Tolerance, however, does occur. Tolerance to LSD develops rapidly, requiring abusers to increase the dosage to achieve the same psychological effects achieved with previous doses. The tolerance lasts only a few days. Cross tolerance between hallucinogens has also been noted; for example, mescaline and psilocybin produce cross tolerance. There is no evidence for cross tolerance between the hallucinogens discussed in this chapter and marijuana.[50]

PCP appears to be unique among the hallucinogens in that its use is reinforcing, because it has been shown to produce self-administration in monkeys. In other words, when given the opportunity, monkeys continue to self-administer PCP, whereas they do not with any of the other hallucinogens. This finding indicates the likelihood that PCP produces some form of chemical dependence. No crossover recognition between PCP and reinforcing drugs, such as stimulants or depressants, has been detected, further confirming the uniqueness of PCP.

Compared with other drugs, mortality reports and emergency department mentions of hallucinogens are infrequent. In 1995, most of the reported hallucinogen-related deaths involved PCP. These deaths were either violent (homicides) or they involved the use of PCP and heroin. The cities reporting the highest rates per 100,000 population of PCP emergency-department mentions were Washington, D.C. (14.2), Chicago (8.9), Los Angeles (7.1), Philadelphia (6.0), New York City (5.3), and San Francisco (4.7). The cities with the highest rates per 100,000 population of LSD emergency-department mentions were Seattle (8.4), San Francisco (5.5), and Denver (4.5). LSD reports appear to be rising.[51]

User descriptions of PCP intoxication vary greatly, even though they may share some of the same features of several other groups of abused drugs. The uniqueness of PCP suggests that treatment programs designed for abusers of other substances may not be effective for the treatment of PCP abusers.

In some areas of the country where PCP use has become epidemic, up to one-third of the abusers are women of childbearing age.[52] The effects of PCP on fetal development have been documented. Newborns of PCP-using mothers develop deviant neurobehavioral symptoms within the first 24 hours after birth. They exhibit "rapid changes in their levels of consciousness, with lethargy alternating with irritability."[53] They are highly sensitive to auditory stimuli and exhibit tremors and facial grimacing. Follow-up studies show that these PCP infants have more medical problems and slower growth and de-

SOLUTIONS

Rick grew detached from his life on campus. He was frustrated in his attempts to communicate with his friends and professors. He quit school and moved home for a short time until his parents hassled him about his apathetic attitude and continual drug use. He bought a bus ticket and returned to the West to stay with a friend. They talked about going to Alaska for the summer to live in a tent and work on a fishing boat but never followed through on the idea.

Rich continued to trip whenever he could. He lived on the road, staying with one friend or acquaintance after an-

other. Sometimes he took a job laying sod, pouring concrete, or doing other manual labor, but he always quit when it became too much trouble. After drifting around, he settled in a small college town. In a coffee house, he was befriended by an eccentric group of intellectuals. These were people with whom he could communicate and share ideas without needing to tap into the chemical world of an altered reality. He slowly began to accept responsibility for himself and to realize that the future was up to him to create with all he had before him.

velopment than average,[54] but research so far has failed to demonstrate long-term effects comparable with those of fetal alcohol syndrome.[55]

The health risks of designer drug abuse were mentioned previously. They include not knowing what you have been given or sold, occasional bad trips, and with MDA and MDMA, the possible destruction of certain neurotransmitter receptor sites on nerve cell membranes. To this should be added the potential of serious infection if these drugs are injected and possible arrest and prosecution if caught with these illegal substances.

SUMMARY

The hallucinogens comprise a broad group of natural and synthetic psychoactive substances that produce hallucinations and changes in perception of color, place, and time. Hallucinations and changes in perception are the result of interference by these drugs with neurotransmitters, principally serotonin, norepinephrine, dopamine, and acetylcholine. Although the members of this group of drugs all produce hallucinations and none have approved medical uses, they vary in their physiological action.

Psilocybin, mescaline, DMT, and several other natural hallucinogens have long histories of use, but LSD, PCP, and other synthetic hallucinogens are relatively recent phenomena. The hallucinogens reached the height of their popularity in the 1960s. LSD use declined throughout the 1980s but has increased again in the 1990s.

PCP, a dissociative anesthetic, is the most dangerous and unpredictable of the hallucinogens. The hallucinogenic amphetamines, such as DOM, MDA, and MDMA,

share properties of both the amphetamines and the hallucinogens. These dangerous drugs belong to a larger group of illegally manufactured "designer drugs." The hallucinogens, with the exception of PCP, do not produce physical dependence but do produce tolerance and cross tolerance.

REVIEW QUESTIONS

1. Write a definition for the term *hallucinogen*.
2. How are hallucinogenic drugs classified? What effects caused by the hallucinogens led to their use in primitive religions?
3. Who first synthesized LSD?
4. What are the plant sources of psilocybin and mescaline? How do their effects on the user differ, and in what respects are they similar?
5. What natural hallucinogen is referred to as the "businessman's LSD"? Why?
6. Who was the counterculture Harvard professor who advocated the use of first psilocybin and then LSD in the 1960s? For what purpose did he advocate their use?
7. What is the term for the blending of sensory inputs, such as occurs during LSD use? What is a relatively common adverse side effect associated with LSD use?
8. As opposed to other hallucinogens, MDA is known to produce permanent tissue change among some users. What is the nature of this change? What synthetic hallucinogen is known by the street name "ecstasy," or "XTC"? How is it related to MDA?
9. What is meant by the term *designer drug*? How did designer drugs complicate the enforcement of

existing drug laws? How did the analog drug act counteract this problem? What are the health risks associated with the abuse of designer drugs?

10. PCP was once thought to have potential use as an anesthetic for humans. What was its unique property? Why was it withdrawn from human trials? As an illicit drug, how is PCP most often used? What effects are to be expected with PCP abuse? What is "special K?"

11. To what extent is physical dependence a component of hallucinogen use? What effect does PCP abuse by a pregnant woman have on the development of the fetus?

12. What is the recent trend in LSD use among high school and college students? Why is the outlook bleak for a decline in use over the next few years?

REFERENCES

1. E. M. Breecher, "Licit and illicit drugs," In *The Consumer's Union Report* (Boston: Little Brown, 1972.

2. Anonymous: "Wow, Man," *USA Today*, 16 April, 1993, p. D1.

3. Breecher, "Drugs."

4. P. Kurtzweil, "Medical Possibilities for Psychedelic Drugs, *FDA Consumer*, (September 1995): 25–28.

5. Ibid.

6. R. M. Julien, *A Primer of Drug Action*, 6th ed. (New York: Freeman & Co., 1992.

7. S. Nadis, "After Lights," *Omni*, (February 1990): 24.

8. Breecher, "Drugs."

9. Julien, *Drug Action.*

10. R. E. Schultes, and A. Hofmann, *The Botany and Chemistry of the Hallucinogens*, (Springfield, Ill.: Charles C Thomas, 1973).

11. Breecher, "Drugs."

12. Schultes and Hofmann, *Hallucinogens.*

13. Ibid.

14. Breecher, "Drugs."

15. Julien, *Drug Action.*

16. Ibid.; Schultes and Hofmann, *Hallucinogens.*

17. Drug Enforcement Administration, *Drugs of Abuse: 1996 Edition* (Arlington, VA: Department of Justice, 1996).

18. J. Alrazi, and K. Verebey, *MDMA Biological Disposition in Man: MDA Is a Biotransformation Product*, Research Monograph no. 90 (Rockville, Md.: National Institute on Drug Abuse, 1988).

19. Drug Enforcement Administration, *3,4-methylenedioxymethamphetamine (MDMA): October, 1996*, Pub. No. (DEA 96054) (Arlington, Va.: Department of Justice, 1996).

20. DEA, *MDMA.*

21. Alrazi and Verebey, *MDMA Biological Disposition.*

22. Ibid.

23. G. Garcia, "Ripping the Night Fantastic, *Time*, 17 August, 1992, p. 60; T. Randall, "Ecstasy-Fueled 'Rave' Parties Become Dances of Death for English Youths, *JAMA* 268, no. 12 (1992):1505.

24. DEA, *MDMA.*

25. Randall, "Dances of Death."

26. Julien, *Drug Action.*

27. M. Carroll, "PCP: The Dangerous Angel, in *The Encyclopedia of Psychoactive Drugs* (New York: Chelsea House, 1985).

28. Julien, *Drug Action*; Schultes and Hofmann, *Hallucinogens.*

29. R. L. Linder, S. E. Lerner, and R. S. Burns, *PCP: The Devil's Dust; Recognition, Management and Prevention of Phencyclidine Abuse* (Belmont, Calif.: Wadsworth, 1981).

30. Ibid.

31. M. M. McLarron, "Phencyclidine Intoxication," in *Phencyclidine: An Update*, Research Monograph no. 64 (Rockville, Md.: National Institute on Drug Abuse, 1986).

32. Linder, Lerner, and Burns, *PCP.*

33. L. Abood, "Receptor-Transductive Mechanisms for Drugs of Abuse," in *Problems of Drug Dependence*, Research Monograph no. 90 (Rockville, Md.: National Institute on Drug Abuse, 1988).

34. R. Seymour, et al., *The New Drugs: Look Alikes, Drugs of Deception, and Designer Drugs* (Center City, Minn.: Hazeldon Foundation, 1989).

35. Carroll, *PCP.*

36. McLarron, "Intoxication."

37. Seymour, *New Drugs.*

38. Julien, *Drug Action*; Schultes and Hofmann, *Hallucinogens.*

39. *Physicians' Desk Reference*, 51st ed. (Montvale, N.J.: Medical Economics Company, 1997).

40. Schultes and Hofmann, *Hallucinogens.*

41. Julien, *Drug Action.*

42. Substance Abuse and Mental Health Services Administration, Office of Applied Studies, *National Household Survey on Drug Abuse: Main Findings 1994*, Pub. No. (PHS) (Rockville, Md.: USDHHS, 1996).

43. Substance Abuse and Mental Health Services Administration, Office of Applied Studies, *National Household Survey on Drug Abuse: Population Estimates 1995*, Pub. No. (OHS) (Rockville, Md.: USDHHS, 1996).

44. Ibid.

45. *National Survey Results on Drug Use from the Monitoring the Future Study, 1975–1994*, vol. 2, *College Students and Young Adults* (Rockville, Md.: USDHHS, 1996).

46. *The Rise in Drug Use among American Teens Continues in 1996*, Press Release 19 December, 1996, University of Michigan, Ann Arbor.

47. Ibid.

48. Ibid.

49. *Epidemiologic Trends in Drug Abuse*, vol. 1, *Highlights and Executive Summary*, NIH Pub. No. 96-4128 (Rockville, Md.: NIDA, 1996).

50. Julien, *Drug Action*.

51. *Epidemiological Trends*.

52. SAMHSA, *Survey on Drug Abuse 1995*.

53. J. Howard, V. Kropenske, and R. Tyler, *The Long-Term Effects on Neurodevelopment in Infants Exposed Prenatally to PCP*, in *Phencyclidine: An Update*, Research Monograph, no. 64 (Rockville, Md.: National Institute on Drug Abuse, 1986).

54. Ibid.

55. T. A. Fico, and C. Venderwende, "Phencyclidine During Pregnancy: Behavioral and Neurochemical Effects in the Offspring," in *Prenatal Abuse of Licit and Illicit Drugs, Ann Acad Sci* 562 (1989):319.

SOURCES FOR HELP

Do It Now Foundation
P.O. Box 5115
Phoenix, AZ 85010
(602) 257–0797

The Native American Rights Fund
1506 Broadway Street
Boulder, CO 80302
http://www.narf.org/

Intelligence Production Unit
Intelligence Division
DEA Headquarters
Washington, D.C. 20537
(202) 307–8726

Division of Epidemiology and Preventive Research
National Institute on Drug Abuse
5000 Fishers Lane
Rockville, MD 20857
http://www.nida.gov/

OVER-THE-COUNTER DRUGS (NONPRESCRIPTION DRUGS)

CHAPTER OBJECTIVES

After studying this chapter, you will be able to:

1. Describe the role that OTC drugs play in self-diagnosis and self-medication.

2. Describe the history of OTC drugs.

3. List several of the 26 different classes that OTC drugs can be grouped into based on their designated use.

4. Identify the important information contained on the OTC label regarding safe and effective use.

5. Explain how OTC medications can be dangerous in the development of polypharmacy among older adults.

6. Explain the differing opinions concerning the role of homeopathics, herbal preparations, and dietary supplements in today's health care.

7. Explain why college students should refrain from using stimulants, diet pills, laxatives, and emetics.

8. List the important considerations for the safe use of OTC drugs.

9. Explain why cosmetics and foreign-manufactured OTC drugs pose potential problems for consumers.

PROFILE

Jannelle raced for the subway and darted in just as the door closed on the man behind her. The train lurched forward and she lost her balance. As she grabbed the hand rail above, her briefcase fell open, spilling its contents around the feet of the morning commuters. Jannelle felt her heart pound as she scrambled to collect the report she had spent most of the night putting together. Downtown, her report intact save for a heel print or two, she exited the subway.

She climbed the stairs to the street in a slow jog as best she could in a business suit and pumps. Suddenly Jannelle became dizzy. She seemed to be caught in a time warp and felt that she was sweating simultaneously from every pore of her skin. Seconds seemed to drag into minutes, and the walls of her heart painfully strained to expand.

Jannelle slumped to the stairs, overcome by nausea, and curled up with her head between her knees. She struggled laboriously to breathe. "I'm too young for this," she panicked, "I can't be having a heart attack."

Was Jannelle really having a heart attack, or was there some other explanation? What over-the-cuonter products might contribute to this sort of reaction? Keep Jannelle's episode in mind as you study this chapter, and then take a look at the solutions box on page 179.

People have always used the services of health professionals in treating and preventing illness. Village elders, medicine men or women, priests, barbers, midwives, apothecaries, and physicians have been available in the community to provide services and preparations intended to restore health. Throughout history, people have also attempted to diagnose and treat themselves. Today, self-diagnosis and self-treatment are more common than ever before because of the availability of *over-the-counter (OTC)* drugs, or nonprescription drugs. Thousands of nonprescription pills, capsules, suspensions, powders, creams, and gels are on the drug store and grocery shelves awaiting those who decide to self-diagnose and self-medicate. However, it is important to recognize that a wellness lifestyle might significantly reduce the need for OTC medications. For example, a balanced diet reduces the need for nutritional supplements, such as vitamins; a diet with ample fruits and vegetables promotes bowel regularity, thus minimizing laxative use; effective coping skills reduce the frequency and severity of stress-induced headaches, reducing the need for pain relievers; and careful, frequent handwashing during the cold season minimizes the need for cold and cough products.

HISTORY

The history of nonprescription drugs dates back to ancient times. In fact, today's intense interest in herbal medications, homeopathics, and dietary supplements can be traced to the health practices of ancient civilizations, including China 3,000 years ago.

Early History

Since antiquity, healing preparations in various forms have been gathered, harvested, dispensed, sold, and traded. Forerunners of our modern drug stores existed in the larger cities of the ancient world, and material evidence of the "healing arts" has been discovered among the archeological findings of ancient peoples. For many of the world's cultures, the shaman, medicine man, or witch doctor was the source of healing powers. Those who had no medicine man or witch doctor relied on folk cures or mysticism in times of illness.

The development of many of the OTC products sold in the United States is closely associated with the evolution of Western medical practice. This evolution occurred in Europe over several hundred years. Four groups of practitioners were once involved in trying to meet people's health needs. These were physicians (who treated illness with medications), surgeons (who treated disease by cutting out body tissue), barbers (who supplemented their income through bloodletting and surgery), and apothecaries (who were forerunners of today's pharmacists, who dispense formulated medicines, principally for physicians).[1]

It is through the apothecaries' quest for an increased scope of practice (including diagnosis and treatment) that OTC preparations have their origin. We see evidence of this broad range of activities in the following description of an apothecary from Thackeray's *Pendennis*, written in 1898:

> There were those alive who remember having seen his name painted on a board, which was surmounted by a gilt pestle and mortar over the door of a very humble little shop in the city of Bath [England], where Mr. Pendennis exercised the profession of apothecary and surgeon; and where he not only attended gentlemen in their sickrooms, and ladies at the most interesting periods in their lives, but would condescend to sell a brown paper plaster to a farmer's wife across the counter—or to vend toothbrushes, hair powder, and London perfumery.[2]

As the role of apothecaries was evolving in England and western Europe, a similar movement was occurring

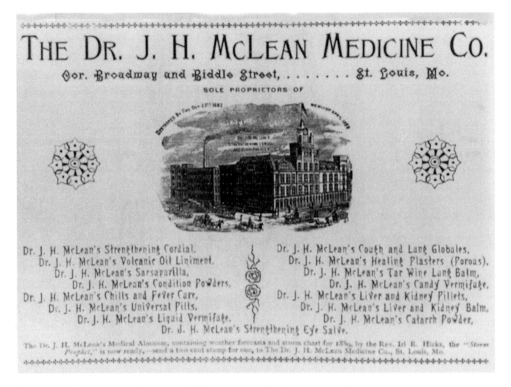

The apothecary shop of the late 1880s sold medications for all ills, formulated and dispensed drugs prescribed by physicians, and printed almanacs.

among physicians in America. Physicians began to engage not only in the diagnosis of illness, but also in the performance of surgery and the formulation and dispensing of medications. Over time, however, physicians began to rely on the local pharmacists or apothecaries for the formulation of many of the prescribed drugs. Increasingly, medications were prescribed by physicians and formulated and dispensed by pharmacists. By the end of the 1880s, the apothecary shop (drug store) had become a common site in the community.[3]

Appearance of OTC Drugs in the American Marketplace

As the modern apothecary shop was being established at the turn of the century, pharmacists began producing and marketing nonprescription preparations intended for the self-medication of self-diagnosed illnesses and conditions. A growing variety of medications, usually composed of "secret" ingredients and often containing ample quantities of alcohol, began to find its way into the hands of consumers.[4] These medications were often prepared by pharmacists for sale in their own shops or by a rapidly expanding number of small drug companies. These small drug companies were operated by "home chemists" with little knowledge of physiology, pathology, or chemistry. Nonetheless, the OTC drug industry—projected to have sales of $19 billion by the year 2000[5]—had been born.

A 1951 amendment of the Food, Drug, and Cosmetic Act of 1938 (see chapter 11), the Durham-Humphrey

Amendment,[6] marked the "official" recognition of medications that could be purchased for self-treatment as being OTC drugs. OTC drugs were formally identified as drugs that were not habit forming, did not have harmful side effects when used according to directions, and did not require professional expertise in order to be used appropriately.

Although primarily applicable to prescription medication, the Kefauver-Harris Amendment of 1962, an amendment to the 1938 Food, Drug, and Cosmetic (FDC) Act, required evidence of both *safety* and *effectiveness* before an OTC drug could be marketed. In 1972, the FDA embarked on a long-range regulatory program to apply these drug efficacy amendments to all nonprescription medications.[7]

As a result of the 1972 actions, OTC drugs were placed in three categories on the basis of the safety and effectiveness of their active ingredient(s). Drugs assigned to category I were those whose active ingredients were deemed both safe and effective. The acronyms **GRAS** (generally regarded as safe), **GRAE** (generally regarded

GRAS an acronym for OTC drugs generally regarded as safe

GRAE an acronym for OTC drugs generally regarded as effective

GRAHL an acronym for OTC drugs generally regarded as honestly labeled

as effective), and **GRAHL** (generally regarded as honestly labeled) were applied to these products.

Category II products were deemed either not safe and effective or untruthfully labeled and were to be removed from shelves within six months. Category III was reserved for products for which there were insufficient data to determine their safety and/or effectiveness. Category III drugs were sold until 1981, when the FDA dropped this classification entirely.[8] Today, only safe and effective drugs that are truthfully labeled can be marketed in the United States.

Since 1981, in an attempt to remove all ineffective and unsafe OTC formulations from the marketplace, the FDA has undertaken an evaluation of the 85 treatment categories into which they classify OTC products. To date, 58 of the 85 categories have been fully evaluated in terms of active ingredients, permissible inactive ingredients, dosage, and labeling. Each fully evaluated treatment category has generated a monograph for distribution to the health care community. Products in the 27 not yet fully evaluated categories are marketed on a provisional basis, subject to changes that may appear in the final published monograph.[9] Consumers should be cautioned that while currently marketed OTC products are safe and effective, very old versions of a current brand name product may be formulated differently. Clearly, old OTC products should not be used or even retained in the medicine cabinet.

Reclassification of Prescription Drugs as OTC Drugs

For reasons most likely related to the well-established self-care movement in the United States and the lack of a national health care system that pays for both physicians' visits and prescription medications, Americans use OTC medications in the treatment of illness more often than in any other country.[10] Further, Americans appear to be extremely satisfied with the OTCs to which they have access. Accordingly, pharmaceutical companies are assigning increasing numbers of prescription medications to OTC status each year. Today, over 56 active ingredients and dosages that were formerly restricted to prescription use have been cleared for OTC use by the FDA, and an additional 25 are anticipated.[11] Although this path is more expensive to pursue than waiting for clearance of the active ingredient, it does afford a period of protected sales. Regardless of the path taken, however, this progressive conversion of prescription drugs to OTC use has resulted in over 600 products that were formerly capable of being used only under a physician's direction being made available as OTCs in the last 20 years.[12] Some of the most recently reassigned products include nicotine-containing chewing gum (Nicorette), transdermal nicotine patches (Nicotrol and Nicoderm CQ), hydrogen ion inhibitors for heartburn relief (Zantac 75, Axid AR, and Pepcid AC), and a hair growth stimulant (Rogaine). The cost effectiveness of this trend for consumers is clearly

evident when the average OTC price ($4.00) is compared with the average prescription price ($25.00).[13]

In spite of the recent trend of reformulating prescription medications for the OTC market, a drug may occasionally be transferred in the other direction. Recently, cough suppressants containing both codeine and terpin hydrate were reassigned to schedule V status when it was decided that terpin hydrate was ineffective. (See chapter 1 for a discussion of drug schedules.) This left codeine, a prescription drug, as the only effective ingredient. Instances such as this one are the exception. Normally, should an OTC formulation be found to be effective but unsafe because of the risk of toxicity, dependence formation, or drug interaction, it would be reformulated to meet OTC standards rather than transferred into the highly regulated and competitive prescription drug market.

CLASSIFICATION AND USE

In comparison to the 2,500 prescription drugs available, there are approximately 300,000 OTC drugs.[14] The 1972 amendment to the 1938 FDC Act led to the establishment of 26 different classes of OTC drugs (see the box below). In addition to this classification system, the FDA also categorizes OTCs into 81 different treatment categories. A specific product can, of course, appear in more than one of these treatment categories if its active

CLASSES OF OTCs*

Antacids	Laxatives
Antimicrobials	Contraceptive and vaginal
Sedatives and sleep	products
aids	Stimulants
Analgesics	Hemorrhoidals
Cold remedies and	Antidiarrheals
antitussives	Dandruff and athlete's
Antihistamines and	foot preparations
allergy products	Bronchodilators and
Mouthwashes	antiasthmatics
Topical analgesics	Antiemetics
Antirheumatics	Emetics
Hematinics	Ophthalmics
Vitamins and minerals	Miscellaneous internal
Antiperspirants	products
Dentifrices and dental	Miscellaneous external
products	products
Sunburn treatments	
and preventives	

*Each class is divided into multiple subclasses. The *Physicians' Desk Reference for Nonprescription Drugs* provides detailed information on each subclass and the specific brand name products within each.

ingredient is both safe and effective for more than one condition.

Some of the most commonly purchased OTC drugs are described in the box below. Almost everyone has used at least one of these products. They are topical analgesics (external); analgesics (internal); antacids; antidiarrheals; cold, cough, and allergy remedies; hemorrhoidal products; laxatives; ophthalmic preparations; cures for lice (pediculicides); and topical antiinfectives.

LABELING

Current **labeling** of nonprescription drugs reflects the regulatory process established by the Kefauver-Harris Act of 1962. The OTC label is intended by the FDA to provide the consumer with all of the information neces-

---

SOME COMMON OTC DRUGS*

Analgesics, external: pain relievers that are applied topically, on the skin (Absorbine, Ben-Gay, Mentholatum)

Analgesics, internal: pain relievers that are swallowed (Tylenol, Anacin, Advil)

Antacids: for relief of acid stomach, indigestion, heartburn (Alka-Seltzer, Pepcid AC, Mylanta, Zantac 75)

Antidiarrheals: for control of frequent and watery stools (Kaopectate, Pepto-Bismol)

Cough, cold, allergy medications: for relief of the symptoms of colds, hay fever, allergies (This is a broad category that includes (1) oral drugs for coughs [Benylin, Vick's Formula 44, Robitussin] and decongestants and antihistamines [Actifed, Allerest, Chlor-Trimeton, Contac, Dimetapp, Sudafed, Comtrex, Dristan], (2) nasal drops and sprays [Dristan, Neo-Synephrine], and (3) lozenges [Cepacol, Chloraseptic, Sucrets].)

Hemorrhoidal preparations: for relief of temporary discomfort from inflamed or strained hemorrhoidal blood vessels (Preparation H, Tucks)

Laxatives: for relief from constipation, to assist in the movement of bowels, or stimulation of defecation (Correctol, Ex-Lax, Fleet, Phillips Milk of Magnesia)

Ophthalmic preparations: for relief of temporary dryness or itching of the eyes (Murine, Visine)

Pediculicides: to exterminate head, body, or pubic lice (R & C, Rid)

Topical antiinfectives: to prevent or retard infection of an open wound or sore (Betadine, Cortaid, Neosporin)

*Appendix G lists some interactions that can occur when using different OTC medications or when combining them with prescription medications.

---

sary for the appropriate selection and safe use of a product. As shown on the sample label (fig. 10.1), an OTC drug label includes the following information:

1. Product name
2. Statement of identity
3. List of active ingredients
4. Net quantity of contents
5. Name and address of the manufacturer, packer, or distributor
6. Indications for use
7. Directions for use and dosage indications
8. Warnings
9. Cautionary statements
10. Drug interaction precautions
11. Expiration date

In addition to the 11 elements listed, which are required on OTC labels, OTC manufacturers routinely include additional consumer-friendly information on their product labels. A few of these optional elements include "label flags," used when a product has been slightly changed from an earlier version, complaint procedures, instructions for claims on money-back guarantees, explanations of safety closures for products that may be harmful to children, disclosure of the quantities of active ingredients, and disclosure of inactive ingredients.

In spite of the current labeling requirements, it is important to remember that OTC drugs that have been in the medicine chest for some time may appear to be the same as the currently marketed brand, but may, in fact, have a different formulation. It is always safest to periodically discard old OTC medications. Also, when more detailed information is needed than that listed on the OTC drug label, reference books are helpful. One useful example is the *Physicians' Desk Reference for Nonprescription Drugs.*[15]

OTC DRUGS AND POLYPHARMACY

Polydrug use, or *polypharmacy*, is the use of several medications at the same time to treat different health problems.[16] The current concern over this practice stems from the detrimental interactions that can occur among the drugs being taken. Today, it is recognized that depression, mental confusion, malnourishment, and falls may be the result of taking several medications at the same time.

Polypharmacy is of particular concern among the elderly.[17] By later adulthood, it is not uncommon for five or six different diagnosed health problems to exist at the same time (a condition called **comorbidity**). Three or four physicians may be involved in the treatment of these illnesses, and several different drug stores may be used in

FIGURE 10.1

OTC drug labels are required to provide important information for the consumer.

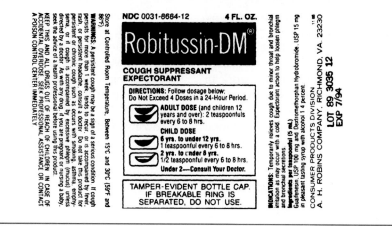

filling prescriptions. Often, there is little coordination of the use of various prescription drugs. Occasionally, changes brought about by the interactions among these drugs may be treated as a "new" health problem by yet another physician, leading to additional prescriptions.

In comparison to prescription medications, the role of OTCs in polypharmacy is somewhat difficult to determine. However, it can be assumed that a variety of OTC drugs are used by people who have comorbidity. In addition, it is unlikely that all of the physicians involved in the treatment of various conditions are aware that OTC medications are being taken in addition to the prescription medication; thus, medication use is even less coordinated. Appendix G lists several of the more common adverse interactions that can occur when OTCs are used with prescription medications and other OTCs.

Patients (or family members) should volunteer information about medication use, including OTCs, to physicians involved in the treatment of comorbidity. The patient should complete a list of medications being used and take it to doctor appointments. On a positive note, many pharmacies are using newly available computer programs to track medication use and to identify drug interactions and interactions between a particular medication and conditions other than the one for which the medication was prescribed. Physicians are increasingly likely to request information from patients about their medical and medication history.

ALTERNATIVE OTC MEDICATIONS

In addition to the more familiar OTC medications sold in drug stores, supermarkets, convenience stores, and even vending machines, homeopathic medications, herbal medications, and dietary supplements are sold for the prevention and treatment of a variety of health conditions. The use of these products is not new, but their movement into the mainstream of the **self-care movement** is more recent. In most cases, consumers decide to use these forms of over-the-counter products with little or no guidance from professionally trained health care providers, many of whom believe strongly that these products are ineffective.

Origin of Homeopathic Medicine

Homeopathic medicines are, according to the principles of homeopathy, substances that produce specific symptoms of illness when taken in large quantity but cause these same symptoms of illness to disappear when taken in highly diluted form (microdoses). Further, these highly diluted natural drugs return the body to a state of desired balance (homeostasis) rather than simply "masking" symptoms of disease and illness, as proponents of homeopathy claim is done by the "synthetic wonder drugs" used by physicians who practice *allopathic* (conventional, scientific, Western) medicine.[18] Based on the law of similars, attributed to Hippocrates, the modern use of homeopathic medicines can be traced to the tenets of Dr. Samuel Hahnemann (1755–1843), a German physician. Hahnemann's search for a more humane approach

labeling printed information supplied with an OTC drug, including that printed on the packaging, container, and insert

comorbidity more than one diagnosed illness or disease occurring at one time

self-care movement health care based on the principles of self-diagnosis, self-treatment, and self-directed health promotion

to the treatment of illness and disease, and thus his concoction of medications that lack virtually any active ingredient, was a reaction to the widespread practice of bloodletting, cauterizing (burning), use of leeches, and the administration of highly toxic chemical compounds that characterized medical practice at that time.

Homeopathic medicine's roots in this country stem from the gradual acceptance of Hahnemann's work in Europe. By the 1880s, word of seemingly safe and effective drugs that presented an alternative to established medical procedures reached the United States and found a receptive audience. The scope of this acceptance resulted in 14,000 practitioners and 22 school of homeopathic medicine by the turn of the century.[19] However, with the rapid advances in biological sciences made in the early decades of this century, homeopathy rapidly lost favor to scientific medicine. Schools of homeopathic medicine closed or merged with allopathic medical schools, and by the mid-1920s, there were no schools remaining and few homeopathic physicians in practice. More recent interest in self-medication, however, has renewed interest in homeopathy.

Preparation of Homeopathic Medications

In the formulation of a homeopathic medication, a careful dilution process is followed in which one part of a particular herb, mineral, glandular extract, or body fluid is mixed vigorously (with impact) with 10 parts of distilled water or ethyl alcohol to obtain a dilution of 1:10, represented by the roman numeral X. When one part of this dilution is again mixed with 10 parts of water or alcohol, a dilution of 2X, or 1:100, results. This process may then be repeated over and over again, leading to dilutions as great as 6X (1 part active ingredient to 1,000,000 parts water or alcohol) or even 24X (1 part to 10^{24} parts water or alcohol).[20] At this latter level of dilution, there is a complete absence of active ingredient in virtually every sample of the solution. To the homeopathist, however, this extremely limited level (or absence) of active material is of little importance, since it is the "essence" of the active ingredient imparted to the solution by the method of preparation, not the active ingredient itself, that makes the medication effective. (It should also be noted that an initial dilution of 1 part active ingredient to 100 parts of distilled water or ethyl alcohol can be used and is noted with the roman numeral C, rather than X. Accordingly, dilutions of 1C (1:100), 2C (1:10,000), 3C (1:1,000,000), and higher are also marketed.)

The very process described, leading to the near or total absence of active substance in homeopathic medications, is the basis on which allopathic medicine questions the effectiveness of such medication in the cure or prevention of illness and disease. Proponents of homeopathy usually respond with a number of arguments. For example, they contend that "homeopathic medicines work because people who use them report that they work," "the effectiveness of a particular homeopathic medication is different for each individual; therefore, they work better for some than for others," and "people who use homeopathic medication know they are safe because they are not getting overdosed as they would if they were using a medicine prescribed by a traditional doctor." Despite the absence of credible proof of effectiveness, the use of homeopathic medicine appears to be growing, and the availability of homeopathic products in drug stores and supermarkets suggests that mainstream consumers are increasingly interested in buying them. Most likely, according to medical scientists, what is being sold and purchased is nothing more than the **placebo effect**.

HERBAL MEDICATIONS

The use of plant material directly as food or as flavorings in the preparation of other foods is familiar to everyone. Perhaps somewhat familiar too is *herbalism*, or the use of **herbs** for the prevention of illness and disease. Herbalism can be traced to the dawn of recorded history, although, like homeopathy, it too lost favor during the scientifically oriented twentieth century. Today, however, the gradual resurgence of herbs as a medical alternative to the mass-produced "synthetic" medicine preferred in the West may be traced to the "back-to-nature" movement of the 1960s and the more recent self-care movement. Herbalists market herbs in several forms, including pastes, infusions, juices, pills, extracts, liniments, powders, teas, and as whole plant parts.

The Role of Plants in Modern Medicine

Throughout this century, the Western scientific community has recognized that a wide array of plant materials possess compounds that are **biologically active** in humans and effective in curing or preventing illness or disease. A wide variety of these botanicals have been carefully studied, their specific active ingredients identified, and synthesized versions of these active ingredients produced in mass quantities as prescription medications. Continued subtle modification of these molecular structures of plant origin has given rise to an increasingly larger number of other effective drugs whose chemical structures are nearly identical to the original drugs of plant origin. Since the human body reacts in the same way to any particular active ingredient, regardless of whether it is naturally occurring or synthetically produced, Western medicine has chosen for financial and quality control reasons to limit the use of actual plant material to basic research in the discovery of new drugs. In fact, so completely is this trend followed that today no legal standards exist regarding the effectiveness and safety of herbs when used as medications in the cure and prevention of illness and disease. People who wish to use herbs as medications must, therefore, be extremely careful regarding the sources of information they consult and the manner in which they actually use herbal preparations. People who use herbs in the most careful manner possible are said to be practicing rational herbalism.

Rational Herbalism

Two important factors must be considered in deciding whether to use herbs as an alternative to (or in addition to) prescription medications. The first is effectiveness. Many of the biologically active compounds known to exist in plants have not yet been evaluated for effectiveness in treating diseases or illnesses for which it *seems* possible that they could be effective. Therefore, to be a rational herbalist in this sense, only those herbs that have been carefully studied by the pharmaceutical industry and have been used in the formulation of effective prescription medications should be considered reasonably effective in herb form.

The second criterion that must be considered by the rational herbalist is safety. Two indicators of safety are fairly reliable. The first is whether or not a long history of safe use of an herbal preparation (of exactly the same type and in the exact formulation that one has access to) can be securely established. When this validation is possible, the question of safety is less problematic. This is particularly true when long-term use can be fully substantiated.

The second indicator of safety concerns the accuracy of the diagnosis of the condition for which a particular herb is to be used. To this end, the rational herbalist would consult a reliable physician to confirm the diagnosis of the condition to be treated, rather than using self-diagnosis. Once this has been done, herbal

A physician should monitor the use of herbal medications to help ensure their safety and effectiveness.

medications could be used as the sole basis of treatment or used in combination with medications or other therapies prescribed by the physician. The physician should be willing to monitor the safe and effective use of *all* sources of biologically active ingredients, including herbs. Certainly, to use apparently safe herbal preparations for the wrong condition because of a distrust of modern medicine would be an error of potentially serious consequences.

Paraherbalism

There is little dispute that a vast array of plants contain one or in some cases dozens of biologically active compounds that can positively influence the course of illness and disease. Thus, it makes some sense to better use plants than Western medicine appears to do. However, the return to herbalism as an alternative to medicines produced by the pharmaceutical industry may be based on commonly held misconceptions about both herbalism and Western medicine. In his book *Herbs of Choice: The Therapeutic Use of Phytomedicinals*, Varro Tyler, a professor of pharmacognosy at Purdue University, cautions readers about the reasons some people promote a less rational, unscientific form of herbalism that he calls **paraherbalism**.[21] Following is a list of these questionable reasons, followed by Tyler's response to them:

1. *A conspiracy by the medical establishment discourages the use of herbs.* There is no conspiracy. Very few health care practitioners have any knowledge of the field because the subject is not included in most academic curricula. The pharmaceutical industry generally views phytomedicinals (plant medicines) as unprofitable products.
2. *Herbs cannot harm, only cure.* On the contrary, some of the most toxic substances known—amatoxins, convallatoxin, aconitine, strychnine, abrin, ricin—are derived from plants.
3. *Whole herbs are more effective than their isolated active constituents.* For every example cited in support of this thesis, there is at least one example that opposes it. Furthermore, many herbs contain toxins in addition to useful compounds.
4. *"Natural" and "organic" herbs are superior to synthetic drugs.* Wohler disproved the claim about "natural"

placebo effect psychological and physiological effects associated with the patient's expectations about a drug

herb a plant reported to be capable of curing or preventing illness or disease

biologically active capable of influencing metabolic or regulatory processes at the cellular level

paraherbalism an irrational, unscientific form of herbalism based on questionable beliefs

herbs in 1828. Today, established limits on pesticide residues render treated plants no more harmful than "organic" plants.

5. *The Doctrine of Signatures is meaningful.* This ancient belief postulates that the form of a plant part determines its therapeutic value. If this were true, kidney beans should cure all types of renal (kidney) disease, and walnuts, which look similar to the human brain, should cure various types of cerebral malfunction.

6. *Reducing the dose of a medicine increases its therapeutic activity.* There is no proof that this is generally true, as claimed by practitioners of homeopathy. Positive results obtained by homeopathic treatment are demonstrations of the placebo effect.

7. *Astrological influences are significant.* No scientific evidence supports this assertion.

8. *Physiological tests performed on animals are not applicable to human beings.* Differences do exist, but there is a high probability of significance and applicability when diverse animal species, especially those from different orders, have similar responses.

9. **Anecdotal evidence** *is highly significant.* It is extremely difficult to assess the reliability of such evidence. Consequently, it must be viewed simply as one of many factors (animal tests and clinical trials, for example) that may indicate the therapeutic reliability of an herb.

10. *Herbs were created by God specifically to cure disease.* This claim is not testable and should not be used as a substitute for scientific evidence.

DIETARY SUPPLEMENTS

Dietary supplements compose a large group of OTC products that encompasses many homeopathic medications and all herbal preparations taken orally. The 1994 Dietary Supplements Health and Education Act initially defined dietary supplements as:

- Products (other than tobacco) that are intended to supplement the diet, including vitamins, amino acids, minerals, glandular extracts, herbs, and other botanicals, such as fungi
- Products that are intended for use by people to supplement the total daily intake of nutrients in the diet
- Products that are intended to be ingested in pill, capsule, tablet, or liquid form
- Products that are not in themselves to be used as conventional foods or as the only items of a meal or diet
- Products that are to be labeled as a "dietary supplement"
- Products, such as prescription drugs, certified antibiotics, or licensed biologics, that were originally marketed as dietary supplements (unless the Secretary of Health and Human Services waives this provision)[22]

In addition to defining dietary supplements, this law also established the conditions under which the FDA would remove "adulterated" (unsafe) supplements, in spite of having initially left the formulation of standards defining safety to the discretion of manufacturers. Further, the law established the right of manufacturers to display literature regarding the beneficial role of active ingredients in places where supplements are sold, as long as the material was written by people not associated with the manufacturing of products containing these ingredients. It also prevented manufacturers from making label claims regarding effectiveness (such as using the words *prevent, mitigate, treat,* or *cure*) except for products containing calcium (which helps prevent osteoporosis) and folic acid (which helps prevent neural tube [spinal cord] defects in infants). Also, the specificity of other information on labels, such as exact ingredients and specific amounts of each, was established. Lastly, the law created a Commission of Dietary Supplements, to begin the process of bringing control and standardization to the manufacturing and marketing of supplements, and an Office

Many women take OTC calcium supplements to help prevent osteoporosis.

DRUGS IN YOUR WORLD

DHEA: A Fountain of Youth?

Are we truly on the threshold of having the ability to reverse many of the changes associated with aging, including changes in skin elasticity, joint flexibility, muscular strength, sexual interest and potency, and endurance? Is there an easy way to protect ourselves against heart disease? Many people, including some physicians, believe that the hormone **DHEA** (dehydroepiandrosterone), now available in synthetic form as a dietary supplement, can make this possible.

DHEA is an adrenal gland hormone that is converted by the body into the anabolic steroids testosterone and estrogen, which are principal players in development of the youthful adult body. With age, however, the natural production declines from its maximum level at age 25 until it virtually disappears from the body by age 85. This decline, in the opinion of DHEA proponents, is a significant reason for the appearance of age-related changes leading to frailty and eventual death. Accordingly, they argue, a return of DHEA levels to those seen in younger adults should postpone or even reverse the aging process. Initial research in rats and anecdotal accounts from long-time users of DHEA provide some support for this contention. Some side effects, however, such as acne and the development of ex-

cessive body hair, have also been reported, although these apparently regress when use is discontinued.

As is generally the case when a dietary supplement is advanced as a curative or preventive agent of previously unrecognized value, the FDA responds in a predictable manner, suggesting that two things must be considered before rushing to the health food store in the mall. First, research done on animals, particularly nonprimates, cannot always be applied to humans, particularly in the absence of controlled clinical trials using human subjects. Second, since DHEA is presently classified as a dietary supplement rather than a drug, the FDA has never had authority to oversee the several levels of research and clinical trials required when a new pharmaceutical product is presented for approval. In the absence of the data obtained through the rigorous approval process applicable to prescription medication, little is known about the product's safety or effectiveness, particularly for long-term use.

In the absence of any form of approval beyond having met the labeling requirements for a dietary supplement, the users of DHEA are proceeding at their own risk. The usual dosage of 20 to 25 mg per day is at this time considered minimal, but many people may far exceed this dosage, the health consequences of which are unknown.

of Dietary Supplements within the National Institutes of Health to explore the scientifically valid role of supplements in improved health care for Americans.

Introduction of the bill in early 1994 was met by one of the most intense lobbying campaigns seen in recent times. Manufacturers of popular dietary supplements, such as vitamins, amino acid preparations, and herbs, tried to convince segments of the American public that, if passed in its present form, this legislation would effectively remove all of the familiar and trusted products, such as vitamins and mineral supplements, from the OTC market. Largely because of these lobbying efforts, a much weaker version of the bill was passed into law in October 1994. Efforts are now under way in the Congress to allow manufacturers to directly communicate truthful, nonmisleading information to consumers concerning the nutritional content and disease prevention benefits of their products and to clarify other rules enacted by the original legislation.

Regardless of the final outcome of these legislative efforts, consumers of food supplements should remember that at this time these products are not drugs by definition; thus, their manufacturers have never been required to substantiate either safety in the form in which

the products are marketed or effectiveness, in spite of the glowing recommendations that can be made by promotional materials widely available to the general public.[23] For example, the hormone DHEA has been touted as a miracle product that can slow or even reverse the aging process. This claim is considered in the box above.

OTC PRODUCTS ON THE COLLEGE CAMPUS

Four classes of OTC drugs seem to be particularly popular among college students and are at times misused to the point of abuse. These classes of drugs are stimulants, diet pills, laxatives, and emetics.

1. **Stimulants.** Although at one time OTC stimulants contained more than one ingredient, today there is only a single ingredient approved for use as an OTC

anecdotal evidence evidence that is not based on controlled studies, but on personal experience

stimulant. This ingredient is caffeine, the psychoactive agent in coffee, tea, chocolate, and many popular soft drinks. When dispensed as an OTC drug, caffeine is found under such brand names as No-Doz and Vivarin. No-Doz is sold as a 100 mg tablet; Vivarin comes in a 200 mg tablet. A 100 mg dose of caffeine is equivalent to one cup of strong black coffee.

2. **Diet pills.** A second popular OTC product on the college campus is diet pills. Unlike the "stay awake" products described previously, diet pills contain phenylpropanolamine (PPA) as their active ingredient. Even at its approved dose (75 mg), PPA is not considered safe by some experts. When combined with coffee or caffeine-based pills, diet pills may be too stimulating to the central nervous system to be used as an unsupervised medication. While research continues on the overall safety of PPA, these products continue to be marketed, and the demand for them is high.

3. **Laxatives.** Laxatives are a third class of OTC drugs commonly used on campuses. Their use is associated with the purge component of the eating disorders bulimia and anorexia. Laxatives are used to speed up movement of ingested food through the digestive tract, thereby reducing the opportunity for the absorption of nutrients. Chronic excessive laxative use can lead not only to malnourishment, but also to a gradual dependence that proves extremely difficult to overcome when discontinuation of laxative use is attempted.

4. **Emetics.** Emetics are drugs that promote vomiting. In contrast to laxatives, emetics such as syrup of ipecac act to remove food from the stomach before it can be digested and absorbed into the body. Although emetics are useful as a first aid agent in some poisoning cases, habitual use to induce vomiting is certainly considered abuse. The danger to one's health includes destruction of teeth, esophageal ulcers and bleeding, and potassium loss brought about by the changes in body chemistry caused by the loss of fluids through vomiting. Deaths caused by cardiac failure have been reported in people with bulimia and anorexia who have misused emetics. These deaths are an ironic contrast to the intended life-saving role of emetics in countering poisoning emergencies. Today, pharmacists are "pulling back" emetics from easily accessible shelves so that they can more closely supervise their sales.

COSMETICS

Although not often thought of as OTC products, cosmetics represent one of the most highly advertised and profitable product lines on the nonprescription market. For example, in 1993, the cosmetic industry spent $810 million on magazine advertisements, while in 1994, it spent close to $2 billion on television commercials.[24] Skin care products, fragrances, eye makeup, shampoos, bath oils, and shaving products (plus hundreds of similar products) are used by people of all ages. Concern exists, of course, about the safety of products that are used daily on the body.

On the basis of consumer injury reports filed by the 5,000 cosmetics manufacturers, it would be reasonable to assume that very few cases of injury from cosmetic use occur. For example, in 1990, fewer than 100 reports were filed with the FDA.[25] Most of these were related to allergic reactions and eye infections caused by the introduction of bacteria into the eye from contaminated brushes used to apply eye makeup. Some consumer groups, however, are concerned that such cases are grossly underreported by the industry.

Regardless of the actual extent of user injury, cosmetics do contain potentially toxic ingredients and can be contaminated by sharing with others or by careless handling. The consumer should remember that these familiar products are drug-related in composition and, therefore, are a possible source of adverse reactions and injury. Answer the questions in the self-assessment box on page 177 to determine whether you use cosmetics safely.

SAFETY

In addition to the safety-related information found on OTC product labels (see p. 171) and in various reference books, users of OTC products should regularly consider all of the following issues of special concern:

Polypharmacy. As discussed earlier, OTC drugs can be dangerous when they are taken in combination with other medications. Concerns regarding the use of multiple drugs, both OTC and prescription, should be expressed to a physician or pharmacist.

Contraindications. An OTC drug should not be taken when the label identifies a **contraindication** or condition that applies to the user that could be worsened by taking the drug.

Dosage. The amount of medication taken should be carefully monitored, particularly with OTC medications that can impair alertness or cause drowsiness. Information about overdose can be obtained from a local, state, or national poison control center.

Adverse reactions. In a given individual, a particular OTC drug can produce an adverse reaction, such as nausea or an irregular heartbeat. When an adverse reaction occurs, use of the OTC drug should be discontinued immediately. A physician should be consulted if the reaction continues.

SELF-ASSESSMENT

Do You Use Cosmetics Safely?

Cosmetics can be dangerous if not used properly. Consumers should follow several precautions to protect themselves and the quality of their cosmetics. If you answer no to any of the following, you may not be using cosmetics safely:

Do you keep cosmetics containers tightly closed except when in use?

Do you keep cosmetics out of sunlight? (Light can degrade preservatives.)

Do you avoid using eye cosmetics if you have an eye infection, such as conjunctivitis, and do you throw away all cosmetics you were using when you first discovered the infection?

Do you avoid adding any liquid to bring a cosmetic product back to its original consistency? (Adding water or, even worse, saliva could introduce bacteria that could easily grow out of control.)

Do you avoid sharing cosmetics with friends?

Do you throw cosmetics away if the color changes or an odor develops? (Preservatives can degrade over time and may no longer be able to fight bacteria.)

Modified from *FDA Consumer* 25, no.9 (1991):18.

Length of use. Because of the potential for a toxic effect from an extended period of use and the possibility that prolonged use of an OTC drug might delay consultation with a physician, OTC drug use should not extend beyond the period recommended on the label.

Side effects. Every drug has multiple effects on physiology. For example, aspirin relieves pain but also thins the blood and can cause stomach ulcers. Many antihistamines produce drowsiness, in addition to the intended effects.

Storage. For safety and effectiveness, medications should not be kept beyond the expiration date on the label. All medications should be stored in a cool, dry place, out of reach of children and household pets.

Disposal. Most households have at least some OTC drugs that have expired or are no longer needed. Periodically, medicine cabinets should be checked, and drugs that are no longer needed or whose expiration dates have passed should be flushed down the toilet.

Look-alikes. Many prescription and OTC drugs look alike. Taking medications in the dark is especially risky because many OTC drugs and prescription drugs are packaged similarly. The wise consumer reads the label before each use. Also, drugs should always be stored in their original containers so that they can be easily identified.

Children. The correct dosage for children as well as adults is clearly stated on the label. The label should be read carefully before an OTC preparation is given to a child so that the child will not be given an adult dose by accident.

Tampering. Another important aspect of OTC safety involves awareness of the intentional tampering with OTC products. A tragic tampering case involving Tylenol capsules that resulted in seven deaths in 1982 prompted the FDA to require "tamper-resistant" packaging for OTC drugs, liquid oral hygiene products, vaginal preparations, and contact lens solutions. A more recent case of tampering involving Sudafed (1991) in "tamper-resistant" packaging has led to renewed emphasis on the consumer's continued vigilance in looking for signs of product adulteration.

Recognizing that it is impossible to entirely prevent tampering with products as readily available to the public as the OTC medications sold on drug store and supermarket shelves, in more recent years the OTC industry has attempted to redefine its packaging as being "tamper-evident." This concept is slightly different from that of "tamper-proof" or even "tamper-resistant" in that it places the responsibility for actively looking for signs of tampering on the consumer's shoulders. It is hoped that a proactive public, who is *actively looking* for evidence of tampering, will discourage people thinking about tampering with OTC products from actually doing so. Complete the self-assessment on page 178 to see whether you are taking responsibility for using OTC products safely.

OTC DRUGS MANUFACTURED OUTSIDE THE UNITED STATES

How likely is the consumer to encounter foreign-manufactured OTC drugs? FDA requirements concerning safety and effectiveness make marketing drugs in this country very demanding and, as a consequence, no OTC drugs are imported for sale.

contraindication a condition or characteristic of a person that makes the use of a particular medication by that person unwise or dangerous

SELF-ASSESSMENT

Do You Use OTC Products Properly?

In the space provided, select the response that most closely reflects your pattern of OTC medication use by assigning the item 1 point (never), 2 points (usually), or 3 points (always).

_____ 1. When symptoms of an illness first appear, are you confident of your ability to self-diagnose?

_____ 2. On the basis of your ability to self-diagnose, are you comfortable with your ability to select a safe and effective OTC product?

_____ 3. Do you read package instructions on OTC products before you leave the store so that areas of confusion or misunderstanding can be clarified by talking with the pharmacist?

_____ 4. At the time you purchase an OTC medication, do you know whether the product could result in a drug interaction with or in some way reduce the effectiveness of other medications being taken?

_____ 5. Is there a knowledgeable person, such as a pharmacist, at the store at which you usually purchase your OTC medications to answer your questions and address your concerns?

_____ 6. When you are taking multiple medications (OTCs and prescription), do you keep a record of use in order to avoid excessive or inadequate intake?

_____ 7. Do you use a pill box or other device that compartmentalizes OTC medications, thus providing greater control over the time and amount of medication taken?

_____ 8. For OTC medications that you take frequently (but not continually), do you reread package directions to refresh your memory regarding safe and effective use?

_____ 9. Before actually using an OTC medication for the first time, do you check the product's seal and inspect the container for pinhole-sized punctures?

_____ 10. Do you store all OTC medications in a cool, dry place unless directed by the label or the pharmacist to store them differently?

_____ 11. Are your medications stored in a manner that makes them inaccessible to children?

_____ 12. For medications that are to be taken during the night, do you always turn on a light or have a plan for taking the medication safely in a darkened room?

_____ 13. Do you dispose of expired or no longer needed OTC medications on a regular basis?

Interpretation

Score range

30–39 points . . . You are a careful user of OTC medication and should be able to avoid most potentially serious problems with the use of these products.

20–29 points . . . You are a reasonably careful user of OTC medications, but there are areas in which you should be more cautious.

13–19 points . . . You are far from a careful user of OTC medications and should make a serious effort to improve your practices in the areas suggested by the items in which you scored only 1 point.

When traveling outside the United States, however, a consumer may have occasion to purchase and use foreign-manufactured OTCs. Many experts in the field of OTC drugs believe that products manufactured and sold in Canada and most of western Europe are very similar to their American counterparts in terms of both safety and effectiveness.[26] Of course, directions for use should be understood before taking any OTC drug. In contrast, the safety and effectiveness of OTC products manufactured and sold in other regions of the world are in many cases unproven. It is recommended that Americans take OTC products with them when traveling abroad.

For Americans traveling outside the country who have purchased foreign-made OTC products and wish to bring them home, it is recommended that the original package be retained in order to substantiate the type of medication in the traveler's possession. Even with this, however, the medication is likely to be confiscated by customs authorities upon return to the United States.

SOURCES OF CONSUMER INFORMATION ABOUT OTC DRUGS

Inherent in the use of OTC drugs is the need for the consumer to make a self-diagnosis. The consumer is then able to select the product most likely to bring temporary relief of symptoms. Knowledge of the appropriate medi-

SOLUTIONS

Jannelle didn't have a heart attack. In fact, she was breathing normally and felt a little better by the time the paramedics arrived and began to administer oxygen. During the course of a medical interview, Jannelle related that she had skipped supper the night before as well as breakfast that morning. Before leaving for work she had taken three times the recommended amount of an over-the-counter appetite suppressant. Jannelle found that taking a larger amount of this drug not only kept her from getting hungry all day but also gave her an amazing "energy boost."

The paramedics took Jannelle to the emergency room for observation. The ER physicians determined that she had had an intense adverse reaction to the increased dosage of the over-the-counter drug. They advised her to eat better and to make her exercise routine more regular as a safer alternative to losing weight and increasing her energy level.

Jannelle was discharged from the hospital at 1:05 that afternoon. That evening on the way home from work, Jannelle stopped by her favorite bookstore and purchased a fitness and nutrition book designed for young business people on the run. This text offered a number of quick and easy recipes for eating healthfully on the go and working fitness into her life without going too far out of her way. She stopped using the appetite suppressant and began taking the stairs instead of the elevator and getting off the train a stop or two away from home (dependent on the weather) and walking the rest of the way. As she became more fit, she had more energy to pursue interests outside of the demands of her office job. Her frightening experience had led her to take the much-needed first steps toward a healthful new lifestyle.

cation can be obtained from a variety of sources, including family, friends, advertisements, health practitioners, medical reference books, and the programs developed by health educators.

Obviously, objectivity and credibility of information vary from source to source. Some of these sources may not be very reliable. An excellent source of information about OTC medications is the *Physicians' Desk Reference for Nonprescription Drugs.* It should be noted, however, that the information in this publication, although detailed, is provided by the manufacturer and might not be completely objective. A pharmacist is also a good source of information about both prescription and nonprescription drugs.

In the area of herbal medications, two books may be especially useful. The first, *Herbs of Choice: The Therapeutic Use of Phytomedicinals,* by Varro Tyler of the Purdue University School of Pharmacy and Pharmacal Sciences, is considered a book suitable for both professionals in the health care field and laypeople. A second book in the area of herbalism is *Vis Medicatrix Naturae* (The Healing Power of Nature), by Rick Schmitt.[27] This book is often the principal source of information used by pharmacists to respond to questions about herbs and herbal medication.

LIMITATIONS OF OTC MEDICATION USE

When used according to the manufacturer's instructions, OTC drugs are considered safe and effective for the ma-

jority of the population. It is important to note, however, that with few exceptions OTC drugs provide only **symptomatic relief,** relief from the discomfort of the signs and symptoms of the disease, and do not cure the underlying cause of the disease or discomfort. (Notable exceptions are antifungal cream for athlete's foot and topical antibiotic ointment for a minor cut or scrape.)

Therefore, it is important for the consumer to note carefully the duration and severity of signs and symptoms, and consult a physician if these persist. Next, the consumer must read and understand the entire label, check the manufacturer's claims, use the drug according to directions, and evaluate the results. If these results are unsatisfactory, the consumer should recheck the label and then consult a pharmacist or physician.

SUMMARY

When confronted with illness, many people self-diagnose the problem and treat themselves with over-the-counter (OTC) medications. The origin of many of these nonprescription drugs can be traced to European apothecaries, the forerunners of today's pharmacists. Early OTC medications were often unsafe and of limited effectiveness in treating the condition for which they were intended. Accordingly, federal regulation of the OTC drug market eventually became necessary.

symptomatic relief alleviation of discomfort or other signs and symptoms of a condition or disease without curing the cause of the disease or condition

Today, regulation of OTC medications is the responsibility of the Food and Drug Administration (FDA), an agency of the United States Public Health Service. The FDA's power to require that all OTC products be safe, effective, and truthfully labeled before they can be legally sold stems from a series of laws and regulations dating back to the Pure Food and Drug Act of 1906. Today, the Food, Drug, and Cosmetic Act of 1938, with its numerous amendments, serves as the basis of the government's regulatory power. At this time, 58 of the 85 categories of active ingredients have been fully evaluated by the FDA.

The 300,000 OTC products now on the market fall into 26 classes based on intended use. Reformulation of prescription drugs into OTC medications has added brand names to several classes of OTC drugs. Today, 56 active ingredients that were previously limited to prescription use have been released for use in OTC products.

The misuse of OTC products is a continuing concern. To reduce the likelihood of misuse, the labels and the package inserts that accompany all OTC drugs provide information about appropriate use. At least 11 areas of concern should be considered in association with safe use of OTC drugs. Among these are contraindications, recommended dosage, adverse reactions, and proper disposal of expired or unwanted OTC products.

Polypharmacy, the use of several drugs at the same time, is also a concern, particularly in older adults. OTCs can contribute significantly to the total number of drugs being taken at a given time. In addition, the growing interest and use of homeopathics, herbal products, and dietary supplements is seen by many as an area of concern. This concern is principally related to the questionable value of homeopathic medications and the limited control that the FDA has over the effectiveness and safety of dietary supplements, including herbal products. Certainly, a rational use of herbal products is recommended over a less cautious form of use known as paraherbalism. Dietary supplements are intentionally not marketed as drugs; thus, little information needs to be submitted to the FDA regarding effectiveness or safety.

Misuse and abuse of four classes of OTC products (stimulants, diet pills, laxatives, and emetics) among some college students are also of concern to health professionals.

Although not often thought of as OTC products, cosmetics are a potential area of concern regarding safe use. Sharing cosmetics is particularly unsafe. The safety of OTCs manufactured outside the United States is unsubstantiated. Travelers should consider taking necessary American-made OTCs along with them, rather than buying products made abroad.

For consumers who want additional information about OTC medications, such reference books as the *Physicians' Desk Reference for Nonprescription Drugs* are available at libraries and bookstores.

REVIEW QUESTIONS

1. Describe the development of OTC drugs from their initial appearance in eighteenth-century Europe to their current availability in drugstores and supermarkets. What roles did the Food and Drugs Acts of 1906, the Federal Food, Drug, and Cosmetic Act of 1938, the Durham-Humphrey Amendment (1951), and the Kefauver-Harris Amendment (1962) play?

2. What levels of safety and effectiveness can today's consumers be assured of, and who is responsible for providing that assurance?

3. Identify 10 of the 26 classes of OTC drugs, describe the intended use of each, and give some examples of each by brand name. Of the 85 categories of active ingredients used in OTC formulations, how many categories has the FDA fully evaluated and released monographs regarding?

4. The labeling of OTC drugs is tightly regulated. What information must be supplied to consumers on the label? What areas of information are optional?

5. What is polypharmacy? Why is it a particular concern among the elderly? How do OTC drugs contribute to the problem of polypharmacy?

6. What are the principles of homeopathy, and why did it gain popularity in Europe and then in the United States? How do homeopathic medications differ in formulation from the medications used in Western allopathic medicine?

7. In comparison to homeopathy, what are the principles of herbalism? What relationship exists today between botanical products and the development of synthetic pharmaceutical products? How would rational herbalism be practiced? What is paraherbalism?

8. What are the qualifications that make a biologically active substance capable of being defined as a dietary supplement rather than a drug? What was the intent of the 1994 Dietary Supplements Health and Education Act, and why was it so strongly opposed by the makers of vitamins and other dietary supplements?

9. What are the four classes of OTC drugs most frequently misused by college students? What relationship exists between eating disorders and two of these classes?

10. In addition to information on the labels of OTC drugs regarding safe use, what other aspects of safety should be considered in ensuring the safe use of OTC drugs?

11. What countries or regions of the world other than the United States manufacture OTC drugs that are generally considered safe? What recommendation was made regarding returning to the United States with OTC drugs purchased abroad?

12. What is the *Physicians' Desk Reference for Nonprescription Drugs*? Who supplies the information con-

tained in each year's publication? Where would you expect to find a copy?

REFERENCES

1. B. Inglis, *A History of Medicine* (Cleveland: World Publishing, 1965).
2. Ibid.
3. Ibid.
4. J. H. Young, *The Medical Messiahs: A Social History of Health Quackery in Twentieth-Century America* (Princeton, N.J.: Princeton University Press, 1967).
5. M. Segal, "Rx to OTC," *FDA Consumer* 25, no. 2 (1992):9.
6. FDA consumer memo, *Milestones in U.S. Food and Drug Law History*, DHHS Pub. No. 85-1063 (Washington, D.C.: U.S. Government Printing Office, 1985).
7. Ibid.
8. O. Ray and C. Ksir, *Drugs, Society, and Human Behavior*, 7th ed. (St. Louis: WCB/McGraw-Hill, 1997).
9. *Physicians' Desk Reference for Nonprescription Drugs*, 17th ed. (Montvale, N.J.: Medical Economics Data Production, 1996).
10. *Health Care, Self-Care, and Self-Medication.* World Federation of Proprietary Medicine Manufacturers, 1991.
11. *Physicians' Desk Reference for Nonprescription Drugs.*
12. Ibid.
13. Ibid.
14. Ibid.
15. Ibid.
16. *Mosby's Medical, Nursing, and Allied Health Dictionary*, 4th ed. (St. Louis: Mosby, 1994).
17. W. Abrams, and R. Berkow, eds., *The Merck Manual of Geriatrics*, 2nd ed. (Rahway, N.J.: Merck and Co., 1995).
18. *Homeopathics: History of Homeopathics* (Kihei, Hawaii: Mindbody, Inc., 1994).
19. Stephen Barret, et al., *Consumer Health—A Guide to the Intelligent Decisions* (St. Louis: WCB/McGraw-Hill, 1997).
20. M. Clark, *On-Line Campus of Homeopathy* (London: British Institute of Homeopathy, 1996).
21. V. E. Tyler, *Herbs of Choice: The Therapeutic Use of Phytomedicinals* (New York: Pharmaceutical Products Press, 1994).
22. Dietary Supplement Health and Education Act of 1994, U.S. Food and Drug Administration, Center for Food Safety and Applied Nutrition, 1 December 1995, Hypertext by *dms*.
23. Leclair J. Command, Personal Interview, 10 September, 1996.
24. *Statistical Abstract of the United States 1995: The National Data Book*, U.S. Department of Commerce, Bureau of the Census.
25. D. Stehlin, "Cosmetic Safety: More Complex than the First Blush," *FDA Consumer* 25, no. 9 (1991):18.
26. B. Clayton, Personal Interview, 2 July 1993.
27. R. Schmitt and K. Bond, *Vis Medicatrix Naturae* (United States: Wal-Mart Pharmacy, 1994).

SOURCES FOR HELP

American Pharmaceutical Association
2215 Constitution Ave. NW
Washington, D.C. 20037
(202) 628–4410

National Association of Retail Druggists
205 Dangerfield Rd.
Alexandria, VA 22314
(703) 683–8200

Food and Drug Administration
5600 Fishers Lane
Rockville, MD 20857
(301) 443–3170
http://www.fda.gov/

PRESCRIPTION DRUGS

11

1. Explain the role of a health-enhancing lifestyle in reducing the need for prescription medications.

2. Describe the general history of prescription drugs from ancient times to the present.

3. Explain the process of developing new or modified prescription medications, including the involvement of the FDA in monitoring drug research and development.

4. List several reasons why prescription drugs are not consistently effective for all users.

5. Define the term *placebo* and explain the importance of placebos in vaccine and drug trials.

6. Describe what kind of information appears on a prescription's label and on the product's accompanying package insert.

7. Define the terms *bioavailability, bioequivalence,* and *therapeutic equivalence* as they relate to generic drugs.

8. Explain why it is important to regularly consult both the physician and the pharmacist regarding all aspects of appropriate drug use.

9. Describe the problem of polypharmacy among older adults.

Prescription drugs are ordered by physicians or dentists and dispensed by registered pharmacists. By definition, these drugs are to be used under the supervision of highly trained health care specialists—physicians, dentists, nurses, physician assistants, pharmacists, and some medical technologists. This method of distribution is intended to protect the consumer from misusing these powerful substances, either accidentally or intentionally. Because these drugs are usually stronger or more concentrated than over-the-counter (OTC) drugs, they are dispensed in limited amounts through a precise prescription. Each prescription order specifies the name of the patient, the dosage, and the number of refills allowed.

Examples of types of prescription medications and their effects include antibiotics (which destroy certain disease-producing microorganisms, especially bacteria), narcotic analgesics (for relief of pain), birth control pills (for the prevention of unwanted pregnancy), and anticoagulants (which increase blood clotting time to reduce the likelihood of clot formation). Two groups of drugs that have made important contributions to the health of some people are the antidepressants and the antipsychotics, a new drug for weight management, and several new HIV/AIDS-related medications (see the boxes on pages 185 and 191). Clearly, prescription medications play an important role in our lives.

REDUCING THE NEED FOR PRESCRIPTION MEDICATIONS

Much as an automobile or house requires routine care and preventive maintenance to avoid the need for costly repairs, so too does the body require a health-enhancing lifestyle and preventive medical care to minimize the need for prescription medications. Appropriate levels of rest, exercise, nutrition, use of stress reduction strategies, and avoidance of tobacco, in combination with a compliant approach to medication use, are the keys to limiting prescription medication use.

This proactive approach to lessening the need for prescription medication can be taken in several ways. For example, learning effective coping skills can eliminate the need for tranquilizer use during periods of excessive stress. Quitting smoking, or not starting in the first place, allows freedom from the use of bronchodilators and antibiotics used in the treatment of chronic obstructive pulmonary disease. Following safer sex practices, paying attention to personal hygiene, such as proper handwashing, and completing childhood immunizations can help prevent the spread of infectious disease, thus reducing the need for antibiotics. In addition, regular exercise and a healthful diet can reduce the need for cholesterol-lowering medications, expensive "clot busters" used to treat myocardial infarctions (heart attacks), and insulin used to treat type II diabetes mellitus.

HISTORY

The history of prescription drugs, like that of OTC drugs, has its origins in antiquity. The oldest known written prescriptions are those appearing on a clay tablet belonging to the Sumerian civilization that existed in the Middle East about 2000 B.C.[1] Most of the approximately one dozen prescriptions on the tablet contain references to certain plants.

An Egyptian scroll, dated about 1500 B.C., lists more than 800 prescriptions. Although most of the early prescriptions were of unknown usefulness, some, such as those referring to opium and castor oil, were effective.

In recent times, particularly the last 100 years, so many useful and effective agents have been discovered or developed that this era has been called the "modern drug revolution." Paul Ehrlich's discovery of arsenic as a cure for syphilis in 1910, Alexander Fleming's discovery of penicillin in 1928, and Gerhard Domagk's discovery of the first **sulfa drug** in 1935 are just a few examples of the many great contributions made during the early part of this period.

Unfortunately, not all discoveries were as beneficial as these, and some were even dangerous. Eventually, the safety and effectiveness of new drugs became an important issue, and laws were passed to regulate the drug industry. The first of these laws, the Federal Food, Drug, and Cosmetic (FD&C) Act of 1938, required, for the first time, that a drug manufacturer prove the safety of a medication before it could be marketed. Further, the law established ranges of tolerance for unavoidable toxic substances in drugs and strengthened the seizure laws through the use of court injunctions. It also removed an earlier requirement that the FDA prove intent to defraud before actions could be brought in drug mislabeling cases.[2]

A 1951 amendment to the FD&C Act, the Durham-Humphrey Amendment, marked the "official" recognition of prescription drugs as medications that could be dispensed only by the prescription of a licensed practitioner.[3] OTC drugs were formally identified as drugs that were not habit forming, did not have harmful side effects when used according to directions, and did not require professional expertise to be used appropriately.

An even more recent modification of the laws pertaining to the manufacturing of prescription medications was the 1962 Kefauver-Harris Amendment. This legislation required that a manufacturer prove not only the safety of

prescription drugs drugs and medications dispensed by pharmacists on orders from a patient's health care provider

sulfa drugs a general category of sulfonimide-based drugs that produce an antibacterial action

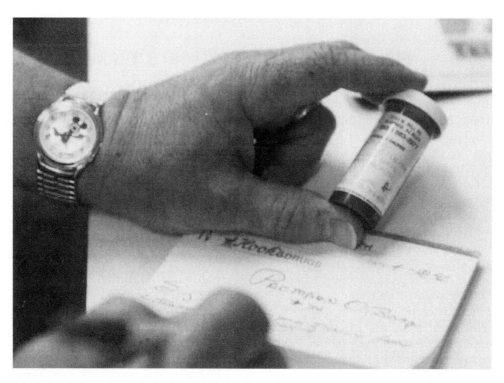

Pharmacists dispense prescriptions on the orders of a patient's physician or dentist.

a drug but also its effectiveness in treating the condition for which it was marketed. Further, the legislation provided for the National Academy of Sciences and the National Research Council to conduct needed reviews of **efficacy** (effectiveness) on a contractual basis. In addition, the Kefauver-Harris Amendment required that the FDA be provided with adverse-reactions reports and that advertisements appearing in medical journals contain complete information regarding the benefits and risks of the drug being advertised.

In more recent years, a variety of acts have been passed to broaden and refine the drug manufacturing process. These laws establish policies regarding orphan drugs (see p. 190), generic drugs, the establishment of drug user fees to pay for additional FDA staff, and various changes in the laws regarding human subjects and in the New Drug Application process. Several of these policies are discussed later in the chapter.

CLASSIFICATION

Although most people will never need more than perhaps a dozen different prescription drugs during their lifetime, more than 2,500 different medications are listed in each annual edition of the *Physicians' Desk Reference for Prescription Drugs (PDR)*, a widely used reference book containing detailed information about each drug.[4] Prescription medications are classified into approximately 170 groups based on their function. The box on this page

---

REPRESENTATIVE CLASSES OF PRESCRIPTION DRUGS

Analgesics	Diuretics
Antacids	Fertility agents
Antibiotics	Gallstone dissolution
Anticoagulants	agents
Antihistamines	Hemorrhoidal
Antimetabolites	preparations
Antiparasitics	Hyperglycemic agents
Bone metabolism	Monoclonal antibodies
regulators	Muscle relaxants
Cardiovascular agents	Ophthalmologics
Central nervous system	Penicillin adjuvants
stimulants	Respiratory stimulants
Contraceptives	Sedatives
Decongestants	Thyroid agents
Diagnostics	Tranquilizers

---

lists 26 representative groups from the PDR's classification scheme. Drugs used to treat depression are discussed in the box on page 185. Also, see the self-assessment on page 186 for help in recognizing the signs of depression.

At any point in time, only about 200 medications make up the bulk of the more than 2 million new and refilled prescriptions ordered annually.[5] Among the most frequently prescribed drugs are those for ulcers, cardiovascular disease, arthritis, anxiety, infectious diseases,

DRUGS IN YOUR WORLD

Drugs and Emotional Health

Depression is by far the most common emotional disorder that occurs among adults. Depression occurs in two forms: *bipolar disorders* (manic-depressive disorders) and *unipolar disorders* (called endogenous, major, or primary depression and exogenous, minor, secondary, or reactive depression).

Unipolar Disorders

Unipolar depression is the more common of the two types. People with unipolar depression enter periods during which they lack motivation and are virtually incapable of, or at least uninterested in, participating in daily activities. Exogenous depression is related to a specific event, such as a divorce or job layoff, and can be treated reasonably well with psychotherapy, sometimes in combination with antidepressant medications. Endogenous depression, on the other hand, is caused by neurological dysfunction. Patients generally do not respond well to psychotherapy if antidepressive medications are not used. This type of depression may result from a genetic predisposition and can be expressed with or without a triggering event. Endogenous depression, therefore, can "run in families" and may occur without warning. It is more common among women.

Bipolar Disorders

Bipolar disorders are characterized by periods of mania, during which the person is highly excited, easily distracted, and very confident, followed by periods of depression, during which the person lacks motivation, withdraws from interpersonal involvement, harbors negative feelings of self-worth, and may even consider suicide. Patients with bipolar disorder have traditionally been treated with the drug lithium, which tends to normalize mood swings more effectively than antidepressants.

Treatment of Depression

The treatment of endogenous or major depression is increasingly based on the use of antidepressant drugs. These drugs affect the action of neurotransmitters responsible for CNS excitation. Interestingly, when taken by people who are not depressed, antidepressants have few or no mood-altering effects.

Types of Antidepressant Medications. There are four main types of antidepressant medications: monoamine oxidase (MAO) inhibitors, trycyclic antidepressants, tetracyclic antidepressants, and the recently introduced serotonin-specific antidepressants, such as Prozac.

The MAO inhibitors, such as Marplan, Nardil, and Parnate, block the activity of monoamine oxidase, an enzyme that breaks down the neurotransmitters serotonin, norepinephrine, and dopamine. The tricyclic antidepressants, such as Tofranil, Janimine, Elavil, and Endep, are believed to interfere with the reuptake of neurotransmitters into the synaptic terminal on the presynaptic side of the synapse. Tetracyclic antidepressants, such as Ludiomil and Asendin, function in a manner similar to that of the tricyclics but have a shorter delay between initial use and evidence of improvement.

Fluoxetine hydrochloride (Prozac), a popular antidepressant drug, is neither a tricyclic nor a tetracyclic, but functions by enhancing the ability of the neurotransmitter serotonin to sustain an excitatory effect at the synapse. Prozac is now among the most frequently prescribed of all medications, attesting to its effectiveness in reversing the symptoms of depression. Early controversy regarding the drug's association with an increased risk of suicide and fetal damage when taken by pregnant women appears to have subsided as reports supporting its safety and effectiveness have accumulated. In addition, previously "off-label" uses of Prozac for the management of obsessive-compulsive disorders and eating disorders have now been approved by the FDA. It has also been used, off-label, as an appetite suppressant in conjunction with weight management efforts.

Prozac is now nearing the end of its patent-protected period of sales. Several slightly different serotonin-specific antidepressants, such as Zoloft, Effexor, and Paxil are already on the market, and generic versions of Prozac will appear as soon as patent protection ends.

and birth control to prevent pregnancies. A list of the top 20 prescription drugs by brand name, based on the number of units sold, is shown in table 11.1.[6] The name of the manufacturer is also given for each drug.

Obviously, there is a significant amount of money to be made in the pharmaceutical field, and drug companies continue experimenting with thousands of chemical compounds each year in search of new marketable products. The nearly $400 million price tag associated with the development of a single new prescription drug must reflect a reasonable chance of finding a financially successful prescription drug.[7]

efficacy the capacity to produce the intended and desired effect or result

SELF-ASSESSMENT

Recognizing Depression

In the scope of adult health problems, depression may be one of the most common conditions that physicians fail to recognize. This may occur because depressed people do not present themselves for evaluation or because symptoms of depression may be masked by, or confused with, symptoms associated with other conditions. Today, this is particularly unfortunate, since depression can be treated with both medications and psychotherapy. Have you experienced any of the following symptoms?

1. Persistent sad moods
2. Feelings of hopelessness or pessimism
3. Loss of interest or pleasure in ordinary activities, including sex
4. Sleep or eating disorders
5. Restlessness, irritability, or fatigue
6. Difficulty concentrating, remembering, or making decisions
7. Thoughts of death or suicide
8. Persistent physical symptoms or pains that do not respond to treatment

If you have experienced any of these symptoms, have you considered seeking the advice of a physician?

TABLE 11.1 The Top 20 Drugs: Drugs Dispensed Most Often in U.S. Community Pharmacies*

1995 Rank	1994 Rank	Product	Company	Total Rxs (000)
1	1	Premarin Tabs	Wyeth-Ayerst	39,125
2	3	Trimox	Apothecan	31,593
3	5	Synthroid	Knoll	26,334
4	2	Amoxil	SK Beecham	25,612
5	4	Zantac	Glaxo Wellcome	25,150
6	6	Lanoxin	Glaxo Wellcome	21,616
7	7	Procardia XL	Pfizer	19,757
8	8	Vasotec	Merck & Co	19,262
9	9	Prozac	Eli Lilly	18,021
10	11	Proventil Aerosol	Schering	15,570
11	10	Cardizem CD	Hoechst Mar R	14,635
12	25	Hydrocodone/APAP	Watson	14,454
13	24	Zoloft	Pfizer	12,951
14	13	Coumadin Tabs	Du Pont Ph	12,589
15	12	Augmentin	SK Beecham	12,222
16	14	Amoxicillin	Biocraft	11,846
17	33	Triamterene w/HCTZ	CibaGeneva	11,581
18	23	Zestril	Zeneca Phrm	11,556
19	30	Acetaminophen w/Codeine	Lemmon	11,069
20	19	Cipro	Bayer Pharm	10,913

Modified from: "The Top 20 Drugs," *American Druggist* 213(2): 18–26, February 1996.

*Total prescriptions (new and refill) 2,140,799 in sample

RESEARCH AND DEVELOPMENT

Each year, drug companies collectively explore the potential of more than 125,000 compounds. Less than 1% of these compounds can be expected to be found suitable for more intense study. Eventually, less than 100 new prescription medications reach the medical marketplace annually.

Pharmaceutical companies must take these drugs through a long, rigorous process before they can be marketed. This process is overseen by the FDA (fig. 11.1). The process of developing a new prescription drug be-

FIGURE 11.1

A significant amount of time, effort, and money is required to develop a new drug for the market.

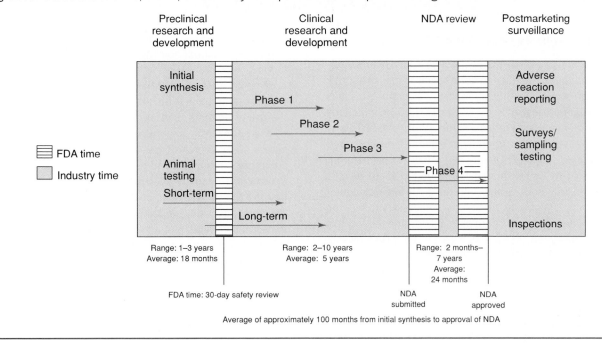

Average of approximately 100 months from initial synthesis to approval of NDA

gins when a pharmaceutical company identifies a compound that has preventive or curative potential. This determination is based on many months of research using cell cultures, laboratory animals (see the box on p. 188), and computer simulations. Upon successful completion of these initial studies, the company must prepare a lengthy preliminary document, called an Investigational New Drug (IND) application, for submission to the FDA. This document requests permission to conduct further studies, including human trials.

Human experimental trials conducted after submitting the IND application are aimed at determining the efficacy of the compound for human subjects (table 11.2). The first phase of these studies, *phase 1*, involves healthy volunteer subjects, often selected from volunteer populations of medical students, the urban poor, or prison inmates. It has recently come to light that some groups of people in past decades took part in human trials without their knowledge or consent. See the box on page 189 for more information.

The second round of human subject studies, *phase 2*, is undertaken on a relatively small number of people who have the condition for which the compound is thought to be effective but who are free from other possible complicating conditions. Phase 3 studies are greatly expanded versions of phase 2 studies, often involving thousands of people for each compound being evaluated.

These clinical trials may last from 2 to 10 years. On completion of *phase 3*, a New Drug Application (NDA)

must be submitted. The FDA has 180 days to review the application and either approve or reject it. Once approved for marketing, a fourth investigational phase, *phase 4*, is begun. In this phase, experiences of clinicians using the drug in their practices are reported to the FDA. During this phase, the FDA monitors clinical reports on long-term complications.

Only through the successful completion of this time-consuming and expensive process can a proposed compound receive approval by the FDA for distribution and sale in the United States as a prescription medication (fig. 11.1). An average of seven years is normally required to complete the development of a marketable prescription drug. For each drug that reaches the market, the manufacturer can expect, on average, approximately 10 years of patent-protected sales in the lucrative prescription medication marketplace. During this time, the drug is protected from competition because it cannot be produced in generic form by another pharmaceutical manufacturer. Although drug patents are in effect for 17 years, approximately 7 of those protected years are used up in the process of clinical trials and other aspects of obtaining FDA approval.[8]

To decrease the time required to move a new drug through the approval process, the FDA has been authorized to charge drug companies fees that are used to hire additional investigators.[9] Any shortening of the time required before a new drug can be marketed will mean a longer period of protected sales for that drug, as well as

WHAT DO YOU THINK?

Should Animals Be Used in Drug Research?

In the quest for new, safe, and effective drugs, pharmaceutical companies conduct extensive research to identify new molecular structures that show medical promise. It has been estimated that only six of the 100,000 compounds examined each year ever reach the marketplace. This is because each drug must undergo extensive research and pass numerous tests for safety and effectiveness before it can be sold for use in humans. The first of these tests is conducted in cell or tissue cultures or through computer simulations. Eventually, though, it is necessary to test the drug on living organisms, and animals become the focus of extensive research. In fact, as a part of the FDA's Investigational New Drug (IND) approval procedure (see p. 187), toxicological studies must be conducted on at least two different species of animals. Usually several hundred rats and mice of both sexes will be used for such studies, but occasionally it is necessary to use other animals, such as chickens, cats, dogs, sheep, pigs, or even primates (monkeys and chimpanzees).

Because of the importance of animals in research, several branches of the federal government, some state governments, and organizations such as the American Association for the Accreditation of Laboratory Animal Care (AAALAC) have issued guidelines for the housing, feeding, handling, veterinary care, and disposal of animals used in pharmaceutical research. In order to monitor compliance with these guidelines, research proposals to federal agencies are carefully reviewed to make certain that the proposed procedures comply with the guidelines. Also, under the guidelines of The Animal Welfare Act of 1966 and its many amendments, the USDA carries out unannounced inspections of animal housing facilities that receive federal funds.

In spite of the scientific community's contention that drug research cannot be successfully undertaken without the use of animals, animal rights activists protest the use of any animals for pharmaceutical and other medical research. They contend that epidemiological databases and computer simulation models are sufficient to adequately determine the safety and effectiveness of new drugs, including the complexities of drug interactions in living organisms. They believe that any use of animals for this purpose is immoral and unnecessary. Perhaps the most familiar of these groups is People for the Ethical Treatment of Animals (PETA). Information about how to contact PETA appears in the Sources for Help list on page 199.

What is your opinion about the use of animals in drug development? Would you feel comfortable using a drug that had not been tested on living organisms? Are there some animals you feel are more appropriate to use in testing than others?

NIH Animal Care and Use Committee, NIH Training Center: *Using Animals in Intramural Research: Guidelines for Investigators* (Washington, D.C.: U.S. Government Printing Office, 1992). U.S. Congress, Office of Technology Assessment: *Alternatives to Animal Use in Research, Testing, and Education,* OTA Pub. No. BA-273 (Washington, D.C.: U.S. Government Printing Office, February 1986). U.S. Department of Health and Human Services, Public Health Service, National Institutes of Health: *Guide for the Care and Use of Laboratory Animals,* NIH Pub. No. 85-23 (Washington, D.C.: U.S. Government Printing Office, Revised 1985).

TABLE 11.2 Investigational Drug Testing in Humans

	Number of Patients	Length	Purpose	Percent of Drugs Successfully Tested*
Phase 1	20–100	Several months	Mainly safety	70
Phase 2	Up to several hundred	Several months to 2 years	Some short-term safety but mainly effectiveness	33
Phase 3	Several hundred to several thousand	1–4 years	Safety, dosage, effectiveness	25–30

Source: "New Drug Development in the United States," in *From Test Tube to Patient: New Drug Development in the United States,* DHHS Pub. No. 95-3168, January, 1995, Food and Drug Administration.

*For example, of 100 drugs for which investigational new drug applications are submitted to FDA, about 70 will successfully complete phase 1 trials and go on to phase 2; about 33 of the original 100 will complete phase 2 and go to phase 3; and 25 to 30 of the original 100 will clear phase 3 (and, on average, about 20 of the original 100 will ultimately be approved for marketing).

DRUGS IN YOUR WORLD

The Use of Human Subjects in Drug Research

During the first half of this century, the use of human subjects to test new drugs, devices, and treatment procedures was, at best, poorly supervised. Frequently, subjects were recruited for studies involving substantial health risks that were known to the researchers but never disclosed to these human "guinea pigs." For example, military personnel were exposed to radiation, chemical poisons designed for drug warfare, and the drug LSD. In the civilian community, African-American men were infected with syphilis in order to study the course of this disease and to test possible treatments. In another study, cancer cells were injected into human subjects to test their immune response. The consequences of some of these early experiments are only now coming to light.

As a result of public outcry over these unethical practices, the federal government formulated regulations to control the use of human subjects in federally funded research. These regulations, which began to appear in the early 1970s, and which are annually disseminated to researchers in the appropriate parts of the Code of Federal Regulations, are now standard procedures and are followed by drug companies and the FDA[a].

Of particular importance are regulations detailing the establishment and function of Institutional Review Boards (IRBs). Any institution that conducts research using human subjects must establish an IRB, whose responsibility is the approval and supervision of human subject research carried out within that institution. Before approving research, the IRB must have proof that the proposed project meets the following rules:

1. Risks to subjects are minimized: first, procedures are used that are consistent with good research design and that do not expose the subjects to unnecessary risks; second, if the subject is a patient, procedures are used that are already being performed on the subject for diagnostic or treatment purposes.
2. Informed consent is obtained and documented from each subject or the subject's legal representative.
3. Selection of subjects is fair and equitable, and there are safeguards to protect subjects, such as the mentally retarded, who may not be able to look out for their own interests.
4. Risks to subjects are reasonable in relation to expected benefits to those subjects and the importance of the knowledge that may be gained.
5. The plan provides for monitoring the data as it is collected to ensure continued safety of the subjects.
6. There are provisions to protect the privacy of subjects and to maintain the confidentiality of the data.[b]

In addition, the IRB will require that researchers give subjects adequate information about the study, answer subjects' questions fully, and allow subjects to withdraw from the study at any time.

Perhaps the most recent concern regarding human subject research has been the inadequate representation of women and children as research subjects. Critics point out that many drugs used in the treatment of women were developed using relatively few women as subjects or using only women beyond childbearing years as subjects. In response to these concerns, renewed consideration is being given to the use of greater numbers of women, women of childbearing age, and even, in some cases, pregnant women. An initial response to these concerns regarding female representation occurred in July 1993, when the FDA lifted many of the age restrictions on the use of female subjects.

In regard to the expanded use of children in clinical trials, the FDA has moved more cautiously. In 1994, new rules were published regarding the appropriate use of the term *pediatric use* as it currently appears on drugs that were tested almost exclusively on adults. This new rule allows the FDA to request pediatric-specific information, although this information is most likely based on experience rather than on carefully controlled studies using children. The formulation of specific policies and guidelines that will expand the use of children in clinical trials is currently being reviewed by the FDA in cooperation with the National Institute of Child Health and Human Development.[c]

[a]Office of the Federal Register, National Archives and Records Administration, *1992 Code of Federal Regulations (CFR), Foods and Drugs,* parts 1–99 (21), Revised April 1 (Washington, D.C.: U.S. Government Printing Office, 1992).

[b]"Protecting 'Human Guinea Pigs'," *From Test Tube to Patient: New Drug Development in the United States,* DHHS Pub. No. 95-3168 (Washington, D.C.: Food and Drug Administration, January, 1995).

[c]"Why FDA is Encouraging Drug Testing in Children," in *From Test Tube to Patient: New Drug Development in the United States,* DHHS Pub. No. 95-3168 (Washington, D.C.: Food and Drug Administration, January, 1995).

WHAT DO YOU THINK?

Are Drug Companies Wining and Dining Physicians Too Much?

How does your physician learn about the availability of new prescription medications? Traditionally, medical doctors learned about new pharmaceutical products through pharmaceutical sales representatives, who routinely make calls at physicians' offices. During these visits, new products are explained in detail and samples are left for use by the physicians. These same sales representatives also schedule visits to hospitals, where they display their newest medications, often near the physicians' lounge. Another way physicians learn about new prescription drugs is through attractive full-page advertisements in well-known medical journals, such as the *Journal of the American Medical Association (JAMA)* and the *New England Journal of Medicine.* These advertisements are designed not only to catch the physician's eye, but also to educate him or her about the medication, perhaps reinforcing the message provided by sales representatives. However, some concern exists about the accuracy of these advertisements. Finally, physicians learn about newly available medications by visiting drug company displays at national professional meetings.

Although all of the previously mentioned advertising techniques are considered ethical and professional, newer approaches to marketing have raised serious concerns about their appropriateness. Included among these newer approaches are the sponsorship of "dinner symposiums"

for which physicians are paid an "honorarium" to attend a professional presentation and have dinner courtesy of a drug company; the underwriting of costs of Continuing Medical Education (CME) courses by drug companies; and the sponsorship by drug companies of "grand rounds" for residents and medical students, in which well-recognized experts detail the treatments (and medications) that they use. While these activities appear to be primarily educational, they have also proven to be effective marketing tools for the drug companies.

In addition to the newer marketing strategies described, the pharmaceutical industry has also begun to advertise prescription medication directly to consumers through the placement of expensive advertisements in popular magazines or on television. Through advertisements, consumers are made aware of new products. Most recently, detailed information about prescription medications is being sent through the mail to individuals at their residences. The intent of these practices is to inform consumers about a new product so that the consumer will prod his or her physician to prescribe the product.

How do you feel about the practice of drug companies treating physicians to meals or vacations as an enticement to try their products? How do you feel about the practice of marketing prescription drugs to physicians indirectly by directing advertisements at their patients?

being beneficial to patients. The debate about the marketing practices used by pharmaceutical companies is addressed in the box above.

Approval of Experimental Drugs

Pressure by AIDS activists for effective medications to fight AIDS has moved the FDA to speed up the process for bringing new prescription medications to the marketplace (see the box on p. 191). Rule changes made in 1987 have allowed experimental drugs for terminal illnesses, such as AIDS, Alzheimer's disease, and certain forms of cancer, to be more widely and quickly available than they would have been under the above-mentioned schedule. American drug companies are being allowed by the FDA to market drugs in foreign countries now before the drugs are approved for sale in the United States.

Orphan Drugs

Another important change in the U.S. drug laws occurred in 1983, when Congress passed the Orphan Drug Law.[10]

This law has enabled drug companies to develop and market drugs for rare diseases—ones that affect less than 200,000 Americans. It is not normally profitable for companies to market drugs for rare diseases because sales are correspondingly low. The Orphan Drug Law made available certain financial incentives to manufacturers willing to develop these "unwanted" or "orphan" drugs. Examples of drugs that fall into this category are the AIDS drug AZT; a drug used to treat severe combined immunodeficiency (SCID); and DDI, DDC, and paclitaxel (Taxol) for the treatment of ovarian cancer. To date, 108 new orphan drugs have been developed under the Orphan Drug Law.[11]

FACTORS INFLUENCING EFFECTIVENESS

In spite of the careful research and development associated with prescription medications and the reasonably faithful compliance of most patients, the effectiveness of

DRUGS IN YOUR WORLD

Medications for the Treatment of HIV/AIDS

Since the first appearance of HIV/AIDS in 1981, the American (and international) pharmaceutical industry has labored to develop medications that are effective in stopping (or slowing) the disease. Several medications, generally used in combination, have now been approved for use. Unfortunately, none has been found capable of completely stopping the progression of the disease, and most eventually lose their effectiveness as the HIV organism mutates into less susceptible forms.

Nucleoside Analogs

The first antiviral medication approved for use in treating HIV/AIDS was zidovudine, Retrovir, or more commonly, AZT. This drug functions by inhibiting replication of the HIV virus by incorporating its DNA by viral reverse transcriptase, thus altering the DNA and depriving the virus of its ability to enter not-yet-infected immune system cells. Use of AZT as a single treatment modality has been found to slow the progression of the illness by reducing the likelihood of developing opportunistic infection, but it has not been found to extend life expectancy. Further, use of AZT is associated with a wide array of side effects, including muscle loss, anemia, white cell depression, and many uncomfortable but less serious adverse reactions.

Following the development of AZT, additional nucleoside-analog type medications became available. Among these are ddI (didanosine, Videx), ddC (zalcitabine, Hivid), d4T (stavudine, Zerit), and 3TC (lamivudine, Epivir). The first two of these medications, ddI and ddC, have been found to be most effective when used in combination with AZT in patients who have not previously used AZT or in patients who used only ddI or ddC. Both drugs, like AZT, produce a number of side effects. These include stomach pain, diarrhea, and pancreatitis when used with ddI, and changes in nerve innervation to the extremities (peripheral neuropathy) when used with ddC.

The third nucleoside analog, d4T, is more often used as an alternative to AZT in patients who cannot take AZT or have developed a resistance to it. Occasionally, d4T is combined with the fourth drug, 3TC, for AZT-resistant people. Like ddC, peripheral neuropathy has been reported in pa-

tients who used d4T. Clearly, this drug is not only capable of slowing the decline of T-cell levels in the blood associated with AIDS but has also been associated with the return of T-cell counts to higher levels than those that existed at the time treatment began.

The fourth drug in the AZT-related family is 3TC. When combined with AZT, this medication has been shown to significantly increase T-cell count and to reduce the amount of HIV in the blood. The drug is also used in patients who have already begun AZT-ddI or AZT-ddC use. Side effects associated with 3TC resemble a combination of those seen with AZT and ddI.

Protease Inhibitors

The most recent type of medication approved for use in treating HIV/AIDS is the protease inhibitors. Drugs in this category, saquinavir (Invirase), ritonavir (Norvir, ABT-538), and indinavir (Crixivan, MK-669), block the activity of protease, an enzyme necessary for HIV to infect immune system cells. In patients treated with these drugs, HIV replication is altered, resulting in an HIV that is incapable of invading T-cells. Studies of protease inhibitors suggest that these drugs both improve T-cell count (even when initially as low as zero) and lower the level of HIV in the blood. When combined with nucleoside analogs, particularly AZT and 3TC, large reductions in blood HIV levels are noted. Unfortunately, recent studies also report that HIV can develop resistance to the protease inhibitors, making it important that they be used in the most effective manner possible.

Because long-term use of the protease inhibitors (alone or in combination) has not occurred, the side effects of their use over time are not known. It is known that with short-term use these drugs produce, in addition to resistance, relatively fewer of the side effects seen with the nucleoside analogs. However, while saquinavir produces only slight gastrointestinal side effects, ritonavir may influence liver enzymes slightly, and indinavir use may be associated with kidney stone development in a small percentage of users. Regardless, the protease inhibitors hold promise for extending the life expectancy of HIV/AIDS-infected people.

these medications may vary from person to person and day to day, depending on the user factors discussed in chapter 4. These factors include the age, sex, and physiological condition of the patient. For example, pregnancy, nutritional status, body weight, and percentage of body fat can influence the effectiveness of a drug. Individual differences in sensitivity to certain compounds,

illnesses, and the taking of concurrent medications can also affect the action of prescription medications and can sometimes lead to adverse reactions.

In addition to the factors that influence drug effectiveness already mentioned, *compliance*, or the patient's willingness and ability to take medication in the prescribed manner, also influences the effectiveness of medication-based treatment. When patients are *noncompliant*, they fail to follow directions related to the appropriate medication use or, in some cases, they simply stop using the medication that has been prescribed to them.

Noncompliance may take one of two basic forms, depending on the patient involved. *Intentional noncompliance* generally occurs when a patient either stops taking a medication or in some fashion alters the dosage-related directions that they have been given. This willful failure to follow the physician's direction is, however, ultimately thought by the patient to be "rational" in that he or she "knew" or "felt" that the medication was not working properly or that it was no longer needed. A physician is particularly likely to see intentional noncompliance in an older patient who seems to "know the body" under certain circumstances better than the physician.

The second form of noncompliance is the more familiar *unintentional noncompliance* in which the patient discontinues or alters medication use in a way that detracts from the effectiveness of treatment. This form of noncompliance is caused by misunderstood directions from the physician, absence of trust in the physician, difficulty in opening childproof containers, lack of transportation to the pharmacy, or the inability to pay for the medication prescribed. In this form of noncompliance, the physician or pharmacist could have assisted the patient had they been made aware of the situation. Note that this form of noncompliance may occur because of the inability or unwillingness of the physician or pharmacist to communicate effectively with the patient.[12]

Adverse Reactions

Adverse reactions to prescription drugs can occur for a variety of reasons.[13] Pharmacological reactions to a drug occur when some property of the drug is incompatible with a patient's disease. These are also known as *toxic reactions.* For example, vaginal yeast infections, if mistakenly identified as vaginitis caused by other organisms, may be worsened by the use of wide-spectrum antibiotics, which disrupt the microbial balance of the area, leading to an environment favorable to a secondary infection.

A second kind of adverse reaction is an *allergic reaction.* An allergic reaction may occur as a result of an unexpected immune response to a drug. These reactions may take the form of anaphylaxis (an acute, potentially fatal, overwhelming sensitivity response of the airways), **serum sickness,** tissue reactions (such as an increase in blood pressure), skin reactions (such as a rash), fever, or a combination of these reactions. Such an allergic reaction is seen when a person with no previous history of asthma develops a hypersensitivity to aspirin and experiences an asthma attack upon a second use of this common OTC analgesic.

The last of the adverse reactions to prescription drugs are classified as drug interactions, which were first discussed in chapter 4. In these reactions, two or more medications taken at the same time interact to cause an adverse or unwanted effect. This can occur when one drug alters another drug or the physiological process associated with it. An example of a drug interaction is when an acetylcholinesterase inhibitor, being taken to control hypertension (high blood pressure), reacts with an NSAID (nonsteroidal anti-inflammatory drug), such as ibuprofen, in a manner that reduces the effectiveness of the antihypertensive drug. Although it is impossible to prevent all of the adverse drug reactions that can occur, careful cooperation between physicians and patients can minimize these reactions. Clearly, it is important that patients be prepared with questions about prescription medications (see the self-assessment box on p. 193).

In addition, people may experience one or more other unexpected reactions to prescription medications. These general responses, such as weight gain when using steroid-based medication and mouth dryness with some antidepressants, are referred to as **side effects.** In most cases, side effects are anticipated and thus are discussed on the drug information sheets provided by pharmacies. In other cases, of course, highly unusual, unanticipated responses occur. In such cases, the person having the adverse reaction should consult a physician immediately or if necessary seek emergency care.

Placebo Effect

A **placebo** is a chemically inactive substance that, when given in place of an active ingredient, occasionally elicits physiological responses in the same manner as the active ingredient. This ability of inert materials to perform as if they were medically active is called the **placebo effect.**

The use of placebos in vaccine and drug trials is very important. For a particular drug to be deemed effective, it must not only perform better than no treatment, but it must also perform better and more consistently than a placebo, or blank treatment. For example, in a drug trial some test subjects receive a yellow pill containing the actual test drug, whereas other subjects receive an identical-looking yellow pill that does not contain the drug. If the experiment is carried out correctly, neither the subjects nor the scientists reading the results know which subjects received the actual drug treatment and which received the placebo until after the conclusion of the trials. This *double-blind trial* is a standard method used to determine whether a test drug actually performs better than a placebo.

The use of placebos in drug trials also assures researchers that observed results are a result of the active ingredient and not the process of applying the medication or otherwise handling the research subjects. Pla-

SELF-ASSESSMENT

Should I Have This Prescription Filled?

The cost of prescription medications is a significant expense in the management of many illnesses. In this regard, patients may have a valid reason to question physicians and pharmacists regarding the prescriptions they are given. Have you ever asked any of the following questions in an attempt to reduce the medication-related costs associated with a particular diagnosis?

1. Is this the most frequently prescribed medication for my condition, or are there other medications that are effective? Would any of the latter be less costly? Am I purposely not being placed on an effective medication because of its high cost?
2. Is the regimen to be followed more extensive than that usually prescribed?
3. If I can find this medication available locally for less than your pharmacy charges, will your pharmacy match that pharmacy's price?
4. Is this drug available in a generic form? Have you written the prescription so that the generic equivalent can be substituted?
5. Is there a nondrug approach to managing this condition that you have not yet discussed with me?
6. Is the cost of the prescribed drug high enough to warrant spending the time and money required to get a second opinion?

7. If a reformulation of this prescription medication is available as an OTC product, could I be adequately helped by using the OTC version rather than the prescription medication?

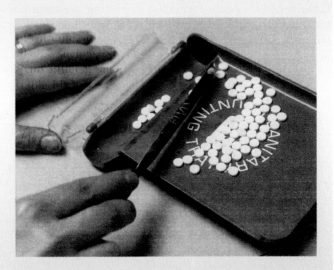

The decision to have a prescription filled rests with the patient.

---

cebos produce the anticipated effects in some patients even though they contain no active ingredients.

An explanation of the placebo effect cannot be given with certainty. Some believe the effect is the result of conditioned responses of users, brought about by past experiences or by the anticipation of changes that have been described by others. Regardless, the effects are quite real for those who experience them, and sometimes these effects can even be measured physiologically.

CONSUMERS AND PRESCRIPTION DRUGS

People taking prescription drugs are consumers of some of the most costly and dangerous products encountered in the health care field. Accordingly, it is important to understand why these drugs have been prescribed and how they are to be used.

The Prescription

A **prescription** conveys instructions from a physician or other health care provider to a pharmacist regarding the dispensing of a prescription medication. Most prescriptions include terms that are highly abbreviated and

serum sickness a hypersensitivity reaction to a foreign protein

side effects undesirable effects caused by prescription medications or other drugs

placebo a medically inert substance formulated to mimic the appearance of an active substance

placebo effect psychological and physiological effects associated with the patient's expectations about a drug

prescription written instructions (using abbreviated Latin symbols) from a health care provider to a pharmacist regarding the dispensing of a prescription medication written in Latin. Table 11.3 lists some instructions frequently used by physicians. Clearly, the use of these terms in prescriptions restricts the average citizen from easily interpreting them. Whether this traditional method of providing instructions on prescription forms will someday be replaced by a simpler method remains to be seen.

Package Inserts

Considerably more information regarding prescription medications is available from manufacturers' inserts than from information provided by physicians. Unlike those

for many OTC drugs, these inserts do not routinely accompany individual prescriptions.

Inserts such as that shown in figure 11.2 can generally be obtained from pharmacists on request. Even more detailed descriptions of prescription medications are available in the *PDR*, which can be found in bookstores and libraries.

Generic versus Brand Name Drugs

When a new prescription drug is ready for the marketplace, it carries three names: a chemical name, a generic name (usually an abbreviated form of the chemical

TABLE 11.3 Common Latin Inscriptions

Latin Word or Phrase	Latin Abbreviation	English Meaning
Ad libitum	*ad lib*	Freely, as needed
Ante cibum	*a.c.*	Before meals
Bis in die	*b.i.d.*	Twice a day
Capsula	*cap.*	Capsule
Dispensa	*disp.*	Dispense
Gutta	*gt.*	Drop
Hora somni	*h.s.*	At bedtime
Per os	*P.O.*	By mouth
Quaque 4 hora (a.4h)	*q.4h.*	Every four hours
Quater in die	*q.i.d.*	Four times a day
Signa	*Sig.*	Written on label
Ter in die	*t.i.d.*	Three times a day
Ut dictum	*ut dict. or u.d.*	As directed

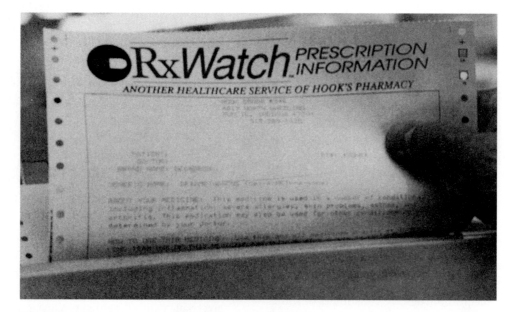

Computerized systems such as this one assist pharmacists in detecting potential problems with prescription drug interactions in patients.

FIGURE 11.2

Package inserts, available from pharmacists, provide detailed information about prescription drugs.

Brand name ——— **CARAFATE® Tablets**
Generic name ——— **(sucralfate)**

INDICATIONS AND USAGE
CARAFATE® (sucralfate) is indicated in
1 Short-term treatment (up to 8 weeks) of active duodenal ulcer While healing with sucralfate may occur during the first week or two, treatment should be continued for 4 to 8 weeks unless healing has been demonstrated by x-ray or endoscopic examination
2 Maintenance therapy for duodenal ulcer patients at reduced dosage after healing of acute ulcers

No conditions are believed to exist that would prevent use of this product
CONTRAINDICATIONS
There are no known contraindications to the use of sucralfate

Limitation of effectiveness ———
PRECAUTIONS
Duodenal ulcer is a chronic, recurrent disease. While short-term treatment with sucralfate can result in complete healing of the ulcer, a successful course of treatment with sucralfate should not be expected to alter the post-healing frequency or severity of duodenal ulceration
Special Populations: Chronic Renal Failure and Dialysis Patients: When sucralfate is administered orally, small amounts of aluminum are absorbed from the gastrointestinal tract Concomitant use of sucralfate with other products that contain aluminum, such as aluminum-containing antacids, may increase the total body burden of aluminum. Patients with normal renal function receiving the recommended doses of sucralfate and aluminum-containing products adequately excrete aluminum in the urine. Patients with chronic renal failure or those receiving dialysis have impaired excretion of absorbed aluminum. In addition, aluminum does not cross dialysis membranes because it is bound to albumin and transferrin plasma proteins. Aluminum accumulation and toxicity (aluminum osteodystrophy, osteomalacia, encephalopathy) have been described in patients with renal impairment. Sucralfate should be used with caution in patients with chronic renal failure

Medications whose effectiveness is lowered when taken in combination with this product
Drug Interactions: Some studies have shown that simultaneous sucralfate administration in healthy volunteers reduced the extent of absorption (bioavailability) of single doses of the following drugs cimetidine, ciprofloxacin, digoxin, norfloxacin, phenytoin, ranitidine, tetracycline, and theophylline. The mechanism of these interactions appears to be nonsystemic in nature, presumably resulting from sucralfate binding to the concomitant agent in the gastrointestinal tract In all cases studied to date (cimetidine, ciprofloxacin, digoxin and ranitidine), dosing the concomitant medication 2 hours before sucralfate eliminated the interaction Because of the potential of CARAFATE to alter the absorption of some drugs, CARAFATE should be administered separately from other drugs when alterations in bioavailability are felt to be critical In these cases, patients should be monitored appropriately.

Based on animal studies, this product is not known to stimulate formation of cancer or genetic mutations, nor does it impair fertility
Carcinogenesis, Mutagenesis, Impairment of Fertility: Chronic oral toxicity studies of 24 months' duration were conducted in mice and rats at doses up to 1 gm/kg (12 times the human dose) There was no evidence of drug-related tumorigenicity A reproduction study in rats at doses up to 38 times the human dose did not reveal any indication of fertility impairment Mutagenicity studies were not conducted
Pregnancy: Teratogenic effects. Pregnancy Category B. Teratogenicity studies have been performed in mice, rats, and rabbits at doses up to 50 times the human dose and have revealed no evidence of harm to the fetus due to sucralfate. There are, however, no adequate and well-controlled studies in pregnant women. Because animal reproduction studies are not always predictive of human response this drug should be used during pregnancy only if clearly needed

Limitation on product's use ———
Nursing Mothers: It is not known whether this drug is excreted in human milk. Because many drugs are excreted in human milk, caution should be exercised when sucralfate is administered to a nursing woman

Caution when being considered for use with children
Pediatric Use: Safety and effectiveness in children have not been established

Side effects ———
ADVERSE REACTIONS
Adverse reactions to sucralfate in clinical trials were minor and only rarely led to discontinuation of the drug In studies involving over 2700 patients treated with sucralfate tablets, adverse effects were reported in 129 (4.7%)
Constipation was the most frequent complaint (2%) Other adverse effects reported in less than 0.5% of the patients are listed below by body system
Gastrointestinal: diarrhea, nausea, vomiting, gastric discomfort, indigestion, flatulence, dry mouth
Dermatological: pruritus, rash
Nervous system: dizziness, sleepiness, vertigo
Other: back pain, headache

OVERDOSAGE
There is no experience in humans with overdosage Acute oral toxicity studies in animals, however, using doses up to 12 gm/kg body weight, could not find a lethal dose Risks associated with overdosage should, therefore, be minimal

Recommended dosage ———
DOSAGE AND ADMINISTRATION
Active Duodenal Ulcer: The recommended adult oral dosage for duodenal ulcer is 1 gm four times a day on an empty stomach
Antacids may be prescribed as needed for relief of pain but should not be taken within one-half hour before or after sucralfate
While healing with sucralfate may occur during the first week or two, treatment should be continued for 4 to 8 weeks unless healing has been demonstrated by x-ray or endoscopic examination
Maintenance Therapy: The recommended adult oral dosage is 1 gm twice a day

Packaging ———
HOW SUPPLIED
CARAFATE (sucralfate) 1-gm tablets are supplied in bottles of 100 (NDC 0088-1712-47) 120 (NDC 0088-1712-53) and 500 (NDC 0088-1712-55) and in Unit Dose Identification Paks of 100 (NDC 0088-1712-49) Light pink scored oblong tablets are embossed with CARAFATE on one side and 1712 bracketed by C s on the other
Issued 4/90

Manufacturer ——— MARION MERRELL DOW INC.
KANSAS CITY, MO 64114

name), and a brand name under which it will be marketed. During the remainder of the patent period, the **brand name drug,** or **pioneer drug,** will be protected from competition because competing pharmaceutical companies are not permitted to sell drugs with the same chemical formula. When the patent period expires, however, competing drug companies can manufacture and sell chemical and therapeutic equivalents of the pioneer drug. These chemical- and therapeutic-equivalent drugs are known as **generic drugs.**

The role of generic drugs in the practice of medicine has increased steadily since Congress passed the 1984 Drug Price Competition and Patent Term Restoration Act. Since 1984, an average of 15 pioneer drugs a year have lost their patent protection; however, this average should increase rapidly, since nearly 200 pioneer drugs are now nearing the end of their protected sales period. These drugs, too, will encounter stiff competition from generic counterparts. In 1992, it was estimated that by 1995 generic drug sales would approach $15 billion annually. To date, sales figures to substantiate that estimate are not available. Since FDA regulations ensuring equivalency were strengthened in 1990, patients routinely insist on purchasing the considerably less expensive generic drugs rather than brand name drugs, and physicians feel increasingly more comfortable prescribing generics. The reasons for the high cost of brand name drugs are discussed in the box on page 197.

To be approved for marketing, generic drugs must be the bioequivalent of the pioneer drugs that they will compete against. To achieve bioequivalency, generics must have the same **bioavailability** as pioneer drugs. Bioavailability refers to the speed and extent of absorption of biologically active molecules, and thus the amount of active ingredients reaching the bloodstream for distribution to the target sites of action (see chapter 4). In addition to bioavailability, **bioequivalence** requires that generic drugs, once they reach their target sites, exert their active effects with the same speed as pioneer drugs. It should be noted, however, that FDA regulations allow slight variations in the speed of absorption between the generic drugs and their equivalent pioneer drugs, as long as the labels of the generics state that difference in absorbency exists.[14] This latter characteristic imparts therapeutic equivalence to generic drugs. When **therapeutic equivalence** is achieved, approval for marketing is granted.[15]

Since 1990, the approval process for generic drugs has become more rigorous. The following summarizes this process:

During inspections, the FDA reviews the step-by-step manufacturing process and monitors how much and what kind of active ingredients, excipients (material added to make the product a suitable consistency), flavorings, and other substances will be used. Sponsors must even identify the type of machinery that will be used in each step of the manufacturing process. Just as it does with brand name drugs, the agency closely regulates generic makers' production sites and blocks the marketing of any drugs produced in substandard facilities. Agency inspectors also review on-site production records, examine exhibit batches, and determine whether the plant is capable of producing the drug properly.[16]

Samples are taken on a regular basis and tested to determine whether the generic drug complies with standards of potency, dissolution, content uniformity, product identification, moisture content, and purity. Currently, the FDA approves approximately 250 generic drugs annually.[17]

Misuse of Prescription Drugs

According to some estimates, half of the 1.7 billion medicines prescribed annually are taken improperly. This misuse of prescription drugs results in many unnecessary illnesses and deaths. It is estimated that 10% of all hospital admissions are related to the misuse of prescribed medications. The most common misuses are taking too much or too little medicine, stopping medication use before indicated, and simply not taking the prescribed medicine at all.

One segment of the population that is at increased risk for the misuse of prescription medications is the elderly, particularly the "older elderly," those people 75 years of age or older. As these elderly adults age, they often develop multiple illnesses and sometimes come under the care of more than one physician. It is not unusual, in fact, for the typical older elderly person to have four or five different diagnosed illnesses and to be taking eight to twelve different medications that were prescribed by several different physicians. Too frequently, one physician is unaware of the prescriptions written by another for his or her patient.

Complicating this **polypharmacy** is the fact that many seniors also take several OTC drugs, food supplements, and even home remedies. Because physicians do not always ask about these other drugs, they are often unaware of the extent of their use.

Further complicating polypharmacy among the older elderly population is the nature of pharmacokinetics in an aging body. Aging alters the body's metabolism such that absorption, distribution, biotransformation reactions, and excretion occur at different rates than they do in younger adults. One result is that drug-induced confusion and depression can occur, causing these elderly people to miss doses, take extra doses, or otherwise misuse their medication. Pharmacists, physicians, and nurses should be ready to assist the elderly in determining whether any of their medications is contraindicated and whether each of their medications is necessary.

The successful use of prescription medications is a cooperative effort between health care providers and pa-

What Do You Think?

Is the Cost of Prescription Drugs Too High?

One of the most frequently heard complaints regarding the high cost of health care in this country is about the exorbitant prices of prescription medications. In comparison, a prescription that costs $10.00 in the United States would cost $6.16 in Canada, $4.80 in the United Kingdom, $2.44 in France, and only $2.34 in Spain. Since 1980, drug prices in the United States have increased nearly 130%, with only 22% of the increase related to inflation.

Many consumers believe that the explanation for these price increases is simple—drug companies make huge profits and pay high dividends to their stockholders. Consumer groups support this contention by pointing out that the 3.2% average profit earned by Fortune 500 companies pales in comparison to the 12% to 15% profit range enjoyed by the prescription drug industry. In the opinion of these consumer groups, only strong action on the part of the public, health care providers, or the government will force prices down to the point where most people will be able to afford their prescription medications.

In response to the charges levied by consumers, drug companies contend that large profit margins on prescription drugs are necessary in order to pay for the substantial costs associated with research, including the research done on formulations that never reach the marketplace. Opponents argue that some of the research is funded by government grants. Further, research and development ac-count for only about 15% of the retail cost of drugs. In fact, approximately 30% of the cost of drugs can be attributed to marketing and advertising, including expensive dinners for physicians, continuing education seminars of questionable scientific objectivity, and other incentives for those who prescribe drugs. Much of the remaining portion of the price, after production costs, goes into the profits earned by the drug companies and their stockholders.

Drug companies are now beginning to alter their pricing policies in an attempt to forestall some type of government-mandated price control and to avoid confrontation with well-organized consumer groups. Some companies are even giving drugs free to people without health insurance. Drug companies are also stepping up their efforts to educate the American public about the value of prescription drugs. One approach has been to claim that the cost of prescription drugs is justifiable because of the long-range savings that are provided when the need for surgery or more expensive treatment is avoided.

A second explanation for the high cost of prescription drugs is that drug companies need money to fight liability suits filed by consumers. As was the case with Eli Lilly and Company's antidepressant Prozac, these suits can be both expensive and time-consuming to defend.

What are your feelings about these issues? In your opinion, is prescription medication too expensive? Who, if anyone, is at fault?

tients. Poor judgment based on misinformation can have serious consequences for all. The following list contains several precautions for people who use prescription medications:

1. Take the exact amount of the drug prescribed, and follow the dosage schedule as closely as possible.
2. Never take drugs prescribed for a friend or relative, even though your symptoms may be similar.
3. Always tell your physician about past problems with drugs. Keep a record of any drug allergies you have or may have had in the past.
4. Keep a daily record of all medications you are taking. Tell your physician about all other prescription and nonprescription (OTC) drugs you use.
5. Make sure you understand all the directions printed on the drug container. If you have a vision problem, ask the pharmacist to use large type.
6. Discuss any possible side effects with your health

brand name drug (pioneer drug) another term for the original patent-protected drug

generic drugs drugs that are the chemical and biological equivalents of brand name drugs but are sold under the common chemical name

bioavailability the extent to which biologically active molecules are absorbed and distributed to the target site

bioequivalence the extent to which biologically active molecules enter cells, where they exert their effects

therapeutic equivalence the extent to which biologically active molecules produce the equivalent effect on cell function

polypharmacy the use of multiple prescription medications, as well as OTC and dietary supplements, for the treatment of various health problems that exist at the same time

care provider. Find out if there are any reactions that you should report quickly. Ask whether the drug will interfere with any specific type of OTC medication you take, such as aspirin.

7. Store all drugs in a cool, dry place. The bathroom medicine cabinet is often too warm and humid for proper storage. Be sure to store drugs where children cannot get into them. Always keep drugs in their original containers.
8. Ask your physician or pharmacist about the special storage requirements of each medicine; for example, ask whether a medicine must be refrigerated.
9. Ask when the drug should be taken in relation to eating or drinking. Find out whether the medication can be taken on an empty stomach or with alcohol.
10. Never take a prescription drug in the dark. Turn on a room light to be certain you are taking the correct drug in the proper dose.
11. Dispose of all medicines you no longer need or use by flushing them down the toilet.
12. Ask whether a generic drug can be prescribed instead of a brand name.

Maximum effectiveness is possible when medications are (a) prescribed by experienced physicians who are fully informed of their patients' medical histories, (b) properly labeled and dispensed by pharmacists, and (c) carefully used by patients who communicate well with their health care providers and comply with carefully stated directions. To assist patients in proper use, pharmacists often apply precautionary labels to drug containers.

SUMMARY

At some time during their lives, most people will need to use a prescription medication. These drugs are prescribed by a variety of health care providers. Unlike over-the-counter drugs, which primarily relieve the symptoms of illness, prescription medications are often designed to actually cure illness. More than 2,500 prescription drugs are in use today and are classified into 170 groups on the basis of function. In 1995, 2,140,799 prescriptions were filled (or refilled).

The research and development of a new prescription drug is a time-consuming and costly undertaking. In accordance with FDA policies, drug companies conduct a variety of animal and computer-simulated trials and carefully controlled human trials before marketing a new drug. For a drug to be proved effective, it must perform better than a placebo. It takes approximately seven years to bring a drug to market. Efforts have been successful in shortening the time required to approve drugs to treat certain life-threatening illnesses. Drug companies have been given new government incentives to develop and

market orphan drugs. In addition, a new fee schedule developed by the FDA will add staff to speed the approval of all prescription medications.

The effectiveness of drugs can vary depending on the physical and psychological status of the user. In addition, several types of adverse reactions can occur. For various reasons, some people use medication in a noncompliant manner that can compromise safety and effectiveness.

Generic drugs are less expensive alternatives to pioneer, or brand name, drugs. The unique "language" physicians use in writing prescriptions is understood and honored by pharmacists.

Misuse of prescription drugs is common in the United States. Particularly among the elderly, the use of several prescription medications in addition to OTC drugs and dietary supplements leads to the existence of polypharmacy. The safe use of prescription medications requires the cooperation of the health care provider, pharmacist, and patient. Instructions for safe drug taking and precautionary labels are available from pharmacists.

REVIEW QUESTIONS

1. Describe the differences between prescription drugs and OTC drugs. What has generally happened when a prescription drug appears in the marketplace as an OTC medication?
2. Describe the steps required in the development of a new prescription drug before an NDA is approved by the FDA. What is meant when a prescription drug is said to be under "patent protection"?
3. Under what circumstances can a new prescription medication be made available to patients more quickly than normal? What is an orphan drug, and how does the FDA support its development?
4. What factors account for the fact that some prescription medications work differently for some people than for others? What is a placebo?
5. What information is included in a prescription that a physician (or dentist) writes to a pharmacist? What are some of the more familiar Latin abbreviations used in medicine and pharmacy?
6. What is a generic drug? In what ways are generic and brand name drugs different? In what ways are they similar? How can a generic drug be classified as being the bioequivalent of its pioneer counterpart when it is technically not?
7. Beyond the interaction of the several drugs being used, what other factors can complicate the polypharmacy observed in a large segment of the elderly population?
8. Drug safety is a concern of health care providers, pharmacists, and the general public. What can patients do to ensure that they use prescription medications safely?

REFERENCES

1. E. F. Cafruny, "Drugs," in *The World Book Encyclopedia* (Chicago: World Book, 1986).
2. "New Drug Development in the United States," in *From Test Tube to Patient: New Drug Development in the United States*, DHHS Pub. No. 95-3168, January, 1995, Food and Drug Administration.
3. *Milestones in U.S. Food and Drug Law History*, HHS Pub. No. (FDA) 85-1063 (Washington, D.C.: U.S. Government Printing Office, 1985).
4. *Physicians' Desk Reference*, 51st ed. (Montvale, N.J.: Medical Economics Data Production, 1997).
5. "The Top 200 Drugs," *American Druggist* 213, no. 2 (February, 1996):18–26.
6. Ibid.
7. "Drug Development Costs," *PhRMA Facts*, (February 1996).
8. "New Drug Development in the United States," in *Benefits vs. Risks: How FDA Approves New Drugs*, DHHS Pub. No. 95-3168, January, 1995, Food and Drug Administration.
9. "New Drug Development in the United States," in *FDA Finds New Ways to Speed Treatments to Patients*, DHHS Pub. No. 95-3168, January, 1995, Food and Drug Administration.
10. "New Drug Development in the United States," in *Orphan Products: New Hope for People with Rare Disorders*, DHHS Pub. No. 95-3168, January, 1995, Food and Drug Administration.
11. Office of Orphan Products Development, Food and Drug Administration, Telephone Interview, 21 October, 1996.
12. A. F. Ferrini, and R. L. Ferrini, *Health in the Later Years* (Madison, Wis.: Brown & Benchmark Publishers, 1997).
13. B. L. MacDermott, and J. H. Deglin, *Understanding Basic Pharmacology: Practical Approaches for Effective Application* (Philadelphia: F. A. Davis Company, 1994).
14. "New Drug Development in the United States," in *FDA Ensures Equivalence of Generic Drugs*, DHHS Pub. No. 95-3168, January, 1995, Food and Drug Administration.
15. Ibid.
16. "New Drug Development."
17. Ibid.

SOURCES FOR HELP

Contact Information Regarding Clinical Trials and Other Drug-Related Questions

In many cases, the following phone numbers will function as initial contact points for beginning a more focused search for researchers and clinical trial locations. It should be noted that the FDA is prevented by law from releasing information regarding clinical trials until such information has been made public by manufacturers or the medical institutions conducting the trials.

AIDS Clinical Trials Information Service
(800) 847–2572

The Clinical Trials Mailing List
majordomo@world.std.com

Pharmaceutical Research and Manufacturers of America
Fax-On-Demand Document Index
(202) 985–6060

National Multiple Sclerosis Society
(800) Fight–MS/(800) 244–4867

Office of Orphan Products Development—Drug List
(800) 300–7469

PETA
501 Front Street
Norfolk, VA 23510
(757) 622-PETA
FAX: (757) 622-1078

Prescription drug information can be found on the World Wide Web at: http://www.rxlist.com/

NICOTINE 12

1. Recount the history of tobacco use in this country, including the relatively recent popularity of cigarettes.

2. Explain the changing nature of cigarette consumption in this country and the tobacco industry's export-oriented response to it.

3. Contrast the positions taken by the tobacco industry and antismoking advocates over the role of advertising in the marketing of tobacco products.

4. Describe the restrictions proposed by the Clinton administration on cigarette marketing, as well as the position taken by the FDA.

5. Explain the physiological dynamics of nicotine, including absorption, distribution, and excretion, as well as the drug's influence on synaptic function.

6. Differentiate between the two components of dependence, including various theories of development and the challenges each presents to smoking cessation.

7. List the specific health consequences of tobacco use, including those unique to men and women of various ages.

8. Compare the various types of tobacco smoke, how they are generated, and the relative dangers that each presents to the nonsmoker.

9. Describe and evaluate the various approaches to smoking cessation.

10. Identify the dangers associated with the use of smokeless tobacco.

PROFILE

Elaine was an attractive college freshman of average weight, but like many women she felt pressured to attain the idealized body type that society dictated as "slim" or fashionable. She skipped meals often in the cafeteria because they were usually high in calories and fat. Many of her sorority sisters smoked, and at a party her friend Alyssa offered her a cigarette. "No, I don't smoke, thanks." Elaine declined.

"Suit yourself," Alyssa replied. "Me, I can't survive without one."

"Why is that?" Elaine asked curiously, her interest piqued by Alyssa's emphatic tone.

"Well, not only does a cigarette *make* a conversation," Alyssa gestured dramatically, cigarette in hand, "but it relaxes me, and I don't have as much of an appetite when I smoke." She offered Elaine the pack again.

By her sophomore year, Elaine was smoking more than a pack of cigarettes a day. Even as she became more and more dependent on cigarettes, Elaine promised herself she would quit smoking as soon as she lost a little weight. When the weight came off, she decided she would quit smoking as soon as her habit became inconvenient. Now, a year and a half later, she is not so confident that she can quit. She has noticed that she gets out of breath easily playing intermurals, and sustained aerobic activity gives her a deep, phlegmy chest cough.

Are Elaine's cough and lack of physical stamina likely to be the only health problems she will develop if she continues smoking? Do you think Elaine can quit smoking easily if she decides to do so? Consider these questions as you read about smoking and nicotine addiction in this chapter. Then take a look at the solutions box at the end of the chapter.

In this chapter, we discuss **nicotine,** a dependence-producing, central nervous system stimulant that is readily available in the marketplace. Because nicotine is derived from tobacco and tobacco is legally sold, except to people under 18 years of age, nicotine has enjoyed a long history of use. Conversely, the use of tobacco, with its naturally occurring nicotine and many other toxic components, has been shown to represent a serious threat to human health. At a cost of 418,690 lives in 1990, cigarette smoking is easily the single deadliest drug habit in the United States.

In the remainder of the chapter, the drug nicotine will be discussed where it is of specific interest. In addition, tobacco use will be comprehensively addressed because it not only supplies the body with nicotine but is, in itself, such a significant health concern.

TOBACCO

Tobacco and its primary psychoactive ingredient, nicotine, are products of the New World. When Christopher Columbus arrived at San Salvador, the natives, who were in the habit of smoking tobacco as a gesture of friendship, offered him some of the dried leaves.[1] Nicotine is derived from the leaves of two species of plants in the genus *Nicotiana*, which contains approximately 60 species of plants worldwide.[2] These two species are *Nicotiana tobacum*, a large-leaf species native to South America, and *Nicotiana rustica*, which has smaller leaves and was native to the West Indies and eastern North America. Both of these species, already under cultivation in the New World at the time of Columbus, are now grown in many countries throughout the world.[3]

HISTORY OF TOBACCO USE IN AMERICA

Between the time of the arrival of Columbus (1492) and the beginning of the American Revolutionary War (1776), tobacco use spread throughout much of Europe.[4] Some at first thought that tobacco had medicinal value, but others doubted such claims. Nonetheless, tobacco financed much of the Revolutionary War, because France was willing to lend money to the American Colonies based on production of this product.[5]

During and immediately after the Revolutionary period, the primary form of tobacco being used was **snuff,** a powdered tobacco that was snuffed or snorted. Snuff was most popular in England and other parts of Europe,

---

nicotine the primary, dependence-producing central nervous system stimulant in the tobacco plant; also, a mild euphoriant and a toxicant

snuff finely shredded or powdered smokeless tobacco, used for dipping (placing between the cheek and gum) or, in the case of powder, sniffing through the nose

DRUGS IN YOUR WORLD

The Tobacco Industry Under Fire

The year 1996 will be remembered as a bad one for the tobacco industry in its ongoing battle against public and private sector forces attempting to regulate and restrict cigarette smoking. In August, a liability suit in the amount of $750,000 was won by a plaintiff who charged a cigarette manufacturer with failure to adequately warn him of the dangers of using its product, thus resulting in his development of lung cancer. Although later reversed by a higher court, the initial judgment marked only the second time the industry had lost such a suit. In addition, the tobacco industry was sued by a growing list of states (41 presently) and by some individual cities (including San Francisco), attempting to recoup money spent through their respective Medicaid programs in treating the illnesses resulting from tobacco use. Further, in information released by tobacco industry insiders, we learned more about the tobacco industry's early awareness of the lung cancer risks associated with smoking, its targeting of adolescents through cigarette design and marketing, and its own research on the addictive nature of nicotine, in spite of contentions to the contrary.

Last, of course, was the FDA's stated desire to declare cigarettes to be drug-delivery devices. At the same time, President Clinton was proposing restrictions on the marketing of cigarettes in ways that attract children.

As this textbook goes to press, the tobacco industry appears to be on the verge of a total collapse of its collective defense against liability. Specifically, Ligget and Meyer, a major American tobacco company, appears to be willing to provide unrestricted access to documents related to the tobacco industry's understanding of the health damages associated with smoking and its plans to counter public awareness of this damage in exchange for immunity from the class action suits being brought by states to recoup Medicaid-related costs. In response to the growing animosity toward tobacco by some members of Congress, FDA officials, and the President, the tobacco industry increased its lobbying efforts in Washington and its financial support of candidates whom they believed were "sensitive" to their concerns about regulation. Figures available through 1995, the year before the formal campaign for President began, show that during the period 1986 to 1995, the tobacco industry gave $20.6 million ($4.7 million in 1995 alone) to candidates from both parties, but most generously to Republicans ($4 million in 1995) and members of committees whose decisions affect the tobacco industry. Common Cause reported that legislators from tobacco states serving on committees with clear roles in the potential regulation of tobacco, such as Agriculture and Commerce, received amounts ranging from $75,000 to nearly $125,000. Perhaps the most interesting example of these efforts was the nearly $300,000 in money and corporate jet rides provided to the campaign of Senator Dole, a strong supporter of the tobacco industry.

J. Drinkard, "Tobacco Lobby Spending Millions," *USA Today,* 9 September 1996, p. 8a.

Common Cause, "Following the money," Common Cause: analysis of campaign records, *USA Today,* 10 July 1996, p. 10a.

"Dole on Smoking," (Washington column) *USA Today,* 14 June 1996, p. 4a.

where it was used mostly by the upper classes and even royalty.[6] People became addicted to snuff during this period in the same manner that people have become addicted to cigarettes today. It was said that Napoleon used about seven pounds of snuff each month.

By the early part of the nineteenth century, chewing began to gain popularity as a method of tobacco use. Smoking was not a popular method of use in the United States during this period and was even banned in many places, perhaps because of the fire hazard it created. In 1860, at the beginning of the Civil War, only 7 of the 348 American tobacco factories made smoking tobacco.[7] Throughout the remainder of the 1800s, chewing tobacco was the most common form of tobacco used.

By 1911, however, sales of smoking tobacco had surpassed those of chewing tobacco. The reasons for the success of cigarettes over chewing tobacco are many, but an important one is that the use of chewing tobacco requires spitting. Tuberculosis was a major cause of death at the turn of the century, and the efforts of antituberculosis groups may have contributed to the unpopularity of spitting (a source of tuberculosis contamination) and the use of the **spittoon (cuspidor).**

As cigarettes and chewing tobacco fought for popularity, a third method of tobacco use surpassed them both. By 1904, Americans were spending more for cigars than for any other form of tobacco.[8] This trend continued until 1920, the last year that cigar sales topped cigarette sales.[9] After this date, however, cigarettes were never seriously challenged as the dominant form of tobacco use. Interestingly, however, cigar smoking is enjoying a resurgence. In 1995, cigars generated sales of $1 billion,

One hundred years ago, the popularity of chewing tobacco necessitated the distribution of numerous receptacles (spittoons) for tobacco juice and saliva.

mainly to younger adults, including a very small but growing percentage of women, and the magazine *Cigar Aficionado*, an upscale publication devoted to cigar smoking, is now enjoying rapid growth in readership.[10]

Cigarette Production, Sales, and Exportation

The production of cigarettes in this country has fluctuated in the last two decades. In 1981, the annual production of cigarettes in the United States reached a peak of 744 billion. From that point, production declined each year through 1986, when only 658 billion were produced. Today, production is again higher, with 719 billion cigarettes produced in 1992.[11] In terms of consumption patterns, however, the per capita consumption of cigarettes declined from 4,287 cigarettes per person in 1966 to 2,493 per person in 1994.[12] Regardless of decreasing domestic use, the tobacco industry continues to enjoy strong sales, as noted in 1994, when $46.2 billion was spent on cigarettes.[13]

The upward trend in cigarette production, coupled with the decreased consumption of cigarettes in this country, reflects the growing role of American manufacturers in supplying cigarettes to the international marketplace. Today, this country is both the world's leading importer of unprocessed tobacco and its leading exporter of manufactured tobacco products, with much of the latter going to the most underdeveloped countries in the world. The box above addresses this trend and its potentially serious health implications.

MARKETING OF TOBACCO PRODUCTS

Shredded plant material, wrapped in paper or leaf, ignited with a flame, and then placed on or near the delicate tissues of the mouth . . . what other human behavior does this resemble? If you answered *None!*, then you understand how unique smoking is, and, therefore, that it must be learned, because it is unnecessary for daily survival. How it is learned currently is not fully understood. This process likely requires a variety of stimuli, ranging from modeling to actual experimentation. The role of advertising as a source of models has been long suspected and intensely debated. Today, as in the past, the intent of the tobacco industry's advertising is controversial. Do the hedonistic commercials and familiar logos seen in a variety of media challenge the "brand loyalty" of those who have already decided to smoke, as the industry claims? Do they attempt to entice new smokers, older children and young adolescents, in sufficient numbers to replace the 3,000 smokers who die each day from the consequences of tobacco use?

Over the years, the tobacco industry has used all types of mass media, including radio, television, print, billboards, and sponsorship of televised athletic events and

spittoon (cuspidor) large bowl-like container used as a receptacle for saliva or spit containing tobacco juice

WHAT DO YOU THINK?

The Tobacco Industry Pursues New Markets

The growing, processing, and manufacturing of tobacco and its related products is big business. Thus the American tobacco industry requires markets, both old and new. As the American market for tobacco products, particularly cigarettes, has decreased (see p. 203), the industry has pursued new markets, largely in Africa, Asia, and China. Today, carefully tailored advertising uses virtually every medium, including television, emphasizing a Western lifestyle that includes the independence of women, creating an explosive demand for American cigarettes. In addition, political intervention from the highest levels in Washington has lessened restrictions on the marketing of American tobacco products, resulting in an annual per capita increase in cigarette consumption of nearly 1.7% worldwide. For every cigarette no longer being smoked in a developed country, three additional cigarettes are being smoked in a developing country. Since 1985, cigarette smoking in the United States has decreased by 13%, while increasing by 20% in China. That country alone now has 300 million smokers, some 25% of the world's total cigarette users.

The human costs of these trends are as predictable for these new markets as they are in this country: longer periods of debilitation from chronic illnesses, significant increases in specific diseases, such as cancer and cardiovascular diseases, and, of course, reduced life expectancy. In China alone, 50 million young smokers who are alive today will die prematurely from the effects of smoking. The annual number of deaths from smoking-related conditions worldwide will rise from 3 million today to 10 million by the year 2020, with 70% occurring in developing countries. The cost to individuals, dependent families, particularly children, and developing countries through lost productivity is currently estimated at over $200 billion annually.

In addition to these health concerns, the importation of raw tobacco from developing countries into the United States is equally problematic. For example, the curing process required to prepare tobacco for shipment abroad requires the use of wood fires. As a result, deforestation increases with little likelihood that reforestation will be undertaken.

In addition, the growing of tobacco to export requires the use of powerful fertilizers and pesticides, both of which can cause environmental harm. Further, the processing of raw tobacco in preparation for shipping is very labor intensive, resulting in the employment of children at very low wages and the discontinuation of their much-needed formal education. Even the developing countries' food supply is diminished as women are drawn from the fields and kitchens to work in tobacco production.

At the time of this writing, the World Health Organization is attempting to stem the tide of cigarette smoking and tobacco exporting in developing countries but is making little progress. As American citizens, we should begin to ask our federal government and the tobacco industry to justify their actions in light of the experience we have gained at home about the long-term consequences of cigarette smoking. What do you think?

The Farming of Tobacco and Its Environmental Impact: the Economics of Tobacco Production, World Health Organization, World No Tobacco Day.

Tobacco and Health: The Facts, World Health Organization, World No Tobacco Day.

Costs of Tobacco Use: The Causes and Consequences of a Lucrative but Dangerous Trade, World Health Organization, World No Tobacco Day

---

concerts, to sell its products. In addition, the industry has often distributed free samples and sold merchandise bearing the company or product logo.

Today, the tobacco industry has been denied access to television and radio, and it can no longer distribute free samples, but the industry continues to actively use other channels of the mass media. For example, Philip Morris has introduced an upscale, quarterly lifestyle magazine, *Unlimited: Action, Adventure, Good Times.* Intended for young men, the free publication is mailed to 1.5 million smokers and is offered through promotions. Topics such as fashion, rock climbing, and camping link healthful activity and various Philip Morris tobacco products.[14]

The industry also promotes smoking by having bartenders supply cigarettes to patrons of bars and restaurants who try to "bum" cigarettes from neighboring customers. In this approach, tobacco companies provide new brands of cigarettes that are not yet being marketed and pay establishments to "introduce" these new blends. Because the product being given away is not currently being marketed, this practice does not technically violate laws restricting the free distribution of cigarettes. To date, several hundred establishments in several major cities are participating in this unique form of advertising.[15]

A final current example of tobacco's subtle but effective presence in the public mind is tobacco use in motion

WHAT DO YOU THINK?

Should Tobacco Industry Marketing Be Regulated?

With the United States finally waking up to the health consequences of cigarette smoking, the tobacco industry has been forced to alter its advertising approaches. One tobacco company has attempted to target two groups: minorities from inner cities and undereducated "virile females."

The RJ Reynolds Tobacco Company unsuccessfully tried to test-market a cigarette brand called Uptown. This cigarette was aimed principally at urban minorities. Opposition to this product came quickly from antismoking groups and Dr. Louis Sullivan, then Secretary of the Department of Health and Human Services. Under heavy pressure, Reynolds withdrew Uptown cigarettes in early 1990. Reynolds also introduced a cigarette called Dakota. The targeted group for this cigarette was to be "virile females," an 18- to 24-year-old female group with no education beyond high school that holds entry-level service or factory jobs.[a] The Philip Morris Tobacco Company targeted a different group with its super-thin, low-smoke cigarette, Superslims.

Apparently, Superslims has been aimed at a more sophisticated woman who is conscious of her body weight.

Furthermore, U.S. cigarette companies are coping with declining consumption in the United States by increasing their sales abroad, especially in developing nations. In the industrialized world, smoking is decreasing about 1% each year. However, in Asia and Latin America, smoking is growing 7% faster than the population. In Africa, smoking is growing 18% faster.[b]

U.S. tobacco companies are fueling this increase in smoking. With few restrictions on advertising and the lure of revenue through taxation, these developing countries allow the unrestrained marketing of tobacco products. Over time, the health effects of cigarette smoking will begin to be seen in these developing countries.

Do you think companies should be allowed to promote an addictive yet legal product in developing countries or to target population segments already strapped by financial and educational burdens? Who will take the responsibility for the sickness and death that will certainly follow?

[a]G. Will, "Today's Question: Do Daughters of Tobacco Execs Smoke?" *Muncie Star,* 25 February 1990, p. A12.

[b]S. Chapman, and J. Richardson, "Tobacco Excise and Declining Tobacco Consumption: The Case of Papua, New Guinea," *Am J Pub Health* 80, no. 5 (1990):537.

---

pictures. In spite of a 1990 film industry policy preventing "brand placement" of tobacco products in films, cigarette and cigar smoking continues to be disproportionately represented in current films. A survey conducted by *USA Today* of the 18 top-grossing films of late 1996 revealed that 10 of the 18 films featured at least 15 separate scenes in which cigarettes or cigars were smoked. In most of the films depicting tobacco use, the characters seen smoking were among the films' central characters, most of whom were cast in very "powerful" roles.[16]

Many health professionals believe that the advertising messages about tobacco are misleading because they fail to fully inform customers about health risks. Further ethical questions are raised by the marketing strategies that apparently aim subtle but powerful messages toward children and adolescents who have not yet become dependent on cigarettes. The models shown in cigarette advertisements portray youthful, attractive, healthy people enjoying "the good life." Smokers are never presented as unattractive, old, poor, or sick. This might lead children and adolescents to believe that, by smoking the advertised brand, they can become like the models in the advertisements.

Absurd as it may seem, cartoon characters make highly seductive models. RJ Reynolds's "Joe Camel" advertising campaign for Camel cigarettes has been so successful that Joe is now as familiar to American youngsters as Mickey Mouse.[17]

Preference for the Camel brand among ninth-graders soared from 2% before the Joe Camel ad campaign to nearly 30%, or five times more than the market share for the adult population.[18] Reynolds and Philip Morris, the maker of Marlboro, use another marketing ploy to appeal to youth: the sale of promotional items, such as magazines, calculators, T-shirts, baseball caps, and posters announcing sporting events. These items are purchased with special coupons like the one shown in Fig. 12.1.

Evidence is growing that the tobacco industry purposely targets young nonsmokers and novice smokers. Internal tobacco documents made public during 1996 indicate that, in spite of industry contentions to the contrary, adolescents were surveyed as recently as the early 1980s to determine their preferences in packaging, tobacco flavor, and factors influencing brand loyalty.

Further evidence for the power of tobacco industry advertising to influence teenage smoking is seen in a study reported in April 1996, suggesting that as the level

FIGURE 12.1

A Camel Cash coupon.

of advertising for a particular brand increased, the likelihood of teens purchasing that brand increased by a factor of threefold.[19] This study also reported that 80% of all teen smokers select the three most heavily advertised brands. Such findings do not surprise professionals in the advertising industry. When 300 top advertising executives were recently polled, 52% thought that tobacco advertising was directed at adolescents, and 71% thought current tobacco advertisements were capable of persuading adolescents to smoke more.[20] Members of the group polled have, in fact, undertaken an advertising campaign to counter the influence of the tobacco industry's efforts.

Perhaps as a result of the advertising profession's concerns or because of the pending federal restrictions on tobacco advertising (see the box on page 208), the FTC reports that the tobacco industry reduced its advertising and promotional efforts in 1994 (the last year for which data are available) to $4.8 billion from the 1993 amount of $6 billion, a decrease of nearly 20%. This is still 40 times the amount spent on antismoking campaigns by the federal government (fig. 12.2).

PHARMACOLOGY OF NICOTINE

The primary active (and addictive) ingredient in tobacco is nicotine. In its purest state, nicotine is an extremely toxic, clear, oily liquid with a characteristic odor.[21] At low doses, it acts as a stimulant; at high doses it is a poison.

ADMINISTRATION AND ABSORPTION

Nicotine enters the body through a variety of routes. Inhalation of smoke (heated air containing nicotine va-

Cigarette advertising by major companies has been shown to be attractive to children as well as adults.

FIGURE 12.2

Tobacco companies spend approximately $40 advertising and promoting cigarettes for every $1 the federal government spends on antismoking campaigns.

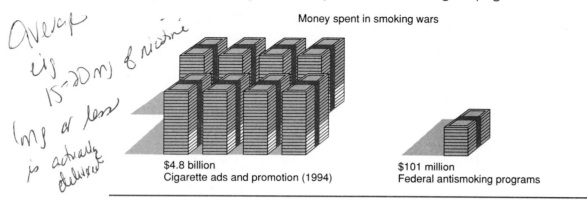

Money spent in smoking wars

$4.8 billion
Cigarette ads and promotion (1994)

$101 million
Federal antismoking programs

Handwritten note in margin: Average cig 15-20 mg of nicotine 1 mg or less is actually delivered

por) from a cigar, cigarette, or pipe is perhaps the most common route. During smoking, some nicotine is absorbed through the membranes of the mouth, throat, and bronchi, as well as the alveoli of the lungs. In the case of snuff and chewing tobacco, nicotine reaches the bloodstream by absorption through the mucous linings of the mouth, nose, and throat. For those who swallow nicotine-containing pills, the drug is absorbed through the lining of the stomach and intestines.

DISTRIBUTION

Inhalation is the quickest and most effective delivery method. Experts estimate that 90% of the nicotine that reaches the alveoli of the lungs in each breath is absorbed into the bloodstream. Although an average cigarette contains 15 to 20 mg of nicotine, only about 1 mg or less (a range of 0.1 to 2 mg) from each cigarette smoked is actually delivered to the mouth.[22] About 25% is immediately carried to the brain, where it easily crosses the blood-brain barrier and interferes with normal brain biochemistry. In addition, many drugs, including nicotine, easily cross the placenta and affect the fetus.[23]

EXCRETION

As with other foreign substances, excretion begins as soon as the first molecules enter the body. A small amount of nicotine is exhaled in air that leaves the lungs. Another small portion is excreted unchanged by the kidneys. The primary mechanism of excretion is **biodeactivation** by enzymes of the liver; 80% to 90% of the nicotine is eliminated in this way.[24] The products of this biodeactivation are then excreted by the kidneys. About 50% of the nicotine in the body is removed in less than 30 minutes.[25]

NEUROHORMONAL INFLUENCES OF NICOTINE

As with other substances, nicotine affects many tissues and systems of the body. Nicotine produces both acute (immediate) and chronic (long-term) effects.

Acute Effects of Nicotine on the Central Nervous System

In the CNS, nicotine activates receptors within the brain. This stimulation of the brain is seen in changes in electroencephalogram (EEG) patterns, reflecting an increase in the frequency of electrical activity. This is part of a general arousal pattern signaled by the release of the neurotransmitters norepinephrine, dopamine, acetylcholine, and serotonin. Heavy use of tobacco products, resulting in high nicotine levels in the bloodstream, eventually produces a blocking effect as more and more receptor sites are filled. The result is a generalized depression of the CNS. When blood levels of nicotine reach a critical point, the brain's vomiting center may be activated. This response is a built-in mechanism of protection against poisoning.

The level of plasma nicotine associated with normal levels of heavy smoking (one to two packs per day), would not likely produce the depressive effect previously described. However, in chain smokers (four to eight packs per day), plasma nicotine levels would be sufficient to depress nervous system function.[26] In fact, some have suggested that chain smoking is driven by the fruitless effort to counter the depressive influence of chronically high levels of nicotine.

biodeactivation biochemical alteration of a drug in the body that makes the drug less reactive

WHAT DO YOU THINK?

How Much Should the Marketing of Tobacco Be Restricted?

Over the past decade, Americans have become familiar with many restrictions on smoking. Public settings of virtually every type, including prisons, prohibit smoking except in a few carefully selected areas. Various types of public transportation, the vast majority of restaurants, work sites of all types and sizes, and even some outdoor arenas restrict smoking as well. In fact, smokers have increasing difficulty finding any locations, other than their homes and some individual office areas, in which they may smoke.

In addition to these restrictions, 1996 marked a period of increased interest in restricting access to tobacco or lessening the public awareness of its availability. Driven by concern over the addictive nature of nicotine and the sudden upturn in adolescent smoking, the federal government proposed additional restrictions.

Former FDA Commissioner David Kessler considered asking Congress for legislation that would allow the FDA to define nicotine as addictive and cigarettes as a "drug delivery system." Once so defined, cigarettes would become controlled in much the same way as prescription medications are today. To date, the FDA has not made this request to the Congress.

The second area of increased restriction was proposed by the Clinton administration and focused on the marketing and advertising of tobacco products, particularly cigarettes. In this set of proposed changes, the marketing of tobacco products to the general public, particularly children, would be curtailed in the following ways:

1. Limit tobacco advertising in publications that appeal to teens, and restrict billboards with tobacco-related content to no closer than 1,000 feet of schools and playgrounds. (An August 1995 study in California found that stores near schools displayed significantly more tobacco-related advertisements than those farther from schools.)
2. Restrict the use of logo and other tobacco-related images on nontobacco products such as towels, T-shirts, and caps.
3. Require merchants to obtain proof of age when selling tobacco products to adolescents (newly adopted laws require that merchants request photo identification for all customers purchasing tobacco products who appear to be 27 years of age or less).

4. Bar certain sources of access to tobacco products, such as mail order sales, the distribution of free samples, and vending machines.
5. Halt sponsorship of high-visibility events, such as auto racing and athletic contests, in which brand names appear on such highly televised surfaces as hoods, fenders, uniforms, and arena sign boards. (It is estimated that the Marlboro logo is seen 5,933 times during the course of a 90-minute televised Winston Cup auto race.)

The tobacco industry has announced its intention to fight such restrictions in the courts, while proposing a set of industry-designed steps that are similar in many ways to those already described. Critics contend that the tobacco industry threatens massive lawsuits against FDA for its involvement in the control of nicotine and nicotine delivery. They also charge that the industry promotes restrictions on advertising and sponsorship that are carefully watered-down versions of the restrictions proposed by the federal government.

How do you see the government's proposals and the tobacco industry's responses in the efforts to control exposure to tobacco products? To what extent do you feel that tobacco sponsorship of sporting events, such as auto racing, is so "imprinted" on the American mind that removal of all sponsorship would be ineffective in reducing sales of cigarettes or making them less appealing to children? How would you suggest that the outdoor advertisers (billboards), vending machine manufacturers, and convenience store owners respond to these proposals?

Unfortunately, no federal agency has been given the responsibility of determining whether the marketing activities of the tobacco industry are appropriate, including Alcohol, Tobacco, and Firearms (AFT), the only federal agency with tobacco in its title. In fact, this agency within the Treasury Department deals only with issues of federal taxation of tobacco products.

Regardless, after people exposed to tobacco advertising become dependent on tobacco, the advertising is no longer required to maintain them as customers. Nicotine dependence takes over as the primary force in their choice to smoke. In addition, there is a continuing supply of young, susceptible people to whom tobacco products can be marketed.

In carefully controlled studies involving both animals and humans, nicotine increased the ability of subjects to concentrate on a task.[27] The duration of this improvement was limited. Most would agree that this brief benefit is not enough to justify the health risks associated with chronic tobacco use.

Non-CNS Acute Effects of Nicotine Use

Outside the central nervous system (CNS), nicotine affects the transmission of nerve signals at the neuromuscular junction by mimicking acetylcholine (see chapter 4). It occupies receptor sites at the end plate and prevents the transmission of nerve impulses from neuron to muscle cell. Because of its ability to act in this manner, nicotine has been successfully used as an insecticide in greenhouses.

Nicotine also causes the release of epinephrine from the adrenal medulla, which increases respiration rate, heart rate, blood pressure, and coronary blood flow. It also causes the constriction of the blood vessels beneath the skin, a reduction in the motility in the bowel, loss of appetite, and changes in sleep patterns.

Although a lethal dose of nicotine could be obtained through the ingestion of a nicotine-containing insecticide, to "smoke oneself to death" in a single intense period of cigarette use would be highly improbable. In humans, 60 mg is a lethal dose.[28] As noted previously, a typical cigarette supplies less than 2 mg of nicotine, and that nicotine is relatively quickly biotransformed for removal from the body.

Chronic Effects of Nicotine Use

The chronic effects of nicotine use include the development of dependence. This phenomenon causes the user to consume greater quantities of nicotine over extended periods of time, further endangering the user's health.

Dependence can have both physical and psychological components. Particularly with cigarettes, physical dependence or addiction, with its associated tolerance, withdrawal, and **titration,** is strongly developed by 40% of all smokers.[29] Most of the remaining population of smokers will experience lesser degrees of physical dependence. Psychological dependence, or habituation, with its accompanying psychological components of compulsion and indulgence, is almost universally seen.

Compulsion is a strong emotional desire to continue tobacco use despite restrictions on smoking and the awareness of health risks. Very likely, the user is compelled to engage in uninterrupted tobacco use in fear of the unpleasant physical, emotional, and social effects that result from discontinuing use. In comparison with compulsion, indulgence is seen as "rewarding" oneself for aligning with a particular behavior pattern, in this case, smoking. Indulgence is made possible by the various reward systems built around the use of tobacco, including a perceived image, group affiliation, and even appetite suppression intended to foster weight control.

Much to the benefit of the tobacco industry, dependence on tobacco is easily established. Many experts believe that physical dependence on tobacco is far more easily established than is physical dependence on alcohol, cocaine (other than crack), or heroin. Of all people who experiment with cigarettes, 85% develop various aspects of a dependent relationship.[30]

A small percentage of smokers, known as "chippers," can smoke a few cigarettes a day without becoming dependent. Experts believe that they are less likely to use tobacco to influence their mood and thus do not "require" cigarettes to feel a sense of pleasure.[31] They may, in fact, truly be "social smokers" in that they smoke only with a few selected friends or in a very limited number of places. Unfortunately, many inexperienced smokers feel that they too are only "social smokers"; however, a few months of this type of occasional smoking could move the smoker into a dependence pattern of tobacco use.

THEORIES OF NICOTINE ADDICTION

Each individual develops and maintains physical dependence or addiction in a personal and complicated way. Experts have proposed several theories to explain the development of dependence. We will briefly describe some of the more familiar theories. Other aspects of dependence formation were discussed in the previous section.

In the **bolus theory** of nicotine addiction, each inhalation of smoke releases into the blood a concentrated quantity of nicotine (a ball or bolus) that reaches the brain and results in a period of neurohormonal excitement.[32] Smokers perceive this period of stimulation as pleasurable but, unfortunately, it is short-lived. Thus, smokers attempt to reestablish this pleasurable feeling by again inhaling and sending another bolus of nicotine on its way to the brain. The 70,000 or more inhalations during the first year of smoking condition the novice smoker, resulting in a lifelong pattern of cigarette dependence. The level needed for arousal is different for each smoker, depending on the length of addiction, the level of tolerance, inherited characteristics, and other factors.

A second theory of dependence suggests that nicotine stimulates the release of adrenocorticotropic hormone (ACTH) from the anterior pituitary, or "master gland" of the endocrine system. Researchers have shown that

---

titration a particular level of nicotine in the blood that is maintained by adjusting cigarette or other tobacco use

bolus theory a theory to account for tobacco dependence based on the body's response to periodic "balls" of nicotine after each inhalation of cigarette smoke

ACTH causes the release of **beta endorphins** (naturally occurring opiatelike chemicals), which produce mild feelings of euphoria. Perhaps this stresslike response mechanism involving ACTH also may account for the increased energy expenditure seen in smokers and thus their tendency to maintain lower body weight than nonsmokers.

When we view these physiological responses collectively, we may see nicotine as biochemically influencing brain activity by increasing the extent and strength of various forms of "communication" between different brain areas[33] and even glands of the endocrine system. If this is the case, we see why, once a smoker is addicted, the functioning of the smoker's control systems is radically changed in comparison with those of nonsmokers.

Yet another explanation, called *self-medication*, suggests that nicotine, through the effects of mood-enhancing neurotransmitters, may allow smokers to "treat" feelings of tiredness and lack of motivation. In other words, a "smoke" lifts the spirits, if only briefly. Eventually, however, smokers depend on tobacco as a "medication" to make then feel better. Because tobacco is a legal drug, smokers prefer it over equally effective illegal drugs, such as cocaine and stimulants.

Although this discussion of nicotine addiction focuses on the smoking of tobacco, snuff and chewing tobacco also deliver nicotine to the bloodstream and brain and thereby produce similar dependence.

OTHER COMPONENTS OF CIGARETTE SMOKE

Nicotine is only one of the factors in considering the effects of smoking. Other components of the smoke are the gases and particulates. Experts estimate that the number of compounds in tobacco smoke exceeds 4,000. Many of these are considered physiologically active, toxic, and carcinogenic.

Gases

Carbon monoxide (CO) is one of the most abundant gases in cigarette smoke. We have known the mechanism of its toxicity for many years. Carbon monoxide molecules replace oxygen molecules at binding sites on the hemoglobin molecules in red blood cells. In this way, the blood becomes less able to transport oxygen to the tissues and cells where it is needed, such as brain cells and heart cells.

Although it is true that natural body metabolism always keeps an irreducible minimum of CO in the blood (0.5% to 1%), the blood of smokers may have levels of 5% to 10% CO saturation. We are exposed to additional CO from environmental sources, such as automobiles,

buses, and other combustion of fossil fuels. By combining a smoker's CO with environmental CO, smokers become more easily "out of breath" than nonsmokers. Compared with nicotine, the half-life of CO combined with hemoglobin is much longer, approximately four hours.

The gaseous phase of tobacco smoke also contains other harmful compounds, such as benzopyrene, hydrogen cyanide, vinyl chloride, ammonia, nitrosamines, pyridine, formaldehyde, and many others. At least 43 of these compounds have been determined to be **carcinogenic,** that is, they cause cell changes leading to cancer.[34]

Tar

The total of all the solid materials (particulates) that are inhaled as part of the tobacco smoke, less nicotine and water, is called **tar.** Many of these particulates have also been shown to be carcinogenic. A person who smokes one pack of cigarettes per day will collect 4 oz of tar in his or her lungs in a year. Only the gases and the smallest particles reach the small sacs of the lungs, the **alveoli,** where oxygen exchange occurs. The larger particles are deposited somewhere along the air passage leading to the lungs.

Many particles are deposited on the ciliated epithelium of the bronchi, air tubes leading from the larynx (voice box) to the lungs. Cilia, the tiny hairlike structures that line the bronchi, normally remove these particles through their constant wavelike motion. This ciliary escalator carries particles up to the throat, where they can be coughed up and spat out or swallowed and excreted through the gastrointestinal tract.

Chronic smoking may eventually overload and permanently damage the cilia's natural cleaning system. Tar that can no longer be removed efficiently from the air passages remains in contact with epithelial cells lining the respiratory tract. This contact may cause cellular changes, and these cellular changes may result in the development of a cancerous tumor.

HEALTH CONSEQUENCES OF SMOKING

Three decades ago, the famous 1964 *Report by the Surgeon General* concluded that "smoking increases overall mortality (death) in men, causes lung and laryngeal cancer in men, and causes chronic bronchitis." In 1989, the Surgeon General's report, *Reducing the Health Consequences of Smoking—25 Years of Progress,* reported significant advances in our knowledge of the health hazards of smoking. For example, we now have evidence that smoking increases the morbidity and mortality of both men and women. A causal association has also been demonstrated between smoking and coronary heart disease, atherosclerotic peripheral vascular disease (blockage of blood

DRUGS IN YOUR WORLD

Smoking Harms the Nonsmoker

After many years of increasing restrictions on smoking, we have heard complaints that it is becoming harder and harder to be a smoker, at least in public. However, we have not seen clear evidence of how smoking could damage other aspects of our public and private lives, including parenting and employment.

Based on the growing body of evidence that **passive smoking** harms the growth and development of children, some are beginning to assert that parental smoking is a form of child neglect. Particularly when a pregnant woman smokes immediately before and during her pregnancy, the detrimental effects on the developing baby suggest a low level of concern, if not neglect, by the woman. Of course, the same can be said for other family members who continue to smoke near a pregnant woman regardless of her desire to be smoke-free to protect herself and her developing child.

Thus, smoking by a parent can affect custody decisions made in a divorce. In one custody case, a nonsmoking father attempted to establish his home as the primary residence for his two young children over the home of his former wife, who was a heavy smoker. He contended that the smoking would damage the children's health if they resided with their mother continuously.

A final concern affects employees who must work in establishments with smoking sections, such as bowling alleys, bars, and restaurants. Current issues include whether an employee can request (or demand) assignment to only the nonsmoking area of such a work site and the responsibility for illnesses an employee may develop while working in a business that allows customers to smoke.

passive smoking the inhalation by nonsmokers of air containing tobacco smoke

---

flow into the legs), lung and laryngeal (throat) cancer in women, oral (mouth) cancer, esophageal (food tube) cancer, chronic obstructive pulmonary disease, and intrauterine (fetal) growth retardation leading to low-birthweight babies.[35]

In addition, many experts consider smoking to be the probable cause or a contributing cause for other conditions, such as unsuccessful pregnancies, increased infant mortality, peptic ulcer disease, chronic bronchitis, emphysema, and cancers of the bladder, pancreas, and kidney. Increasing evidence suggests that cigarette smoking in combination with alcohol or certain types of occupational exposures increases the risk of cancer. Smoking also seems to be associated with cerebrovascular disease (stroke) and cancer of the uterus (womb).

The 1964 Surgeon General's report labeled smoking as "habituating," but the 1989 report declared that cigarettes (and other forms of tobacco use) are "addicting." Despite the warnings on each package of cigarettes (fig. 12.3), an estimated 48 million Americans (or 25.5% of the adult population) were smokers in 1994.[36] The four leading causes of death in the United States (heart disease, cancer, cerebrovascular disease, and lung diseases) are all related to cigarette smoking.[37]

A 1993 report attributed 418,690 deaths in the United States in 1990 (about one in five) to smoking. During this same year, premature deaths (deaths before the age of 65) resulted in 1,152,635 years of potential life lost.[38] These grim statistics are summarized in the now-familiar statement, "Cigarette smoking is the single most preventable cause of premature death in the United States."[39]

Perhaps the only exception that can be made about the strong association between smoking and virtually every form of illness and disease is in Alzheimer's disease (AD). Recent studies suggest that smokers may be less susceptible to developing AD for reasons related to the increased level of nervous system (synaptic) functioning reported in smokers.

CURRENT TRENDS IN CIGARETTE SMOKING

After the Surgeon General's 1964 report, smoking prevalence (the number of current smokers per 100 people) in the United States began a 25-year decline. This

beta endorphins naturally occurring opiatelike substances within the CNS, thought to create a euphoric effect to which the smoker becomes conditioned

carcinogenic cancer causing

tar solid materials (particulates) present in tobacco smoke

alveoli thin, saclike structures in the lungs where gases are exchanged between the blood and inhaled air

FIGURE 12.3

One of these four health warning labels must appear on every package of cigarettes and on promotional materials sold or distributed in the United States.

> **SURGEON GENERAL'S WARNING:** Smoking causes lung cancer, heart disease, emphysema, and may complicate pregnancy.

> **SURGEON GENERAL'S WARNING:** Smoking by pregnant women may result in fetal injury, premature birth, and low birth weight.

> **SURGEON GENERAL'S WARNING:** Quitting smoking now greatly reduces serious risks to your health.

> **SURGEON GENERAL'S WARNING:** Cigarette smoke contains carbon monoxide.

decline ended in 1991, when the smoking prevalence ratio began leveling off.[40]

Cigarette Smoking among Adults

Much of the decline in smoking **prevalence** from 1965 to 1990 can be traced to decreases in the percentage of adult smokers (18 years of age and older). For example, in 1991, of the 89.8 million (49.8%) adults who had ever smoked, only 46.3 million (51.5%) were current smokers. Thus, 48.5% of all adults who had ever smoked were former smokers during 1991. The proportion of former smokers among those who had ever smoked was higher among men (51.6%) than women (44.7%), and it was higher for those with at least 16 years of education (66.1%) than those with 12 years of education or less (41.8%).[41] Data reported for 1994 (see p. 211) indicate that levels of smoking remain relatively similar to those reported in 1991, although the actual number of smokers in each category is slightly larger because of population increases and because of the increasing rate of young adult smokers reported below.[42]

In 1994, smoking was most prevalent in the 25- to 44-year-old age group, in which 30% of adults smoked. In the youngest category of smokers studied, the 18- to 24-year-old age group, the rate of increase (+2.2%) was greatest. Among adult men, 28.2% (25.3 million) smoke; among adult women, 23.1% (22.7 million) were current smokers. Smoking among Asians and Pacific Islanders is lower than the national average (13.9%), but it is higher among Native Americans and Alaskan Natives (42.2.4%). Again, as in 1991, higher levels of edu-

cation and income were associated with lower levels of smoking.[43]

Cigarette Smoking among Women

According to the Surgeon General's report, smoking by women has declined more slowly than for men, although it has always been at a lower level than that of men. In 1994, 20 million women (23.1%) were current smokers, compared with 25.3 million men (28.2%).[44] The disparity in smoking rates between the genders can be attributed to higher smoking rates for older men.

Some of the health consequences of these trends are already evident. Since 1987, more women have died each year from lung cancer than from breast cancer. Recent studies show that cigarette smoking raises the risk of heart attack and stroke and increases cervical cancer in women.[45] Cigarette smoking combined with the use of birth control pills in women over 35 years of age increases the risk of heart attack.[46] Smoking is also an important cause of low birthweight and infant mortality. Experts have also correlated maternal smoking and an elevated rate of infant deaths caused by sudden infant death syndrome (SIDS).[47] Osteoporosis (loss of calcium from the bone) and premature facial wrinkling have also been associated with cigarette smoking.

Cigarette Smoking among College Students and Young Adults

Smoking among college students and young adults dropped significantly between 1977 and 1981 and then

Children and adolescents are sometimes led to believe that smoking cigarettes will make them appear more attractive and mature.

remained relatively constant until 1991. In 1991, the rates of daily smoking actually increased in both groups. Young adults aged 19 to 28 who were not students had higher smoking rates (21.7%) than college students (13.8%).[48] Most of these smokers began smoking as teenagers.

Cigarette Smoking among Teenagers

As encouraging as it is that adults have moved away from smoking in recent decades, the most current data about smoking by adolescents are discouraging. Based on 1994 statistics, 19% of eighth-grade students and 31% of high school seniors reported smoking at least once within the past month, and 9% of eighth-grade students and 19% of high school seniors report smoking daily.[49] Because 14- to 17-year-old young people model most closely the behavior of 18- to 24-year-olds, this upward trend does not bode well for the future.

The factors that have contributed to the recent increase in adolescent tobacco use, particularly smoking, are multifaceted and could prove difficult to reverse, particularly because long-term consequences are difficult to envision and immediate rewards are appealing. Regardless, the pattern is distressing for several reasons. Current smokers miss more school, enjoy school less, and do worse in school than nonsmokers. Teenage smokers also know more people who use other drugs, such as alcohol, marijuana, and cocaine. In addition, teenagers who smoke overestimate their ability to quit smoking after they begin.[50] In particular, smokers who begin before 14 years of age will demonstrate little ability (4.4%) to quit before the age of 30.[51] For those who cannot, the negative consequences of tobacco use for both themselves and others will soon begin to overwhelm whatever earlier rewards they gained.

Involuntary (Passive) Smoking

The smoke generated by the burning of tobacco can be classified as either **mainstream smoke** (the smoke inhaled and then exhaled by the smoker) or **sidestream smoke** (the smoke that comes from the burning end of the cigarette, pipe, or cigar). When either form of tobacco smoke is diluted and stays within a common source of air, it is called **environmental tobacco smoke (ETS)**. All three forms of tobacco smoke lead to involuntary smoking and can present health problems for both nonsmokers and smokers.[52]

Surprisingly, mainstream smoke makes up only 15% of our exposure to involuntary smoking. This is because much of the nicotine, carbon monoxide, and particulate matter is retained within the active smoker.[53]

Sidestream smoke is responsible for 85% of our involuntary smoke exposure. Because it is not filtered by the tobacco, the filter, or the smoker's lungs, sidestream smoke contains more free nicotine and produces higher yields of both carbon dioxide and carbon monoxide. Much to the detriment of nonsmokers, sidestream smoke has 20 to 100 times the quantity of highly carcinogenic substances (*N*-nitrosamines) than mainstream smoke.[54]

Current scientific opinion suggests that smokers and nonsmokers are exposed to much the same smoke when tobacco is used within a common airspace. The important difference is the quantity of smoke inhaled by smokers and nonsmokers. For each pack of cigarettes smoked by a smoker, nonsmokers who must share a common air supply with the smokers likely will involuntarily smoke the equivalent of three to five cigarettes. Because of the small size of the particles produced by burning tobacco, environmental tobacco smoke cannot be completely removed from an indoor site by even the most effective ventilation system.

By the beginning of the 1990s, passive smoking both in the home and in the workplace was revealed to be a definite health risk to all who shared a common air source. More recently, a scientific study found that nonsmokers living with smokers had a 20% greater mortality rate than nonsmoking partners of nonsmokers, resulting in 65,000 premature deaths per year.[55] In a second study,

prevalence the number of events, cases of disease, or instances of behavior in a given population at a given time
mainstream smoke smoke that is drawn through the cigarette, inhaled, and then exhaled by the smoker
sidestream smoke smoke rising from the burning tip of the cigarette; contains more dangerous chemicals than mainstream smoke
environmental tobacco smoke (ETS) all tobacco smoke in the ambient air

DRUGS IN YOUR WORLD

Restrictions on Tobacco Smoking

Smoking is now prohibited or restricted in almost all public places. Most commercial retail establishments, public transportation systems, and schools have banned smoking. Smoking in malls and airports is limited to a few designated areas, some with separate ventilation systems. Smokers must stand outside or go to a smoking lounge in most workplaces when they want to light up. Even hotels have designated smoking and nonsmoking rooms. In fact, bars and bowling alleys seem to be the only places in which smoking is still unrestricted.

These bans on smoking result from concerns about the health effects of environmental tobacco smoke. Accordingly, nonsmokers are pressuring legislatures to respond to a health threat that the U.S. Environmental Protection Agency describes as "a serious and substantial public health risk."

In opposition to these bans, smokers and representatives of the tobacco industry contend that restricting smoking is of questionable legality because the sale and use of tobacco are legal. Further, they contend that restrictions are largely unenforceable and that smokers are reasonable people who know how and when to control their own behavior.

Sidestream smoke contains more nicotine, carbon monoxide, and carbon dioxide than mainstream smoke.

nonsmoking wives of husbands who smoked were found to be at greater risk of developing lung cancer, by a factor of approximately 1.75, than wives of nonsmoking husbands.[56] Other recent studies have reported health complications ranging from low-birthweight babies and children with more respiratory problems than normal to increased risks of developing cervical cancer.[57] In January 1993, the EPA released a report on the health effects of passive smoking in which it concluded that passive tobacco smoke is a "serious and substantial public health risk" and classified it as a group A carcinogen.[58] Group A is reserved for compounds or mixtures that have been shown to cause cancer in humans.

In addition to passive smoke's role in respiratory conditions, including cancer, the EPA further found that exposure to passive smoke also increases the risk of asthma and such lower-respiratory tract infections as bronchitis and pneumonia in children, as well as increasing the prevalence of middle ear disease and reduced lung function in children.[59]

Responding to growing concern over passive smoking, in 1994, the Occupational Safety and Health Administration (OSHA) proposed sweeping rules regulating indoor air quality in the workplace. Although six months of hearings on these proposed regulations were conducted in 1995, at the time of this writing, no specific action has been taken on the proposals. The OSHA rules would have forced most employers to ban smoking rather than simply setting aside specific areas in which smoking could occur.

In spite of the lack of federal regulation, the private sector has taken clear action to reduce passive smoke exposure. In one highly visible instance in 1994, McDonald's announced that all 1,400 company-owned stores would be smoke-free in the interest of children and because the majority of their customers preferred such an environment. Arby's and Wendy's followed suit soon after. Nowhere, however, is smoking more noticeably prohibited than in the U.S. airline industry. Currently, smoking is banned on all domestic flights and international flights of less than six hours. Individual airlines have banned smoking entirely, even on their longest international flights.

Outside the public sector, the United States Army and Air Force have moved to reduce exposure to smoke by ending their long-time subsidy of tobacco products sold on posts and bases.

SMOKING CESSATION

Assuming that adults quit smoking in the same proportions that we see today, by the year 2000 the number of adult ex-smokers will equal the number of adult smokers. Contributing to the decline are (1) warning labels on cigarette packages, (2) physicians' advice to quit, (3) antismoking advertising, (4) worksite smoking-cessation programs, (5) increased restrictions on places to smoke, (6) reduced insurance premiums for nonsmokers, and (7) increased taxes on cigarettes.[60]

Experts believe that the campaign against smoking by the Public Health Service, other governmental agencies, and many volunteer agencies and individuals has played an important role in reducing the number of adult smokers. Smoking cessation avoided or postponed an estimated 789,000 smoking-related deaths by 1991. Projecting into the future, as many as 2.1 million lives may be saved from premature death by the year 2000.

Clearly, cessation of smoking and preventing initiation of smoking is an important goal. Statistics show that one in four people who smoke will be able to quit before the age of 60. Of course, one should attempt to stop at the youngest age possible, as a great deal of damage, some irreparable, occurs with each year of smoking. Better yet, one should never start smoking rather than hope to be able to quit. Nevertheless, for those who have managed to quit or will quit, after about 10 years, death rates approach those for nonsmokers.

STOPPING TOBACCO USE

Experts in health behavior contend that before people will discontinue harmful health behaviors, such as tobacco use, they must understand fully what they are expecting of themselves. This understanding grows in relationship to the following:

1. *Knowledge* about the health risks associated with tobacco use
2. *Recognition* that these health risks are applicable to all tobacco users
3. *Familiarity* with steps that can be taken to eliminate or reduce these risks
4. *Belief* that the benefits to be gained by no longer using tobacco will outweigh the pleasures gained through the use of tobacco
5. *Certainty* that one can start and maintain the behaviors required to stop or reduce the use of tobacco

On closer examination, we see that these steps combine both knowledge and desire (or motivation). Being knowledgeable about risks will not always stop behaviors that involve varying degrees of psychological and physical dependence. The 75% failure rate thought to be common among tobacco cessation programs suggests that maintaining the motivation to discontinue tobacco use is not as easy as many people believe. In spite of this, however, only one successful attempt is necessary for one to enjoy a healthier and longer life.

Among the variety of smoking cessation programs, some use a highly organized format, with or without the use of prescription or OTC nicotine-replacement systems. In past years, most of the 1.3 million people who managed to quit smoking each year did so by throwing away their cigarettes (going **cold turkey**) and paying the physical and emotional price of waiting for their bodies to adjust to life without nicotine. Today, however, nicotine-replacement products are combined with external programs or programs accompanying the nicotine replacement product itself.

Smoking cessation programs come in a variety of formats, including educational programs, behavior modification, aversive conditioning using noxious stimuli, hypnosis, acupuncture, and various combinations of these approaches. Programs are offered in both individual and group settings by hospitals, universities, health departments, voluntary health agencies, churches, and private practitioners. The better programs have limited success, at 20% to 50% as measured over one year (with self-reporting), whereas the remainder have even poorer results.

cold turkey abrupt cessation of the use of a drug, such as tobacco; refers to the "gooseflesh" sometimes experienced during withdrawal

ALTERNATIVE CHOICES

Alternatives to Complete Cessation of Tobacco Use

If you are a tobacco user who recognizes the serious health risks involved with smoking but do not think you can quit, you have some alternatives. In support of your health, you can:

1. Replace your current high-tar and high-nicotine cigarette brand with a low-tar and low-nicotine brand.
2. Reduce your consumption of cigarettes, regardless of brand, by smoking fewer cigarettes, inhaling less often and less deeply, and smoking only half the cigarette.
3. Practice both the preceding alternatives.

Another alternative is to obtain nicotine through a nontobacco source. Nicorette, the nicotine-containing chewing gum, is designed to assist those who wish to reduce and even eventually stop smoking. When one chews this gum, the nicotine is released and absorbed through the mucous membrane of the mouth into the bloodstream. Proper use of the gum results in nicotine levels sufficiently high to discourage cigarette use. Studies in both the United States and England have demonstrated a long-term success rate of 40% or more when gum is used with other smoking-cessation therapies. Its use is contraindicated in people with certain forms of cardiovascular disease.

Another nontobacco source of nicotine that has been shown to be effective is the nicotine transdermal patch (see chapter 4). As with all transdermal delivery systems, a steady supply of the active drug is provided to the body as long as the patch is worn.

Two tools for weaning smokers from cigarettes to a nontobacco source of nicotine are nicotine-containing chewing gum (Nicorette), in either prescription or OTC versions, and transdermal patches (Nicoderm, Nicotrol, Habitrol, Prostep), in either prescription or OTC versions, using either single-strength or step-down formats. Following are brief descriptions of gum and the transdermal patch. However, prescription and OTC formulations vary, and brands vary:[61]

Nicotine-containing chewing gum. Correct use of nicotine-containing chewing gum requires an immediate cessation of smoking, an initial determination of dosage (4 mg or 2 mg of nicotine per piece), the appropriate manner of chewing each piece of gum, the appropriate time to chew each piece, the maximum number of pieces to be chewed each day, and time to begin withdrawal from the therapy. When used with physician guidance or program support provided by the manufacturer, nicotine-containing gum may have a success rate of 40% or more. Nicotine-containing chewing gum therapy ranges in cost from an initial $50 kit to weekly refills of approximately $30.

Transdermal nicotine patches. The more recently developed transdermal (through the skin) nicotine patches appear to be less effective (25%) than the gum just described but in many ways are more easily used. If the smoker uses a step-down version (21 mg, 14 mg, 7 mg), one must determine the appropriate initial dosage (based on number of cigarettes smoked per day and body weight), the length of time at the initial dosage before stepping down, and the manner of withdrawal after a usual 8- to 12-week treatment period. The single dose (15 mg) versions, of course, eliminate the step-down component. The cost of the transdermal nicotine-replacement therapy is similar to that of the gum-based program.

In all delivery forms and concentrations, nicotine-replacement therapy carries with it contraindications and adverse reactions, including skin irritations, redness, and irregular heart rate.

A recently developed prescription medication, mecamylamine, used in combination with the transdermal nicotine patch, improves the latter's effectiveness rate to the 40% level reported for nicotine-containing chewing gum. The drug affects receptors in the CNS, reducing the pleasurable effects of nicotine and decreasing dependence.

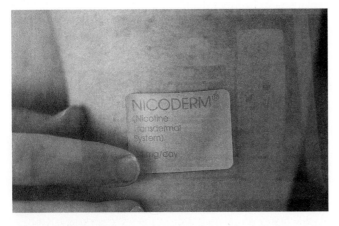

Transdermal nicotine patches have been shown to be effective in helping people quit smoking.

FIGURE 12.4

This newly approved nicotine replacement inhalation device is an alternative to transdermal patches and chewing gum.

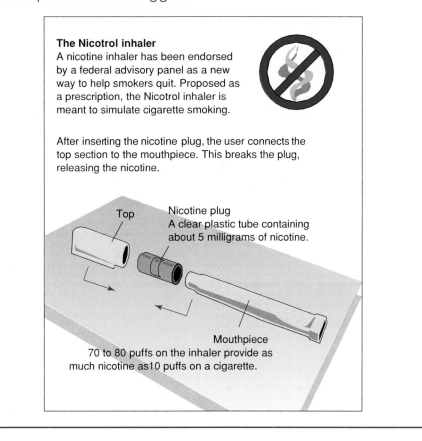

The Nicotrol inhaler
A nicotine inhaler has been endorsed by a federal advisory panel as a new way to help smokers quit. Proposed as a prescription, the Nicotrol inhaler is meant to simulate cigarette smoking.

After inserting the nicotine plug, the user connects the top section to the mouthpiece. This breaks the plug, releasing the nicotine.

Top

Nicotine plug
A clear plastic tube containing about 5 milligrams of nicotine.

Mouthpiece
70 to 80 puffs on the inhaler provide as much nicotine as 10 puffs on a cigarette.

In addition to mecamylamine, a nicotine-replacement therapy using inhalation has just been endorsed (in prescription form) by a federal advisory group to the FDA. Figure 12.4 depicts a "cigarette holder" device and describes its method of use. Because of the large surface area of the lungs and rapid absorption into the blood, inhalation-based delivery of nicotine should become a very attractive alternative to transdermal and oral routes of replacement.

RJ Reynolds unsuccessfully attempted to develop a safer cigarette, *Premier*, in the early 1990s and is currently developing another attempt. *Eclipse* heats rather than burns tobacco to reduce the amount of smoke and alter the composition of the smoke generated by the cigarette.[62] Test marketing results suggest less than a burning interest in the product, principally because of the difficulty in lighting the cigarette and the limited effect of its reduced nicotine.

Very few insurance programs will cover the cost of smoking-cessation programs and nicotine-replacement treatment, particularly without physician involvement.

SMOKELESS TOBACCO

Thanks to the resurgence of smokeless tobacco, no longer are professional baseball players the only Americans to know the value of an empty coffee can or empty soft drink cup. These discarded containers are becoming standard equipment for people who dip and chew smokeless tobacco. Both the NCAA and National Association of Professional Baseball Leagues (minor leagues), however, have banned the use of smokeless tobacco, although the NAIA and Major League Baseball have not.

As the term implies, smokeless tobacco is not burned; rather, it is placed in the mouth. Once the tobacco is in place, the physiologically active nicotine and other soluble compounds are absorbed through the mucous membranes and into the blood. Within a few minutes, nicotine levels in the blood reach concentrations equivalent to those of cigarette smokers. The user of smokeless tobacco experiences the effects of nicotine without being exposed to the carbon monoxide and tar generated by burning tobacco.

A recent survey by the Centers for Disease Control and Prevention estimated that in 1994, 6.1 million men (6.1%) and 735,000 women (0.7%) 18 years of age or older used moist snuff or other smokeless tobacco products during the month the survey was taken.[63] Unfortunately, many who choose to use "spit tobacco," as former Surgeon General Antonia Novello prefers to call it, begin long before adulthood. In the study cited above, 599,000 young people between 12 and 17 years old also had used smokeless tobacco during the same period.[64] Young males were much more likely to be users than were females.

Although smokeless tobacco would seem to free the tobacco user from some of the health risks of smoking, smokeless tobacco does not represent a safe alternative to smoking. Both chewing tobacco and dipping (using snuff) carry substantial health risks. These include the development of **periodontal disease**, a gum disease that may result in the loss of teeth, abrasive damage to the enamel of the teeth caused by the tobacco, tooth decay from the sugar added to the tobacco during processing, and oral cancer.

In 1979, the Surgeon General's report revealed an association between the use of smokeless tobacco and oral cancer.[65] In 1986, seven years later, a definite causal link was established. In the 1989 report, carcinogenic tobacco-specific nitrosamines were reported in high concentrations in smokeless tobacco. Oral cancer is believed to result from the frequent contact of cheek and gum epithelium cells with these carcinogenic agents in the tobacco.

Two early signs of impending disease are the formation of precancerous **leukoplakia** (white spots) and **erythroplakia** (red spots), precursors to oral cancer (see

> ### SMOKELESS TOBACCO: SIGNS OF IMPENDING DISEASE*
>
> 1. Lumps in the jaw or neck area
> 2. Color change in lumps inside the lips
> 3. White, smooth, or scaly patches in the mouth or throat or on the lips or tongue
> 4. A red spot or sore on the lips or gums or inside the mouth that does not heal in two weeks
> 5. Difficulty or abnormality in speaking or swallowing
>
> *When any of these indicators of change are noted, users should stop using smokeless tobacco and promptly notify a dentist or physician.

the box above). In smokeless tobacco users who develop oral cancer, delayed treatment can allow the tumor to spread to the jaw, neck, or brain. In addition to the damage to the tissues of the mouth and throat, the need to process the inadvertently swallowed saliva that contains dissolved carcinogens places both the digestive and urinary systems at risk of cancer.

Clearly, those who use smokeless tobacco have chosen a dangerous product. Continued use of tobacco in this form is a serious threat to health.

SUMMARY

Cigarettes, cigars, pipe tobacco, and smokeless tobacco are familiar tobacco products. The history of tobacco reflects changes in consumer preference for various tobacco products. The production, sale, and export of

Smokeless tobacco (sometimes called "spit tobacco") is not a safe alternative to cigarette smoking.

SOLUTIONS

Elaine went to the campus health center after suffering for a week with a case of bronchitis that she couldn't seem to shake. The doctor gave her a few pamphlets to read about the effects of smoking on the body. He also gave her an easy-to-follow 12-step program for smoking cessation.

Elaine read over the materials she got from the doctor and talked to Alyssa about how they could work together to quit smoking. The first steps of the program were designed to make smoking inconvenient—something they would have to go out of their way to do. However, Elaine was surprised at what she would do to have a cigarette, such as walking 10 minutes across campus in bitter cold, windy weather to get the pack of cigarettes she had left in the car and then standing outside the lecture hall to smoke one.

Elaine and Alyssa stopped and then started smoking again several times. Each time they quit they noticed a few immediate improvements—their clothes and hair didn't smell of smoke, food tasted better, and they could breathe more easily. On her fourth attempt, Elaine gave up cigarettes cold turkey. She found herself avoiding Alyssa, who still smoked, because being around her made cigarettes too tempting. After the first few days, her cravings became tolerable, and by the end of her first smoke-free month, Elaine could declare proudly that she had kicked the habit for good.

---

tobacco is changing as the American market remains relatively slow, while demand for American tobacco products abroad increases.

The marketing of cigarettes is under attack because of concerns that tobacco is being marketed to adolescents in spite of tobacco industry contentions that it is not. Specific restrictions proposed by the Clinton administration are under review.

Nicotine is the primary psychoactive component of tobacco. It enters the body through inhalation, in the case of smoking, and through mucous linings of the mouth, in the case of dipping and chewing. Nicotine readily crosses both the blood-brain barrier and the placental barrier. Most of the nicotine dose absorbed is eventually biodeactivated by liver enzymes and excreted through the kidneys.

Both short-term effects on CNS function and the long-term effects of chronic use can be observed. Nicotine produces dependence in humans, resulting in both addiction and habituation. It affects physiological function within the nervous system by interfering with normal neurotransmitter activity. The cardiovascular, respiratory, and gastrointestinal systems are also affected by the presence of nicotine.

Cigarette smoke is a complex mixture of gases and particles, most of which are biologically active. The gaseous component of tobacco smoke includes carbon monoxide, benzopyrene, and many other gases. The particulate component is called tar. Cigarette smoke reduces the oxygen-carrying capacity of the blood, constricts vessels, alters epithelial tissue, and otherwise harms the body. Several forms of cancer are directly related to tobacco use, and virtually all remaining forms of cancer are influenced by tobacco use. Cardiovascular

and cerebrovascular disease are also strongly influenced by tobacco use, as are several respiratory diseases.

According to 1994 statistics, smoking prevalence has peaked for both adult males and females and is lowest among people with more formal education. On a more distressing note, however, the incidence of smoking among 12- to 18-year-olds has increased each year since 1991. The public is becoming concerned about this demographic trend.

Concern over the health risks of passive smoking is also growing. Mainstream, sidestream, and environmental tobacco smoke collectively contribute to several clearly documented types of illnesses that are more frequently seen in the partners and children of tobacco users than nontobacco users. Smoking is now a factor in charges of child neglect and in the awarding of child custody in divorces.

Reducing tobacco use by Americans is a goal of public health officials. A variety of programs and practices can help smokers stop the use of tobacco. Nicotine-replacement therapies once available only as prescription medications are now available over the counter. When one stops smoking, positive changes in physiological

---

periodontal disease disease of the tissue supporting the teeth

leukoplakia white, smooth or scaly patches in the mouth or on the lips, tongue, or throat suggesting precancerous cellular changes

erythroplakia red patches (similar to the white patches of leukoplakia) suggesting advanced changes in precancerous cells

function can be observed. The tobacco industry continues its limited efforts to produce a "safer" cigarette.

Smokeless tobacco, including snuff and chewing tobacco, is popular with many younger tobacco users. Although smokeless tobacco users are free from the effects of carbon monoxide and inhaled particles, the risks of using smokeless tobacco remain unacceptably high. Oral cancer, in particular, is a serious health threat to smokeless tobacco users.

REVIEW QUESTIONS

1. Briefly describe how the public's preferences for tobacco products have changed through the years. How have these changes influenced the export of tobacco products?
2. What group does the tobacco industry say is the target audience of its advertising? Why is the health-care community concerned about the goal of this advertising?
3. What restrictions on tobacco advertising and sales have the Clinton administration proposed?
4. How is nicotine taken into the body, distributed, and removed? Describe nicotine's distribution in the body, including the blood-brain and placental barriers.
5. What is the acute influence of nicotine on CNS function? What additional acute effects are seen in other body systems during exposure to nicotine?
6. What are the explanations suggested for nicotine addiction and habituation?
7. How does the carbon monoxide found in the gaseous portion of smoke affect cardiorespiratory function? What body tissue is particularly damaged by the particulate matter (tar) found in cigarette smoke?
8. Name several disease processes that are strongly affected by cigarette smoking and tobacco use.
9. What are some of the factors that have contributed to the decline in smoking among adults. What direction is tobacco use taking among today's adolescents?
10. What techniques for stopping smoking are currently available to smokers who want to quit? What is the current status of nicotine-replacement therapy in this country?
11. Is smokeless tobacco a positive alternative to other forms of tobacco use? What are the health consequences of long-term smokeless tobacco use?

REFERENCES

1. G. Arents, Jr., *Tobacco: Its History, Illustrated by Books, Manuscripts, and Engravings*, vol. 1 (New York: Rosenbach, 1937).
2. T. H. Goodspeed, *The Genus Nicotiana: Origins, Relationships, and Evolutions of Its Species in Light of Their Distribution, Morphology and Cytogenetics* (Waltham, Mass.: Chronica Botanica, 1954).
3. Ibid.
4. Arents, *Tobacco*.
5. J. M. Price, *France and the Chesapeake: A History of the French Tobacco Monopoly, 1774–1791, and of Its Relationship to the British and American Tobacco Trades* (Ann Arbor: University of Michigan Press, 1973).
6. E. M. Brecher, *Licit and Illicit Drugs: The Consumers Union Report on Narcotics, Stimulants, Depressants, Inhalants, Hallucinogens, and Marijuana—including Caffeine, Nicotine, and Alcohol* (Boston: Little, Brown, 1972).
7. O. Ray, and C. Ksir, *Drugs, Society, and Human Behavior*, 7th ed. (St. Louis: Mosby, 1997).
8. The Encyclopedia Americana, *Cigars* (Danbury, Conn.: Grolier, 1988).
9. U.S. Department of Commerce, Bureau of the Census, *Statistical Abstract of the United States 1960*, 81st ed. (Washington, D.C.: U.S. Government Printing Office, 1960).
10. M. Wells, "Women Fire Up Cigars, Put 'She' in Hedonism," *USA Today*, 25 June 1996, p. 1b.
11. U.S. Department of Commerce, Bureau of the Census, *Statistical Abstract of the United States 1995*, 115th ed. (Washington, D.C.: U.S. Government Printing Office, 1995).
12. G. Giovino, M. Schooley, et al., "Surveillance for Selected Tobacco-Use Behavior—United States, 1900–1994," *MMWR* 43(SS-3):6–7, 18 November 1994.
13. U.S. Department of Commerce, Bureau of the Census, *Statistical Abstract of the United States 1996*, 116th ed. (Washington, D.C.: U.S. Government Printing Office, 1996).
14. M. Wells, "Philip Morris Fires Up New Magazine," *USA Today*, 24 July 1996, p. 1b.
15. "Thank You for Smoking: Tobacco Firms Hoe Friendly Turf in Taverns," *USA Today*, 1 July 1996, p. 8b.
16. K. Thomas, "Lighting Up: Tobacco Has a Role in Most Movies," *USA Today*, 7 November 1996, p. 6d.
17. "Cigarette Ads: A Matter of Life and Death," *USA Today*, 25 March 1992, p. 11a.
18. Ibid.
19. "Marketing Study of Teen Smoking by Tobacco Industry," *Journal of Marketing*, 4 April 1996.
20. D. Enrico, "Survey: Tobacco Ads Reach Teens," *USA Today*, 18 December 1996.
21. D. J. K. Balfour, ed., "Nicotine and the Tobacco Smoking Habit," in *International Encyclopedia of Pharmacology and Therapeutics* (New York: Pergamon, 1984).
22. N. L. Benowitz, *The Use of Biologic Fluid Samples in Accessing Tobacco Consumption*, Research Monograph

48 (Rockville, Md.: National Institute on Drug Abuse, USPHS, 1983).

23. H. H. Szeto, "Maternal-Fetal Pharmacokinetics and Fetal Dose-Response Relationships," *Ann N Y Acad Sci* 562 (1989):42.

24. R. M. Julien, *A Primer of Drug Action*, 6th ed. (New York: W. H. Freeman, 1992).

25. B. R. Kuhnert, and P. M. Kuhnert, *Placental Transfer of Drugs, Alcohol, and Components of Cigarette Smoke and Their Effects on the Human Fetus*, Research Monograph 60 (Rockville, Md.: National Institute on Drug Abuse, 1985).

26. Personal Interview, Nicki Turner, M. D., Ball Memorial Hospital, Muncie, Ind., 2 January 1996.

27. "Improved Concentration, Neurological Basis," *Nature*, 4 November 1996.

28. R. Lehne, L. Crosby, D. Hamilton, and L. Moore, *Pharmacology for Nursing Care* (Philadelphia: W. B. Saunders, 1990).

29. Personal Interview, Art Ulene, M. D., NBC News, New York, 6 November 1995.

30. D. Hahn, and W. Payne, *Focus on Health*, 3rd ed. (St. Louis: Mosby Publishing, 1997).

31. S. Shiffman, "Chippers—Individual Differences in Tobacco Dependence," *Psychopharmacology*, 97, no. 4 (1989):539–47.

32. M. Russell, "Cigarette Smoking: Natural History of a Dependency Disorder," *Br J Med Psych* 44 (1971):1.

33. D. McGehee, "Nicotine Enhancement of Fast Excitatory Synaptic Transmission in CNS by Presynaptic Receptors," *Science* 269:1692–96, 22 September 1995.

34. Centers for Disease Control, "The Surgeon General's 1989 Report on Reducing the Health Consequences of Smoking: 25 Years of Progress (Executive summary), *MMWR* 38 (1989):1(Suppl 5-2).

35. Ibid.

36. G. Giovino, M. Schooley, et al., "Surveillance for Selected Tobacco-Use Behavior—United States, 1900–1994," *MMWR* 43(SS-3):6–7, 18 November 1994.

37. National Center for Health Statistics, "Advance Report of Final Mortality Statistics, 1991," *Monthly Vital Statistics Report* 42(2):21, Suppl., Hyattsville, Md., 1993.

38. Centers for Disease Control and Prevention, "Cigarette Smoking—Attributable Mortality and Years of Potential Life Lost—United States, 1990," *MMWR* 42, no. 33 (1993):645.

39. Centers for Disease Control, *Surgeon General's 1989 Report*.

40. Centers for Disease Control and Prevention, "Cigarette Smoking among Adults: United States, 1991," *MMWR* 42, no. 12 (1993):230.

41. Ibid.

42. Centers for Disease Control and Prevention, "Cigarette Smoking among Adults: United States, 1994," *MMWR* 45, no. 27 (1996):588–90.

43. Ibid.

44. Ibid.

45. M. I. Slattery, et al., "Cigarette Smoking and Exposure to Passive Smoke Are Risk Factors for Cervical Cancer," *JAMA* 261, no. 11 (1989):1593.

46. R. A. Hatcher, et al., *Contraceptive Technology: 1988–1989*, 5th ed. (New York: Irving Publishing, 1988).

47. B. Haglund, and C. Sven, "Cigarette Smoking as a Risk Factor for Sudden Infant Death Syndrome: A Population-Based Study," *Am J Pub Health* 80, no. 1 (1990):29.

48. L. S. Johnston, P. M. O'Malley, and J. G. Bachman, *Smoking, Drinking, and Illicit Drug Use among American Secondary School Students, College Students and Young Adults, 1975–1991*, vol. 2, *College Students and Young Adults*, NIH Pub. No. 93-3481 (Rockville, Md.: National Institute on Drug Abuse, USDHHS, USPHS, 1992).

49. *The Monitoring the Future Study* (Ann Arbor: The University of Michigan, 1995).

50. Hahn and Payne, *Focus on Health*.

51. **American Journal of Public Health** . . . ability of young smokers to quit . . . **03/11/96**

52. Hahn and Payne, *Focus on Health*.

53. Ibid.

54. Ibid.

55. **Circulation** . . . risks of smoke to nonsmoking partners . . . **08/15/96**.

56. K. Uberlaik, "Lung Cancer from Passive Smoking: Hypothesis or Convincing Evidence?" *Int Arch Occup Environ Health* 59, no. 5 (1987):421.

57. Slattery, et al., *Contraceptive Technology*.

58. Environmental Protection Agency (EPA), *Respiratory Health Effects of Passive Smoking, Fact Sheet* (Washington, D. C.: 1993).

59. Hahn and Payne, *Focus on Health*.

60. Centers for Disease Control and Prevention, "Trends in Cigarette Smoking: Wisconsin, 1950–1988, *MMWR* 38, no. 44 (1989):752.

61. **PDR** (prescription) . . . **1996.** **PDR**(OTC) . . . **1996.**

62. "Eclipse Doesn't Light Up Smokers," *USA Today*, 26 March 1996, p. 4d.

63. U.S. Department of Health and Human Services, *National Household Survey on Drug Abuse: Population Estimates 1994*, DHHS Pub. No. (PHS) 95-3063, 1995.

64. Ibid.

65. U. S. Department of Health, Education, and Welfare, *Smoking and Health: A Report of the Surgeon General*, U.S. DHEW, Office of Assistant Secretary for Health, Office of Smoking and Health, DHEW Pub. No. (PHS) 79-50066, 1979.

SOURCES FOR HELP

American Lung Association
1740 Broadway
New York, NY 10019
(212) 315–8700

Action on Smoking and Health (ASH)
2013 H St., N.W.
Washington, D.C. 20006
(202) 659–4310

Council for Tobacco Research
900 Third Ave.
New York, NY 10022
(212) 421–8885

Smoking Control Advocacy Resource Center
1730 Rhode Island Ave., N.W.
Washington, D.C. 20036
(202) 659–8475

Tobacco Institute
1875 I St., N.W.
Washington, D.C. 20006
(202) 457–4800

Campaign for Tobacco-Free Kids
1707 L St. N.W.
Suite 800
Washington, D.C. 20036
(800) 284–KIDS

THE METHYLXANTHINES: CAFFEINE AND RELATED COMPOUNDS

CHAPTER OBJECTIVES

After studying this chapter, you will be able to:

1. Identify the specific compounds that comprise the methylxanthines.

2. List the wide array of beverages through which caffeine is available.

3. Describe the long history associated with tea and coffee consumption.

4. Explain the pharmacological effects of the methylxanthines.

5. Differentiate between the acute responses to caffeine and those associated with chronic use.

6. Describe the relationship between caffeine consumption and several health-related areas, including heart and vascular disease, cancer, athletic performance, and suicide.

7. Define the term *caffeinism*.

8. Describe techniques that can be used to reduce or eliminate dependence on caffeine.

PROFILE

Ray's restaurant opened at 5:00 in the morning and ministered to the nutritional, social, and spiritual needs of countless working men and women, some children, an occasional dog at the back door, and a middle-aged professor who talked too much about health.

Ray was never without a cup of coffee in hand, even as he turned the bacon, flipped the hot cakes, or rang up a sale on the cash register. Without missing a beat he would regularly draw a cup of coffee whenever he passed the giant coffee urn that was visible from each stool at his lunch counter. Daily from 5:00 A.M. until the restaurant closed at 2:00 P.M., Ray would consume the equivalent of 20 to 25 full cups of coffee that were drawn in quarter- to half-cup increments.

One day the middle-aged professor talked to him about the many health concerns associated with such a high intake of caffeine and the fact that caffeine is highly addictive. After hearing about how his coffee consumption could be responsible for his high blood pressure and his increasingly poor night's sleep, Ray decided to try and cut back a bit. He tried several times but in the end failed to reduce his coffee intake.

How important is it for Ray to reduce his caffeine consumption? How do you think he might be able to do so? After learning more about this familiar drug by reading this chapter, turn to the solutions box on page 000 to find out how Ray was able to break his coffee habit.

THE METHYLXANTHINES: CAFFEINE, THEOPHYLLINE, AND THEOBROMINE

In comparison to all other types of drugs discussed in this book, none is as frequently used, as readily available, and as socially acceptable as the **methylxanthines.** Clearly, you know the methylxanthines if you have drunk a cup of coffee, enjoyed a caffeinated soft drink, ordered iced tea with a meal, or eaten a piece of chocolate candy. In fact, the newest consumer product with a methylxanthine added to its formulation is plain water, marketed under the label *Water Joe.*[1]

The methylxanthines are a family of chemicals that includes three compounds: caffeine, theophylline, and theobromine. Chemically, these compounds are soluble alkaloids with similar structures and similar stimulatory effects. Since caffeine has the greatest effect on the CNS, most of our discussion will refer to this compound.

Caffeine can be found in coffee, tea, cocoa, many soft drinks, several groups of OTC drugs (see chapter 11), and as mentioned previously, in specially formulated water. The tendency of Americans toward liberal consumption of coffee and soft drinks and their willingness to use OTC drugs means that many Americans consume significant amounts of caffeine each day. In fact, in the minds of many, drinking a caffeine-based beverage or taking a caffeine-containing OTC medication is an effective way to offset the effects of boredom and tiredness associated with work and school.

Of the remaining two methylxanthines, theophylline is the primary methylxanthine in tea. This substance is a less potent CNS stimulant than caffeine. Theobromine is the predominant methylxanthine in chocolate.

Many people rely on caffeine to lessen feelings of fatigue and boredom.

Theobromine is also not as strong a CNS stimulant as caffeine.

HISTORY OF CAFFEINE

The consumption of beverages containing caffeine is, as you might imagine, by no means of recent origin. Tea, according to legend, was discovered by the Chinese emperor Shen Nung in 2737 B.C. when, while boiling water, leaves from a local plant, *Camellia sinensis*, landed in the water. The tea leaves imparted a new and pleasing taste to the emperor's familiar drink of plain hot water and left the emperor with "vigor of body, contentment of mind, and determination of purpose."[2]

Tea quickly became China's national beverage. Today in the United States, 2.25 billion gallons of tea are consumed annually, mostly in the form of iced tea.[3]

The history of coffee, the principal source of caffeine for Americans, is also antiquated. Coffee, in nonbeverage form, was first used as a form of currency and consumed as a food in Africa in approximately A.D. 600. Somewhat later, in the same area of Africa, coffee began being used as a beverage.

The habit of coffee consumption appears to have slowly moved northward toward the Mediterranean regions of Africa, reaching the Arab world by the eleventh century. Soon after, it was introduced into wide areas of southern Europe, including Spain. Its arrival in the Americas may have occurred in conjunction with Spanish exploration and conquests. Regardless of the exact route that coffee took in reaching modern America, its presence is well established. Today, nearly 2 billion pounds of roasted coffee is imported into this country annually, with the majority coming from Brazil, Colombia, and Mexico.[4] Per capita coffee consumption in this country fell from 3.12 cups per day in 1962 to 1.75 cups per day in 1991.[5] Now, however, the popularity of coffee is surging, with coffeehouses springing up across the country.

SOURCES OF CAFFEINE

In addition to coffee and tea, caffeine is an important component of many commercial soft drinks, and the caffeine content of some of these beverages is significant (table 13.1). (The designation of "cola" or "sugar-free cola" does not indicate the caffeine content of the drink.) Likewise, many OTC drugs contain significant amounts of caffeine. These OTC products include not only stimulants, such as No-Doz and Vivarin, but also analgesics (pain killers), such as Anacin, Excedrin, and Vanquish (table 13.2).

PHARMACOLOGY OF CAFFEINE

Caffeine and the other methylxanthines are ingested in water-soluble form and are absorbed into the bloodstream primarily through the small intestine. Absorption is rapid and essentially complete.[6] Effects can be felt in 30 minutes, and peak levels of CNS activity usually occur within two hours of ingestion.[7] Caffeine is evenly distributed throughout the tissues of the body, including the brain and the placenta and fetus of a pregnant woman. Biodeactivation is accomplished by liver enzymes before excretion by the urinary system. About 10% of the caffeine ingested is excreted unchanged. The half-life of caffeine in the body ranges from three to seven hours.[8]

MECHANISM OF ACTION OF CAFFEINE AND OTHER METHYLXANTHINES

It is believed that caffeine inhibits an enzyme, cAMP phosphodiesterase, that breaks down cyclic adenosine monophosphate (cAMP). Cyclic adenosine monophosphate, a **second messenger,** is a component of the internal cellular communication process that allows cells to respond in an excitory manner to various stimuli.[9] Because less than a normal amount of cAMP is broken down due to caffeine's inhibitory influence on the enzyme, a build-up of cAMP increases cellular activity, resulting in a generalized excitation of the nervous system.

Iced tea is the most popular form of tea in the United States.

methylxanthines a family of chemical compounds that includes caffeine, theophylline, and theobromine

second messenger a regulatory chemical compound within cells that is activated by the presence of a hormone (first messenger) or other chemicals

TABLE 13.1   Caffeine Content of Selected Beverages

Soft Drinks	mg Caffeine per 12-Oz Can	
Jolt	100.0	
Sugar-Free Mr. Pibb	58.8	
Mountain Dew	54.0	(0 in Canada)
Mello Yellow	52.8	
Tab	46.8	
Coca-Cola	45.6	
Diet Cola	45.6	
Shasta Cola	44.4	
Shasta Cherry Cola	44.4	
Shasta Diet Cola	44.4	
Mr. Pibb	40.8	
Dr. Pepper	39.6	
Pepsi Cola	38.4	
Aspen	36.0	
Diet Pepsi	36.0	
RC Cola	36.0	
Diet RC	36.0	
Diet Rite	36.0	
Canada Dry Cola	30.0	
Canada Dry Diet Cola	1.2	
7 Up	0	

Coffee	mg per 7-Oz Cup
Drip	115–175
Espresso—1 serving (1.5–2 oz)	100
Brewed	80–135
Instant	65–100
Decaf, brewed	3–4
Decaf, instant	2–3

Tea	
Iced (12 oz)	70
Brewed, imported	60
Brewed, U.S.	40
Instant	30

Data from the National Soft Drink Association and Bunker and McWilliams: *J Am Diet Assn* 74:28.

ACUTE EFFECTS OF CAFFEINE

In the CNS, caffeine stimulates the brain's cortex, resulting in increased mental awareness, alertness, and a quickening of thought processes. At higher doses, restlessness, agitation, tremors, and cardiac dysrhythmias can occur. At extremely high doses, convulsions and death can occur. This is extremely rare, however, because a lethal dose would require the drinking of about 100 cups of coffee. At normal doses, the stimulatory effects of caffeine are much weaker than those of amphetamines or cocaine. Fortunately, the poststimulatory period of depression is also much milder.

Caffeine and the methylxanthines impart a stimulatory effect on the CNS and, thus, a variety of different muscle tissues. Caffeine affects respiration rate and skeletal musculature. Theophylline, present in tea, affects the heart and smooth muscles and is the most potent diuretic. Theobromine, found in chocolate, exhibits the weakest effects on the CNS and skeletal muscles and only moderately affects the heart and smooth muscles.

Caffeine Intoxication

Independent of these acute effects, some people can consume caffeine so excessively in a short period of time that

TABLE 13.2 Caffeine Content of Selected OTC Drugs

Drug	mg Caffeine per Tablet
Stimulants	
No-Doz tablets	100
Vivarin tablets	200
Pain Relievers	
Anacin	32
Excedrin	65
Excedrin P.M.	0
Midol	32
Vanquish	33
Cold Remedies	
Coryban-D	30

Data from FDA's Center for Drugs and Biologics.

it results in caffeine intoxication. Although very unlikely to result in death, since 100 or more cups of coffee would be needed to do that, heavy consumption of coffee can, nevertheless, produce a toxic response encompassing restlessness, nervousness, excitement, insomnia, flushed face, excessive urination, gastrointestinal disturbances, muscle twitching, incoherent thought and speech, and excessively rapid heart rhythm.[10] When such an extreme response to coffee consumption occurs, medical attention is required, as medication and appropriate emergency care may be necessary.

Safe Dosage Levels for Adults

Because individuals differ greatly in their level of sensitivity to caffeine, determining a safe amount of caffeine is open to speculation. However, it is very likely that a daily consumption up to 600 mg (the equivalent of five to six cups of coffee) is relatively safe for most adults.[11] For people with preexisting health conditions, such as irregular heart beat patterns, as little as two cups of coffee (or the equivalent of one or two OTC "stay awake" pills or three soft drinks) could be unsafe. In children, because of their smaller size, a single soft drink could have harmful effects.

HEALTH CONSEQUENCES OF CHRONIC CAFFEINE USE

The chronic effects of caffeine are controversial and include the questions of tolerance and dependence and possible health consequences. In the section that follows, a review of the health concerns related to caffeine use is presented.

Because of the heavy use of caffeine in America and other countries, a great deal of research has been aimed at determining the role of caffeine in certain diseases.

Efforts have been made to link caffeine to a wide variety of conditions in both adults and children, including heart disease, various forms of cancer, pregnancy-related conditions, and even sleep patterns in older adults and edginess in children. To date, results remain inconclusive. It remains wise, however, to consume caffeine only in moderation.

Heart and Vascular Diseases

To date, this country's first and third leading causes of death (cardiovascular disease and cerebrovascular disease) do not seem to be negatively influenced by moderate consumption of caffeine. Several extensive studies, conducted both in this country and abroad, and involving both male and females subjects, report no **causal relationship** between moderate caffeine consumption and cardiovascular disease, including coronary artery disease, high blood pressure, and irregular heart beat patterns.[12] Of particular interest is a recent study from England showing that tea consumption in males may actually reduce the risk of stroke.[13]

Panic Attack

For nearly two decades the relationship between **panic attack** and caffeine consumption has been recognized. More specifically, in people who have previously experienced these periods of extreme anxiety and fear, moderately heavy consumption of coffee (five to six cups) delivered enough caffeine to precipitate, in a quarter of

causal relationship a relationship between two or more factors in which the occurrence of one factor depends upon the existence of another (causal) factor

panic attack an acute mood disorder characterized by episodes of extreme anxiety and fear

the group being tested, such an attack shortly after the consumption had ended.[14] On the basis of this study, it might be concluded that a first panic attack could occur following caffeine consumption and that people with a history of panic attack should reduce their caffeine consumption in all forms.

Sleep Disturbances

Few people are unaware of the commonly held belief that caffeine consumption late in the evening interferes with sleep. This is, of course, attributable to the stimulatory effect of caffeine on the nervous system, leading to restlessness prior to sleep and the uncomfortable "hangover" upon arising due to the dehydrating effect of caffeine on brain cells. Regardless of the specific mechanism involved in caffeine's influence on sleep, reference books predictably report that insomnia is associated with chronic caffeine use. In support of this contention is a recent study on use of caffeine-containing OTC products among older adults. In this study, it was reported that nearly one-fourth of the participants had greater difficulty falling asleep, had a tendency to sleep less soundly, and were more likely to awaken earlier than they intended.[15] On the other hand, this study failed to double-blind the caffeine status of the beverages or medications being given to subjects. Thus, it is difficult to separate the psychological effect of knowing (or believing) that caffeine was being consumed prior to sleeping from the physiological influence that the caffeine actually delivered.

HEALTH CONSEQUENCES FOR WOMEN

Although caffeine influences the physiological function of men and women in much the same manner, caffeine can affect women in ways unique to their gender. In the section that follows, the relationship between caffeine consumption and breast cancer, ovarian cancer, infertility and pregnancy, and osteoporosis will be explored.

Breast Cancer

Perhaps no caffeine-related cancer topic has received more attention than the influence of caffeine on breast cancer in women. This interest stems perhaps from concerns regarding caffeine consumption and fibrocystic breast condition. In regard to breast cancer and caffeine consumption, postmortem assessment of over 100,000 women who died of breast cancer cannot support an association between caffeine consumption and this second leading form of cancer deaths in women.[16] In fact, a 1987

medical study involving thousands of nurses suggests that caffeine consumption might actually provide some protection from breast cancer.[17]

Ovarian Cancer

As with breast cancer, the relationship between caffeine consumption and ovarian cancer has received recent attention. Again, no positive association could be identified.[18] In fact, the American Cancer Society does not include caffeine consumption as a factor associated with any form of cancer in either its discussion of cancer-related risk factors or dietary-related cancer prevention.[19]

Fibrocystic Breast Condition

Many women are affected by cystic activity within the breast tissue during certain portions of the menstrual cycle. This fibrocystic breast condition results in swelling, tenderness, and the appearance of breast masses resulting from the formation of fluid-filled pockets or cysts. Anecdotal reports of relief of symptoms when caffeine consumption is stopped have been common since the 1970s. Accordingly, many people assumed that the reverse was also true—caffeine consumption worsened fibrocystic breast condition. To date, little support for this assumption has been evident through carefully controlled research.[20]

Infertility and Pregnancy-Related Health Concerns

The association between caffeine consumption and various aspects of pregnancy has been clarified in the last few years; however, questions in this area remain. For example, a recent study found no relationship between caffeine consumption and infertility when caffeine intake was low to moderate (less than 300 mg, or three cups of coffee per day). With heavier consumption, however, caffeine users were more than two times less likely to become pregnant than women who consumed less caffeine.[21]

Once a pregnancy has been established, the effects of caffeine may depend on the level of consumption. For example, a 1993 study reported that even low doses of caffeine (as little as one cup of coffee per day) were associated with miscarriage.[22] Other studies, however, have suggested that risk exists with heavy use but that caffeine consumption has little or no influence on the course of pregnancy when coffee intake is low.[23]

Caffeine's effects on fetal development and breastfeeding have also been frequently examined over the past 25 years. Early animal studies suggested that consuming too much caffeine during pregnancy might be detrimental to the fetus.[24] However, a recent study in humans failed to show any risk to the fetus when mothers drank less than three 8-oz cups of coffee per day. Babies born to women who drank more than three cups of coffee per day (heavy consumption) had a slightly increased risk of bearing infants with low birthweight and smaller head size.[25] In regard to breastfeeding, caffeine does appear in breast milk; thus, nursing infants share caffeine consumption with their mothers.[26]

The most recent studies, involving careful analysis of all earlier studies, failed to demonstrate a negative influence on fetal development or birthweight with light to moderate caffeine consumption. The studies also failed to find any impairment of early infant development in women who consumed caffeine in moderate amounts and breast fed their infants. However, in spite of these more recent studies, most physicians continue to recommend that women who are attempting to become pregnant within the month, or are pregnant, or are breastfeeding should stop, or at least moderate, caffeine consumption.

Osteoporosis

The loss of bone mass (calcium resorption) caused by decreased estrogen availability in menopausal women is called osteoporosis. As loss of bone occurs, women (and some men) become increasingly susceptible to fractures of the hip, wrist, and cervical spine, in addition to chronic pain and discomfort. The potential for developing this debilitating condition is slightly more evident in people who consume large amounts of caffeine before and during the menopausal years. In this regard, women who consume caffeine should be particularly certain to include a milk product (or other good source of calcium, such as calcium-fortified orange juice) in their diet, as the loss of calcium attributed to caffeine can be offset by little more than an ounce of milk.[27]

EFFECTS OF CAFFEINE ON CHILDREN AND ADOLESCENTS

Principally because of soft drink consumption, many children, even young children, and adolescents consume more caffeine than adults might imagine. Caffeine consumption in people of these ages is associated with a positive increase in attention span and manual dexterity, both of which would seem to be beneficial in school-related activities, such as test taking.[28] However, reasoning ability, short-term memory, and numerical reasoning are not generally improved by caffeine consumption.[29] Perhaps, in a test situation, caffeine keeps students awake, but it does not ensure enhanced performance. More worrisome is the edginess and nervousness reported with even moderate caffeine consumption,

particularly in young children after drinking a soft drink or two.[30]

ATHLETIC PERFORMANCE

Athletic performance certainly requires high-level health, which can be affected by caffeine consumption. Current research suggests that for people engaged in endurance activities, caffeine consumption prior to beginning activity can prolong participation, apparently by slowing glycogen depletion by enhancing the body's ability to use fat as a source of energy.[31] On the less desirable side, the gastric disturbance, diuretic effect, and possible diarrhea caused by caffeine consumption may decrease performance, particularly later in the course of activity. In international athletic competition, including the Olympics, caffeine is considered to be a performance-enhancing drug if levels in the body exceed accepted standards.

SUICIDAL BEHAVIOR

Common sense might suggest that people who consume high levels of caffeine are also likely to use alcohol, smoke cigarettes, and feel stress, all factors associated with a higher likelihood of suicide. Several earlier studies attempting to demonstrate this occurrence found, however, that moderate caffeine consumption was associated with lower-than-normal levels of suicide. Most recently, data collected during the large Harvard Nurses Study, mentioned earlier, were used to again test this hypothesis. As had been found in earlier studies, a lower level of suicide was found among people who consumed moderate amounts of caffeine.[32] A lower level of fatal traffic

Heavy caffeine users are more likely to use alcohol, smoke cigarettes, and feel stress.

accidents was also found among caffeine users.[33] No specific explanation of these two findings can be made at this time. It is possible, however, that caffeine consumption reduces emotionally centered stress, thus reducing thoughts of suicide by structuring more relaxed behavior patterns, including "time-out" coffee breaks and periods of planned social interaction with trusted friends. In terms of fatal traffic accidents, caffeine does, of course, increase alertness and, thus, perhaps, improve driving skills. In addition, the use of a car as a means of suicide might be negated by the stress-reducing influence of caffeine consumption.

DEPENDENCE AND TOLERANCE

In spite of the fact that caffeine is a relatively benign drug for most people, it can produce dependence in some people.[34] Chronic consumption of high levels of caffeine is called **caffeinism.** For these caffeine-dependent people, it may be difficult to stay away from coffee for more than a very short period of time. Most of the studies on caffeine dependence have been carried out with coffee. One careful study demonstrated that tolerance to caffeine develops quickly, in as few as four days, and can persist for at least 24 hours. Withdrawal symptoms begin from 6 to 19 hours after the beginning of abstinence from caffeine and peak at about 48 hours. Headache is the most commonly reported physical symptom, and this may be accompanied by depression, fatigue, sleepiness, lethargy, runny nose, persistent yawning, tension, or anxiety.[35] Other studies have reported instances of leg and muscle pain upon withdrawal. When caffeine consumption is resumed, individuals report the cessation of the headache within one to three hours.

caffeinism physical and psychological dependence on caffeine

BREAKING THE CAFFEINE HABIT

Chronic heavy coffee and caffeinated cola drinkers can experience difficulty breaking the caffeine habit. As with those who are attempting to stop smoking, proven approaches may assist caffeine users who wish to leave their dependence behind.

An initial step to take prior to beginning a self-directed weaning from coffee is to make certain that a wellness-oriented lifestyle is in place or can be put into place. This should, of course, include adequate sleep, regular exercise, and healthful dietary practices. Once in place, the following techniques could result in the less frequent use of caffeinated beverages and products or even the complete discontinuation of their use:[36]

A coffee break, with or without a caffeinated beverage, can provide an opportunity for pleasant social interaction.

SOLUTIONS

Ray still started his day with a few regular cups of coffee, but as the morning progressed he tried to work the extra steps into his routine that would bring him over to the decaf pot. This threw everything off—it was the very regularity of his routine that gave him the time and composure to run the counter, grill, and cash register on his own. There is an art to being a short order cook, and Ray was the best.

One day the professor challenged Ray to a friendly wager, "Ray, I'll bet you $100 you can't give up coffee for one year." A few weeks later, when the professor showed up for his "usual," he noticed something different about Ray—he had no coffee cup in hand.

Ray greeted the professor with a wry wink and a smile. "Fill you up, doc? Regular or unleaded? None for me, mind you, and you'd better start saving your pennies. I've gone two weeks now without coffee or caffeine. The headaches are gone, and I'm sleeping like a baby."

"How did you do it?" the professor asked in amazement. He really hadn't expected Ray to take him up on the bet.

"Every day I put my coffee mug in the sink a half hour earlier than I had the day before. It was so gradual that I almost didn't notice that I was cutting back. Now I start my day with a few cups of decaf," he said proudly, "Before you know it, I'll be collecting my hundred bucks!"

1. Keep a record of all caffeine consumption, including type, amount, place, time, and specific circumstances associated with its use.
2. Slowly reduce consumption, by a cup, can, or pill per day.
3. Gradually reconstitute the coffee supply from fully caffeinated to partially caffeinated, and then to decaffeinated coffee.
4. Replace caffeinated tea with decaffeinated tea and replace caffeinated soda with caffeine-free soda.
5. Use smaller cups and glasses.
6. Increase the use of milk in coffee and tea to reduce the absolute amount of caffeinated beverage being consumed.
7. Consider a true alternative to a caffeinated beverage, such as bouillon, cider, herbal tea, and grain-based beverages, such as Postum.
8. Do not restructure home and work routines to avoid caffeine so much that the healthful aspects of a coffee break or evenings out on the town are lost. Remember that noncaffeinated beverages are available; just plan ahead.
9. During times when a caffeine-based beverage would "feel right," substitute another activity, such as taking a walk, jogging, or even taking a short nap.
10. Establish a reward system for yourself as a source of positive motivation. For example, for each week that you remain caffeine free, treat yourself to a movie or other favorite activity.

When the above activities are incorporated into a wellness-oriented lifestyle, dependence on caffeine can be reduced or eliminated without the loss of the more pleasant aspects of having been a regular caffeine user.

SUMMARY

Caffeine and other methylxanthines are the psychoactive components of coffee, tea, cocoa, chocolate candy, many soft drinks, some OTC medications, and even one brand of bottled water. Caffeine and other methylxanthines are CNS stimulants. They are believed to influence CNS function by inhibiting an enzyme that normally reduces the level of cAMP, a second messenger that increases the level of cellular activity. Tolerance and dependence develop with use, and withdrawal symptoms can be observed in people who use methylxanthines, particularly caffeine. Predictable effects, both acute and chronic, can be observed in association with caffeine consumption.

The health consequences of light to moderate caffeine use do not appear to be significant. Usage that exceeds five or six cups of coffee per day raises several health concerns such as those associated with heart and vascular disease, cancer, fibrocystic breast condition, pregnancy and fetal development, osteoporosis, athletic performance, panic attack, and sleep. Acute caffeine intoxication can occur with a single episode of heavy use.

Because of the dependence-forming nature of caffeine, many people attempt to reduce or even eliminate their caffeine use. Several techniques can be employed to aid this process without forcing the caffeine user to completely disengage from the pleasant activities with which caffeine consumption is often associated.

REVIEW QUESTIONS

1. What specific compounds comprise the methylxanthines?

2. Describe the widespread use of caffeine in this country.

3. What is known about the history of tea and coffee? What is the current direction of coffee consumption at this time? In what form is tea often consumed?

4. In terms of absorption, distribution, biodeactivation, and excretion, how does the body process caffeine? What is the influence of caffeine on cAMP, an important second messenger in cellular response to stimuli? What influence does caffeine exert on cardiac and smooth muscle?

5. What are the acute effects of caffeine use? What is caffeine intoxication? What amount of coffee represents the upper limits of safe daily consumption? How dangerous is a single episode of moderately high to heavy caffeine use? Is there a lethal dose for caffeine consumption?

6. What is our current understanding of the association between chronic caffeine consumption and several health conditions, including cardiovascular disease, cancer, athletic performance, sleep disturbances, panic attacks, and suicide? In what manner does caffeine consumption influence breast cancer and ovarian cancer development, osteoporosis, infertility and pregnancy-related problems in women?

7. What are the symptoms of caffeine intoxication? How should it be responded to?

8. To what extent is it possible to become dependent on caffeine? How can caffeine dependence be described?

9. What techniques can be employed to aid in reduction or elimination of caffeine use?

REFERENCES

1. "Just Add Caffeine: Waking Up to Water Joe," *Newsweek*, 127(21):67, 20 May 1996.

2. "Tea: A Story of Serendipity," *FDA Consumer*, 30(2): 22–26, March, 1996.

3. Ibid.

4. Specialty Coffee Association, "Where Our Coffee Comes From," *USA Today*, 8 August 1994, p. 1B.

5. FIND/SVP, "Coffee Cup Doesn't Runneth Over," *USA Today*, 10 February 1994, p. 1D.

6. R. M. Julien, *A Primer of Drug Action*, 7th ed. (New York: W. H. Freeman, 1995). J. E. James, *Caffeine and Health* (New York: Academic Press, 1992).

7. R. Seeley, T. Stephens, and P. Tate, *Anatomy and Physiology*, 3d ed. (St Louis: Mosby Publishing, 1995).

8. Ibid.

9. Ibid.

10. "What Happens When You Overdose?," *Caffeine and Your Health* (November 1996), http://www.seas.upenn.edu/~cpage/caffeine/FAQ4.html

11. "*The Big Picture on Caffeine*," Http:net-abuse.org/lizardo/caff.big.pict.html November, 1996.

12. *Caffeine and Women's Health*, International Food Information Council/Association of Women's Health, Obstetric, and Neonatal Nurses, June, 1994, http://www.social.com/health/ific/food_additives/caff-wh.html

13. S. O. Keli, M. G. Hertog, E. J. Feskens, and D. Kromhout, "Dietary Flavonoids, Antioxidant Vitamins, and Incidence of Stroke: The Zutphen Study," *Archives of Internal Medicine*, 156(6):637–42, 25 March 1996.

14. R. Ray, and C. Ksir, *Drugs, Society, and Human Behavior*, 7th ed. (St Louis: Mosby, 1996).

15. S. L. Brown, et al., "Occult Caffeine as a Source of Sleep Problems in an Older Population," *Journal of the American Geriatics Society* 43(8):860–64, 9 August 1995.

16. *Cancer Facts and Figures—1996* (Atlanta: American Cancer Society, 1996).

17. *Harvard Nurse's Health Study*, W. C. Willett, M. J. Stampfer, G. A. Colditz, et al. Dietary fat and the risk of breast cancer, **NEJM**, 316(1):22–28, January 1987.

18. *Caffeine and Women's Health*.

19. Cancer Facts and Figures

20. *Caffeine and Women's Health*.

21. F. Grodstein, M. B. Goldman, and R. L. Cramer, "Relation of Female Infertility to Consumption of Caffeinated Beverages," *American Journal of Epidemiology* 137(12):1353–60, 15 June 1993.

22. C. Infante-Rivard, et al., "Fetal Loss Associated with Caffeine Intake before and during Pregnancy," *JAMA* 270(24):2940-2943,

23. *Caffeine and Women's Health*.

24. T. J. Sabotka, "Neurobehavioral Effects of Prenatal Caffeine: Prenatal Abuse of Licit and Illicit Drugs," *Ann N Y Acad Sci* 562(1989):327.

25. J. L. Mills, et al., "Moderate Caffeine Use and the Risk of Spontaneous Abortion and Intrauterine Growth Retardation," *JAMA* 269, no. 5 (1993):593.

26. *Caffeine and Women's Health*.

27. "Osteoporosis: Boning Up on the Latest Facts," *Dairy Council Digest* 67, no. 1 (February 1996):1–5.

28. G. A. Bernstein, et al., "Caffeine Effects on Learning, Performance, and Anxiety in Normal School-Age Children," *Journal of Child and Adolescent Psychology* 33, no. 3 (March–April 1994):407–15.

29. *Caffeine's Effects on Academics and Athletics*, October, 1996, http://net-abuse.org/~lizardo/caff.acad.ath.html

30. Bernstein, et al., "Caffeine Effects."

31. T. E. Graham, and L. L. Spriet, "Caffeine and Exercise Performance," *Sports Science Exchange* 9, no. 1 (1996), 1996, Graduate Sports Science Institute.

32. I. Kawachi, et al., "A Prospective Study of Coffee Drinking and Suicide in Women," *Archives of Internal Medicine* 156(5):521–25, 11 March 1996.

33. Ibid.

34. E. C. Strain, G. K. Mumford, K. Silverman, and R. R. Griffiths, "Caffeine Dependence Syndrome: Evidence from Case Histories and Experimental Evaluations," *JAMA* 272(13):1043–48, 5 October 1994.

35. R. J. Gilbert, "Caffeine: The Most Popular Stimulant," in *Encyclopedia of Psychoactive Drugs*, (New York: Chelsea House, 1986); R. R. Griffith, G. E. Bigelow, and I. A. Liebson, "Human Coffee Drinking: Reinforcing and Physical Dependence Producing Effects of Caffeine," *J Pharmacol Exp Ther* 239, no. 2 (1986):416; K. Silverman, "Withdrawal Syndrome after the Double-Blind Cessation of Caffeine Consumption," *N Engl J Med* 327, no. 16 (1992): 1109.

36. *Tips for Breaking the Caffeine Habit*, November, 1996, http://net-abuse.org/~lizardo/caff.tips.html

ANABOLIC DRUGS

14

1. Define the term *anabolic drug* and explain the difference between the two major types.

2. Explain how anabolic-androgenic steroids affect human physiology, and list the physical changes that result from using these drugs.

3. Describe the acute and chronic psychological effects of the nonmedical use of anabolic-androgenic steroids.

4. List and discuss the health risks associated with chronic anabolic-androgenic steroid abuse.

5. Describe the approved medical uses of anabolic-androgenic steroids.

6. Describe the current trends in steroid abuse in the United States.

7. Define human growth hormone and explain its origin and its medical uses.

8. Describe the risks associated with the nonmedical use of human growth hormone.

9. Discuss the use of steroids in competitive sports and the concept of fair competition.

10. Discuss the features of a comprehensive steroid abuse prevention program.

11. Briefly discuss the unique features of steroid abuse treatment.

12. Briefly review recent federal laws regulating anabolic-androgenic steroids.

PROFILE

Andrea glided through the water inches below the surface. As she neared the wall, she stretched forward, tucked, rolled, and snapped around to place her feet squarely on the wall of the pool. In a fluid explosion, she sprang off the wall a full two seconds before anyone else in her heat finished the first lap.

Andrea's days began at 4:30 A.M., as her team gathered in the predawn gray to run 7 miles. After the run, they had an hour of pool time, followed on alternating days by Nautilus workouts or 30 miles on the bike, and this was just the morning session. It was an intense pace, but for Andrea, with her eye on the Olympic trials, it was the lifestyle she craved.

A year and a half earlier, Andrea and a few other members of her swim team had researched the effects of anabolic steroids on an intensive training program. They went to a medical library and tried to evaluate all the pros and cons of steroid use. Based on their research, she and another team member decided to go on a 3-week cycle of steroid use every 4 months. Their goal was to enhance their training program by increasing muscle mass and power.

Do you think this plan will work for Andrea and her teammate? What physical side effects of steroid use might they experience? What are the potential consequences for participation in their sport if steroid use is detected? Keep Andrea's decision in mind as you learn about anabolic drugs in this chapter. Then turn to the solutions box at the end of the chapter.

Athletes searching for a competitive edge, body builders looking for a quick way to increase muscle mass, and teenage boys wishing to hasten their physical development are among those tempted by anabolic drugs. One path to achieving these goals is patience and a great deal of hard work (see the box on p. 000). A quicker and more dangerous path is to use anabolic drugs, which accelerate muscle growth and development.

As with other drugs discussed in this text, abuse of anabolic drugs carries the risk of unpleasant and sometimes dangerous side effects. In this chapter, we review the classification, history, pharmacology, physiological and psychological effects, and medical and nonmedical uses of anabolic drugs. We also discuss their current legal status and offer suggestions for abuse control and prevention.

CLASSIFICATION

Anabolic drugs are performance-enhancing drugs that include two types of compounds: **anabolic-androgenic steroids** (hereafter referred to simply as **steroids**), which are synthetic compounds that mimic the action of the male hormone testosterone; and **human growth hormone (hGH),** a protein produced by the human pituitary gland. These compounds can be considered performance enhancing because they accelerate the rate at which the body builds proteins; thus, they increase muscle size and strength and promote muscle-injury repair among athletes who use them. Both types of anabolic drugs are legally available only with a physician's or veterinarian's prescription.

Most of the illicit anabolic steroids available in the United States are smuggled into the country. Some of the most commonly encountered are boldenone (Equipoise), ethylestrenol (Maxibolin), fluoxymesterone (Haloestin), methandriol, methandrostenolone (Dianabol), methyltestosterone, nandrolone (Durabolin, Deca-Durabolin), oxandrolone (Anavar), oxymetholone (Anadrol), stanozolol (Winstrol), testosterone, and trenbolone (Finajet).[1] Many bogus or counterfeit products are sold as anabolic-androgenic steroids. Many of these contain dangerous impurities.

HISTORY

Anabolic-androgenic steroids first appeared in the 1930s. Their first medical uses were to speed recovery from starvation, burns, and major surgery.[2] Because of their remarkable effects, use of steroids soon spread to the healthy population. For example, during the Second World War, Hitler's secret police were rumored to be taking steroids to increase their size and aggressiveness.

The first successful uses of steroids in athletic competition were those by the Soviet weight-lifting teams in

---

anabolic drugs drugs that accelerate muscle growth and development

anabolic-androgenic steroids (steroids) synthetic steroids that mimic the action of the male hormone testosterone

human growth hormone (hGH) a protein produced by the human pituitary gland that accelerates physical growth

ALTERNATIVE CHOICES

Better Ways to Build Muscles

Are there truly effective alternatives to steroid use for those who wish to increase their performance? Or are steroids the only option for those who "want the very best"? Consider the following alternatives to the risk of using illegal, dangerous anabolic drugs:

Training. Use the most current and effective nondrug-based training routines available in your sport. Ask successful and competent coaches, trainers, exercise scientists, and performers for their nondrug-based approaches to training in your sport.

Equipment. In conjunction with the above, use the most complete facilities and equipment available to you. Make certain that you use these facilities in the ways your advisors suggested.

Nutrition. Carefully follow the dietary practices recommended by nutritionists who have specialized in the relationship of nutrition to conditioning and performance. To better understand these practices, take a basic nutrition course.

Health. Maintain a high level of health in all of its dimensions: physical, emotional, social, intellectual, and spiritual. Find a balance among employment, education, socialization, relaxation, and avocations.

Assessment. Regularly assess your goals in relation to your past accomplishments and your growing understanding of your abilities and remaining potential for improvement.

---

the 1950s.[3] After this success, steroid use spread among athletes in other countries and in other sports, such as track and field, particularly in the shot put and the hammer throw, and to football. After that, their use spread to endurance events, including distance running and swimming. Eventually, they found their way into recreational use, where they were used by those seeking the "ripped" or "chiseled" look of a highly trained athlete. Use and abuse of steroids continues in all of these areas today.

ANABOLIC-ANDROGENIC STEROIDS

Steroids are a class of lipid molecules that contain four carbon rings with various attached side chains of chemicals. Examples include cholesterol, cortisol, and aldosterone. Some of these steroids, such as hydrocortisone, have important medical uses either in replacement therapy for adrenocortical deficiency or for their potent anti-inflammatory effects in disorders of many organ systems.[4]

Two important steroids are the female hormone estrogen, produced in the ovaries, and the male hormone testosterone, produced in the testes. These two hormones have only small chemical differences but large differences in their effects on growth and development.

Steroids also can be produced synthetically. Synthetic steroids that produce testosteronelike effects are called **androgenic steroids** because they cause the expression of male secondary sex characteristics, including a deep-

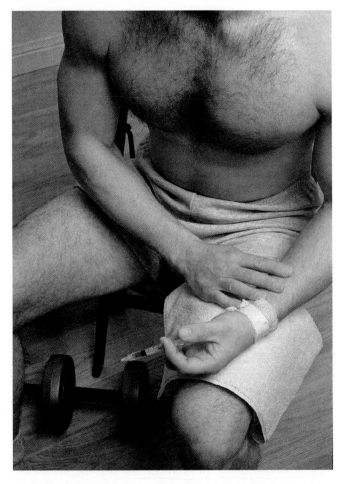

Anabolic-androgenic steroids are sometimes abused by young men as a short cut to achieving the "ripped" look.

of the voice, growth of facial and body hair, and ...ased aggressiveness. They also are called **anabolic steroids** because they stimulate protein synthesis, resulting in increases in muscle size and strength. Although researchers have attempted to increase the anabolic properties and decrease the androgenic properties of these synthetic steroids, they have not completely dissociated anabolic effects from androgenic effects; that is, the masculinizing effects always accompany the muscle-building effects.[5]

Pharmacology of Anabolic-Androgenic Steroids

Anabolic-androgenic steroids can be taken orally or injected directly into the muscle. Although testosterone itself is not effective when taken orally because it is quickly biodeactivated by the liver, synthetic steroids have been chemically altered to resist rapid breakdown. Furthermore, injected steroids are often suspended in oil, a technique that increases their half-lives.[6]

Whether absorbed through the lining of the stomach or from the muscle, steroids circulate in the bloodstream in bound and unbound forms. Only unbound molecules, perhaps 1% of the total, are free to leave the bloodstream and diffuse to sites of action. Sites of action include special receptor sites on the membranes of various types of cells, including skeletal muscle cells, hair follicle cells, sebaceous gland cells, and certain endocrine gland and brain cells. These receptor sites specifically bind testosterone and to varying degrees its synthetic relatives, the steroids.

Inside the cell, anabolic steroids interact with the cell's DNA to accelerate the synthesis of various proteins involved in muscle building or other male hormone actions, such as beard growth and enlargement of the larynx. The type of action induced depends on the type of cell exposed. Another effect of anabolic-androgenic steroids is a blocking of normal **catabolic processes** (processes that break down excess muscle). Still another type of action occurs in the brain, where the presence of steroids is detected in the hypothalamus, causing a drop in the levels of gonadotropin-releasing hormone. The result is a decrease in the production of testosterone and sperm. For this reason, some researchers have proposed that certain anabolic steroids should be tested as candidates for male contraception.

Like testosterone itself, steroids are biotransformed into other compounds by the liver. Some of these compounds are eliminated quickly, but others remain in the body for longer periods. Steroids dissolved in water are eliminated more quickly than those suspended in oil; the latter can remain in the body for weeks or months.[7] The products of steroid biotransformation reactions are removed from the blood by the kidneys and excreted in the urine.

Neurohormonal Influences of Anabolic-Androgenic Steroids

Anabolic-androgenic steroid use causes several physiological and psychological changes. Some of these changes begin immediately, but others normally appear only after long-term use. Some of these changes are temporary; others are permanent.

Physiological Effects.   The physiological effects of using anabolic-androgenic steroids are increased weight and muscle mass, increased water retention, and decreased body fat.[8] Researchers recently demonstrated in a carefully controlled study that "supraphysiologic doses of testosterone, especially when combined with strength training, increase fat-free mass and muscle size and strength in normal men."[9]

Do steroids actually improve performance? The answer depends on how one defines performance. In some sports, such as body building, where muscle size is performance, steroids do improve performance. With proper nutrition and training, strength is also increased.[10] Endurance is thought to be improved because steroids promote red blood cell proliferation, thereby increasing the blood's oxygen-carrying capacity. However, controlled studies showing improvement in aerobic capacity have not been conducted.[11] Steroids do reduce recovery time after injury or exhaustion, enabling athletes who abuse steroids to train longer and harder than they would otherwise. However, these athletes risk injury and permanent disability from such overtraining. In addition, athletes may lose flexibility or become "muscle bound." Abuse of anabolic-androgenic steroids results in several physiological side effects in both sexes, including male pattern baldness, acne, and edema in the feet and legs. When adolescents take steroids, these agents can prematurely stop the lengthening of bones, resulting in stunted growth. Steroid abuse by males can result in sore or swollen breast tissue, testicular shrinkage, hair loss, and impotence. For females, unwanted effects include a deepening of the voice, menstrual irregularities, reduction in breast size, and enlargement of external genitals.[12]

---

steroids a class of lipid molecule exhibiting four carbon rings and an assortment of molecular side chains; examples are cholesterol, estrogen, and testosterone.

androgenic steroids synthetic steroids that cause the expression of male secondary sex characteristics, such as growth of facial hair and deepening of voice

anabolic steroids synthetic steroids that stimulate protein synthesis, resulting in increases in muscle size and strength

catabolic processes physiological processes that break down muscle

The short-term physiological effects of using steroids are increased weight and muscle mass, increased water retention, and decreased body fat.

Chronic steroid abuse produces a variety of irreversible health problems, including long-bone fusion in children; changes in physical appearance; damage to organs and organ systems, including liver tumors; and prostate cancer in males. All oral and some injectable steroids reduce high-density cholesterol while increasing low-density cholesterol, increasing the risk for atherosclerosis (clogging of blood vessels) and myocardial infarction (heart attack).[13] Chronic use of steroids also causes hypertension (chronic high blood pressure), thereby increasing the risk for cerebrovascular accidents (stroke).

Psychological Effects. In addition to the physiological effects already discussed, steroid abuse causes significant psychological changes in both men and women. Initially, users report feelings of well-being, euphoria, inflated feelings of self-esteem, increases in energy and sex drive, and improvement in appetite. These feelings may be accompanied by increased aggression and decreased tolerance to pain. Users often have difficulty controlling their emotions, especially anger, and many experience sudden mood swings, aggressive behavior, and combativeness. Such instances of mania are sometimes called "steroid rages" or simply "roid rages."[14]

When abusers discontinue their steroid abuse, they report dysphoria, depression, fatigue, decreased sex drive, insomnia, lack of energy, and dissatisfaction with body appearance.[15] Some experience severe depression and thoughts of suicide. A recent placebo-controlled prospective study confirmed adverse mood and behavioral effects from anabolic steroid use.[16] Another study found that adolescent steroid users reported significantly higher levels of depression, anger, vigor, and total mood disturbance while on a cycle of steroid use.[17] Steroids also increase the likelihood that the user will develop social problems as a result of personality or attitudinal changes. These problems could include disrupted and damaged interpersonal relationships, misuse and abuse of other prescription and illicit drugs, aggressive and antisocial behaviors resulting in trouble with the law (fines and imprisonment), and disqualification or disbarment from athletic competition.

Tolerance and Dependence. Tolerance to the presence of steroids begins to develop with the first dose. In men, the body reduces its own production of testosterone in response to the presence of adequate male hormone. Sperm production also decreases and, with continued steroid abuse, the testes shrink. As the body adjusts to the continued doses of steroids, these drugs become less effective. To overcome problems of tolerance, those abusing steroids resort to three dose-management techniques: stacking, cycling, and pyramiding.[18]

Stacking refers to taking high doses of several different types of steroids so that tolerance to one type might be overcome by the anabolic presence of another. **Cycling** is the taking of steroids for a period of 4 to 12 weeks, followed by an equal or longer period of absti-

Both physio & psycho depend.

nence to allow one's tolerance to decline. **Pyramiding** refers to a gradual increase then decrease in doses during a single cycle. The purpose of gradually increasing the dose is to overcome tolerance; the goal in decreasing the dose at the end of the cycle is to lessen the physiological and psychological effects of withdrawal.

Strong evidence suggests that steroids produce both physical and psychological dependence. A study of weight lifters revealed that two criteria for dependence were met: continued use despite adverse consequences and the presence of the withdrawal symptoms described in the previous section.[19]

Other Health Risks.   Because all nonmedical use of steroids is illegal, both the Food and Drug Administration and the Drug Enforcement Administration closely monitor the production and distribution of these drugs. Therefore, the primary source of anabolic drugs is the black market. Drug enforcement agents estimate that 30% to 50% of the steroids available on the black market are either contaminated with impurities or totally counterfeit, even though their labels often appear to be genuine.[20]

Another unsafe source of street steroids is the veterinary market. Winstrol-V is an injectable veterinary steroid that is heavily abused. Veterinary drugs are not screened as carefully as human drugs and thus present unknown risks for the user.

Until recently, observers assumed that those using steroids were training for competition or otherwise focused on their physical conditioning and were thus unlikely to concurrently abuse other drugs. However, a recent study found that this is not the case. Instead, the study found that the factors that contribute to the abuse of steroids are similar to or the same as those that contribute to the abuse of other drugs. Specifically, the study revealed that the frequency of steroid use in 14-year-olds was associated with the use of cocaine, injectable drugs, smokeless tobacco, and to a lesser extent cigarette and alcohol use. Perhaps more disturbing was the finding that among these young steroid users, 25% reported sharing needles to inject drugs, a practice that put them at risk for HIV and other blood-borne infections.[21]

Current Use Patterns   *Schedule III*

Anabolic-androgenic steroids are classified as schedule III drugs and have legitimate medical uses. They are also subject to abuse because of their performance-enhancing characteristics.

Medical Uses.
There are several well-known, commercially prepared anabolic-androgenic steroids and many that are less known. Among the best-known products are Anadrol-50 (oxymetholone), manufactured by Syntex,

Withdrawal from steroid use may be accompanied by feelings of dysphoria, depression, fatigue, decreased sex drive, insomnia, and dissatisfaction with body appearance.

Deca-Durabolin (nondrolone decanoate), by Organon, and Winstrol (stanozolol), by Winthrop.[22]

Anabolic-androgenic steroids have a limited number of valuable medical uses. These include treatment for certain types of anemia (iron deficiency), hereditary angioedema (accumulation of fluid in the heart), replacement therapy for males with congenital or acquired deficiency of testosterone production, certain kinds of

stacking the taking of high doses of several different types of anabolic-androgenic steroids so that tolerance to one type might be overcome by the presence of another, slightly different steroid

cycling alternating periods of steroid use with equal or longer periods of abstinence for the purpose of decreasing one's tolerance   *4-12 wk.*

pyramiding gradually increasing and then decreasing doses during a single cycle

gynecological conditions, and abnormal protein synthesis. They may also be used as an adjunct to other therapies in the treatment of constitutional growth delay, osteoporosis, and advanced breast cancer. All medical uses combined are believed to account for fewer than 3 million prescriptions per year in the United States.[23]

Patterns of Abuse. The nonmedical use (and abuse) of steroids has increased dramatically in recent years and now occurs at virtually all levels of sports—professional, collegiate, and high school—and among a growing number of people who do not participate in organized, competitive sports. The black market trade in performance-enhancing drugs was estimated in 1992 at $400 million.[24] More than 1 million Americans have used anabolic-androgenic steroids for nonmedical purposes at least once in their lives.[25] In 1996, 1.9% of high school seniors reported having used steroids at least once, and more than 40% said that steroids would be "fairly easy" or "very easy" to get.[26] While this 40% perceived-availability rate seems high, it represents a highly significant decline from the 45% rate of 1995, when in Phoenix, for example, the cost of an oral dose was $2.25 and an injectable dose was $15 to $18.[27] Senior males are four times as likely to abuse steroids as their female counterparts (2.4% vs. 0.6%).[28]

The reasons competitive athletes give for using steroids include getting bigger, increasing their ability to lift heavier weights, and competing better in sports. Many young people take them just to "look better" or simply because "everyone else is taking them." One common myth is that those who use steroids are health conscious and do not normally take other drugs. Recent studies have found the opposite is true.[29] The frequency of steroid use among adolescents was significantly associated with the use of other illegal drugs, such as cocaine, amphetamines, and heroin, as well as the use of tobacco and alcohol. Students who perceived that they performed below average academically and those who reported injected drug use also reported higher anabolic-androgenic steroid use.[30]

Steroid abusers typically take mega-doses equal to 10, 100, or even 1,000 times the medical dose.[31] The body of a typical adult male produces 2.5 to 10 mg of testosterone each day. An appropriate medical dose for anabolic steroid replacement therapy is about the same, 5 to 10 mg per day. Those who abuse steroids to improve athletic performance may take as much as 25 to 50 mg orally each day and 100 to 200 mg by injection weekly for 10 to 12 weeks before a competition. Steroid abuse for power lifting or body building might involve a regimen of 100 mg orally a day and 200 mg by injection three times per week. This dosage is taken using the previously discussed techniques of stacking, cycling, and pyramiding.[32]

HUMAN GROWTH HORMONE (HGH)

Human growth hormone (hGH) is not a steroid but a large protein secreted by the brain's pituitary gland. The function of hGH in the healthy body is to promote normal growth, primarily during childhood and adolescence. It does this by stimulating the production of growth factors known as somatomedins.[33]

The specificity of growth hormones is greater than that for steroids. Thus, only hGH and not the growth hormones of other animals can promote growth in humans.

Human growth hormone is prescribed medically to promote growth in children who are judged to be significantly below specific height-for-age standards. The cost of hGH is high, up to $1,500 for a two-week supply.[34] Thus, insurance companies have strict standards about the physiological conditions that constitute "medical need." However, because hGH can now be manufactured synthetically, prices may eventually decline, which should enable more widespread medical use.

Human growth hormone has no known medical uses in adults, but abuse of the drug has already begun (see the box on p. 241). When new substances appear for the first time, they are often surrounded by mythical beliefs that contribute to their popularity. Such is the case with hGH. Athletes who use hGH do so in the belief that it is free from side effects and is safer and even more effective than steroids. These ideas are not accurate.

The side effects from the use of hGH are serious and include acromegaly (a thickening of the bones, especially apparent in the face, hands, and feet); organomegaly (enlargement of internal organs); diabetes; heart and thyroid diseases; menstrual disorders; decreased sexual desire; and a shortened life span.[35]

Another possible side effect of hGH use that does not occur with steroid use has to do with the body's immune system. Because hGH is a protein, it is more likely to stimulate antibody production by the immune system. Antibodies produced will attack hGH and perhaps other, similar endogenous proteins, a process that could result in an **autoimmune condition.**

There is no solid evidence that hGH works better than steroids, because most athletes who have used hGH have used it in conjunction with steroids. Because most of the hGH available on the black market is of questionable origin, the safety claim is also unfounded.

One claim that seems to be true is that hGH is hard to detect in the body. This factor has made hGH popular among users who are subject to random, unannounced testing in spite of the dangers (see the box on p. 242). Although the potential for abuse of hGH is substantial,

WHAT DO YOU THINK?

Recapturing Youth: Human Growth Hormone

As our population ages and more people face the likelihood of spending some time as a "frail" older adult, many are tempted to try to slow or even reverse the aging process. The latest fuel for this interest is our ability to synthesize human growth hormone (hGH) through bioengineering techniques. Produced in the pituitary gland, hGH is a natural hormone that stimulates tissue growth and repair and increase in muscle in adolescents and younger adults.

Studies conducted over the last 10 years tested hGH in older adults. The result has been altered body composition (less fat and more lean tissue), increased muscle mass and strength, and thickened skin. These changes, say some researchers, suggest a de-aging of the body. However, significant changes in daily functional ability have not yet been reported. Studies specifically using frail elderly people are only now beginning.

Some question the wisdom of using hGH extensively. A primary concern is the cost. Costing $14,000 or higher annually, hGH treatment is currently affordable only by the rich. As synthesis expands on a large scale, however, hGH will become available to more people. Perhaps a greater concern is that hGH therapy probably promises far more than it can deliver and is not without side effects. Professionals point out that the physical changes associated with aging are not the only consequence of having lived a long time. They say hGH cannot offset the effects of disease, life-long exposure to one's environment, and the emotional burden of being near the end of life. Less fat, more muscle, and thicker skin may seem to be improvements when viewed through the eyes of young researchers, but to older adults, they may represent only minor interruptions on the path of aging and eventual death. In addition, making hGH available for routine use by the elderly could result in more abuse by all ages. What do you think? When and to what extent should hGH be introduced into an already drug-dependent world?

Modified from S. Lehrman, "Human Growth Hormone: The Fountain of Youth?" *Harvard Health Letter* 17, no. 8 (1992):1.

no studies reporting the number of people currently abusing this substance have been published.

ANABOLIC DRUGS AND FAIR COMPETITION

Is anabolic drug use by competitive athletes unethical? Shouldn't the athlete decide whether the benefits (the competitive advantage, for example) outweigh the health risks? Sports such as football, soccer, and skiing also carry injury risks. Other artificial enhancements that give a competitive edge are perfectly legal, such as improved equipment and advanced training techniques, both physiological and psychological. Isn't the outlawing of drug use and its enforcement through drug testing a paternalistic approach to competition?

A strong argument for the prohibition of anabolic drug use and for the drug testing of those participating in athletic competition was made by Don Catlin and Thomas Murray.[36]

Elite athletes such as those competing in the Olympic Games couple extraordinary natural gifts with intense discipline and commitment. It is partly a function of the sport, but chances are that the athlete began his or her climb to elite status while young. It is likely that he or she has had to forsake may other aspects such as the development of other talents, a rich social life, and education to perfect the athletic abilities. At some point along this arduous climb, perhaps after many years of effort, the athlete may discover that his or her competitors hold an advantage based on their willingness to use performance-enhancing drugs. At that point, athletes are faced with the following 3 choices: they may abandon their athletic quest, unwilling to use drugs, but reluctant to give up what may be a decisive competitive edge; they may elect to compete without using drugs, knowing that they may lose to competitors with fewer scruples; or they may be unwilling to either quit or to accept a competitive disadvantage, and so find themselves feeling compelled to use performance-enhancing drugs to level the playing field.

Thus, one athlete's decision to use anabolic drugs affects other athletes in the competition and the competition itself. Athletes are free to choose whether to violate

autoimmune condition a health condition in which the body's immune system destroys its own tissue as if it were foreign

DRUGS IN YOUR WORLD

Are You Willing to Take the Risk?

One of the less positive results of the Omnibus Crime Control Act of 1990, which placed most anabolic-androgenic steroids under the supervision of the Drug Enforcement Administration as schedule III drugs, has been the movement of users away from steroids toward other performance-enhancing drugs. This abandonment of steroids in favor of so-called steroid substitutes risks problems at least as serious as those associated with the anabolic steroids.

Four popular steroid substitutes are clenbuterol, a veterinary drug used to build muscle mass and strength in large animals; gamma hydroxybutyric acid (GHB), an investigational drug that induces sleep but that users think stimulates growth hormone production; human growth hormone (hGH), a natural hormone approved for use in treating pituitary dwarfism; and erythropoietin (EPO), a drug that fosters red blood cell formation and is used as an adjunct to AZT treatment in people with AIDS.[a] The use of EPO by athletes means that blood testing, in addition to urine testing, eventually may be required for certain athletes.[b] In addition, a growing variety of food supplements, including various combinations of amino acids, are taken as "growth/

performance enhancers." Because these supplements are not regulated by the FDA, they appear in nutrition stores in every shopping mall, often advertised as working like steroids. At least one outbreak of clenbuterol poisoning has been reported.[c]

These new drugs are not as well understood as the steroids. Most experts believe these drugs could produce changes in the structure and function of the body, including tumors, high blood pressure, abnormal growth in all areas of the body, and many of the other problems caused by anabolic steroids. Steroid-substitute users should remember that the anabolic-androgenic steroids, available only by prescription, were approved for human use only after rigorous testing and then only in amounts equivalent to those occurring naturally. Most of these steroid substitutes were not tested in this way.

Some users appear to be willing to test the untested in a quest for the elusive "perfect body." How do you assess the safety of your own drug-taking behavior? Have you ever taken an unknown drug because someone promised that it would produce some effect you desired? Have you ever taken a drug even though you suspected that no medical authority had approved the drug for this particular purpose? Have you ever offered such a drug to another person?

[a] K. L. Ropp, "Steroid Substitutes: No-Win Situation for Athletes," *FDA Consumer,* (December 1992) p. 8.

[b] D. H. Catlin, and T. H. Murray, "Performance-Enhancing Drugs, Fair Competition, and Olympic Sport," *JAMA* 276, no. 3 (1996): 231–37.

[c] L. Salleras, et al., "Epidemiologic Study of an Outbreak of Clenbuterol Poisoning in Catalonia, Spain," *Pub Health Rep* 110 (1995):338–42.

Clenbutrol
hGH GHB, EPO

the rules (or ethics) of fair competition but are not free to pursue their dreams with the confidence that the best athlete will win. Observers have said that ". . . the staunchest supporters of drug testing are the athletes of the Olympic movement."[37] In addition, fans should know that the athletes who succeed did so on a level playing field; otherwise, why should one be a fan?

For these reasons, many professional organizations and bodies have published statements prohibiting the use of anabolic steroids. A list of some of these organizations appears in the box on page 243.

PREVENTION AND CONTROL

With a steroid use epidemic in junior and senior high schools, authorities have made several attempts to increase students' knowledge about the risks of steroid use. Unfortunately, the result has sometimes been increased interest in steroids instead of a decrease in their use.[38]

Two lessons have been learned: (1) programs must provide information about healthy alternatives to steroid use (such as nutrition and strength training), and (2) educational programs must begin earlier. The latter finding was based on the discovery that 2% of athletes 10 to 14 years old had used anabolic steroids but knew little of their side effects.[39]

Community prevention efforts should target schools and local health clubs that may be distribution points for steroids. A comprehensive steroid prevention and control program has several components.[40] It should have a clearly written policy statement prohibiting the possession, use, or distribution of steroids. It should adequately train coaches and supervisors in the recognition and dangers of steroid use. Parents should also receive this information. Athletes and parents should be required to sign a comprehensive statement describing the school's policy and philosophy about athletics and the use of the facilities, including a no-drug-use policy.[41] Lastly, a total drug-prevention program should include a student

DRUGS IN YOUR WORLD

Professional Organizations that have Published Position Statements Prohibiting the Use of Anabolic Steroids

American Academy of Pediatrics
American College of Sports Medicine
American Osteopathic Academy of Sports Medicine
International Amateur Athletic Federation
International Federation of Body Builders
National Athletic Trainers Association
National Collegiate Athletic Association

National Federation of State High School Associations
National Football League
National High School Athletic Coaches Association
National Strength and Conditioning Association
United States Olympic Committee

N. J. Kennedy, *Prevention of Anabolic Steroids: Is It Possible?* presentation to the Alcohol, Tobacco and Other Drugs section, American Public Health Association, 31 October 1994, Washington, D.C.

---

assistance program (SAP) that counsels and supports students who need peer support in working through drug related or other personal problems.

Testing for steroids is technically more difficult than testing for drugs such as marijuana, heroin, or cocaine. It requires the use of gas chromatography/mass spectrometry (see chapter 4) and is expensive. Even when performed by the best and most efficient laboratories, testing one urine sample for anabolic steroids costs about $100.[42] This puts the cost of routine testing for steroids out of the financial reach of most high schools and many colleges. The NCAA conducts tests at certain national events, and the NCAA and NFL conduct unannounced tests.[43]

When properly performed, drug tests can be an effective deterrent against steroid abuse. To be effective, such a program should include: (1) year-round, random, unannounced testing; (2) strict chain-of-custody guidelines for handling specimens; (3) testing by a qualified, certified laboratory; and (4) simultaneous testing for masking drugs and diuretic agents that might be taken to conceal steroid abuse.[44]

TREATMENT

Our society feels a renewed urgency for treatment of anabolic-androgenic steroid dependence because of the revelation that many users are sharing needles with other drug users and are, therefore, at risk for acquiring blood-borne diseases. Long-term dependence also may increase one's risk of developing serious physical and psychological damage. Obviously, a prerequisite to treatment is accurate diagnosis, which may be difficult given the variety of different possible symptoms. Physical symptoms as diverse as acne, high blood pressure, and liver tumors may be accompanied by psychological disorders, including mood disorders, such as mania, depression, and irrita-

bility, or other mental disorders, such as paranoia, hallucinations, and psychosis. Not all of these symptoms appear at the same time.

Medical tests, such as those that show a lowered sperm count, might motivate some male athletes to quit steroid abuse.[45] Treatment for steroid dependence requires acute intervention and long-term follow-up and may require nonsteroid alternatives that help maintain body fitness and positive self-esteem.[46] Another treatment approach is psychotherapy, focusing on body image and self-image, in a program that works closely with the individual's authority figure (often a coach) to remove perceived stressors that could cause a relapse.[47]

ANABOLIC DRUGS AND THE LAW

The use of anabolic-androgenic steroids to improve competitive performance is unethical and has been censured by various groups, including the National Strength and Conditioning Association, the National Collegiate Athletic Association, the National Football League, the U.S. Olympic Committee, and the International Olympic Committee. Medical groups opposed to the nonmedical use of steroids include the American Medical Association, the American Academy of Pediatrics, and the American College of Sports Medicine.[48]

In addition to violating the policies of most athletic sanctioning bodies and medical associations, the nonmedical use of steroids is now illegal. The **Omnibus Anti-Substance Abuse Act of 1988** made the unlawful distribution of steroids across state lines a felony under federal law, punishable by one to three years in prison

Omnibus Anti-Substance Abuse Act of 1988 federal law that made it a felony offense to distribute steroids across state lines

SOLUTIONS

When Andrea completed her fourth cycle of steroids, the Olympic trials were just 6 months away. To ensure a clean drug test, this would be her last cycle. In the last 16 months, Andrea had put on 12 pounds of muscle and decreased her body fat from 15% to 11%. As is common among intense female endurance athletes, she had stopped menstruating 7 months earlier.

During the time between her last cycle of steroids and the Olympic trials, Andrea had difficulty staying focused. Her training suffered, and she was often irritable. She had become psychologically dependent on steroids —without them, she was less confident of winning. In the last meet before the trials, Andrea was off her best times in both the 100-meter freestyle and the breast stroke.

Andrea did make it to the Olympic trials but turned in poor times in both qualifying events. She was eliminated after the first round of competition. Discouraged, she stopped using steroids but continued to participate on her college swim team. The next year at nationals, she finished third in her division.

Andrea realized that her decision to use steroids had cost her the chance to be in the Olympics. She would never know whether she could have made it without drugs. She regretted her decision but knew that she could not do it over again. Instead, she took pride in the wins she had achieved without the help of steroids.

and a fine of up to $250,000.[49] State laws governing the possession and distribution of anabolic drugs vary, but a conviction in most states carries a stiff fine and imprisonment.

The **Omnibus Crime Control Act (OCCA) of 1990** placed some anabolic-androgenic steroids in schedule III of the Controlled Substances Act, thus bringing them under the control of the Drug Enforcement Administration. This means that the schedule III provisions for registration, reporting, record keeping, and prescribing, as well as investigation of and penalties for misuse, now apply to steroids. For example, only properly registered practitioners can issue prescriptions, and these prescriptions can be refilled a maximum of five times within six months from the date of issuance.

The OCCA of 1990 also regulates hGH. It establishes criminal penalties under the Federal Food, Drug and Cosmetic Act for distributing hGH for nonmedical uses.[50]

SUMMARY

Anabolic drugs are substances that accelerate muscle growth and development. The use of anabolic drugs for nonmedical purposes is not new but is increasing at all levels of competitive sports and among junior and senior high school students.

> **Omnibus Crime Control Act (OCCA) of 1990** a federal law that added certain anabolic-androgenic steroid substances to schedule III of the Controlled Substance Act of 1970

There are two main types of anabolic drugs: anabolic-androgenic steroids and human growth hormone. Anabolic-androgenic steroids are synthetic molecules with a structure similar to the male hormone testosterone. Human growth hormone is a complex protein that stimulates growth in children and adolescents.

Anabolic-androgenic steroids have profound physical and psychological effects that include both masculinizing and protein-building effects. They have legitimate medical use as replacement therapy for those with deficient testosterone production. The nonmedical use of steroids has increased dramatically in recent years. Steroid abuse initially produces feelings of well-being and increased aggressiveness. It produces many unpleasant side effects, however. Among the most dangerous are liver tumors, hypertension, and heart disease. Psychological side effects include mood swings, dependence, and depression upon withdrawal.

Human growth hormone is not a safe alternative to steroid use. Known side effects include acromegaly, diabetes, and heart disease.

Experts make solid arguments for prohibiting steroid use from athletic competition. Elite athletes themselves are among the staunchest supporters of drug testing to ensure fair competition.

Programs to prevent steroid abuse among youth should begin at an early age and should target schools and health clubs. Sports programs should have a written policy prohibiting steroid use, and parents as well as athletes should help implement the policy.

Testing for steroids is technically difficult and too expensive for many school districts. When properly performed, however, drug testing can deter steroid abuse.

Treatment for steroid abuse begins with quick and accurate diagnosis and intervention. Effective treatment usually requires long-term follow-up and may require the use of nonsteroid alternatives to help maintain self-esteem and positive body image.

The nonmedical use of anabolic drugs is illegal. Violations of the laws carry severe penalties. The abuse of these drugs can be prevented through education, testing, enforcement, and treatment.

REVIEW QUESTIONS

1. What are the two types of anabolic drugs?
2. Exactly how do anabolic-androgenic steroids work?
3. List the physiological and psychological effects of the nonmedical use of steroids.
4. List the physiological side effects of steroid use in males and in females.
5. What is the evidence that steroids produce tolerance and dependence?
6. What are the health risks of the nonmedical use of steroids?
7. What are the approved medical uses of anabolic-androgenic steroids?
8. What is human growth hormone, and where does it come from?
9. Does the nonmedical use of hGH have any side effects or health risks? If so, what are they?
10. Is the use of steroids in competitive sporting events unethical? Defend your answer.
11. What are some features of a comprehensive steroid abuse prevention program?
12. How does the Omnibus Anti-Substance Abuse Act of 1988 affect the possession and distribution of steroids?
13. How does the Omnibus Crime Control Act of 1990 affect the use of anabolic-androgenic steroids?

REFERENCES

1. Drug Enforcement Administration, *Drugs of Abuse, 1996 Edition*, United States Department of Justice, Arlington, Va., U.S. Government Printing Office, Superintendent of Documents, Mail Stop: SSOP, Washington, D.C. 2402-9328.
2. R. H. Strauss, and C. E. Yesalis, "Anabolic Steroids in the Athlete," *Ann Rev Med* 42 (1991):449.
3. Ibid.
4. *Physicians' Desk Reference*, 51st ed. (Montvale, N.J.: Medical Economics Company, 1997).
5. Ibid.; Council on Scientific Affairs, American Medical Association, "Medical and Nonmedical Uses of Anabolic-Androgenic Steroids," *JAMA* 264, no. 22 (1990):2923.
6. Strauss and Yesalis, "Steroids in the Athlete."
7. Ibid.
8. K. Friedl, et al., "What the Coach, Athlete and Parent Need to Know About Anabolic Drugs: A Fact Sheet," *Nat Strength Condit Assoc J* 11, no. 6 (1989):10.
9. S. Bhasin, et al., "The Effects of Supraphysiologic Doses of Testosterone on Muscle Size and Strength in Normal Men," *N Engl J Med* 335, no. 1 (1996):1–7.
10. Strauss and Yesalis, "Steroids in the Athlete"; Bhasin, et al., "Testosterone."
11. Strauss and Yesalis, "Steroids in the Athlete."
12. Strauss and Yesalis, "Steroids in the Athlete"; AMA, "Anabolic-Androgenic Steroids"; Friedl, et al., Anabolic Drug Fact Sheet."
13. Friedl, et al., "Anabolic Drugs Fact Sheet."
14. J. M. Schrof, "Pumped Up," *U.S. News & World Report*, 1 June 1992, p. 55; O. Fultz, "Roid Rage," *American Health* (May 1991): 60.
15. Schrof, "Pumped Up"; R. D. Daigle, "Anabolic Steroids," *J Psychoactive Drugs* 22, no. 1 (1990):77.
16. T. P. Su, et al., "Neuropsychiatric Effects of Anabolic Steroids in Male Normal Volunteers," *JAMA* 269, no. 21 (1993):2760.
17. K. J. Brower, et al., "Evidence for Physical and Psychological Dependence on Anabolic-Androgenic Steroids in Eight Weight Lifters," *Am J Psychiatr* 147, no. 4 (1990):510.
18. Daigle, "Anabolic Steroids."
19. K. F. Burnett, and M. E. Kleiman, "Psychological Characteristics of Adolescent Steroid Users," *Adolescence* 29 (113):81–89.
20. DEA, *Drugs of Abuse*; Daigle, "Anabolic Steroids."
21. Daigle, "Anabolic Steroids."
22. *Physicians' Desk Reference*.
23. Ibid.; AMA, "Anabolic-Androgenic Steroids."
24. Fultz, "Roid Rage"; National Institute on Drug Abuse: *Anabolic Steroids: A Threat to Body and Mind*, NIDA Research Report Series, NIH pub. no. 96-3721, (Rockville, Md.: National Clearinghouse on Alcohol and Drug Information, 1996).
25. Substance Abuse and Mental Health Services Administration, Office of Applied Studies, *National Household Survey on Drug Abuse: Main Findings 1994*, U.S. Public Health Service, USDHHS Pub. No. (SMA) 96-3085 (Rockville, Md.: USDHHS, 1996).
26. *The Rise in Drug Use Among American Teens Continues in 1996*, Press Release, 19 December 1996, University of Michigan, Ann Arbor.
27. National Institute on Drug Abuse, *Epidemiologic Trends in Drug Abuse*, vol. 1, *Highlights and Executive Summary*, NIH Pub. No. 96-4126 (Rockville, Md.: Community Epidemiology Work Group, June, 1996).
28. L. D. Johnston, P. M. O'Malley, and J. G. Bachman, *National Survey Results on Drug Use from the Monitoring the Future Study, 1975–1995*, vol 1, *Secondary*

School Students, NIH Pub. No. (PHS), 99-4139 (Rockville, Md.: USDHHS, 1996).

29. R. H. DuRant, et al., "Use of Multiple Drugs Among Adolescents Who Use Anabolic Steroids," *N Engl J Med* 328, no. 13 (1993):922; R. H. DuRant, L. F. Escobedo, and G. W. Heath, "Anabolic-Steroid Use, Strength Training, and Multiple Drug Use Among Adolescents in the United States," *Pediatrics* 96, no. 1 (1995):23–28.

30. DuRant, et al., "Use of Multiple Drugs."

31. AMA, "Anabolic-Androgenic Steroids."

32. DEA, *Drugs of Abuse*; Daigle, "Anabolic Steroids."

33. Friedl, et al., "Anabolic Drugs Fact Sheet."

34. Daigle, "Anabolic Steroids."

35. Friedl, et al., "Anabolic Drugs Fact Sheet"; "The Fountain of Youth," *Harvard Health Letter* 17, no. 8 (1992):1–3.

36. D. H. Catlin, and T. H. Murray, "Performance-Enhancing Drugs, Fair Competition, and Olympic Sport," *JAMA* 276, no. 3 (1996): 231–37.

37. Ibid.

38. V. S. Cowart, "Blunting 'Steroid Epidemic' Requires Alternatives, Innovative Education," *JAMA* 264, no. 13 (1990):1641.

39. Ibid.

40. J. R. Olsen, and G. L. Landry, "Health Education: School Districts Need a Plan of Action to Prevent Use of Anabolic Steroids," *Interscholastic Athletic Administration*, 19, no. 4 (1993):15–17.

41. Ibid.

42. G. L. Landry, and P. K. Kokotailo, "Drug Screening in the Athletic Setting," *Curr Prob Pediatr* 24, no. 10 (1994):344–59.

43. Strauss and Yesalis, "Anabolic Steroids."

44. Friedl, et al., "Anabolic Drugs Fact Sheet."

45. NIDA, *Threat to Body and Mind*.

46. Ibid.; A. J. Giannini, and G. B. Collins, "Substance Abuse and Thought Disorders," in *Dual Diagnosis in Substance Abuse*, M. S. Gold and A. E. Slaby, eds. (New York: Marcel Dekker, 1991).

47. Indiana Prevention Resource Center for Substance Abuse, The Facts about Steroids, *Prevention Information Series* 7 (1989):1.

48. AMA, "Anabolic-Androgenic Steroids."

49. IPRCSA, "The Facts about Steroids."

50. S. Nightingale, "Anabolic Steroids as Controlled Substances," *JAMA* 265, no. 10 (1991):1229.

SOURCES FOR HELP

Entertainment Industries Council, Inc.
Reston Ave.
Reston, VA 22090
(703) 481–1414

NCAA Drug Testing/Drug Education Coordinator
6201 College Blvd.
Overland Park, KS 66211-2422
(913) 399–1906

Turn It Around Campaign
(David M. Winfield Foundation)
2050 Center Ave.
Ft. Lee, NJ 07024
(201) 461–5535

INHALANTS

PROFILE

I t was her first year out of college, and Nikki Kostopolous was enjoying every minute of teaching. Her class was a joy, and although her training couldn't prepare her for every situation, she often consulted her peers or one of her old teachers when a special problem arose. Such was the case today. She had discovered a group of boys "bagging" at lunch recess on the far side of the playground. They had wandered back to the ball fields, which were off limits except during PE class. There they had coated a handkerchief with spray paint, put it inside a plastic bag, and took turns "huffing" the contents.

When caught, the boys implicated Carlos Diaz as the instigator. Ms. Kostopolous took the matter to the principal of her school, who simply dismissed it by ordering a week's suspension for all the children involved.

Wanting to do more, Ms. Kostopolous asked her favorite professor for help. Dr. Michaels had been her advisor throughout her student teaching, and the two had become friends. Dr. Michaels recommended that Ms. Kostopolous set up a meeting with all the students' parents to discuss the seriousness of what the children had done.

Do you think Ms. Kostopolous should intervene or let the matter drop? How do you think the boys' parents will react to the news of their sons' drug use? Turn to the solutions box after you read this chapter.

Inhalants are volatile substances that produce physiological and psychological changes when breathed or inhaled and are rarely, if ever, administered in any other way. These substances are legally available products that serve useful purposes in our society and can be found in homes, offices, workshops, and stores. Their nearly universal availability makes them the drug of choice for many adolescents. Inhalants are considered a gateway drug because they are legal, easy to get, inexpensive and difficult to detect, and they may lead to other illicit drug use.[1] (See chapter 2 for a discussion of gateway drugs.)

CLASSIFICATION

Inhalants can be classified as volatile solvents (such as gasoline, glue, paint, and polishes), anesthetics (such as chloroform, ether, and nitrous oxide), and nitrites.[2]

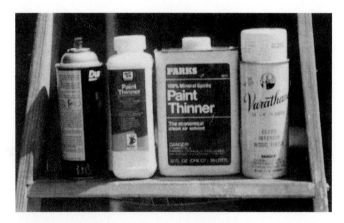

A variety of common household products can become dangerous inhalants.

Among the most popular sources of these chemicals are household and industrial solvents, including paint thinners; adhesives and cleaning agents; aerosols, such as hair sprays, deodorants, and fabric sprays; aerosolized food products, such as whipped cream; anesthetic gases; and the nitrates, sometimes called room deodorizers.[3] Table 15.1 lists the chemicals commonly found in the three major categories of products.[4]

Inhalants are easy to use and, aside from occasional headaches, are relatively free from acute side effects. The best hope of reducing inhalant abuse lies in campaigns based on education of adolescents, their parents, and their teachers. In addition, because of their availability, reducing supply as a method of control does not work.

HISTORY

Inhalant abuse is not new. One hundred years ago people had ether parties in which participants sniffed ether to feel lightheaded and to change their mood. More recently, inhalant abuse began to make news in the 1950s, when youths reportedly began "getting high" through "glue sniffing."[5] This term is still used today, but the variety of substances that are abused in this manner has expanded markedly.

METHODS OF ABUSE

Inhalants are a unique group of drugs, and they are grouped here by route of administration rather than their effects on the central nervous system. Nonetheless, in-

TABLE 15.1 Inhalants and Their Chemical Contents

Volatile Substances	
Adhesives	
Airplane glue	Toluene, ethyl acetate
Other glues	Hexane, toluene, methyl chloride, acetone, methyl ethyl ketone, methyl butyl ketone
Special cements	Trichloroethylene, tetrachloroethylene
Aerosols	
Spray paint	Butane, propane (U.S.), fluorocarbons, toluene, hydrocarbons, "Texas shoe shine," (a spray containing toluene)
Hair spray	Butane, propane (U.S.), CFCs
Deodorant; air freshener	Butane, propane (U.S.), CFCs
Analgesic spray	Chlorofluorocarbons (CFCs)
Asthma spray	Chlorofluorocarbons (CFCs)
Fabric spray	Butane, trichloroethane
PC cleaner	Dimethyl ether, hydrofluorocarbons
Cleaning Agents	
Drycleaning fluid	Tetrachloroethylene, trichloroethane
Spot remover	Xylene, petroleum distillates, chlorohydrocarbons
Degreaser	Tetrachloroethylene, trichloroethane, trichloroethylene
Solvents and Gases	
Nail polish remover	Acetone, ethyl acetate
Paint remover	Toluene, methylene chloride, methanol acetone, ethyl acetate
Paint thinner	Petroleum distillates, esters, acetone
Correction fluid and thinner	Trichloroethylene, trichloroethane
Fuel gas	Butane, isopropane
Lighter fluid	Butane, isopropane
Fire extinguisher	Bromochlorodifluoromethane
Food Products	
Whipped cream	Nitrous oxide
Whippets	Nitrous oxide

Anesthetics	
Gaseous	Nitrous oxide
Liquid	Halothane, enflurane
Local	Ethyl chloride

Nitrites	
"Room Deodorizers"	
Locker Room, Rush, Poppers	Isoamyl, isobutyl, isopropyl or butyl nitrite (now illegal), cyclohexyl

C. W. Sharp, "Introduction to Inhalant Abuse," in *Inhalant Abuse: A Volatile Research Agenda,* Research Monograph, No. 129 (Rockville, Md.: National Institute on Drug Abuse, 1992).

halant abusers vary in their abuse practices. Some of these methods are called "sniffing," "snorting," "huffing," and "bagging." In **sniffing** or **snorting,** the nose is placed close to the container holding the substance (can of paint, tube of glue), and the user inhales repeatedly. In

inhalants volatile substances that produce effects when breathed or inhaled

sniffing, snorting inhaling volatile substances directly from their containers

DRUGS IN YOUR WORLD

Telltale Signs of Inhalant Abuse

Runny nose or nosebleeds
Sores or rashes around the mouth and nose
Nausea and headaches
Chronic cough
Sudden memory loss and lack of concentration
Unusual odor on breath, in bedroom, or on clothes
Stains on skin or clothing
Plastic bags, soft drink cans, or rags with chemical smell
Empty butane lighters

Signs of inhalant abuse may be accompanied by such general signs of drug abuse as the following:

Extremes in mood swings
Changes in personal hygiene
Abrupt changes in school performance or attendance
A sudden loss of interest in friends, sports, hobbies
Red, irritated eyes
Sudden weight loss

---

bagging, the user sprays or otherwise empties the substance into a plastic bag, then holds the bag to the nose and mouth, and breathes. Sometimes a rag is soaked with a mixture and placed in the mouth so that fumes can be inhaled; this is called **huffing.** Sometimes a user sprays a substance directly into the mouth.[6]

Users of inhalants can often be identified by various telltale signs, including odor and appearance. Signs of inhalant abuse are presented in the box above.

PATTERNS OF USE

According to a 1995 national survey, more than 12 million Americans had used inhalants at least once in their lifetimes, and nearly 1 million were current users (had used an inhalant within the month before the survey). Tragically, more than half of current users belonged to the 12- to 17-year-old age group (fig. 15.1).[7] Males make up 60% of those abusing inhalants (fig. 15.2).

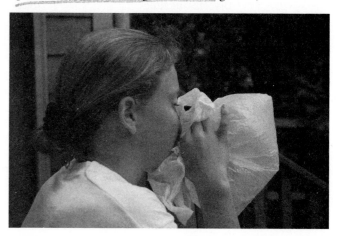

Bagging is a dangerous form of inhalant abuse among adolescents.

FIGURE 15.1

Current inhalant abuse (within previous 30 days) by age group.

18–25 years
23%

26–34 years
13%

35+ years
11%

12–17 years
53%

FIGURE 15.2

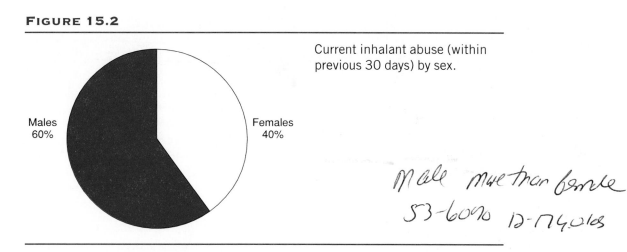

Current inhalant abuse (within previous 30 days) by sex.

Males 60%

Females 40%

[handwritten notes: Male more than female 53-60% 12-17 y old]

Substance Abuse and Mental Health Services Administration (SAMHSA), Office of Applied Studies: *National household survey on drug abuse: population estimates 1995,* DHHS pub no (SMA) 96-3095, 1996, Rockville, MD.

Among eighth graders, inhalants are the most abused substances after alcohol, tobacco, and marijuana. One in every five eighth graders (21%) has used inhalants, and more than one in 20 (5.8%) say they have used them in the past month.[8] Among eighth-graders interviewed in 1995, 7% said they had used inhalants before the end of the fifth grade.[9]

The percentages of eighth, tenth, and twelfth graders reporting any inhalant use in the previous 12 months are 12%, 10%, and 8%, respectively.[10] After 4 years of increasing inhalant abuse among American youth, abuse seems to be steadying and even declining in 1996. Experts have attributed this decline to an increase in the proportion of eighth and tenth graders who in 1996 said that trying inhalants once or twice are at "great risk" of harming themselves.[11]

HEALTH CONSEQUENCES OF INHALANT ABUSE

The health consequences of inhalant abuse include both acute and chronic health risks.

Acute Health Consequences of Inhalant Abuse

The acute or short-term effects of inhalant abuse include heart palpitations, breathing difficulty, dizziness, and headache. Inhalant abuse has been likened to a quick "drunk."

Although acute, high-level exposure to most solvents induces short-term effects that are usually reversible, in some instances secondary effects produced irreversible damage and sudden death. Deaths directly attributed to inhalants have been connected to the following agents: gasoline, nitrous oxide, Freon 12, the solvent combination found in typewriter correction fluid, butane, and propane.[12] Most deaths among inhalant abusers are not the direct result of an unintentional acute toxic overdose. Rather, the leading causes of death among this population are suicides, unintentional injury deaths, and homicides. In cases where death was the direct result of acute inhalant abuse (an event known as "sudden sniffing death"[13]), the physiological cause of death was usually heart arrhythmia.[14] Other causes of death are asphyxiation, suffocation, choking on vomitus, and careless behaviors that result in fatal injuries.[15]

Health Consequences of Chronic Inhalant Abuse

The health effects of chronic abuse of inhalants include damage to the nervous system, heart, liver, lungs, kidneys, blood-forming system, and adrenal glands. Nervous system damage is not limited to the brain but can also include cranial nerves and the peripheral nervous system. Loss of nervous system function can produce mental retardation, loss of coordination of muscle movements, parkinsonism (rigidity and tremor), and visual loss.

Substances that can produce structural and functional damage in adults can be considered harmful to developing fetuses. Some evidence suggests that such damage

bagging the practice of spraying an inhalant into a plastic bag and then breathing from the bag

huffing soaking a rag with a volatile liquid, such as gasoline or toluene, and inhaling from the rag, or even placing the rag in the mouth

ALTERNATIVE CHOICES

Prevention Tips

Know the facts.

Be able to communicate the facts clearly.

Explain that inhalants are not drugs. They are deadly chemicals and poisons.

The facts will prevent curiosity and the temptation to experiment.

Inhalant prevention is a community solution:

Involve media

Involve retailers

Involve schools

Involve churches

Involve health-care providers

Involve civic and volunteer organizations

Involve elected officials

Involve law enforcement and the legal community.

Inhalant abuse prevention is everybody's business.

Get them involved.

Synergies, National Inhalant Prevention Coalition, 1996.

indeed occurs, resulting in a "fetal solvent syndrome." Although problems have been reported in infants born to mothers who chronically abuse inhalants, these mothers also drank alcohol, which could have contributed to the abnormalities. Further studies are needed to establish the neonatal toxicity of the various inhalants.[16]

PREVENTION

More than 1,000 legal and useful products in our society can be abused as inhalants. Many of these products are free or very inexpensive, can be used without complex paraphernalia, and are easy to conceal. Thus, prevention efforts should include a strong demand-reduction component. Ed-

ucational programs must teach the facts about inhalants, change attitudes and beliefs about these substances, and teach and reinforce appropriate skills among youth.

Community-based inhalant abuse prevention programs must involve a wide variety of stakeholders to produce the best results. Such programs should include participation by the media, retailers, schools, churches, health care providers, civic and volunteer organizations, the law enforcement and legal communities, and elected officials.[17] An important component of a community-based program is the school-based substance abuse prevention program. The foundation of any school-based program is the school's written policy clearly stating "no drug use." Table 15.2 shows some guidelines for a school-based program.[18]

TABLE 15.2 Do's and Don'ts of School-Based Inhalant Abuse Prevention

Do	Don't
Review school policy regarding drug use:	Glamorize or promote usage
Provide training for all school staff and parents	Rely on scare tactics
Start prevention efforts by age 5	Tell too much too soon
Link inhalants to safety or environmental issues	Give details on "how to use"
Ascertain current level of knowledge	Discuss trendy products being abused
Teach and reinforce the following appropriate skills:	Limit prevention to secondary schools
Reading labels	Link inhalants with drugs or a drug unit
Safety precautions	
Following instructions	
Decision-making skills	
Recognition of poisons/toxins	
Refusal skills	
Awareness of physical symptoms	

I. Burk, School Based Prevention Programs, National Inhalant Prevention Coalition, Austin, Tex., *ViewPoint* 6 no. 1 (Fall/Winter 1996):7.

SOLUTIONS

At the meeting with the boys' parents, Carlos's father was defensive and dismissed his son's actions as "boys will be boys."

Ms. Kostopolous diplomatically pointed out that the boys' behavior was more serious than it might seem and could lead to abuse of other drugs. She gave the parents a pamphlet from the National Institute of Drug Abuse on warning signs and symptoms of inhalant abuse and urged the parents to talk to their children about the harmful consequences of even experimental use.

Two weeks later, Carlos's mother called to thank Ms. Kostopolous for the materials. During the time she had spent with her son while he was suspended, Mrs. Diaz had recognized a number of symptoms in him of a regular user.

Carlos's mom contacted the National Institute of Drug Abuse, and a counselor referred her to the National Inhalant Prevention Coalition in Austin, Texas. This organization sent her information on how to conduct a local media/awareness campaign and how to form partnerships with other parents concerned about the risks of inhalant abuse.

With the help of Ms. Kostopolous and a few of the other mothers of children in Carlos's class, Carlos's mother organized a community-wide campaign to raise awareness of inhalant abuse. Her first priority, however, was to spend more time with Carlos and help him understand the dangers of inhalant abuse. Their time together was rewarding, and Carlos was the first student in the school to sign the "I promise not to use inhalants" pledge.

SUMMARY

Inhalants are volatile substances that produce their effects when breathed and are rarely abused by any other route. They include such things as adhesives, aerosols, cleaning agents, food products, anesthetics and room deodorizers. The availability of many of these substances and their ease of use contribute to their popularity among adolescents. More than one million Americans are current users of inhalants. Inhalant abuse carries substantial acute and chronic health risks, including death. Community-based inhalant abuse prevention programs are most likely to be successful when they involve a wide variety of stakeholders.

REVIEW QUESTIONS

1. What are inhalants? Can you provide some examples? Which age group seems to be at greatest risk for inhalant abuse?
2. What are the characteristics of inhalants that result in their classification as gateway drugs?
3. What are some acute and chronic health risks associated with inhalant abuse?
4. What are the signs of inhalant abuse?
5. Describe the components of a successful inhalant abuse prevention program.

REFERENCES

1. *Inhalants—The Silent Epidemic* (Austin, Tex.: Synergies-National Inhalant Prevention Coalition, 1997).
2. C. W. Sharp, "Introduction to Inhalant Abuse," in *Inhalant Abuse: A Volatile Research Agenda*, Research Monograph, no. 129 (Rockville, Md.: National Institute on Drug Abuse, 1992).
3. *Inhalants.*
4. Sharp, "Inhalant Abuse."
5. National Institute on Drug Abuse, *Inhalant Abuse: Its Dangers are Nothing to Sniff At*, Research Report Series, NIH Pub. No. 94-3818 (Rockville, Md.: 1994).
6. Sharp, "Inhalant Abuses."
7. Substance Abuse and Mental Health Services Administration (SAMHSA), Office of Applied Studies: *National Household Survey on Drug Abuse: Population Estimates, 1995*, USDHHS Pub. no. (SMA) 96-3095 (Rockville, Md.: USDHHS, 1996).
8. *The Rise in Drug Use Among American Teens Continues in 1996*, University of Michigan News and Information Service, Press Release, 19 December 1996, Ann Arbor, Mich.
9. L. D. Johnston, P. M. O'Malley, and J. G. Bachman, *National Survey Results on Drug Use from the Monitoring the Future Study, 1975–1995*, vol. 1, *Secondary School Students*, NIH Pub. No. 96-4139 (Rockville, Md.: USDHHS, 1996).
10. *Rise in Drug Use*, Press Release.
11. Ibid.
12. J. C. Garriot, *Death Among Inhalant Abusers*, Research Monograph, no. 129 (Rockville, Md.: National Institute on Drug Abuse, 1992); E. Siegel, S. Wason, *Sudden Sniffing Death Following Inhalation of Butane and Propane: Changing Trends*, Research Monograph, no. 129 (Rockville, Md.: National Institute on Drug Abuse, 1992).
13. Sharp, "Inhalant Abuse."

14. Siegel and Wason, *Sudden Sniffing Death.*
15. Substance Abuse and Mental Health Services Administration, Center for Substance Abuse Prevention, *Tips for Teens about Inhalants*, pamphlet (Rockville, Md.: DHHS, 1992).
16. N. L. Rosenberg, and C. W. Sharp, *Solvent Toxicity: A Neurological Focus*, Research Monograph, no. 129 (Rockville, Md.: National Institute on Drug Abuse, 1992).
17. *Inhalants.*
18. I. Burk, "School Based Prevention Programs," National Inhalant Prevention Coalition, Austin, Tex., *ViewPoint* 6 no. 1 (Fall/Winter 1996):7.

SOURCES FOR HELP

Aerosol Education Bureau
1001 Connecticut Ave., NW, Suite 1120
Washington, D.C. 20036

American Council for Drug Education
204 Monroe Street, Suite 110
Rockville, MD 20850
(800) 488–drug (3784)
(301) 294–0600

Drug Abuse Information and Treatment Referral
Hotline SAMHSA
(800) 662–HELP

Families in Action
2296 Henderson Mill Rd., Suite 204
Atlanta, GA 30345
(404) 934–6364

International Institute for Inhalant Abuse
799 East Hampden Avenue, Suite 500
Englewood, CO 80110
(800) 832–5090

SYNERGIES
National Inhalant Prevention Coalition (NIPC)
1201 West Sixth Street, Suite C-200
Austin, TX 78703
(800) 269–4237
(515) 480–8953
FAX (515) 477–3932

Solvent Abuse Foundation for Education
(SAFE)
750 17th Street, NW, Suite 250
Washington, D.C. 20006
(202) 332–7233
FAX (202) 429–0655

16

ALCOHOL: HISTORY, PHYSIOLOGY, AND PHARMACOLOGY

CHAPTER OBJECTIVES

After studying this chapter, you will be able to:

1. Identify how alcohol has been used since prehistoric times.

2. Understand that alcohol is produced through fermentation or distillation of cereal grains or fruits.

3. List the many forms of alcoholic beverages and their various strengths.

4. Understand how drinking patterns vary considerably among people.

5. List the many factors affecting the absorption of alcohol.

6. Explain how alcohol depresses physiological function and behavior through its effects on the central nervous system (CNS).

7. Recognize the signs and symptoms of acute alcohol intoxication.

8. Identify a variety of health problems attributed to alcohol consumption.

9. Define fetal alcohol syndrome and explain how it can be prevented.

Hardly a day goes by that we fail to see, read, or hear about alcohol's effects on our lives. Despite the positive images portrayed in alcohol advertising, most of what we learn about alcohol is negative. We read about fetal alcohol syndrome, cancer's connection with alcohol use, or how alcohol use can destroy families. We see on television the horrible aftermath of a fatal car accident involving a drunk driver. We hear that a friend or colleague is missing work or classes because of alcohol-related problems. We see adult children of alcoholics having a difficult time forming relationships or coping with their own adulthood.

Although it is easy to find evidence of the negative effects of alcohol use, it is becoming difficult to find ways that the careful, judicious use of alcohol might be a positive influence on the lives of people. In the next two chapters, we explore alcohol from many perspectives. Chapter 16 focuses on the influence of alcohol on the body. We will examine the way alcohol is absorbed, distributed, and removed from the body, the physiological effects of alcohol, and the immediate and chronic health effects of alcohol.

Chapter 17 focuses on problem drinking and alcoholism. We will explore the developmental roots of drinking problems, alcoholism's impact on friends and families, and intervention and recovery for alcoholics. Health benefits that can be attributed to moderate drinking also will be identified. As authors and educators, we realize that two chapters cannot completely explore alcohol problems. However, we believe that these chapters enable readers to understand the principal issues surrounding our nation's number one drug.

For some, alcohol consumption is a natural accompaniment for an enjoyable social outing.

HISTORY

Alcohol (also known as ethyl alcohol, grain alcohol, or ethanol) is not a new product. Alcohol was probably first discovered in prehistoric times when people drank the juices of a berry mash that had been exposed to airborne yeast. When users realized that this drink produced pleasant, even euphoric, feelings and reduced discomfort, early civilizations began the purposeful production of crude wine. Thus, alcohol has been consumed for more than 4,000 years and used medically for hundreds of years as a sedative and an analgesic.[1]

Through the process of **fermentation**, yeast cells act on the sugar content of fruits and grains to produce alcohol and carbon dioxide (fig. 16.1). Until about 500 years ago, two main beverages were made with alcohol: wine (from fruit sources) and beer (from grain sources). These beverages contained maximum alcohol concentrations of 10% to 14%. Fermentation alone could not yield stronger concentrations of alcoholic beverages.

Not until the process of **distillation** was developed in fifteenth-century Europe did alcoholic beverages contain a higher percentage of alcohol. This process used a

FIGURE 16.1

The chemical process of fermentation produces ethyl alcohol and carbon dioxide.

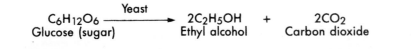

$$C_6H_{12}O_6 \xrightarrow{\text{Yeast}} 2C_2H_5OH + 2CO_2$$

Glucose (sugar)   Ethyl alcohol   Carbon dioxide

Police enforcement during Prohibition. Here the contents of an illegal brewery were dumped into the street.

device called a still to gather the concentrated vapors of the heated, fermented mixture. These liquids were called distilled spirits and contained alcohol concentrations that exceeded 50%. Over the years, people developed other distilled beverages (whiskey, rum, vodka, and gin) that could contain even higher concentrations of alcohol. Distilled spirits are often called by their common name, liquor.

Alcoholic beverages have been available in the United States since the earliest days of colonialism. However, it was not until the early 1800s that a movement to restrict alcohol consumption began to reach organized levels. This movement was called the temperance movement, because the initial goal was to temper (meaning "to curtail or moderate") the use of distilled spirits. The temperance movement gathered more public support during the mid-1800s. Temperance advocates expanded their targets to include beer and wine consumption in addition to distilled spirits. Facing growing pressure, individual states began to enact Prohibition laws. These laws banned the sale of alcoholic beverages in individual states. Finally, in 1920, the U.S. government ratified the Eighteenth Amendment to the Constitution, which prohibited the manufacture, sale, and transportation of alcohol.

Throughout the 1920s, the United States, at least officially, was a "dry" country. Although evidence suggests that alcohol use and alcohol-related problems were somewhat reduced during Prohibition, alcohol was still being manufactured and sold illegally during Prohibition. Enforcing prohibition became increasingly difficult and expensive. With mounting public pressure to control crime

and to collect taxes on alcohol, the United States ratified the Twenty-first Amendment to the Constitution in 1933. The Twenty-first Amendment repealed the Eighteenth Amendment, allowing individual states to regulate alcohol production and sales.

ALCOHOL: THE BEVERAGE

In spite of the potential problems associated with their use, alcohol-based beverages are consumed by millions of Americans. Today, as in the past, people seek these beverages, often preferring them to readily available alternatives.

Today's Alcoholic Beverages

The three principal alcohol-containing beverages used today are beer, wine, and distilled spirits. However, because of the production measures used, variations can be found within these categories. For example, forms of beer include ale (5% alcohol per unit volume), malt beverage or malt liquor (7%), regular beer (4%), light beer

---

fermentation chemical process in which plant products are converted into alcohol by the action of yeast on carbohydrates

distillation process of heating a fermented alcohol mixture to produce vapors that are then cooled and collected as a stronger alcohol solution

(4%), low-alcohol beer (1.5%), and nonalcoholic brew (0.5%). Wine is marketed in several forms, including fortified (containing distilled spirits that raise the alcohol concentration to 18%), natural or common (12%), champagne (12%), light wines (8%), or wine coolers (6%). Distilled spirits are manufactured in the form of liqueurs (25% to 40%), regular distilled spirits or liquor (40% to 80%), or liquor coolers (15% to 25%).

The alcohol concentration in distilled beverages is expressed by the term **proof**. The proof of a distilled spirit is equal to twice its alcohol concentration. Thus, a bottle of 80-proof liquor is a beverage that is 40% ethyl alcohol. The proof of most distilled beverages ranges from 80 to 160 proof. *Pure grain alcohol* has a proof that approaches 200.

Ethyl alcohol has little taste. When consumed alone, this clear fluid usually produces an initial burning sensation in the mouth and esophagus. The various flavors found in alcoholic beverages are byproducts of the type of fruit or grain used and any additional flavorings added to the fermenting mixture. Table 16.1 lists the types of alcoholic beverages and sources.

Alcoholic beverages cannot be considered a valuable source of nutrition because they are high in **empty cal-** ories. One fluid ounce of 100-proof distilled spirits contains 100 calories, whereas a 12-oz can of regular beer has about 150 calories. Alcohol products contain only simple carbohydrates, few minerals, and no vitamins, fats, or protein. To help put the caloric impact of alcohol into perspective, from your study of nutrition, you probably already know that fats produce about 9 calories per gram, while carbohydrates and protein produce about 4 calories per gram. Alcohol produces about 7 calories per gram, nearly as many calories per gram as fats.[2]

Alcohol can, however, be considered a food because it does supply calories.[3] As a food, alcohol is unique because it does not require digestion to be absorbed into the bloodstream.

Alcohol Use Patterns

Nearly 60% of all American adults (age 18 and older) consume alcoholic beverages.[4] However, in the college population, various surveys report that nearly 90% of students drink alcohol. Unfortunately, for some students, these years will also be the entry to a lifetime of problem drinking or alcoholism. They will join the estimated 12% of the adult population classified as heavy drinkers

TABLE 16.1 Categories of Alcoholic Beverages

Category	Alcohol Content (%)*	Serving Size (in Ounces)*	Sources
Beer			
Regular beer	4	12	Barley malt, rice, or corn. (Hops added during the brewing process.)
Light beer	4	12	
Low-alcohol beer	1.5	12	
Malt liquor	7	12	
Ice beer	5–7	12	
Ale	5	12	
Nonalcoholic brew	0.5	12	
Wine			
Natural: red/white	12	5	Grapes or other fruit.
Fortified (dessert)†: port, sherry, muscatel, Madeira	18–20	3	
Wine cooler‡	6	12	
Champagne	12	4	Wine with added carbon dioxide.
Distilled Spirits			
Whiskey: bourbon, Scotch, Irish, rye	45	1	Corn, rye, wheat, or malted barley mash distilled and stored in charred oak barrels for up to 10 years.
Brandies, liqueurs, cordials	25–40	1–2	Distilled from various fruits.
Rum, gin, vodka	45	1	Rum—distilled from fermented sugar cane or molasses; Gin—distilled from rye, wheat, corn, or barley and flavored with juniper berries; Vodka—distilled from various grains and kept free of flavors.

*Amounts given are typical, but may vary.

†Wine with added alcohol.

‡Wine flavored with fruit juice.

SELF-ASSESSMENT

Are You Missing Out Because of Alcohol?

We know that some students are alcoholics and an even larger group of students have serious problems with alcohol. Another significantly large group of students, however, suffer from alcohol-induced "miss out." If you frequently experience any of the following because of the effects of alcohol, you may be among those who will miss out on much of what college life is all about:

1. Skip classes and labs
2. Miss assignments or deadlines
3. Fail to show up for work
4. Avoid group activities or projects
5. Sleep in the library, in class, or during the day
6. Alienate friends

More than likely you can manage to balance frequent alcohol use and school for some time. However, eventually you will depend on others to cover for you, and finally the school experience will become so fragmented that you will depart or be dismissed. Are you in the process of "drinking yourself out of college?"

It can be difficult to recover from alcohol-induced miss out.

Alcohol use is associated with many enjoyable social activities.

(many of whom can be considered alcoholics). Other students will suffer from alcohol-induced "miss out" (see box above).

One final, frightening statistic about alcohol use patterns is the astounding disparity in the consumption

proof twice the percentage of alcohol by concentration; 100-proof alcohol is 50% alcohol

empty calories calories consumed from a food source lacking in important nutrients

levels among adults who drink. Experts estimate that 70% of the drinking population consumes only 20% of the alcohol sold. The other 30% of the drinking public consumes the other 80% of the alcohol sold. Furthermore, one-third of this 30% of drinkers consumes about half of all alcohol sold. Thus, just 10% of the drinkers consume roughly half of all the alcohol sold in the United States.[5]

These figures might have more meaning if you imagined a group of 10 people representing an actual cross-section of the adult population, including, of course, both drinkers and abstainers. If you had 10 beers to distribute among these people according to adult drinking patterns, you would divide the beers as follows:

Three people abstain (reflecting the one-third who do not drink)

Five people share two beers (70% of drinkers drink 20% of the alcohol)

Two people share eight beers (30% of drinkers drink 80% of the alcohol) However, of these two drinkers, one drinks two beers and the other drinks six beers.[6]

OTHER ALCOHOLS

Ethyl alcohol is not the only form of alcohol. Among the other familiar forms are methyl alcohol (wood alcohol), isopropyl alcohol (rubbing alcohol), and butyl alcohol. Only ethyl alcohol can be consumed relatively safely by humans. All other forms are toxic and unsafe for use in beverages. Consuming alcohols other than ethyl has caused serious injury and death. Be careful that you never consume alcohol unless you are certain of its form.

PHARMACOLOGY OF ALCOHOL

Alcohol is a very strong CNS depressant. When consumed in large quantities, alcohol eventually shuts down brain functioning, respiration, and circulation to the point that death is inevitable. In small doses, alcohol appears to produce stimulating effects, and some users may act more jubilant, less rigid, and more talkative than normal. These behavioral changes are caused by alcohol's ability to produce disinhibition.

As a person continues to drink alcohol faster than it can be oxidized by the liver, the **blood alcohol concentration (BAC)** rises, and the depressant effects become more apparent and dangerous. A fairly predictable sequence of physiological and behavioral effects takes place when a person drinks alcohol at a rate faster than one drink every hour. When the BAC reaches 0.05%, everyday tensions appear to be released, and judgment and critical thinking are somewhat impaired. A 160-lb person

consuming about two drinks would reach this BAC in an hour.

The drinker typically loses significant motor coordination when the BAC level reaches 0.10% (one part alcohol to 1,000 parts blood). Every state considers a drinker legally intoxicated and incapable of operating a vehicle safely at this level of intoxication, even though studies show that driving skills are impaired before this point. By October 15, 1996, 13 states (Alabama, California, Florida, Hawaii, Kansas, Maine, New Hampshire, New Mexico, North Carolina, Oregon, Utah, Vermont, and Virginia) had established 0.08% as the legal BAC limit.[7] In addition, at this time, New Jersey is considering a 0.08% law. An additional 24 states had planned to introduce similar legislation in 1997.

The health risk of acute alcohol intoxication increases rapidly as a person continues to elevate the BAC from 0.20% to 0.50%. A BAC of 0.20% is characterized by the loud, boisterous, obnoxious drunk who staggers. A 0.30% BAC produces stuporous behavior during which the drinker becomes incapable of understanding external stimuli (such as verbal commands). The 0.40% or 0.50% BAC produces unconsciousness, if this has not already occurred. Survival at BAC levels this high may be tenuous, because brain centers that control body temperature, heartbeat, and respiration can virtually shut down.

Chronic heavy drinkers may not exhibit the behavioral and motor symptoms typically seen in less-experienced drinkers, despite having similar BACs. After drinking five or more drinks, these heavy drinkers may appear to be in full control of themselves. This phenomenon may reflect the high tolerance to alcohol that heavy drinkers can develop. Heavy drinkers also may learn how to conceal certain nervous system disruptions.[8] However, these drinkers are likely to be unable to reason clearly and to control their physical movements as much as they might appear. For this reason, they pose a threat to themselves and other people.

Factors Related to Alcohol Absorption and Distribution

When it is consumed, alcohol is not digested but instead is absorbed into the bloodstream, primarily through the walls of the stomach and small intestine. Approximately 20% of the alcohol is absorbed into the bloodstream through the walls of the stomach, whereas the remaining 80% is absorbed through the walls of the small intestine.

Alcohol is absorbed by the principle of diffusion, or the movement of a substance from an area of greater concentration to an area of lesser concentration. Several factors influence alcohol absorption, most of which the drinker can control. These factors include the following:

1. *Strength of the beverage.* Beverages with higher concentrations of alcohol will produce higher BACs than

FIGURE 16.2

A typical serving of an alcoholic beverage (beer, wine, or distilled spirits) contains one-half ounce of pure alcohol.

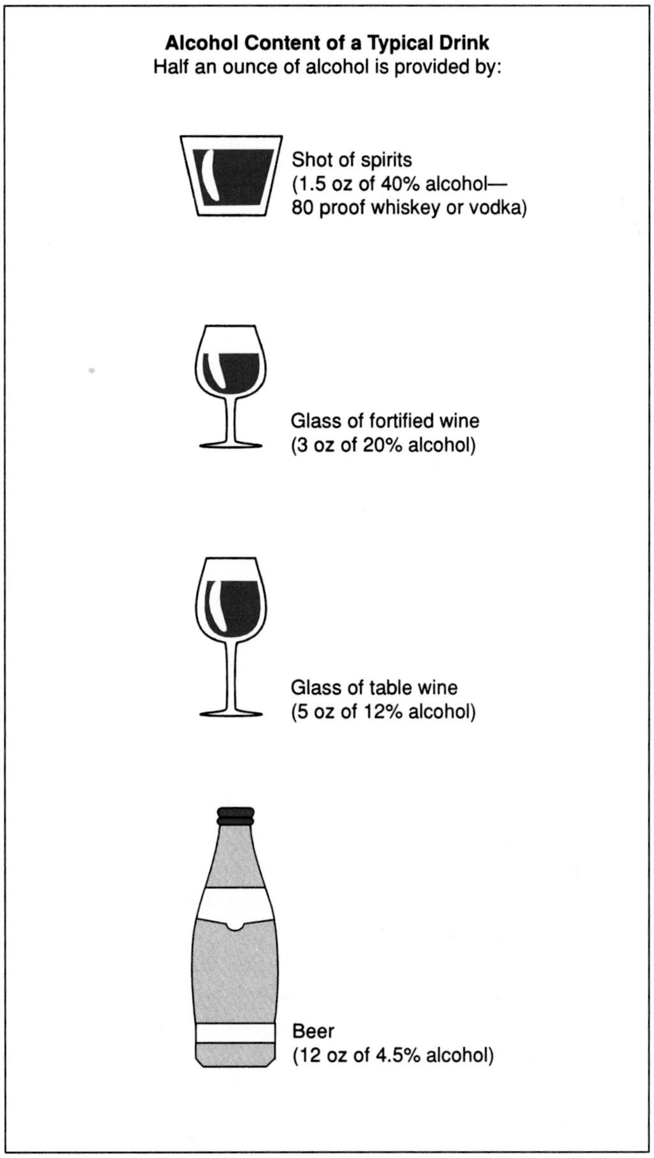

Alcohol Content of a Typical Drink
Half an ounce of alcohol is provided by:

Shot of spirits
(1.5 oz of 40% alcohol—
80 proof whiskey or vodka)

Glass of fortified wine
(3 oz of 20% alcohol)

Glass of table wine
(5 oz of 12% alcohol)

Beer
(12 oz of 4.5% alcohol)

beverages with lower concentrations; thus, 3 oz of vodka will produce a higher BAC than 3 oz of wine or beer. Evidence also suggests that the higher the concentration of alcohol in a beverage, the more rapidly absorption will occur; thus, the alcohol in a mixed drink (for example, a daiquiri, a cocktail made of rum, sugar, and lime or lemon juice) is absorbed more slowly than the alcohol in a full-strength drink (for example, straight Scotch whiskey).

2. *Number of drinks consumed.* This may seem simplistic, but the greater the number of drinks consumed, the greater the absorption of alcohol. Unfortunately,

many people are unaware that a typical "serving" from each of the three categories of alcoholic beverages (distilled spirits, wine, or beer) contains about the same amount of pure alcohol, about half an ounce (fig. 16.2). Thus, they assume that they can drink more servings of certain beverages than other types of beverages. This just isn't true.

blood alcohol concentration (BAC) proportion of alcohol in a measured volume of blood, given as a percentage

FIGURE 16.3

Absorption, distribution, and oxidation of alcohol.

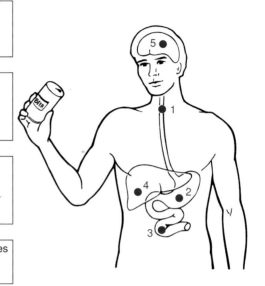

1. When it is swallowed, alcohol travels through the esophagus to the stomach.

2. Absorption of alcohol begins in the stomach. Approximately 20% passes directly into the venous drainage of the stomach wall. Food in the stomach wall will delay passage of the remaining alcohol into the small intestine.

3. The majority of alcohol (80%) is absorbed into the venous drainage of the small intestine. Absorption is proportional to the concentration of alcohol within the small intestine. Once in the venous drainage, alcohol is transported throughout the body and eventually reaches the liver for oxidation.

4. When it arrives in the liver, alcohol undergoes oxidation. The liver is capable of oxidizing approximately 1/4 to 1/3 oz of alcohol per hour. Surplus alcohol is circulated throughout the body and BAC rises. Blood alcohol concentration gradually falls as the liver oxidizes the remaining alcohol.

5. As BAC rises in the blood reaching the brain, predictable changes occur. At levels approximating 0.5%, central nervous system function can be so depressed that death can occur.

3. *Rate of consumption.* The rate of drinking affects the rate of absorption of alcohol. If consumed rapidly, even relatively few drinks can produce high BACs. Slower consumption results in lower BACs.

4. *Presence of food in the stomach.* If the stomach contains food, the absorption of alcohol is slowed. This slower absorption will help slow a rising BAC and permit alcohol already circulating in the bloodstream to be oxidized. The presence of carbon dioxide in the stomach from such drinks as sparkling wines and champagne hastens, rather than slows, the rate of alcohol absorption. Drinking alcohol with carbonated soft drinks also speeds the absorption of alcohol.

5. *Body chemistry.* Each person has an individual pattern of physiological functioning that can affect the way alcohol is absorbed and removed from the body. Because of this, some people may not fit the "typical picture" of alcohol absorption and resulting behavioral responses. In addition, the movement of alcohol from the stomach to the small intestine can be influenced by stress, anger, fear, illness, and the condition of the stomach tissues.

Other than body chemistry, the drinker can control all factors related to absorption. Many of the problems associated with alcohol use stem from alcohol misuse based on one or more of these factors.

When alcohol is absorbed into the circulatory system, it is distributed throughout the body (fig. 16.3). One important factor affecting distribution and resultant BAC is body size. Because larger people have a greater blood volume than smaller people, identical amounts of alcohol consumed the same way will produce different BACs. The smaller person has less blood into which alcohol can be distributed and, as a result, develops a higher BAC.

Body composition also affects the distribution of alcohol. Alcohol does not absorb as well in fatty tissues as it does in muscle tissues; thus, more alcohol remains in the bloodstream. Because of this, two people of equal body weight (but with different percentages of body fat) who drink identical amounts of alcohol will not show identical BACs. The person with the higher percentage of body fat will have a higher BAC than the leaner person with a greater percentage of muscle tissue.

This factor also helps explain why men and women of equal weight are unlikely to have identical BACs after drinking identical amounts of alcohol. Women's BACs likely will be higher than men's BACs.[9] Because of their potential roles as childbearers, women's bodies typically have a higher percentage of body fat than men's. Of course, these generalizations do not apply in comparisons of women who have lean bodies with men who have bodies with excessive fat tissue.

FIGURE 16.4

The multistage process of alcohol oxidation.

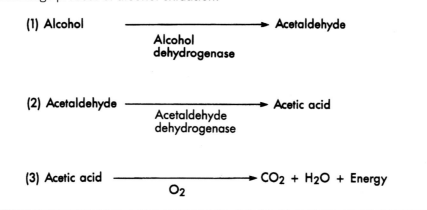

(1) Alcohol $\xrightarrow[\text{Alcohol dehydrogenase}]{}$ Acetaldehyde

(2) Acetaldehyde $\xrightarrow[\text{Acetaldehyde dehydrogenase}]{}$ Acetic acid

(3) Acetic acid $\xrightarrow[\text{O}_2]{}$ CO_2 + H_2O + Energy

Like many other drugs, alcohol can cross the blood-brain barrier and exert its pharmacological effect on brain function. The familiar behavioral changes associated with various levels of alcohol consumption reflect the progressive anesthetizing of brain centers.

In addition to distribution across the blood-brain barrier, alcohol can also cross the placental barrier.[10] The tragic consequence of this characteristic is described in a later section on fetal alcohol syndrome.

Alcohol Oxidation

Because the body recognizes alcohol as a toxic substance, the body begins to break it down and remove it as soon as it reaches the liver. Approximately 5% of the alcohol consumed leaves the body unchanged through sweat, urine, or the breath. Breathalyzers work because a person's BAC is directly related to the proportion of alcohol in the exhaled air.

The remaining 95% of alcohol in the body must first be chemically altered, or metabolized, before it can be removed. This process is known as **alcohol oxidation**. Alcohol is oxidized in a multistage process using two liver enzymes: alcohol dehydrogenase (ADH) and acetaldehyde dehydrogenase (ACDH). ADH converts alcohol into acetaldehyde, the toxic breakdown product that is responsible for many of the unpleasant side effects of hangovers. ACDH metabolizes the acetaldehyde into acetic acid. Acetic acid leaves the liver and travels throughout the body. Virtually any body cell or tissue can break down acetic acid into carbon dioxide and water, the final products of alcohol metabolism (fig. 16.4).

Within the past decade, the scientific literature has reported that women tend to produce less **gastric ADH** than men.[11] This helps explain why a significant percentage of women tend to process alcohol less efficiently than men, even when other factors, such as body size and

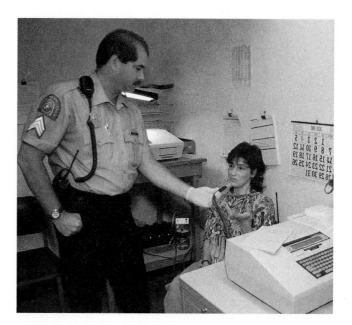

Breathalyzers measure the proportion of alcohol in exhaled air.

amount of alcohol consumed, are similar. This finding may help explain why female drinkers tend to become intoxicated more quickly and develop liver disease more rapidly than males.

Although the rate of absorption of alcohol can vary (see p. 260), alcohol is oxidized at a constant rate of one-quarter to one-third ounce of pure alcohol per hour.[12]

alcohol oxidation the removal of alcohol from the bloodstream

gastric ADH ADH that functions in the stomach to break down alcohol before it reaches the bloodstream

FIGURE 16.5

In most states, a BAC of 0.10% represents legal intoxication. However, a lower BAC can impair functioning enough to lead to a serious accident.

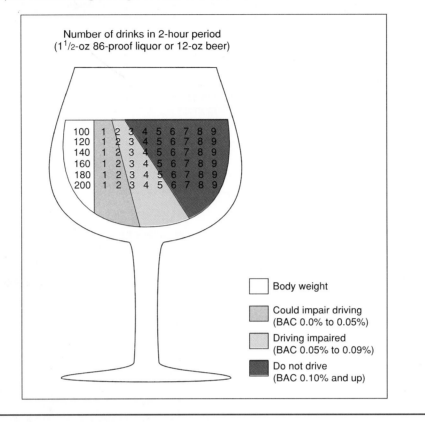

Number of drinks in 2-hour period
(1 1/2-oz 86-proof liquor or 12-oz beer)

100	1 2 3 4 5 6 7 8 9
120	1 2 3 4 5 6 7 8 9
140	1 2 3 4 5 6 7 8 9
160	1 2 3 4 5 6 7 8 9
180	1 2 3 4 5 6 7 8 9
200	1 2 3 4 5 6 7 8 9

☐ Body weight

▨ Could impair driving
(BAC 0.0% to 0.05%)

▨ Driving impaired
(BAC 0.05% to 0.09%)

■ Do not drive
(BAC 0.10% and up)

(Recall that each typical serving of beer, wine, or distilled spirits contains about half an ounce of pure alcohol.) Thus, the body takes about two hours to fully oxidize one typical alcoholic drink. Because of this constant rate, alcohol that has not yet been oxidized continues to circulate and influence brain activity and resultant body functions and behavioral responses. Despite what many people may think, exercise, cold showers, body size, caffeine intake, or food in the stomach do not affect the removal (oxidation) of alcohol from the bloodstream. Thus, although various factors affect the absorption of alcohol into the bloodstream, the removal of alcohol from the bloodstream depends solely on enzyme activities within the liver. (See fig. 16.5 for an approximate timetable for removal of alcohol from the bloodstream.)

NEUROHORMONAL INFLUENCES OF ALCOHOL

As a CNS depressant, alcohol affects brain chemistry, causing sedation. Both acute and chronic effects of alcohol intoxication can be life-threatening.

Mode of Action

Like the depressants discussed in chapter 6, alcohol is thought to produce its effects by increasing the activity of one of the neurotransmitters, gamma-aminobutyric acid (GABA). Experts believe that as BAC levels increase, GABA action is increased, leading to increased sedation and the familiar signs of intoxication.[13]

Acute Effects of Alcohol Intoxication

The dangerous effects of alcohol use can be seen in people who consume large amounts of alcohol relatively quickly. College students frequently engage in this type of drinking behavior. Because high BACs are life-threatening, one must be able to recognize the signs and symptoms of acute alcohol intoxication (alcohol poisoning) and get medical help for anyone suspected of being in this condition. (See the box on p. 265.)

The first true danger signs are those typical of **shock.** By the time shock signs are evident, a drinker will already have advanced to a stuporous or unconscious stage of intoxication. The drinker's BAC likely will be reaching

DRUGS IN YOUR WORLD

Responding to Acute Alcohol Intoxication

If you encounter a person experiencing acute alcohol intoxication, you must intervene to minimize the risk of death. The first of the following recommendations ensures the greatest degree of protection for the intoxicated person, but the remaining recommendations also are valuable when professional care is unavailable:

1. Transport the intoxicated person to a hospital emergency room, and remain at the hospital until he or she has been seen, treated, and released by the hospital.
2. In the absence of hospitalization, monitor the person regularly for signs of respiratory distress or nausea. Position the person on his or her side to minimize the chance of airway obstruction. If breathing becomes labored, get emergency assistance (dial 911).
3. If the person begins vomiting, make certain that the person's head is positioned lower than the rest of the upper body. This minimizes the possibility that vomitus will obstruct the air passages.

Clearly, a person who has stopped drinking because of unconsciousness is not yet free of the life-threatening risks of alcohol consumption.

or exceeding 0.25% or 0.30%. He or she will be difficult or impossible to arouse and likely will have a weak, rapid pulse (over 100 beats per minute). The skin will be cool or damp, and breathing will be increased to once every 3 or 4 seconds. These breaths may be shallow or deep and probably irregular. Skin color will be pale or bluish gray in the case of people with light-toned skin. People with dark-toned skin who are in acute alcohol intoxication will display these color changes of shock more noticeably in the fingernail beds or the mucous membranes inside the mouth or under the eyelids. Whenever any of these signs is present, seek help immediately.

Involuntary regurgitation (vomiting) can be another potentially life-threatening emergency for a person who has consumed too much alcohol. This is one of the body's protective measures. Additional alcohol remains in the stomach and irritates the stomach lining. Unconscious victims who regurgitate may be lying in such a position that the airway becomes obstructed with vomitus from the stomach. Such victims can die from asphyxiation, because they are unable to change positions voluntarily. As a first-aid measure, you should place unconscious intoxicated people on their sides, not on their backs or in prone (face-down) positions.

Aside from acute alcohol intoxication, several additional effects can stem from acute overconsumption of alcohol. One well-known effect in men is an increase in **impotence** among those who have been drinking. Drinking may bring on disinhibition and promote a desire for sexual activity. However, the depressant effects of alcohol may render a man unable to perform sexually.

Being intoxicated also places drinkers at much greater risk of death or injury from violence, accidents, and disease. These and other social problems associated with alcohol use are discussed further in the next chapter.

Chronic Effects of Alcohol Consumption

The relationship of chronic alcohol use to the structure and function of the body is reasonably well understood. Alcohol affects virtually every organ system in the body, either directly or indirectly.[14] Heavy alcohol use causes a variety of changes to the body that lead to an increase in death and disability. Table 16.2 lists many of these changes.

In some health conditions, such as serious changes in the liver, alcohol alone is the culprit. In other health conditions, including various forms of cancer and heart conditions, alcohol acts in concert with other elements or risk factors to promote debilitative changes. For example, smoking and alcohol seem to work together to promote cancers of the mouth and throat. Heavy alcohol use, smoking, genetic predispositions, and hormonal changes caused by unresolved stress can work together to encourage heart and blood vessel changes.

In addition to the more specific changes listed in table 16.2, research clearly shows that chronic alcohol use changes the immune system and the nervous system. Thus chronic users are at higher risk for infections and neurological complications.[15] Research continues to suggest a reasonably strong correlation between heavy alcohol consumption and an increased risk for developing breast cancer in women. This cancer connection does not appear to be as strong for women who are not heavy drinkers. The National Institute on Alcohol Abuse and Alcoholism (NIAAA) contends that "moderate drinking

shock a potentially life-threatening depression of vital bodily functions (especially respiration, circulation, and temperature control)

ALTERNATIVE CHOICES

Nonalcoholic Beer

Nonalcoholic beer is a brewed beverage that contains very little or no alcohol. The alcohol content in nonalcoholic beers must not exceed the 0.05% level established by the U.S. Bureau of Alcohol, Tobacco, and Firearms. Introduced in the late 1980s, nonalcoholic beers now make up about 2% of all beer sales in the United States. Top-selling brands include O'Doule's, Sharps, Cutters, and Pabst N/A. Brewers of imported beers (Beck's and Heineken) also have begun to market nonalcoholic choices. Nonalcoholic beers are packaged in bottles and cans that resemble typical beer bottles and cans. Prices for nonalcoholic beers are similar to those of regular beers.

These beverages provide an alternative product for those who wish to consume beer without the accompanying alcohol. They can be an alternative for those who wish to reduce their alcohol consumption at a party, perhaps by drinking nonalcoholic beers exclusively or by alternating a regular beer with a nonalcoholic beer. These beers allow businesspeople to remain alert over a business lunch or dinner. Certainly, they reflect a user's concern for health.

Professionals in the alcohol-treatment community have some concerns about nonalcoholic beer, however. The fact that these beverages do contain some alcohol makes them problematic for some alcoholics in recovery. Drinking non-alcoholic beer can make it easier for an alcoholic to make the transition (perhaps even "accidentally") to regular beer. Furthermore, the associated beer-drinking activities (such as the companionship, the games, the bar scene, and the party scene) can subtly stimulate a former drinker into a relapse.

Nonalcoholic beers are not the same as low-alcohol beers. Low-alcohol beers typically contain about 2% to 2.5% alcohol, about half the amount as in regular beer, but considerably more than in nonalcoholic beers.

TABLE 16.2 Health Problems Related to Chronic Alcohol Use

Organ or Body System	Debilitative Changes
Liver	Chemical imbalance: altered protein production, blood sugar imbalance, fat accumulation in the liver tissue
	Inflammation: impaired circulation, scar tissue formation, alcohol-related hepatitis
	Cirrhosis: impaired circulation, kidney failure, death
	Cancer
Digestive tract	Oral cavity: especially when combined with smoking, alcohol use promotes cancer of mouth, tongue, and throat
	Esophagus: irritation, impaired swallowing, cancer
	Stomach: irritation, gastritis, ulceration
	Pancreas: inflammation (pancreatitis)
	Digestion: impaired absorption, malnutrition
	Nausea, diarrhea, vomiting
Endocrine system	Nutritional and metabolic disorders: incomplete absorption of important nutrients; increase in osteoporosis
Cardiovascular system	Cardiomyopathy: shortness of breath, heart enlargement
	Hypertension: increase in hemorrhagic stroke
	Dysrhythmias: cardiac insufficiency
	Coronary artery disease: angina pectoris, myocardial infarction
Reproductive system	Women: Amenorrhea, infertility, miscarriage, fetal alcohol syndrome, early onset of menopause
	Men: Impotence, low testosterone levels, low sperm count, testicular shrinkage

Modified from W. A. Payne and D. B. Hahn, *Understanding Your Health,* 5th ed. (St. Louis: WCB/McGraw-Hill, 1998).

may be weakly related to female breast cancer."[16] Women who consume two drinks of alcohol per day have a 25% higher rate of breast cancer than women who drink only occasionally.[17]

Alcohol and Other Drug Interactions

By itself, alcohol can be a dangerous drug. When used with other drugs, alcohol can be especially dangerous. The table of common OTC drug interactions in appendix G shows many interactions between alcohol and non-prescription drugs. Alcohol-drug interactions may occur because alcohol can influence (by speeding up or slowing down) the metabolism of other drugs by the liver. In addition, alcohol can combine with other depressant drugs or prescription medications to produce life-threatening additive effects (see chapter 4 for a review of drug interactions).

Fetal Alcohol Syndrome

Research data gathered over the last two decades clearly show that alcohol use by pregnant women can cause a variety of birth defects in developing fetuses. When alcohol crosses the **placenta,** it enters the fetal bloodstream in a concentration equal to that in the mother's bloodstream. The underdeveloped fetal liver cannot oxidize the alcohol, and as a result, the fetal brain becomes bathed in alcohol until the mother's BAC drops.

This exposure to alcohol is capable of producing disastrous consequences. Low birthweight, facial abnormalities (small head, widely spaced eyes, depressed nasal bridge, thin upper lip), mental retardation, learning disabilities, behavioral dysfunctions, joint problems, and heart abnormalities are often seen in such affected infants. Recognized first in 1973, this combination of defects is known as **fetal alcohol syndrome (FAS).**

Estimates of the prevalence of FAS vary. The worldwide incidence of FAS has been estimated at one to three cases per 1,000 births. Partial expression, or **fetal alcohol effects (FAE),** has been estimated at three to nine cases per 1,000 births. In the United States, the Centers for Disease Control and Prevention reported that the 1992 rate of FAS was .37 cases per 1,000 live births.[18] FAS is now recognized as the "leading environmental cause of mental retardation in the Western World."[19] FAS is completely preventable.

Although any alcohol exposure might produce difficulties, FAS is most likely to occur in babies whose mothers were heavy drinkers during pregnancy. In addition, alcohol consumed during the first trimester of pregnancy may be especially critical to the health status of the fetus. **Binge drinking,** the rapid consumption of large amounts of alcohol, is thought to be especially harmful, because this behavior produces high BACs.[20]

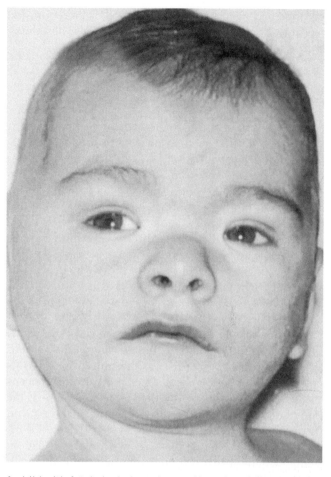

A child with fetal alcohol syndrome. Note the widely spaced eyes, thin upper lip, and depressed nasal bridge.

Most health professionals now recommend total abstinence from alcohol during pregnancy. For couples who are trying to achieve a pregnancy, a safe course is for the woman to avoid alcohol use during periods of unprotected intercourse. In this sense, prevention begins

impotence the inability to achieve and maintain an erection of the penis

placenta structure through which nutrients (and drugs, including alcohol) pass from the bloodstream of the mother into the bloodstream of the developing fetus

fetal alcohol syndrome (FAS) a collection of characteristic birth defects observed in some children of women who consume alcohol during pregnancy

fetal alcohol effects (FAE) a limited number of the characteristic birth defects associated with fetal alcohol syndrome

binge drinking the consumption of large amounts of alcohol in a short time; often defined as five or more drinks at a sitting

before a pregnancy. Expectant fathers (or fathers-to-be) might show support for their partners by also abstaining before and during the pregnancy.

SUMMARY

Alcohol use can be traced to the dawn of history. Fermentation was the first method of alcohol production, followed in time by distillation. Today's alcoholic beverages come in a variety of forms, including beer, wine, and distilled spirits. The concentration of alcohol in a beverage depends on the type of product, but the amount in a normal serving of each is about the same.

Nearly 60% of all adult Americans consume alcoholic beverages. The percentage of drinkers is nearly 90% on college campuses. The majority of those who drink consume only light to moderate amounts of alcohol, whereas about 10% of the drinkers consume about half of the alcohol sold.

Alcohol affects the function of the body primarily through its ability to depress functioning of the nervous system. Impairment increases as the concentration of alcohol in the blood increases. The blood alcohol concentration (BAC) is affected by the amount consumed, the rate of its absorption from the gastrointestinal tract, and its distribution by the circulatory system. Alcohol is removed from the body primarily through oxidation. Acute alcohol intoxication occurs when the BAC is elevated to dangerous levels.

Alcohol consumption causes or worsens a variety of health problems. Fetal alcohol syndrome is sometimes seen in the children of women who consumed alcohol during pregnancy. Interactions between alcohol and other drugs can have serious health consequences.

REVIEW QUESTIONS

1. Define the processes of fermentation and distillation. What is the relationship between the proof of distilled spirits and the percentage of alcohol per unit volume?
2. Approximately when did the temperance movement take place in the United States? When was prohibition enacted in the United States? How effective was prohibition?
3. Describe the nature of CNS decline as the BAC increases. What factors influence the rate of alcohol absorption into the bloodstream?
4. How is alcohol removed from the body? What enzymes are responsible for this? Why are women who drink likely to have higher BACs than men of equal weight?
5. Describe acute alcohol intoxication. What first-aid measures should you take for people who may be in this condition?

6. Identify some of the health consequences of chronic alcohol consumption.
7. What is fetal alcohol syndrome (FAS)? What is fetal alcohol effects (FAE)? Which is more common? How can these conditions be prevented?

REFERENCES

1. O. Ray, and C. Ksir, *Drugs, Alcohol, and Human Behavior*, 6th ed. (St. Louis: Mosby, 1993).
2. G. M. Wardlaw, *Contemporary Nutrition: Issues and Insights*, 2nd ed. (St. Louis: Mosby, 1997).
3. Ibid.
4. *Alcohol and Health: Eighth Special Report to the U.S. Congress*, DHHS Pub. No. (ADM) 94-3699 (Washington, D.C.: U.S. Government Printing Office, 1994).
5. J. Kinney, and G. Leaton, *Loosening the Grip: A Handbook of Alcohol Information*, 5th ed. (St. Louis: Mosby, 1995).
6. Ibid.
7. Phone Correspondence, Mothers Against Drunk Driving (MADD) National Headquarters, Irving, Texas, 14 October, 1996.
8. Ray and Ksir, *Human Behavior*.
9. National Institute on Alcohol Abuse and Alcoholism, *Alcohol Alert–Moderate Drinking*, DHHS Pub. No. 16, PH 315, April, 1992.
10. *Alcohol and Health*.
11. M. Frezza, et al., "High Blood Alcohol Levels in Women: The Role of Gastric Alcohol Dehydrogenase Activity and First-Pass Metabolism," *N Engl J Med* 322, no. 2 (1990):95.
12. Ray and Ksir, *Human Behavior*.
13. *Alcohol and Health*.
14. Ibid.
15. Ibid.
16. NIAAA, *Alcohol Alert*.
17. P. Gillyatt, "Lowering Breast Cancer Risk," *Harvard Health Letter* 21, no. 11 (1996):7–8.
18. Centers for Disease Control and Prevention, "Fetal Alcohol Syndrome—United States, 1979–1992, *MMWR* 42, no.17:339.
19. *Alcohol and Health*.
20. D. B. Hahn, and W. A. Payne, *Focus on Health*, 3rd ed. (St. Louis: Mosby 1997).

SOURCES FOR HELP

Alcohol and Drug Problems
Association of North America
444 North Capitol St., NW, Suite 706
Washington, D.C. 20001
(202) 737-4340

Alcohol Research Information Service
1106 East Oakland
Lansing, MI 48906
(517) 485–9900

American Health and Temperance Society
6830 Eastern Ave., NW
Washington, D.C. 20012
(202) 722–6736

The Johnson Institute
7151 Metro Blvd.
Minneapolis, MN 55435
(612) 944–0511

Licensed Beverage Information Council
1250 I St., NW, Suite 900
Washington, D.C. 20005
(202) 628–3544

National Alcohol Hotline
(800) ALCOHOL

National Women's Christian Temperance Union
1730 Chicago Ave.
Evanston, IL 60201
(312) 864–1396

Mothers Against Drunk Driving (MADD)
511 E. John Carpenter Freeway
Suite 700
Irving, TX 75062
(800) 438–6233

ALCOHOL: SOCIAL, ECONOMIC, AND LEGAL ISSUES

17

CHAPTER OBJECTIVES

After studying this chapter, you will be able to:

1. Identify alcohol as one of the nation's primary drugs of choice.

2. Understand that a high percentage of college students consume alcohol, and many college students binge drink.

3. List a variety of negative consequences that result when college students consume alcohol.

4. Describe alcoholism as a disease that is often progressive and fatal, and that has genetic, environmental, and psychosocial causes.

5. Define denial and enabling, psychological processes that are frequently related to the development of alcoholism.

6. Explain how alcoholism damages the lives of drinkers, their families, their coworkers, and society.

7. Explain why dependent relationships between alcoholics and their relatives or friends tend to delay intervention and treatment.

8. Describe how various alcoholism treatment and recovery programs differ in their approaches.

9. Evaluate alcohol advertisements for their encouragement of heavy consumption and underage drinking and for the targeting of women, minorities, and college students.

PROFILE

Gabe Santinelli arrived for class late and utterly unprepared to give a lecture, but he fancied that his disheveled look and unreliability added to his mystique as an eccentric creative writing professor.

"Take out your homework," he instructed, and the class read aloud from last week's assignment. Gabe occasionally made a comment to encourage discussion. With his thumb and index finger, he massaged the bridge of his nose and rubbed his eyes, commanding his headache to subside.

Gabe dismissed class early and retired to his office, where he fortified his morning coffee with a dollop of whisky. After the second cup, his headache was gone, but he asked the department secretary to cancel his remaining classes for the day anyway. It was too nice a day to be stuck in the classroom, and besides, he needed another drink.

As he left campus, he ran into Dr. Auden, the elderly chairman of the English department. In a rich and well-trained voice, Dr. Auden announced gravely, "Gabe, I must speak to you about a matter of serious concern. After last week's department meeting, Dean Whitacker asked me about the quality of your work. Your class reviews have always been excellent, and it seems you develop a fine rapport with your students. It is your absences and cancellations lately that have raised a bit of a red flag. Is anything wrong?"

"No, nothing is wrong, not really," Gabe responded uncomfortably. "There are just a few personal issues I'm working through." He excused himself and hurriedly walked to his car.

Can Dr. Auden do anything to help Gabe face his drinking problem? If so, what? Do you think Gabe is ready to enter a recovery program? Do you know anyone in a situation similar to Gabe's? Read this chapter to learn more about alcoholism, and then turn to the solutions box to find out what Dr. Auden decided to do about Gabe's problem.

This is the second of two chapters that examine alcohol. Chapter 16 centered on alcohol's effect on the human body. This chapter focuses on the psychosocial dynamics of alcohol use. We will look first at drinking patterns among adults and college students. Then we will examine the development of drinking problems and alcoholism, as well as alcohol-related social problems, alcohol recovery programs, and responsible alcohol use.

ALCOHOL: THE DRUG OF CHOICE

Alcohol remains our nation's most popular drug. (With the exception of caffeine, alcohol is used by more Americans than any other legal or illegal drug.) This chapter is designed to prompt you to reflect on yourself, a family member, or someone you know whose life has been touched in some serious way by alcohol. Indeed, more lives are affected by alcohol than any other licit or illicit drug. Despite headline stories about cocaine, methamphetamine, or heroin, our country's biggest drug problem remains the misuse and abuse of alcohol.

This fact may seem difficult for the typical college student to accept. For a large majority of students, alcohol remains a symbol of the independence that college life offers. The evidence is convincing. Alcohol is typically at center stage at college parties and student gatherings. Advertising for alcohol is pervasive in student newspapers. Alcohol is associated with the weekend, a time to kick back and forget about a difficult week of work. Alcohol's connection to sexual attraction and relationships further solidifies its effect on college students' lives.

We hope this chapter will encourage you to examine alcohol's influence on people's lives, especially your own.

Adult Drinking Patterns

Recall from chapter 16 that in the United States approximately 60% of the adult population (age 18 years and older) consumes alcohol. The most recent National Household Survey on Drug Abuse reported that almost two-thirds of the population age 12 and older reported drinking alcohol at least once in the past year.[1]

Within this drinking population, the average drinker consumes 2.43 gallons of pure alcohol annually.[2] This amount of pure alcohol consumed annually per capita equals 576 12-oz cans of beer (that is, 24 cases of beer), or viewed another way, a combination of 29.1 gallons of beer, 2.7 gallons of wine, *and* 1.85 gallons of liquor. Of course, as we learned in chapter 16, the distribution of alcohol among drinkers is very uneven, with a large percentage of drinkers consuming much less than these amounts and a small percentage of drinkers consuming much more than these amounts.

College Student Drinking Patterns

A large national survey reported that nearly 90% of college students drink alcohol.[3] For some drinkers, this is a "rite of passage," and their drinking is not especially heavy. However, 41% of American college students

Do you believe that drive-up windows such as this one contribute to impaired driving?

reported binge drinking, or the consumption of five drinks or more in a row, at least once in the previous two-week period. This heavy drinking frequently takes place on weekends. However, 4% to 5% of college students also said that they drink on a daily basis.[4]

Binge Drinking.   A second large study, "Alcohol and Drugs on American College Campuses: A Report to College Presidents," sheds light on current college drinking behavior. In this national study of college students, important information about the drinking patterns of college students emerged.[5]

By most standards, many college students can be called heavy drinkers. How much do students drink on a weekly basis? They average 5.11 drinks per week, while 7.8% drink an average of 16 or more drinks per week, and 17.8% drink 10 or more drinks per week (fig. 17.1).[6]

The study "Alcohol and Drugs on American College Campuses: A Report to College Presidents" reported specific data about binge drinking. As shown in figure 17.2, 42% of the college students in this national study reported drinking five or more drinks in a row in the two weeks before the study. Perhaps more revealing is the finding that 28% reported having binged more than once in the two weeks before the study.

These figures should be especially alarming to faculty members, administrators, and of course, parents. College administrators consistently report the connection between binge drinking and residence hall damage, sexual assault, fights, and drunk driving. Student alcohol use clearly has major implications for the educational process and the quality of life on college campuses.

Drinking and Academic Performance.   The Report to College Presidents study also gave some interesting insights into the relationship between alcohol use and academic performance. Quite simply, the more alcohol college students drink, the lower their grades are likely to be (fig. 17.3). Students averaging 3.45 drinks per week earned As, while students averaging 10.87 drinks a week earned Ds or Fs. If you know someone who drinks heavily and earns high grades, this person is clearly the exception to the rule.

Other Negative Consequences.   What other negative consequences might affect students who consume alcohol? The Report to College Presidents study asked college students what negative consequences resulted from their alcohol (and other drug) use within the past year. Figure 17.4 reports the top 10 negative consequences that affected students after alcohol or other drug use.[7]

Professors' Thoughts.   When we present this generally negative information about campus alcohol use to our students, many of them believe we sound like their "nagging parents." In the classroom, some students minimize the problems alcohol can cause among their peers. They say, "We're supposed to have fun, aren't we?" Certainly

FIGURE 17.1

Average number of drinks per week.

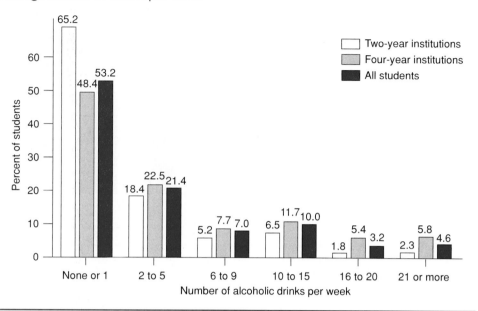

(From C. A. Presley and P. W. Meilman: *Alcohol and drugs on American college campuses: a report to college presidents,* Southern Illinois University Student Health Program Wellness Center, June, 1992, US Department of Education.)

FIGURE 17.2

Frequency of consumption of five or more drinks (binge drinking) in the past two weeks.

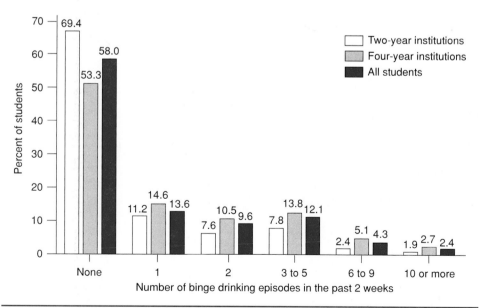

(From C. A. Presley and P. W. Meilman: *Alcohol and drugs on American college campuses: a report to college presidents,* Southern Illinois University Student Health Program Wellness Center, June, 1992, U.S. Department of Education.)

FIGURE 17.3

Average number of drinks per
week, by GPA.

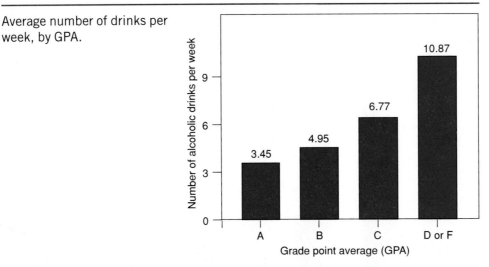

(From C. A. Presley and P. W. Meilman: *Alcohol and drugs on American college campuses: a report to
college presidents,* Southern Illinois University Student Health Program Wellness Center, June, 1992,
US Department of Education.)

FIGURE 17.4

Negative consequences of alcohol and drug abuse within the past year.*

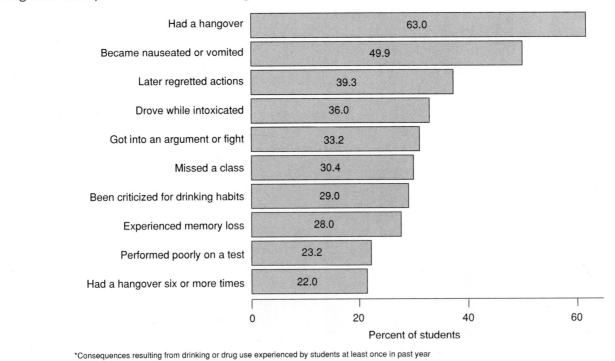

*Consequences resulting from drinking or drug use experienced by students at least once in past year

(From C. A. Presley and P. W. Meilman: *Alcohol and drugs on American college campuses: a report to
college presidents,* Southern Illinois University Student Health Program Wellness Center, June, 1992,
US Department of Education.)

Alcohol education uses a variety of teaching approaches.

we believe that college should be an enjoyable experience in the fullest sense. However, we see alcohol as a potentially double-edged sword.

For many students, the college years are the time they drink most heavily. As many students graduate and move into the "real world," their drinking moderates. However, like the rest of the population, approximately 12% will be unable to moderate their alcohol consumption. They will continue to drink alcohol and will eventually be unable to control their drinking behavior. Clearly, they will face significant problems. They will eventually hurt themselves or others around them. Ironically, they will also hurt those they love. This is why we take seriously the information we provide about alcohol and its potential for harm.

ALCOHOLISM

A Definition

The definition of *alcoholism* has evolved over many years. Professionals in the areas of alcohol treatment, alcohol research, medical management, and psychiatry have offered various versions to fit their particular focus, and the general public has its own definition of the term alcoholism.

In the early 1990s, a 23-member multidisciplinary committee of the National Council on Alcoholism and Drug Dependence and the American Society of Addiction Medicine finished its two-year study to define alcoholism. This committee tried to define alcoholism in light of the most current concepts concerning the disease:

> Alcoholism is a primary, chronic disease with genetic, psychosocial, and environmental factors influencing its development and manifestations. The disease is often progressive and fatal. It is characterized by impaired control over drinking, preoccupation with the drug alcohol, use of alcohol despite adverse consequences, and distortions in thinking, most notably denial. Each of these symptoms may be continuous or periodic.[8]

Some of the wording in this new definition of alcoholism might need to be discussed. "Primary" suggests that alcoholism is a disease in and of itself and not a symptom of another underlying disease. "Often progressive and fatal" suggests that alcoholism frequently persists over time and that the negative effects of alcoholism are cumulative. Further, the negative consequences can worsen over time and lead to premature death in a variety of ways.

"Impaired control" implies that the drinker is consistently unable to limit the duration of drinking, the amount of alcohol consumed, and/or the behavioral consequences that follow the drinking episode. "Preoccupation with the drug alcohol" reflects a person's

Should Chronic Heavy Users of Alcohol Receive Liver Transplants?

As a result of the escalating cost of health care in this country (now above $1 trillion per year), policy makers are looking with renewed interest at the idea of rationing care. The possibility of restricting medical procedures that are highly expensive, because of their technical complexity or the need for donor organs, is particularly interesting to those who wish to hold down medical costs. Heart, kidney, lung, and liver transplants would be carefully screened because of the technical expertise and donor organs required.

Because chronic heavy consumption of alcohol leads to progressive deterioration of liver function, many relatively young heavy alcohol users experience liver failure to the point that they need a liver transplant to survive. This need for expensive care and rare transplant organs raises questions about who deserves access to the money that is needed for such a procedure.

What is your position on public financing of care required by individuals who have damaged themselves through chronic heavy alcohol use, particularly when others have equally critical needs because of conditions that did not involve excessive alcohol use?

excessive, focused attention on alcohol and its effects. This preoccupation often leads a person to divert attention and energy from other life concerns that once were considered important.[9]

"Adverse consequences" refers to alcohol-related problems in several areas. Alcoholics continue to use alcohol despite serious personal health problems (such as alcohol withdrawal syndrome, liver disease, or gastritis); psychological problems (major changes in mood and behavior); interpersonal problems (marital conflicts, child abuse, and deteriorating social relationships); occupational problems (employment problems or academic failures); and legal, financial, or spiritual problems. Indeed, alcoholics continue to drink despite consistently hurting themselves and others.[10]

"Denial" is a characteristic manifestation of alcoholism that refers to a wide range of psychological maneuvers that drinkers use to convince themselves that alcohol is not the cause of their problems. In fact, many alcoholics can convince themselves that alcohol is the *solution* to their problems. (In a later section, we discuss denial in greater detail.)

Alcohol Withdrawal Syndrome

Many alcoholics experience the phenomenon of **alcohol withdrawal syndrome.** Alcohol is a highly addictive depressant drug. When deprived of alcohol, alcoholics characteristically display both physical and mental withdrawal symptoms.[11] Mental symptoms include increased levels of agitation and vigilance. The alcoholic becomes concerned about how and when the next drink will be found. Physical symptoms of alcohol withdrawal syn-

drome can be life-threatening. These include uncontrollable shaking, nausea, vomiting, hallucinations, shock, and ultimately cardiac and pulmonary failure. Uncontrollable shaking combined with irrational hallucinations during an alcoholic's withdrawal is termed **delirium tremens (DTs).**

Like diabetes and hypertension, alcoholism is now considered an incurable disease. Indeed, it can be controlled only through abstinence. Alcoholics who have gone through treatment and recovery programs consider themselves alcoholics for the rest of their lives. Alcoholics realize that taking that first drink will almost assuredly start them back on a pattern of alcoholic behavior. Thus, alcoholism must be considered a lifelong disease.

Some of the characteristic behaviors exhibited by individuals who are progressing toward alcoholism are shown in table 17.1. If any of these behaviors fits your alcohol use patterns or those of your friends, you have reason for concern about alcohol use.[12]

Problem Drinking

The definition of alcoholism presented earlier stresses that alcoholism is a disease. This does not mean that a person can have problems with alcohol only when he or she develops alcoholism. The term **problem drinking** refers to any drinking pattern that produces difficulties in a person's life. These difficulties may appear in the person who rarely consumes alcohol. A major difficulty can result from just one problem exposure to alcohol, such as a situation in which a nondrinker is encouraged to have a few drinks and then has a car accident. For some, problem drinking may be a precursor to the devel-

TABLE 17.1 Progressive Stages of Alcohol Dependence

Early	Middle	Late
Escape drinking	Loss of control	Prolonged binges
Guilt feelings	Self-hate	Alcohol used to control withdrawal symptoms
Sneaking drinks	Impaired social relationships	Alcohol psychosis
Difficulty stopping once drinking has begun	Changes in drinking patterns	Nutritional disease
Increased tolerance	Temporary sobriety	Frequent blackouts
Preoccupation with drinking	Morning drinking	
Occasional blackouts	Dietary neglect	

From W. A. Payne and D. B. Hahn, *Understanding Your Health,* 5th ed. (St. Louis: WCB/McGraw-Hill, 1998).

opment of alcoholism. However, problem drinkers rarely are so dependent on alcohol that they suffer withdrawal symptoms when they are deprived of it.

Perhaps the factor that separates problem drinkers from nonproblem drinkers is that when problem drinkers drink, they frequently lose control over their drinking and their behavior. They may not be physically addicted to alcohol, but when they drink, they cause problems for themselves and others. The self-assessment on page 278 lists criteria by which you might judge whether you are a problem drinker.

DEVELOPMENT OF ALCOHOLISM

Alcoholism is a multifaceted disease process with genetic, environmental, and psychosocial components. The scientific literature suggests that alcoholism is not caused by just one factor but that it develops from the interaction of all three factors.

Problem drinkers frequently lose control over their behavior.

Genetic Factors

Studies in both humans and animals produce compelling evidence that genetics does play a role in some cases of alcoholism. However, inherited alcoholism is a controversial topic among health professionals. The argument that people are genetically vulnerable, or "at risk," to alcoholism is countered by the argument that a person's environment (e.g., family, socioeconomic status, role models) plays the central role in a person's developing alcoholism. Perhaps both of these factors are important in the development of the disease.

Despite the debate, two forms of alcoholism are thought to be inherited: **Type 1 (or milieu-limited alcoholism)** and **Type 2 (or male-limited alcoholism).** Type 1 is a less severe form and seems to be inherited by sons or daughters of an alcoholic parent of either sex. Type 1 alcoholism is thought to take years to develop and

alcohol withdrawal syndrome the collection of characteristic signs and symptoms experienced by alcohol-addicted people when they are deprived of alcohol; also called alcohol abstinence syndrome

delirium tremens (DTs) uncontrollable shaking and hallucinations associated with withdrawal from heavy chronic alcohol use

problem drinking a pattern of alcohol use (abuse) in which a drinker's behavior creates personal difficulties for the drinker or for others

Type 1 alcoholism an inherited form of alcoholism that is thought to be primarily influenced by environmental factors; also known as milieu-limited alcoholism

Type 2 alcoholism an inherited form of alcoholism that is thought to pass primarily from alcoholic fathers to their sons; also known as male-limited alcoholism

SELF-ASSESSMENT

Could You Be a Problem Drinker?

As the term implies, problem drinkers are people whose use of alcohol frequently leads to problems for themselves or others. Answer each of the following questions according to your own alcohol use pattern:

1. Do you drink to cope with difficult situations?
2. Do you frequently drink to a state of intoxication? Is the word "intoxication" used by others to describe your condition?
3. Do you drive while under the influence of alcohol?
4. Do you fight when drinking? Have you ever injured someone or been injured while drinking, to the extent that medical attention was required?

5. Do you do things while drinking that you later believe you would not have done had you not been drinking?
6. Do you display any of these additional signs of problem drinking?

   Need to drink before facing certain situations
   Engage in frequent drinking sprees
   Require increasingly more alcohol to feel "satisfied"
   Drink alone
   Drink early in the morning

   If you have answered yes to any of these questions, then you have shown behavior generally associated with problem drinking.

---

may not surface until the midlife years. Whether a person with a Type 1 profile develops into an alcoholic depends heavily on environmental factors.[13]

Type 2 alcoholism is the more severe form and appears to be passed along primarily from fathers to sons. This form of alcoholism frequently develops earlier in a person's life and may appear during the adolescent years. The person often has a history of petty criminality. Type 2 alcoholism may account for 25% of the cases of alcoholism in men in the general population.[14] Sons of alcoholics with this genetic predisposition may be more seriously affected by initial episodes of drinking than sons with a Type 1 genetic profile. Environmental factors do not play a major role in the expression of Type 2 alcoholism. For at-risk men, abstinence from alcohol is the critical factor in preventing the development of alcoholism.

Other evidence supports a genetic basis for alcoholism development. Many Asian people seem to have an alcohol intolerance that is caused by low levels of the enzyme ADH, which is necessary for the biodeactivation of alcohol. In addition, some Native Americans may be predisposed to alcoholism because of a hypothesized genetic difference in the rate of absorption of alcohol in the small intestine.

Most recently, scientists have been searching for a single gene that is a marker for alcoholism vulnerability. Studies currently suggest more than one gene probably is related to increased alcoholism vulnerability. If the genetic markers for alcoholism vulnerability could be identified, then high-risk individuals could be identified,

intervention could be initiated at an earlier time, and new treatment protocols could be developed.

However, one must not assume that genetics holds the key to the prediction of alcoholism. As Dr. Enoch Gordis, Director of the National Institute on Alcohol Abuse and Alcoholism (NIAAA) stated, "Based on our current understanding, it is probable that environmental influences will be at least as important, and possibly more important, than genetic influences."[15]

Environmental Factors

A wide variety of environmental factors shape the lives of people. Certainly the central environmental influence for most people is the family. Children learn from the behavior of their parents and siblings. Family relationships, socioeconomic status, and family patterns are factors that can shape the behavior of youths. Children are also influenced by friends of the family and peers in their neighborhood. School, athletic, and church experiences also play central roles in the developmental lives of youths. Certainly you can think of other environmental influences that could affect drinking behavior.

Environmental factors continue to affect individuals throughout a lifetime. The experiences people have in college, the friends they choose, and the mentors they admire all play a part in the development of lifelong adult behavior. Employment experiences (successes and failures), the availability of close friendships, and the concern employers show for healthy or unhealthy behavior can further affect drinking patterns. Maintaining a marriage and family presents people with a myriad of environmental influences. The experiences people have as they move through midlife and elderly years continue to shape their entire lives.

Psychosocial Factors

Certain psychosocial factors that predispose people to the development of alcoholism have been identified. Experts have described factors ranging from an unusually low level of self-esteem to an **antisocial personality.** Additional factors that might increase a person's susceptibility to alcoholism are excessive reliance on denial, hypervigilance, compulsiveness, and chronic anxiety.[16]

Always complicating the study of psychosocial factors and personality traits is the uncertainty of whether the factor or trait is a predisposing factor (perhaps from inheritance or influences before alcohol use) or is caused by the alcoholism itself. In addition, the complexity of sorting out family dynamics, economic factors, and living conditions further clouds any profile of genetics and personality factors alone.

Denial and Enabling

Two of the most powerful psychological processes contributing to the development of alcoholism are denial and enabling. Although both processes can be observed in the progression of alcoholism, denial is found primarily in alcohol abusers and enabling in alcohol abusers' families, friends, and coworkers.

Denial. Alcoholics (and even some problem drinkers) often use the psychological defense mechanism of **denial** to maintain their drinking behavior. (You will recall that denial was a major concept in the definition of alcoholism given on p. 275.) Denial includes a wide range of maneuvers that people use to convince themselves that alcohol is not the cause of their problems. Using denial, many alcoholics can convince themselves that alcohol is the solution to their problems. A drinker's denial is an unconscious process that is apparent only to rational observers.

Of course, this kind of thinking encourages alcoholics to continue drinking and to avoid seeking treatment for their addiction. In the past, alcoholics were required to admit that their denial was no longer effective before they could be admitted into a treatment program. Alcoholics had to "hit bottom" and realize for themselves that they needed help.

This is not the case today. Currently, family members, friends, or coworkers of chemically dependent people are encouraged to intervene and virtually force people into treatment before they hit bottom. For treatment to be

Children of alcoholics can become caregivers. Enablers can be an alcoholic's worst enemy.

successful, patients must break through their denial and convince themselves that alcohol controls their lives.

Enabling. For family and friends of chemically dependent people, **enabling** can perpetuate the process of denial. In this process, people close to the drinker inadvertently support his or her behavior by denying that the drinker has a problem. Enablers unconsciously make excuses for the drinker and try to keep the drinker's work and family life intact. By covering up for the drinker through enabling behaviors, these people, in effect, support the continued abuse of alcohol. Addiction counselors contend that enablers may be some alcoholics' worst enemies, because their efforts delay entry into a treatment program. Even on the college campus, one can identify enablers. Have you noticed any such people at your college?

ALCOHOL-RELATED SOCIAL PROBLEMS

As we have already seen, the misuse and abuse of alcohol are influenced by a variety of social problems that affect both the drinker and his or her family. These problems

antisocial personality a personality profile characterized by behaviors opposed to acceptable social norms

denial contention by alcoholics that they have no problems with alcohol use; denial maintains drinking behavior and delays treatment

enabling the inadvertent support that some people provide to alcohol abusers or other drug abusers

affect the quality of interpersonal relationships, employment stability, and financial security on which both the individual and family depend. Clearly, alcohol's negative social effects reduce our quality of life. In financial terms, experts have estimated the cost of alcohol abuse and dependence at $136.3 billion for 1990 and $150 billion for 1995.[17]

We see the effects of alcohol consumption on social problems in the following critical areas: accidental deaths, crime and violence, and suicide.

Accidental Deaths

The four leading causes of accidental death (motor vehicle crashes, falls, drownings, and fires and burns) have significant statistical connections to alcohol use. Until the mid-1980s, approximately half of all fatal traffic crashes were alcohol-related. Public outrage over alcohol-related traffic deaths resulted in a gradual lowering of this percentage to below 40% in the early 1990s.[18] However, after a decade of progress at lowering the number of alcohol-related traffic deaths, 1995 saw an increase in the number of such deaths. In 1995, 17,274 people died in alcohol-related traffic crashes, an increase of 4% over 1994.[19] The likelihood of a fatal crash is about eight times higher for a drunk driver (0.10% blood alcohol content [BAC]) than for a sober one.[20]

Many people are surprised to find that falls are the second leading cause of accidental death in the United States, causing about 13,000 deaths per year. Alcohol use increases the risk for falls. Various studies suggest that alcohol is involved in 17% to 73% of deadly falls.[21]

Drownings are the third leading cause of accidental death in the United States. Studies have shown that alcohol use is implicated in 47% to 65% of adult drowning deaths. Alcohol appears in over half of all drowning fatalities associated with swimming, boating, and rafting. In addition, increasing evidence suggests that alcohol use plays a role in a significant number of diving-related spinal cord injuries.[22]

Fires and burns are responsible for an estimated 6,000 deaths each year. This fourth leading cause of accidental death is also connected to alcohol use, with studies showing that nearly half of burn victims have BACs above the legal limit.

Crime and Violence

You may have noticed at your college that most of the violent behavior and vandalism on university campuses is related to alcohol use. Indeed, the connection of alcohol to crime has a long history. Prison populations have large percentages of alcohol abusers and alcoholics. People who commit crimes are more likely to have alcohol problems than people in the general population. This is especially true for young criminals. Alcohol use has been reported in 67% of all homicides, with the victim, the perpetrator, or both found to be drinking. In rapes, rapists are intoxicated 50% of the time and victims 30% of the time.[23]

Because of research methodological problems, pinpointing alcohol's connection to family violence is difficult. Among many families, however, alcohol is clearly associated with violence and other negative interactions,

Drinking and driving can lead to horrific accident scenes.

SELF-ASSESSMENT

Codependence: Are You at Risk?

Alcoholism frequently affects not only the alcoholic but other people as well, such as a spouse, children, friends, and coworkers. These affected people are often considered codependent on the condition of alcoholism, and in fact, can prolong it. If the following situations describe your experiences, you may be involved in a codependent relationship. Do you:

1. Feel responsible for the feelings, thoughts, and actions of the alcohol-dependent person?
2. Feel guilty when you observe the alcoholism of a spouse, child, friend, or coworker?
3. Feel a compulsion to help the alcoholic?
4. Experience a sense of anger when you see or think about the alcoholism of another person?

5. Feel a sense of duplicity about another person's alcoholism? For example, would you like him or her to undergo treatment and recovery but feel uncertain about what the future would be like if the alcoholic regained sobriety?
6. Feel most secure when you are giving to the alcoholic rather than receiving from them?
7. Feel attracted to people who are needy or recognize that these people are attracted to you?
8. Feel sadness that you have spent your whole life giving and no one has reciprocated?

Experts contend that these feelings often underlie the unique relationships between alcoholics and those who live and work with them.

---

including physical abuse, child abuse, psychological abuse, and abandonment.[24]

Suicide

Alcohol's relationship to suicide is not surprising. Between 20% and 36% of suicide victims have a history of alcohol abuse or were drinking shortly before their suicides. In addition, alcohol use is associated with impulsive suicides rather than with premeditated ones. Drinking is also connected with more violent and lethal forms of suicide, such as those involving the use of firearms.[25]

For many of these social problems, alcohol use impairs critical judgment and allows a person's behavior to quickly become reckless, antisocial, and deadly.

ALCOHOLISM AND THE FAMILY

Rarely does alcoholism harm only the drinker. Family life can be seriously affected by alcoholism, so much so that some experts consider alcoholism a family disease. Addiction to alcohol tends to make relationships difficult for alcoholics, especially relationships with family members. Instead, alcoholics develop relationships with alcohol. Families are disrupted not only by the consequences of the drinking behavior (such as violence, illness, or unemployment), but also by individual members' uncertainties about their roles in causing and prolonging the situation.

Family members often assume a variety of new roles that enable them to cope with the presence of an alco-

holic in the family. The more commonly seen roles are the "family hero" (the responsible one who manages the household), the "lost child" (the adjuster who takes things in stride), the "family mascot" (the placator who soothes hurt feelings), and the "scapegoat" (the defiant one who gets into trouble).[26] Without appropriate counseling, these roles can last throughout a person's lifetime.

Codependence

The term **codependence** began appearing in alcohol and drug-addiction literature several years ago. Codependence is a condition characterized by an unusual set of behaviors exhibited by one who is in a close relationship with a drug-dependent person. Codependent people may or may not be chemically addicted themselves, but their behaviors indicate that they are "addicted" to the chemically dependent person.

Codependents frequently exhibit enabling and denial behaviors that tend to delay intervention and treatment for a considerable period. People who find themselves in codependent relationships often share similar behavioral traits with the chemically dependent person. These traits seem to predispose them to codependence. (See the self-assessment above.)

> **codependence** a condition characterized by an unusual set of behaviors by a person who is in a close relationship with a chemically dependent person; these behaviors may include "enabling" and "denial"

DRUGS IN YOUR WORLD

Common Traits of ACAs

Adult children of alcoholics often:

1. Guess what normal behavior is
2. Have difficulty following a project from beginning to end
3. Lie when it would be just as easy to tell the truth
4. Judge themselves without mercy
5. Have difficulty having fun
6. Take themselves very seriously
7. Have difficulty with intimate relationships
8. Overreact to changes over which they have no control
9. Constantly seek approval and affirmation
10. Feel that they are different from other people
11. Are super-responsible or super-irresponsible
12. Are extremely loyal, even in the face of evidence that the loyalty is undeserved.
13. Tend to lock themselves into a course of action without giving consideration to consequences

Modified from J. G. Woititz, *Adult Children of Alcoholics* (Pompano Beach, Fla.: Health Communications, 1983).

Fortunately, most treatment and recovery programs for alcoholics encourage family members (some of whom may exhibit codependence) to participate in many aspects of the recovery. This helps them better realize how they have been affected by alcoholism. Family members are encouraged to participate in support groups related to Alcoholics Anonymous, such as Al-Anon and Alateen.

Adult Children of Alcoholics (ACAs)

At about the same time that the phenomenon of codependence was discovered, another effect of alcoholism was recognized—the unusually high prevalence of alcoholism in the **adult children of alcoholics (ACAs)**. These adult children are estimated to be about four times more likely to develop alcoholism than children whose parents were not alcoholics. In the United States, there are an estimated 28 million ACAs.[27] Clearly, many of these ACAs do not become alcoholics or even have major life crises, but even ACAs who do not become alcoholics may have a difficult time adjusting to everyday living patterns. Janet Geringer Woititz, author of the landmark book *Adult Children of Alcoholics*, describes 13 traits that most ACAs exhibit to some degree (see the box above).[28]

Many of the difficulties that ACAs have can be traced to the years of living in an alcoholic family. When they were children, ACAs had to learn survival behaviors to cope with the complexities of living in a dysfunctional family. Many of these behaviors were probably compulsive ones that permitted the child to adjust to the inconsistencies, embarrassment, shame, denial, secrecy, and lying, as well as feelings of being trapped, isolated, or different.[29] However, as these children grew up and moved into a more healthy environment, the behaviors they learned in the dysfunctional family were unable to serve them well.

Many ACAs have a difficult time discovering what "normal" behavior really is. For this reason, they tend to marry alcoholics. ACAs are familiar with the chaos of living with an alcoholic.

In response to the concern about ACAs, support groups have been formed to assist adult sons and daughters in understanding their situations. Through support groups, ACAs can better learn about themselves. They learn to be honest with themselves and others and to identify unhealthy patterns in their lives. They learn that they did not cause their parents' drinking problems. They learn that there are other ACAs who have had similar struggles and that help is available through both professionals and support groups. Finally, ACAs must learn to take charge and seek help.[30]

ALCOHOL TREATMENT AND RECOVERY

Recovery from alcoholism is certainly possible. Most college students and professors know friends or relatives who have been successfully treated for alcohol problems. Recovery works best when the alcoholic internalizes the concept that alcoholism is a treatable (but incurable) illness, not a form of moral weakness. Recovery is further improved when the patient has a good emotional support system, including concerned family, friends, and employers. The alcoholic's chances for recovery are considerably lower when this support system is not well established.

As mentioned earlier in this chapter, alcohol-treatment professionals have generally discarded the notion that an alcoholic must "hit bottom" before he or she can successfully enter a treatment program. Thus, family members and concerned friends are increasingly using **confrontation** to encourage or even force an alcoholic

ALTERNATIVE CHOICES

You Can Choose to Help or Look the Other Way

Because of the many people who have problems with alcohol, each of us probably will be confronted by someone who needs professional help for an alcohol problem. We can then choose whether to help this person or to look the other way. The following story, titled The Starfish Man, gives an analogy to how you can empower yourself to help someone else gain safety and freedom:

One morning at dawn a young boy went for a walk on the beach. Up ahead he noticed an old man stooping down to pick up starfish and fling them into the sea. Finally, catching up with the old man, the boy asked

him what he was doing. The old man answered that the stranded starfish would die unless they were returned to the water. "But the beach goes on for miles, and there are millions of starfish," protested the boy. "How can what you're doing make any difference?" The old man looked at the starfish in his hand and then threw it to safety in the waves. "It makes a difference to this one," he said.

Modified from Alcohol, Drug Abuse, and Mental Health Administration, Office of Substance Abuse Prevention, *Faculty Member's Handbook: Strategies for Preventing Alcohol and Other Drug Problems*, U.S. DHHS Pub. No. (ADM) 91-1843, 1991.

to seek treatment. Users of the confrontation approach try to break through an alcoholic's denial by presenting the facts about his or her behavior in a face-to-face meeting with the alcoholic. Confrontation combined with loving support and concern are leading many alcoholics into earlier treatment and recovery. (See the box above for one view of our need to help others.)

Treatment Approaches

Methods of treating alcoholism vary according to the specific needs of the patient. Detoxification, the medical management of chronic health problems associated with alcohol abuse, and individual, group, and family counseling sessions are all parts of alcoholism treatment.

Most treatment programs combine inpatient and outpatient care. Inpatient treatment in hospitals, clinics, or chemical dependence centers often lasts for about four weeks and may cost $10,000 to $30,000. Long-term aftercare may last for months.

A variety of therapeutic approaches can be used. Sometimes the drug **Antabuse** is given to recovering alcoholics. Antabuse inhibits an enzyme (acetaldehyde dehydrogenase) from breaking down acetaldehyde (see fig. 17.4). People who take Antabuse and then drink alcohol experience a toxic buildup of acetaldehyde in their systems. This toxic buildup produces a violent reaction, including nausea, vomiting, flushed skin, chest pain, blurred vision, heart palpitations, headache, and weakness.[31] Obviously, this reaction deters the use of alcohol.

Another drug was recently approved for use in helping alcoholics reduce their cravings for alcohol. Naltrexone (brand name ReVia) works by blocking certain opioid receptors in the brain; thus, ReVia is a pure opioid antagonist. ReVia seems to reduce the pleasurable effects one

receives when consuming alcohol.[32] Used in conjunction with other therapeutic approaches, ReVia is prescribed to be taken in 50 mg capsules once a day for up to 12 weeks.[33] The extent to which this drug will be routinely prescribed is not yet known.

Most but not all health insurance programs have provisions for alcoholism treatment. Increasing evidence shows that expensive inpatient treatment may not be significantly more effective than less-expensive outpatient treatment. However, individuals who resist treatment or fail at outpatient treatment may find that inpatient treatment is the best option for them.

The fastest-growing approach to medically supervised treatment is the *intensive outpatient program*. This approach uses an aggressive combination of inpatient and outpatient treatment strategies. Patients spend considerable time in comprehensive therapy sessions during the day but still reside in their own homes at night.

12-Step Programs

Some people who seek recovery from alcohol addiction join 12-step programs. These programs may be run independently or jointly with the traditional medical

adult children of alcoholics (ACAs) adults whose parents were alcoholics and who are thus at risk themselves of becoming alcoholics

confrontation a face-to-face intervention meeting with a drug-dependent person to convince him or her to enter treatment

Antabuse a drug prescribed to some recovering alcoholics that produces a violent illness if alcohol is consumed

management procedures just described. The best-known 12-step program is **Alcoholics Anonymous (AA).** AA is a voluntary fellowship of men and women whose primary purpose is to get sober, stay sober, and help others achieve sobriety. AA was started by two recovering alcoholics in 1934 in Akron, Ohio.[34]

Alcoholics Anonymous's only membership requirement is a person's desire to stop drinking. AA charges no dues for membership and is self-supported by personal contributions. It is not organized around any sect or religious denomination and is not involved with politics. AA does not support or oppose any causes. Its only purpose is to help members remain sober.[35]

The term *12 step* comes from the 12 steps to recovery from alcoholism that AA members follow (see the box on p. 285). Keys to accomplishing the 12 steps are a belief in personal humility coupled with a belief in a "higher power." Each member develops his or her own definition of higher power (see the box below). According to AA, to achieve sobriety an alcoholic must admit that there is a power greater than himself or herself.[36] In this sense, AA has a strong spiritual component, although this spiritual component is defined solely by the alcoholic.

AA members do not attempt to scientifically understand their drinking behaviors. Rather, they rely on simple slogans or sayings to help them remain sober "one day at a time." The three most common slogans of AA are "first things first," "easy does it," and "live and let live." Most AA members have sponsors.[37] These are sober men and women who have significant experience with AA and serve as confidants or mentors to newer AA members.

There are more than 96,000 AA groups throughout the world, with members in 134 countries. The average member attends three AA meetings per week. AA has served as a model for other treatment programs, including Narcotics Anonymous and Cocaine Anonymous. You can find AA programs in your area in the telephone book or in the classified ads section of your local newspaper. See the Sources for Help box at the end of this chapter for information on how to reach the national AA office.

Secular Recovery Programs

Despite the significant benefits that AA and other 12-step programs have had for many alcoholics, a growing number of people feel uncomfortable with the concept of having to admit that their lives are ultimately controlled by a higher power. They feel uncomfortable with notions of divine intervention and spiritual guidance.

For these people, **secular recovery programs** may be the answer to their alcoholism. These programs are based on the idea that the key to maintaining sobriety comes from within the alcoholic. Secular programs place major emphasis on self-reliance and self-determination. During their group meetings, they encourage rational thinking and attempt to identify the irrational thoughts some members have about their alcoholic behavior. Members reject the notion of "powerlessness" that some groups propose.

Unlike most 12-step programs, secular recover programs have no sponsor systems. Personal independence is encouraged. Like 12-step programs, however, secular recovery programs do not criticize any other recovery programs, do not have a political agenda, and are self-supported through voluntary contributions from members.

Two secular recovery programs are especially notable. Secular Organizations for Sobriety (SOS) was begun in 1985 by James Christopher, a recovering alcoholic. This organization can be reached at (310) 821-8430 or at 5521 Grosvenor Boulevard, Los Angeles, CA 90066.

AA MEMBERS' OCCUPATIONS

Professional/Technical	13%
Retired	11%
Other (including self-employed)	11%
Manager/Administrator	10%
Laborer	9%
Unemployed	7%
Health professional	6%
Craft worker	5%
Disabled	5%
Service worker	4%
Sales worker	4%
Clerical worker	4%
Educator	3%
Homemaker	3%
Student	3%
Transportation (equip. oper.)	2%

Alcoholics Anonymous, *1996 Membership Survey*, Alcoholics Anonymous World Services (brochure), 1997.

Support groups can help alcoholics who seek sobriety.

ALTERNATIVE CHOICES

The 12 Steps of Alcoholics Anonymous

1. We admitted we were powerless over alcohol—that our lives had become unmanageable.
2. Came to believe that a Power greater than ourselves could restore us to sanity.
3. Made a decision to turn our will and our lives over to the care of God as we understood Him.
4. Made a searching and fearless moral inventory of ourselves.
5. Admitted to God, to ourselves, and to another human being the exact nature of our wrongs.
6. Were entirely ready to have God remove all these defects of character.
7. Humbly asked Him to remove our shortcomings.
8. Made a list of all persons we had harmed, and became willing to make amends to them all.
9. Made direct amends to such people wherever possible, except when to do so would injure them or others.
10. Continued to take personal inventory and when we were wrong promptly admitted it.
11. Sought through prayer and meditation to improve our conscious contact with God, as we understood Him, praying only for knowledge of His will for us and the power to carry that out.
12. Having had a spiritual awakening as a result of these steps, we tried to carry this message to alcoholics, and to practice these principles in all our affairs.

Alcoholics Anonymous, *This Is AA: An Introduction to the AA Recovery Program*, Alcoholics Anonymous World Services (brochure), 1992.

A second well-known secular recovery program is called Rational Recovery Systems (RRS), or simply Rational Recovery. This program can be reached at RRS, P.O. Box 800, Lotus, CA 95691. Because these programs are relatively new, you may have to search carefully to find out about local meetings. For more information, see the sources for help list at the end of this chapter.

Al-Anon and Alateen

Al-Anon and **Alateen** are parallel organizations that support people who live with alcoholics. Al-Anon is aimed at spouses and other relatives, and Alateen focuses on teenage children of alcoholics. Both groups help members realize that they are not alone and that they can successfully adjust to nearly every alcoholic-related situation. Al-Anon and Alateen chapter organizations are usually listed in the telephone book or in the classified sections of local newspapers.

ARE THERE ANY BENEFITS OF ALCOHOL USE?

Can alcohol use benefit our health? Scientific research has never concluded that heavy alcohol consumption benefits a person's health, but what about moderate drinking? Some studies have reported that moderate drinkers live longer than teetotalers (nondrinkers). For years evidence has suggested that moderate drinking reduces the risk of heart disease. Moderate drinking (two drinks or less per day) was thought to raise high-density lipoprotein (HDL) cholesterol, the type of cholesterol that protects one from heart disease. (Note the most recent definition of moderate drinking in the box on p. 286.)

Recently, an overview of research in the *Harvard Heart Letter* has further supported the notion that risk for coronary artery disease is reduced among men and women who drink in moderation.[38] This report suggests that moderate alcohol consumption raises HDL cholesterol levels while reducing the blood's ability to clot easily. Nevertheless, some health professionals still argue that this health benefit may be more attributed to various combinations of lifestyle factors than to alcohol consumption alone.

Health experts caution readers not to start drinking to gain this possible beneficial effect. The risk of coronary heart disease can be reduced through other activities (such as healthy eating, physical activity, smoking cessation, and lowering blood pressure and cholesterol levels).

Alcoholics Anonymous (AA) voluntary support group for recovering alcoholics

secular recovery programs alcohol or drug recovery approaches that do not encourage members to believe in a god or higher power

Al-Anon voluntary support group for families of recovering alcoholics

Alateen voluntary support group for teenage children of recovering alcoholics

DRUGS IN YOUR WORLD

Moderate Drinking Redefined

Alcohol Alert, a publication of the National Institute on Alcohol Abuse and Alcoholism, defines moderate drinking as no more than two drinks each day for most men and no more than one drink each day for women. These consumption levels are based on the amount of alcohol that can be consumed without causing problems, either for the drinker or society. (The gender difference is due primarily to the higher percentage of body fat and the lower amount of an essential stomach enzyme in women.) Elderly people are limited to no more than one drink each day, again because of the higher percentage of body fat in older people.

These consumption levels are for most people. Indeed, people who plan to drive, women who are pregnant, recovering alcoholics, people under age 21, people taking medications, and those with medical concerns should not consume alcohol. In addition, although some studies have shown that low levels of alcohol may promote minor psychological and cardiovascular benefits, the NIAAA does not advise nondrinkers to start drinking.

From National Institute on Alcohol Abuse and Alcoholism, "Moderate Drinking," *Alcohol Alert* no. 16, (1992)315:1.

These activities are not linked to the negative consequences of alcohol consumption. Moderate drinking is also statistically linked to certain health risks (such as stroke, motor vehicle crashes, interactions with medications, cancer, birth defects, and the shift to heavier drinking).

The one remaining health benefit that might be attributed to alcohol use is alcohol's ability to function as a **social lubricant.** Used in moderation, alcohol reduces personal inhibitions and helps some people relax. For some drinkers, words appear to come more easily, and they act more confident around others. Thus, some would contend that when alcohol is used in moderation it can temporarily enhance one's emotional and social health.

There are many social lubricants besides alcohol, however. Dining, conversing, dancing, walking, attending an artistic or sporting event, and working together are all avenues that serve as social lubricants. Those who use alcohol as a social lubricant must clearly realize that their relaxation is an artificially induced state. Such users may just think they are more sociable when they drink; they may be deceiving themselves.

ALCOHOL ADVERTISING

Alcohol manufacturers in the United States spend more than $1 billion annually marketing their products in the print and broadcast media. Understandably, these marketing images show alcohol as a safe and effective social lubricant, not the source of one of the nation's most serious drug problems. Alcohol ads promise the "good life": a carefree, fun-loving environment composed of handsome men and attractive, playful women. Some alcohol ads encourage blue-collar workers to "drink like a man" and be a "real American." Other ads focus on the relaxation that their product can bring someone after a long day of stressful activity. Certain alcohol ads increasingly target women, minority populations (including young African-Americans and Hispanics), college students, and heavy drinkers.

Public health advocates have become concerned that the images created by alcohol ads encourage not only brand loyalty but also chronic heavy consumption. Some suggest that the ads also encourage underage drinking. These concerns have led some health officials to push for restrictions on alcohol advertising that include a ban on television advertising, a reduction in the number of billboards that target minorities in the inner city, and the elimination of alcohol advertising in college publications and at college sporting events. The recent reintroduction of liquor advertisements on television has added to the concerns of health advocates.[39] (See the box on p. 287.)

Some suggest that alcohol advertising creates a major dilemma. On one hand, alcohol is the foundation for many of the country's greatest drug problems. The use of alcohol creates more personal, social, economic, and legal problems than all other drugs used in the United States. On the other hand, alcohol is a legally available product whose sales are controlled primarily by individual states and local communities. Alcohol producers also support many worthy community causes.

This dilemma poses several questions. Should the fact that alcohol is a legal product make it difficult to restrict alcohol advertising? Is targeting a segment of the market illegal or unethical? Is it acceptable for your college or university to accept alcohol advertising? We must address all these questions as we look at alcohol advertising in the future.

WHAT DO YOU THINK?

Liquor Ads On Television

In 1936, the producers of distilled spirits stopped advertising their products on the radio. Twelve years later, the liquor companies decided to stop broadcasting ads over the new medium of television. The liquor industry was not required by law to take these measures, but did so voluntarily.[a]

All this changed in late 1996, when some companies began to run liquor ads on independently operated television stations in selected markets. All four of the major broadcast networks reportedly refused to allow liquor ads to be shown. The Distilled Spirits Council of the United States said that the companies were breaking no laws and were exercising their free-speech rights. The advertisers attempted to protect young people by not using images or cartoons that might attract children.

[a]R. A. Serrano, "Clinton Condemns Broadcast Liquor Ads," *Lexington (KY) Herald Leader,* 10 November 1996, p. A1.

Public health professionals were understandably alarmed with this action. Even President Bill Clinton denounced the move, claiming that liquor ads could be as harmful as cigarette ads in luring children into unhealthy behaviors. Whether the public outcry over this issue will curtail liquor ads on television and radio is uncertain. (Interestingly, in a move to curb underage drinking, Anheuser-Busch decided in December 1996 to switch its beer advertising from the teen-oriented MTV station to VH1, a music channel geared more to adult viewers.)

Have you seen any of these liquor advertisements on T.V.? Do you believe that liquor ads encourage underage drinking or irresponsible drinking? Are the messages in liquor ads different from ones that come from beer or wine ads?

RESPONSIBLE ALCOHOL USE

Is there such a thing as responsible alcohol use? Some argue that any drinking is irresponsible. Others disagree, believing that there are responsible ways to consume alcohol. Responsible drinking might be described as follows:

Drinking that does not jeopardize one's health, life satisfaction, occupational status, or legal status. This includes legal consumption that leads only to mild intoxication on an irregular basis. This includes never drinking and driving, drinking in a manner that affects job performance, or drinking and taking other major risks. Responsible drinking encompasses the ability to remain in control of one's behavior and to be able to stop drinking at a specified time or number of drinks.

Drinking that does not harm or injure someone else. This includes drinking behavior that does not injure one's family members, fellow employees, or friends. It also includes behaviors that provide good role models for young children. Of course, this behavior also includes never drinking and driving and never drinking and taking other risks that could hurt others.

Hosting a Party Responsibly

Social events where alcohol is served are never totally safe when one considers the possibility of unexpected drug synergism, overconsumption, and the consequences of released inhibitions. Responsible party hosting is becoming more and more the rule rather than the exception. The impetus for this trend has come from new respect for an individual's right to choose not to drink alcohol, the growing recognition of alcohol's role in automobile accidents, and the legal threats related to **host negligence.** Some important guidelines for being a responsible host if alcohol is served at your party are listed in the box on p. 288.

In addition to these suggestions, the use of designated drivers is an important component of responsible alcohol use. By planning to abstain or carefully limit their own alcohol consumption, designated drivers can safely transport friends who have been drinking. This may be especially important during times of generally heavy alcohol consumption, such as Super Bowl Sunday, New Year's Eve, or St. Patrick's Day.

social lubricant any factor that allows or promotes social interaction

drug synergism the heightened or exaggerated effect produced by the concurrent use of two or more drugs

host negligence failure to act with reasonable care in serving alcohol to others, resulting in injury to other people, thereby incurring potential liability

ALTERNATIVE CHOICES

How to Be a Responsible Host

Provide other activities as a primary focus when alcohol is served.

Respect an individual's decision about alcohol, whether that decision is to abstain or to drink responsibly.

Provide equally attractive and accessible nonalcoholic drinks when alcohol is served.

Recognize that drunkenness is neither healthy nor safe; one should not excuse unacceptable behavior.

Provide food when alcohol is served.

Serve diluted drinks, and do not urge that glasses be kept full.

Avoid intoxication yourself, and encourage others to do the same.

Make contingency plans for intoxication. If someone becomes intoxicated in spite of your efforts to prevent it, assume responsibility for the health and safety of the guest. Provide overnight accommodations or safe transportation home.

Serve alcohol only in places conducive to pleasant and relaxing behavior.

From *Task Force on Responsible Decisions about Alcohol, Interim Report No. 2* (Denver: Education Commission of the States, 1975).

Organizations That Support Responsible Alcohol Use

The serious consequences of irresponsible alcohol use have led concerned citizens to form several groups. Although each organization has its specific approach, all attempt to deal objectively with two indisputable facts: alcohol use is part of the fabric of our society and irresponsible alcohol use can be deadly. Some of the best-known groups follow:

Mothers Against Drunk Drivers (MADD). This group attempts to educate people about alcohol's effects on driving and to encourage legislation and enforcement of laws related to drunk driving. In the late 1980s, MADD clearly had a major role in the passage of laws enacted by states to raise the legal drinking age to 21.

Students Against Driving Drunk (SADD). SADD is an organization composed primarily of high school students whose goal is to reduce drinking-related deaths among teenagers. In this organization, students help educate other students about the consequences of drinking and driving. SADD encourages students and parents to sign contracts agreeing to provide transportation for each other if either is unable to drive safely after consuming alcohol.

Boost Alcohol Consciousness Concerning the Health of University Students (BACCHUS). Managed by student volunteers, this college-based national organization promotes responsible drinking among university students who choose to drink. BACCHUS supports responsible party hosting that includes the provision of food and nonalcoholic beverages. BACCHUS members often participate in alcohol education efforts on their campuses. Is there a chapter of BACCHUS on your campus?

Some college student organizations have collaborated with bars near campus to produce passcards that permit designated drivers to receive a limited number of nonalcoholic drinks when they accompany their drinking friends to these bars. Designated driver passcards are controversial. Generally, they have been well received as a way to keep sober drivers on the road. On the other hand, designated driver passcards have been criticized because they allow nondrivers to consume more alcohol than they might have otherwise; thus, they may encourage heavy drinking. What do you see as the pros and cons of these passcards?

One additional point was discussed in chapter 16. More and more states are passing laws that establish 0.08% as the legal blood alcohol limit. As of October 15, 1996, 13 states had established this new BAC limit. Legislation to lower the BAC to 0.08% was expected to be introduced in 24 additional states in 1997. Has this occurred in your state?

SUMMARY

Alcohol remains the country's drug of choice. Drinking patterns of the general public and of college students differ. Approximately 60% of American adults consume alcohol, but nearly 90% of college students drink. A relatively high percentage of college students binge drink (that is, they drink five or more drinks in a row). Alcohol use on the college campus is directly related to academic performance and a wide range of negative health and social consequences.

Alcoholism is defined as a "primary, chronic disease with genetic, psychosocial, and environmental factors influencing its development and manifestations." Alcohol-

SOLUTIONS

Dr. Auden had taken an interest in Gabe not only because he believed that Gabe's presence in the department added a new vitality to the curriculum, but because alcoholism was something Dr. Auden himself had struggled with many years ago. Dr. Auden asked a substance abuse counselor at the university hospital how to best approach the topic of alcoholism with a friend or colleague. Together they talked to Dean Whitaker and then to Gabe's wife. All were in agreement about what had to be done.

The next Sunday morning they all met at Gabe's house before he awoke to begin the intervention. When Gabe stumbled out of the bedroom, bleary-eyed from a long Saturday night of drinking, he was astonished to see everyone there. First, his wife confronted him about his drinking problem. Gabe angrily denied any problem. Then, Dr. Auden and Dean Whitaker confronted him with a litany of absences, missed deadlines, and other incidents caused by his continual drinking. When Gabe still refused to acknowledge any difficulty, Dean Whitaker gave him an ultimatum, "Gabe, either you enter a treatment program today, or you will not teach at the college next year."

With all eyes on him, Gabe began to shake and cry. He reluctantly admitted that his drinking had gotten a little beyond his control, and he agreed to enter treatment. Gabe's road to recovery was not smooth, even with the support of his family and colleagues. Nevertheless, after completing an intensive outpatient treatment program, Gabe has remained sober with the help of AA. He has since become a mentor and role model for many students struggling with alcohol abuse.

ism is considered an incurable disease. The physical symptoms of alcohol withdrawal syndrome can be life-threatening. One need not be an alcoholic to have problems with alcohol.

The development of alcoholism is rooted in genetic, environmental, and psychosocial factors. No one factor can fully explain why someone becomes an alcoholic; rather, a combination of factors probably affects the progression toward alcoholism. Alcohol consumption has a major role in some of our greatest social problems, including accidents, crime, and suicide.

One of the most tragic consequences of alcoholism is the way it hurts families. In this chapter, we discussed the effect of alcoholism on families and included sections on codependence, adult children of alcoholics, denial, and enabling.

Treatment and recovery programs are essential for alcoholics and their families. Options for help in recovery include 12-step programs, secular recovery programs, and support programs for families and children.

Two possible benefits of alcohol use are a reduction in risk of coronary artery disease and alcohol's ability to act as a social lubricant. Responsible alcohol use may include hosting a nonalcohol-based party. Organizations that promote responsible alcohol use include MADD, SADD, and BACCHUS.

REVIEW QUESTIONS

1. What percentage of all adults drink alcoholic beverages? What percentage of college students?
2. Define *binge drinking*. What percentage of college students binge drink? What negative consequences do college students face when they drink alcohol?
3. Define *alcoholism*. Why is alcoholism considered a primary disease? What are some of the proposed causes of alcoholism? What social problems are connected directly to alcohol use?
4. What is meant by the term *denial*? Can you give examples of an alcoholic's denial? What is meant by the term *enabling*? Describe some enabling behavior patterns.
5. Why do people develop codependent behaviors? Who are ACAs, and what is the their concern regarding alcohol use?
6. How do 12-step programs function? How do they differ from secular recovery programs? How is Antabuse used in the treatment of alcoholism?
7. Discuss the two benefits suggested for moderate alcohol use. Should people start drinking to gain these benefits?
8. What groups are especially targeted by alcohol marketing campaigns?
9. What are the goals of MADD, SADD, and BACCHUS?

REFERENCES

1. U.S. Department of Health and Human Services, *National Household Survey on Drug Abuse: Population Estimates 1995*, DHHS Pub. No. (SMA) 96-3095 (Washington, D.C.: U.S. Government Printing Office, 1996).
2. U.S. Department of Health and Human Services,

Alcohol and Health: Eighth Special Report to the U.S. Congress, NIH Pub. No. 94-3699 (Washington, D.C.: U.S. Government Printing Office, 1994).

3. U.S. Department of Health and Human Services, *Smoking, Drinking and Illicit Drug Use among American Secondary School Students, College Students, and Young Adults, 1975–1992*, vol. 2, NIH Pub. No. 93-3598 (Washington, D.C.: U.S. Government Printing Office, 1993).

4. Ibid.

5. C. A. Presley, and P. W. Meilman, *Alcohol and Drugs on American College Campuses: A Report to College Presidents*, Southern Illinois University Student Health Program Wellness Center, June, 1992, U.S. Department of Education.

6. Ibid.

7. Presley and Meilman, *Alcohol and Drugs.*

8. R. M. Morse, et al., "The Definition of Alcoholism," *JAMA* 268, no. 8 (1992):1012.

9. Ibid.

10. Ibid.

11. D. B. Hahn, and W. A. Payne, *Focus on Health*, 3rd ed. (St. Louis: Mosby, 1997).

12. Ibid.

13. DHHS, *Alcohol and Health, Eighth Report.*

14. U.S. Department of Health and Human Services, *Alcohol and Health: Seventh Special Report to the U.S. Congress*, DHHS Pub. No. (ADM) 90-1656 (Washington, D.C.: U.S. Government Printing Office, 1990).

15. National Institute on Alcohol Abuse and Alcoholism, "The Genetics of Alcoholism," *Alcohol Alert* 18, no. 328 (1992):1.

16. DHHS, *Alcohol and Health, Seventh Report.*

17. DHHS, *Alcohol and Health, Eighth Report.*

18. National Institute on Alcohol Abuse and Alcoholism: "Drinking and Driving," *Alcohol Alert* 31, no. 362 (January 1996).

19. C. J. Castaneda, "Drunken Driving Deaths Rising Again," *USA Today*, 27 November, 1996, p. 3A.

20. DHHS, *Alcohol and Health, Seventh Report.*

21. J. Kinney, and G. Leaton, *Loosening the Grip: A Handbook of Alcohol Information*, 5th ed. (St. Louis: Mosby, 1995).

22. DHHS, *Alcohol and Health, Eighth Report.*

23. DHHS, *Alcohol and Health, Seventh Report.*

24. Kinney and Leaton, *Loosening the Grip.*

25. DHHS, *Alcohol and Health, Seventh Report.*

26. Kinney and Leaton, *Loosening the Grip.*

27. M. Maris, *Adult Children of Alcoholics*, Alcohol Education Program, AT Wood Student Health Center, Ball State University (brochure).

28. J. G. Woititz, *Adult Children of Alcoholics* (Pompano Beach, Fla.: Health Communications, 1983).

29. Maris, *Adult Children.*

30. Ibid.

31. *Physicians' Desk Reference*, 51st ed. (Oradell, N.J.: Medical Economics Data Production, 1997).

32. National Institute on Alcohol Abuse and Alcoholism: "Neuroscience Research and Medications Development," *Alcohol Alert* 33, no. 366 (July 1996).

34. Alcoholics Anonymous, *AA in Treatment Facilities*, Alcoholics Anonymous World Services (brochure), 1991.

35. Alcoholics Anonymous, *This Is AA: An Introduction to the AA Recovery Program*, Alcoholics Anonymous World Services (brochure), 1992.

36. Ibid.

37. Ibid.

38. "Alcohol and the Heart: Consensus Emerges," *Harvard Heart Letter*, 6, no. 5 (January 1996): 1–3.

39. R. A. Serrano, "Clinton Condemns Broadcast Liquor Ads," *Lexington (KY) Herald-Leader*, 10 November, 1996, p. A1; "Anheuser-Busch Drops Beer Ads from MTV," *Muncie Star-Press*, 25 December, 1996, p. 3A.

SOURCES FOR HELP

Alcoholics Anonymous (AA)
P.O. Box 459, Grand Central Station
New York, NY 10163
(212) 686–1100

Al-Anon Adult Children Groups
One Park Ave.
New York, NY 10016
(212) 302–7240

Al-Anon Family Groups
P.O. Box 862, Midtown Station
New York, NY 10018
(212) 302–7240

American Council on Alcoholism
5024 Campbell Blvd., Suite H
Whitemarsh Business Center
Baltimore, MD 21236
(301) 529–9200

BACCHUS of the U.S. (Boost Alcohol Consciousness Concerning the Health of University Students)
P.O. Box 10430
Denver, CO 80210
(303) 871–3068

Children of Alcoholics Foundation, Inc.
200 Park Ave., 31st Floor
New York, NY 10010
(212) 351–2680

Mothers Against Drunk Driving (MADD)
511 E. John Carpenter Freeway
Suite 700
Irving, TX 75062
(800) 438–6233

National Association for Children of Alcoholics
31582 Coast Highway, Suite B
South Laguna, CA 92677
(714) 499–3889

National Council on Alcoholism (NCA)
12 West 21st St.
New York, NY 10010
(212) 206–6770

Rational Recovery Services
P.O. Box 800

Lotus, CA 95691

Remove Intoxicated Drivers (RID)
P.O. Box 520
Schenectady, NY 12301
(518) 372–0034

SOS National Clearinghouse
P.O. Box 5
Buffalo, NY 14215
(716) 834–2922

Students Against Driving Drunk (SADD)
P.O. Box 800
Marlboro, MA 01752

DRUG ABUSE PREVENTION: EDUCATION AND TREATMENT

18

CHAPTER OBJECTIVES

After studying this chapter, you will be able to:

1. Explain the concepts of primary, secondary, and tertiary prevention as they apply to drug abuse prevention and give examples of each.

2. Discuss the goals of drug abuse prevention and the nature of comprehensive drug abuse prevention.

3. Describe the characteristics of an effective school-based drug abuse prevention program.

4. Describe the characteristics of an effective community-based drug abuse prevention program.

5. Discuss the settings of drug abuse treatment.

6. Discuss a variety of approaches that drug abuse treatment programs use.

7. Discuss special issues for women in drug abuse treatment.

This chapter is the first of three chapters on the prevention and control of drug abuse. As stated in chapter 2, **prevention** is "the sum of our actions to ensure healthy, safe, and productive lives for all Americans."[1] Prevention is more than telling people what not to do. It also means helping people say "yes" to healthy choices. Prevention of drug abuse and dependence has many benefits, including: (1) saving lives, (2) containing health care costs, and (3) reducing social costs, such as violence, crime, unemployment, and lost productivity.[2]

Prevention is employed at three levels: primary, secondary, and tertiary. **Primary prevention** includes measures aimed to prevent the onset of drug use. **Secondary prevention** includes detection, screening, intervention, and treatment of early drug abuse so that those who are just beginning to use drugs can avoid further use. **Tertiary prevention** includes treatment and rehabilitation of people with more serious or chronic drug problems so that they will no longer need or want drugs.

THE GOALS OF DRUG ABUSE PREVENTION

Prevention aims to reduce both individual and environmental risk factors for drug abuse and dependence.[3] Some prevention programs are designed to influence personal attitudes and beliefs, interpersonal skills or skill deficiencies, and unmet developmental needs (prevention of individual risk factors). Other prevention programs aim to influence the home and family, school, peers, and the community at large (prevention of environmental risk factors). Some prevention programs address both individual and environmental risk factors for drug abuse and dependence and thus are comprehensive. **Comprehensive drug abuse prevention** targets the individual as well as the environment, including the family, peer group, neighborhood, school, workplace, colleges and universities, and community. Prevention targeted at the individual often takes the form of social skills education and resistance training or counseling. Family interventions focus on parenting education and encouraging parents to be positive role models for their children.

Peer group prevention strategies include training peers as leaders to attempt to change the norms for drug use. Neighborhood prevention often includes efforts to maintain safety, promote a sense of loyalty to the neighborhood, and discourage drug trafficking. Schools educate teachers, enabling them to recognize high-risk youths, develop policies to involve parents, implement student assistance programs (SAPs), and improve self-esteem among students.

Workplace prevention measures include employee assistance programs (EAPs) and drug-free workplace poli-

Many prevention programs target youths at risk for drug abuse.

cies. College and university leaders focus on reducing the availability of drugs on campus and limiting the marketing of alcohol. Community strategies include creating drug-related policies and media campaigns and providing comprehensive treatment, education, and law enforcement services. Law enforcement is discussed in chapter 20.

By its nature, a comprehensive drug abuse prevention plan builds networks among key community agencies and individuals. This networking enables communities

prevention the sum of all efforts to reduce drug abuse and dependence

primary prevention measures that prevent the onset of drug use

secondary prevention measures involving the detection, screening, early intervention, and treatment of drug abuse

tertiary prevention treatment and rehabilitation of people with more serious or chronic drug problems

comprehensive drug abuse prevention activities and programs that aim to reduce both individual and environmental risk factors for drug abuse and dependence

to develop task forces, or coalitions, that represent many sectors of the community to address drug abuse and dependence problems. These coalitions may influence public policy to reduce the harmful effects of drug use. Public policy is discussed in chapter 19.

One example of a comprehensive drug abuse prevention program that targets the individual, as well as the environment, is the Midwestern Prevention Project (MPP). This federally funded project has operated since 1984 in Kansas and Missouri and has more recently been expanded to include Indiana. MPP uses five prevention strategies: school-based peer resistance training, media campaigns, parent/family involvement, community organization activities, and health policy change. In the first 2 years of MPP, 22,500 sixth and seventh graders attended a school-based educational program that involved parents and included media campaigns. This broad-based combination of individual, family, school, and community strategies has reduced drug use and abuse among youths.[4]

The four major elements of alcohol, tobacco, and other drug prevention strategies are (1) education, (2) treatment, (3) public policy, and (4) law enforcement. The first two of these four elements, education and treatment, reduce the demand for drugs and are the topics of this chapter.

EDUCATION

As stated in chapter 2, drug abuse prevention education limits the demand for drugs by disseminating information about drugs of abuse, changing attitudes and beliefs about drugs, providing the skills necessary to abstain from drugs, and ultimately changing drug abuse behavior. Education is an example of primary prevention and a crucial component of comprehensive drug abuse prevention. Education occurs in school and community settings. To be effective, education must be specific to the age and life stage of the individual, and it must target the community. The following list depicts particular groups and examples of potential drug education activities.

Prenatal: Work with mothers to encourage nonuse
Preschool: Educate about positive family communication
School-age: Develop social skills necessary to resist peer pressure
Teenagers: Cope with identity and sensation-seeking needs
College: Identify social consequences of drug abuse
Athletes: Educate about the dangers of smokeless tobacco
Workplace: Adjust to independence and demands of employment

Elderly/Disabled: Identify interactions between medications and other drugs

School-Based Education

A critical component of any comprehensive drug abuse prevention program is **school-based drug abuse education.** The most effective kind of school-based drug abuse education program is one that is an integral part of a comprehensive school health education curriculum. A quickly purchased or thrown-together, stand-alone drug abuse prevention education program is less likely to produce the desired behavioral changes needed to reach drug abuse prevention objectives. To be successful, school-based programs must also address social influences, such as peer pressure and the effects of alcohol and tobacco advertisements, and include parental and community involvement.

Drug education has traditionally been provided primarily in schools. Nearly all states mandate some form of drug education in kindergarten through twelfth grades. Most health educators believe that a comprehensive school health program, including drug education, is more effective than a separate drug class that focuses on illicit drug use. *Here's Looking at You 2000* is an example of one K-12 school health curriculum that integrates drug education into a comprehensive health education curriculum at each grade level.

From the old motion picture *Reefer Madness* to the anti-alcohol essay contests of the 1950s to the "Just Say

Drug abuse prevention through education should be an ongoing aspect of school curricula.

ALTERNATIVE CHOICES

The Seventh Generation Project

The seventh generation has a special meaning among members of the Lakota tribe. The seventh generation is a time of healing. Today's Native American children are considered to be the seventh generation.

The prevalence of alcohol drinking among Native American youth is the same as that of their Caucasian counterparts, but they start drinking at a younger age, drink more frequently, and drink greater quantities of alcohol. The average age of drinking among Native American youth is 12 years, and the average age of first becoming drunk is 13 years of age. Although many Native American youths drink alcohol, the idea that all Native Americans are predisposed to alcohol abuse is a myth. There is no evidence that Native Americans are genetically predisposed to alcohol dependence.

The Seventh Generation Project is an after-school alcohol prevention program for fourth and fifth grade students in Denver, Colorado. The 14-week program establishes nonuse of drugs as a norm and encourages Native American values, including harmony, respect, generosity, courage, wisdom, humility, and honesty.

Source: *The Prevention Pipeline,* Center for Substance Abuse Prevention, 10:1, 3–6, 1997.

No" programs of the 1980s, drug education has been familiar to generations of Americans. Most recently, however, school-based drug education has moved from an information-only, "scare tactics" approach, such as those previously mentioned, to programs that improve social skills. Research has found that giving information alone has little or no effect on drug use.[5] School-based drug prevention programs that address social influences and that are comprehensive have been found to be most successful in preventing the onset of drug use.[6]

Social influence programs include resistance skills, life skills, and normative beliefs.[7] Resistance skills training teaches children how to resist pressure from peers and the media to use drugs. Children not only learn to say "no" to drugs, but they also learn and practice different ways to refuse the temptation to try drugs. Life skills training teaches children how to be assertive, how to resolve interpersonal conflict, and how to communicate with others. **Normative beliefs** are the perceptions among young people that drug use is common and acceptable. Social influence programs show children the rates of drug use among young people and help them compare their beliefs with those of others in the group.

Social influence programs are designed to promote resilience by actively teaching children the resistance and life skills needed to protect themselves against drug use. Building resilience, or protective immunity against drug involvement, is an important goal of programs that aim to increase social competence.[8]

For school-based drug education to be successful, schools, parents, students, and communities must work together. The best school-based curriculum will be ineffective without a supportive environment outside the school. Project DARE (Drug Abuse Resistance Education) is one example of a school-based drug abuse prevention program using schools, students, and the community (see the box on p. 296). Keep a Clear Mind

(KACM), a program that involves the school, family, and community, fosters communication that reduces the role of drugs in the lives of children.[9] BABES (Beginning Alcohol and Addiction Basic Education Studies), a drug prevention curriculum for young children ages 4 to 8 years and their families, teaches the skills needed to make healthy decisions and avoid drug use, such as refusal skills and positive communication.[10] BABES increases children's drug knowledge and reinforces negative attitudes toward drugs.[11] Alternative programs, such as alcohol-free parties on college campuses, offer socially acceptable ways of having fun and seeking sensation for people who may be at risk for drug abuse.

Community-Based Education

Community-based drug abuse education outside the school setting may include formal programs, such as those conducted in public child-care facilities and public housing facilities, and informal activities, such as incidental learning through advertisements and television programming.

Formal community-based drug education programs may be ineffective in reaching the public because of low

---

school-based drug abuse education social influence programs offered in kindergarten through twelfth grade that emphasize resistance training, life skills, and normative beliefs to protect children from drug use

normative beliefs beliefs about cultural norms or standards of acceptable behavior

community-based drug abuse education formal and informal programs and activities in the community designed to involve individuals and organizations in the prevention of drug abuse and dependence

ALTERNATIVE CHOICES

Project DARE: A School-Based Drug Abuse Prevention Program

Project DARE began in 1982 as a collaborative program between the Los Angeles Police Department and the Los Angeles Unified School District. DARE uses uniformed law enforcement officers as classroom teachers. DARE officers teach students (primarily in fifth and sixth grades) how to resist peer pressure to use drugs, stress management skills, self-esteem, and alternatives to drug use.

In addition to providing classroom instruction, the program offers teacher orientation, officer-student interaction, parent education evenings, and the development of school-based teams composed of both school and community members.

Studies have shown that on a short-term basis, DARE has improved students' attitudes about themselves and increased their sense of responsibility for themselves and to police. However, DARE has not been shown to strengthen peer resistance to drugs.

The most effective way to foster prevention is through education.

participation levels, apathy, and a lack of cultural sensitivity. However, community-based drug education is effective when it addresses broader issues, such as coping and learning skills, and when it is coordinated with other community activities and organizations. Red Ribbon Week and the American Lung Association's Great American Smokeout are examples of community-based drug education. Race Against Drugs (RAD) is a nationwide program that links motor sports with drug abuse prevention.[12] RAD works with recognized auto racing heroes to convince young people that drug use cannot be casual or harmless. To be successful, programs must overcome cultural barriers by using appropriate language and reading levels and using spokespeople similar to the target group. Doctors Ought to Care (DOC) educates young people in humorous and refreshing ways using a community-based approach. To call attention to the

The crash test dummies visit campus as part of Alcohol Awareness Week activities.

ALTERNATIVE CHOICES

Girl Power!

The Department of Health and Human Services has designed a community-based prevention program to encourage and empower 9- to 14-year-old girls to make the most of their lives. This national public education campaign targets underage tobacco use, physical fitness, mental health, and teenage pregnancy. Girls who use drugs are at greater risk for physical and sexual abuse, pregnancy, and HIV/AIDS than girls who do not use drugs. The Girl Power! campaign provides messages and materials about the harmful effects of drug use. Materials include baseball caps, bookmarks, fact sheets, posters, t-shirts, a media kit, and press releases. Find more information about Girl Power! at (800) 544–7467 or gpower@health.org.

Girl Power!
We've Got the Power to Be Drug Free!

---

devastating health and economic effects of alcohol, tobacco, and other drugs, DOC sponsored the Emphysema Slims Tennis Tournament and the Dead Man Chew Softball Tournament.

Informal community-based education also disseminates information about drug use through the media, music, movies, and billboards. On the other hand, "unintentional" positive images of drug use send mixed messages to young people at the same time people and communities are working to encourage healthy lifestyles. Antidrug media campaigns, lectures, films, and bumper stickers are forms of counteradvertising that can educate the public about the dangers of drugs.

A recent example of informal community-based education is the Reality Check Campaign sponsored by the U.S. Department of Health and Human Services. Reality Check is a nationwide effort to prevent and reduce the problems associated with marijuana use among youth. Teens who use marijuana generally do not think the drug is harmful and believe it boosts creativity. Reality Check increases awareness of the harmful effects of marijuana, teaches teenagers how to refuse the drug or quit using, involves adults in delivering prevention messages, and changes the perception that marijuana is not harmful. The Reality Check Community Kit contains ready-to-use media materials, public service announcements, parent guides, posters, and novelty items and is available to local groups.[13]

TREATMENT

Treatment is another component of prevention. As discussed in chapter 2, treatment is the act of providing medical and/or psychological care to someone with an injury, illness, or disorder. The goal of drug dependence treatment is to remove the physical, emotional, and environmental conditions that have contributed to the dependence. Treatment not only benefits the abuser, but it also reduces health and welfare costs and makes communities safer. For every $1 spent on drug dependence treatment programs, an average of $7 is saved in health costs and crime reduction.[14]

Like education, treatment attempts to limit the demand for drugs. Treatment for drug dependence is considered either secondary or tertiary prevention. It is secondary prevention if the drug-dependent individual is evaluated and treated before physical and mental problems become severe. More commonly, however, treatment requires successful rehabilitation to prevent the recovering person from relapsing into a former pattern of abuse. Unfortunately, more than 50% of patients treated for alcoholism relapse within the first 3 months after treatment.[15]

Relapse prevention programs target drug-dependent individuals and families and are designed to help recovering individuals maintain drug-free lifestyles. Because most drug-dependent people require multiple treatment attempts, treatment is usually considered to be tertiary prevention.

There is no single treatment for alcohol and other drug dependence. Because the symptoms, intensity of use, drug of addiction, and background of the abuser vary from person to person, treatment programs differ. For example, methadone treatment is

relapse prevention programs to help drug-dependent individuals and families stay drug-free and avoid former patterns of abuse

ALTERNATIVE CHOICES

Crime and Drug Abuse: Treatment Works!

Drug use and crime are strongly associated. Of adult males who are arrested in the United States, 54% to 81% test positive for drugs. Of adult females who are arrested, 42% to 83% test positive. The good news is that treating a criminal for substance abuse can greatly reduce crime. Criminal activity declines 66% after treatment. The longer the person remains in treatment, the greater the reduction in criminal activity.

Some arrestees receive treatment from Treatment Alternatives for Special Clients (TASC), a court-approved program designed to provide treatment, education, and job training for nonviolent drug offenders. In Illinois, less than 5% of criminals who participate in TASC are reincarcerated. TASC costs only $39 per day, compared with $89 per day to jail drug offenders. In Texas, drug-addicted prison inmates participate in a 9-month in-prison treatment program, followed by a 4-month outpatient program. One year after release, only 7% of those completing the program returned to prison.

Source: *Substance Abuse, Crime, and Treatment: Treatment Works Fact Sheet,* Center for Substance Abuse Prevention, Rockville, Md., 1997 (http://www.health.org).

offered only to people addicted to narcotics. Because most drug-dependent people are addicted to multiple drugs, treatment for alcohol and other drugs is very similar. In fact, the diagnoses of substance dependence, abuse, and withdrawal are not specific to the drug of addiction.[16]

In general, drug treatment is provided in a variety of settings and includes many approaches, including counseling; drug therapy; educational and vocational services; urine testing; relapse prevention; and family, social, and community support. Treatment is often ordered by a court, as with many drunk-driving cases.

Unfortunately, drug treatment is available only to less than 10% of prison inmates who need it.[17] Experts estimate that the number of people in the United States who need treatment is three or four times the number of people who actually receive drug treatment.[18] Furthermore, too few treatment programs are tailored to pregnant

Treatment programs can be found in a variety of settings within the community.

women, women with children, those on parole or probation, and youth. Clearly, we need to increase the availability of drug treatment in the United States.

Settings for Drug Dependence Treatment

Treatment setting is the location in which treatment takes place and is either nonresidential (outpatient) or residential (inpatient). More than half of those receiving treatment are in **nonresidential treatment,** or outpatient programs.[19] They live at home and receive treatment at a community facility. Outpatient treatment is less disruptive to family life and job responsibilities. The drug-dependent person often visits the facility several times per week for 2 to 4 weeks and then returns once a week for a designated period of time. Family members and other support people are usually encouraged to join the recovering person at certain times during treatment.

In **residential treatment,** or inpatient programs, the recovering person lives at the facility. Residential facilities can be found in hospitals, special treatment facilities, correctional institutions, therapeutic communities, group homes, or halfway houses. Although more expensive than nonresidential programs, inpatient care is warranted by the severity of the condition or when outpatient treatment has been ineffective. Abusers tend to refuse residential treatment. Most drug-dependent people are in denial and are often unwilling to give up employment and other obligations to enter residential treatment. The expense of inpatient treatment is also a real concern for many abusers and their families. In addition, some people believe that residential programs breed dependence on the staff and give the patient unrealistic protection from societal stress.

Aftercare is continuing care for recovering substance abusers who have successfully completed outpatient or inpatient treatment and must now return to their homes, jobs, and communities. Aftercare may include periodic counseling sessions alone or with family members, employers, family health care providers, clergy, or other professionals. Aftercare usually includes mandatory or voluntary attendance at support group meetings, in which individuals at different stages in their recovery meet to help each other remain drug free.

Treatment Approaches

The term **treatment approach** refers to "the theoretical underpinning that the treatment professional brings to the therapeutic situation."[20] Before active treatment can begin, the drug-dependent person must undergo **detoxification,** the elimination of a drug (and its major byproducts) from the body through a period of planned withdrawal of drug use. The severity of the physical symptoms and time needed for withdrawal depend on the specific drug being abused. With narcotic addiction, a medication (e.g., methadone) is usually required to ease the symptoms of withdrawal illness. With alcohol addiction, medications are usually not a part of the detoxification process. Detoxification is complete when symptoms of acute physical dependence are absent.

In the past, detoxification was often the sole form of treatment and often occurred in jails or sanitoriums, where alcohol-dependent people could "dry out" before being released. The amount of counseling varied. We now know that detoxification alone usually results in relapse and readmission. Today, detoxification is usually considered little more than a prerequisite for entrance into an active treatment program.

Treatment approaches include psychoanalytic, behavioral, counseling, substitute dependence, and support group approaches, as well as many others. Some of these approaches are performed on an individual basis, while others involve in families and groups. After detoxification, most programs employ individual, group, or family counseling. The approach varies from program to program; however, the most effective treatment combines several approaches to produce long-lasting change.[21]

In the psychoanalytic approach, the abuser's childhood and early life experiences are examined to help the abuser understand his or her drug abuse problem. In the behavioral approach, positive behavior (including abstinence from drugs) is rewarded, with the goal of extinguishing destructive (drug-abusing) behavior. This approach may include techniques such as character building, behavioral self-control training, and assertiveness training.

Counseling attempts to get abusers to alter their current paths of behavior. One approach, motivational interviewing, replaces the more common technique of confrontation with the notion that the abuser is responsible for making treatment choices based on information

---

treatment setting the location in which treatment takes place

nonresidential treatment outpatient programs that are less disruptive to family life and job responsibilities

residential treatment inpatient programs requiring drug-dependent individuals to live at the facility

aftercare continuing care for recovering substance abusers who have successfully completed inpatient or outpatient treatment and must now return to their homes, jobs, and communities

treatment approach the theoretical underpinning that the treatment professional brings to the therapeutic situation

detoxification elimination of a drug from the body through a planned withdrawal from drug use

Support groups such as this one help individuals remain in recovery.

from the interviewer's assessment.[22] **Intervention** is a counseling approach that targets high-risk individuals who are abusing and may be dependent on drugs. This approach is considered secondary prevention because it employs early detection and treatment before problems become severe. Intervention includes crisis telephone hotlines, peer counseling, individual and family counseling, workplace training, and student and employee assistance programs.

Substitute dependence is defined as the redirection of addiction to a less harmful substance. The use of methadone for heroin dependence (see chapter 7) and the nicotine transdermal patch for smoking cessation (see chapter 11) are examples of substitute dependence treatment. For greatest effectiveness, substitute dependence treatment is combined with counseling.

Support group approaches include peer group therapy, family therapy, and self-help support group therapy. Group therapy with peers offers immediate feedback and support to the abuser along with peer pressure to remain in recovery. Family therapy extends treatment to the home so that family members can participate. Self-help

support groups may serve as a link to the larger community and continue as a part of aftercare in the recovery period. Examples of self-help support groups are Alcoholics Anonymous (AA), Narcotics Anonymous (NA), and Secular Organizations for Sobriety (SOS). Support groups are usually nonprofessional, self-regulating, nondenominational, multiracial, and nonpolitical.[23] They provide an environment of mutual support among those with similar experiences. AA and NA are called "12-step programs." One hallmark of 12-step programs is reliance on spirituality, or a higher power, for successful recovery. SOS also forms local support groups of recovering people but does not rely on spirituality.[24] SOS focuses on sobriety as an issue separate from spirituality and supports the use of the scientific method to understand addiction.

Women and Treatment

Drug dependence treatment programs have traditionally been designed by and for men. Substance abuse has been viewed as a man's disease. Women have drug use patterns, reasons for use, and consequences that differ from the male experience,[25] yet women are underserved in both prevention and treatment programs.

Many female drug abusers are victims of violence and sexual abuse, and often the men in their lives oppose their treatment. To be successful, drug dependence treatment for women must increase their self-esteem and self-confidence by creating a safe, nurturing, and sup-

---

intervention a counseling approach for early detection and treatment of drug-dependent individuals

substitute dependence the redirection of an addiction to a less harmful substance

support group a group of individuals in recovery who come together to help each other remain drug free

More depression

portive environment. The treatment staff should be sensitive to women's issues, and women-only treatment sessions should be offered. Because women are usually busy caring for children and families, the treatment must accommodate women's schedules and relationships with their children. Female drug abusers are also more likely to experience depression than male drug abusers; thus, women may need mental health care as well as drug dependence treatment.[26]

Although the treatment needs of pregnant women have been paid the most attention, women may use alcohol and other drugs throughout their lives. Women experience many stressors, role and relationship changes, and hormonal and physiological adjustments throughout their lives. Drug dependence treatment programs are beginning to address the special needs of women of all ages who are addicted to drugs. Women's treatment centers usually offer both residential and nonresidential treatment, child care, and parenting classes. Of women in substance abuse treatment, 95% report drug-free births, and 75% who complete treatment remain drug-free.[27]

SUMMARY

Prevention of drug abuse helps people say "yes" to healthy choices. Comprehensive drug abuse prevention aims to reduce individual and environmental risk factors for drug abuse and dependence. Prevention includes both education and treatment. Education to prevent drug abuse includes school- and community-based approaches. It is best if drug abuse prevention education is specific to the age and life stage of the individual and targeted to the specific community. School-based programs that teach resistance skills, life skills, and normative beliefs are the most effective in preventing drug abuse. Community-based programs are both formal and informal, including planned programs in child care and housing facilities and incidental learning through advertisements and television programming. Treatment for drug dependence aims to remove the physical, emotional, and environmental conditions that have contributed to the problem. Like education, treatment attempts to limit the demand for drugs.

Treatment occurs in both nonresidential and residential settings and includes a combination of approaches such as detoxification, intervention, substitute dependence, and aftercare, including support groups. Women experience drug use patterns, reasons for use, and consequences that differ from the male experience. Drug treatment must address the special needs of women of all ages who are addicted to drugs.

REVIEW QUESTIONS

1. Give examples of primary, secondary, and tertiary prevention of drug abuse.
2. What is the goal of drug abuse prevention?
3. What does comprehensive drug abuse prevention include?
4. Why should school-based drug abuse education be integrated into every school's health curriculum?
5. What are social influence programs and what components do they include?
6. In what ways are community-based education programs both formal and informal?
7. What is the goal of drug dependence treatment?
8. In what ways is treatment both secondary and tertiary prevention?
9. How accessible is drug dependence treatment in the United States?
10. What are the different treatment settings?
11. What approaches are used in combination for successful treatment?
12. Why do drug-abusing women need special consideration in treatment?

REFERENCES

1. *Prevention Works: A Discussion Paper on Preventing Alcohol, Tobacco and Other Drug Problems*, Center for Substance Abuse Prevention, DHHS, PHS, SAMHSA (Rockville, Md., 1993).
2. Ibid.
3. J. D. Hawkins, et al., *Communities that Care* (San Francisco: Jossey-Bass, 1992).
4. W. J. Bukoski, *A Framework for Drug Abuse Prevention Research*, NIDA Monograph, No. 107, 1991; D. Cahalan, *An Ounce of Prevention: Strategies for Solving Tobacco, Alcohol, and Drug Problems* (San Francisco: Jossey-Bass, 1991); M. A. Pentz, et al., "A Multicommunity Trial for Primary Prevention of Adolescent Drug Abuse: Effects on Drug Use Prevalence," *JAMA* 261, no. 22 (1989):3259.
5. D. R. Gerstein and L. W. Green, ed., *Preventing Drug Abuse: What Do We Know?* (Washington, D.C., National Academy Press, 1993).
6. W. B. Hansen, "School-Based Substance Abuse Prevention: A Review of the State of the Art in Curriculum, 1980–1990," *Health Education Research* 7, no. 3 (1992):403.
7. W. B. Hansen, "School-Based Alcohol Prevention Programs," *Alcohol Health & Research World* 17, no. 1 (1993):54.
8. Hawkins, et al., *Communities that Care.*

9. C. E. Werch, et al., "Effects of a Take-Home Prevention Program on Drug-Related Communication and Beliefs of Parents and Children," *J Sch Health* 61, no. 8 (1991):346.

10. *BABESWorld, Lower Elementary Basic BABES Teaching Guide* (available from BABESWorld, 33 E. Forest, Detroit, Michigan 48201), 1990.

11. E. J. Hahn, "Parent Participation and Preschool Drug Prevention Programs," *Addictions Nursing Network* 3 (1991):4, 115–120.

12. "Race against Drugs (RAD)," *The Prevention Pipeline* 9 (1996):6, 15–18.

13. N. Hadi, "The Reality Check Campaign," *The Prevention Pipeline* 9(1996):4, 5–6.

14. *A Look at Successful and Cost-Effective State Treatment Programs: Treatment Works Fact Sheet*, Center for Substance Abuse Prevention, Rockville, Md., 1997 (http://www.health.org).

15. *National Institute on Alcohol Abuse and Alcoholism (NIAAA) Reports on Main Findings of Project MATCH*, NIAAA, 1997 (http://www.jointogether.org/).

16. L. Friedman, et al., *Source Book of Substance Abuse and Addiction* (Baltimore, Md.: Williams & Wilkins, 1996).

17. *Substance Abuse, Crime, and Treatment: Treatment Works Fact Sheet*, Center for Substance Abuse Prevention, Rockville, Md., 1997 (http://www.health.org).

18. U.S. Department of Justice, Office of Justice Programs, *Drugs, Crime, and the Justice System* (Washington, D.C., U.S. Government Printing Office, 1992).

19. Alcohol, Drug Abuse, and Mental Health Administration, *National Drug and Alcoholism Treatment Unit Survey: 1989 Main Findings Report* (Washington, D.C., U.S. Government Printing Office, 1990).

20. P. E. Hall and D. P. Greenfield, "An Overview of Treatment," *Prescription Drug Abuse and Dependence: How Prescription Drug Abuse Contributes to the Drug Abuse Epidemic*, ed. D. P. Greenfield (Springfield, Ill.: Charles C Thomas, 1995).

21. *AA at a Glance* (New York: AA General Service Office, 1992).

22. J. A. Lewis, "Treating People with Alcohol Problems," *Addictions: Concepts and Strategies for Treatment*, ed. J. A. Lewis (Gaithersburg, Md., Aspen Publishers, 1994).

23. *AA at a Glance.*

24. *SOS Home Page: Secular Organizations for Sobriety (SOS)*, 1997, http://www.codesh.org/sos/.

25. N. Finkelstein, et al., *Gender-Specific Substance Abuse Treatment*, National Women's Resource Center (http://www.nwrc.org/), Center for Substance Abuse Prevention (CSAP), Rockville, Md., March, 1997.

26. Ibid.

27. *Substance Abuse and Treatment: Treatment Works Fact Sheet*, Center for Substance Abuse Prevention, Rockville, Md., 1997 (http://www.health.org).

SOURCES FOR HELP

Al Anon/Alateen Family Group Headquarters, Inc.
1600 Corporate Landing Parkway
Virginia Beach, VA 23454
(800) 356–9996
http://www.al-anon.org/

Alcoholics Anonymous
475 Riverside Dr.
New York, NY 10015
(212) 870–3400
Fax: (212) 870–3003
http://www.alcoholics-anonymous.org/

Center for Substance Abuse Treatment
http://www.samhsa.gov/csat/csat.htm

Girls, Inc.
Resource Center
441 West Michigan St.
Indianapolis, IN 46202-3233
(800) 374–4475

Narcotics Anonymous
P.O. Box 9999
Van Nuys, CA 91409
(818) 773–9999
Fax: (818) 700–0700
http://www.wsoinc.com/

National Association for Children of Alcoholics
(NACoA)
11426 Rockville Pike
Suite 100
Rockville, MD 20852
(301) 468–0985
Fax: (301) 468–0987
http://www.health.org/nacoa/

National Clearinghouse for Alcohol and Drug
Information Prevline
P.O. Box 2345
Rockville, MD 20847-2345
(800) 729–6686
http://www.health.org

National Women's Resource Center
515 King St., Suite 410
Alexandria, VA 22314
(800) 354–8824 (information and referral)
(703) 836–8761
Fax: (703) 836–7256
http://www.nwrc.org/

Parents Resource Institute for Drug Education
   (PRIDE)
3610 DeKalb Technology Parkway
Suite 105
Atlanta, GA 30340
(404) 577–4500

Robert Wood Johnson Foundation
P.O. Box 2316
Princeton, NJ 08543
(609) 452–8701
http://www.rwjf.org

SOS National Clearinghouse
The Center for Inquiry-West
5521 Grosvenor Boulevard
Los Angeles, CA 90066
(310) 821–8430
Fax: (310) 821–2610
http://www.sosla@loop.com

DRUGS AND PUBLIC POLICY

CHAPTER OBJECTIVES

After studying this chapter, you will be able to:

1. Discuss public policy and its effect on drug use.

2. Describe three major policy categories for successful prevention of drug abuse.

3. Discuss the relationship between drug prices and consumption.

4. Explain the importance of counteradvertising to deglamorize drug use.

5. Discuss harm reduction as an unpopular U.S. policy strategy.

6. Describe drug testing as a policy strategy that plays an important role in education, treatment, and law enforcement.

7. Explain the legal issues related to drug testing as a policy strategy.

8. Discuss ways that coalitions change public policy.

Public policy and its role in drug abuse prevention is the focus of this chapter. Designing and implementing health-related public policy is an important community-based prevention strategy. To be truly effective, drug abuse prevention must be comprehensive, that is, it must incorporate education, treatment, public policy, and law enforcement. As explained in chapter 2, public policy includes the principles and courses of action pursued by governments to find solutions for practical problems that affect society. With respect to drug abuse prevention, public policy includes the enactment of drug laws and zoning ordinances, the regulation of advertising and labeling of legal drugs, the regulation of over-the-counter and prescription drugs, and drug testing. Public policy also influences the proportion of the federal, state, or local government's budget that is used to address drug problems.

As discussed in chapter 2, a variety of individual and environmental risk factors increase one's vulnerability to drug abuse. Public policy attempts to reduce environmental risk factors, such as the availability and appeal of alcohol, tobacco, and other drugs. Public policy is aimed at reducing both the supply of and demand for drugs. Laws that limit access to tobacco and alcohol products are examples of policies that reduce the supply or availability of drugs. Governmental regulations that restrict advertising and promotion of alcohol and tobacco products aim to reduce the demand for or appeal of drugs by limiting prodrug messages.

HOW PUBLIC POLICY AFFECTS DRUG USE

Public policy involves communities taking action to reduce the damaging effects of drug use. Public policy efforts have succeeded in reducing drunk driving, closing crack houses, restricting smoking in public places, and finding jobs for troubled teens. These successes have not come from waiting for others to act; rather, public policy changes occur when communities take action. People of all ages and from all walks of life must be involved, including parents, children, police, ministers, government officials, media, teachers, and business leaders.

The best examples of how public policy affects drug use are the alcohol laws enacted to reduce drunk driving. Over 14,000 lives have been saved as a result of raising the legal drinking age to 21. In addition, 37 states have enacted license revocation laws for drunk driving.[1] The percent of fatally injured teen drivers with an illegal blood alcohol concentration declined from 53% in 1980 to 26% in 1994.[2] **Zero tolerance laws** are estimated to have reduced teen alcohol-related fatalities by 30 percent or more. These laws set the maximum blood alcohol concentration (BAC) allowable for drivers under age 21

at nearly zero, rather than the 0.08% or 0.10% for older drivers. Many states have also successfully reduced nighttime fatal crashes by establishing sobriety checkpoints, such as North Carolina's "Booze It and Lose It" campaign. In addition, many states are enacting graduated driver licensing systems restricting nighttime driving for the first year.

HEALTHY PUBLIC POLICIES

The federal government has developed a blueprint for healthy public policies by creating Healthy People 2000, a national effort to identify specific ways to promote health and prevent death and disabilities.[3] Healthy People 2000 outlines goals for reducing alcohol, tobacco, and other drug use. Among these are promoting incentives to the hospitality industry for alcohol server training programs, increasing the tobacco excise tax to 50% of the retail price, and increasing the number of workplace alcohol and drug policies.

Five policy objectives are recommended for successful reduction and prevention of drug abuse:[4]

1. Make drug abuse prevention an urgent priority in every community.
2. Increase taxes on alcohol and tobacco.
3. Require counteradvertising to portray the health risks associated with drug abuse.
4. Require substance abuse treatment for criminal offenders.
5. Ensure that every addicted person gets treatment.

This chapter describes the first three objectives: public policy that makes prevention an urgent priority, increases the price of alcohol and tobacco products, and creates counteradvertising to communicate the health risks associated with drug abuse. Chapter 18 discusses treatment as an important component of drug abuse prevention.

Making Prevention an Urgent Priority

One example of making prevention an urgent priority is President Clinton's plan to reduce underage tobacco use by giving the Food and Drug Administration (FDA) authority to regulate the use, sale, distribution, and display of tobacco products. The goal is to cut tobacco use by

---

public policy the principles and courses of action pursued by governments to find solutions for practical problems that affect society

zero tolerance laws legislation that requires the maximum blood alcohol concentration (BAC) to be nearly zero for drivers under age 21

ALTERNATIVE CHOICES

Campaign for Tobacco-Free Kids

The National Center for Tobacco-Free Kids is the largest private organization to fight underage tobacco use by changing public policy. Established in 1996 in Washington, D.C., the center is funded by the Robert Wood Johnson Foundation and the American Cancer Society. The center counters tobacco industry tactics, aims to change public policy, and tries to increase public awareness that tobacco company ads target children. The goal is to ensure that children get information about tobacco from parents and caring adults, not Joe Camel. The center is well-known for its Campaign for Tobacco-Free Kids print public service announcements that appear in the *New York Times* and *Washington Post.* These ads expose the tobacco companies for directly marketing to children. In 1997, the center was asked by the attorneys general from 40 states to participate in negotiations with the tobacco companies to settle state and class action lawsuits and propose sweeping reforms to reduce underage tobacco use. The center's representative, Matt Myers, was the only public health voice at the table. The center encourages participation by adults and youth. To get involved, call the National Center for Tobacco-Free Kids at 1(800) 284–KIDS.

teenagers in half by 2004. FDA regulation of tobacco products has been called the most significant public health initiative of our generation.[5] The FDA rules reduce access to tobacco products and limit advertising. The regulations to reduce access designate age 18 as the minimum age of sale, require retailers to check identification of anyone age 26 or younger, restrict vending machine sales, ban free samples and single cigarettes, or "loosies," and eliminate self-service displays and mail ordering free or discounted cigarettes. The FDA regulations to limit the appeal of tobacco products prohibit outdoor advertising within 1,000 feet of public playgrounds and schools; require tobacco advertising to be in black and white, text-only format in publications read by youth; ban distribution of promotional items, such as t-shirts and caps; and ban tobacco company sponsorship of sporting events.

The FDA regulations have sparked much protest from the tobacco companies, tobacco growers, and advertising agencies. The four largest tobacco companies and the major tobacco-growing states filed a motion in a North Carolina court to appeal the FDA ruling. FDA jurisdiction over tobacco products was upheld. Some advertising agencies claim that the FDA advertising restrictions violate freedom of speech. In response to the threat of FDA regulation, the leading tobacco companies created and distributed "It's the Law" programs to educate retailers and encourage them not to sell tobacco products to people under 18 years of age. These programs include educational materials and stickers for retailers to post in their stores. "It's the Law" programs do not reduce illegal sales of tobacco products.[6] However, illegal sales to minors have been reduced by passing strict local ordinances and consistently enforcing the law.

The federal government uses another very effective tool to make prevention an urgent priority. With both alcoholic beverages and tobacco products, the federal government requires states to either pass laws or lose federal funds. In 1995, Congress mandated that states pass some type of zero tolerance law or risk losing federal highway funds. In 1992, Congress enacted Section 1926 of the Public Health Service Act (the Synar Amendment), which required states to reduce youth access to tobacco products or risk losing substance abuse treatment and prevention funds. In some states, the Synar Amendment has not only reduced youth access to tobacco products but has also led to more restrictive tobacco laws, such as requiring licensing of tobacco retailers in Maine.[7] Legislation restricting the sale of tobacco products to minors has been enacted in all 50 states and the District of Columbia.[8]

Raising Taxes on Alcoholic Beverages and Tobacco Products

Studies show that the price of alcoholic beverages, tobacco products, and illicit drugs is directly associated with consumption. The higher the price, the lower the consumption. This is especially true with youth. With every 10% increase in the price of cigarettes, there is a 14% drop in the rate of smoking among teenagers.[9] Illicit drug use is also sensitive to price. For every 10% increase in the price of illicit drugs, there is an estimated 10% drop in consumption.[10]

Some experts say that raising the excise tax on alcohol and tobacco is the most effective way to reduce underage alcohol and tobacco use. For this reason, tobacco companies and tobacco growers oppose any effort to raise the cigarette excise tax, and they are usually successful. Tobacco companies, often called "Big Tobacco," are known for influencing public policy, partly by contributing to campaigns, political parties, and legislators' favorite charities (see chapter 12).[11]

Federal and state excise taxes on alcohol and tobacco products generate billions of dollars and contribute to lower consumption. Although the federal excise tax on

ALTERNATIVE CHOICES

Taking Action Against Broadcast Liquor Ads

Since 1936, the U.S. Distilled Spirits Council has urged the alcohol industry not to advertise on the radio. In 1948, the ban was extended to television. Recently, however, ads for scotch, whiskey, and gin have appeared on both television and radio. Many of the radio stations that air alcohol ads also feature youth-oriented rock and roll. In 1995, radio and television advertising for beer and wine totaled $700 million. Children learn how, when, where, and why to drink from broadcast ads for alcoholic beverages.

You can make a difference by visiting managers of local television and radio stations. Tell them to stop running alcohol ads or urge them not to accept ads if they are offered. If the radio or television station runs ads for distilled products, demand equal time to discourage underage drinking. Write letters to the editor of the local newspaper. Hold a youth rally outside the radio or T.V. station protesting liquor ads or praising those who refuse to accept alcohol ads. Contact the Federal Communications Commission to investigate questionable liquor ads (1 888 CALL–FCC).

Action Packet: Stop Broadcast Liquor Ads, Join Together, 1996, http://www.jointogether.org/.

cigarettes has risen since 1983, tax as a percent of the retail price per pack has declined dramatically. Interestingly, tobacco company profits have risen sharply during the same time period.[12]

Taxes on alcoholic beverages and tobacco products vary by state. For example, cigarette excise taxes range from 2.5 cents per pack in Virginia to 82.5 cents in Washington.[13] Alcohol taxes range from 2 cents per gallon in Wyoming to 77 cents in South Carolina.[14] Despite recent increases in state cigarette taxes, the real price of cigarettes in most states has not kept up with inflation.[15] States also use tax revenues for different purposes. Some states earmark tax revenues to fund prevention programs or health care.

Counteradvertising

Advertising and promotion of alcoholic beverages and tobacco products influence teenagers' decisions to begin smoking more than does peer pressure.[16] Prodrug images are communicated in many ways: outdoor billboards, sponsorship of sporting events, rock concerts, point-of-sale displays, and promotional items. **Counteradvertising** aims to provide health messages, balancing the glamorized view of drinking and smoking promoted by company advertising. The Partnership for a Drug-Free America warns youth about the hazards of illegal drug use and motivates youth to reject illegal drugs via anti-drug announcements on radio, television, and print media. The 1997 National Drug Control Strategy aims to create partnerships with media, the entertainment industry, and professional sports organizations to reduce the glamorization of illegal drugs, alcohol, and tobacco use.[17]

Professional sports teams and community action groups are beginning to work with their communities to deglamorize alcohol and tobacco use by using counteradvertising. The New Jersey Nets run antismoking ads in their game programs, message board, and fan magazine.

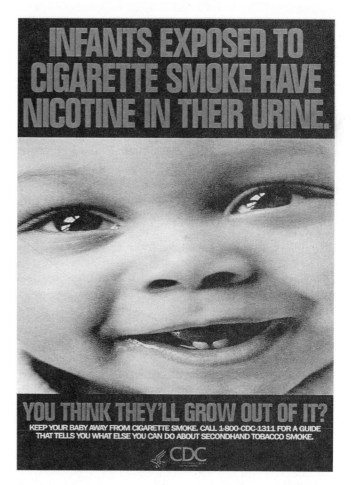

Government agencies and other public health organizations use counteradvertising in an effort to balance the glamorous images of smoking and drinking promoted by industry advertising.

counteradvertising health messages designed to balance the glamorized view of drinking and smoking promoted by company advertising

Some sports stadiums are refusing billboard advertising of tobacco products. Since many rodeos promote tobacco products, some communities in the Southwest are counteradvertising by using the slogan, "Yes to sports and health. . . . No to tobacco pushers and oral cancer."[18]

Some states and localities require alcohol and tobacco health warning signs. Posters are mandatory wherever alcoholic beverages and tobacco products are sold. The signs are required to be posted in a conspicuous place. Governments usually localize the message. For example, if the community is multilingual, the warnings appear in several different languages. If the population consists largely of college students, the warnings address the issue of binge drinking. Warning signs provide a low-cost means of advertising the health-damaging effects of drugs. They also reinforce the federally mandated warning labels on alcohol and tobacco products. One problem with the federally required warning labels is that the message never changes and consumers often lose interest. In some cases the messages are barely legible, printed in small type, or made to blend into the background.

Controversial Public Policies Related to Drugs

Public debate about legalization or decriminalization of drugs continues in the United States. Marijuana use for medical purposes is currently permitted in Arizona and California. Many substance abuse professionals believe permitting medical use of marijuana will increase availability and lead to greater marijuana use. In addition, the medical use language is misleading. Many young people mistakenly believe marijuana cures cancer; actually, marijuana reduces the nausea and pain associated with terminal illness but does not cure the disease.

Another controversial drug policy strategy is **harm reduction.** This approach modifies the behaviors of drug users and the conditions under which they use drugs.[19] Examples of harm reduction strategies are needle exchange programs for intravenous drug users and school condom programs to reduce unintended pregnancies and sexually transmitted disease. Although needle exchange programs have been shown to greatly reduce the incidence of HIV/AIDS,[20] very few such programs exist in the United States. The United States has generally resisted harm reduction policies for fear of "sending the wrong message." Instead, drug policies continue to focus on use reduction rather than harm reduction.

DRUG TESTING

Drug testing plays an important role in a comprehensive, community-based prevention program and has become a popular policy strategy. Whether in the workplace or at school, it can be considered a primary, secondary, or tertiary prevention measure. When used to forestall initial use, drug testing can be considered primary prevention because some people who might be tempted to try drugs may decide not to if the possibility of drug testing exists. If a person must be drug free to work, participate in athletics, or stay out of jail, drug testing acts as a powerful deterrent to drug use. When used to detect drug use that has already begun, drug testing is a form of secondary prevention. Drug testing for chronic drug abusers, who have already suffered the health effects of long-term drug

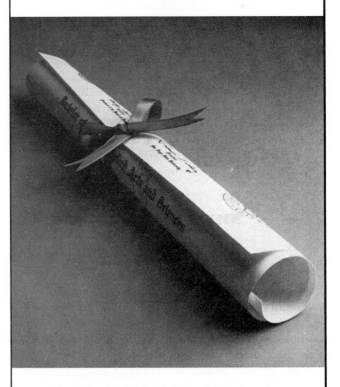

There's one sure way to see your future go up in smoke. Do drugs.

This year, most of the *Fortune 500* will be administering drug tests. If you fail the test, you may be out of a job.

The message is simple. Doing drugs could blow your whole education.

Most companies now require job applicants to submit to pre-employment drug screening. This ad reminds students that drug use could cost them a job.

WHAT DO YOU THINK?

Is Preemployment Drug Testing Justified?

Drug abuse in the workplace is a continuing concern. In factories, stores, and offices, employee drug abuse is suspected to be the cause of a significant portion of all absenteeism, accidents, medical claims, insubordination, thefts, and loss of productivity.

In response to the growing concern over drug abuse, more than 87% of America's businesses have instituted mandatory preemployment drug screening.[a] Prospective employees of these firms are required to pass one or more drug screenings to be considered for employment. A positive test result or failure to submit to screening may mean rejection. Preemployment screening is also becoming more common in the public employment sector.

Needless to say, there is controversy over mandatory preemployment drug screening. Supporters of mandatory screening point out that employers have an obligation to provide a safe and healthy work environment. They also contend that the cost of health care insurance, already too high, is being driven even higher by drug-related illnesses

[a]"Drug Testing in the Workplace," *Prevention Pipeline*, 9(1996): 4, 3.

and accidents. Worker's compensation costs are also high, perhaps in part because of an increase in drug-related accidents and the chronic nature of drug-related illnesses. According to companies, profits are declining and production costs are rising beyond acceptable levels because of drug and alcohol abuse in the workplace.

In addition, employers point out that those who have taken drugs and have failed a drug screening have already broken the law by using illegal drugs. They have, therefore, forfeited their right to be considered for employment.

Opponents of preemployment drug screening express two concerns. Their first concern is that the validity and reliability of screening tests are too low. Too often, they contend, potential employees are rejected when in fact they have not used drugs. Their second concern regards the invasion of individual privacy by the companies that assume applicants are guilty until proven innocent by the testing laboratory.

In light of positions held by both sides, do you feel that mandatory preemployment drug screening is justified? In your opinion, are students who use drugs aware of the impact that their use can have on future employment opportunities?

use, is considered tertiary prevention. If chronic drug users must be drug free to successfully complete treatment or to remain in recovery, drug testing offers an objective measurement of sobriety.

Workplace Drug Testing

In 1986, President Ronald Reagan passed Executive Order Number 12564, mandating a Drug Free Federal Workplace. As a result of this policy, drug testing programs for federal employees in safety-sensitive jobs were initiated. The Drug Free Federal Workplace order suggests procedures for drug testing programs and creates employee assistance programs to provide counseling and rehabilitation for workers with drug problems.

In 1988, the Drug Free Workplace Act extended the drug free federal policy to include all federal grantees (including universities) and most federal contractors. Although the Drug Free Workplace Act did not directly mandate drug testing, it encouraged tougher, planned approaches to prevent and deal with drug problems at the worksite.

Private businesses and industries have developed drug testing procedures similar to those used by federal agen-

cies. The percentage of businesses testing employees and job applicants jumped from 22% in 1987 to 87% in 1996.[21] The percentage of employees testing positive for drug use dropped from 4.2% in 1990 to 1.9% in 1995.

Since 1981, the U.S. military has conducted random drug testing. In the Navy and Marine Corps, members can expect to be tested randomly an average of three times per year. Mandatory drug testing in the military has been credited with sharply reducing drug use, improving duty performance, and reducing injuries and accidents. Furthermore, it may prevent first use of drugs by countless troops and employees (primary prevention) and contribute to the voluntary discontinuation of use by many others (secondary prevention). In substance abuse treatment centers, mandatory drug testing enables those running the program to monitor patient drug use and helps the patient confront denial and perhaps prevent relapse (tertiary prevention).

> **harm reduction** a policy approach to drug prevention that minimizes harm by modifying the behaviors of drug users and the conditions under which they use drugs

How Drug Testing Programs Work

Drug testing is usually either "for cause" or random, without cause or suspicion.[22] "For cause" testing is usually performed when there is probable cause or suspicion of drug use and is scheduled on specific dates and times. Random drug testing is unscheduled, or unannounced, and gives the person short notice to produce a urine or hair sample. Random testing is the type most criticized by civil libertarians, who argue that unannounced drug testing violates an individual's right to privacy.

If the **drug screening test** is positive for drugs, most programs perform a **confirmatory test** to verify the results. GC/MS is usually used as the confirmatory test because it is the most accurate. Figure 19.1 outlines the typical drug testing procedure.

Drug testing programs using urine samples have strict chain-of-custody guidelines for collecting, identifying, handling, and storing the samples. It is critical that urine samples are not tampered with and that test results are properly matched with the donor. A comprehensive drug testing program includes three components: (1) a policy statement that outlines drug testing procedures, (2) plans for staff training and employee education regarding drug testing, and (3) an employee assistance program (EAP) that ensures confidentiality and assists employees who test positive for drugs.[23]

Populations Being Tested

Although it is unlikely that all people will be tested for drug use, the groups already undergoing testing are large and diverse. Widespread support exists for mandatory testing of all employees involved in occupations that affect the public's safety. For example, 8 million transportation workers (airline, rail, truck, and maritime) undergo mandatory drug testing each year.[24] Fewer safety-sensitive industries have also adopted testing because of concerns about problems at work, national

publicity, and high-risk work environments. Many company executives are convinced that drug testing can improve productivity, enhance public trust, and assist employees who may be at risk for drug abuse. However, some companies have quit drug testing because it was not cost effective. On average, companies spend $50,000 per year on drug testing.[25] Companies that combine education programs with drug testing report lower positive-test rates than companies that do not offer any help for employees.

Mandatory drug testing has been adopted by the International Olympic Committee (IOC), National Football League (NFL), National Collegiate Athletic Association (NCAA), and other amateur athletic sanctioning bodies. The criminal justice system uses drug testing as a way to monitor drug use, deter future drug use, and reduce criminal activity. Drug testing is often used at the time of arrest, during the pretrial release period, in jails, and during probation and parole. The National Institute of Justice Drug Use Forecasting (DUF) Program is an example of an initiative designed to measure recent drug use among booked arrestees. Established in 1987, DUF also measures drug use trends among criminal offenders. DUF obtains anonymous urine samples and interviews booked arrestees in 24 sites across the United States. In 1996, the U.S. Congress passed a law requiring prisons to drug-test inmates eligible for release and those free on parole. States not adhering to the law will lose federal prison grant money.[25]

The Drug Testing Controversy

If the only purpose of drug testing were to identify people who need treatment so that on completion they would remain drug free, little controversy would exist regarding its appropriateness. Unfortunately, however, drug testing can be used for purposes that could ultimately influence employment opportunities and career advancement. Even when issues of public safety or national security are considered, many question whether mandatory drug testing violates an individual's right to privacy. Although the American Civil Liberties Union (ACLU) has tried to argue against drug testing on the grounds that it constitutes illegal search and seizure, the judicial branch of government views most drug testing programs as legal within the Constitution. In 1989, the U.S. Supreme Court upheld federal regulations that mandate drug testing for public workers in safety-sensitive jobs. In that same year, a U.S. Circuit Court of Appeals in Chicago upheld a Tippecanoe County, Indiana, random drug testing program for high school athletes and cheerleaders. There is little doubt that there will be additional court cases over drug testing.

---

drug screening test assessment of urine, blood, or hair for evidence of the presence of drugs or their metabolites; used to determine the necessity of further drug testing

confirmatory drug test an assessment of urine, blood, or hair for the presence of drugs or their metabolites; used after drug screening to confirm the results of drug testing

coalition an alliance of individuals and groups in the community who join together to prevent a communitywide problem such as alcohol, tobacco, and other drug abuse

FIGURE 19.1

Drug testing procedure.

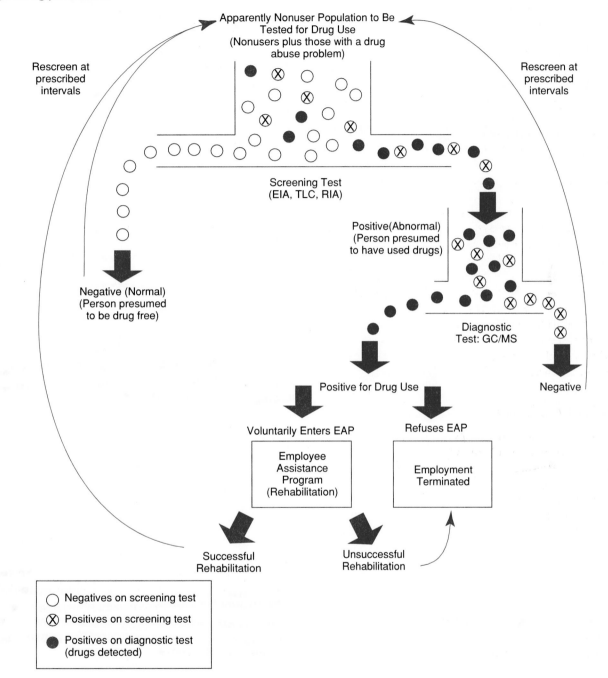

Legend:
- ◯ Negatives on screening test
- ⊗ Positives on screening test
- ● Positives on diagnostic test (drugs detected)

Beyond the legality issue are concerns about the quality of the tests and the care taken to ensure that no mistakes occur. For example, the methods used in collecting urine samples, the security of samples, and the confidentiality of results make drug testing a controversial topic.

HOW TO INFLUENCE PUBLIC POLICY

Individuals often feel powerless to influence policy, but community **coalitions** have been successful in changing

TO ALL THE SIGNS THAT MAKE
DRIVING A LITTLE SAFER,
WE'D LIKE TO ADD ONE MORE.

Even though your ability to drive a car is seriously impaired at a
blood alcohol level of .08, most states only prosecute at .10 or higher.

We'd like every state to make .08 the blood alcohol limit.

If you want to help, please call or write your state legislators.

Together we can make this a sign of life.

MADD
Mothers Against Drunk Driving

MADD relies on both grassroots and grasstops strategies to
influence public policy.

grassroots efforts to change public policy that involve
local people who are close to the issue

grasstops efforts to change public policy that involve
influencing key policymakers or legislators

drug-related public policy. Coalitions are **grassroots** efforts to change public policy, meaning that local people who are close to the issue are involved in solving the problem. Although most coalitions have depended almost solely on federal funds, many are relying on more than one funding source to continue their activities. Cuts in federal dollars for drug prevention have had a negative effect on coalitions and public policy. Some private foundations, such as the Robert Wood Johnson Foundation, are funding alcohol and tobacco prevention coalitions. Many of these coalitions have been so successful that the motto "think globally, act locally" has been transformed into concrete results at the local level.

Community coalitions often address negative media messages by designing counteradvertisements. For example, some communities have been successful in requiring alcohol retail outlets to post warning signs about the dangers of alcohol. Others have been successful in raising the state cigarette excise tax. The Coalition to Reduce Binge Drinking urges university newspaper editors to reject advertisements by local bars that promote "bar crawls," all-you-can-drink specials, or weekend discounts. These ads encourage abusive alcohol consumption, which leads to serious consequences for the college community.

For successful public policy, **grasstops** efforts are also important. Grasstops strategies are those that influence key policymakers or legislators. Many groups hire lobbyists to inform and persuade legislators about key policy issues. The alcohol beverage and tobacco industries depend on highly skilled and well-connected lobbyists to protect their special interests in Washington and in each state capitol. Health groups traditionally have not been able to compete with the wealthy alcohol and tobacco companies. Lobbyists for the alcohol and tobacco industries vastly outnumber lobbyists that represent health interests.[27]

Another example of a grasstops strategy is surveying candidates and legislators about drug policy. The Community Anti-Drug Coalitions of America (CADCA) polled candidates for U.S. House and Senate.[28] A majority (65%) ranked prevention above treatment, interdiction, and law enforcement as the most effective means of handling the drug crisis. CADCA conducted the survey as a larger effort to raise awareness among national leaders about the drug issue. CADCA involves congressmen in developing their own local antidrug coalitions.

SUMMARY

Public policy plays an important role in community-based drug prevention. It involves individuals and communities taking action to reduce and prevent drug abuse.

Policies that make prevention an urgent priority, raise alcohol and tobacco taxes, and promote counteradvertising are most successful. Drug testing is an important weapon in the fight against drug abuse. Drug testing has become more common in both public and private workplaces. Military personnel, transportation workers, and professional athletes undergo regular mandatory drug testing. Drug testing is a controversial issue but one that is apparently here to stay. Individuals may feel powerless to influence public policy, but coalitions have been successful in changing drug-related policy.

REVIEW QUESTIONS

1. How does public policy limit both the supply of and demand for drugs?
2. In what ways do public policies affect drug use? Give two examples.
3. What are some Healthy People 2000 goals to reduce drug use?
4. How is the FDA regulation of tobacco products designed to affect underage tobacco use?
5. What happens to alcohol, tobacco, and other drug consumption when prices rise?
6. How does counteradvertising deglamorize drug use? Give two examples.
7. How might legalization of marijuana affect drug use?
8. Why have harm reduction policies been unpopular in the United States?
9. What is the difference between drug screening and confirmatory drug testing? Which is less costly? Which is more accurate? What are the basic technologies used in each?
10. Which public and private groups are most likely to undergo mandatory drug testing?
11. What are some of the factors that make drug testing controversial?
12. Compare and contrast grassroots and grasstops efforts to influence public policy.

REFERENCES

1. *Healthy People 2000: Midcourse Review and 1995 Revisions* (Boston, Ma: Jones and Bartlett, 1996).
2. B. M. Sweedler, "Risk-Taking Behavior and Young Adults in Transportation Operations," *Prevention Pipeline* 9 (1996):5, 19–23.
3. *Healthy People 2000.*
4. "Join Together, Take Action," 1996, http://www.jointogether.org/.
5. "A Giant Leap Forward in Tobacco Control," *Prevention Pipeline* (1997) 10:2, 4–6.
6. J. DiFranza, et al., "Youth Access to Tobacco: The Effects of Age, Gender, Vending Machine Locks, and 'It's the Law' Programs, *American Journal of Public Health* 86 (1996):2, 221–24.
7. L. A. Downey and J. A. Gardiner, *Reducing Youth Access to Tobacco: A Partial Inventory of State Initiatives* (Chicago, Ill.: University of Illinois at Chicago, 1996).
8. State Cancer Legislative Database Program, *Youth Access to Tobacco Fact Sheet* (Bethesda, Md.: National Cancer Institute, March 1997).
9. B. S. Lynch and R. J. Bonnie, *Growing Up Tobacco Free: Preventing Nicotine Addiction in Children and Youths* (Washington, D.C.: National Academy Press, 1994).
10. "The Utility of Drug Prices," *Drug Policy Research Center Newsletter,* 6 (1997):1, 7–8.
11. *Comprehensive Framework and Analysis of Tobacco Industry Strategies and Tactics,* (Washington, D.C.: The Advocacy Institute, 1994).
12. Substance Abuse: The Nation's Number One Health Problem: Key Indicators for Policy, Institute for Health Policy, Brandeis University, Waltham, Ma., October 1993.
13. State Cancer Legislative Database Program, *Tobacco Use Fact Sheet* (Bethesda, Md.: National Cancer Institute, March 1997).
14. Substance Abuse.
15. U.S. Department of Health and Human Services, *Preventing Tobacco Use among Young People: A Report of the Surgeon General* (Atlanta, Ga.: Centers for Disease Control and Prevention, Office on Smoking and Health, 1994).
16. N. Evans, et al., "Influence of Tobacco Marketing and Exposure to Smokers on Adolescent Susceptibility to Smoking," *Journal of the National Cancer Institute* 87 (1995):1538–45.
17. The National Drug Control Strategy, 1997, Office of National Drug Control Policy, Washington, D.C.
18. D. Morris, "Kick tobacco out of rodeos," *Tobacco-free Youth Reporter,* 9 (1997):1, 4.
19. R. J. MacCoun, "The Psychology of Harm Reduction: Comparing Alternative Strategies for Modifying High-Risk Behaviors," 1997, RAND Drug Policy Research Center.
20. D. C. Des Jarlais, et al., "Harm Reduction: A Public Health Response to the AIDS Epidemic among Injecting Drug Users, *Annual Review of Public Health,* 14 (1993):413–50.
21. "Drug Testing in the Workplace," *Prevention Pipeline,* 9 (1996):4, 3.
22. D. C. Walsh, L. Elinson, and L. Gostin, "Worksite Drug Testing," *Ann Rev Public Health* 13 (1992):197.

23. National Institute on Drug Abuse, *Comprehensive Procedures for Drug Testing in the Workplace: A Process Model of Planning, Implementation, and Action*, DHHS Pub. No. (ADM)91-1731 (Washington, D.C.: U.S. Government Printing Office, 1991).

24. Join Together, "Clinton Mandates Drug Tests," 1996, http://www.jointogether.org/.

25. "Drug Testing in the Workplace."

26. Join Together, "Clinton Mandates."

27. "Utility of Drug Prices."

28. Join Together, "CADCA Survey Reveals that Congressional Candidates Support Different Drug Strategy than Presidential Candidates," 1996, http://www.jointogether.org/.

SOURCES FOR HELP

Advocacy Institute
1707 L St., NW
Suite 400
Washington, DC 20036
(202) 659–8475

Join Together
441 Stuart Street
Sixth Floor
Boston, MA 02116
(617) 437–1500
http://www.jointogether.org

The National Center for Tobacco-Free Kids
Washington, DC
1(800) 284–KIDS

Office of National Drug Control Policy
Executive Office of the President
Washington, DC 20503

RAND Drug Policy Research Center
1700 Main Street
P.O. Box 2138
Santa Monica, CA 90407-2138
(310) 451–7002
http://www.rand.org

LAW ENFORCEMENT

20

CHAPTER OBJECTIVES

After studying this chapter, you will be able to:

1. Explain how law enforcement can be considered both a secondary and a tertiary prevention measure.

2. Outline the four primary goals of law enforcement as a drug-prevention strategy.

3. Discuss the role of law enforcement in reducing the supply of drugs.

4. Discuss the process of drug interdiction.

5. Describe the types of alcohol and tobacco laws.

6. Identify the federal agencies that enforce drug-control laws.

7. Describe community policing as a current trend in local law enforcement.

8. List the main goals of Clinton's 1997 National Drug Control Strategy.

Comprehensive community-based prevention includes not only education and treatment (discussed in chapter 18) and public policy (discussed in Chapter 19), but also strict law enforcement. While education and treatment reduce the demand for drugs, law enforcement controls the supply of drugs by reducing drug trafficking and protecting neighborhoods from drug-related crime.

Strict law enforcement that produces arrests of drug dealers and seizures of large quantities of drugs may reduce the availability of drugs and the number of first-time drug users. Although enforcement is a necessary component of a comprehensive community-based prevention program, enforcement alone as a form of primary prevention is expensive and inefficient. Primary prevention includes measures aimed at preventing the onset of drug use. Law enforcement is generally viewed as either a secondary prevention measure when it involves early detection, arrest, and referral for treatment of drug users, or a tertiary prevention strategy when it leads to incarceration and rehabilitation.

LAW ENFORCEMENT

Law enforcement is the application of federal, state, and local laws to arrest, jail, bring to trial, and sentence those who break laws. In 1995, the **Drug Use Forecasting (DUF) Program** found that the majority of male and female arrestees tested positive for drugs, most commonly cocaine and marijuana.[1] The primary goals of law enforcement as a drug-prevention strategy are (1) to con-trol drug use; (2) to control crime, especially crime associated with **drug trafficking,** the buying, selling, manufacturing, or transporting of illegal (illicit) drugs; (3) to prevent the establishment of crime organizations; and (4) to protect neighborhoods.[2]

The Role of Law Enforcement in Illegal Drug Control

The role of law enforcement is to control the supply of illegal drugs by interrupting the source, transit, and distribution of drugs. In 1994, law enforcement agencies

law enforcement the application of federal, state, and local laws to arrest, jail, bring to trial, and sentence those who break laws

Drug Use Forecasting (DUF) Program a federal program that surveys arrestees and criminal offenders in major metropolitan areas across the United States to determine drug use trends and prevalence

drug trafficking the buying, selling, manufacturing, and transporting of illegal drugs

money laundering the process of converting illegally earned assets or cash to other forms of wealth to conceal true ownership or illegal acquisition

precursor (essential) chemicals chemicals required for the extraction and synthesis of all major illegal drugs except marijuana

interdiction the process of denying the drug smuggler the use of air, land, and maritime routes

Law enforcement aims to control the supply of drugs. Here a police officer inspects marijuana plants prior to their removal.

DRUGS IN YOUR WORLD

Double-Breasted Dealing

Until very recently, drug dealers rarely sold more than one type of drug. Cocaine or crack dealers were not likely to sell heroin. Likewise, heroin dealers would carry only small amounts of cocaine for customers who liked to "speed ball." Traditionally, cocaine or crack dealers tend to associate with nonusers and sell their drugs to strangers in a businesslike manner. On the other hand, heroin dealers often sell to friends, are drug users themselves, and are often paid in drugs.

Street drug sales are increasingly being managed by young nonusers who sell both heroin and cocaine, known as double-breasting. In 1994, the Drug Enforcement Administration noticed double-breasted dealing when raiding stash houses in New York, Florida, and Chicago. Double-breasted dealers are known for their bold approach. In a recent New York raid, heroin dealers retreated to selling indoors, but the double-breasted dealers continued selling both heroin and cocaine in open areas. This new breed of dealers reports pressure from Colombian cocaine distributors to sell heroin. Dealers often "front" heroin for their distributors; that is, they are not required to pay in advance for supplies they take to sell.

This new joint marketing structure for drug dealing presents new problems. Cocaine/crack dealers have no experience in "cutting" or diluting heroin and often combine the drug with unusually potent substances. These powerful mixtures, called heroin cocktails, caused a dramatic increase in 1996 drug-related emergency room visits in Philadelphia and Baltimore.

"Developments in the Heroin Trade," *Pulse Check,* Spring 1996 (http://www.ncjrs.org)

worldwide seized 275 tons of cocaine.[3] The seizure of illegal drugs, however, is only one drug-control strategy that law-enforcement agencies use. Law-enforcement officials also aim to disrupt **money laundering** operations, the process of converting illegally earned assets or cash to other forms of wealth to conceal true ownership; break up drug distribution networks; destroy crops; and control **precursor (essential) chemicals** used in the production of cocaine, heroin, LSD, PCP, and methamphetamine.[4]

Recently, law enforcement has focused on gangs, which are often involved in sophisticated drug production and distribution networks. Most jail inmates who were involved in gangs say they manufactured or distributed drugs.[5] Gangs including the Crips, Bloods, Dominicans, Gangster Disciples, and others have migrated from urban areas to smaller cities and rural communities, increasing drug-related crime.

Interdiction is the process of denying the drug smuggler the use of air, land, and maritime routes. Federal law-enforcement officials seize drugs and drug trafficker's assets and arrest the traffickers. In 1993, the Drug Enforcement Administration (DEA), FBI, and United States Customs and Coast Guard authorities seized more than 238,000 pounds of cocaine, 3,300 pounds of heroin, and more than 750,000 pounds of marijuana.[6] After more than a decade of focus on drug seizures, the DEA recently shifted to a "kingpin strategy," focusing on destroying drug-smuggling organizations in selected countries.[7] Cocaine is smuggled almost solely from South America, through Mexico, and into the United States across the Southwest border.[8] Larger shipments are often concealed in commercial ships or cargo planes.

The Department of Justice has the largest drug control budget of any federal agency. A significant portion of DOJ's budget is used to maintain prisoners and prisons.

DRUGS IN YOUR WORLD

Bringing Illegal Drugs into Your World

During emergency surgery to stop internal bleeding caused by injuries received in the Avianca Flight 52 crash of the preceding day (in January 1990), doctors found 70 condoms of cocaine in the intestinal tract of Jose Figueroa.[a] Fortunately for Mr. Figueroa, none of the condoms had burst, for if they had, Mr. Figueroa would have died from massive cocaine overdose. Such is the potential fate of cocaine and heroin "mules," who use their bodies to transport illicit drugs into the United States.

Who are these "mules" who attempt to carry illegal drugs? They may be tourists returning from vacation, students returning to the United States after holidays, or in some cases, professional smugglers. If successful, mules can earn $3000 for bringing one pound of South American cocaine valued at $500,000 or one pound of heroin valued at $1 million into the United States.[b]

The method is simple. The first step is swallowing condoms, balloons, or the fingertips of surgical gloves that have been filled with drugs and tied closed with dental floss. Mules often lubricate the "packets" before swallowing or use a topical anesthetic to deaden the throat. The mule then boards a plane bound for the United States. On arrival, the mule must pass through U.S. Customs and wait until the contraband passes safely through the body.

[a]J. Kelley, "Narcotics Smuggled Internally: Mules Ingest Sealed Packets," *USA Today,* 1 February 1990, p. 3A.

[b]K. Carter, "Drugs' Hidden Route to USA," *USA Today,* 1 February 1990, p. 3A.

[c]Kelley, "Narcotics Smuggled."

Each year U.S. Customs agents intercept hundreds of pounds of drugs being carried by mules.[c] Mules are most often identified by their suspicious behavior. Suspects must consent to being X-rayed; if not, they are sent, under guard, to a hospital, where they are monitored until the packets have a chance to pass from the rectum. The most cocaine intercepted in one person was 156 bags, containing 4.6 pounds of cocaine. The most condoms swallowed was 445, containing a total of 2.5 pounds of hashish. U.S. customs agents have arrested mules as young as 14 and older than 60.

In light of the physical discomfort and great danger in being mules, why do people undertake this high-risk crime?

Each year U.S. customs agents, with the help of specially trained dogs, intercept thousands of pounds of drugs being smuggled into the U.S.

In 1994, 840 tons of cocaine were produced in Bolivia, Colombia, and Peru.[9] Opium production has nearly doubled since 1986. During most of the past decade, most of the world's heroin came from Burma, with an increasing amount produced in Colombia.[10] In 1995, for the first time, more heroin entered the United States from South America than from Asia.[11]

Drug Laws and Enforcement Agencies

The enactment and enforcement of laws designed to prevent the misuse and abuse of drugs have a long history. Some of the specific drug-related laws have been mentioned in earlier chapters. In general, there are five major categories of drug laws. Drug laws focus on (1) new and casual users, (2) current users, (3) organized crime,

(4) supply networks, and (5) street dealers. The trend in drug legislation is to stiffen criminal statutes and add legislation to combat increasingly sophisticated drug trafficking. Many states have adopted drug laws mandating stricter penalties for drug trafficking, drug crimes committed within 1,000 feet of a school, drug transactions involving minors, and criminal enterprise, focusing on arresting drug kingpins.[12]

The Controlled Substances Act (CSA) of 1970 is the legal basis for U.S. drug laws. The CSA outlines penalties

asset forfeiture laws provisions in international, federal, state, and local laws that allow authorities to seize cash, property, vehicles, and other assets when they make drug arrests

SELF-ASSESSMENT

Where Do You Draw the Line?

Would you be a "mule" in the distribution and sale of drugs? How likely would you be to participate in one or more of the following activities?

Would you give to, or purchase cigarettes or other tobacco products for, a person younger than 18 years old? A 15-year-old? A 10-year-old?

Would you give alcohol to, or buy alcohol for, your 20-year-old roommate? For someone who was 15?

Would you rent (or share) an apartment with someone who used marijuana a few times a year? If your roommate wanted to smoke a joint and you didn't, would you leave or ask him or her to stop? Would you notify authorities? What would you do if it were crack?

Would you allow a classmate or friend to "park" illegal drugs in your backpack, dorm room, or car until it was safe, even if it were for only a few minutes?

Would you transport illegal drugs (for money or as a favor) across campus? Across the city? Across state lines? Into this country? If so, how much is enough money for you to risk arrest or even potential death?

Would you notify a law enforcement agency if you suspected a friend, family member, or co-worker of selling or transporting illegal drugs?

TABLE 20.1 Federal Drug-Trafficking Penalties, 1996

	Quantity	First Offense	Second Offense
Marijuana	Less than 50 kg	Not more than 5 years Fine not more than $250,000	Not more than 10 years Fine $500,000
	50–99 kg or plants	Not more than 20 years If death or serious injury, not less than 20 years Fine $1 million	Not more than 30 years If death or serious injury, not more than life Fine $2 million
	100–999 kg or plants	5–40 years If death or serious injury, not less than 20 years Fine not more than $2 million	10 years to life in prison If death or serious injury, not more than life Fine not more than $4 million
	1,000 kg (or more) or plants	10 years to life in prison If death or serious injury, 20 years to life Fine not more than $4 million	20 years to life in prison If death or serious injury, not more than life Fine not more than $8 million
Cocaine	500–4,999 gm	5–40 years If death or serious injury, 20 years to life Fine not more than $2 million	10 years to life in prison If death or serious injury, life in prison Fine not more than $4 million
	5 kg or more	10 years to life in prison If death or serious injury, 20 years to life Fine not more than $4 million	20 years to life in prison If death or serious injury, life in prison Fine not more than $8 million

Source: U.S. Department of Justice, Drug Enforcement Administration, *Drugs of Abuse, 1996* (Washington, D.C.: U.S. Government Printing Office, 1996).

for the unlawful manufacture and distribution of controlled substances, such as marijuana, heroin, and cocaine. Table 20.1 summarizes federal trafficking penalties for marijuana and cocaine. **Asset forfeiture laws** are used by international, federal, state, and local law enforcement to seize cash, property, vehicles, and other assets when drug arrests are made. In 1995, the Drug Enforcement Administration seized over $640 million in cash, real estate, vehicles, vessels, aircraft, and other assets.[13]

Alcohol Laws. With the repeal of Prohibition, the U.S. Constitution granted states the right to regulate the distribution and sale of alcohol. Most states have agencies, usually called alcoholic beverage control (ABC) agencies, that regulate the manufacture, distribution, and sale of alcoholic beverages in each state. States require vendors to obtain licenses to sell alcohol. In 1991, approximately 560,000 retail licenses were issued in the United States.[14] Thirty-nine states have **"local option" provisions,** allowing local communities to regulate where and when alcohol is sold. In these states, local communities can choose to be "dry" or to ban the sale of alcohol.

The **National Minimum Drinking Age Act of 1984** required all states to raise their minimum alcohol purchase and public possession age to 21 years. Because states that did not conform risked losing federal highway dollars, all states complied. Raising the minimum legal drinking age has reduced alcohol consumption, traffic crashes, and related fatalities among those under 21 years of age.[15] However, many state laws contain loopholes that permit underage drinking. For example, many states allow minors to possess alcohol with parental permission or in private settings. Some states make alcohol purchase illegal only if the minor intends to consume the alcohol. Twenty-one states have no laws that make consumption by minors specifically illegal, although the minor may be charged with possession. Twenty-three states do not make it illegal for a minor to attempt to purchase alcohol.[16]

Some states have adopted and enforced creative laws to deter underage drinking. Many states delay, suspend, or revoke driver's licenses for alcohol-related violations. Experts agree that penalizing a minor by taking away the driver's license is an effective strategy for reducing drunk driving. Some states prohibit alcohol advertising that appeals to youth. Others mandate server training, requiring all alcohol servers and sellers to undergo training about state laws and penalties, and how to identify an underage drinker.

Some states have adopted **zero-tolerance laws** that set maximum blood alcohol concentration (BAC) limits for drivers under 21 years of age at 0.02% or lower. States with zero-tolerance laws have fewer single-vehicle nighttime crashes among young drivers.[17]

Tobacco Laws. Federal and state governments have increasingly enacted legislation to protect nonsmokers from environmental tobacco smoke and to reduce youth access to tobacco products. Many states and local communities have passed laws restricting smoking in public places and workplaces, banning the sale of cigarettes in vending machines, restricting advertising, increasing tobacco excise taxes, and requiring licensing of tobacco-product vendors. Although most states restrict smoking in some manner, laws range from limited prohibition (e.g., banning smoking on school buses) to comprehensive clean-indoor-air laws that ban smoking in all public places, including restaurants and private workplaces. Under federal law, facilities that routinely deliver services to children must prohibit indoor smoking, including schools, libraries, day care facilities, and health care settings.[18] Smoking also is prohibited on all domestic air flights and most U.S. international flights.

Excise taxes on cigarettes vary by state, ranging from 2.5 cents per pack in Virginia to 81.5 cents per pack in Washington.[19] Tobacco advertising is not allowed on television or radio, and health warnings are required on advertisements for all tobacco products, except billboards for smokeless tobacco products.

Under a federal regulation called the **Synar Amendment** (Section 1926 of the Public Health Service Act), all states are required to adopt legislation that prohibits the sale and distribution of tobacco products to people under age 18.[20] States are required to have an enforcement plan that includes both random and targeted unannounced inspections of over-the-counter sales and vending machine sales. States that do not comply with these regulations lose federal dollars for alcohol, tobacco, and other drug prevention and treatment programs.

On August 28, 1996, the Food and Drug Administration (FDA) adopted the most comprehensive federal law to reduce the access, and the appeal of, tobacco products to children.[21] The FDA regulation has been called the most important public health initiative of our generation. The FDA rule sets a minimum age of 18 to buy tobacco products, bans most vending machines and self-service displays, prohibits "kiddie packs" or free samples, prohibits billboards within 1,000 feet of schools, limits outdoor and in-store advertising to black-and-white text only, restricts magazine advertising in publications with significant youth readership, bans tobacco company sponsorship of sporting events, and prohibits brand names on promotional items, such as hats and t-shirts.[22]

Enforcement Agencies. Many federal, state, and local agencies are responsible for drug control. At all levels of government, many programs attempt to reduce either the supply of or the demand for drugs. Table 20.2 lists

---

"local option" provisions provisions in state laws that allow local communities to regulate where and when alcohol is sold

National Minimum Drinking Age Act of 1984 a federal law that required all states to raise their minimum alcohol purchase and public possession age to 21 years

zero-tolerance laws regulations that set maximum blood alcohol concentration (BAC) limits for drivers under 21 at 0.02% or lower

Synar Amendment federal law that requires all states to adopt legislation that prohibits the sale and distribution of tobacco products to people under age 18

multijurisdictional drug-control task forces coalitions of local and state law-enforcement agencies (usually five or more) that work closely with federal enforcement agencies

TABLE 20.2 Federal Agencies That Enforce Drug-Control Laws

Name of Agency	Function
Department of Justice (DOJ)	
Drug Enforcement Administration (DEA)	Identifies, arrests, and prosecutes violators; maintains prisons and prisoners; manages treatment, education, and rehabilitation programs for prisoners.
Federal Bureau of Investigation (FBI)	FBI investigates multinational organized crime networks; deports alien drug traffickers.
Immigration and Naturalization Services	
Organized Crime Drug Enforcement Task Force	
Department of the Treasury	
U.S. Customs Service	U.S. Customs interdicts drugs at our borders.
Internal Revenue Service (IRS)	IRS investigates money laundering and prosecutes tax evasion cases.
Bureau of Alcohol, Tobacco, and Firearms (BATF)	BATF regulates alcohol and tobacco.
Department of Transportation (DOT)	Works with other agencies to interdict drugs.
U.S. Coast Guard	
Federal Aviation Administration	
National Highway Traffic Safety Administration (NHTSA)	NHTSA regulates and enforces drunk driving laws.
Department of State (DOS)	Provides diplomatic and military assistance to foreign countries.
Bureau of International Narcotics Matters	
Agency for International Development	Attempts to reduce the production and shipment of illegal drugs to the United States.
U.S. Information Agency (USIA)	
Food and Drug Administration (FDA)	Regulates the use, sale, and distribution of nicotine-delivery devices (cigarettes).

selected federal agencies involved in enforcing drug control laws.

The primary responsibility for the enforcement of federal drug laws falls upon the Department of Justice (DOJ). The lead DOJ agency responsible for the development of overall drug enforcement strategy, programs, planning, and evaluation is the Drug Enforcement Administration (DEA). The mission of the DEA is to enforce the controlled substances laws and regulations and to use the criminal and civil justice system to restrict and punish those organizations, and the principal members of those organizations, involved in the growing, manufacture, or distribution of controlled substances appearing in, or destined for, illicit traffic in the United States. As of June 1996, the Agency had about 7,500 employees and a budget of more than $1 billion.[23]

While not truly a law enforcement agency, the Department of Health and Human Services (DHHS) receives billions of dollars for drug-prevention education, treatment, and research. Unlike the other federal agencies focusing on drug control, most DHHS funds are spent to reduce the demand for drugs. The lead agency within DHHS is the Substance Abuse and Mental Health Services Administration (SAMHSA). Within SAMHSA are three centers: (1) the Center for Substance Abuse Prevention (CSAP), (2) the Center for Substance Abuse Treatment (CSAT), and (3) the Center for Mental Health Services (CMHS). Another agency within DHHS is the National Institute on Drug Abuse (NIDA), which is devoted to drug-abuse research. Also within DHHS is the Food and Drug Administration (FDA), which is responsible for regulating all prescription and nonprescription drugs.

While the federal government provides tremendous economic support and direction to drug-control efforts, state governments are increasingly directing and implementing statewide initiatives in schools, neighborhoods, and homes. Although initiatives are almost always implemented at the local level, state agencies provide expertise and limited funding for law enforcement, drug education, and drug treatment. State police, departments of health and mental health, offices of education, and other state agencies work in drug control.

Current Trends in Law Enforcement

Data reported routinely by the Federal Bureau of Investigation (FBI) and other government agencies suggest that the enforcement approach to drug abuse prevention is still being actively pursued. At the local level, about 85% of police and sheriff's departments in the nation have special drug-enforcement units.[24] Half of those work in **multijurisdictional drug-control task forces,** coalitions of five or more local and state law-enforcement agencies that work closely with federal enforcement agencies.[25] Observers estimate that state and local authorities make most drug arrests, about 1.1 million in 1993, up 59% since 1984.[26] Public sentiment also increasingly favors stricter prosecution of drug dealers and increased efforts to keep drugs out of the country. The general public believes that stricter enforcement is an important step in countering the current drug problem.

Clearly, however, law enforcement alone cannot win the "war on drugs." We need a comprehensive, community-based effort that involves federal, state, and local governments, educational institutions, and the public. For example, the Public Housing Drug Elimination Program provides funds through the U.S. Department of Housing and Urban Development (HUD) for collaborative antidrug efforts of police and local housing authorities.[27]

One trend in local law enforcement is **community policing.**[28] Crime prevention is the basic mission of community policing. Local police maintain a visible presence in neighborhoods and attempt to resolve disputes before they escalate into crimes. Community policing is a proactive rather than a reactive strategy of law enforcement. Community policing aims to form partnerships between police and citizens and give police important information about neighborhoods. Community policing encourages citizens to take an active role in preventing and solving crimes.

Community policing takes various forms in different communities. Some communities have increased foot patrols, and others have opened storefront police offices in high-risk areas, often called "COP (community-oriented policing) Shops." **Weed and Seed** is a comprehensive federal initiative implemented by a coalition of federal agencies. Weed and Seed helps communities remove drug traffickers and violent criminals from their neighborhoods and offers social and economic incentives to keep communities drug free.

National, state, and local law enforcement agencies have joined forces to reduce the availability of drugs. Organized Crime Drug Enforcement Task Forces are reorganizing regions of the United States to respond to changing drug-trafficking patterns.[29] Federal funds have been targeted to high-intensity drug trafficking areas by linking local, state, and federal enforcement efforts. In a joint effort, the FBI and DEA formed DRUGX, an automated database containing drug intelligence information.

Tampa, Florida, developed a unique approach to street drug trafficking. **QUAD (Quick Uniform Attack on Drugs)** emphasizes community cooperation and neighborhood cleanup. Officers respond quickly to every community complaint, attempting primarily to inconvenience, but not necessarily jail, drug traffickers. QUAD works with local policy makers to strengthen loitering laws in areas of high drug activity. QUAD also enlists the cooperation of the media to increase community awareness and involve citizens.[30]

National Drug Policy

In 1989, the first National Drug Control Strategy was designed to address the problem of drug abuse. Federal, state, and local agencies; all 535 members of Congress; and other experts and organizations worked together to review the current efforts and recommend policy changes. The 1989 National Drug Control Strategy united government and the private sector in a national partnership committed to increasing resources for law enforcement, treatment, and education.

The national drug control budget is divided into four main categories: (1) demand reduction, (2) law enforcement, (3) international/border control, and (4) drug interdiction. Federal spending for drug control has increased sixfold since 1985 (fig. 20.1).[31] In fiscal year 1996, the federal government spent more than $13 billion on drug control, with about 55% of that allocated to domestic law-enforcement efforts. The second-largest component was demand reduction, including Safe and Drug-Free Schools, community partnerships, and expanded treatment programs.

President Clinton's 1997 National Drug Control Strategy has the following major goals:[32]

1. *Educate and enable America's youth to reject illegal drugs, as well as alcohol and tobacco.* Clinton's plan increases the number of community organizations, schools, and community drug coalitions focusing on prevention. The 1998 drug control budget includes money for a national media campaign to target illegal drug consumption by youth and an 11% increase in money for drug and violence prevention in schools.

2. *Increase the safety of America's citizens by substantially reducing drug-related crime and violence.* Drug users are more likely to commit crime than nondrug users. In 1994, drug offenders made up 60% of the prison population, compared with only 25% in 1980.[33] In the 1998 drug-control budget, money for community-oriented policing is up 9%.

3. *Reduce health and social costs to the public of illegal drug use.* Experts estimate the societal cost of drug abuse at more than $66 billion a year.[34] These costs include

---

community policing a cooperative approach by local police to working with citizens and other agencies based on the concept of shared responsibility for community security

Weed and Seed a federal program that helps communities remove drug traffickers from their neighborhoods and offers incentives for communities to remain drug free

QUAD (Quick Uniform Attack on Drugs) a program that emphasizes quick response by enforcement officers to every community complaint, combined with neighborhood cleanup efforts

FIGURE 20.1

National Drug Control Spending by Function, FY 1985–1998

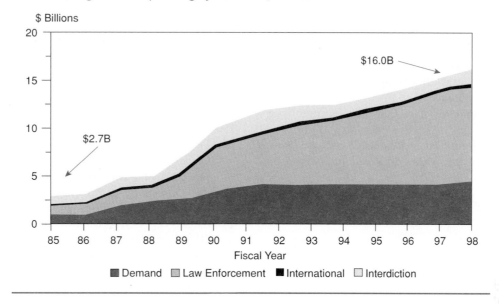

unnecessary health care, extra law enforcement, auto accidents, crime, and lost productivity. Clinton's plan encourages access to drug treatment, reduces the spread of infectious disease related to drug abuse, expands drug prevention in the workplace, and supports research on prevention and treatment of drug abusers.

4. *Shield America's air, land, and sea frontiers from the drug threat.* One of President Clinton's most important initiatives is to increase enforcement efforts on the southwest border, where the majority of cocaine and heroin enters the United States. Efforts to stop smuggling by commercial air, maritime, and land cargo routes have been increased.

5. *Break foreign and domestic drug sources of supply.* Since 1995, the national drug-control strategy has shifted the interdiction focus from drug transit areas to countries that are the primary sources of illegal drugs. Interdiction in source countries has successfully disrupted cocaine production. The 1998 budget includes funds for international narcotics control, as well as money to curb domestic sources.

Compared with other federally funded programs, the war on drugs is less expensive than farm support, NASA, food stamps, Medicare, and national defense. However, we do not know whether any amount of money spent on enforcement, without adequate support for education, treatment, and poverty reduction, can reduce the illicit drug supply and demand.

Some policy experts believe that the national drug policy has outlawed some drugs while encouraging the use of others.[35] For example, the government supports tobacco growers, even though tobacco contributes to

more than 400,000 deaths a year.[36] Alcohol marketing and lenient drunk and drugged driving laws have encouraged the use of alcohol, America's drug of choice. Is a war on drugs aimed at the substances that cause fewer than 5% of all drug-related deaths warranted and just?

SUMMARY

Law enforcement, the application of laws to prevent illicit drug use, is an important component of a comprehensive community-based prevention program. Countless federal, state, and local agencies help enforce drug laws. Clinton's 1997 National Drug Control Strategy includes plans to reduce demand for drugs, enforce drug-trafficking laws, and interdict drugs from across our borders. Community policing is a law-enforcement strategy that encourages citizens to become involved. Without strict law enforcement, treatment and education programs could not prevent many drug-related problems.

REVIEW QUESTIONS

1. Why is law enforcement to control drugs considered a secondary prevention measure? Give an example. How can it also be considered as tertiary prevention? Give an example.
2. What are the four primary goals of drug-control law enforcement?
3. How does law enforcement reduce the supply of illegal drugs? How does it reduce minors' access to legal, social drugs?

4. What is interdiction, as applied to the control of illegal drugs?
5. The distribution and sale of alcohol is regulated by which level of government—federal, state, or local? What was the National Minimum Drug Age Act of 1984?
6. What was the Synar Amendment? How is the Food and Drug Administration attempting to regulate tobacco products?
7. Identify the federal agencies that help enforce drug laws.
8. What makes community policing a unique law-enforcement strategy? What do Weed and Seed programs do?
9. What are the five main goals of President Clinton's National Drug Control Strategy?

REFERENCES

1. U.S. Department of Justice: *1995 Drug use forecasting annual report on adult and juvenile arrestees*, Washington, DC, 1996, U.S. Government Printing Office.
2. Bureau of Justice Statistics: *Drugs, crime and the justice system 1992*, Washington, DC, 1992, U.S. Government Printing Office.
3. B. R. McCaffrey, *Reducing drug use and its consequences in America*, Washington, DC, August 16, 1996, Office of National Drug Control Policy.
4. Controlling chemicals used to make illegal drugs: the chemical action task force and domestic chemical action group, National Institute of Justice: *Research in brief* 137862:1, 1993.
5. *Drugs and crime facts, 1994*, Rockville, MD, 1995, Bureau of Justice Statistics.
6. Ibid.
7. "DEA Shifts to 'Kingpin Strategy,'" *USA Today*, p 3A, May 10, 1993.
8. Office of National Drug Control Policy: *National drug control strategy-1997*, Washington, DC, 1997, U.S. Government Printing Office (NCJ163915).
9. McCaffrey, *Reducing Drug Use*.
10. Ibid.
11. Drug Enforcement Administration Intelligence Division, Intelligence Bulletin: *The 1995 Heroin Signature Program*, DEA-96042, August 1996, Washington DC.
12. "DEA 'Kingpin Strategy.'"
13. Bureau of Justice statistics, U.S. Department of Justice, *Sourcebook of Criminal Justice Statistics-1995, 1996*, U.S. Government Printing Office, Washington DC.
14. U.S. Department of Education: *Use and alcohol: selected reports to the Surgeon General*, Washington, DC, 1993, U.S. Government Printing Office.
15. Preventing alcohol abuse and related problems, *Alcohol Alert*, 34:3, October, 1996.
16. Dept. of Education, *Use and Alcohol*.
17. R. Hingson, T. Heeren, and M. Winter, Lower legal blood alcohol limits for young drivers, *Public Health Reports* 109(6):738-744, 1994.
18. Centers for Disease Control and Prevention: *State tobacco control highlights—1996, 1996*, Atlanta, GA, Office on Smoking and Health (CDC pub no 099-4895).
19. Ibid.
20. Department of Health and Human Services: Substance abuse prevention and treatment block grants: sale or distribution of tobacco products to individuals under 18 years of age: proposed rule, *Federal Register Part II* 45:96, August 26, 1993.
21. Saving our children from tobacco, *FDA Consumer*, 30(8):7–8, October, 1996.
22. Ibid.
23. U.S. Department of Justice, Drug Enforcement Administration (http://www.usdoj.gov/dea/agency/mission.htm)
24. Bureau of Justice Statistics: *National Update* 2(1):1, 1992.
25. J. R. Coldren, Implementing multijurisdictional drug control task forces: case studies in six jurisdictions. In National Institute of Justice & Bureau of Justice Assistance: *Second annual evaluating drug control initiatives: conference proceedings*, p 35, Washington, DC, 1991, Justice Research and Statistics Association.
26. *Drugs and Crime Facts.*
27. B. Webster and E. F. Connors, The police, drugs, and public housing, *Research in brief*, Washington, DC, 1992, National Institute of Justice.
28. Community policing in the 1990s, *National Institute of Justice Journal* 225:2, 1992.
29. Office of National Drug Control Policy, 1997.
30. D. M. Kennedy, Closing the market: controlling the drug trade in Tampa, Florida, National Institute of Justice Journal 139963:1, April, 1993.
31. Office of National Drug Control Policy, 1997.
32. Ibid.
33. Ibid.
34. Ibid.
35. M. A. Smith, The drug problem: is there an answer? *Federal Probation* 52(1):3.
36. CDCP, *State Tobacco Control.*

SOURCES FOR HELP

Bureau of Justice Statistics (BJS)
http://www.ojp.usdoj.gov/bjs/

Drug Enforcement Administration (DEA)
U.S. Department of Justice (DOJ)
1405 I St., NW
Washington, D.C. 20537
(202) 786–4096
http://www.usdoj.gov/dea/

International Committee on Alcohol, Drugs, and
    Traffic
National Safety Council
444 North Michigan Ave.
Chicago, IL 60611-3991
(312) 527–4800

Juvenile Justice Clearinghouse
Box 6000
Rockville, MD 20850
(301) 251–5307

National Crime Prevention Council
Substance Abuse Prevention Programs
733 15th St, NW, Room 540
Washington, D.C. 20005
(202) 393–7141

Office of National Drug Control Policy (ONDCP)
Drugs and Crime Clearinghouse
P.O. Box 6000
Rockville, MD 20849-6000
(800) 666–3332
askncjrs@aspensys.com
http://www.ncjrs.org

Partnerships Against Violence Network (PAVNET)
NCJRS
Box 6000
Rockville, MD 20849-6000
http://www.pavnet.org

RAND Drug Policy Research Center
1700 Main St.
P.O. Box 2138
Santa Monica, CA 90407-2138
(310) 451–7002
http://www.rand.org/centers/dprc/

Law Enforcement Listservs:

Criminal Justice Discussion List is a forum for a wide range of criminal justice issues. To join cjust-1, send the following message to <listserv@cunyvm.cuny.edu>:
    subscribe cjust-1 your name

Victim Assistance List is for the staff and volunteers of victim assistance programs. To subscribe, send the following message to <listserv@pdomain.uwindsor.ca>:
    subscribe victim-assistance your name

APPENDIX A
SCHEDULE OF CONTROLLED SUBSTANCES

SCHEDULE I

Guidelines

The drug or other substance has

- a high potential for abuse.
- no currently accepted medical use in treatment in the United States.
- a lack of accepted safety for use of the drug or other substance under medical supervision.

Examples

| Type of Drug | Name | Trade or Street Name | Dependence | | Tolerance |
			Physical	Psychological	
Narcotic	Heroin	Horse, Smack	High	High	Yes
Marijuana	Marijuana	Pot, Grass	Unknown	Moderate	Yes
Hallucinogen	LSD	Acid, Microdot	None	Unknown	Yes
Hallucinogenic Amphetamines	MDA, MDMA, DOM, DOB, others	Ecstacy, Adam	Possible	High	Yes

SCHEDULE II

Guidelines

The drug or other substance has

- a high potential for abuse.
- a currently accepted medical use in treatment in the United States or a currently accepted medical use with severe restrictions.
- a risk for severe psychological or physical dependence.

Examples

Type of Drug	Name	Trade Name	Dependence Physical	Psychological	Tolerance
Narcotic	Morphine	Morphine	High	High	Yes
Depressant	Pentobarbital	Nembutal	High	Moderate	Yes
Stimulant	Cocaine	Cocaine	Possible	High	Yes
Stimulant	Amphetamine	Dexedrine	High	High	Yes
Stimulant	Methylphenidate	Ritalin	Possible	High	Yes
Cannabis	Dronabinol	Marinol	Moderate	Moderate	Yes

SCHEDULE III

Guidelines

The drug or other substance has

- a potential for abuse less than the drugs or other substances in schedules I and II.
- a currently accepted medical use in treatment in the United States.
- a risk for moderate or low physical dependence or high psychological dependence.

Examples

Type of Drug	Name	Trade Name	Dependence Physical	Psychological	Tolerance
Narcotic	Codeine	Tylenol with Codeine	Moderate	Moderate	Yes
Stimulant	Phendimetrazine	Bontril	Moderate	Moderate	Yes
Anabolic drugs	Nadrolone	Durabolin	Unknown	Unknown	Unknown

SCHEDULE IV

Guidelines

The drug or other substance has

- a low potential for abuse relative to the drugs or other substances in schedule III.
- a currently accepted medical use in treatment in the United States.
- a risk for limited physical dependence or psychological dependence relative to the drugs or other substances in schedule III.

Examples

Type of Drug	Name	Trade Name	Dependence Physical	Psychological	Tolerance
Depressant	Barbiturate	Phenobarbital	High-Moderate	High-Moderate	Yes
Depressant	Diazepam	Valium	Moderate	Moderate	Yes
Stimulant	Pemoline	Cylert	Possible	Possible	Yes

SCHEDULE V

Guidelines

The drug or other substance has

- a low potential for abuse relative to the drugs or other substances in schedule IV.
- a currently accepted medical use in treatment in the United States.
- a more limited risk of producing physical dependence or psychological dependence relative to the drugs or other substances in schedule IV.

Examples

| Type of Drug | Name | Trade Name | Dependence | | Tolerance |
			Physical	Psychological	
Narcotic	Codeine	Tussar-2	Moderate	Moderate	Yes

Data from *Physicians' Desk Reference,* 51st ed. (Montvale, N.J.: Medical Economics Company, Inc., 1997); Indiana Board of Pharmacy, *Compilation of pharmacy and controlled substance statutes and regulations,* Indianapolis, 1997; Drug Enforcement Administration, Department of Justice, *Drugs of Abuse, 1996 Edition,* Washington, D.C., 1996.

APPENDIX B

THE STRUCTURE AND FUNCTION OF THE BRAIN

The divisions of the brain are the **cerebrum,** the **diencepahalon,** the **cerebellum,** and the **brain stem.** The functions of each of these divisions were briefly discussed in chapter 3. Additional information on the diencephalon and the brain stem is provided here for interested students.

The **thalamus** is an area of the diencephalon that lies just above the hypothalamus. Information coming to the brain through incoming sensory nerve fibers is directed to the correct sensory association areas in the cerebrum by the thalamus. The **hypothalamus** lies below the thalamus and serves as a connection point between the brain and the endocrine system through the pituitary gland which lies just below it. The hypothalamus has centers associated with eating, temperature control, sexual behavior, and fluid intake and balance. It controls homeostasis via the involuntary nervous system. There are also reward centers in the hypothalamus that contain norepinephrine secreting cells. Amphetamines and many other psychoactive drugs are believed to affect the hypothalamus.

Another structure is the **limbic system,** which itself is made up of several smaller structures. The limbic system helps integrate emotion, expression of emotion, learning, and memory. It interacts with both the hypo-

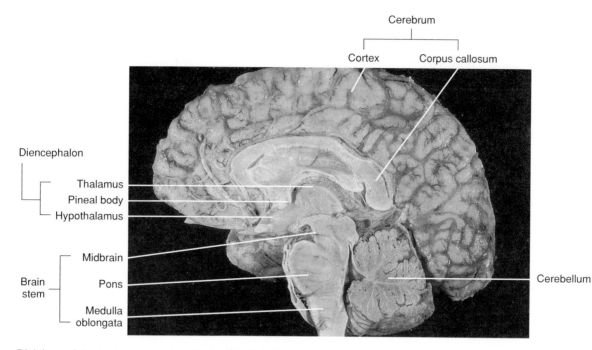

Divisions of the brain as seen in a midsagittal section.

Functions of Major Divisions of the Brain

Brain Area	Function
Brain Stem	
Medulla oblongata	Two-way conduction pathway between the spinal cord and higher brain centers; cardiac, respiratory, and vasomotor control center
Pons	Two-way conduction pathway between areas of the brain and other regions of the body; influences respiration
Midbrain	Two-way conduction pathway; relay for visual and auditory impulses
Diencephalon	
Hypothalamus	Regulation of body temperature, water balance, sleep-cycle control, appetite, and sexual arousal
Thalamus	Sensory relay station from various body areas to cerebral cortex; emotions and alerting or arousal mechanisms
Cerebellum	Muscle coordination; maintenance of equilibrium and posture
Cerebrum	Sensory perception, emotions, willed movements, consciousness, and memory

thalamus and the cerebrum. The limbic system is affected by tranquilizers, such as chlordiazepoxide (Librium) and diazepam (Valium) and by marijuana, which affects memory. Clearly, drugs that affect the diencephalon affect higher brain functioning, including reasoning, memory, and feelings. Interestingly, drugs that affect the diencephalon also influence critical survival controls of the brain, such as temperature, fluid balance, and metabolism.

The **brainstem,** which lies below the diencephalon and connects the rest of the brain with the spinal cord, has three parts: the midbrain, the pons, and the medulla oblongata. The **midbrain,** the uppermost part, is a passageway for information from the spinal cord to the diencephalon, cerebrum, and cerebellum. Contained in the midbrain are the substantia nigra, pigmented bodies that produce the neurotransmitter dopamine, essential for muscle movement. It is also the site of interpretation of hearing and vision, thus, the midbrain is particularly affected by drugs that produce visual or auditory hallucinations.

The **pons**—the word means bridge—lies between the midbrain and the medulla oblongata. It contains a network of fibers that connect higher brain regions with the medulla oblongata and spinal cord. The effects of drugs on the pons are unknown.

The **medulla oblongata** connects the brain with the spinal cord. Control over several basic physiological functions, such as respiration, heart rate, and sleeping and waking occurs in the medulla oblongata. Its central core is made up of a complex network of neurons that extend through the pons and midbrain and carry incoming information to the cerebrum. All psychoactive drugs are believed to affect the medulla in some way. Narcotics that depress respiration are believed to do so by acting on the medulla oblongata.

APPENDIX C

NEUROTRANSMITTERS: THEIR LOCATION, FUNCTIONS, AND EXAMPLES OF INTERACTING DRUGS

Transmitter	Location	Functions	Interacting Drugs
Acetylcholine	Brain and parasympathetic branch of the autonomic nervous system	Excitation/Inhibition of brain and autonomic nervous system; can affect memory	Nicotine
Norepinephrine	Brain and sympathetic branch of autonomic nervous system	Excitation or Inhibition; regulates sympathetic effectors; regulation of emotional response	Amphetamine
Dopamine	Brain; autonomic nervous system	Mostly inhibition; emotions, moods and motor control	Amphetamines
Serotonin	Brain and spinal cord	Mostly inhibition; affects moods and emotions; sleep	LSD, Antidepressants
Histamine	Brain, spinal cord peripheral nervous system	Mostly excitatory; affects thirst, body temperature, emotions	Antipsychotics
Glutamic acid	Brain, spinal sensory neurons	Excitation	Hallucinogens
GABA	Brain (cerebrum and cerebellum) and spinal cord	Inhibition	Sedative/hypnotics

Modified from G. A. Thibodeau, and K. T. Patton, *Anatomy and Physiology*. (St. Louis: Mosby-Year Book, Inc., 1996).

APPENDIX D
DOSE-RESPONSE FORMULAS

Dose-response formulas express relationships between the amount of drug administered and its observable effect. When a drug is administered to a specific population, individuals in that population respond differently.

Sensitive individuals show effects to very low doses, whereas more resistant individuals respond only to high doses. If the number of individuals who respond to each dose level is plotted on a graph, it is possible to determine

A simplified dose-response curve. As the dose increases, the percentage of the population responding increases.

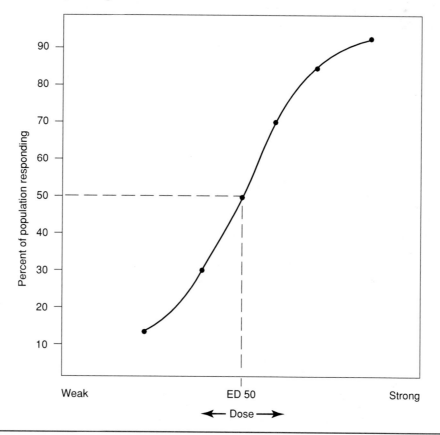

the dose that produces a response for one-half (50%) of the population. This is known as the median effective dose (ED50) for the population. The ED50 is the dose level above which drug effects can be observed in 50% of the test population. If the test substance is a pesticide, a toxic dose for 50% (TD50) or lethal dose for 50% (LD50) of the population might be of interest.

The safety of a particular drug can be calculated by the ratio of its LD50 to its ED50. The greater the ratio, the safer the drug. This index of drug safety, the therapeutic index (TI), is calculated using the formula, TI = LD50/ED50. To be even safer, scientists may use the following formula for the margin of safety of a substance: Margin of Safety = LD1/ED99. LD1 is the minimal dose needed to cause one death in a hundred test cases, and ED99 is the dose of drug that is therapeutically effective for 99% of the cases in a population.

C. D. Klaassen, and D. L. Eaton, "Principals of Toxicology," in Casserett and Doull's *Toxicology: The Basic Science of Poisons* (New York: McGraw-Hill, 1993).

APPENDIX E

TYPES OF INHIBITORY INTERACTIONS BETWEEN DRUGS

There are several types of inhibitory interactions, including functional, dispositional, and receptor-based interactions. Functional inhibition refers to the phenomenon in which two drugs have the opposite effect on some function of the body, such as blood pressure. Although barbiturates might lower blood pressure, amphetamines taken simultaneously might raise it. Dispositional inhibition means that the absorption, distribution, biotransformation, or excretion of the drug is altered so that a less active compound reaches the target organ, or the active compound is present there for a shorter time. Using syrup of ipecac, which induces vomiting, to remove an ingested drug before it is completely absorbed is an example of dispositional inhibition. Activated charcoal dispositionally inhibits the action of drugs by binding with them and preventing their absorption from the intestinal tract. Receptor inhibition occurs when two drugs that bind to the same receptor site produce a lower effect than either does alone. This can be represented mathematically by $3 + 4 = 5$ or $0 + 4 = 1$.

APPENDIX F

DURATION OF DETECTIBILITY OF DRUGS IN THE URINE

Detectibility of Drugs in the Urine

Substance	Duration of Detectibility*
Amphetamine	48 hrs
Methamphetamine	48 hrs
Barbiturates	
Short-acting	24 hrs
Intermediate-acting	48–72 hrs
Long-acting	7 days or more
Benzodiazepines (therapeutic dose)	3 days
Cocaine metabolites	2–3 days
Methadone	3 days
Codeine/morphine	48 hrs
Propoxyphene/norpropoxyphene	6–48 hrs
Cannabinoids (marijuana)	
Single use	3 days
Moderate use (four times/week)	4 days
Heavy use (daily)	10 days
Chronic heavy use	21–27 days
Methaqualone	7 days or more
Phencyclidine (PCP)	8 days

*These figures are approximate numbers of hours or days. Modified from *American Probation and Parole Association's Drug Testing Guidance and Practices for Adult Probation and Parole Agencies,* Pub. No. (NCJ) 129199, July 1991, Bureau of Justice Assistance.

APPENDIX G
COMMON OTC DRUG INTERACTIONS

The following lists interactions that have been reported in the literature between nonprescription (OTC) products and other OTC products and prescription (Rx) drugs. The information presented here can be useful to patients.

The information listed here does not include all reported interactions. For further information, refer to standard drug interaction textbooks and publications.

I. Acetaminophen (and acetaminophen-containing products) with:

1. Alcohol (and alcohol-containing products):
   Reports of severe liver damage in chronic alcoholics even with therapeutic doses of acetaminophen. Use of another analgesic is suggested.

2. Anticoagulants, oral (Coumadin, warfarin):
   Increase effect of an anticoagulant with chronic or high doses of acetaminophen. (Acetaminophen is a better choice than aspirin for analgesic therapy for patients on anticoagulants.)

3. Aspirin, salicylates (and aspirin-containing products):
   Long-term concomittant use of acetaminophen and salicylates may adversely effect the kidneys.

II. Aspirin, Salicylates (and aspirin-containing products) with:

1. Acetaminophen (and acetaminophen-containing products):
   Long-term simultaneous use of aspirin and acetaminophen may adversely effect the kidneys.

2. Alcohol (and alcohol-containing products):
   There is an increased risk of gastrointestinal bleeding and ulcerations in patients taking large amounts of aspirin and alcohol.

3. Anticoagulants, oral (Coumadin, Dicumarol, warfarin):

Aspirin will potentiate the effects of anticoagulants. This combination should be avoided. If an analgesic is needed, suggest acetaminophen.

4. Antidiabetic agents, oral (Diabinese, Orinase, Tolinase, Diabeta, Micronase, Glucotrol):
   Large doses of aspirin have been reported to enhance the effects of oral antidiabetic agents (sulfonylureas).

5. Corticosteroids (prednisone, methylprednisolone):
   a. Serum salicylate levels may be reduced during costicosteroid therapy. Patients on long-term corticosteroid therapy for asthma, arthritis, etc., should be aware of a decreased aspirin effect.
   b. Concomittant use of aspirin with an oral corticosteroid may increase the risk of gastrointestinal side effects, such as nausea, gas, or possible ulceration.

6. Nonsteroidal anti-inflammatory drugs, (ibuprofen, Naprosyn, Motrin, Anaprox, Tolectin, Nalfon, etc.):
   Simultaneous use of aspirin with a nonsteroidal may increase the risk of gastrointestinal side effects with no apparent additional benefit to the patient.

III. Nonsteroidal Anti-Inflammatory Drugs (NSAIDs) with:

1. Alcohol (and alcohol-containing products):
   There is an increased risk of gastrointestinal bleeding and ulcerations in patients taking NSAIDs and alcohol.

2. Anticoagulants, oral (Coumadin, warfarin, Dicumarol):
   A possible increase of the effects of an anticoagulant by NSAIDs.

3. Antidiabetic agents, oral, (Diabinese, Orinase, Tolinase, Diabeta, Micronase, Glucotrol):
   NSAIDs can enhance the effects of oral antidiabetic agents. Watch for signs of hypoglycemia.

4. Aspirin, salicylates (aspirin-containing products):
Simultaneous use may increase the risk of gastrointestinal side effects without apparent additional benefit.
5. Diuretics, loop-type (furosemide-Lasix, bumetanide-Bumex, etha crynic acid-Edecrin):
The literature has reported incidents of ibuprofen reducing the effects of certain diuretics, namely, the loop diuretics.
6. Corticosteroids (prednisone, methylprednisolone):
Simultaneous use of NSAIDs with an oral corticosteroid may increase the risk of gastrointestinal side effects, such as nausea, gas, or possible ulceration.

IV. Antihistamines (antihistamine-containing products) with:
1. Alcohol (alcohol-containing products):
This combination may cause increased sedation (drowsiness). Avoid driving or performing other tasks that require alertness.
2. Anticholinergic agents (Bentyl, Probanthine, Artane, Cogentin, Donnatal):
This combination may increase the incidence of dry mouth, urinary retention, blurred vision, rapid heartbeat, etc.
3. Antidepressants (Triavil, Elavil, Tofranil, Norpramin, Desyrel, etc.):
Simultaneous use may cause additive CNS depressant and/or anticholinergic effects. Watch for increased incidence of dry mouth, urinary retention, blurred vision, rapid heart beat. Avoid driving or performing other tasks requiring alertness.
4. CNS depressants (Valium, Ativan, Halcion, Restoril, Dalmane, also narcotics, antipsychotic drugs, etc.):
Patients may become extremely drowsy. Avoid this combination: a significant increase in the action of the antihistamine occurs.

V. Antacids with:
Generally, antacids should not be taken with oral medications because of the effects antacids have on the rate and extent of drug absorption. In some cases, it is beneficial that antacids be given directly with the drug product. If a patient must use an antacid and is on other medication, the patient should take the medication 1 to 2 hours before or after the antacid.

Drugs that Should Not Be Given Directly with Antacids
Anticoagulants (Coumadin, warfarin, Dicumarol)
Cation-exchange resins (Questran, Colestid)
Digoxin (Lanoxin)

Iron
Isoniazid (INH)
Phenothiazines (Mellaril, Thorazine, Stelazine, etc.)
Sodium Fluoride
Tetracyclines (Achromycin, Sumycin, Panmycin)

VI. Kaolin and Pectin Products (Kaopectate) with:
These products will reduce the absorption of certain drugs when given at the same time. If these products are needed and the patient is taking other medication, the patient should take the medication 1 to 2 hours before or after the Kaolin/pectin product.

Drugs That May Be Affected
Anticholinergic products: Donnatal, Bentyl, Pro-Banthine, Artane, Cogentin
Digoxin (Lanoxin)
Phenothiazines: Mellaril, Thorazine, Stelazine, etc.

VII. Mineral Oil with:
1. Anticoagulants, oral (Coumadin, warfarin, Dicumarol):
Patients taking mineral oil chronically with anticoagulants may either reduce or increase the effect of the anticoagulant when taken at the same time. If both are needed, space the products 2 hours apart.
2. Vitamins (fat-soluble-A,D,E; vitamin K):
Mineral oil may interfere with the absorption of the fat-soluble vitamins. If mineral oil must be used, take the vitamins several hours before or after mineral oil ingestion.

VIII. Phenylpropanolamine, Pseudoephedrine with:
1. Antihypertensive drugs (Procardia, Aldomet, Minipress, Vasotec):
Simultaneous use may decrease the effect of the antihypertensive agent. Blood pressure may increase.
2. Beta-Blockers (Inderal, Corgard, Lopressor, etc.)
Effect of the antihypertensive medication may be reduced. Blood pressure may increase.
3. CNS stimulants (amphetamines, Ritalin, Cylert):
Simultaneous use may increase CNS stimulation causing nervousness, insomnia, and agitation. Avoid this combination if possible.
4. Monocaine oxidase inhibitors (Parnate, Marplan, Nardil):
Simultaneous use may cause a sudden rise in blood pressure (hypertensive crisis) and adverse cardiac effects. This combination should be avoided.

Modified from *Drug Store News*, Lebhar-Friedman Inc., 1990.

DRUG INFORMATION ON THE WEB

The world wide web contains a wealth of information about drugs. If you have access to the Internet and web browser software, such as Netscape Navigator or Microsoft Internet Explorer, you can investigate many of the topics presented in this chapter.

CHAPTER 1 DRUGS AND DRUG USE IN AMERICA

Activity 1

Abuse of legal and illegal drugs has become a national problem that costs this country thousands of lives and billions of dollars each year. The Substance Abuse and Mental Health Services Administration (SAMHSA) of the United States Public Health Service has the stated missions of assuring that quality substance abuse and mental health services are available to the people who need them and that drug abuse prevention and treatment knowledge is used more effectively in the general health care system. Visit the SAMHSA web site at http:// www.samhsa.gov/ to find out more about current happenings. Scroll down to "more about SAMHSA" and click. Select "Weekly Report," and select three current topics for the week, and write a brief summary for each.

Activity 2

Data on the drug use patterns of American youth are available from a variety of sources. The National Survey Results on Drug Use from the Monitoring the Future is a nationwide survey of a sample of high school seniors. Since 1991, the project has also included nationwide samples of eighth and tenth grade students. In addition, annual follow-up surveys are mailed to a sample of each graduating class for a number of years after their initial participation. The study is conducted by the Institute for Social Research at the University of Michigan and is supported by research grants from the National Institute on Drug Abuse. Visit their web site at http:// www.isr.umich.edu/src/mtf/index.html to find out the latest trends in drug use among youth in the United States. Click on "Health Risks during Adolescence" and then scroll down to MTF Press Releases and Data Tables/Figures. Select two different drugs and briefly describe teenage use patterns.

Activity 3

Drug abuse permeates all aspects of our society, cutting across all age levels, occupations, and social settings. Visit the Schaffer Drug Policy Library at http:// 206.61.184.43/schaffer/index.htm to learn about the impact of drug abuse on our society. Select "Charts and Graphs of Drug War Statistics," choose three different topics, and write a one-paragraph report on the impact of drug abuse on our society.

CHAPTER 2 DETERMINANTS OF DRUG ABUSE AND ELEMENTS OF PREVENTION

Activity 1

The cost to society of alcohol, tobacco, and drugs was nearly $400 billion in 1993. Preventing substance abuse could substantially decrease many of the Nation's problems and counter a tremendous drain on our human and economic resources. The booklet, *Making Prevention*

Work, provides data and information to show that prevention is working and encourages all sectors of society to become involved in this exciting public health challenge. Visit the *Making Prevention Work* web site at http://www.health.org/pubs/mpw-book/mpw-book.htm, and click on "Risk Factors" and "Protective Factors," and write a one-page paper describing three factors that increase the risk of drug use and three factors that are considered protective in reducing drug use.

Activity 2

The National Center on Addiction and Substance Abuse at Columbia University (CASA) provides an interdisciplinary approach (health policy, medicine and nursing, communications, economics, sociology and anthropology, law and law enforcement, business, religion, and education) in studying all forms of substance abuse. CASA's mission is to inform the American people of the cost of abuse of all substances. Visit the CASA web site at http://www.casacolumbia.org/ and take the New National Substance Abuse I.Q. Quiz.

Activity 3

Teen Challenge World Wide Network is a nonprofit organization dedicated to educating teens and adults alike about the dangers of drug abuse. The Network also focuses on drug abuse prevention and provides a message of hope and a new way of life for those already trapped or affected by this terrible epidemic. Visit the Teen Challenge web site at http://www.teenchallenge.com/index.html, and select "web site objectives." Choose "signs" and a write a one-page paper on some of the common signs that teenagers may be using drugs.

CHAPTER 3
NEUROPHYSIOLOGY: HOW DRUGS AFFECT YOUR NERVOUS SYSTEM

Activity 1

The Center for Human Simulation (CHS) is located in the School of Medicine at the University of Colorado Health Sciences Center in Denver, Colorado. The CHS created the Visible Human Male and Female Data sets under contract with the National Library of Medicine, as part of the Visible Human Project. Visit their web site at http://www.uchsc.edu/sm/chs/ to review the general organization of the nervous system in anatomical detail. It is defined digitally in three dimensions, which brings about endless possibilities in visualization and simulations—Virtual Reality.

Activity 2

Understanding brain function requires the integration of information from the level of the gene to the level of behavior. At each of these many and diverse levels there has been an explosion of new scientific information. The "Human Brain Project" supports neuroinformatics research and development of cutting-edge computer-based tools and approaches to acquire, store, manipulate, analyze, integrate, synthesize, disseminate, and utilize information about the brain and behavior. Visit the Human Brain Project web site at http://WWW-hbp.scripps.edu/, and read more about the program under "General Information."

Activity 3

The Division of Neuroscience and Behavioral Science at the National Institute of Mental Health supports behavioral, biomedical, and neuroscience research and research training to develop and expand basic knowledge relevant to the understanding, treating, and preventing of mental illnesses. Visit their web site at http://www.nimh.nih.gov/about/dnbs/dnbs.htm for descriptions of branch programs and other topics listed, and select an area you would like to know more about. Write a brief summary of what you read.

CHAPTER 4 PHARMACOLOGY: HOW THE BODY PROCESSES DRUGS

Activity 1

Pharmacology is the study of the way drugs interact with the physiology of the body. To learn more about the terms and symbols used in Pharmacology, visit the web site of Department of Pharmacology and Experimental Therapeutics at the Boston University School of Medicine at http://med-amsa.bu.edu/pharmacology/Programmed/framedGlossary.html. Using the letters of the alphabet listed on the lower part of the page, select the first letter of several terms you would like to know more about and read the descriptions. Write a brief summary of what you found.

Activity 2

The National Institute for Drug Abuse (NIDA) is expanding its research on women to gain a better understanding of the impact of drug abuse and addiction on women's health. According to NIDA Director Dr. Alan I. Leshner, "Drug abuse may present significantly different challenges to women's health, may progress differently in women than in men, and may require different treatment approaches." Visit the NIDA web site at http://165.112.78.61/NIDA_Notes/NNVol10N1/WomenAdd.html to learn more about gender differences in drug addiction.

Activity 3

Drug testing technology has evolved rapidly in the past two decades and so have workplace policies to test workers. An example is the Omnibus Transportation Employee Testing Act of 1991, which requires alcohol and drug testing of safety-sensitive employees in the aviation, motor carrier, railroad, and mass transit industries. To read more about this Act visit the Indiana Prevention Resource Center at http://www.drugs.indiana.edu/druginfo/dotrules.html. Select from the topics listed on the act. Write a brief summary of why you think this Act is important.

CHAPTER 5 THE STIMULANTS: COCAINE, THE AMPHETAMINES, AND THE CATHINOIDS

Activity 1

Chronic cocaine abuse results in tolerance. More and more cocaine is needed with each successive use to achieve the same level of euphoria achieved by a previous dose. Visit the Cocaine Anonymous web site at http://www.ca.org/, and select and complete the "self-test for cocaine addiction."

Activity 2

Cocaine Anonymous is an organization concerned solely with the personal recovery and continued sobriety of individual drug addicts who turn to the CA Fellowship for help. They do not engage in the fields of drug addiction research, medical or psychiatric treatment, drug education, or propaganda in any form. Membership in CA is open to any individual who desires to stop using cocaine. Visit the Cocaine Anonymous web site at http://www.ca.org/, select "Membership Survey," and write a brief summary on the demographic characteristics of this organizations membership.

Activity 3

The Addiction Research Foundation (ARF) provides detailed information on amphetamines, including their short-and long-term effects, withdrawal symptoms, and potential for abuse. Visit the ARF web site at http://www.arf.org/isd/pim/list.html to obtain public information on amphetamines. Select "Facts about Amphetamines" to learn more about them. Write a brief summary of what you learned.

CHAPTER 6 DEPRESSANTS

Activity 1

Barbiturates are among the most familiar of the depressant drugs and continue to play an important role in modern medical care. However, because of their potential for misuse and abuse barbiturates are among the most dangerous of all prescription medications. Visit the U.S. Drug Enforcement Administration web site at http://www.usdoj.gov/dea/pubs/abuse/contents.htm to learn more about barbiturates. Select "Depressants" and then select "Barbiturates," and write a brief summary of what you read.

Activity 2

Taking methaqualone, or "luding out," while drinking wine, was a popular college pastime a few years ago. Excessive use leads to tolerance, dependence, and withdrawal symptoms similar to those of barbiturates. Visit the U.S. Drug Enforcement Administration web site at http://www.usdoj.gov/dea/pubs/abuse/contents.htm to learn more about Methaqualone and Glutethimide. Select "Depressants" and then select "Methaqualone," and write a brief summary of what you read.

Activity 3

Benzodiazepines are used therapeutically to produce sedation, induce sleep, relieve anxiety and muscle spasms, and to prevent seizures. Of the drugs marketed in the United States that affect CNS function, benzodiazepines are among the most widely prescribed medications and, unfortunately, are frequently abused. Visit the U.S. Drug Enforcement Administration web site at http://www.usdoj.gov/dea/pubs/abuse/contents.htm to learn more about benzodiazepines. Select "Depressants" and then select "benzodiazepines," and write a brief summary of what you read.

CHAPTER 7 NARCOTICS

Activity 1

Opiates have a long and interesting history that spans thousands of years. Those who become dependent on opiates expose themselves to many health risks, including death from overdose. The Addiction Research Foundation (ARF) is one of the preeminent institutions for research into alcohol, tobacco, and other drug problems in North America. Visit the ARF web site at http://www.arf.org/isd/pim/opiates.html to find out more about opiates and dependency. Scroll down to "Tolerance and Dependence," and write a brief two-paragraph summary of the effects of opiate abuse and dependence.

Activity 2

The National Institute of Neurological Disorders and Stroke (NINDS) is conducting research on chronic pain. Visit the NINDS web site at http://www.nih.gov/health/chip/ninds/cronpain/. Scroll down to the table of contents, select "The brain's own opiates," and read the information. Briefly explain how endogenous substances such as enkephalins reduce pain.

Activity 3

Narcotics Anonymous (NA) is an international, community-based association of recovering drug addicts. Started in 1947, the NA movement is one of the world's oldest and largest of its type, with nearly 20,000 weekly meetings in seventy countries. Visit the NA web site at http://www.wsoinc.com/ and click on "Basic info about NA." Write a one-page report on NA's program and organization.

CHAPTER 8   MARIJUANA

Activity 1

The question of physiological dependence regarding *Cannabis* use is uncertain. The cessation of *Cannabis* use in humans gives rise to a desire to resume use. Visit the Marijuana Anonymous web site at http://www.marijuana-anonymous.org/index.shtml, and scroll down to "Am I An Addict?", and answer the questions.

Activity 2

While a number of approved medical uses of the prescription form of THC, Marinol, now exist, the medical use of crude preparations of *Cannabis sativa* remains highly controversial. Visit the Marijuana as Medicine web site at http://www.calyx.net/olsen/MEDICAL/medical.html, select "Medical Journals and Other Publications," and write a one-page summary of reports of various studies cited. What do think about the use of marijuana for medical purposes?

Activity 3

The National Institute on Drug Abuse (NIDA) was established in 1974, and in October 1992, it became part of the National Institutes of Health, Department of Health and Human Services. The Institute is organized into divisions and offices, each of which plays an important role in drug abuse research. Visit the National Drug Institute web site at http://www.nida.nih.gov/MarijBroch/MarijIntro.html to find out more information on facts about marijuana. Select "Marijuana: Facts for Teens," and write a brief summary about what you learned.

CHAPTER 9   HALLUCINOGENS

Activity 1

Recent data indicate an increase in the use of LSD (and related hallucinogens) in recent years. This information was included in a lecture given by Laura F. McNicolas, M.D., Ph.D. to the medical students of the University of Pennsylvania. Visit the following web site at http://www.med.upenn.edu/recovery/ to read the electronic version of this presentation. Write a brief summary about what you learned.

Activity 2

The hallucinogens comprise a broad group of natural and synthetic psychoactive substances that produce hallucinations. One form that is on the rise is Ketamine. Ketamine, a veterinary anesthetic, is a legitimately manufactured product that is being diverted from its intended use and abused with increasing frequency. On the street, the drug is often called "K" or "Special K." It produces effects similar to those produced by phencyclidine (PCP), and the visual effects of LSD. Visit the following web site (http://www.usdoj.gov/dea/programs/diverson/divpub/substanc/ketamine.htm) to learn more about Ketamine. Why do drug users prefer "Special K" over PCP or LSD?

Activity 3

Lysergic Acid Diethylamide (LSD) is the most potent mind-altering drug known. This hallucinogen is one of the most potent mood-changing chemicals. LSD is classified under schedule I of the Controlled Substances Act, a classification that includes drugs with no medical use and/or high potential for abuse. Visit the following web site (http://www.nida.nih.gov/NIDACapsules/NCLSD.html) to find out more about the effects and the current use patterns of LSD. Write a one-page report about what you learned.

CHAPTER 10   OVER-THE-COUNTER DRUGS (NONPRESCRIPTION DRUGS)

Activity 1

The Center for Drug Evaluation and Research (CDER) in the U.S. Food and Drug Administration (FDA) is the largest of FDA's five centers, with a staff of about 1,800. It has responsibility for both over-the-counter and prescription drugs. Other centers have responsibility for medical and radiological devices, foods, cosmetics, biologics, and veterinary drugs. The center's job is to ensure that drugs are safe and effective. Visit the CDER web site at http://www.fda.gov/cder/. Select "Drug Info," scroll down to "over-the-counter drug page: information for consumers and industry about non-prescription drugs," and check this area for updates, changes, and announcements. Select an area that interests you, and write a brief summary of what you learned.

Activity 2

Aspirin is one of the most widely used OTC drugs, but it still may not be used widely enough. Visit the Medicine Sciences Bulletin section pertaining to analgesic and anesthetic drug reviews at the PharmInfoNet web site at http://pharminfo.com/pubs/msb/msbana.html. Select "America's 80 Billion-aspirin Habit," and read more about aspirin. What do you think about using aspirin to protect against certain diseases and illnesses?

Activity 3

The Food and Drug Administration (FDA) sets health and safety standards for all foods, drugs, and cosmetics. Since 1981, in an attempt to remove all ineffective and unsafe Over-the-Counter (OTC) formulations from the marketplace, the FDA has undertaken an evaluation of the 85 treatment categories into which they classify OTC products. To read some of the most recent press releases on nonprescription drugs, visit the FDA web site at http://www.fda.gov/fdahomepage.html, select "Search," type in "nonprescription drugs," and then click on the submit button. Click on any press release regarding non-prescription drugs. After reading it, write a brief summary of what you found most interesting.

CHAPTER 11 PRESCRIPTION DRUGS

Activity 1

We are fortunate to live in an age where prescription medicines are readily available to cure and treat a wide variety of illnesses, diseases, and conditions. Every day, millions of Americans rely on these medicines to live longer, healthier, more productive lives. However, studies show that up to 50% of prescriptions are not taken properly, so people aren't getting the full therapeutic benefit of these drugs. To learn more about how to achieve the full value of prescription medicine, visit the America's Pharmaceutical Companies web site at http://www.phrma.org/ and select "Getting the most from medicines." Write a brief summary of what you learned from this activity.

Activity 2

For many years, scientists have known that high cholesterol levels in the blood contribute significantly to atherosclerosis. By following a diet plan, many people can lower their cholesterol levels. However, some people will not respond at all to dietary changes and may need to take cholesterol-lowing medications. Visit the PharmInfo home page at http://pharminfo.com/disease/cardio/chol_iq.html to test your knowledge about high blood cholesterol using the questions on this page. For each question, click on the circle to the left of the answer that you think is correct (TRUE or FALSE). You will get a report that tells you how well you did and shows you the correct answers. How well did you do?

Activity 3

Although most people will never need more than perhaps a dozen different prescription drugs during their lifetime, more than 2,500 different medications are listed in each annual edition of the *Physicians' Desk Reference for Prescription Drugs* (PDR). At any point in time, only about 200 medications make up the bulk of the 2,140,799 new and refilled prescriptions ordered by practitioners. Visit the RxList web site at http://www.rxlist.com/ and select the "Top 200" prescriptions used in the United States last year. Write a brief summary of five of the most commonly prescribed drugs. Indicate the conditions for which they are prescribed and what the drug does.

CHAPTER 12 NICOTINE

Activity 1

Tobacco use remains the leading preventable cause of death in the United States, causing more than 400,000 deaths each year. Tobacco use also generates more than $50 billion in direct medical costs annually. Visit the Centers for Disease Control and Prevention Tobacco web site at http://www.cdc.gov/tobacco/ to learn more about this major public health problem. Select the Surgeon General's reports, and write a brief summary of one of these reports.

Activity 2

Quitting smoking is not a simple task. In fact, very few people succeed on their first try. If you are looking for help in making it through the quitting process, the following web site (http://192.12.191.51/QuitTools/index.html) offers several suggestions to make it easier. Remember, these tools and techniques can't make quitting painless, but they do increase the likelihood of success. Write a summary describing the various methods discussed.

Activity 3

Action on Smoking and Health (ASH) is a national, non-profit, legal action and educational organization fighting for the rights of nonsmokers against the many problems resulting from smoking. ASH attorneys represent non-smokers in courts and before legislative bodies and regulatory agencies. Visit their web site at http://ash.org/. Select "About ASH," and review their 30 years of progress. What do you think were some of their greatest accomplishments to reduce cigarette smoking in the United States?

CHAPTER 13 THE METHYLXANTHINES AND RELATED COMPOUNDS

Activity 1

Caffeine can be found in coffee, tea, cocoa, many soft drinks, and in certain OTC drugs. The tendency of Americans toward liberal consumption of coffee and soft drinks and their willingness to use OTC drugs means that many Americans consume significant amounts of caffeine each day. Have you wondered whether excess caffeine is adversely affecting your health? Can caffeine affect fertility? Is moderate caffeine consumption harmful during pregnancy? The Virtual Health Store provides answers to these questions and many more. Visit their web site at http://www.vhs.com/caffeine.html to learn more. Select an area of concern to you and study the information provided. Do you plan to alter your caffeine intake in any way as a result of this new knowledge?

Activity 2

Chronic heavy coffee and caffeinated cola drinkers can experience difficulty breaking the caffeine habit. Visit the abuse organizations web site at http://net-abuse.org/~lizardo/caffeine.html to learn more about breaking the caffeine habit. Scroll down the page to "Tips for Breaking the Caffeine Habit" and read. What recommendation did you find the most beneficial and why?

Activity 3

Caffeine and other methylxanthines are ingested in water-soluble form and are absorbed into the bloodstream primarily through the small intestine. The amount of caffeine in various drinks can be found at a University of Pennsylvania web site, http://www.seas.upenn.edu/~cpage/caffeine/FAQmain.html. Select "How much caffeine is there in drink/food/pill?" According to the list provided, what are some of the items that contain the highest levels of caffeine?

CHAPTER 14 ANABOLIC DRUGS

Activity 1

According to the National Institute on Drug Abuse, the nonmedical use of anabolic/androgenic steroids among adolescents and young adults continues to be a serious concern. As many as half a million Americans under age 18 may be abusing these drugs to improve athletic performance, appearance and self-image. However, a growing body of evidence suggests that steroid abuse poses severe risks to physical and psychological health. You can read more about why people use anabolic drugs at the NIDA web site at http://www.nida.nih.gov/Research Reports/Steroids/AnabolicSteroids.html. Scroll down to "The Price of Perfection," and read the information contained in this file. Write a brief summary of about what you read.

Activity 2

Anabolic/androgenic steroids are frequently abused by athletes. Visit the medical students' web site at http://www.medstudents.com.br/sport/sport2.htm to learn more about why athletes use steroids and some of the serious side effects. Write a one-page summary of what you learned from this debate.

Activity 3

Gateway drugs are drugs that serve as the "gate" or path to the use of illicit drugs, such as crack cocaine and heroin. The use of gateway drugs, such as nicotine, alcohol, and marijuana seems to increase the likelihood of the adoption of the drug-using lifestyle. Gateway drugs, or drugs-of-entry, initiate a novice user into the drug-using world.

Recently, the use of anabolic steroids by some students has been shown to produce the gateway drug effect. Visit the Indiana Prevention Resource Centers web site at http://www.drugs.indiana.edu/publications/iprc/factline/gateway.html to read more about gateway drugs. Write a brief summary of what you learned about gateway drugs, and explain how you think about anabolic steroids being considered a gateway drug.

CHAPTER 15 INHALANTS

Activity 1

The National Inhalant Prevention Coalition (NIPC) is funded in part by the Robert Wood Johnson Foundation. The remainder of funding comes from support from individuals and organizations who use NIPC resources. Visit the NIPC web site at http://www.inhalants.org/, select "index," and then scroll down to "What Can You do if Someone You Know is Huffing?" Understanding what to do when someone is abusing inhalants may assist you in saving their life. Write a brief summary of what you found.

Activity 2

Inhalants come in many different shapes and sizes, colors, odors, and names. Because of their accessability, inhalants are very popular with elementary and middle school children. According to a 1993 University of Michigan study for the National Institute on Drug Abuse, one in five eighth graders has used inhalants. This makes inhalants, as a group, the third most abused substance in the United States. Visit the Wisconsin Clearinghouse for Prevention Strategies at http://www.uhs.wisc.edu/wch/paper2.htm to read more about how to reduce inhalant use and abuse. List some of the strategies mentioned.

Activity 3

The National Clearinghouse for Alcohol and Drug Information has a listing of materials and programs on inhalants that have been reviewed for accuracy by the Center for Substance Abuse Prevention of the Public Health Service. Visit their web site at http://www.health.org/pubs/resguide/inhalan.htm to review these materials. Write a brief summary describing the materials you would select if you were responsible for educating today's youth.

CHAPTER 16 ALCOHOL: HISTORY, PHYSIOLOGY, AND PHARMACOLOGY

Activity 1

Blood-alcohol concentration (BAC) can be defined as the ratio of alcohol to total blood volume. In 1937, Dr. Glenn C. Forrester discovered and patented a process for capturing alcohol from a breath sample. The result was the development of a portable, roadside instrument used to collect evidence in suspected drunk driving cases. Breath sampling was an innovative technique for blood alcohol determination at that time. The world's leading manufacturer of alcohol breath testing instruments, Intoximeters, Inc., has a web site (http://www.intox.com/) where you can instantly measure your BAC. Select "Drink Wheel" and complete the form listed. Upon completion, they will instantly compute your estimated BAC based on the information you have provided and return that estimate to you. It is presented as a public service to Intoximeters web site visitors. Its primary purpose is to provide useful information about the responsible use of alcohol.

Activity 2

Alcohol is a very strong CNS depressant. When consumed in large quantities, alcohol eventually shuts down brain functioning, respiration, and circulation resulting in coma and perhaps death. Visit the Intoximeters, Inc. web site at http://www.intox.com/Drink_Wheel.html to read a more detailed discussion of the pharmacology and the stages of intoxication. Scroll down the page and click on "Pharmacology and Disposition of alcohol in humans." Write a brief summary of the information you read.

Activity 3

Alcoholic beverages cannot be considered a valuable source of nutrition because they are high in empty calories. During the oxidation process, alcohol yields about 7 calories per gram, nearly as many calories per gram as fats. These extra, empty calories can lead to obesity. Visit the following web site (http://realbeer.com/brewery/library/AlClbinger.html) to find the "Alcohol and Calorie Content of over 200 Popular Beers." Write a brief summary regarding what you read.

CHAPTER 17 ALCOHOL: SOCIAL, ECONOMIC, AND LEGAL ISSUES

Activity 1

Research has suggested that moderate drinking may be beneficial because it provides certain psychological benefits and may lower your risk of coronary artery disease. Moderate drinking is difficult to define because it means different things to different people. The National Council on Alcoholism and Drug Dependence provides recommendations concerning drinking from the U.S. Dietary Guidelines and the Surgeon General. Visit their web site at http://www.ncadd.org/, scroll down to "Health Information," and click. Then, select "Dietary Guidelines for Americans." Write a brief summary on how moderate drinking is defined for people who choose to drink alcohol and what types of people should not drink alcohol at all.

Activity 2

As you have read in this chapter, the misuse and abuse of alcohol are related to a variety of social problems that affect both the drinker and his or her family. Visit the National Council on Alcoholism and Drug Dependence web site at http://www.ncadd.org/factsdir.html to read more about alcohol's impact on our society. Select one of topics listed, and write a brief summary about the facts related to that topic.

Activity 3

Some persons who seek recovery from alcohol addiction involve themselves with 12-step programs. Twelve-step programs are best represented by Alcoholics Anonymous (AA). Visit the AA web site at http://www.alcoholics-anonymous.org/enghp.html and select "Is A.A. for You?" Answer the 12 questions listed.

CHAPTER 18 DRUG ABUSE PREVENTION: EDUCATION AND TREATMENT

Activity 1

Alateen is a support group for young people whose lives have been affected by someone else's drinking. Visit their web site at http://www.al-anon.org/, scroll down to "Alateen: young people helping young people," and click. Answer the 20 questions listed to decide whether Alateen is for you.

Activity 2

The National Association for Children of Alcoholics (NACoA) is the only national nonprofit membership organization working on behalf of children of alcoholics. Their mission is to advocate for all children and families affected by alcoholism and other drug dependencies. Visit their web site at http://www.health.org/nacoa/, click on "Just for KIDS," and then click on "Kit for Kids." Scroll down to and read "What can kids do?" Write a brief summary regarding some of the recommended "do's and don'ts."

Activity 3

It is important to understand that Alcoholism affects the entire family. The Al-Anon program can help resolve problems if you lived with the disease as a child. Visit their web site at http://www.al-anon.org/probquiz.html, and answer the 20 questions regarding "Did you grow up with a problem drinker?"

CHAPTER 19 DRUGS AND PUBLIC POLICY

Activity 1

In this chapter, you learned about the federal government's blueprint for healthy public policies Healthy People 2000 and its goals for reducing alcohol, tobacco, and other drug use. Visit the Healthy People 2000 web site at http://158.72.20.10/pubs/hp2000/, select "Progress Re-

views," and scroll down to the priority area "Substance Abuse: Alcohol and Other Drugs." After reading this information, write a summary pertaining to the successes in this area.

Activity 2

In this chapter, you read about how the Partnership for a Drug-Free America is a nonprofit coalition of professionals from the communications industry whose mission is to reduce the demand for illegal drugs through media communication. Visit their web site at http://www.drugfreeamerica.org/, select "Frequently asked questions: on drug-related topics," and read about the Partnership's position on issues related to drug legislation. Then, write a response on why you agree or disagree with their stand.

Activity 3

Join Together is a national resource center and meeting place for communities working to reduce substance abuse and gun violence. Visit their web site at http://www.jointogether.org/, and select "Public Policy." Select from one of the categories listed to learn more about a specific area related to public policy. Share what you have learned by writing a brief, one-page summary.

CHAPTER 20 LAW ENFORCEMENT

Activity 1

The Office of National Drug Control Policy (ONDCP) was established by Act of Congress in 1988 and is organized within the Executive Office of the President. ONDCP is authorized to develop and coordinate the policies, goals, and objectives of the Nation's drug control program for reducing the use of illicit drugs. Visit the ONDCP web site at http://www2.whitehouse.gov/WH/EOP/ondcp/html/ondcp.html, and write a brief summary on ONDCP's four priority areas for drug control.

Activity 2

The stated mission of the Drug Enforcement Administration (DEA) is to enforce the controlled substances laws and regulations of the United States and to bring to the criminal and civil justice system of the United States or any other competent jurisdiction, those organizations, and principal members of organizations, involved in the growing, manufacture, or distribution of controlled substances appearing in the United States. The DEA has a long and proud history. Visit their web site at http://www.usdoj.gov/dea/, select "The Agency" icon, and then select "History." Read about their history, and write a one-page report about the DEA.

Activity 3

FDA proposes to regulate cigarettes and smokeless tobacco as nicotine-delivery devices, pursuant to the Agency's statutory authority under the Federal Food, Drug, and Cosmetic Act. State and local requirements pertaining to cigarettes and smokeless tobacco may be preempted under Section 521(a) of the FDC Act. The FDA's web site on children and tobacco at http://www.fda.gov/opacom/campaigns/tobacco/tobpreempt.html offers a wealth of information about preemption of State and Local requirements. Scroll down and click on "FAQs: Frequently Asked Questions About Preemption and FDA's Final Rule on Tobacco." Write a one-page summary of what you learned.

EXAM PREP GUIDE

CHAPTER 1 DRUGS AND DRUG USE IN AMERICA

Multiple Choice

1. An example of a psychoactive drug is:
   A. Nicotine
   B. LSD
   C. Alcohol
   D. All of the above

2. The term used to describe the taking of prescription or nonprescription medication in an inappropriate way is:
   A. Drug abuse
   B. Drug misuse
   C. Drug use
   D. Drug dependence

3. Prohibition took place in the decade of the:
   A. 1910s
   B. 1920s
   C. 1930s
   D. 1940s

4. A classification system for potentially dangerous drugs was established by the:
   A. Comprehensive Drug Abuse Control Act of 1970
   B. Substance Abuse Prevention Act
   C. National Drug Control Strategy
   D. National Institute on Drug Abuse

5. Drugs with no approved medical use and a high potential for abuse, such as heroin, are classified as:
   A. schedule I drugs
   B. schedule II drugs
   C. schedule III drugs
   D. schedule IV drugs

6. Drugs with an approved medical use but high potential for abuse, such as morphine, are classified as:
   A. schedule I drugs
   B. schedule II drugs
   C. schedule III drugs
   D. schedule IV drugs

7. An example of a legal drug is:
   A. Caffeine
   B. Nicotine
   C. Alcohol
   D. All of the above

8. The agency that evaluates the safety and effectiveness of OTC drugs is the:
   A. Substance Abuse and Mental Health Services Administration
   B. Health and Human Services Administration
   C. Food and Drug Administration
   D. Federal Trade Commission

9. Cigarette smoking causes how many deaths in the United States each year?
   A. 400,000
   B. 80,000
   C. 2.2 million
   D. 160,000

10. Use of an illegal drug within the past month by all age groups in the United States is:
    A. Up
    B. Steady
    C. Down
    D. Unknown

11. The drug most commonly used by school-age children in the United States is:
    A. Marijuana
    B. Alcohol
    C. Amphetamines
    D. Nicotine

12. What percentage of college students have reported binge drinking at least once in the previous 2 weeks?
    A. 22%
    B. 40%
    C. 65%
    D. 80%

13. The drug most commonly used by college students in the United States is:
    A. Marijuana
    B. Alcohol
    C. Amphetamines
    D. Nicotine

Critical Thinking

1. What are some of the costs of drug misuse and abuse in the United States?

2. Define the terms *drug use, misuse,* and *abuse,* and give an example of each.

3. Have you seen the effects of drug misuse and abuse in a friend or family member? How did drugs affect this person's life?

4. What are the current trends in drug abuse among school-age children in the United States? Among college students?

5. What is your opinion of the classification system used for narcotics and other drugs in the United States? Would you make any changes to the classifications for any individual drugs?

Chapter 2 Determinants of Drug Abuse and Elements of Prevention

Multiple Choice

1. Individual attributes, situations, and environmental contexts that reduce the probability of drug use are called:
   A. Risk factors
   B. Genetic predisposition
   C. Protective factors
   D. Unmet developmental needs

2. The neurotransmitter associated with the brain's reward system is called:
   A. Dopamine
   B. Phenylalanine
   C. Acetylcholine
   D. Methadone

3. An easily obtainable legal or illegal drug that serves as the drug user's first experience with a mind-altering drug is called a(n):
   A. Gateway drug
   B. Enabling drug
   C. Hallucinogen
   D. Stimulant

4. Treatment and rehabilitation of people with serious or chronic drug problems is called:
   A. Primary prevention
   B. Secondary prevention
   C. Tertiary prevention
   D. None of the above

5. Studies have shown that people with addictive and compulsive disorders have a common chemical imbalance called:
   A. Obsessive-compulsive disorder
   B. Reward deficiency syndrome
   C. Tourette's syndrome
   D. Attention deficit disorder

6. The adaptive model of drug dependence suggests that drug dependence
   A. is a primary disease over which an individual has no control
   B. results primarily from inherited genetic factors
   C. results from an effort to deal with environmental stressors
   D. results from a desire to adopt the behavior of a role model

7. The process of personal growth through adulthood is supported by mastering developmental tasks, including all of the following except:
   A. Attracting followers
   B. Living independently
   C. Pursuing intimacy
   D. Developing social skills

8. Using a negative image of drug-taking to influence people not to take drugs is called:
   A. Modeling
   B. Negative advertising
   C. Resistance
   D. Reverse modeling

9. A form of drug experimentation that occurs when one is suffering from an illness is described as:
   A. Over-the-counter medication
   B. Self-care
   C. Modeling
   D. Overmedication

10. All of the following are essential elements of drug prevention except:
    A. Treatment
    B. Education
    C. Law enforcement
    D. Judicial review

11. One's vulnerability to drug use may be influenced by one's:
    A. Personality type
    B. Temperament
    C. Attitudes toward drugs
    D. All of the above

12. The well-known support group Alcoholics Anonymous subscribes to the:
    A. Rational model of drug dependence
    B. Adaptive model of drug dependence
    C. Genetic model of drug dependence
    D. Disease model of drug dependence

13. Children who are at greatest risk of drug abuse are those:
    A. In families in which both parents work.
    B. In families with clearly defined roles for adults and children.
    C. Whose parents exhibit antisocial behavior or criminality.
    D. All of the above.

14. Research on peer groups has found that:
    A. Peer group drug-taking behavior has no measurable effect on individual behavior
    B. Peer group drug-taking behavior discourages drug-taking by the individual
    C. Peer group drug-taking behavior encourages drug-taking by the individual
    D. The effects of peer group drug-taking behavior cannot be measured

15. One factor that may put people at risk for developing a drug-dependence problem is a
    A. Trend toward greater responsibility for maintaining one's health
    B. Movement toward alternative forms of health care
    C. Greater societal emphasis on physical fitness
    D. Reliance on technological advances to eliminate pain and suffering

Critical Thinking

1. Explain how a child's home and family life can affect his or her risk for drug abuse.

2. Describe the influence of peer groups on an individual's drug-taking behavior.

3. Describe how the trend toward self-care and an overreliance on medical technology can increase the potential for drug abuse.

4. What are some of the ways that you feel society encourages you to use drugs?

5. Describe some of the ways young people can develop resistance to drug abuse.

CHAPTER 3   NEUROPHYSIOLOGY: HOW DRUGS AFFECT THE NERVOUS SYSTEM

Multiple Choice

1. The tendency of the body's physiological system to maintain internal stability is called:
   A. Metabolism
   B. Homeostasis
   C. Equilibrium
   D. Wellness

   B

2. The spinal cord is part of the:
   A. Central nervous system
   B. Cardiorespiratory system
   C. Peripheral nervous system
   D. Gastrointestinal system

   A

3. One of the four major parts of the brain, sometimes called the upper brain, is the:
   A. Cerebellum
   B. Diencephalon
   C. Cerebrum
   D. Brainstem

   A

4. The portion of the brain that coordinates movement with spatial judgment is the:
   A. Thalamus
   B. Limbic system
   C. Cerebellum
   D. Brainstem

    D

5. The part of the peripheral nervous system that allows intentional movement is known as the:
   A. Autonomic nervous system
   B. Involuntary nervous system
   C. Reflex arc
   D. Voluntary nervous system

   D

6. The portion of the involuntary nervous system that helps the body return from an excited state to a resting state is the:
   A. Parasympathetic branch
   B. Sympathetic branch
   C. Ganglia
   D. Fight-or-flight center

7. The portions of a nerve cell designed to receive chemical messages from adjacent nerve cells are the:
   A. Axons
   B. Neurons
   C. Cell bodies
   D. Dendrites

8. The junctions between axons and dendrites are called the:
   A. Motor neurons
   B. Synapses
   C. Glia
   D. Electrical impulses

9. The chemicals contained within synaptic vesicles in nerve cell endings are:
   A. ATPs
   B. Soma
   C. Neurotransmitters
   D. Hormones

10. Psychoactive drugs affect the nervous system primarily through changes at the:
    A. Axon
    B. Dendrite
    C. Neurotransmitter
    D. Synapse

11. The synaptic function that can generate an action potential is called:
    A. Depolarization
    B. Polarization
    C. Hyperpolarization
    D. Inhibition

12. After the neurotransmitter has achieved its purpose, it can be removed from the synapse by:
    A. Active transport back into the axon
    B. Enzymatic breakdown
    C. Diffusion into surrounding areas
    D. All of the above

13. The term *reabsorption* describes the ability of a psychoactive drug to:
    A. Bind with receptor sites on the presynaptic membrane
    B. Bind with receptor sites on the postsynaptic membrane
    C. Destroy enzymes that break down neurotransmitters
    D. None of the above

Critical Thinking

1. What are the major components of a neuron, or nerve cell? What is the role of each?

2. What are the two major components of the nervous system, and what are the roles of each?

3. What are the four anatomical parts of the brain?

4. Describe the sympathetic and parasympathetic branches of the peripheral nervous system.

5. Describe the three ways psychoactive drugs can affect the transmission of nerve impulses.

CHAPTER 4 PHARMACOLOGY: HOW THE BODY PROCESSES DRUGS

Multiple Choice

1. The branch of science that studies the interactions of drugs with the body is called:
   A. Pharmacology
   B. Biology
   C. Psychokinetics
   D. Psychiatry

2. The quickest of the following routes of administration is:
   A. Ingestion
   B. Inhalation
   C. Absorption through the skin
   D. Absorption through mucous membranes

3. A common route of drug injection is:
   A. Intramuscular injection
   B. Intravenous injection
   C. Subcutaneous injection
   D. All of the above

4. The primary route of administration of smokeless tobacco is:
   A. Inhalation
   B. Absorption
   C. Ingestion
   D. Injection

5. A foreign substance that can enter the body by absorption through the skin is:
   A. Pesticides
   B. Nicotine
   C. Mercury
   D. All of the above

6. Substances that are easily dissolved in fats and oils are said to be:
   A. Lipophilic
   B. Aqueous
   C. Hydrophilic
   D. Water-based

7. When a drug reaches the bloodstream, it is first distributed to the:
   A. Site of storage
   B. Site of excretion
   C. Site of action
   D. All of the above

8. The primary site of action for psychoactive drugs is the:
   A. Gastrointestinal system
   B. Lymphatic system
   C. Peripheral nervous system
   D. Central nervous system

9. The placental barrier prevents the following substance from entering the fetal circulation:
   A. Morphine
   B. Cocaine
   C. Alcohol
   D. None of the above

10. All of the following are types of drug action *except*:
    A. Antidepressive
    B. Restorative
    C. Narcotic
    D. Stimulative

11. The point at which the concentration of drug molecules is high enough for the drug's effect to be observed is called the:
    A. Point of maximum response
    B. Point of administration
    C. Threshold
    D. Point of maximum concentration

12. A drug interaction in which a drug that does not exhibit a significant effect by itself increases the effects of another drug is called:
    A. Additive effect
    B. Synergism
    C. Potentiation
    D. Subtractive effect

13. Giving an injection of naloxone to a patient who is unconscious with a heroin overdose illustrates a(n):
    A. Synergistic effect
    B. Inhibitory effect
    C. Additive effect
    D. Depressive effect

14. A symptom of withdrawal illness upon quitting use of a narcotic is:
    A. Fever
    B. Extreme anxiety
    C. Sweating
    D. All of the above

15. A drug test in which antibodies are used to detect the presence or absence of drugs in urine or hair is called:
    A. Mass spectrometry
    B. Chromatography
    C. Immunoassay
    D. Genetic testing

Critical Thinking

1. Identify and describe each of the four ways drugs can enter the body.

2. Describe the various types of drug interactions, including additive, synergistic, potentiating, and inhibitory.

3. Describe how alcohol is altered by the body and excreted.

4. Describe the various methods of drug testing and how they are used.

5. Explain the differences between psychological dependence and physical dependence.

CHAPTER 5   THE STIMULANTS: COCAINE, THE AMPHETAMINES, AND THE CATHINOIDS

Multiple Choice

1. Cocaine is the primary psychoactive substance found in the leaves of the:
   A. Ephedra plant
   B. Cocoa plant
   C. Khat plant
   D. Coca plant
2. Cocaine was first labeled a narcotic by the:
   A. Pure Food and Drugs Act of 1906
   B. Harrison Act of 1914
   C. Comprehensive Drug Abuse Control Act of 1970
   D. Substance Abuse Prevention Act
3. Cocaine was supplied to the United States for many years by two powerful drug cartels in the South American country of:
   A. Venezuela
   B. Bolivia
   C. Colombia
   D. Ecuador
4. An injected mixture of heroin and cocaine, carrying an increased risk of overdose, is called:
   A. A speedball
   B. Crack cocaine
   C. Free-basing
   D. A mainline
5. Cocaine affects:
   A. Only the brain
   B. The entire central nervous system
   C. The peripheral nervous system
   D. Both the central and peripheral nervous systems
6. Large doses of cocaine can produce:
   A. Improved coordination
   B. Congestive heart failure
   C. Increased strength
   D. Reduced blood pressure
7. A phenomenon in which more and more cocaine is needed to achieve the same level of euphoria achieved by a previous dose is called:
   A. Physical addiction
   B. Tolerance
   C. Psychological habituation
   D. Withdrawal
8. An empty or flat feeling experienced by recovering cocaine users, characterized by an absence of pleasure or meaning in one's life, is called:
   A. Cocaine addiction cycle
   B. Manic depressive syndrome
   C. Anhedonia
   D. Recovery response
9. Women who use cocaine while pregnant tend to have pregnancies resulting in more:
   A. Sudden infant deaths
   B. Low-birthweight babies
   C. Premature deliveries
   D. All of the above
10. Amphetamines are biotransformed by the:
    A. Kidneys
    B. Liver
    C. Lungs
    D. Digestive system
11. Amphetamines produce their stimulatory effect by interfering with the normal activity of:
    A. Acetylcholine
    B. Neurotransmitters
    C. Ketogenesis
    D. Peptides
12. The chronic effects of amphetamine use can include:
    A. Increased sensitivity to pleasurable psychological effects
    B. Increased appetite
    C. Episodes of psychosis
    D. All of the above
13. The valid medical use of amphetamines is currently limited to:
    A. Obesity
    B. Attention deficit disorder
    C. Narcolepsy
    D. All of the above
14. The khat plant has been used for medicinal and social purposes for many centuries in:
    A. Africa
    B. Southeast Asia
    C. Europe
    D. South America
15. The chronic effects of habitual use of the cathinoids can include all of the following except:
    A. Weight loss
    B. Anxiety
    C. Increased sleeping
    D. Depression

Critical Thinking

1. Describe the mode of action of stimulants, and give examples of three types of stimulants.

2. Describe the various ways cocaine can be administered and the time required for it to reach the brain by each route.

3. Describe the effects of chronic cocaine use.

4. Describe the acute and chronic effects of amphetamine abuse.

5. Explain the background of the cathinoids and describe their effects.

CHAPTER 6   DEPRESSANTS

Multiple Choice

1. Depressants such as barbiturates are known as:
   A. Hallucinogens
   B. Central nervous system stimulants
   C. Sedative-hypnotics
   D. Appetite suppressants

2. The duration of action of the different barbiturates depends on their:
   A. Lipid solubility
   B. pH level
   C. Blood solubility
   D. Water solubility

3. An example of a benzodiazepine is:
   A. Valium
   B. Seconal
   C. Nembutal
   D. Tuinal

4. The effects of an oral dose of a benzodiazepine begin:
   A. In about 20 minutes
   B. In 30 to 60 minutes
   C. In 1 to 2 hours
   D. In 2 to 4 hours

5. The process by which the body biotransforms a drug to an inactive substance is called:
   A. Administration
   B. Distribution
   C. Biodeactivation
   D. Excretion

6. Physical dependence on benzodiazepines:
   A. Occurs with 1 to 2 weeks of daily use
   B. Occurs with 4 to 6 weeks of daily use
   C. Occurs with 2 to 4 months of daily use
   D. Does not occur

7. Other than taking a drug, an alternative way of dealing with stress is:
   A. Relaxation training
   B. Biofeedback
   C. Physical exercise
   D. All of the above

8. A drug used recently to incapacitate victims in sexual assaults is:
   A. Halcion
   B. Librium
   C. Miltown
   D. Rohypnol

9. Compared with other drugs, barbiturates are abused:
   A. About as much as other drugs
   B. More than any other drugs
   C. Less than other drugs
   D. Not at all

10. The benzodiazepines and the barbiturates both function by:
    A. Stimulating the central nervous system
    B. Increasing the inhibitory neurotransmitter GABA
    C. Increasing respiration and heart rate
    D. Stimulating the release of dopamine from the brain

11. Barbiturate compounds are excreted by the:
    A. Lungs
    B. Sweat glands
    C. Liver
    D. Kidneys

12. The withdrawal symptoms of benzodiazepines can be compared with those of barbiturates as follows:
    A. Benzodiazepines have more severe symptoms.
    B. Benzodiazepines have about the same symptoms.
    C. Benzodiazepines have less severe symptoms.
    D. Benzodiazepines do not cause withdrawal symptoms.

13. Benzodiazepines are usually administered:
    A. By inhalation
    B. Orally
    C. Intravenously
    D. Transdermally

14. Because it has no medical use and high potential for abuse, methaqualone is classified under:
    A. schedule I
    B. schedule II
    C. schedule III
    D. schedule IV

Critical Thinking

1. Explain how depressants affect the central nervous system and affect behavior.

2. Describe the effects of chronic depressant use, including both barbiturates and benzodiazepines.

3. Do any of the depressants have accepted medical uses? If so, which drugs and how are they used?

4. Describe the misuse and abuse of depressants in the United States today.

5. Have you known anyone who chronically used barbiturates, benzodiazepines, or other depressants? How did this affect the person?

CHAPTER 7   NARCOTICS

Multiple Choice

Correct ans

1. The substance opium is derived from the dried juice of what plant?
   A. Psilocybin
   B. *Cannabis*
   C. Oriental poppy
   D. Nightshade

   C   more   C

2. The primary pharmacological component in opium is:
   A. Dopamine
   B. Heroin
   C. Cocaine
   D. Morphine

   D

3. How many Americans are estimated to have used heroin in the past year?
   A. 400,000
   B. 750,000
   C. 1.3 million
   D. 4 million

   A   A

4. By 1995, the following South American country had become a major supplier of heroin to the U.S. market:
   A. Bolivia
   B. Colombia
   C. Ecuador
   D. Venezuela

   B   B

5. The following synthetic narcotic is used in withdrawal and maintenance programs for heroin dependence:
   A. Methadone
   B. Meperidine
   C. Hydromorphone
   D. Dihydromorphone

   A   A

6. The rate of absorption of narcotics depends on their:
   A. Lipid solubility
   B. Region of origin
   C. Route of administration
   D. A and C

   D   A&C

7. The primary route of excretion of heroin is the:
   A. Kidneys
   B. Sweat glands
   C. Lungs
   D. Intestines

   A   A

8. The primary cause of death in cases of narcotic overdoses is:
   A. Cardiac arrest
   B. Respiratory arrest

   B   B

C. Stroke
D. Asphyxiation on vomitus

9. In addition to a "high," a typical result of a first use of heroin is:
   A. Cross-tolerance to other narcotics
   B. Physical dependence
   C. Nausea and vomiting
   D. Resolution of personal problems

   C

10. Most programs for withdrawal from narcotics include the following step:
    A. Aftercare
    B. Active treatment
    C. Detoxification
    D. All of the above

    B   D

11. Success rates for narcotic treatment programs are:
    A. High, over 75%
    B. Moderate, about 50%
    C. Low, less than 25%
    D. Are unknown

    C

12. Narcotics can be classified as what type of drug?
    A. Natural
    B. Quasi-synthetic
    C. Synthetic
    D. All of the above

    D

13. People who no longer feel the desire for heroin may discontinue using heroin without treatment through a process called:
    A. Substitute dependence
    B. Detoxification
    C. Cross-tolerance
    D. Maturing out

    D   B

14. Endorphins are defined as a:
    A. Natural derivative of opium
    B. Natural painkiller produced by the body
    C. Synthetic form of heroin
    D. Substitute for narcotics administered in withdrawal programs

    B

15. Compounds that compete with morphinelike substances for receptor sites can be described as:
    A. Euphoriants
    B. Enkephalins
    C. Agonists
    D. Antagonists

    D   D

Critical Thinking

1. What are the three types of narcotics? How are they produced?

2. Explain the mode of action of narcotics.

3. What are the effects of chronic narcotic abuse?

4. Describe the "cycle of addiction" for many narcotic abusers.

5. Discuss the factors that motivate narcotic addicts to seek treatment and the factors that affect success rates.

CHAPTER 8   MARIJUANA

Multiple Choice

1. What is THC?
   A. A hallucinogen derived from the peyote cactus plant
   B. A drug popular in the 1960s
   C. The active ingredient in marijuana
   D. A new "designer drug"

2. *Cannabis* was introduced to North America primarily for its:
   A. Medicinal value
   B. Psychoactive properties
   C. Use in making rope
   D. Use as an anesthetic

3. The Drug Enforcement Administration classifies marijuana under what category?
   A. schedule I
   B. schedule II
   C. schedule III
   D. schedule IV

4. In 1996, these two states passed state laws permitting the medical use of marijuana:
   A. Oregon and Hawaii
   B. New Mexico and Washington
   C. Hawaii and New Mexico
   D. California and Arizona

5. The chronic effects of marijuana use are similar to those of:
   A. Barbiturates
   B. Cocaine
   C. Solvents
   D. Tobacco

6. The physiological symptoms of withdrawal from chronic marijuana use are:
   A. Severe
   B. Moderate
   C. Mild
   D. Unknown

7. At high doses, marijuana can produce:
   A. Hallucinations
   B. Improved concentration
   C. Paranoia
   D. A and C

8. One of the most serious effects of chronic marijuana use is:
   A. Amotivational syndrome
   B. Escalation to harder drugs
   C. Reduced appetite
   D. Anxiety

9. Marijuana's popularity among illegal drugs is:
   A. Second after cocaine
   B. First
   C. Third after cocaine and amphetamines
   D. Unknown

10. Most recently, marijuana use among college students has been reported to be:
    A. Decreasing sharply
    B. Decreasing slowly
    C. Holding steady
    D. Increasing

11. Marijuana use has been shown to have the following effect on driving:
    A. Increases concentration
    B. Slows reaction time
    C. Enhances coordination
    D. Has no noticeable effect

12. The first legal attempt to outlaw marijuana use was:
    A. The Controlled Substances Act (CSA) of 1970
    B. The Marijuana Tax Act of 1937
    C. California Proposition 215
    D. The Public Health Service Act

13. Like other drugs, marijuana's mode of action appears to be:
    A. Depression of the cardiorespiratory control centers
    B. Interference with neurotransmitter activity
    C. Stimulation of the lymphatic system
    D. Stimulation of the peripheral nervous system

14. Currently, the only prescription medication containing THC is:
    A. Marinol
    B. Phencyclidine
    C. Dilaudid
    D. Methadone

Critical Thinking

1. What are the two varieties of *Cannabis sativa*? Describe their use throughout history.

2. Describe the acute and chronic effects of marijuana use.

3. What are the currently proposed medical uses of marijuana?

4. How are the health risks of smoking marijuana like those of smoking tobacco?

5. Do you think that marijuana laws should be changed in the United States? If so, how?

CHAPTER 9 HALLUCINOGENS

Multiple Choice

1. The blending of perceptions and interpretations of visual and auditory images is called:
   A. Delusion
   B. Synesthesia
   C. Phantasm
   D. Panic reaction

2. The use of hallucinogens can produce:
   A. Tolerance
   B. Cross-tolerance
   C. Physical dependence
   D. A and B

3. An example of a natural hallucinogen is:
   A. Psilocybin
   B. DMT
   C. LSD
   D. A and B

4. LSD was first isolated by:
   A. Parke, Davis, and Company
   B. Aldous Huxley
   C. Timothy Leary
   D. Albert Hofmann

5. The rate of death from overdose of LSD compared with other drugs is:
   A. High
   B. Moderate
   C. Low
   D. Nonexistent

6. A group of mushrooms with psychoactive ingredients, found in the Central America, is commonly known as:
   A. Cohoba
   B. Psilocybin
   C. Peyote
   D. Mescaline

7. Mescaline is typically absorbed through the:
   A. Mucous membranes
   B. Liver
   C. Cardiorespiratory system
   D. Gastrointestinal tract

8. Phencyclidine is classified as a:
   A. Hallucinogen
   B. Hallucinogenic anesthetic
   C. Hallucinogenic stimulant
   D. Narcotic

9. PCP can act as a:
   A. Hallucinogen
   B. Depressant
   C. Stimulant
   D. All of the above

10. Atropine, scopolamine, and muscarine primarily affect which neurotransmitter pathways?
    A. Dopamine
    B. Serotonin
    C. Acetylcholine
    D. Norepinephrine

11. This neurotransmitter alters pain perception, helps control mood, and is affected by LSD, psilocybin, and DMT:
    A. Dopamine
    B. Serotonin
    C. Acetylcholine
    D. Norepinephrine

12. A recent study found that most of the hallucinogen-related deaths reported involved:
    A. MDA
    B. DMT
    C. PCP
    D. LSD

13. The percentage of school-age children who reported using LSD:
    A. Has increased
    B. Has remained steady
    C. Has decreased
    D. Is unknown

14. Native Americans in the United States have fought to retain the right to use the following drug in their religious ceremonies:
    A. Marijuana
    B. Psilocybin
    C. Peyote
    D. Cohoba

15. PCP is unique among the hallucinogens in that:
    A. It appears to produce chemical dependence
    B. It has approved medical uses in humans
    C. It remains legal
    D. Chronic use appears to have few negative effects

Critical Thinking

1. What is a hallucinogen? Give five examples.

2. What are the four neurotransmitters?

3. Which neurotransmitter does LSD primarily affect? Which neurotransmitter does PCP primarily affect?

4. What are the recent trends in hallucinogenic drug use in the United States?

5. What are the special risks in using PCP?

CHAPTER 10   OVER-THE-COUNTER DRUGS (NONPRESCRIPTION DRUGS)

Multiple Choice

1. The forerunners of today's pharmacies were:
   A. Dispensaries
   B. Barbers
   C. Surgeons
   D. Apothecaries

2. Evidence of both safety and effectiveness of an OTC drug was mandated by the:
   A. Durham-Humphrey Amendment
   B. Food, Drug, and Cosmetic (FDC) Act of 1938
   C. Kefauver-Harris Act of 1962
   D. FDA actions of 1972

3. According to the 1972 actions of the FDA, OTC products in category I are:
   A. Safe, effective, and honestly labeled
   B. Either not safe and effective or untruthfully labeled
   C. Of unknown safety and effectiveness
   D. Effective but unsafe for self-administration

4. A product that recently moved from prescription-only to OTC status is:
   A. Hydrogen ion inhibitors for heartburn relief
   B. Hair growth stimulant
   C. Nicotine-containing chewing gum
   D. All of the above

5. The number of OTC drugs on the market is approximately:
   A. 120,000
   B. 18,000
   C. 600,000
   D. 2,000

6. The label on an OTC drug must contain all of the following information except:
   A. The expiration date
   B. Warnings
   C. The generic equivalent
   D. A list of active ingredients

7. A condition in which a person has multiple health problems at the same time is known as:
   A. Polypharmacy
   B. Self-care
   C. Comorbidity
   D. Drug interaction

8. An alternative health care system that prescribes highly diluted natural drugs to return the body to a state of balance is:
   A. Homeopathy
   B. Naturopathy
   C. Allopathy
   D. Ayurveda

9. Plant materials that are biologically active in humans are known as:
   A. Hallucinogens
   B. Drugs
   C. Botanicals
   D. Vitamins

10. Dietary supplements can include:
    A. Fungi
    B. Vitamins
    C. Amino acids
    D. All of the above

11. The primary active ingredient of diet pills is:
    A. Norepinephrine
    B. A laxative
    C. Caffeine
    D. Phenylpropanolamine

12. Chronic use of laxatives can lead to:
    A. Overhydration
    B. Malnutrition
    C. Dependence
    D. Both B and C

13. If an OTC product causes an adverse reaction in a person, he or she should:
    A. Gradually taper usage
    B. Discontinue usage
    C. Switch to a different brand
    D. Both A and C

14. Most OTC products provide:
    A. An effective cure of the underlying condition
    B. An effective cure and symptomatic relief
    C. A partial cure and symptomatic relief
    D. Symptomatic relief only

15. An OTC drug type commonly misused by college students is:
    A. Laxatives
    B. Stimulants
    C. Diet pills
    D. All of the above

Critical Thinking

1. Describe the history of OTC drugs.

2. Explain how older adults are at risk of developing polypharmacy.

3. Explain the principle underlying the practice of homeopathy.

4. Explain the risks to college students of abusing popular OTC drugs.

5. Describe the information that must be included on OTC drug labels.

CHAPTER 11   PRESCRIPTION DRUGS

Multiple Choice

1. The central piece of legislation that defines which drugs will be prescription drugs and which will be OTC drugs is the:
   A. Comprehensive Drug Abuse Control Act of 1970
   B. Harrison Act of 1914
   C. Federal Food, Drug, and Cosmetic (FD&C) Act of 1938
   D. Pure Food and Drugs Act of 1906

2. The 1962 Kefauver-Harris Amendment required drug manufacturers to:
   A. Prove purity of the drug
   B. Include comprehensive labels
   C. Prove safety of the drug
   D. Prove effectiveness of the drug

3. The process of approving a new drug is overseen by the:
   A. AMA
   B. Department of Health and Human Services
   C. U.S. Congress
   D. FDA

4. A new prescription drug carries all of the following types of names except:
   A. Brand name
   B. Generic name
   C. Chemical name
   D. Compound name

5. The ability of generic drugs, once they reach their target sites, to exert their active effects with the same speed as pioneer drugs is called:
   A. Bioavailability
   B. Bioequivalence
   C. Biodeactivation
   D. Bioactivity

6. Polypharmacy is a risk especially to:
   A. College students
   B. Infants
   C. The elderly
   D. Minorities

7. To be approved, a drug must perform better than:
   A. A placebo
   B. The current brand-name equivalent
   C. The generic equivalent
   D. Its OTC equivalent

8. Prescription medications should be taken:
   A. Until the symptoms are eradicated
   B. Until the underlying disease is eliminated
   C. Until the prescription is finished
   D. Both A and B

9. Prescription medications should be stored:
   A. In an easily accessible location
   B. In a warm, humid location, such as a medicine chest in a bathroom
   C. In a container with other prescription medications
   D. In a cool, dry location

10. Dispose of medications you no longer need or use by:
    A. Throwing them away
    B. Donating them to a charity
    C. Flushing them down the toilet
    D. Returning them to a pharmacy

11. Approximately how many prescriptions were filled per year in the mid-1990s?
    A. 800,000
    B. 2 million
    C. 5 million
    D. 12 million

12. Drugs for rare diseases—those that affect fewer than 200,000 Americans—are called:
    A. Pioneer drugs
    B. Trade-name drugs
    C. Orphan drugs
    D. Experimental drugs

13. Anaphylaxis is an example of what type of adverse reaction to a drug?
    A. Allergic reaction
    B. Drug interaction
    C. Rejection
    D. Toxic reaction

14. A general category of drugs that produce an antibacterial action are:
    A. Antitussives
    B. Antihistamines
    C. Analgesics
    D. Sulfa drugs

15. Of the 100,000 compounds examined each year, about how many are estimated to reach the marketplace?
    A. 25
    B. 200
    C. 80
    D. 6

Critical Thinking

1. Describe the general history of prescription drugs from ancient times to the present.

2. Describe the process of developing and gaining approval of a new prescription medication.

3. Explain why placebos can be as effective as a prescription drug.

4. Describe the questions you would ask your physician when he or she wishes to prescribe a medication to you.

5. Do you feel that animals should be used in drug research? Why or why not?

CHAPTER 12 NICOTINE

Multiple Choice

1. Which factor most affects a person's decision to smoke?
   A. Gender
   B. Age
   C. Education
   D. Race

2. Psychosocial factors of tobacco dependence include:
   A. Manipulation
   B. Advertising
   C. Modeling
   D. Both A and C

3. On which consumer group is the FDA focusing its education efforts to discourage increased tobacco use?
   A. Women
   B. African-American men who attend predominately black universities
   C. Teens
   D. Older adults who began smoking before health risks were known

4. Which phase of tobacco smoke includes nicotine, water, and a variety of powerful chemical compounds known collectively as tar?
   A. Active phase
   B. Particulate phase
   C. Gaseous phase
   D. Nicotine phase

5. What signals the beginning of lung cancer?
   A. Changes in the basal cell layer resulting from constant irritation by the tar accumulating in the airways
   B. An inability to breathe normally
   C. A "smoker's cough"
   D. Mucus swept up to the throat by cilia, where it is swallowed and removed through the digestive system

6. What is COLD?
   A. Chronic obstructive lung disease
   B. A chronic disease in which air flow in and out of the lungs becomes progressively limited
   C. A disease state made up of chronic bronchitis and pulmonary emphysema
   D. All of the above

7. Which of the following statements is *false*?
   A. Women who smoke are strongly urged not to use oral contraceptives.
   B. Chewing tobacco and snuff generate blood levels of nicotine in amounts equivalent to those seen in cigarette smokers.
   C. Contrary to some claims, secondhand smoke is not a serious health threat.
   D. Children of parents who smoke are twice as likely to develop bronchitis or pneumonia during the first year of life.

8. Which of the following statements is true?
   A. Chewing tobacco is a safe alternative to smoking.
   B. Sidestream smoke makes up only 15% of our exposure to involuntary smoking.
   C. Spouses of smokers may have a 30% greater risk of lung cancer.
   D. The only effective way to quit smoking is to go "cold turkey."

9. Which is more effective as a means of quitting smoking?
   A. Nicotine-containing chewing gum
   B. Transdermal patch
   C. Neither A nor B
   D. A and B are equally effective.

10. What is the main debate concerning smoking today?
    A. The validity of health warnings
    B. The rights of the nonsmoker vs. the rights of the smoker
    C. The rights of young adults to buy cigarettes
    D. None of the above

11. Dependence on tobacco is more easily established than dependence on:
    A. Alcohol
    B. Heroin
    C. Cocaine
    D. All of the above

12. Tobacco cessation programs are thought to have a failure rate of:
    A. 25%
    B. 33%
    C. 50%
    D. 75%

13. The most damaging component found in the gaseous phase of tobacco smoke is:
    A. Carbon monoxide
    B. Ammonia
    C. Acetone
    D. Acetaldehyde

14. Compared with mainstream smoke, sidestream smoke contains:
    A. Much greater concentrations of carcinogenic substances
    B. About the same levels of carcinogenic substances
    C. Much lower levels of carcinogenic substances
    D. No carcinogenic substances

15. The following statement(s) about smoking and pregnancy are true:
    A. The fetus of a mother who smokes is exposed to carbon monoxide and nicotine.
    B. Children born to mothers who smoked during pregnancy tend to have lower birthweights.
    C. The fetus of a mother who smokes is more likely to be stillborn, miscarried, or born prematurely.
    D. All of the above

Critical Thinking

1. What advertising tactics do tobacco companies use to offset the potential decline in sales resulting from reports of health risks?

2. In what ways is tobacco addictive?

3. How does smoking adversely affect health?

4. Why should a pregnant or breastfeeding woman refrain from smoking?

5. Do you think smoking should continue to be banned from public places? Why or why not?

CHAPTER 13   THE METHYLXANTHINES AND RELATED COMPOUNDS

Multiple Choice

1. The methylxanthine family includes all of the following except:
   A. Theophylline
   B. Caffeine
   C. Epinephrine
   D. Theobromine

2. Caffeine can be found in:
   A. Coffee
   B. Chocolate
   C. Some OTC drugs
   D. All of the above

3. The primary methylxanthine in tea is:
   A. Theobromine
   B. Caffeine
   C. Theophylline
   D. None of the above

4. According to legend, tea first gained popularity as a beverage in:
   A. England
   B. Korea
   C. China
   D. Japan

5. Caffeine and the other methylxanthines are ingested in water-soluble form and absorbed into the bloodstream primarily through the:
   A. Small intestine
   B. Stomach
   C. Large intestine
   D. Liver

6. Caffeine produces its excitatory effect by preventing the breakdown of:
   A. Adrenaline
   B. Cyclic adenosine monophosphate
   C. Dopamine
   D. Enkephalin

7. The effects of caffeine intoxication can include:
   A. Depression
   B. Improved concentration
   C. Rapid heart rate
   D. Reduced urination

8. Studies have shown a link between caffeine consumption and the risk of:
   A. Coronary artery disease
   B. High blood pressure
   C. Stroke
   D. Panic attack

9. Researchers have proved a link between caffeine consumption by women and:
   A. Ovarian cancer
   B. Fibrocystic breast condition
   C. Breast cancer
   D. None of the above

10. Recent studies of moderate coffee drinkers found that they had:
    A. Much higher-than-normal levels of suicide
    B. Somewhat higher-than-normal levels of suicide
    C. Normal levels of suicide
    D. Lower-than-normal levels of suicide

11. Symptoms of caffeine withdrawal can include:
    A. Headache
    B. Anxiety
    C. Lethargy
    D. All of the above

12. All of the following are methods of reducing caffeine consumption except:
    A. Switching from coffee to a caffeinated cola drink
    B. Using smaller cups and glasses
    C. Keeping a record of all caffeine consumption
    D. Substituting physical activity for a coffee break

13. Heavy caffeine users are more likely to:
    A. Use alcohol
    B. Smoke cigarettes
    C. Feel stress
    D. All of the above

Critical Thinking

1. What are the three methylxanthines?

2. What is the primary methylxanthine in coffee? Tea? Chocolate?

3. What are some methods of reducing one's consumption of caffeine?

4. Describe the current state of research on the link between caffeine and diseases.

5. What is your current level of caffeine consumption? Does caffeine consumption interfere with your life?

CHAPTER 14   ANABOLIC DRUGS

Multiple Choice

1. The anabolic compound produced naturally by the human body is called:
   A. Leutinizing hormone
   B. Human growth hormone
   C. Parathyroid hormone
   D. Follicle-stimulating hormone

2. Anabolic-androgenic steroids:
   A. Increase muscle size and strength
   B. Improve emotional wellness
   C. Accelerate the rate at which the body builds proteins
   D. Both A and C

3. The first successful use of steroids in athletic competition was by:
   A. U.S. professional football teams in the 1960s
   B. The Chinese swimming team in the 1980s
   C. The Soviet weightlifting team of the 1950s
   D. The East German track teams of the 1970s

4. All of the following are examples of steroids except:
   A. Aldosterone
   B. Hydrocortisone
   C. Epinephrine
   D. Cholesterol

5. The products of steroid biotransformation are removed from the body by:
   A. The lungs
   B. The kidneys
   C. The liver
   D. The gastrointestinal system

6. Steroid use by males can produce:
   A. Swollen breast tissue
   B. Testicular shrinkage
   C. Hair loss
   D. All of the above

7. An on-and-off technique of taking steroids to avoid building tolerance is called:
   A. Pyramiding
   B. Rhythm
   C. Cycling
   D. Stacking

8. Human growth hormone:
   A. Has several important medical uses in adults.
   B. Has no medical uses in adults.
   C. Has serious side effects in adults.
   D. Both B and C.

9. The nonmedical use of steroids to improve athletic performance:
   A. Is neither unethical nor illegal
   B. Is unethical but not illegal
   C. Is illegal but not unethical
   D. Is unethical and illegal

10. To be effective, a steroid drug-testing program should include:
    A. Testing by a qualified, certified laboratory
    B. A posted schedule of tests
    C. Testing for steroid use only
    D. All of the above

11. Processes that break down excess muscle are called:
    A. Metabolic processes
    B. Anabolic processes
    C. Catabolic processes
    D. None of the above

12. Steroids can remain in the body for long periods when they are suspended in:
    A. Water
    B. Oil
    C. Saline
    D. All of the above

13. Chronic use of steroids can increase the risk of:
    A. Low blood pressure
    B. Heart attack
    C. Both A and B
    D. Neither A nor B

Critical Thinking

1. What is an anabolic drug? What are the two major types?

2. Describe the acute and chronic effects of the nonmedical use of steroids.

3. What are some of the approved medical uses of steroids?

4. What do you think should be the features of a program to prevent steroid use?

5. Why do you think young people risk the long-term consequences of steroid use?

CHAPTER 15 INHALANTS

Multiple Choice

1. The typical abuser of inhalants is:
   A. 5 to 7 years old
   B. 8 to 12 years old
   C. 12 to 17 years old
   D. 18 to 24 years old

2. Young people can get access to inhalants:
   A. Only through a prescription
   B. Easily, because of their widespread commercial availability
   C. Only through a dealer in illegal drugs
   D. Only with a prescription or by purchasing over-the-counter drugs

3. The acute, or short-term, effects of inhalant abuse can include:
   A. Dizziness
   B. Headache
   C. Death
   D. All of the above

4. The chronic, or long-term, effects of inhalant abuse can be particularly damaging to the:
   A. Lymphatic system
   B. Circulatory system
   C. Nervous system
   D. All of the above

5. In cases of sudden death as a direct result of acute inhalant abuse, the physiological cause of death was usually:
   A. Liver dysfunction
   B. Asphyxiation
   C. Heart arrythmia
   D. Stroke

6. The practice of soaking a rag with an inhalant and then inhaling from the rag, or even placing the rag in the mouth, is called:
   A. Snorting
   B. Bagging
   C. Sniffing
   D. Huffing

7. Telltale signs of inhalant abuse include all of the following except:
   A. Increased interest in school or hobbies
   B. Nausea and headaches
   C. Mood swings
   D. Unusual odor on breath or clothes

8. An example of an anesthetic inhalant is:
   A. Lighter fluid
   B. Chlorofluorocarbons
   C. Nitrous oxide
   D. Butyl nitrate

9. An example of a solvent inhalant is:
   A. Dry cleaning fluid
   B. Paint thinner
   C. Butane
   D. Airplane glue

10. A school-based inhalant-abuse prevention program should do all of the following except:
    A. Begin prevention efforts by age 5
    B. Give details on how inhalants are abused
    C. Determine the student's current level of knowledge
    D. Teach the student to read and follow label instructions

11. An example of a cleaning agent inhalant is:
    A. Chlorofluorocarbons
    B. Petroleum distillates
    C. Toluene
    D. Butane

12. Deaths have been directly attributed to the following inhalant:
    A. Gasoline
    B. Nitrous oxide
    C. Typewriter correction fluid
    D. All of the above

13. The short-term effects of inhalant abuse can include:
    A. Breathing difficulty
    B. Improved concentration
    C. Increased aerobic capacity
    D. Both A and B

Critical Thinking

1. Give five examples of inhalants.

2. Describe the typical user of inhalants in the United States today.

3. Describe the potential short-term, or acute, consequences of inhalant abuse.

4. Describe the potential long-term, or chronic, consequences of inhalant abuse.

5. Discuss some of the characteristics of an effective school-based program to prevent inhalant abuse.

CHAPTER 16 ALCOHOL: HISTORY, PHYSIOLOGY, AND PHARMACOLOGY

Multiple Choice

1. The process of gathering the concentrated vapors of a heated, fermented mixture is called:
   A. Brewing
   B. Fermentation
   C. Distillation
   D. Winemaking

2. A liquor that is described as 80 proof is:
   A. 80% ethyl alcohol
   B. 40% ethyl alcohol
   C. 20% ethyl alcohol
   D. 10% ethyl alcohol

3. Heavy drinkers make up what percentage of the adult population of the United States?
   A. 4%
   B. 12%
   C. 20%
   D. 33%

4. Alcohol is oxidized by the:
   A. Liver
   B. Lungs
   C. Kidneys
   D. Intestines

5. Many states have begun changing the legal definition of intoxication from .10% blood alcohol concentration to:
   A. .12%
   B. .09%
   C. .08%
   D. .07%

6. Death can occur at blood alcohol concentrations of:
   A. .40% to .50%
   B. .30% to .40%
   C. .20% to .30%
   D. .10% to .20%

7. Alcohol is unlike other foods in that:
   A. It is a nutritious source of calories.
   B. It contains a variety of vitamins.
   C. It does not need to be digested to be absorbed.
   D. It is a good source of hydration when one is thirsty.

8. Which of the following does not affect the absorption of alcohol from the stomach?
   A. Use of birth control pills
   B. Presence of food
   C. Gender
   D. Quality of the liquor

9. All of the following are danger signs of acute alcohol intoxication except:
   A. Cool or damp skin
   B. Breathing increased to once every 3 to 4 seconds
   C. Pale or bluish gray skin color
   D. A strong, steady pulse

10. Fetal alcohol syndrome can cause a baby to be born with:
    A. Facial abnormalities
    B. Mental retardation
    C. Heart abnormalities
    D. All of the above

11. The occurrence of fetal alcohol syndrome is estimated to be:
    A. .5 to 1 case per 1,000 live births
    B. 1 to 3 cases per 1,000 live births
    C. 4 to 6 cases per 1,000 live births
    D. 7 to 10 cases per 1,000 live births

12. Alcohol can be especially damaging to fetuses when consumed by women:
    A. In the first trimester of pregnancy
    B. In the second trimester of pregnancy
    C. In the third trimester of pregnancy
    D. In the postpartum period

13. What percentage of the U.S. adult population consumes alcoholic beverages?
    A. 90%
    B. 80%
    C. 70%
    D. 60%

14. When a couple is attempting to conceive a child:
    A. The woman should abstain from alcohol after pregnancy is confirmed.
    B. The woman should abstain from alcohol when she suspects she is pregnant.
    C. The woman should abstain from alcohol during periods of unprotected sex.
    D. A woman who drinks liquor should switch to wine or beer after becoming pregnant.

15. The alcohol content of this type of beer may not exceed 0.5%:
    A. Light beer
    B. Regular beer
    C. Low-alcohol beer
    D. Nonalcohol beer

Critical Thinking

1. What are fermentation and distillation?

2. In what way does alcohol function as a depressant?

3. What are some of the consequences of chronic alcohol consumption?

4. What would you do if your friend passed out from alcohol consumption at a party?

5. What role does alcohol play in your life?

CHAPTER 17   ALCOHOL: SOCIAL, ECONOMIC, AND LEGAL ISSUES

Multiple Choice

1. What is binge drinking?
   A. The practice of drinking and then purging
   B. A harmless activity popular among college students
   C. The practice of consuming five or more drinks in a row, at least once in the previous 2-week period
   D. The practice of consuming two or more drinks in a row, at least once a day

2. What type of drug is alcohol?
   A. Stimulant
   B. Hallucinogen
   C. Depressant
   D. Narcotic

3. What should be done with people who become unconscious as a result of alcohol consumption?
   A. They should be given a cold shower to wake them up.
   B. They should be made to drink coffee.
   C. They should be taken to bed and left undisturbed for several hours.
   D. They should be placed on their side and monitored frequently.

4. Which of the following leading causes of accidental death is associated with alcohol use?
   A. Motor vehicle collisions
   B. Falls
   C. Drownings
   D. All of the above

5. A more severe form of alcoholism, passed from fathers to sons, has been labeled:
   A. Type 1 alcoholism
   B. Type 2 alcoholism
   C. Type 3 alcoholism
   D. Recessive alcoholism

6. Which of the following is a good guideline to follow for responsibly hosting a party?
   A. Make alcohol the primary entertainment, especially with a keg or other popular way to serve alcohol.
   B. Ridicule those who are afraid to drink.
   C. If friends say they are able to drive home even though they have been drinking, let them go.
   D. None of the above

7. Which alcohol-awareness group was created to promote responsible party hosting among university students?
   A. AA
   B. MADD
   C. BACCHUS
   D. SADD

8. The following is a sign of problem drinking:
   A. Drinking to cope with a difficult situation
   B. Fighting while drinking
   C. Driving while under the influence of alcohol
   D. All of the above

9. Which support group appeals to the children of alcoholics?
   A. Al-Anon
   B. Antabuse
   C. Alateen
   D. MADD

10. Which drug, approved by the FDA in 1995, is being used to treat alcoholism?
    A. Naltrexone
    B. Antabuse
    C. Heroin
    D. Maltodextrine

11. The likelihood of being involved in a fatal collision is how many times higher for a drunk (0.10% BAC) driver?
    A. 1.5 times as high
    B. Eight times as high
    C. Twice as high
    D. 15 times as high

12. Alcoholism can dramatically affect which member(s) of the alcoholic's family?
    A. Spouse
    B. Children
    C. Parents
    D. All of the above

13. Which of the following is a common trait of adult children of alcoholics?
    A. Have difficulty identifying normal behavior
    B. Tend to be able to drink alcohol without being affected by it
    C. Have difficulty with intimate relationships
    D. A and C

14. Alcohol use is reported in what percentage of homicides?
    A. 15%
    B. 40%
    C. 67%
    D. 90%

15. A person who is in a close relationship with a chemically dependent person can be at risk of developing:
    A. Type 1 alcoholism
    B. Type 2 alcoholism
    C. Codependence
    D. Independence

Critical Thinking

1. Why do people drink alcohol?

2. What physiological differences in women make them more susceptible to the effects of alcohol?

3. What do you think of the designated driver technique? Do you think it saves lives? Does it encourage heavier drinking among the nondrivers?

4. What role does alcohol use play in violent crime, family violence, and suicide?

5. Explain the terms *denial, enabling,* and *codependence* as they occur with alcoholism.

CHAPTER 18 DRUG ABUSE PREVENTION: EDUCATION AND TREATMENT

Multiple Choice

1. To change perceptions that drug use is acceptable among young people, drug prevention programs focus on:
   A. Resistance skills
   B. Life skills
   C. Normative beliefs
   D. Assertiveness training

2. A patient who lives at home and receives drug treatment at a facility several times a week is said to be receiving:
   A. Residential treatment
   B. Nonresidential treatment
   C. Vocational services
   D. Aftercare

3. Before beginning treatment, a drug-dependent person must undergo:
   A. Orientation
   B. Sentencing
   C. Detoxification
   D. Relapse

4. Treatment and rehabilitation of people with serious or chronic drug problems is called:
   A. Primary prevention
   B. Secondary prevention
   C. Tertiary prevention
   D. None of the above

5. Drug-treatment approaches currently include all of the following except:
   A. Psychoanalysis
   B. Substitute dependence
   C. Support groups
   D. Occupational therapy

6. One difference between male and female drug abusers is:
   A. Men can better manage drug use
   B. Men are less susceptible to physical addiction
   C. Women experience more depression
   D. Women find withdrawal to be easier

7. One difference between SOS programs and AA-type programs is:
   A. SOS programs do not rely on spirituality.
   B. AA-type programs rely more on confrontation.
   C. SOS programs are available at little or no cost.
   D. AA-type programs provide support groups for recovering people.

8. Using the nicotine transdermal patch to quit smoking is an example of:
   A. Secondary prevention
   B. Substitute dependence
   C. Intervention
   D. Aftercare

9. Of those treated for alcoholism, what percentage relapse within 3 months of treatment?
   A. 70%
   B. 50%
   C. 20%
   D. 10%

10. A recent community-based campaign sponsored by the U.S. Department of Health and Human Services and aimed at preventing marijuana use among youth is:
    A. Race Against Drugs (RAD)
    B. Reality Check
    C. Drug Abuse Resistance Education (DARE)
    D. Doctors Ought to Care (DOC)

11. Recently, school-based drug prevention programs have moved toward:
    A. Improving social skills
    B. Scaring children away from drugs
    C. Relying primarily on information about drugs
    D. Identifying and treating drug users

12. Drug education has traditionally been provided to children primarily by:
    A. Health-care providers
    B. Parents
    C. Schools
    D. Community organizations

13. In this treatment approach, the abuser's childhood and early life experiences are examined to help the abuser understand his or her drug abuse problem.
    A. Substitute dependence
    B. Behavioral approach
    C. Support group
    D. Psychoanalysis

Critical Thinking

1. Explain the concepts of primary, secondary, and tertiary prevention as they apply to drug abuse prevention, and give examples of each.

2. How have approaches changed in preventing drug abuse among children? What is the focus of the current approach?

3. What are the different approaches toward drug-abuse treatment?

4. How do women's needs for drug treatment differ from those of men?

5. What are your own beliefs about drug use? Describe your own resistance skills and life skills as they apply to drug use.

CHAPTER 19   DRUGS AND PUBLIC POLICY

Multiple Choice

1. Laws that raised the legal drinking age to 21 are estimated to have saved how many lives?
   A. 2,000
   B. 5,000
   C. 9,000
   D. 14,000

2. Zero tolerance laws are designed to:
   A. Outlaw possession of small amounts of marijuana
   B. Jail drug dealers for their first offense
   C. Prevent underage drinking and driving
   D. Force drug users into rehabilitation programs

3. *Healthy People 2000* is a program sponsored by:
   A. A consortium of health care providers
   B. The federal government
   C. A network of state governments
   D. The Centers for Disease Control and Prevention

4. This agency has attempted to reduce underage smoking by increasing its regulation of tobacco:
   A. Food and Drug Administration
   B. Federal Trade Commission
   C. Department of Health and Human Services
   D. Bureau of Alcohol, Tobacco, and Firearms

5. Needle exchange programs for drug users and school condom distribution programs are examples of:
   A. Interdiction
   B. Harm reduction
   C. Demand reduction
   D. Supply reduction

6. The percentage of businesses testing employees and job applicants for drugs jumped by 1996 to:
   A. 48%
   B. 87%
   C. 33%
   D. 67%

7. Drug testing technology can detect the presence of:
   A. Alcohol
   B. Cocaine
   C. Steroids
   D. All of the above

8. The following drug can be detected through drug testing as long as several weeks after it has been used:
   A. Cocaine
   B. Marijuana
   C. Heroin
   D. Amphetamine

9. The drug testing method that examines a vaporized sample from the individual is called:
   A. Radioimmunoassay
   B. Enzyme-multiplied immunoassay
   C. Gas chromatography
   D. Fluorescent polarization immunoassay

10. Companies report lower rates of drug abuse when they combine drug testing with:
    A. Prosecution
    B. Mandatory treatment
    C. Education programs
    D. Discipline or dismissal

11. Drug prevention strategies that attempt to influence key policymakers or legislators are described as what kind of campaigns?
    A. Global
    B. Grassroots
    C. Grasstops
    D. Propaganda

12. Public policy is most effective when it emphasizes:
    A. Treatment
    B. Interdiction
    C. Prevention
    D. Law enforcement

13. The organization fighting drug testing as a violation of privacy is:
    A. The U.S. Chamber of Commerce
    B. Fortune 500 corporations
    C. The Consumers Union
    D. The American Civil Liberties Union

14. When the price of alcoholic beverages, tobacco products, and illegal drugs rises, demand typically:
    A. Rises
    B. Remains steady
    C. Falls
    D. Cannot be measured

Critical Thinking

1. Describe three major policy categories for successful prevention of drug abuse.

2. Do you believe that employers have the right to require mandatory drug testing? Is it an invasion of privacy?

3. What is your opinion of harm reduction as a policy strategy? Do you think it encourages illegal behavior?

4. What is your opinion of recent efforts to limit the marketing of tobacco?

5. What do you think of the recent decision of distillers to begin running television ads for distilled spirits?

CHAPTER 20 LAW ENFORCEMENT

Multiple Choice

Correct

1. Substances used in the production of cocaine, heroin, LSD, PCP, and methamphetamine are called:
   A. OTC drugs
   B. Fillers
   C. Precursor chemicals
   D. Methylxanthines

2. The process of denying the drug smuggler the use of air, land, and maritime routes is called:
   A. Interdiction
   B. Asset seizure
   C. Confiscation
   D. The "kingpin strategy"

3. The legal basis for U.S. drug laws is:
   A. The Volstead Act
   B. The National Minimum Drinking Age Act of 1984
   C. The Public Health Service Act
   D. The Controlled Substances Act (CSA) of 1970

4. A new trend in which local police maintain a visible presence in neighborhoods and attempt to resolve disputes before they escalate into crimes is called:
   A. Zero tolerance
   B. Community policing
   C. The war on drugs
   D. "Three strikes and you're out"

5. What percentage of the prison population were drug offenders in 1994?
   A. 15%
   B. 33%
   C. 50%
   D. 60%

6. President Clinton's 1997 National Drug Control Strategy includes plans to:
   A. Reduce demand for drugs
   B. Enforce drug-trafficking laws
   C. Interdict drugs from across our borders
   D. All of the above

7. Law enforcement to control drugs can be considered:
   A. Primary prevention
   B. Secondary prevention
   C. Tertiary prevention
   D. B and C

8. The process of converting illegally earned assets or cash to other forms of wealth to conceal true ownership is called:
   A. Drug distribution
   B. Drug trafficking
   C. Organized crime
   D. Money laundering

9. In 1995, for the first time, more heroin entered the United States from this area than from Asia:
   A. Mexico
   B. Europe
   C. South America
   D. Africa

10. The authority to grant licenses to sell liquor is held by:
    A. City governments
    B. The Distilled Spirits Council
    C. State governments
    D. The federal government

11. The following statement about underage drinking is true:
    A. Some state laws have loopholes that allow underage drinking
    B. Raising the minimum drinking age has no effect on traffic fatalities
    C. Taking away a driver's license is not an effective way to deter drunk driving
    D. QUAD (Quick Uniform Attack on Drugs) required all states to raise their minimum alcohol purchase and public possession age to 21 years

12. In fiscal year 1996, how much did the federal government spend on drug control?
    A. About $800 million
    B. More than $2 billion
    C. More than $13 billion
    D. Cannot be determined

13. The societal costs of illegal drug use result from:
    A. Increased health care expenses
    B. Auto accidents
    C. The need for additional law enforcement
    D. All of the above

Critical Thinking

1. What are the primary goals of President Clinton's 1997 National Drug Control Strategy?

2. How does law enforcement reduce the supply of drugs?

3. What are the federal agencies involved in enforcing drug laws? What are their roles?

4. What is your attitude toward underage drinking? What are some of the societal effects of underage drinking?

5. Considering that tobacco contributes to 400,000 deaths each year, how do you think it should be regulated?

ANSWERS

Chapter 1

1. D;   2. B;   3. B;   4. A;   5. A;   6. B;   7. D;
8. C;   9. A;   10. A;   11. B;   12. B;   13. B

Chapter 2

1. C;   2. A;   3. A;   4. C;   5. B;   6. C;   7. A;
8. D;   9. B;   10. D;   11. D;   12. D;   13. C;
14. C;   15. D

Chapter 3

1. B;   2. C;   3. C;   4. C;   5. D;   6. A;   7. D;
8. B;   9. C;   10. D;   11. A;   12. D;   13. A

Chapter 4

1. A;   2. B;   3. D;   4. B;   5. C;   6. A;   7. D;
8. D;   9. D;   10. B;   11. C;   12. C;   13. B;
14. D;   15. C

Chapter 5

1. D;   2. B;   3. C;   4. A;   5. D;   6. B;   7. B;
8. D;   9. D;   10. B;   11. B;   12. C;   13. D;
14. A;   15. C

Chapter 6

1. C;   2. A;   3. A;   4. D;   5. C;   6. B;   7. D;
8. D;   9. C;   10. B;   11. D;   12. C;   13. B;
14. A

Chapter 7

1. C;   2. D;   3. A;   4. B;   5. A;   6. D;   7. A;
8. B;   9. C;   10. D;   11. C;   12. D;   13. D;
14. B;   15. D

Chapter 8

1. C;   2. C;   3. A;   4. D;   5. D;   6. D;   7. D;
8. A;   9. B;   10. C;   11. B;   12. B;   13. B;
14. A

Chapter 9

1. B;   2. D;   3. D;   4. D;   5. D;   6. B;   7. D;
8. B;   9. D;   10. C;   11. B;   12. C;   13. A;
14. C;   15. A

Chapter 10

1. D;   2. C;   3. A;   4. D;   5. C;   6. C;   7. C;
8. A;   9. C;   10. D;   11. D;   12. D;   13. B;
14. D;   15. D

Chapter 11

1. C;   2. D;   3. D;   4. D;   5. B;   6. C;   7. A;
8. C;   9. D;   10. C;   11. B;   12. C;   13. A;
14. D;   15. D

Chapter 12

1. C;   2. D;   3. C;   4. B;   5. A;   6. D;   7. C;
8. C;   9. A;   10. B;   11. D;   12. D;   13. A;
14. A;   15. D

Chapter 13

1. C;   2. D;   3. C;   4. C;   5. A;   6. B;   7. C;
8. D;   9. D;   10. D;   11. D;   12. A;   13. D

Chapter 14

1. B;   2. D;   3. C;   4. C;   5. B;   6. D;   7. C;
8. D;   9. D;   10. A;   11. C;   12. B;   13. B

Chapter 15

1. C;   2. B;   3. D;   4. C;   5. C;   6. D;   7. A;
8. C;   9. B;   10. B;   11. B;   12. D;   13. B

Chapter 16

1. C;   2. B;   3. B;   4. A;   5. C;   6. A;   7. C;
8. D;   9. D;   10. D;   11. B;   12. A;   13. D;
14. D;   15. D

Chapter 17

1. C;   2. C;   3. D;   4. D;   5. B;   6. D;   7. C;
8. D;   9. A;   10. A;   11. B;   12. D;   13. D;
14. C;   15. C

Chapter 18

1. C;   2. B;   3. C;   4. C;   5. D;   6. C;   7. A;
8. B;   9. B;   10. B;   11. A;   12. C;   13. D

Chapter 19

1. D;   2. C;   3. B;   4. A;   5. B;   6. B;   7. B;
8. B;   9. C;   10. C;   11. C;   12. C;   13. D;
14. C

Chapter 20

1. C;   2. A;   3. D;   4. B;   5. D;   6. C;   7. D;
8. D;   9. C;   10. C;   11. A;   12. C;   13. D

GLOSSARY

A

absorption administration of a drug through the skin or mucous membranes

action potential the electrical impulse that travels within a neuron

acute drug action the immediate (short-term) result of a drug's presence in the body

adaptive model of drug dependence drug dependence results from an individual's efforts to adapt to the influences of environmental stressors

addiction a condition characterized by the compulsive abuse of a drug or drugs; drug dependence

addictive behavior behavior that is excessive, compulsive, and destructive psychologically and physically

addictive disorder a physical or psychological abnormality that results in a pattern of addictive behavior

adult children of alcoholics (ACAs) adults whose parents were alcoholics and who are thus at risk themselves of becoming alcoholics

aftercare continuing care for recovering substance abusers who have successfully completed inpatient or outpatient treatment and must now return to their homes, jobs, and communities

agonists drugs, including narcotics, that produce effects by interacting with cell physiology

Al-Anon voluntary support group for families of recovering alcoholics

Alateen voluntary support group for teenage children of recovering alcoholics

alcohol oxidation the removal of alcohol from the bloodstream

alcohol withdrawal syndrome the collection of characteristic signs and symptoms experienced by alcohol-addicted people when they are deprived of alcohol; also called alcohol abstinence syndrome

Alcoholics Anonymous (AA) voluntary support group for recovering alcoholics

alveoli thin, saclike structures in the lungs where gases are exchanged between the blood and inhaled air

amotivational syndrome symptoms or a behavior pattern characterized by apathy, loss of effectiveness, and a more passive, introverted personality; this syndrome can result from chronic marijuana abuse

amphetamines drugs, related in structure to the neurotransmitters norepinephrine and dopamine, that produce stimulatory effects on the nervous system

anabolic drugs drugs that accelerate muscle growth and development

anabolic steroids synthetic steroids that stimulate protein synthesis, resulting in increases in muscle size and strength

anabolic-androgenic steroids (steroids) synthetic steroids that mimic the action of the male hormone testosterone

analgesic agents drugs that relieve pain

analgesics drugs that relieve pain (usually without excessive sedation)

anandamide a natural, endogenous cannabinoid

androgenic steroids synthetic steroids that cause the expression of male secondary sex characteristics, such as growth of facial hair and deepening of voice

anecdotal evidence evidence that is not based on controlled studies but on personal experience

anesthetics depressant drugs used in medical practice to induce a state of general anesthesia, including the loss of sensation and consciousness

anhedonia feelings of emptiness, meaninglessness, and lack of pleasure

Antabuse a drug prescribed to some recovering alcoholics that produces a violent illness if alcohol is consumed

antagonists nonpsychoactive compounds that compete with other compounds, such as the narcotics, for receptor sites

antiepileptic agents depressant drugs used to minimize the occurrence of epileptic seizures

antisocial personality a personality profile characterized by behaviors opposed to acceptable social norms

antitussive a drug that acts on the central and peripheral nervous systems to suppress the cough reflex

anxiolytic agents depressant drugs, usually with long durations of action, that reduce anxiety

aphrodisiac a drug that arouses or increases sexual desire

aqueous having the properties of water

asset forfeiture laws provisions in international, federal, state, and local laws that allow authorities to seize cash, property, vehicles, and other assets when they make drug arrests

atropine and scopolamine hallucinogens derived from *Atropa belladonna* (deadly nightshade), *Datura stramonium* (jimsonweed), and *Mandragora officinarum* (mandrake)

attention deficit/hyperactivity disorder (ADHD) a neurological disorder in which stimulating sensory input is not filtered out by the brain's reticular system, resulting in exaggerated behavioral responses; formerly called *hyperactivity*

autoimmune condition a health condition in which the body's immune system destroys its own tissue as if it were foreign

axon a nerve cell component that conducts electrical impulses (action potentials) away from the cell body and toward the synapses

B

bagging the practice of spraying an inhalant into a plastic bag and then breathing from the bag

barbiturates depressant drugs that share the central chemical structure of barbituric acid

benzodiazepines a group of sedative-hypnotic compounds that includes chlordiazepoxide (Librium) and diazepam (Valium)

benzoylmethylecgonine the chemical name for cocaine

beta endorphins naturally occurring opiatelike substances within the CNS, thought to create a euphoric effect to which the smoker becomes conditioned

binge drinking the consumption of large amounts of alcohol in a short time; often defined as five or more drinks at a sitting

bioactivation a biotransformation reaction that results in compounds more active than the original drug

bioavailability the extent to which biologically active molecules are absorbed and distributed to the target site

biodeactivation a biotransformation reaction that results in the alteration of the drug into a less active compound

bioequivalence the extent to which biologically active molecules enter cells, where they exert their effects

biologically active capable of influencing metabolic or regulatory processes at the cellular level

biotransformation the chemical alteration of drugs into various metabolites before excretion

blood alcohol concentration (BAC) proportion of alcohol in a measured volume of blood, given as a percentage

blood-brain barrier uniquely structured capillaries of the brain that lack pores and thus restrict the movement of some drugs into the brain

bolus theory a theory to account for tobacco dependence based on the body's response to periodic "balls" of nicotine after each inhalation of cigarette smoke

brain the portion of the central nervous system enclosed in the skull; includes the cerebrum, diencephalon, cerebellum, and brainstem

brainstem the portion of the brain that lies below the diencephalon and connects the brain to the spinal cord

brand name drug (pioneer drug) the original, patent-protected drug

bufotenin hallucinogen derived from *Amanita muscaria* and other plants

C

caffeinism physical and psychological dependence on caffeine

cannabinoids chemical compounds unique to the plant genus *Cannabis*; THC is the most familiar cannabinoid

Cannabis sativa the scientific name for the marijuana plant

carcinogenic cancer causing

catabolic processes physiological processes that break down muscle

cathine a secondary (and weaker) stimulant found in leaves and stems of the khat plant, *Catha edulis*

cathinone the primary central nervous system stimulant found in fresh leaves and stems of the khat plant, *Catha edulis*

cathinoids alkaloid chemicals that are unique to the khat plant, *Catha edulis*

cathinone a secondary (and weaker) stimulant found in leaves and stems of the khat plant, *Catha edulis*

causal relationship a relationship between two or more factors in which the occurrence, magnitude, or frequency of one factor depends on the existence or strength of another

cell body (soma) a central nerve cell component that summarizes many impulses into a single action potential

central nervous system (CNS) the brain and spinal cord

cerebellum the second largest part of the brain; lies below the cerebrum at the back of the head; coordinates movement with spatial judgment

cerebrum the uppermost part of the brain, consisting of two halves, the right and left cerebral hemispheres; the center for higher intellectual thought

chronic lasting a long time or recurring often

coalition an alliance of individuals and groups in the community who join together to prevent or solve a community problem such as alcohol, tobacco, and other drug abuse

cocaine a potent peripheral and central nervous system stimulant found in the leaves of the coca plant, *Erythroxylon coca*

cocaine addiction cycle a theoretical cyclical model that describes five stages of drug addiction as they relate specifically to cocaine dependence

codeine a natural narcotic with antitussive properties; a component in many prescription cough medicines

codependence a condition characterized by an unusual set of behaviors by a person who is in a close relationship with a chemically dependent person; these behaviors may include "enabling" and "denial"

cohoba (yopo) native terms for dimethyltryptamine

cold turkey abrupt cessation of the use of a drug, such as tobacco; refers to the "gooseflesh" sometimes experienced during withdrawal

community policing a cooperative approach by local police to working with citizens and other agencies based on the concept of shared responsibility for community security

community-based drug abuse education formal and informal programs and activities in the community designed to involve individuals and organizations in the prevention of drug abuse and dependency

comorbidity more than one diagnosed illness or disease occurring at one time

compensatory behavior behavior that results from "poor choice" rationales used to compensate for shortcomings in one's personality development

comprehensive drug abuse prevention activities and programs that aim to reduce both individual and environmental risk factors for drug abuse and dependence

compulsive users those with a cocaine use pattern characterized by high-frequency and high-dosage use

confirmatory drug test an assessment of urine, blood, or hair for the presence of drugs or their metabolites; used after drug screening to confirm the results of drug testing

confrontation a face-to-face intervention meeting with a drug-dependent person to convince him or her to enter treatment

contraindication a condition or characteristic of a person that makes the use of a particular medication by that person unwise or dangerous

Controlled Substance Act (Comprehensive Drug Abuse Control Act of 1970) key federal legislation that provides the legal basis by which access to certain substances is controlled by the federal government

controlled users those who practice a narcotics use pattern characterized by the absence over time of an increase either in dose or frequency; sometimes called "chippers"

counteradvertising health messages designed to balance the glamorized view of drinking and smoking promoted by company advertising

crack a chunk of solid, smokable, free-base cocaine

craving an overwhelming desire or perceived need to take a drug to feel its positive effects and avoid the negative effects of withdrawal

cross tolerance a condition in which tolerance to one drug results in tolerance to other, related drugs

cycle of addiction a conceptual model that describes changes in self identity and behavior of an addict in relation to drug use and the addict's social setting

cycling alternating periods of steroid use with equal or longer periods of abstinence for the purpose of decreasing one's tolerance

D

d-lysergic acid diethylamide the chemical name for the hallucinogen LSD, the most potent known hallucinogen

decriminalize to lessen the criminal penalties for possession of small quantities of a drug

delirium tremens (DTs) uncontrollable shaking and hallucinations associated with withdrawal from heavy chronic alcohol use

dendrite a nerve cell component that receives chemical impulses and conducts impulses toward the cell body

denial contention by alcoholics that they have no problems with alcohol use; denial maintains drinking behavior and delays treatment

depolarization a loss of electrical potential between the inside and the outside of a cell, resulting in impulse transmission

depressants drugs that produce slowing of mental and physical activity, reduce anxiety, and sedate

designer drugs psychoactive drugs whose chemical formulations are very similar to controlled substances

detoxification elimination of a drug from the body through a planned withdrawal from drug use

developmental tasks processes involved in developing an adult self-identity, independence, responsibility, and social skills that occur during maturation from child to adult

diencephalon the portion of the brain that lies above the brainstem and is enclosed by the cerebral hemisphere

dimethyltryptamine (DMT) hallucinogen derived from the powdered bark, seeds, and leaves of several South and Central American plants

disease model of drug dependence the concept that alcohol or other drug dependence is a primary disease over which an individual has no control, and not the manifestation of some other, psychological disorder

disinhibition the removal of social and personal controls on behavior

distillation process of heating a fermented alcohol mixture to produce vapors that are then cooled and collected as a stronger alcohol solution

distress unhealthy stress; results from unpleasant and unplanned situations

DOM hallucinogenic amphetamine with a potency approximately 100 times that of mescaline, also known as STP

dose-response curve a graphic depiction of the response range of a test population to a drug

drug any substance, aside from food, that upon entering the body, alters its function

drug abuse any use of an illegal drug or the use of a legal drug when it is detrimental to one's health or the health of others

drug action the observed response that occurs as drug molecules exert their influence on particular body tissues

drug addiction a condition characterized by the compulsive abuse of a drug or drugs; chemical dependence

drug cartels groups of illegal independent drug dealers who join forces for the purpose of controlling the production, distribution, and marketing of illegal drugs

drug dependence a psychological and sometimes physical state resulting from interaction between the body and a drug

drug interaction the effect that the action of one drug can have on the action of other drugs

drug misuse inappropriate use of a prescription or nonprescription drug

drug paraphernalia various devices used to administer drugs

drug screening assessment of urine, blood, or hair for evidence of the presence of drugs or their metabolites; used to determine the necessity of further drug testing

drug synergism the heightened or exaggerated effect produced by the concurrent use of two or more drugs

drug testing the use of chemical analysis to examine urine, hair, blood, or other body fluids or tissues for the presence of drugs or their metabolites

drug trafficking the buying, selling, manufacturing, and transporting of illicit drugs

drug use a general term to describe drug-taking behavior

Drug Use Forecasting (DUF) Program a federal program that

surveys arrestees and criminal offenders in major metropolitan areas across the United States to determine drug use trends and prevalence

E

education the process of providing knowledge, changing attitudes and beliefs, and altering behavior

efficacy the capacity to produce the intended and desired effect or result

empty calories calories consumed from a food source lacking in important nutrients

enabling the inadvertent support that some people provide to alcohol abusers or other drug abusers

endorphins morphinelike substances produced and released naturally in the human body

enkephalins substances that are produced and released naturally that influence the way pain messages are perceived or transmitted

environmental tobacco smoke (ETS) all tobacco smoke in the ambient air

enzymatic tolerance tolerance resulting from increased enzyme production

enzyme-multiplied immunoassay test (EMIT) the use of an enzyme system to detect antibodies to drugs in an immunoassay

erythroplakia red patches (similar to the white patches of leukoplakia) suggesting advanced changes in precancerous cells

eustress stress that results from planned experiences, such as physical exercise or friendly competition

excretion the removal of drug metabolites and other waste products from the body through urine, feces, exhaled air, perspiration, or breast milk

F

fermentation chemical process in which plant products are converted into alcohol by the action of yeast on carbohydrates

fetal alcohol effects (FAE) a limited number of the characteristic birth defects associated with fetal alcohol syndrome

fetal alcohol syndrome (FAS) a collection of characteristic birth defects observed in some children of women who consume alcohol during pregnancy

flashbacks recurrences of visions or other symptoms associated with earlier use of a hallucinogen

flunitrazepam (Rohypnol) a benzodiazepine, illegal in the United States, that achieved notoriety as the "date-rape drug" of the 1990s

fluorescent polarization immunoassay (FPIA) the use of a fluorescent dye to detect the presence of antibodies in an immunoassay

Food and Drug Administration (FDA) federal agency charged with overseeing the safety and effectiveness of drugs and medications

free-basing the act of preparing smokable cocaine from cocaine hydrochloride crystals by dissolving them in ether or mixing them with baking soda or ammonia and water and then smoking (inhaling) the vapors produced from heating the mixture

G

gamma-aminobutyric acid (GABA) an inhibitory neurotransmitter whose action is enhanced by depressant drugs

gas chromatography/mass spectrometry (GC/MS) a highly technical method of drug detection that is 99.9% accurate and involves identifying minute quantities of drugs or drug by-products using a machine called a *mass spectrometer*

gastric ADH ADH that functions in the stomach to break down alcohol before it reaches the bloodstream

gateway drugs easily obtainable legal or illegal drugs (alcohol, tobacco, and marijuana) that represent the drug user's first experience with a mind-altering drug

generic drugs drugs that are the chemical and biological equivalents of brand name drugs but are sold under the common chemical name

GRAE an acronym for OTC drugs generally regarded as effective

GRAHL an acronym for OTC drugs generally regarded as honestly labeled

GRAS an acronym for OTC drugs generally regarded as safe

grassroots efforts to change public policy that involve local people who are close to the issue

grasstops efforts to change public policy that involve influencing key policymakers or legislators

H

half-life the length of time required for the body to excrete one-half of remaining drug, as measured by the drug's concentration in the blood

hallucinogenic amphetamines synthetic hallucinogens that share the same chemical structure with norepinephrine, dopamine, and the amphetamines

hallucinogenic anesthetic anesthetic that produces hallucinations as a part of its pharmacological effect

hallucinogens drugs that produce distortions in perceptions of reality, hallucinations, and blending of perceptions of visual and auditory images

harm reduction a policy approach to drug prevention that minimizes harm by modifying the behaviors of drug users and the conditions under which they use drugs

harmine hallucinogen derived from *Peganum harmala* and other plants

hash oil oily solution of marijuana resins extracted in alcohol, filtered, and reduced by evaporation

hashish dried, smokeable resin from marijuana flowers and leaves

herb a plant; especially a plant reported to be capable of curing or preventing illness or disease

heroin a highly addictive, quasi-synthetic narcotic produced by chemically altering morphine

heroin maintenance A proposed program through which heroin addicts would be supplied heroin by a governmental agency in an attempt to assist them in better managing their condition and to reduce drug-related crimes

homeostasis the tendency of the body's physiological system to maintain internal stability

host negligence failure to act with reasonable care in serving alcohol to others, resulting in injury to other people, thereby incurring potential liability

huffing soaking a rag with a volatile liquid, such as gasoline or toluene, and inhaling from the rag, or even placing the rag in the mouth

human growth hormone (hGH) a protein produced by the human pituitary gland that accelerates physical growth

hydrophilic water loving, a substance that binds easily with water molecules

hyperpolarization an increase in electrical potential between the inside and the outside of cell, resulting in no impulse transmission

I

ice highly purified methamphetamine crystals that can be dissolved and injected or "smoked" as heated vapors in a glass pipe; also called "crystal meth" or "crank"

illegal (illicit) drugs drugs that cannot be manufactured, distributed, or sold legally and that usually lack recognized medical value

immediate environment home and family, school, peers, and the community

immunoassay the use of antibodies to detect the presence or absence of drugs in the urine, hair, or body tissues.

implantation a variation of the absorption route of administration in which a drug is surgically placed under the skin so that the drug can be absorbed into the bloodstream at a controlled rate

impotence the inability to achieve and maintain an erection of the penis

ingestion entry of a drug through the mouth into the digestive tract

inhalants volatile substances that produce effects when breathed or inhaled

inhalation administration of a drug through the lungs

injection use of a needle to insert a drug into the body

institutional enabling failure of official or unofficial community organizations to discourage alcohol, tobacco, and other drug misuse and abuse

intensified users those with a cocaine use pattern involving daily use over a long period of time and who therefore are more likely to have deterioration of function

interdiction the process of denying the drug smuggler the use of air, land, and maritime routes

interpersonal skills communicative and behavioral skills needed to interact successfully with others

intervention a counseling approach for early detection and treatment of drug-dependent individuals

intramuscular into a muscle

intravenous into a vein

involuntary (autonomic) nervous system a division of the peripheral nervous system that controls glands and involuntary muscles

K

ketamine hydrochloride dissociative anesthetic or hallucinogenic anesthetic chemically related to PCP

L

labeling printed information supplied with an OTC drug, including that printed on the packaging, container, and insert

law enforcement the application of federal, state, and local laws to arrest, jail, bring to trial, and sentence those who break laws

legal (licit) drugs drugs that can be manufactured, distributed, and sold legally

leukoplakia white, smooth or scaly patches in the mouth or on the lips, tongue, or throat suggesting precancerous cellular changes

lipid oil or fat

lipophilic fat loving, a substance that binds easily with fats and oils

"local option" provisions provisions in state laws that allow local communities to regulate where and when alcohol is sold

M

mainstream smoke smoke that is drawn through the cigarette, inhaled, and then exhaled by the smoker

marijuana the dried parts or extracts of the *Cannabis sativa* plant, capable of producing a psychoactive effect in the user

maturing out An observed phenomenon in which older heroin addicts discontinue drug use even in the absence of treatment

MDA and MDMA hallucinogenic amphetamines similar in formulation to mescaline but much more powerful; MDMA is also known as "ecstasy"

meprobamate a sedative-hypnotic drug used as an antianxiety agent under the brand names Equanil and Miltown

mescaline hallucinogen derived from the peyote cactus

methadone maintenance A form of therapy in which a legal narcotic, methadone, is prescribed for an addict to replace heroin

methaqualone a sedative-hypnotic drug with no currently accepted medical use in the United States; formerly sold under the brand name Quaalude

methcathinone a synthetic structural analog of cathinone, manufactured in illegal laboratories and abused; a powerful, amphetamine-like stimulate

methylxanthines a family of chemical compounds that includes caffeine, theophylline, and theobromine

microsomal induction a phenomenon in which the presence of a foreign substance increases the number of microsomes (in the liver), which produce enzymes that detoxify the foreign substance

modeling adoption of one person's behavior by another, usually younger, person

money laundering the process of converting illegally earned assets or cash to other forms of wealth to conceal true ownership or illegal acquisition

morphine a natural narcotic, the primary psychoactive ingredient in opium

multijurisdictional drug-control task forces coalitions of local and state law-enforcement agencies (usually five or more) that work closely with federal enforcement agencies

multimodality programs treatment programs that combine several different treatment approaches

muscarine hallucinogen derived from *Amanita muscaria*

N

narcolepsy a disorder characterized by the rapid and uncontrollable onset of sleep

narcotic a morphinelike drug that relieves pain and induces a stuporous state

National Minimum Drinking Age Act of 1984 a federal law that required all states to raise their minimum alcohol purchase and public possession age to 21 years

natural hallucinogens hallucinogenic drugs derived from natural sources, such as plants

neural adaptation tolerance resulting from adjustments in neurotransmitter production or release

neuron a single nerve cell; the smallest functional unit of the nervous system

neurotransmitters chemical messengers within nerve cells that, when released into the synaptic cleft, diffuse across the cleft and produce a postsynaptic response

nicotine the primary, dependence-producing, central nervous system stimulant in the tobacco plant; also, a mild euphoriant and a toxicant

nonprescription drugs drugs that can be legally purchased without a physician's prescription (example, aspirin)

nonresidential treatment outpatient programs that are less disruptive to family life and job responsibilities

NORML National Organization for the Reform of Marijuana Laws

O

ololiuqui hallucinogen derived from *Rivea corymbosa* (morning glory)

Omnibus Anti-Substance Abuse Act of 1988 federal law that made it a felony offense to distribute steroids across state lines

Omnibus Crime Control Act (OCCA) of 1990 a federal law that added certain anabolic-androgenic steroid substances to schedule III of the Controlled Substance Act of 1970

opium the primary psychoactive substance, or "mother drug," extracted from the oriental poppy plant

over-the-counter (OTC) drugs a term interchangeable with nonprescription drugs

P

panic attack an acute mood disorder characterized by episodes of extreme fear and anxiety

panic reaction sudden exaggerated response to initial use of an illicit drug; associated with fear or feeling of loss of control

paraherbalism an irrational, unscientific form of herbalism based on questionable beliefs

parasympathetic branch that portion of the involuntary nervous system, mediated by the neurotransmitter acetycholine, that decreases the intensity of muscular contractions and glandular secretions

passive smoking the inhalation by nonsmokers of air containing tobacco smoke

peer groups people of the same age or social status (age-mates)

periodontal disease disease of the tissue supporting the teeth

peripheral nervous system (PNS) the portion of the nervous system that lies outside the skull and spinal cord

pharmacology the study of interactions of drugs with the physiology of the body

phencyclidine (PCP) hallucinogenic drug initially developed as a veterinary anesthetic

physical dependence a physiological state in which clinical signs of illness appear when one abstains from a drug

pioneer drug (brand name drug) another term for the original, patent-protected drug

placebo a medically inert substance formulated to mimic the appearance of an active substance

placebo effect an observable clinical response to a chemically inert substance

placenta structure through which nutrients (and drugs, including alcohol) pass from the bloodstream of the mother into the bloodstream of the developing fetus

placental barrier the unique circulatory structures of the placenta that restrict the passage of some substances into the fetal bloodstream

plasma proteins proteins circulating in the blood that bind drugs, thereby preventing them from reaching sites of action or from being excreted

polydrug use use of two or more drugs at same time

polypharmacy the use of multiple prescription medications, as well as OTC and dietary supplements, for the treatment of various health problems that exist at the same time

postsynaptic membrane the cellular membrane of the dendrite

preanesthetic agents depressant drugs given before administration of anesthetic drugs

precursor (essential) chemicals chemicals required for the extraction and synthesis of all major illegal drugs except marijuana

prescription written instructions (using abbreviated Latin symbols) from a health care provider to a pharmacist regarding the dispensing of a prescription medication

prescription drugs drugs and medications dispensed by pharmacists on orders from a physician or dentist

presynaptic membrane the cellular membrane of the axon

prevalence the number of cases of a particular condition or behavioral pattern in a given population at a given time

prevention the sum of all efforts to reduce drug abuse and dependence

primary prevention measures aimed at preventing the onset of drug use

problem drinking a pattern of alcohol use (abuse) in which a drinker's behavior creates personal difficulties for the drinker or for others

proof twice the percentage of alcohol by concentration; 100-proof alcohol is 50% alcohol

protective factors genetic or environmental factors that decrease the probability of drug use, abuse or dependence

psilocybin and psilocin primary psychoactive ingredients in the *Psilocybe mexicana* mushroom

psychedelic effects variety of psychological changes produced by hallucinogenic drugs, including heightened perception of sensory input, vivid imagery, and an enhanced sense of awareness

psychoactive drug a drug that alters sensory perceptions, mood, thought processes, or behavior

psychological dependence a psychological state of mind characterized by an overwhelming desire to continue taking a drug, even though clinical signs of physical illness may not be apparent

public policy principles and courses of action pursued by governments to solve practical problems that affect society

pyramiding gradually increasing and then decreasing doses during a single cycle

Q

QUAD (Quick Uniform Attack on Drugs) a program that emphasizes quick response by enforcement officers to every community complaint, combined with neighborhood cleanup efforts

quasi-synthetic narcotics drugs formed by chemically modifying one of the naturally occurring narcotics

R

radioimmunoassay (RIA) the use of small amounts of radioactive material to detect antibodies to drugs in an immunoassay

recovery response a natural reflex of the mind that occurs when specific obstacles are removed from the addict's path to recovery

recreational users those with a cocaine use pattern that includes experimental and social use and that does not cause significant deterioration in function for the user

reflex arc a special arrangement of neurons in the spinal cord that allows for a direct transfer of impulses from sensory to motor neurons

reinforcers drugs that are capable of generating a self-administration response in laboratory animals

reinforcing agent a drug that produces self-administration, usually demonstrated in laboratory animals

relapse prevention programs to help drug-dependent individuals and families stay drug-free and avoid former patterns of abuse

residential treatment inpatient programs requiring drug-dependent individuals to live at the facility

resistance the concept that individuals are endowed with attributes that lower their susceptibility to drug involvement

reverse modeling conscious or unconscious decision to exclude from one's own behavior an observed behavioral pattern judged undesirable

reverse tolerance a phenomenon in which a chronic drug user experiences the effects of a drug at a lower dose than expected

reward deficiency syndrome name for the manifestation of one or more addictive, impulsive, or compulsive behavioral disorders, including drug abuse or dependence

risk factors genetic or environmental factors that increase the probability of drug use, abuse, or dependence

route of administration the pathway by which a drug enters the body

S

school-based drug abuse education social influence programs offered in kindergarten through twelfth grade that emphasize resistance training, life skills, and normative beliefs to protect children from drug use

second messenger a regulatory chemical compound within cells that is activated by the presence of a hormone or other chemical (first messenger)

secondary prevention detection, screening, intervention, and treatment of early drug abuse to avoid further use

secular recovery programs alcohol or drug recovery approaches that do not encourage members to believe in a god or higher power

self-care movement health care based on the principles of self-diagnosis, self-treatment, and self-directed health promotion

serum sickness a hypersensitivity reaction to a foreign protein

shock a potentially life-threatening depression of vital bodily functions (especially respiration, circulation, and temperature control)

side effects undesirable effects of prescription medications or other drugs

sidestream smoke smoke rising from the burning tip of the cigarette; contains more dangerous chemicals than mainstream smoke

sinsemilla female plants that have been protected against fertilization and are therefore without seeds; they produce increased amounts of resin, and therefore more THC, than plants with seeds

site of action body location at which a drug exerts its effects

sniffing, snorting inhaling volatile substances directly from their containers

snuff finely shredded or powdered smokeless tobacco, used for dipping (placing between the cheek and gum) or, in the case of powder, sniffing through the nose

social drugs legally available psychoactive drugs that are used by a large proportion of society (examples: alcohol, nicotine, caffeine)

social lubricant any factor that allows or promotes social interaction

speed freak a person who injects or inhales large amounts of amphetamines

speedball an injectable mixture of heroin and cocaine (or, alternatively, heroin and amphetamine)

spinal cord the part of the central nervous system that lies outside the skull and serves as a passageway for information between the brain and peripheral nervous system

spittoon (cuspidor) large bowl-like container used as a receptacle for saliva or spit containing tobacco juice

stacking the taking of high doses of several different types of anabolic-androgenic steroids so that tolerance to one type might be overcome by the presence of another, slightly different steroid

steroids a class of lipid molecule exhibiting four carbon rings and an assortment of molecular side chains; examples are cholesterol, estrogen, and testosterone.

storage drug deposition in tissue away from the site(s) of action

stress a natural psychological and physiological response resulting from exposure to stressors

stressors environmental stimuli that produce tension and strain

strongly dependence-producing drugs illegal drugs that produce chemical dependence in a high proportion of those who abuse them

subcutaneous under the skin

substitute dependence the redirection of an addiction to a less harmful substance

substitute dependence treatment a component of a treatment program in which a safer drug and/or a safer route of administration is substituted for a more dangerous drug or route of administration

sulfa drugs A general category of sulfonimide-based drugs that produce an antibacterial action

support group a group of individuals in recovery who come together to help each other remain drug free

sympathetic branch that portion of the voluntary nervous system mediated by the neurotransmitters epinephrine and norepinephrine, that increases the intensity of muscular contractions and glandular secretions

symptomatic relief alleviation of discomfort or other signs and symptoms of a condition or disease without curing the cause of the disease or condition

synapse the junction between adjacent neurons or between neurons and muscle or gland cells

synaptic cleft the space that separates the presynaptic membrane of one neuron from the postsynaptic membrane of an adjacent neuron

synaptic vesicles membranous globules containing neurotransmitter molecules

Synar Amendment federal law that requires all states to adopt legislation that prohibits the sale and distribution of tobacco products to people under age 18

synesthesia blending of sensory inputs

synthetic hallucinogens hallucinogenic drugs that are formulated in a laboratory

synthetic narcotics drugs produced entirely in the laboratory and thus not occurring naturally

T

tar solid materials (particulates) present in tobacco smoke

tertiary prevention treatment and rehabilitation of people with more serious or chronic drug problems so they no longer need or want drugs

tetrahydrocannabinol (THC) primary active compound in marijuana

therapeutic equivalence the extent to which biologically active molecules produce the equivalent effect on cell function

titration maintaining a particular level of nicotine in the blood by adjusting cigarette usage

tolerance physiological and enzymatic adjustments made in response to chronic presence of a drug in the body such that ever-increasing doses are required to produce an effect equivalent to prior effects

treatment the act of providing medical and/or psychological care to someone with an injury, illness, or disorder

treatment approach the theoretical underpinning that the treatment professional brings to the therapeutic situation

treatment setting the location in which treatment takes place

Type 1 alcoholism an inherited form of alcoholism that is thought to be primarily influenced by environmental factors; also known as milieu-limited alcoholism

Type 2 alcoholism an inherited form of alcoholism that is thought to pass primarily from alcoholic fathers to their sons; also known as male-limited alcoholism

V

voluntary (somatic) nervous system a division of the peripheral nervous system through which willful control of voluntary (skeletal) muscles occurs

vulnerability the concept that people are differentially at risk for drug abuse

W

weakly dependence-producing drugs illegal drugs that do not produce chemical dependence in a high proportion of those who abuse them

Weed and Seed a federal program that helps communities remove drug traffickers from their neighborhoods and offers incentives for communities to remain drug free

withdrawal illness (abstinence syndrome) occurrence of unpleasant or painful, clinically recognizable symptoms when drug use is discontinued

Z

zero-tolerance laws regulations that set maximum blood alcohol concentration (BAC) limits for drivers under 21 at 0.02% or lower

CREDITS

Chapter 1

photo on p. 2, CLG Photographics; *p. 3*, Redrawn from Office of Substance Abuse Prevention: *Prevention Plus II: tools for creating sustaining drug-free communities*, Rockville, Md, 1989, NCADI; *p. 5*, Modified from Chaiken, MR: Can a drug epidemic be anticipated? National Institute of Justice Journal 226:23, 1993; *photo on p. 8*, CLG Photographics.

Chapter 2

p. 20, Modified from Office of Substance Abuse Prevention: *Prevention plus II: tools for creating sustaining drug-free communities*, Rockville, Md., 1989, NCADI; *p. 24*, Peele, Stanton. Figure 3–1. Competing Models of Addiction. *Adaptive Model, Visions of Addiction: Major Contemporary Perspectives on Addiction and Alcoholism, p. 46*, Lexington Books, an imprint of Jossey-Bass Inc., Publishers.

Chapter 3

p. 40, Modified from Raven P, Johnson G *Biology*, ed 2, St. Louis, 1989, Mosby; *photo on p. 41*, Bushong: Magnetic resonance imaging, 1988, reprinted by permission of the McGraw-Hill Companies; *p. 43*, Alan Peters from Moffett D, Moffett S, Schauf D: Human physiology: foundations and frontiers, ed 2, 1990, reprinted by permission of the McGraw-Hill Companies; *photo on p. 44*, Alan Peters from Moffett D, Moffett S, Schauf D: Human physiology: foundations and frontiers, ed 2, 1990, reprinted by permission of the McGraw-Hill Companies.

Chapter 5

photo on p. 70, Manewal/Superstock; *p. 75*, Modified from Earley PH: The cocaine recovery book. Newbury Park, CA, 1991, Sage Publications; *p. 76*, Modified from Designer Drugs © 1986 by MM Kirsch, Comp-Care Publishers, Minneapolis, MN; *photo on p. 87*, H. Armstrong Roberts.

Chapter 6

p. 98, Redrawn from Julien: A primer of drug, New York, 1988, WH Freeman.

Chapter 7

photo on p. 114, Drug Enforcement Agency 92004; *photo on p. 115*, Drug Enforcement Agency 92031; *photo on p. 115*, St. Louis Mercantile Library, *p. 117*, Modified from Drug Enforcement Agency Pamphlet; *p. 121*, National Institutes of Health; National Institute on Drug Abuse, CEWG Epidemiologic Trends on Drug Abuse, vol 1, Rockville, MD., December 1995; *p. 129*, Hazelden Educational Materials: What is NA? Narcotics Anonymous, 1985, Van Nuys, CA.

Chapter 8

photo on p. 134, Department of Justice; *photo on p. 138*, Drug Enforcement Agency 4640-1 MJ; *photo on p. 139*, Courtesy Smith-Kline Beecham; *photo on p. 143*, Chris Minnick; *p. 145*, Modified from Johnston LD, O'Malley PM, Bachman JG: *National survey results on drug use from monitoring the future study*, 1975–1992, Rockville, Md. United States Department of Health and Human Services, Public Health Services, National Institutes, National Institute on Drug Abuse, 1993.

Chapter 9

photo on p. 153, Superstock; *photo on p. 155*, R. Smolan/FPG International; *photo on p. 155*, AP/World Wide Photos; *photo on p. 157*, Jack Hayes; *photo on p. 158*, Department of Justice; *photo on p. 160*, Department of Justice.

Chapter 10

photo on p. 168, St. Louis Mercantile Library.

Chapter 11

p. 187, Young FE, *The reality behind the headlines*, FDA Consumer Special Report, from Test Tube to Patient. DHHS Pub No. 90-3186, Rockville, Md, 1990, Department of Health and Human Services, Public Health Service, Food and Drug Administration.

Chapter 12

p. 203, Modified from Cigarette ads: A matter of life and death, *USA Today*, March 25, 1992. Reprinted with permission; *photo on p. 203*, St. Louis Mercantile Library; *photo on p. 214*, Peter Arnold, Inc.

Chapter 14

photo on p. 238, CLG Photographics.

Chapter 16

photo on p. 257, Missouri Historical Society, Groups 227A; *photo on p. 259*, CLG Photographics; *p. 262*, Payne W., Hahn D: *Understanding your health*, ed 2, 1989, reprinted by permission of the McGraw-Hill Companies; *p. 264*, Payne W, Hahn D: *Understanding your health*, ed 2, 1989, reprinted by permission of the McGraw-Hill Companies; *photo on p. 267*, Claus Simon/Michael Janner from Thibodeau G, Patton K: The human body in health and disease, ed 1, 1992, Mosby.

Chapter 17

photo on p. 280, Courtesy Master Sergeant Patrick E. O'Neill Vehicle Investigation. Davison, Ill., State Police; *p. 285*, The Twelve Steps are reprinted with permission of Alcoholics Anonymous World Services, Inc. Permission to reprint the Twelve Steps does not mean that A.A. has reviewed or approved the contents of this publication, nor that A.A. agrees with the views expressed herein. A.A. is a program of recovery from alcoholism *only*—use of the Twelve Steps in connection with programs and activities which are patterned after A.A., but which address other problems, or in any other non-A.A. context, does not imply otherwise.

Chapter 18

photo on p. 294, Governor's Committee for a Drug Free Indiana; *photo on p. 296*, Students of Ball State University, Student Health Education Division; *photo on p. 298*, CLG Photographics; *photo on p. 300*, CLG Photographics.

Chapter 19

photo on p. 307, Centers for Disease Control and Prevention; *photo on p. 308*, Partnership for a Drug Free America; *photo on p. 313*, Mothers Against Drunk Driving.

Chapter 20

p. 317, Chris Minnick, Indianapolis; *p. 318*, Nic Howell.

Appendix

Fox S, *Human Physiology*, 5th edition, © 1996 The McGraw-Hill Companies, fig 8.15b.

INDEX

Note: Page numbers followed by *f* and *t* indicate figure and table, respectively.